REVOLUTION AND COUNTER-REVOLUTION

The Revisionist Coup in China and the Struggle in The Revolutionary Communist Party, USA

RCP Publications, Chicago

Published and Distributed by
RCP Publications
P.O. Box 3486 Merchandise Mart
Chicago, Illinois 60654
Bulk Rates Available
Please Prepay all orders to RCP Publications

September 1978

Table of Contents

Introduction

"What does the history of the development of the international communist movement demonstrate?

"First, it demonstrates that like everything else, the international working-class movement tends to divide itself in two. The class struggle between the proletariat and the bourgeoisie is inevitably reflected in the communist ranks. It is inevitable that opportunism of one kind or another should arise in the course of the development of the communist movement, that opportunists should engage in anti-Marxist-Leninist splitting activities and that Marxist-Leninists should wage struggles against opportunism and splittism. It is precisely through the struggle of opposites that Marxism-Leninism and the international working-class movement have developed. And it is also through this struggle that the international working-class movement has strengthened and consolidated its unity on the basis of Marxism-Leninism." (From "The Leaders of the CPSU Are the Greatest Splitters of Our Times," Foreign Languages Press, Peking, p. 11.)

Today these truths stand out sharply. Once more opportunism has arisen in the international working class movement; yet again genuine communists must consolidate a higher level of unity on the basis of determined Marxist struggle against that opportunism.

The documents in this book, written in late 1977 and early 1978, come from the recent struggle in the Revolutionary Communist Party, USA over the stand of communists toward the rightist coup in China that followed the death of Mao Tsetung. But because that question is one of world-historic dimensions, inevitably all the cardinal questions now facing revolutionaries were raised to one degree or another in this struggle. Thus in addition to the main body of the book on China, there is an appendix concerning communist work in the U.S.

The struggle in the RCP, USA happened in the context of a worldwide struggle between Marxism and revisionism. We are publishing the documents from this struggle—which resulted in the defeat of a revisionist headquarters—as an aid to that struggle.

Introduction

Revisionists Seize Power In China

On September 9, 1976 Mao Tsetung—Chairman of the Central Committee of the Communist Party of China, cherished leader of the international proletariat and oppressed peoples, and the greatest Marxist of the contemporary era—died.

Mao never once retreated from battle. At the very end he gave leadership to the struggle against the counter-revolutionary clique of Hua Kuo-feng and Teng Hsiao-ping. Even on his deathbed Mao put principle above an illusory and false unity.

Mao Tsetung closely united in this, as in earlier struggles, with the revolutionary heroes who were later slandered as "the Gang of Four"—Wang Hung-wen, Chang Chun-chiao, Chiang Ching, and Yao Wen-yuan.

The Four had played vanguard roles throughout the Great Proletarian Cultural Revolution, including in the struggle to smash Lin Piao's headquarters. Further—upholding the line of Mao—in the years of the early and mid-seventies they continued to base themselves on and apply the theory and practice of continuing the revolution under the dictatorship of the proletariat.

These struggles came to a head in the last great battle to preserve the gains of the Cultural Revolution, beat back the right-deviationist wind and smash the Hua/Teng headquarters, which had been sponsored and fostered by Chou En-lai.

With Mao's death, however, the capitalist roaders in the Central Committee were strong enough to make their move. On October 6, these counter-revolutionary hack butchers arrested the heroic Four and many other genuine revolutionaries in a reactionary coup d'etat.

To consolidate their power as a new bourgeoisie these rightists began attacking the line and practice of Mao, and the tempo of these attacks—on fundamental theory as well as line and policies on socialist construction; the target of class struggle under socialism; the international united front against imperialism; education; culture; etc.,—increased with every passing week. (See especially the main paper, "Revisionists Are Revisionists and Must Not Be Supported, Revolutionaries Are Revolutionaries and Must Be Supported" for details.)

Precisely because Mao was the greatest Marxist in the contemporary era and the Chinese revolution had a tremendous international significance, these changes sent shock waves throughout the international working class movement. Correctly summing up the lines coming out of China and the entire march of events following Mao's death became the most pressing question facing the international working class movement.

Historical Experience Holds Lessons

Such a situation is not unprecedented in the history of the communist movement. In 1956, at the 20th Congress of the Communist Party of the Soviet Union, N.S. Khrushchev sank into the gutter of slander and character assassination in a vicious attack against the deceased great Marxist-Leninist, Joseph Stalin.

Stalin had for over 30 years upheld the dictatorship of the proletariat and stood for the achievement of communism worldwide. In this sense Stalin came to represent the experience of proletarian dictatorship and the international communist movement. In attacking Stalin, Khrushchev in fact was attacking the Leninist line Stalin upheld and the proletarian dictatorship Stalin defended.

At this same 20th Congress, Khrushchev ran the line that capitalism could be peacefully transformed into socialism and that imperialism could be "peacefully coexisted" out of existence. He was ingratiating himself to the imperialists to buy time while he wrecked socialism and moved to restore capitalism in the USSR.

The communist parties of China, Albania and a number of other countries stood up against tremendous pressure and fought the line of the modern revisionists. But in most parties there was severe demoralization and capitulation to Khrushchev's revisionism.

These parties all had serious problems in the first place. But Khrushchev's attack on Leninism lent the revisionists within these parties the prestige to administer the final blow to whatever revolutionary elements existed within them.

In other words, the external conditions of a revisionist coup and capitalist restoration in the Soviet Union brought the internal struggle between Marxism and opportunism going on in the other parties to a head—and pushed most of these parties over the brink into the abyss of counter-revolution. The serious setback in the Soviet Union was compounded by the loss of many formerly communist parties.

The October Revolution in Russia (with the exception of the short-lived victory of the Paris Commune) was the first great triumph in the history of the international working class. To paraphrase Mao, its salvoes brought Marxism-Leninism and the cause of communism to millions upon millions everywhere.

Because of all that, defending the gains of the October Revolution and the principles it embodied against the jackals and hyenas attacking it became, with Khrushchev's betrayal, the crucial question before the international communist movement.

Great Proletarian Cultural Revolution— An Historic Breakthrough

Though the working class had suffered a crushing setback in the Soviet Union, the struggle that followed to sum it up laid the basis to advance the proletarian cause to new heights.

In 1966, Mao Tsetung launched the Great Proletarian Cultural Revolution, an historic breakthrough in the theory and practice of class struggle under socialism. An article in the October 1, 1976 issue of *Revolution*, the organ of the Central Committee of the RCP, USA, addressed its significance.

> "In 1967 Mao summed up the experience of the struggle against revisionism this way: 'In the past we waged struggles in the rural areas, in factories, in the cultural field, and we carried out the socialist education movement. But all this failed to solve the problem because we did not find a form, a method, to arouse the broad masses to expose our dark aspect openly, in an all-round way and from below.'
>
> "With this experience in mind, Mao personally kindled the fire of the Great Proletarian Cultural Revolution, a movement unprecedented in history."

The article went on to discuss the international significance of the Cultural Revolution.

> "A new generation of revolutionaries rising up to battle the old order, and seeing the USSR wrapped in the banner of Marx and Lenin, yet mirroring the same evils of the system of exploitation they saw in their own countries, were prey to those who claimed that Marxism-Leninism was not the science of revolution and that the working class was no longer the revoutionary class.
>
> "In the midst of this, Mao Tsetung kindled the sparks of the Cultural Revolution. He showed that the degeneration of the Soviet Union came because that country was no longer under the rule of the working class and had become, in fact, a capitalist power. He developed the theory of continuing the revolution under the dictatorship of the proletariat and by rousing the masses in their hundreds of millions demonstrated to the world that the restoration of capitalism could be prevented and that the working class could lead the people in advancing step by step toward the goal of communism.
>
> "Just as Mao had written, 'The salvoes of the October

> Revolution brought Marxism-Leninism to China,' so it can also be said that the reverberations of Mao's call, 'It is right to rebel against reactionaries,' as well as all his other tremendous contributions to Marxism-Leninism and to the struggle of the international proletariat and the world's peoples, has spread Marxism-Leninism, Mao Tsetung Thought throughout the world and fired revolutionaries on every continent with a faith in the ultimate accomplishment of the goal of communism." (Both quotes from "Cultural Revolution: Breakthrough On the Road to Communism," pp. S13, S16.)

The Cultural Revolution was a world-historic event on the scale of the Paris Commune and October Revolution. Because of its profound significance and because of the attack going on now in China against what it represented, correctly summing up and struggling against these new revisionists is the chief question of line facing the international communist movement.

Split In RCP

All this set the stage for the line struggle and split in the RCP that this book documents.

For some time previous to the coup in China, two leading members of the RCP—M. Jarvis and L. Bergman—had been promoting a number of revisionist lines concerning revolutionary work in the U.S. These lines have been well-documented in a series of articles in *Revolution* and stand out glaringly in their papers included in the appendix of this book.

The coup in China meant two things for these Mensheviks.* On the one hand, it encouraged them to step up their activities. Here, they thought, was "revolutionary authority" for their pragmatism, narrowness and downright revisionism.

At the same time, the rightist takeover also forced their hand. For if the Party were to remain true to its principles as developed in *Red Papers 7 (How Capitalism Was Restored in the Soviet Union)*, the Party *Programme* and elsewhere, then outright opposition to the "goulash communism" promoted by Hua Kuo-feng was inevitable. Such going against the tide was an anathema to these

---

*These ex-RCP opportunists have been dubbed Mensheviks because of their striking similarity to a band of renegades who attacked Lenin and the Bolsheviks in the Russian Social Democratic Party at the turn of the century (Mensheviks—Russian for minority). The Jarvis-Bergman headquarters shared a strong brand of right opportunism and a bent toward factionalism with their Russian political ancestors. (See *History of the Communist Party of the Soviet Union [Bolshevik]* and *Revolution*, January, 1978 for more on the original Mensheviks.)

opportunists.

The Jarvis/Bergman clique pursued their aims through factionalism. Their action basically had three phases to it, and illustrated well that, as Wang Hung-wen said, "If one practices revisionism. . . one will inevitably go in for splits, intrigues, and conspiracy."

First the Mensheviks tried to block any decision on the events in China, while they stalled for time to organize for their line outside Party channels. For months they stubbornly opposed convening a Central Committee meeting to deal with the China question. Meanwhile these Mensheviks actively organized for their stand on China everywhere they could and promoted whatever pragmatist trash appeared in *Peking Review* in 1977. But when this failed and a Central Committee meeting was called, these opportunists shifted tactics.

Comrade Bob Avakian, Chairman of the Central Committee of the RCP, submitted to the CC the draft of "Revisionists Are Revisionists and Must Not Be Supported, Revolutionaries Are Revolutionaries and Must Be Supported." (See pages 1-138 of this volume for the final version of this paper, enriched through the two-line struggle at the CC, adopted by the CC and subsequently submitted to the Party's membership. This document was affirmed and adopted by the 2nd Party Congress in 1978.) At the CC Jarvis submitted a short paper that on the one hand preached agnosticism, saying it was too soon to tell what was really going on in China, but on the other hand insisted that the Four were counter-revolutionaries. Bergman for his part accused the Party of "rushing to judgment," and offered his "full support" for all the revisionism coming out of China.

The Jarvis/Bergman clique gave their "theoretician" the thankless task of concocting a feasible explanation for the wholesale reversals going on in China. Since the Party Center led by Comrade Avakian had succeeded in directing some study around the main line questions at issue, hardly anyone could straight up defend Teng Hsiao-ping, the "Three Poisonous Weeds,"* and Hua's anti-Marxist lines on the target of class

*The "Three Poisonous Weeds," concocted by Teng Hsiao-ping, Hua Kuo-feng and other revisionists are "On the General Program for All Work of the Whole Party and the Whole Country" (dubbed the "General Program"), "Some Problems in Speeding Up Industrial Development" (the "20 Points") and "Outline Report on Science and Technology." These papers were drafted and circulated by the revisionist headquarters in China in the mid to late '70s and became a focal point of struggle launched by the revolutionary left. The current Chinese leadership upholds all three poisonous weeds.

struggle under socialism and the relation between revolution and production.

Therefore this scholar declared the lines irrelevant and not concrete enough. Instead he dug through and promoted an incoherent jumble of accusations and rumors. Since it wouldn't do just to parrot such tall tales straight from the *Peking Review,* this fellow had an interesting approach: find the same tall tales reprinted in Hong Kong or from Kuomintang sources on Taiwan and—lo!—he had found "proof" of the stories in *Peking Review*. Mao's clear ideological and political unity with the Four was not what it seemed, according to his herky-jerky logic, and if one plowed through enough garbage put out by Hong Kong gossips and character assassins in the pay of Teng Hsiao-ping, Hua Kuo-feng, et. al., one could find the real truth.

This mishmash of eclecticism and agnosticism was so thoroughly trashed at the Central Committee meeting where it was presented that by the end of the meeting members of this clique were pleading in tears for someone—anyone!—to explain what had happened in China.

Defeated in ideological struggle, these Mensheviks then threatened to split the Party should the CC adopt Comrade Avakian's report. When this too was rebuffed, they backpedaled into several days of phoney self-criticisms, hypocritical pleas for unity, and vows to carry out the line of the Party.

It was the decisive victory of the revolutionaries at the CC and the retreat of the Mensheviks that determined the character of the CC report on rectification, reprinted as part of the Appendix of this volume on page 375. In that paper, Jarvis is referred to as a "comrade" and there is no explicit exposure of Bergman. At that time, the orientation was to unite with their expressed desire for unity and to "cure the disease and save the patient," with no half-stepping in drawing out the severity of the illness. This report (or the points that were later written up into the report) was unanimously approved by the entire CC, Mensheviks included. The report is relatively short since it was decided at the CC meeting that it should only characterize the main points relating to the domestic class struggle, with further elaboration to take place over the course of the Party Rectification campaign which the report called for.

Of course, once out of the meeting these liars set about splitting the Party. They attempted to refine their gobbledygook defense of revisionism in China submitted at the CC, and the product of these labors, "China Advances Along the Socialist

Road—The Gang of Four Were Counter-Revolutionaries and Revolutionaries Cannot Support Them" is reprinted in this volume on page 139. They well understood that the basic question of overall line, and a Marxist interpretation of the facts, all pointed to a revisionist coup.

If they could however produce a mass of seemingly contradictory facts, then perhaps they could shake people's belief in the possiblity of comprehending the essence of those facts, their real interconnections and motion and development. At the least, these Mensheviks hoped they could plant a reasonable doubt in people's minds. And once they could convince people that reality is so complex, that only a "genius" can grasp it, the critical spirit is extinguished and people can only fall back on subjectivity and follow whomever they "trust."

They also wrote a response to the CC report on rectification as a call to the Party's "rank and file" to rise up in "rebellion." This history of the Party from revisionist eyes is characterized by cheap appeals to emotionalism and by its almost astounding lack of substance (except for the careerism and general rightism dripping down the pages). It is reprinted as part of the Appendix on page 393.

Once these splitters pulled what they could, the final phase of their opportunism took shape. Their first papers had called Teng and the Four "opposite poles of the same stupidity," called out Teng for "revisionist errors," and warned against taking *Peking Review* too seriously since the Right had a lot of influence.

Today these pretenses are gone. They have even changed their original papers to try to keep up with their line as it careens from bad to worse. The documents are reprinted here exactly as the Jarvis/Bergman clique originally circulated them at the time they split from the Party. Their latest version of their line—which they opportunistically call, "Red Papers 8"*—criticizes their "earlier antagonistic characterizations of Teng Hsiao-ping, in effect negating the fact that he is a leading figure within the collective leadership of the Chinese Communist Party which is giving correct leadership to the continuing revolution there."

We should thank our Mensheviks. In this one sentence they have given us more in the way of self-exposure of their pragmatism and opportunism than ten pages of our documents could ever hope to reveal. One of the points made in these documents is that Jarvis/Bergman's line is straight pragmatism: Hua & Co. won; the

***Red Papers* 1-7 were theoretical publications of the Revolutionary Union, which played the key role in the formation of the RCP,USA.

"Gang of Four" lost; therefore Hua & Co. are right and we should support them. But this unsolicited Menshevik confession is really too much: Principle be damned! Teng's got the power!

It is greatly due to the tremendous contributions by Mao and the revolutionary left in China that the RCP,USA was able to weather this onslaught by revisionists in our own ranks. The Jarvis/Bergman clique did not fare well in their plans for a "rank and file" rebellion to reverse the decision of the CC. Over 2/3 of the membership held firm behind a revolutionary line as their "Revolutionary Workers Headquarters," as they now call themselves, stumbles down the well worn revisionist road.

In 1978, a Congress of Victory and Unity, the Second Congress of the RCP, USA, was held. The Mensheviks and their line were thoroughly repudiated there, Jarvis and Bergman were expelled and greater unity and clarity was achieved around the proletarian stand on the international situation and our tasks in this country.

Adopted at the Congress were the response to the Jarvis/Bergman clique's defense of China's revisionists, reprinted in this volume on page 265 and "Rectification Is Fine; The Mensheviks' Answer Is Terrible" (see appendix), a response to their paper on rectification. Amendments passed by the Congress to these papers are so noted in footnotes in this edition. (The papers—together with the Mensheviks' attacks—were originally circulated to the membership shortly after the split.)

On the Jarvis-Bergman Clique

The revisionism in the Chinese Party brought to a head but did not create the revisionism of Jarvis and Bergman. What then was the source of their revisionism? Both M. Jarvis and L. Bergman were trained for long years in the old Communist Party USA. Bergman left in the mid-fifties; Jarvis joined in the early '60s and remained a rising star of the CPUSA until sometime in 1969. While both became part of the RCP, neither thoroughly repudiated the revisionist, bourgeois political line and world outlook of the old CPUSA.

Specifically, each retained the pragmatic philosophy and method that permeated the old CP even in its better days. Pragmatism denies the existence of objective laws operating beneath the appearance of events and, of course, denies the possibility of mastering those laws. With such an orientation, immediate experience becomes unmoored from the historical materialist framework necessary to evaluate it and can only be evaluated on immediate, quantitative and inevitably bourgeois terms.

While those claiming to be Marxist-Leninists today cannot openly deny historical materialism and embrace pragmatism, they can objectively do so in any number of ways. For example, members of the Jarvis/Bergman clique were forever opposing efforts to master Marxist theory. They attacked the self study of political economy in the Party begun in 1976 as requiring "genius"and would shake their heads in wondering disapproval at any comrade or party unit that actually "found the time" to study. Lenin's classic work "*What is to Be Done?*" was dismissed as irrelevant, or worse, by members of this clique. Instead, old Comintern documents were substituted and uncritically promoted as recipes for this or that area of work.

In the working class struggle, the Mensheviks dubbed the economic struggle as "potentially revolutionary." They opposed the Party's 1976 campaign to expose the entire trap of bourgeois elections as being too abstract for workers to relate to. They preferred to confine their exposures to what they called "*Carter's* Unemployment Offensive" and *Carter's* policies generally, carrying on with a long standing revisionist line that reduces the Party to a loyal if sometimes strident opposition to the bourgeoisie.

In work among other strata they tried to focus exclusively on cutbacks. When this line was defeated, they pushed bourgeois liberal mush; a recent glaring example is their main chant at the Philadelphia African Liberation Day rally they led—"Hey Rizzo, Have You Heard, Philly Ain't Johannesburg." What an echo of the CP's demand in its 1940's drive to organize Ford Motor Company, "Bring Dearborn back into the United States"!

In sum, mired in the revisionism of the CPUSA, they adopted themselves totally to the conditions of a temporary and partial lull in the mass movement during the mid '70s. Their recent motion is now 100% unvarnished right wing muck and shows where these Mensheviks intended to steer the RCP.

Why, it might be asked, did the split in the RCP,USA occur principally over China's internal nature, rather than its international line which has been the focus of struggle in parties in many other countries?

Certainly China's international line today is thoroughly reactionary. Hua Kuo-feng, Teng Hsiao-ping, et. al., are pushing a line which puts China at the center of the universe and advocates that China and revolutionaries worldwide ally with and rely on imperialist powers, including the United States. It is a line that "forgets" the difference between oppressed nations and imperialist countries and which seeks to outlaw revolution. They have dubbed this line the great, strategic "Theory of the Three Worlds" and have had the nerve to try to pawn it off as Mao Tsetung's theory. This is a lie.

While Mao might perhaps have used the term "three worlds" in a way to describe certain secondary conflicts in the world, and while Mao was not opposed to revolutionaries making use of contradictions in the camp of the enemy, Mao knew the difference between revolution and reaction, between Marxism and imperialism, and he consistently gave support to revolution.

It is not that the ex-RCP opportunists in any way disagreed with the revisionist international strategy of the Three Worlds. In fact they fought to insert important aspects of it into the Party *Programme,* only to be defeated at the Founding Congress. In addition the RCP and the RU before it had consistently exposed the social-chauvinism of the October League (now the CPML) in the Party press and especially through international conferences in 1976 called expressly to sharpen up line struggle on these questions.

Pragmatists that these Mensheviks were, the international line just wasn't that important to them because war wasn't about to break out tomorrow. Being in one of the two superpowers was the material basis that let these opportunists ignore the ramifications of a revolutionary line on the international situation in the short run. (While in the lesser imperialist and underdeveloped countries the impact of superpower contention for domination is more directly felt.)

But beyond that, the cardinal question before the international working class movement is the overall line of the current rulers in China and which class it represents. The international position of the current rulers is an important aspect of their overall revisionist line, but the pivotal event to the international proletariat was not Teng Hsiao-ping's reactionary "Three Worlds" speech at the United Nations in 1974, but the coup that he helped headquarter in 1976.

On the Documents

As stated earlier, these documents were originally internal ones growing out of a split. While they set the line of the Party and created conditions to deepen that line, they are *not* intended to be a conclusive summation of the revisionist takeover in China. In that light, several points need to be made.

First, it should be remarked that the RCP papers stand up extremely well. Many points that the papers could only infer at that time have now been confirmed as the revisionist Chinese leadership has proceeded at breakneck speed in attacking Marxism-Leninism, Mao Tsetung Thought and restoring capitalism. Developments in China since these documents were written—including the destruction of the revolutionary committees in the factories, schools and other basic units, the qualitative leap in the promotion of the Three Worlds theory, the rehabilitation of bourgeois figures to full political life (including 100,000 who had been known as counter-revolutionaries), the continued executions of followers of Mao, and the shameless glorification of Tito and Yugoslavia as socialist coupled with big power chauvinism toward Albania have borne out that indeed revisionists have seized power in China. All this has taken place at a pace even faster than anticipated and today China should be characterized as a revisionist country where capitalism is being restored.

Second, if anything the RCP papers do not give the Four *enough* credit. What Marx said about the communards applies well to the Four:

> "What elasticity, what historical initiative, what a capacity for sacrifice there is in these Parisians!...the present uprising in Paris—even if it should be crushed by the wolves, swine and vile dogs of the old society—is the most glorious deed of our party since the June insurrection in Paris. Just compare these Parisians, storming heaven, with those slaves to heaven of the German-Prussian Holy Roman Empire, with its posthumous masquerades reeking of the barracks, the church, the clod-hopping Junkers and above all, of philistinism..." ("Marx to Ludwig Kugelmann," *Selected Letters*, FLP pp. 36-37)

The Four's contributions in uniting the masses to carry out Mao's line are contributions that the international proletariat will cherish and build on for the rest of its historic struggle.

Third, while this introduction has drawn some parallels between the revisionist takeover of the USSR and that of China, one very important difference must be emphasized. As was pointed to in the CC Report, today, because of the contributions of Mao and other revolutionary leaders, revolutionaries are much better able to analyze what happened in China. Many are not compounding the setback by sinking into revisionism themselves.

Fourth, since the Central Committee Report was written more

evidence of resistance in China has come to light. This includes months of armed struggle in several provinces, resistance on the basic levels to Teng and Hua's country-wide speedup, and the apparent establishment of a clandestine press. This too is a part of Mao's legacy and support for it is a task of revolutionaries everywhere.

The struggle in China is not a source of demoralization but a bitter lesson that must arm all with a deeper understanding of the historic mission of the proletariat. In this light it is fitting to end this introduction with the conclusion of a speech given by Comrade Avakian at a memorial meeting for Mao Tsetung in September, 1976, a month before the counter-revolutionary coup:

> "Yes, there can be temporary setbacks. Until these differences—between mental and manual work, between the more backward countryside and the more developed cities, between the workers in the cities and the working people in the countryside, until these differences and wage differentials—until those things are eliminated; until the political consciousness, knowledge and skill of people in society are raised to a whole new level, and knowledge and skills cannot be monopolized by individuals or small groups of people; until we get society to the point where goods can be produced quickly in great abundance and only a small amount of time has to be spent in producing the basic things that people need to live and providing for further development, and a great part of the time can be spent in education and culture and raising the political consciousness and the grasp of the masses of people of the science that can show them how to change the world; until all that has been accomplished, yes, the possibility of a new class of exploiters arising and turning things back does exist. But it is not inevitable.
>
> "What is inevitable is that people will continue to fight back against their oppression and exploitation, that this system of capitalism is not here to stay, or eternal, that it only developed at a certain stage, . . . and that the very development of capitalism . . . [has] drawn together as capitalism's gravedigger a mighty army from those who were scattered and separated . . .
>
> "So when they raise the question, who will be Mao Tsetung's successors, the working class is ready with its answer: *We* will be Mao Tsetung's successors, in our millions and hundreds of millions, and we will continue the cause for which he fought and in which he led us and to which he devoted his entire life, until that great goal of eliminating exploitation and oppression and achieving communism has finally been achieved."

September, 1978

Revisionists Are Revisionists And Must Not Be Supported, Revolutionaries Are Revolutionaries and Must Be Supported

Report on China by Bob Avakian, Chairman of the Central Committee of the Revolutionary Communist Party, USA, Adopted by the 3rd Plenary of the 1st Central Committee of the RCP, USA (1977), Affirmed and Adopted by the 2nd Congress of the RCP, USA (1978)

Introduction

The question of the developments in China since the death of Mao Tsetung and what direction China is taking, what class the present leadership as opposed to the so-called "Gang of Four" (or rather the Four) represent—this is the most important question of line now confronting the international communist movement, including our Party. There is no way we can, or should want, to ignore this question or fail to make a scientific analysis of it. Nor is there any lack of objective possibility of making a basic analysis of this question.

Further, as the Bulletin, Vol. 2, No. 3 stressed, ". . . how our Party deals with the situation in China will have a very profound effect on the entire development of our Party. The struggle in China is a life and death question for the proletariat and has tremendous implications for the working class and its Party in every country. And the attitude and approach every Party takes in understanding and evaluating the events in China will have much to do with determining whether or not that Party remains a Marxist-Leninist Party or degenerates into one kind of opportunism or another." This is certainly correct and very important.

Basic Assessment, Basic Approach

It has been my opinion, since it became clear that in fact the Four had been arrested by Hua Kuo-feng and Co., that this represented a right-wing coup and a serious blow against the proletariat in China and its revolutionary leadership. To sum up the struggle there and its culmination in a certain stage with the arrest of the Four, one phrase can put it simply—"The wrong side won."

This initial opinion of mine was not based on intuition but on the fact that the articles put out by and under the direction of the Four, as well as what I knew about the Cultural Revolution and the overall role of the Four up to the time of their arrest, indicated clearly that they were revolutionary leaders of the proletariat carrying out and fighting for Mao's line with whatever mistakes they may have made, and that in the midst of a major and (then) continuing struggle against the right, the Four were put down by Hua Kuo-feng—a man whose speech to the 1975 Tachai Conference, a major statement of position, was in my estimation a deviation from and opposed to Mao's line and identified Hua in my opinion with those whipping up the right deviationist wind.

Of course, given the momentous nature of the developments in China and the necessity of arming our whole Party with, and uniting it around, a correct line on this most decisive question, it was not only correct but especially necessary to adopt a serious, scientific attitude of studying further events after the arrest of the Four, and in particular to identify and concentrate on the main questions of line, in order to arrive at a more definite and deep-founded understanding. But I believe that these developments and such an approach have long since confirmed the fact that the present leaders are implementing a revisionist line and that the Four's struggle against them was in the main and decisively a righteous struggle for a correct line to continue China on the socialist road toward communism. And the more that comes out about the situation the more, in my opinion, it confirms this.

This is because of the truth pointed out in the article, "Capitalist-Roaders Are the Bourgeoisie Inside the Party" (*Peking Review,* No. 25, 1976):

> "Some people are of the opinion that it is not easy to discern the capitalist roaders inside the Party because they not only have the title of 'Communist Party members' but are leading persons and some of them have very high posts. It should be admitted that since the capitalist-roaders, who are the bourgeoisie inside the Party, are in power in the Party and have a variety of political 'protective colors' and since they invariably resort to all sorts of wiles and intrigues to deliberately put up a false front, it is therefore much more difficult for us to detect them. But dialectical materialism tells us that all objective things can be known step by step in the course of practice; agnosticism is both idealist and metaphysical. No matter how crafty the capitalist-roaders in the Party are in disguising themselves, they are bound to expose their true colors since they oppose Chairman Mao's revolutionary line and pursue a revisionist line. So long as we really have a good grasp of Marxism-Leninism-Mao Tsetung Thought—the telescope and microscope in political affairs—we will be able to distinguish between right and wrong on cardinal issues from the viewpoint of political line and recognize the reactionary bourgeois essence of the capitalist-roaders." (pp. 10, 24)

Along with this, we should keep in mind what Mao himself wrote to Chiang Ching in 1966, speaking of the danger of a right-wing coup in China and the fact that if this should happen the genuine left could and should rise up and overthrow the right—the bourgeoisie. Specifically, Mao noted (prophetically) that after he died, if the right should come to power, then "The right in power could utilize my words to become mighty for a while. But then the left will be able to utilize others of my words and organize itself to overthrow the right."

This has direct relevance for the situation today. Certain statements attributed to Mao, which are at the least torn out of the overall context in which they were made and blown all out of proportion, are used by the right in power to attack the left they have overthrown. And meanwhile, the main thrust of Mao's words—his line as he continually developed and deepened it as well as the specific guidance he gave to the struggle in China during the last few years of his life—are either omitted or chopped up and distorted by the right in power.

It is definitely true that the right in power has the necessity to use some of Mao's words to cover up its revisionist line. This is because, as those in power put it, the "Gang of Four" (they really mean the "Gang of Five," including Mao) have "spread a great deal of confusion" (they really mean "have spread a great deal of

Marxism-Leninism, Mao Tsetung Thought"), so it is necessary to spread a lot of their own confusion in fact in order to carry out their revisionist aims. And in their use of Mao to oppose Mao two things stand out: one, overwhelmingly the things they cite from Mao are taken from his speeches and writings from before the Cultural Revolution, and in the main even before the Great Leap Forward (1958), and even those are distorted and misused; and two, those which are from the more recent period are more blatantly distorted ("tampered with" is the current phrase, I believe).

Therefore it is especially important for us to have a discerning eye and concentrate exactly on the "cardinal issues," the main questions of line, and to view things in terms of their actual development and how the opposing sides line up on these matters. And it is particularly important to determine how Mao's words are being used—i.e., whether they are being used in the service of creating public opinion for and implementing a revisionist or revolutionary line.

But how can Mao's words be used by the bourgeoisie in the Party for its purposes? The answer is, as Lenin pointed out, "Opportunism can be expressed in terms of *any* doctrine *you like, including Marxism.*" (See *Collected Works*, Vol. 18, p. 363, emphasis Lenin's.) And unfortunately there has been a tendency on all levels of our Party to fall into accepting the use made of Mao's words and Marxism generally in the service of opportunism and to forget, ignore or even oppose the use made of Mao's words and Marxism generally in the service of socialist revolution.

This is important because in order to sort out right from wrong and revolution from counter-revolution it is necessary to go beyond the appearance of things to their essence and to look beyond the mere pronouncement of words or phrases to see what the whole thrust of a statement of position is. For example, the OL (or CP-ML) in its articles on the international situation rarely fails to say that the U.S. working class should overthrow the bourgeoisie in this country; they usually talk about the "special responsibility" of the U.S. working class to oppose our own ruling class and they even make noises about turning an imperialist war into a civil war in this country. On that account we do not say, "Well, they talk about these things, therefore how can we say there is anything wrong with their line on the international situation?" No, we go on to analyze the overall position they put forward and expose the fact that its essence and whole thrust is in direct contradiction to proletarian internationalism and to the correct line of especially opposing our own imperialists and making all necessary preparations to actually turn an imperialist war into a civil war in this country.

Similarly, it is unthinkable that, at this point at least, the current rulers of China can overtly fail to talk about "class struggle as the key link," and the principal contradiction as being between the proletariat and the bourgeoisie in China, etc. They certainly cannot call for an end to the dictatorship of the proletariat, as Khrushchev was able to do 20 years ago. But the fact that they find themselves forced to talk about these things should not keep us from examining and analyzing the essence and thrust of the line they put forward to see if it actually conforms to Mao's revolutionary line and Marxism-Leninism. If we apply the telescope and microscope of Marxism-Leninism, Mao Tsetung Thought to the line put forward by the current rulers and to that of the Four and subject each to Marxist critical analysis, it becomes clear that the line of the Four is Mao's line while that of the current rulers is in fact directly opposed to it.

One other important point on this: the subject of China and particularly the possibility that it is going revisionist is bound to generate a great deal of emotion. This happens in every struggle over major events and questions of line in the revolutionary movement. For example, in the struggle against the Franklin opportunists, in order to cover up the central questions of line, they played up the sentiment that if you supported the Black Panther Party and the Black people's struggle, you had to side with them. Similarly, during the struggle against the Bundists they attacked the RU for trying to "keep the niggers in their place," with the same purpose. And now there are people—the OL and others—who attempt to get over with the same kind of thing, raising "support for China" as some kind of religious duty divorced from and above class and Marxist analysis. As pointed out in the polemics against the Franklins (see *Red Papers 4)*, especially at times like this, in considering such literally soul-stirring questions, it is all the more important to put science above emotion and to be "ruthlessly scientific," or else there is no way to arrive at correct conclusions.

This takes us back to the all-important truth that the decisive thing is ideological and political line. And in order to come to and unite around a correct position on the events in China it is necessary to concentrate on the major questions of line, which the bulk of this paper will address itself to. Of course to answer all the crap that has come out of China in the last year and more, which has found certain echoes in our Party, would require a long book. But fortunately, that is not necessary here. Instead I will present a summation of my position in opposition to what I see as the essence of the incorrect line on the main points and leave the rest for further study and discussion within the Party according to the guidelines set by the Central Committee, which will make it possible to go into the main questions much more deeply and thoroughly.

The remainder of this paper will contain the following major sections: The Line of the Current Rulers and the Four's Line in Opposition to It; Refutation of Certain Erroneous Arguments in Defense of the *Status Quo* and Against the Four; Why Did the Revisionists Triumph in This Battle and What Lessons Should We Draw?; What Do We Do Based on a Correct Understanding of What Has Happened? and The Problem of Bad Tendencies in Our Party Connected with the Line Questions in the Struggle in China.

I. The Line of the Current Rulers and the Four's Line in Opposition to It

To put it simply and in the terms of the struggle in China itself, the present rulers have reversed or are reversing the correct verdicts of the class struggle in China, specifically but not only the verdicts and achievements of the Great Proletarian Cultural Revolution. And in so doing they are taking the capitalist road. This is clear on any number of questions of line and policy as well as in the purging of many revolutionary forces on various levels of the Party and the restoration of numerous leading people who were justly and correctly cast down as die-hard rightists and capitalist-roaders, not only Teng Hsiao-ping himself but also Chou Yang, Lo Jui-ching and many others, including associates of Peng Teh-huai who went down in 1959, whom Mao fought to knock down—and keep down once they had clearly shown that they were hell-bent on carrying out a revisionist line.

To see how far and how fast the current rulers have departed from Mao's line, comrades should go back and read the article in the October 15, 1976 *Revolution* on China and the statement by the Chinese Party Central Committee right after Mao died, which laid out the "behests" of Mao's that the Party and people were pledged to carry out, including among other things, a denunciation of the "counter-revolutionary revisionist line of Liu Shao-chi, Lin Piao and Teng Hsiao-ping," (*Peking Review,* No. 38, 1976, p. 7) and the statement that:

> "We must carry on the cause left behind by Chairman

> Mao and consolidate the great unity of the people of all nationalities under the leadership of the working class and based on the worker-peasant alliance, deepen the criticism of Teng Hsiao-ping, continue the struggle to repulse the Right deviationist attempt at reversing correct verdicts, consolidate and develop the victories of the Great Proletarian Cultural Revolution, enthusiastically support the socialist new things, restrict bourgeois right and further consolidate the dictatorship of the proletariat in our country." (p. 10)

Hua and Co. have carried out none of these—in fact they have done just the opposite.

It is also significant to note that the current rulers are even reversing the verdict on Yugoslavia. The question of whether Yugoslavia is a capitalist (revisionist) country was one of the first major subjects of polemics by the Chinese Party against the Soviets, as far back as 1963. Since then, in recent years, the Chinese have made efforts to establish ties with Yugoslavia as part of the general policy of uniting with forces opposed to Soviet hegemonism. But recently Hua & Co. went a step further, essentially re-establishing Party to Party relations with the Yugoslav revisionists. (See *PR*, Nos. 42, p. 30 and 49, p. 3) This goes along with reports in the *New York Times* and elsewhere that the Chinese are studying the Yugoslav system of management, which is a model for "motivating" workers to produce under capitalist conditions in a fairly backward economy—a model which the revisionist rulers of China no doubt find worthy of study!

The "Three Poisonous Weeds" that were sharply criticized, while Mao was alive and giving at least basic, general guidance to the struggle against the right deviationist wind, are now upheld as "fragrant flowers." They are still poisonous weeds.

And, of course, the whole struggle against the right deviationist wind has not been just stopped but reversed—the right deviationist wind is now the good wind to those in power—which makes perfect sense since they were the ones responsible for whipping it up in the first place. But as the saying goes, a rose by any other name still smells the same, and this wind still smells like a fart to the proletariat and Marxist revolutionaries.

Mao's teachings on the bourgeoisie in the Party and the danger of capitalist restoration are perverted so that they lose their materialist and dialectical basis and life and death character. And in this way, under the conditions of today, the theory of "dying out of class struggle" is promoted.

Mao's line of "grasp revolution, promote production," is replaced with the "theory of the productive forces"—and this will be true no matter how many times the current rulers whine that any time they talked about promoting production they were stuck with this label, because all their talk, their line, about promoting production is in fact the theory of productive forces. The reason these revisionists make loud noises about such charges is because they are stuck pigs, and stuck pigs squeal.

As an article put out under the direction of the Four—and attacked by the current rulers—points out, "However, many living facts show that the Great Proletarian Cultural Revolution is a strong motive force in the development of China's productive forces. Mass criticism of the revisionist line and the theory of the productive forces has promoted substantial development of socialist production and has produced solid fruits. Is it right for the masses of people to label Liu Shao-chi and Lin Piao and their like as 'revisionists' and 'promoters of the theory of the productive forces'? Absolutely right! Lenin said it well: 'The negation of revisionism is aimed at covering up one's own revisionism.' The negation of the criticism of the revisionist theory of the productive forces by that unrepentant capitalist roader in the Party and by his 'General Program' is aimed at inheriting the mantle of Liu Shao-chi and Lin Piao, at continuing to push the counter-revolutionary revisionist line and theory of productive forces." (from an article by Cheng Yueh in *Study and Criticism,* published in Shanghai, April 1, 1976.)

Capitalist-Roaders Are the Bourgeoisie in the Party

But let's back up a second and look at a few particulars of the current rulers' line and the Four's struggle against it. A most important question at issue is the nature, and target, of the class struggle under socialism. Much was already pointed out in the last bulletin (Vol. 2, No. 4) on the question of the bourgeoisie in the Party, but since that bulletin itself represented a compromise and was not supposed to deal with the overall line of Hua and Co., some more remarks should be made here.

Apparently, some confusion has arisen around the question of whether class contradictions in socialist society are concentrated in the Party as opposed to merely reflected and also around the concept of "agents" of the bourgeoisie in the Party—i.e., whether the capitalist-roaders in the Party are the commanders or tools of the bourgeois elements outside the Party. To get at this question more deeply, let's look at an article by Hua Kuo-feng printed in

PR, No. 19, 1977—an article which, by the way, gives no attention to the "theory of the productive forces," while claiming to uphold Mao's line on continuing the revolution under the dictatorship of the proletariat.

Here Hua does say that "the two-line struggle in the Party remains a reflection, and a concentrated reflection at that, of the class struggle in society" and he does talk about "wavering elements inside the Party [who] have been hit by the material and spiritual sugar-coated bullets of the bourgeoisie and have degenerated into agents of the bourgeoisie." (p. 22—it should be noted in passing that in his article Hua basically dismisses the question of bourgeois democrats turning into capitalist-roaders as false "labelling" by the "gang of four"—and I will have more to say about other aspects of this article of Hua's a little later.)

But how does Hua treat this question of "concentrated reflection"? He still presents the bourgeoisie outside the Party as the commander and bourgeois agents inside as the tools. And he does not spell out what the "material" "sugar-coated bullets" of the bourgeoisie are. In other words he does not link the bourgeoisie in the Party directly to the existence of *capitalist productive relations* in socialist society. This is what the Four—and Mao—consistently did, pointing out that where a revisionist line leads and leadership is not in the hands of Marxists and the masses, bourgeois relations of production will actually exist, even in the collective form. The capitalist-roaders in the Party as the representatives of these capitalist relations—this is what the Four and Mao gave emphasis to and what gives the question of the bourgeoisie in the Party its material basis and shows how the capitalist-roaders can turn socialist society into its opposite.

This question of the persistence of capitalist productive relations in socialist society, and the revisionists in the Party as representatives of them, was also given great emphasis in both *Red Papers 7* and the article in *The Communist* exposing Nicolaus (Vol. 1, No. 1). It is what makes clear the very real danger that the capitalist-roaders pose, for if they had no such material and social base for restoring capitalism, then indeed they would pose a minor problem, as Hua wants to say. It is the persistence and constant re-emergence of these relations that explains why it would be "quite easy" for people like Lin Piao to "rig up the capitalist system" if they come to power, something Hua does not like to talk about.

In other words, as Mao emphasized for several years before his death, in many ways the new socialist society is not much different than the old society, especially as regards inequality among the people, the mental/manual contradiction, worker-peasant differences, differences in rank and pay, etc. This provides the basis for capitalist relations and bourgeois elements representing them to constantly emerge. With a revisionist group usurping power and a revisionist line in the leading position, tremendous social forces can be easily unleashed for capitalist restoration.

And, especially at this point in the development of Chinese society, who are most of the people who are in a position to turn their relations with those under their leadership into bourgeois relations?—overwhelmingly it is Party members. As the Bulletin pointed out, it is overwhelmingly Party members who are managers, directors, heads of farms, ministries, institutions, etc. As explained in *RP7* people of this type at the lower levels form a big part of the social base for capitalist restoration while revisionists at the top are the ones strategically placed to unleash this social base around a revisionist line for capitalist restoration. Of course, none of this is "automatic"; it exactly depends on what line leads, but given a revisionist takeover at the top and a revisionist line in command, many forces—strategically placed Party members as well as old and new bourgeois elements outside the Party—can and will be mobilized for capitalist restoration. This is the grave danger Mao warned of and which the Four, taking up his call, mobilized people to combat. (To get a deeper grasp of this,comrades should study over *RP 7*, especially pp. 13 and 21 and the article criticizing Nicolaus in *The Communist.)*

It is all this that is at the heart of the matter and which gives meaning to the question of "concentrated" and to the capitalist-roaders in the Party as the commanders of the social forces in society that can be mobilized for capitalist restoration.

Hua, in opposition to this, puts forward a line that evades the essence of these vital questions. He does this because to make a correct analysis would require him to say, as the Four did, that the capitalist-roaders "are the representatives of the capitalist relations of production which have been vanquished but have not yet been eliminated . . . As individuals, they may not necessarily own capital, run factories and operate banks like the former capitalists, but their political line which energetically upholds the capitalist relations of production reflects in a concentrated way the economic interests and political aspirations of the bourgeoisie." And ". . . *the power to allocate and manage means of production and the power to distribute products are expressed in a concentrated way as the power of political leadership.*" (from an article by Chuang Lan in

Study and Criticism, June 14, 1976, emphasis added) This is exactly why, in opposition to what Hua and Co. insist, the new ruling bourgeoisie, or the main force of it, does indeed emanate from the Communist Party, especially its top levels.

From what has been said it should be clear that the question of analysis of classes in socialist society, and particularly the analysis of the bourgeoisie, is much more complicated than under capitalism. In capitalist society if someone occupies a certain material position—for example president of a corporation, or head of the finance department of the state—it is easy to identify such a person as part of the bourgeoisie. But in socialist society the matter turns not only and not even mainly on social position, but on line—that is, the head of a ministry or manager of a big plant is certainly not part of the bourgeoisie by mere virtue of occupying such a position, but becomes part of the bourgeoisie only if and when he implements a revisionist line, and more than that, persists in taking the capitalist road. Even with those who do take the capitalist road, it is correct and necessary to struggle to win them back to the socialist road. But it is also true that while many can be won over at any given time there will also be some who cannot, and these constitute the bourgeois elements, or bourgeois class, that must be overthrown by the masses. And in general the fact that economic units—and the economy as a whole—can be turned from socialist to capitalist is a result of the fact that the means of production under socialism are still not completely the common property of all of society and that the masses of people still have not yet completely become masters of the economy and society as a whole. These contradictions will exist all the way throughout the long socialist period of transition to communism and will provide the material basis for capitalist restoration and point to the grave danger that revisionism poses, especially as it emerges at the top of the Party, which as Mao often stressed, is "quite likely" for all the reasons spoken to in this paper and the last Bulletin.

Hua basically avoids this whole thrust of Mao's on this question and the emphasis the Four put on the fact that the power of leadership is in fact concentrated power over allocation and management of means of production and distribution, because Hua is a representative of those who want to make use of this power to give free rein to capitalist productive relations—all in the name of "promoting production" and "modernization" and "building a powerful socialist country" of course (more on this later). The article quoted just above from Shanghai makes a very important point in citing how Engels in *Anti-Duhring* analyzed the way in which classes and the state first arose. In primitive society, the author notes, "the work of safeguarding public interests, 'though it was under supervision by all of society, could not but be carried out by individual members.' (*Anti-Duhring*)" Further, the author notes, Engels pointed out that " 'With the appearance of disparities in distribution, class differences also appear. Society is divided into the privileged and under-privileged, the exploiter and the exploited, the ruler and the ruled.' (*Anti-Duhring*)" What is being stressed here is, as Engels also stated in *Anti-Duhring*, "Distribution, however, is not merely a passive result of production and exchange; it has an equally important reaction on both of these." (See the chapter "Subject Matter and Method.")

And the author (Chuang Lan) goes on to make the following very correct and important point: "Because these 'individual members' took advantage of the opportunity accorded by their management of public property and exploited their power to distribute articles of consumption and products to make private gains and own more surplus product than others, sprouts of private ownership appeared on the land under the clan system of public ownership and, as a result, those who were originally 'servants' of society became rulers enjoying all sorts of privileges. Although the birth of capitalist roaders is much more complicated, there are also similarities. When later Engels summed up the historical experience of the Paris Commune, he again stated that after the establishment of the dictatorship of the proletariat, it was necessary to 'prevent the state and state organs from turning from servants of society into its masters' and 'pursuing their own special interests.' ('Engels' Introduction to the 1891 edition of the *Civil War in France*')"

The author of this *Study and Criticism* article points out that Mao further developed Marxist theory and practice on this question and that these teachings of the revolutionary leaders of the proletariat "hit the Party capitalist roaders where it hurts most." He notes that in socialist society, "To extend bourgeois rights in distribution actually smacks of allowing a section of people to possess the labor of another section of people without compensations, which means extending class differences . . . The historical lesson of capitalist restoration in the Soviet Union fully shows how important it is for a socialist state, while consolidating the proletarian dictatorship and public ownership of the means of production, to strive to restrict bourgeois rights in the field of distribution in order to prevent the Party and state from changing color."

What is wrong with this line? To the proletariat and its revolutionary leadership, absolutely nothing—it is fine indeed. But to Hua Kuo-feng and his cohorts it is deadly; or to borrow from Lenin, in regard to such an analysis, Hua and Co. "are like petty thieves who stay away from the place where they have stolen." (See *Imperialism, the Highest Stage of Capitalism.*)

This is why, in his report to the 11th Congress, Hua presents the perverted line that the Four "confounded the differences in distribution between the leading cadres of the Party, the government and the army on the one hand and the broad masses on the other with class exploitation." (See *PR* No. 35, 1977, pp. 35-36.) With this broad statement Hua hopes to write off the real question raised by the Four—and really by Mao, with his whole emphasis on bourgeois right, differences in pay and rank, etc. as important material bases for capitalist restoration. Isn't it obvious that the Four's analysis is right in line with Mao's while Hua's is a repudiation of it?

This is clearly shown in an article by the current rulers in the August, 1977 issue of *Red Flag,* the theoretical journal of the Chinese Party CC, where Mao's line on bourgeois right is not only tampered with but trampled on. The article starts by juggling around a quote from Mao of several years ago, where he stressed that, except for the change in the ownership system, China was not much different than the old society. This article quotes Mao out of context and out of order and even leaves out the statement by Mao that before liberation China "was much the same as a capitalist country," all for the purpose of downplaying the danger of capitalist restoration and the danger posed by expanding rather than restricting bourgeois right. Then this article tells us that in speaking of bourgeois rights under socialism Mao's "brilliant idea" was that they can only be restricted! The whole purpose of this article is essentially to say, not much can be done about bourgeois right under socialism so don't worry about it (this is a consistent line of Hua & Co. which will be examined again later, in analyzing Hua's speech at the 1975 Tachai Conference in particular).

This is why Hua & Co. raise such a stink about the fact that the Four—and Chang Chun-chiao in particular—had the audacity to want to make an analysis of the question of classes in socialist society. Several times in the last year the *Peking Review* has carried blasts at Chang Chun-chiao for saying that even after reading Mao's "Analysis of Classes in Chinese Society" (written in 1926!) and the rest of Mao's four volumes he was "still not clear" on the question of class relations in socialist society and therefore more study and investigation of this should be done. What is wrong with that? Nothing, unless such study and investigation will expose you as the bourgeoisie in the socialist period, as is the case with Hua and the others now ruling China.

Mao Tsetung would be the last one to say that his 1926 analysis of classes in a semi-feudal, semi-colonial China was a sufficient guide to understanding class relations in China today—how could it be!—or that there was no need to study and investigate this question. In fact, Mao stressed just the opposite, saying in 1961, for example, "Now that we have entered the socialist period, a series of new problems has emerged. If we do not produce new writings and form new theories to conform with new needs, it also will not do." (From "Reading Notes on the Soviet Union's 'Political Economics' " printed in a U.S. government collection of Mao's post-1949 writings, speeches and talks.) And Mao would certainly be the last one to suggest that only he should make such analysis and develop such "new theories!" In reality Chang Chun-chiao (and the Four in general) are being attacked by Hua & Co. for nothing other than doing exactly what Marxists should do—and again, this is because to make a Marxist analysis can only expose Hua and his cronies. Comrades should seriously ask themselves—doesn't the material produced by the Four and their followers enrich our understanding of important questions, especially on the nature of classes and class struggle in socialist society? Of course Mao set the basic line, but they did their part in elaborating it as well.

Instead of a Marxist analysis of the question of classes in socialist society and the bourgeoisie in the socialist period in particular, what we get from Hua and Co. is an attempt to write off the danger of capitalist restoration, of capitalist-roaders being the bourgeoisie in the Party and in a strategic position to restore capitalism. What we get is lots of insistence that after all the capitalist-roaders are only a mere handful and are constantly being exposed and weeded out.

Comrades should think over their own discussions with workers and others about the question of socialism. Isn't one of the first and main questions they raise, "Yeah, but how do we know that you guys will be any different once you're in power?" How would they take it if we answered them by saying, "Don't worry about that, the people in power who turn out bad under socialism are only a mere handful and they are constantly being exposed and weeded out"? Wouldn't they tell us to get the hell away from them and come back when we were serious? Wouldn't they think we were trying to put something over on them and sucker them? And they would be right! But this is what we get from the present rulers.

And we get lots of statements such as the following: "In socialist society, the contradictions between the relations of production and the productive forces and between the superstructure and the economic base continue to find expression in class contradictions which consist of contradictions between ourselves and the enemy, although *most are contradictions among the people themselves.* This accordingly requires us to persist in taking class struggle as the key link and make a strict differentiation between the two types of contradictions which are different in nature." (*PR* No. 12, 1977, p. 12, emphasis added)

Here we have a good example of eclecticism—different contradictions are in fact mixed together and there is no distinguishing as to which is principal. This is a way of actually writing off class struggle as the key link and denying the principal contradiction while pretending agreement with it. It is, as Lenin said, "a perfect example of base renunciation of Marxism in practice, while hypocritically recognizing it in words," and as Lenin also noted in that same work (*The State and Revolution*), "Substituting eclecticism for dialectics is the most frequently seen and the most universal phenomenon in dealing with Marxism in the journals of the formal social-democratic parties at present."

In the quote from *PR* above it stresses that "most are contradictions among the people." The question, however, is not "most" but what is principal—what is the principal contradiction in socialist society? On this Mao was very clear—it is the contradiction between the proletariat and the bourgeoisie, which is an antagonistic contradiction as even this *PR* article admits. To talk about "most" is to try to confuse quantity with quality and direct people away from what is the main problem—the principal contradiction—which will remain the principal contradiction until communism is achieved, regardless of how "many" contradictions there are among the people.

To see how the principal contradiction is being subtly tampered with, compare the following two statements (characterizations, not actual quotes), the first which could serve as a summary of Mao's line and the second of the line of Hua & Co. as expressed in the *Peking Review* and elsewhere: 1) The basic contradictions in socialist society give rise to contradictions among the people on a vast scale but the main contradiction they give rise to is the antagonistic contradiction between the proletariat and the bourgeoisie; and 2) The basic contradictions in socialist society give rise to the antagonistic contradiction between the proletariat and the bourgeoisie but most contradictions they give rise to are among the people. Isn't there a world—or world outlook—of difference between these two statements, don't they represent two different class interests, even though on the surface they may seem to be somewhat similar? Aren't Hua & Co. perverting Mao's line on this most important question?

And the political purpose of this becomes even clearer if we pose the all-important question: how will the contradictions between the forces and relations of production and the base and superstructure principally be resolved? According to Hua & Co., as expressed in this article and many other places, by "adjusting that part of the relations of production in disharmony with the productive forces and that part of the superstructure in disharmony with the economic base, and uphold [ing] the principle of grasping revolution and promoting production." The article even sounds very serious about this, for it adds immediately, "On this issue, there must not be the slightest shilly-shallying or else we will lose our bearings." (*PR* No. 12, 1977, p. 12)

But actually those who put forward this line have already "shilly-shallied" into revisionism with their "adjusting" (and their "grasping revolution and promoting production" which really means smashing revolution in the name of promoting production, as I'll show later). Their line is opposed to Mao's correct line on this question. This is in large part because they treat the question of "adjusting" not as principally and essentially the question of class struggle against the bourgeoisie—antagonistic class struggle. In "Correct Handling of Contradictions Among the People," Mao does say that the contradictions between the forces and relations of production and the base and superstructure are "not antagonistic" in socialist society—but he means something very specific by this—that they can "be resolved one after another by the socialist system itself." In other words, to resolve these contradictions in socialist society it is not necessary for the *system itself* to be *overthrown* as in previous systems—though it is ultimately necessary for the system to make the final transition to communism, when there will still be such contradictions, but of a different nature, *not* in the nature of *class* distinctions.

And it should be remembered that at that time (1957) Mao was only beginning to develop his thinking on this question. As he developed it further he formulated the line that throughout the socialist transition period there are classes and class struggle and the danger of capitalist restoration, and that in order (as he said in "Correct Handling") to "resolve all such contradictions" as between forces/relations, base/superstructure, it is necessary to wage the class struggle against the bourgeoisie and *overthrow those portions of power* it will continually usurp until it is eliminated. This was exactly what the Cultural Revolution was for—as much as the present rulers may want to deny it (more on their attitude towards and roles in the Cultural Revolution later).

In short, resolving these contradictions requires not mere "adjustment" but antagonistic class struggle against the bourgeoisie which will at each step stubbornly resist further transformation of the relations of production and the superstructure. This is the line of Mao—and the Four—in direct opposition to Hua and the gang (or gangs) ruling China now.

While they occasionally feel the need to talk about the proletariat overthrowing the bourgeoisie, even in socialist society, it is most significant that the current rulers of China have written this out of the basic programme of the Constitution of the Chinese Communist Party. Comparing the paragraph in the 10th Congress Constitution dealing with the basic program with that in the 11th Congress we find the following striking difference: in the 10th it is stated that the Party's basic programme is "the complete overthrow of the bourgeoisie and all other exploiting classes, the establishment of the dictatorship of the proletariat in place of the dictatorship of the bourgeoisie and the triumph of socialism over capitalism." The corresponding part in the 11th Constitution, reflecting fundamental changes, says that the basic programme "for the entire historical period of socialism is to persist in continuing the revolution under the dictatorship of the proletariat, *eliminate* the bourgeoisie and all other exploiting classes *step by step* and bring about the triumph of socialism over capitalism." (see *PR* No. 36, 1977, p. 16, emphasis added)

Again, this at first may not seem like a significant change, or may even seem more in accordance with present conditions, since it may appear that the task of *overthrowing* the bourgeoisie has already been accomplished in China. But that is not in fact the case—it is a repudiation of Mao's line that, as he said to Mao Yuanhsin ("sworn follower" of the "gang of four") as early as 1964, "At present, the task of the revolution has not yet been completed; it has not been finally determined who, in the end, will overthrow whom. In the Soviet Union, is not Khrushchev in power, is not the bourgeoisie in power? We, too, have cases in which political power is in the grip of the bourgeoisie; there are production brigades, factories and *hsien* committees, as well as district and provincial committees, in which they have their people, there are deputy heads of public security departments who are their men. Who is leading the Ministry of Culture?" (See Stuart Schram's *Chairman Mao Talks to the People,* p. 243)

And Mao was very clear and emphatic that one Cultural Revolution could not solve this problem, that class struggle must consistently be waged against the bourgeoisie, that there would be a need for many Cultural Revolutions and that throughout the entire historical period of socialism who would win out, who would overthrow whom, could not be finally settled, until the bourgeoisie and all other exploiting classes were eliminated and communism finally achieved. Eliminating the bourgeoisie, Mao stressed, meant repeatedly *overthrowing* it, by mobilizing the masses to overthrow *from below* those portions of power the bourgeoisie repeatedly usurps.

It is this that the current rulers, despite any cover elsewhere, have thrown out with their changes in such a key document as the Constitution—specifically its "basic programme"—replacing it with the notion of simply eliminating the bourgeoisie and other exploiting classes step by step without overthrow from below. In other words, they present it as all a question of struggle against the bourgeoisie *from the top down,* which is completely consistent with their attempts to write off the real danger of the bourgeoisie in the Party and the fact that bourgeois headquarters will not only repeatedly emerge within the Party but will repeatedly usurp large portions of power, a situation that can only be dealt with by mobilizing the masses to seize back that power *from below.* This top down character of the present rulers' line runs throughout their whole presentation of what socialism is and how it must be built (more on that later).

Hua & Co. continually pose as big upholders of "non-antagonistic contradictions" among the people. This is for one purpose—to prevent the proletariat from waging class struggle against its enemy, the bourgeoisie, represented right now by Hua & Co. themselves. Meanwhile, they themselves are waging fierce class struggle against the proletariat, as shown by their arrest of the Four and their suppression and purging of anyone who opposes them—I am not complaining about arrests or purges in general and certainly not about suppression of any kind; dictatorship is dictatorship and must be carried out resolutely, but the question is always who is suppressing and dictating to whom? Comrades should study the new fascist Constitution adopted at the 11th Congress, and compare and contrast it with the 10th Party Congress Constitution, especially on the question of ideological struggle within the Party, to see just how "benevolent" the new rulers of China are in fact, how like Confucius theirs is the benevolence of the slave-master.

The key point with regard to this is the fact that in the tasks of the primary organizations of the Party, the Constitution is specifically changed from the 10th Party Congress to *take out* "...wage an active ideological struggle so as to keep Party life vigorous," which is replaced with the instruction to report the opinions and demands of the masses to higher Party organizations and to be concerned about the masses' political, economic and cultural life. (see *Peking Review* No. 36, 1977, page 22, Article 18, point 4 in particular) This is dialectically related to other changes in the Constitution, such as instituting "commissions for inspecting discipline" at various levels of the Party, re-instituting one-year probationary requirements for new members—something previously dropped from the Constitution as a result of the Cultural Revolution—and the direct tying of going against the tide to upholding the "three do's and don'ts," which really means that the last two are the basis for defining the first—that is, anyone who goes against the tide is splitting and conspiring and is therefore a revisionist.

Again, it is the taking out of ideological struggle as a requirement of basic units which most makes clear that what is being called for is absolute obedience to higher levels and unquestioning compliance with orders from above. There is no justification on any basis for this, even if we were to assume that the "gang of four" did all the things accused of them and created anarchy and conspiratorial cliques in the Party. Lin Piao certainly did do this, on a large scale, and yet the 10th Constitution retained the requirement of basic units to wage active ideological struggle and even added going against the tide, without directly tying it to the "three do's and don'ts," and in fact raising it as a principle on the same level with carrying out these three principles. Again, comrades should carefully study over the 11th Constitution and compare and contrast it with the 10th on the points mentioned here, and others, to see clearly how it is a fascist Constitution of a Party guided by a revisionist line.

Hua & Co. are waging class struggle against and suppressing the proletariat and, to cover that, they are putting out a line of: everything is non-antagonistic, you're fine, I'm fine, everybody's fine, we're all "positive factors"; the only problem is that those dirty "gang of four" and their followers keep waging antagonistic struggle, and if we just smash them everything will be fine. In other words, if we just get rid of this "bane" of the proletariat waging struggle against the bourgeoisie we can get on with the real task—boosting production—which means reducing the workers to wage-slaves producing for their new rulers.

But isn't it important to correctly distinguish and handle contradictions between the enemy and the people and contradictions among the people? Didn't Mao stress this many times? Yes, of course, but Mao never meant that this should be used to write off the class struggle of the proletariat against the bourgeoisie, for as he pointed out so many times, so long as it still exists, the bourgeoisie will never for a minute stop waging struggle against the proletariat.

And how did the Four handle this? Undoubtedly in practice they made some mistakes—it would be almost impossible not to, especially under the conditions of such acute class struggle as existed over the past several years and, for example, at the high point of mass upsurge in the Cultural Revolution. Mao himself remarked during this high tide that one of the most difficult things about the Cultural Revolution was that the two different types of contradictions were very hard to sort out. But the point is that the *line* of the Four on this question was correct.

To cite just one of many examples, in another article from *Study and Criticism* also by Chuang Lan, in addition to a basic analysis of the bourgeoisie in the Party, the question of how to deal with people who take the capitalist road and how to unite all who can genuinely be united against the enemy is presented this way:

> "Practice proves that the vast majority of Party members and cadres who made the mistakes of capitalist roaders during the Great Proletarian Cultural Revolution returned to Chairman Mao's proletarian revolutionary line after seriously studying Chairman Mao's theory on continuing the revolution under the dictatorship of the proletariat and with the criticism and help of the masses. Only a very few unrepentant capitalist roaders such as Teng Hsiao-ping and his ilk, continue to stubbornly stick to the capitalist road, and their contradiction with us eventually becomes an antagonistic contradiction. In our struggle against capitalist roaders, we must take account of different conditions and isolate to the maximum extent and strike at a handful of diehard capitalist roaders until they are completely discredited."

What is wrong with this—isn't it quite correct? If anything it's too lenient.

But isn't it possible to say one thing and do another, and isn't that possibly the case with the Four on this question? In fact this is a major charge against the Four, especially on this point. Yes, there are certainly cases where people say one thing and do another—and the present rulers of China are a good example of that, specifically on the question of "non-antagonistic contradictions." But over any period of time it is not possible to consistently propagate an overall correct line and carry out an overall incorrect line. And it is a truth that in order to carry out an incorrect line it is necessary to create public opinion for such a line and it is necessary for opportunists to deviate from Marxism-Leninism, Mao Tsetung Thought in word as well as deed—even while claiming to uphold it.

Such can definitely be shown to be the case with Hua & Co. But with the Four it cannot be shown that their stand deviated from Marxim-Leninism, Mao Tsetung Thought and that they created public opinion for an opportunist line that they were attempting to carry out. The public opinion they created was for a correct line—as in the article quoted above at length. And it should be remembered that this article was written in Shanghai, where according to the present rulers of China, "things they [the Four] dared not say in Peking they said in Shanghai and from there it was disseminated to the rest of the country." (see *China Reconstructs*, November, 1977, page 4)

I would like to call comrades' attention to what was written 20 years ago, by a comrade about Stalin, in the face of denunciations of him by Khrushchev, since I at least believe it applies in essence to the Four, especially in the face of attacks on them by Hua & Co. today:

> "In addition, Stalin authored some the best attacks on the 'cult of the individual,' and his articles on collective work are inspiring. Then what do we have—someone who preached well but practiced badly? Maybe so. I can postulate that a great theoretical physicist might beat his children, but I find it difficult to comprehend that a genius in social science can produce sound and original work dedicated to human advancement without a genuine love for humanity, with self-glorification as his guiding impulse, with a care for self above his fellow. On this basis it is possible that the next great advancement in Marxist science will come from a thorough scoundrel. I do not see it—there is a unity to the whole man; to be great in this field seems precisely not possible for a villain. Of course, as well as unity, there is diversity to the whole man, and even the greatest will have faults, perhaps serious ones . . ." (See *Red Papers 7*, page 154).

Stalin specifically made mistakes, even serious ones, in the sphere of correctly distinguishing and handling contradictions between the enemy and the people and contradictions among the people, but he was, overall, a great Marxist-Leninist, and certainly denunciations of him for being a "tyrant," etc. by Khrushchev should have been and have been repudiated by genuine Marxist-Leninists. Similarly, the Four undoubtedly made *mistakes* in this sphere, as well as others (I will speak to what I see as some of their errors later); perhaps they were not as good as Stalin, and certainly they were not as good as Mao. But overall they fought for and carried out Mao's line on this as well as all other major questions; as with Stalin they should certainly be upheld as Marxist-Leninist leaders of the proletariat, and denunciations of them as "fascists," etc. by Hua Kuo-feng & Co. should certainly be repudiated as well.

Here it should be stressed that Stalin's basic error with regard to contradictions under socialism is that he failed to grasp the persistence of the *antagonistic* contradiction between the proletariat and the bourgeoisie. Stalin certainly did recognize the existence under socialism of non-antagonistic contradictions among the people—for example between workers and peasants. But he failed to recognize the persistence of capitalist productive relations and the fact that even the contradictions among the people contained the seeds of contradictions between the people and the enemy and if not handled correctly would grow into such antagonistic contradictions. Failing to recognize *this* Stalin failed to wage the class struggle correctly and to distinguish between the two different kinds of contradictions. He treated people who represented the bourgeoisie in the Soviet Union as simply agents of foreign capital and often treated people who made serious errors as the same as enemy agents, because he did not correctly grasp how the contradictions existing in socialist society created the basis for capitalism to be restored, for new bourgeois elements to emerge and for people, including even some who could be won over, to take the capitalist road.

Further, on the question of the two different types of contradictions, glossing over the differences among the people—for example between intellectuals and the masses of manual workers—means allowing these contradictions to grow into antagonism. Such contradictions not only exist in socialist society but do indeed contain the seeds of antagonism and do tend to become antagonistic, unless correct leadership is given to narrowing step by step these differences in opposition to "left" and right errors on this question. In China it was the Four, following Mao, who recognized that such differences must be restricted and who gave correct leadership to narrowing these differences in accordance with the material and ideological conditions. It was not they, but the current rulers, who are turning these relationships into antagonistic ones by expanding rather than restricting such differences, putting technicians, intellectuals, etc., in command over the masses (more on this later). Again, comrades should think about their own experience with such contradictions in capitalist society, keeping in mind Mao's insistence that especially with regard to such contradictions China was not much different than capitalism, and ask themselves whether or not these contradictions tend to become antagonistic when the intellectuals, technicians, etc. are allowed, as they are under capitalism, to lord it over the masses of workers.

It would be possible to go on for pages on this one question of class struggle under socialism and the bourgeoisie in the Party. But if comrades study what has been written so far, together with the last Bulletin on this question and the material provided and cited as reference, and apply the Marxist stand, viewpoint and method, it will be clear that the Four's line on this question is correct, is Mao's line, while that of Hua & Co. is a repudiation of Mao's line. To sum up in one sentence the essential points on this question: Hua Kuo-feng & Co.'s line on this is nothing but the line of "dying out of class struggle" in the form in which it has to be put forward in China today (in no small part because of the public opinion created for the correct line by the Four), it opposes the dialectical and materialist analysis of the question of the bourgeoisie in the Party, deliberately downplays the danger of capitalist restoration, and distorts the target and tasks of the proletariat in waging the class struggle under the dictatorship of the proletariat; the Four's line on this question is correct, it is Mao's line.

Putting Revolution First Is the Only Way to Promote Socialist Production

Another major question at issue is the relationship between class struggle and the struggle for production, or revolution and production. In the past year it has been repeatedly charged by the present rulers of China that the Four talked only about revolution and not about production, or that they said that production would "automatically" go up if revolution were carried out well and that in fact all the talk about revolution only served the purpose of sabotaging production.

Is there any truth to this? From all I know and from the investigation I have done—and especially by focusing on the question of line—there is no truth to it at all. The truth is that the Four steadfastly upheld the correct principle of "grasp revolution, promote production," while those now in power really have an "automatically" line—that is, they say that if production goes up that will solve the problem of revolution, and further they equate production with revolution so that boosting production becomes the way to carry out revolution.

Again, this was dealt with in some specifics in the last Bulletin which comrades should study over again on this point, but since that Bulletin was not supposed to deal with the overall line of the Four on the one hand and the present rulers on the other, it is necessary to go into this question, in a deeper and more all-around way here. What is the so-called "automatically" line of the Four? From what I can tell, and from what has been said by some echoing this charge against the Four, it is the line expressed in statements such as the following: "Man is the most important productive force. As long as proletarian politics is placed in command and man's enthusiasm for socialism is fully aroused under socialist conditions, production will flourish at a swift tempo." (From Cheng Yueh's article in *Red Flag*, April 1, 1976).

Is this incorrect, is it opposed to Mao's line? Just the opposite—it is exactly Mao's line, exactly a Marxist-Leninist position on the question. It was Mao, not the Four, who said, "Of all things in the world, people are the most precious. Under the leadership of the Communist Party, as long as there are people, every kind of miracle can be performed . . . We believe that revolution can change everything, and that before long there will arise a new China with a big population and a great wealth of products, where life will be abundant and culture will flourish." (See "The Bankruptcy of the Idealist Conception of History," *Selected Works of Mao Tsetung*, Vol. 4, page 454.) Imagine poor Mao, even when attacking idealism he is so infected with the "gang of four idealism" and their metaphysics that he talks about "miracles" and "revolution can change everything"!

The Four's position was *not* that the class struggle can *replace* the struggle for production or revolution can *replace* production, but that class struggle is the key link and everything—production included—hinges on it (as Mao said) and that revolution must *command* production, not the other way around. Repeatedly, during the struggle against the right deviationist wind to reverse correct verdicts, the articles written under the direction of the Four stressed that not only was it very necessary to promote production but that specifically, "We have always attached importance to economic accounting and accumulation and opposed such erroneous ideas as not estimating the cost, neglecting accumulation and being extravagant and wasteful. Teng Hsiao-ping, however, attacked the criticism of putting profits in command and material incentives as 'one-sided opposition to the making of profits.' " (*Peking Review* No. 24, 1976, page 10). And this article goes on to quote that idealist and metaphysician who said, "Ideological and political work are the guarantee for accomplishing economic work and technical work, and they serve the economic base. Moreover, ideology and politics are the commander, the soul. If our ideological work and political work slacken just a little, economic work and technical work are bound to go astray." (The statement is by Mao, of course—imagine, "*guarantee*" for "accomplishing economic work and technical work"—how "automatically" can you get!)

Along the same lines, the article by Cheng Yueh quoted above stresses that, "The difference between Marxism and the revisionist theory of the productive forces is not the question of whether or not it is necessary to grasp production and do a good job in economic construction. Marxism has always attached great importance to the development of the productive forces, but it has also held all along that the development of productive forces cannot be separated from the reform of the relations of production and the superstructure, and that only by grasping revolution will it be possible to promote production. And the adjustment in the relations of production will pave the way for the development of productive forces." (Of course, there is "adjustment" and "adjustment" and "reform" and "reform"—in this article by Cheng Yueh, as in all the Four's material, it is clear that such transformations in the relations of production and superstructure fundamentally and principally depend on class struggle against the bourgeoisie and overthrow of diehard representatives of the bourgeoisie who hold portions of power in their hands—and in fact it is for promoting such struggle that the Four are repeatedly attacked by the present rulers.)

But is this just a question of "covering your ass" with a few general statements about developing production in a few articles? Again, all the evidence points to the fact that the opposite is the case. Comrades can study, for example, the series of articles in *Peking Review* 16-19, 1976 on "Socialist Industry," where I think the question of the concrete relation between grasping revolution and promoting production is put forward very well (these articles were reprinted as a pamphlet).

More, in practice, in Shanghai, in Liaoning Province where Mao Yuan-hsin, Mao's nephew and a "sworn accomplice" of the Four, played a leading role, and in other places where they had influence the Four gave correct guidance to and led the development of production under the command of revolution (more on that and some history around it a little later). Even the present rulers have to backhandedly admit that. For example Li Hsien-nien (now number 4) said in an interview with foreign correspondents that in Shanghai under the Four production was not disrupted (see *New York Times*, Aug. 30, 1977).

Of course the present rulers, as stated by Li in that interview, and in a number of *Peking Reviews*, try to say that the Four created a stable situation where they had power and chaos where they didn't. But the important fact is that the Four and the present rulers have fundamentally different lines on how to develop production, and where the Four were able to carry out their line production actually went ahead on a socialist basis, and where they didn't they waged struggle for the correct line to keep production from "going astray" because it was not guided by a correct ideological and political line (see Mao's statement on this general question above). Naturally such struggle is bound to cause temporary "disruption" in many places but not as much disruption to *socialism* as the carrying out of an opportunist line (and of course in a situation of complicated and acute struggle many undesirables, including the right deviationists, are bound to get involved and much disruption will result from various forces; it is quite wrong to make the Four the cause of all the disruption as is being done now—more on "disruption" later). So again we are back to the question of line, but in any case it cannot be honestly stated that the Four paid no attention to the concrete problems of developing production, it can only be said that they had a line on this opposed to the present rulers' line. And they should have—the present rulers' line is revisionist, and not to oppose it would be criminal—and the Four certainly did oppose it, with a correct line.

As for the Four's basic line on this question, I have studied over several hundred pages of *Fundamentals of Political Economy* printed in Shanghai, which clearly puts forward the Four's line and criticizes right and "left" opportunist lines on the question. It should be noted that this textbook was printed in 1974, before the right deviationist wind had been whipped up on a big scale (though certainly not before the right deviationists were making real attempts at reversing correct verdicts). It positively and strongly puts forward the need to accomplish the modernization of agriculture, industry, national defense and science and technology (which came to be called the "four modernizations")—and again, this is put forward positively and strongly, that is, not by way of simply saying, "Of course, we want modernization but not at the cost of selling out revolution."

I find the line promoted in this textbook not only correct but enlightening and thought-provoking, not only on the general question of the relation between revolution and production but on a whole series of questions involving how to actually develop production under the command of revolution. The need for enterprises generally to make profit is stressed—but not as an absolute—and "profits in command" is well refuted. There is a whole chapter on "Frugality Is an Important Principle in the Socialist Economy," where among other things it is stated that "all frugality is in fact the economizing of live and embodied labor, or the economizing of labor time. . . In socialist society saving labor time assumes an immense significance. . . To violate the law of frugality is to violate the basic requirement of socialist economic development. . . To practice frugality is an important way to increase accumulation through self-reliance. . . The socialist country can only rely on the diligent labor of its whole laboring people and internal frugality for accumulation. . . To practice frugality is especially important to China's socialist construction. China is a big country but is also an economically backward and poor country. . . Only through diligence and thrift can the laboring masses create wealth and play the greatest possible role and can China soon be developed into a big and strong socialist country. To practice frugality is also necessary if a socialist country is to discharge its obligations to internationalism. Only by saving more can we contribute to world revolution." And, as opposed to the current rulers, the Four, in this textbook and elsewhere, stress that the key to achieving socialist frugality, as well as developing the socialist economy in general, is to mobilize the masses and rely on them as the masters to solve such questions, under the guidance of a correct line.

These are, of course, general statements, but very correct ones, certainly not indicating lack of concern for the problems of developing production and modernizing China. And there are many specific policy statements not only in this chapter but in every one, including on socialist production relations and their relation to the superstructure; commodity production and the operation of the law of value under socialism and the relations between different economic units, regions, etc.; different forms of socialist ownership and the means for resolving the contradictions that arise on this basis; how to carry out the general line for socialist construction; planning (short term and longer term); the relations between agriculture and industry and the worker-peasant alliance and the policy of agriculture as the foundation and industry as the leading factor, grain as the key link in agriculture and steel as the key link in industry; the relation between production and consumption, the state, collective and individual and so on. The textbook also puts forward a correct line on trade, calling for actively developing it while subordinating it to self-reliance and stresses that achieving equality and mutual benefit in trade with non-socialist countries is also a question of *class struggle,* something we hear very little, if anything at all, about from the current rulers.

And all of these are dealt with in terms of how they relate to the ultimate goal of achieving communism in China and worldwide. To me it is clear that those whose line guides such a major work are Marxist revolutionaries and that charges that they only talked about revolution and not about production or that they cared nothing about developing the economy, in fact only wanted to sabotage it, etc. etc. *ad nauseam* are utterly groundless and base attempts to do what Lenin said of Kautsky when the latter tried to cover his own revisionism by distorting the position of the genuine revolutionaries—to attribute to your opponent an obviously stupid position, and then to refute it (Lenin said), is a method used by none too clever people—and none too Marxist either.

Fortunately, in evaluating the two different lines—that of the Four and that of the present rulers—on this all-important question of the relation between revolution and production, we have a good deal of material available to us, on both sides. And the more we compare and contrast it the more it becomes obvious that the line of the present rulers is revisionist trash while that of the Four is correct. Again, to go into all of this would require a long book, so let's look at a few questions in some depth and contrast the two lines on some other points more briefly.

The "Three Poisonous Weeds" (now called "fragrant flowers" by the present rulers) all share in common the position sharply criticized at the 10th Congress of the Chinese Communist Party—that the main task now is to develop production, which was then (1973) correctly called "revisionist trash." (See page 5 of the 10th Congress documents.) One way this "revisionist trash" is put forward in these three documents is in the formulation (directly or indirectly stated) that the "three directives" of Mao's are the "key link." In some cases this is said straight up, in others it is put this way: "The three directives cannot be separated" (or another translation, "are an inalienable entity,"—found in both the "Outline Report" on science and technology and the "20 Points" on accelerating industrial development).

Here is the perfect example where "metaphysics is rampant." Mao always insisted that there is no such thing that "cannot be separated." Everything is divisible, everything divides into two. (If the elementary particle can be separated, why can't the three directives?) But here we have two (or three) into one. And for what purpose?—simply to deny the leading role of class struggle and to put developing the economy on the basis of stability and unity on a par with—in fact above—the class struggle. Again, of course, there is "separated" and "separated." If these documents only meant that the three directives are inter-related and should all be carried out, then there would be no real problem. But clearly they mean that they should be put on a par as one "key link"—an eclectic formulation which serves, again, the purpose of actually raising production above revolution and stability and unity above class struggle—and in fact waging class struggle against the proletariat. This is the whole line that runs through these documents, of that I don't see how there can be any doubt.

The "General Program" starts off by saying that the three directives are the "general program for work in all fields" and that they will "also be the general program in the whole course of struggle for achieving the grand objectives of the next 25 years"—i.e., the "four modernizations." And then we are told, "Carrying out these three important directives is tantamount to carrying out the Party's basic line, the Party's line of unity for victory, and the Party's general line for building socialism."

So this "general program" is no small matter, no incidental thing, and this "three directives are the key link" is no accidental formulation—it is *the line* for the next 25 years. And it is a completely incorrect, revisionist line, specifically repudiated by Mao, as we know, in his blast at "taking the three directives as the key link." Now Mao is no fool, and no hot-headed sectarian who would just jump on one mistaken formulation if it were an isolated thing—no, Mao clearly recognized that this formulation was part of a whole revisionist program, the "general program," and that is exactly why he denounced it so strongly. Mao might have made an offhand blast among comrades against an incorrect formulation without regarding the whole line as rotten, but the point is that he would not allow such a statement of his to be made public in a way that would tag its author(s) as revisionist unless he regarded such a statement, "taking the three directives as the key link," as part of a whole revisionist line, which it clearly was (and is).

But Hua & Co. steadfastly uphold the "General Program" and unabashedly promote and implement its revisionist line and its whole revisionist "vision" if we can call it that. Hua even goes so far as to formulate a new "historical mission of the Chinese working class and the Chinese people to accomplish in the rest of this century"—"making China a powerful and modern socialist country." (See *Peking Review* No. 35, 1977, page 39 and also No. 21, 1977, page 13, both of these are from major speeches by Hua.)

What the "vision" is here is further indicated in an article by Hua where he quotes Mao saying that in agriculture if the capitalist rather than the socialist road is taken production can increase but it would take more time and be more painful, and Hua says the following on the subject of which road to take: "Capitalism enabled many countries to industrialize. . . Socialism is far superior to capitalism. It enables us to go faster than capitalism in expanding production, industrialize the country in a comparatively short period and surpass capitalism in labor productivity step by step." Hua throws in that modernization should be done "in keeping with the orientation of socialism and communism," but this is really quite incidental to and treated essentially as external to the question of promoting production and modernizing. (See *Peking Review* No. 19, 1977, page 24.)

This reminds me of the Bundists that we struggled against several years ago, before the Party was formed; as we pointed out then, to them self-determination was the highest goal and revolution was simply the means to that end and subordinate to it. Similarly, for Hua & Co. industrialization and modernization are the highest goal and "socialism" simply a means to get to them, and revolution is definitely subordinate to them. Since in China capitalism can't bring about rapid industrialization and modernization, then we will have to have socialism—this is the outlook of Hua & Co. And what is the logical extension of Hua's statements when applied to the capitalist countries—since there it "enabled many countries to industrialize" then there is no need for socialism and revolution in these countries. This is really what comes through, despite window dressing about "in keeping with the orientation of socialism and communism."

Hua and Co.'s "orientation" is not in keeping with socialism and communism, and their "socialism" is not socialism at all—it is the revisionist view of socialism which essentially equates it with simply a greater development of the productive forces, essentially does not deal with socialist production as the unity of productive forces and productive relations, essentially ignores the dynamic role of the superstructure and divorces socialism from the real historical mission of the working class, to transform society through socialist revolution and achieve communism, to abolish classes. When we define what communism is, what do we say is the essence of it—that there will be a high degree of development of the productive forces or that classes will be eliminated—both are true but which is the main thing, the essential thing? For a communist, the abolition of classes, but for a revisionist philistine and the "practical men" who promote "goulash communism" and make a fetish of production, it is industrialization and modernization that are essential.

The productive forces in our country are much more highly developed than those in China and this is likely to remain so for many decades—and surely in the years since 1956 (when Mao talked about overtaking the U.S. economically in 50-60 years) Mao came to recognize this. But does that make the system in the U.S. "higher" and "superior" to the socialist system or will it be "superior" until the socialist countries surpass it economically? And will socialism in China be a failure if its economy is not more developed than here by 2000? I remember that after an acquaintance returned from a trip to China he was asked by a worker how it was, and he replied, "It was like going through a time machine." The worker, on the basis of bourgeois spontaneity and prejudices said, "Yeah, they're still a long ways behind us, so it's really like going back in time." "No," the acquaintance replied, "it's like going forward!"

Hua and Co. would find themselves in agreement with the worker in this discussion. Their whole outlook is that of the bourgeois democrat who has turned to "socialism"—i.e. public ownership—because it can bring about modernization faster in their opinion. If this seems unfair or anyone is still unconvinced, listen to the following statement by Yu Chiu-li, in a major speech at the 1977 Taching Conference: "To build our socialist country under the dictatorship of the proletariat into a still more powerful state and catch up with and surpass the most developed capitalist countries economically—*this* is the great call of our great leader and teacher Chairman Mao, the long cherished common aspiration of the people of the whole country and the *lofty ideal* for which countless revolutionary martyrs fought to the last drop of their blood." (*Peking Review* No. 22, 1977, page 16, emphasis added).

Well, if it is wrong to say that the ultimate historical mission for the working class is modernization, can there be such a "historical mission" for the next 23 years in China to achieve modernization? No, there cannot, for this is just another way of saying that modernization, developing production, is the main task—just more "revisionist trash." And fundamentally it is a way of separating the tasks of the proletariat in socialist society from the ultimate goal of communism, a way of walling off the next 23 years from the real historic mission of the proletariat and erecting a "new period of development in our country's socialist revolution and socialist construction," in which the Cultural Revolution is finished (thank Confucious! say Hua and Co.) and we can get on with the real task of promoting production. (See Hua's report to the 11th Congress, *Peking Review* No. 35, 1977, page 39.)

In short, to make modernization the "historical mission" from now till the end of the century, while talking about "socialist revolution" and trumpeting the totally eclectic "key link" of bringing great order across the land in the course of acute struggle against the "gang of four," is just another way of resurrecting the line of "three directives as the key link"—after all, there is more than one way to skin a cat, and as we know, to the present rulers it does not matter whether that cat is black or white so long as it promotes the "historical mission" of modernization. And in fact the "new period" Hua & Co. are gloriously proclaiming is nothing other than the period when Mao's line is being overthrown—the time when the old "era of Chin Shih-Huang" (a well-known reference to Mao Tsetung) is "gone forever," as those reactionaries who hoisted their banner in the Tien An Men incident in April 1976 proclaimed.

In fact and in essence, Hua & Co. have thrown out Mao's correct line on the principal contradiction under socialism and replaced it with the revisionist line that the principal contradiction in China now is between the advanced socialist system and the backward productive forces. They don't say this straight up, of course, since that exact formulation was long ago denounced and exposed in China. As was pointed out at the 10th Congress of the Chinese Communist Party, when Lin Piao came out with this line in 1969, he did not present it in exactly the same form in which it had previously been presented—and repudiated. Instead he just said that the main task then was to develop production, which might have seemed "reasonable," coming off the mass upheaval of the Cultural Revolution in the three previous years. But, as was pointed out at the 10th Congress, Lin's line in 1969 was "*a refurbished version under new conditions*" of the "same revisionist trash." (See again p. 5 of the 10th Congress documents, emphasis added.) So, too, the line of Hua & Co. today is a *refurbished version under new conditions* of the line that the principal contradiction is between the advanced socialist system and the backward productive forces.

The way Hua and Co. formulate it is that the problem in China is that they have the "superior socialist system" but have not surpassed the advanced capitalist countries economically. In other words, the principal contradiction is really between the "superior socialist system" and the lack of modernization—or the backward productive forces. The same "revisionist trash" but a "refurbished version under new conditions." It is not possible to read over any major statement by the current rulers on the situation in China without seeing that this is, despite talk about the class struggle, the way they present the main problem in China, that this is how they actually put forward the principal contradiction. Anyone who is not convinced of this should read over major statements from the current rulers with this question in mind—such as Hua's article in *Peking Review* No. 19, his speech to the 11th Congress, his speech at the Taching conference this year, etc. (see *Peking Review* Nos. 35 and 21)—and apply the Marxist method to get beyond the appearance to the essence of what is being put forward.

But didn't Mao say that building a modern socialist state is a great task and can't you find statements from Mao in which he says "our aim" is to build a powerful or modern socialist country? Yes, such statements can be found, especially from the period before the Cultural Revolution, particularly the 1950s. But two things on this: first, Mao never meant such statements to be used to say that modernization should be put on a par with or raised above revolution and the ultimate goal of communism worldwide; and second, especially through the Cultural Revolution and in the last years of his life in particular, the question of modernization, while certainly not abandoned in Mao's thinking, was most definitely not the uppermost thing on Mao's mind, not the greatest goal that he put forward nor the thing he focused attention on.

In fact in the directives of Mao's that came to be referred to as his "three directives" the one on socialist construction was, as far as I can tell, limited to a general call for "pushing the national economy forward," and was certainly not meant to be put on a par with his instructions on the class struggle, and the theory of proletarian dictatorship and combatting and preventing revisionism in particular, which was the main and decisive directive. When Mao said that class struggle is the key link and everything hinges on it, he meant that it determines the direction of everything else, including along what lines, which road, the economy would be developed—i.e. whether socialist or capitalist development would take place.

Beyond that, it should be pointed out that these "three directives" were not all issued at the same time and under the same circumstances; in other words they were not issued together as one "general program." It was Teng Hsiao-ping—along with Hua Kuo-feng and others—who threw them together as one program and tried to put them on a par in form in order to wipe out the decisive role of class struggle in essence. Certainly nowhere in Mao's different directives and most definitely not in his response to this eclectic trick of putting them on a par together as one "general program " is there any indication that Mao agreed with making modernization the "historical mission" that Hua & Co. are now braying about.

It is most interesting and significant that with all the propaganda of Hua & Co. about how the four modernizations are the "historical mission" of the present era, they have not been able to cite one statement by Mao in recent years which supports this or even one that lays stress on the four modernizations. The most they can come up with is Chou En-lai's statement at the 4th People's Congress that at the 3rd People's Congress 11-12 years earlier Mao set forth the general proposal for modernizing the country in two stages by the end of the century. Chou's speech neither says that this is the most important task nor does it actually say that Mao has recently reiterated the call for the implementation of this plan. Certainly Mao did not agree that the four modernizations were some sort of overriding and almost magical plan that everything else should be subordinated to, or that in order to achieve these modernizations it was necessary and correct to throw out the class struggle and abandon the correct line on developing the economy by adopting a "major policy" of selling out China's resources for advanced technology and other revisionist measures that Teng Hsiao-ping and his fellow right deviationists had cooked up. In fact Mao emphatically said quite the opposite.

In *Peking Review* No. 42, 1977, it is stated that in 1975 Chang Chun-chiao said that the four modernizations " 'means no more than growing several hundred million tons of grain and producing tens of millions of tons of steel.' " Assuming Chang said this, I think he is right in line with Mao. His remark sounds to me very much like what Mao said about the arrogance of the Soviets and how they "are blinded by material gains and the best way to deal with them is to give them a good dressing down." Mao insisted: "What are the material gains? Nothing but 50 million tons of steel, 400 million tons of coal, and 80 million tons of petroleum. Does this amount to much? Not at all. Now at the sight of this much their heads are swelled. What Communists! What Marxists! I say multiply all that tenfold, or even a hundredfold, it still doesn't amount to much. All you have done is to extract something from the earth, turn it into steel and make some cars, planes, and what not. What is so remarkable about that?" (Vol. 5, p. 365) Chang Chun-chiao's meaning, assuming he made this statement, could well be—and in my opinion would be, since it is consistent with his line—the four modernizations after all are not something so great that we should subordinate everything else to them, not something in whose name we should give up revolution and socialism.

Does this mean that striving for modernization by the end of the century is in itself wrong—how should we view this and what was the view of the Four on this matter? No, striving for modernization in itself is not wrong and, if guided by a correct line and under the command of revolution, is a very important and necessary endeavor. But at the same time, it has to be recognized that everything should not be staked on achieving this modernization by the year 2000 and that making a big push for modernization is bound to unleash a lot of forces favoring and favorable to capitalist restoration and, for that reason, it is especially important to insist on the leading role of revolution and to devote special attention to the struggle against revisionism.

This basic stand was laid out clearly by Chang Chun-chiao in an article (pamphlet) written right after the 4th People's Congress in early 1975, where the goal of modernization by the year 2000 was set out in general terms in Chou En-lai's report. Chang begins his article by saying, "Our country is in an important period of its historical development"—note "important period," not "new period" whose "historical mission" is modernization. And Chang goes on to say that "full of militancy, all our people are determined to build China into a powerful socialist country before the end of the century." And then he stresses what is absolutely necessary and correct to stress: "In the course of this effort and in the entire historical period of socialism, whether we can persevere all the way in the dictatorship of the proletariat is a cardinal issue for China's future development. Current class struggles, too, require that we should get clear on the question of the dictatorship of the proletariat." (*On Exercising All-Round Dictatorship Over the Bourgeoisie*, pp. 1-2)

And in criticizing the "Three Poisonous Weeds" the Four and their followers pointed out that in Chou En-lai's report to the 4th People's Congress it is stressed that " 'Only when we do well in revolution is it possible to do well in production.' " (Quoted in an article in *Study and Criticism,* April 14, 1976—I will speak to the "Chou En-lai question" later) This line of the 4th People's Congress is exactly the opposite of that of the "General Program," where the relationship between revolution and production is reversed to say that, "In a place or unit where production is carried out with bad results, it would be deceptive to say that revolution is an excellent success." Instead of the correct principle that only when revolution is carried out well is it possible to do well in production—*socialist* production—the authors of the "General Program" reverse things to say, only when we do well in production can we say we are doing well in revolution.

Further, as the article referred to above also notes, the "General Program" in particular, while taking off from the call in Chou En-lai's report to the 4th People's Congress for modernization by the end of the century, does not base this on what Chou En-lai's report stresses first: " 'Socialist revolution is the powerful engine for developing the social productive forces.' 'While tackling economic tasks, our leading comrades at all levels must pay close attention to the socialist revolution in the realm of the superstructure and keep a firm grasp on class struggle and the struggle between two lines.' " (from the same article in *Study and Criticism)*

Further, another article criticizing the "General Program" points out why on the one hand modernization is an important task but why on the other hand it cannot be the main task. It says, quite correctly in my opinion:

> "Therefore, the basic task for the whole Party and the people of the whole country not only at present but also throughout the entire historical period of socialism, including the next 25 years, is to fight for nothing but the realization of our Party's basic program [see the Constitution of the 10th Party Congress] and the execution of its basic line. Should we develop the national economy? Should we achieve all-around modernization of agriculture, industry, national defense, and science and technology in two stages before the end of the century? Of course we should! However, this is only a task we should

> fulfill in order to realize the basic program of our Party. Although it is a magnificent task, it is not the basic task of the Party, still less the whole task of our Party. Originally the 'four modernizations' were set forth as a plan in connection with the task of developing the national economy. However, to pull off a monumental hoax, the 'General Program' sets forth the realization of 'four modernizations' as a major premise for all work both at present and in the next 25 years, a premise on which all of our work must be based. This fully shows that, in the eyes of that unrepentant capitalist roader in the Party, at present, the only task is to undertake production and construction, there being no need for class struggle, proletarian revolution and the dictatorship of the proletariat. This then completely negates our Party's basic program and thoroughly tampers with the basic task and the orientation of advance for the whole Party and the people of the whole country." (from Cheng Yueh's article in *Study and Criticism,* April 1, 1976)

In sum, then, the Four were in favor of striving for the four modernizations in accordance with Mao's line on revolution and production but they were against what the right deviationists tried to make the "four modernizations" stand for. They were very aware of the danger that making a big push for the four modernizations would give the green light to "production first" revisionists and they were very concerned that in the effort to fulfill the task of modernization, the basic task—class struggle—not be thrown overboard and that in the name of promoting production to achieve modernization the commanding role of revolution not be thrown out. Is there anything wrong with this? No, it is not only not wrong it is very necessary to take such a stand. In fact this is exactly how Mao approached the problem and no doubt a major reason why, at the time when the call for modernization by the end of the century was being made, Mao issued his most important directive—on studying the theory of the dictatorship of the proletariat and combatting and preventing revisionism. The line promoted and implemented by the present rulers of China in the name of modernization shows precisely how justified the great concern of Mao and the Four was.

One final note on this specific point. To set up the four modernizations as an absolute, as the basic task for the whole next 25 years is automatically (!) to have a wrong and disastrous line in regard to the class struggle, both in China and internationally. Won't a big upsurge of class struggle, or a war involving China, disrupt the achievement of these four modernizations? And can it be said that neither will be a necessity in the next 25 years? The only answer, to be true to the four modernizations as the basic and actually only task, is to capitulate—to the bourgeoisie in China and to the imperialists internationally. This is no answer at all.

If it is argued that in fact the four modernizations are necessary exactly in order to get prepared for war, then it can only be said that talk of the "next 25 years" is extremely dangerous and/or a hype to get the Chinese people to produce without being armed with a real and deep understanding of the actual objectives of that production—which by definition will lead to revisionism and to bourgeois principles and practices in command of production. And in any case, if the line is that, by undertaking the four modernizations as the key link China can actually catch up to and surpass the major military powers—specifically the Soviet Union—so as to be able, so to speak, to "fight them on their own terms," this is not only erroneous but will bring disaster to China. Of course China should modernize, of course she should have the most up-to-date weapons possible and be in the strongest position to defeat aggression, but that can never be accomplished by throwing out the class struggle and disarming the masses politically, leaving them in a very weak position to fight the only kind of war they can win—a people's war where they pit their strength—a class conscious politically motivated people—against the enemy's weakness which flows from its aggressive and imperialist nature.

Here a statement by Mao as early as 1961, where he draws a link between modernization of the economy (and national defense) and military line, is most relevant. He says that:

> "We will adopt advanced technology. But we cannot, because of this, negate the inevitability of backward technology in a certain period of time. Since the beginning of history, in revolutionary wars, it has always been people armed with inferior weapons who defeated those with superior weapons. During the civil wars, the anti-Japanese war, and the War of Liberation, we did not exercise power over the whole country and we did not have modernized arsenals. If we must have the newest weapons before we fight, then this is tantamount to disarming ourselves."

And after saying that it will take several decades to achieve overall mechanization in the economy, Mao goes on to insist that:

> "In the coming period, due to a shortage of machinery, we will still be advocating semi-mechanization and reform of tools. At present we are still not advocating universal

> automation. We should discuss mechanization, but we should not do it excessively. Excessive discussion of mechanization and automation will make people have contempt for semi-mechanization and production by native methods. There have been such tendencies in the past. Everybody one-sidedly went in for new technology and new machinery, massive scales and high standards. They looked down upon native methods and medium and small-sized enterprises." (From the U.S. Government collection of Mao's post-1949 speeches, writings and talks)

Here Mao is not advocating backwardness and denying the need for modernization. He is opposing one-sided stress on modernization and *reliance* on modernization either in the economy or in warfare. Can anyone honestly say that the present rulers of China, with their consistent one-sided emphasis on "modern, modern, modern" and "advanced, advanced, advanced" are doing anything other than repudiating Mao's line on these crucial questions? If anyone is confused on this, they should read over the stuff coming out of China, especially on the economy and on science and technology in particular, and use the statements by Mao cited just above as a standard for evaluating the line coming out of China now on these questions.

For all these reasons, while it is correct to strive for the four modernizations this cannot be the basic task or aim, and the general program of the current rulers of China is wrong and, worse,it is revisionist and will bring great harm to China and the international proletariat. The Four were entirely correct in opposing it and they opposed it correctly—with a correct line.

Basic Summations of the Opposing Lines on Other Important Points

In *Peking Review* No. 42, 1977 there is an article whose title asks the question, "Why Did the 'Gang of Four' Attack 'The Twenty Points'?" The answer is simple—the "20 Points" is revisionist. Supposedly a program for accelerating industrial development, it is actually a program for accelerating capitalist restoration. To characterize the "20 Points" it is only necessary to repeat the statement attributed in that *Peking Review* article to Chang Chun-chiao, who is quoted as saying that the "20 Points" has "put forward a revisionist line, complete with principles and policies; it peddles rubbish that has long ago been criticized, such as material incentives, profits in command, direct and exclusive control of enterprises by the ministry concerned, reliance on specialists to run factories, the 'theory of the all-importance of the productive forces,' the 'theory of the dying out of the class struggle'; and its application of eclecticism is really unsurpassed." (See pp. 12-13.)

I have read over a version of the "20 Points" and am convinced not only that it is authentic but is authentically revisionist and that Chang's characterization is right on time. The "20 Points" has to be looked at not only in its particulars, but also in how they fit together into one revisionist line for developing the economy—the line that is being implemented now and has been since Hua & Co. pulled their coup. The basic line is this: to develop the economy and industry especially we must put overwhelming emphasis on and rely on the big, modern and advanced; to get modern and advanced equipment we must rely on the advanced, capitalist countries; we must sell off what we have, raw materials, for what we need from them, advanced technology; to utilize this advanced technology we must rely on specialists, and technicians must be in command; and there must be more not less centralized control (which is what the "20 Points" actually calls for despite double-talk on this point); to repay the advanced countries we must make a big profit in every enterprise, especially, though not exclusively, those using this equipment; and to make such profits we must have "scientific management" that puts managers in command at the enterprise level, under the whip of the central, higher authorities, and we must institute rules and regulations that get the workers to stick to one specific production post to produce this profit, making use of piece-work and luring the workers with bonuses, etc.; and most of all we must have an end to the situation where factories are not only production units but first of all battlegrounds of the class struggle. This is what runs throughout the "20 Points" and gives it its integral character as a line on industrial development—a revisionist line.

More specifically, flying in the face of Mao's directive and guidance on the question of studying the theory of proletarian dictatorship and combatting and preventing revisionism and on restricting bourgeois right and the three great differences, the "20 Points" makes an absolute out of the division of labor in production and society and seeks to expand rather than restrict bourgeois right. It seeks to lure workers with promises of wage increases for harder work, and openly talks about raising the wages of a section of the workers who have more skill and work harder. This policy is now openly proclaimed, for example in *PR* No. 49, 1977 where the policy of bonuses for harder work and wage increases especially for more skilled and intellectual workers, specifically in science and technology, is trumpeted. (see page 3)

The "system of responsibility" called for in the "20 Points," as well as the "General Program," is one which clearly goes against the breakthroughs made by the workers through the Cultural Revolution, where they reformed rules and regulations and achieved a more rational division of labor which broke down conventions and the enslavement of workers to one production post, so that each worker had both a particular post and also many abilities—policies which pushed forward production, along socialist lines, and enabled the masses to further their mastery over production and place it under the command of proletarian politics.

Beyond this, as indicated, the "20 Points," promotes the policy of tying China's industrial development to the coattail of imperialist countries—in the name of trade for "mutual benefit" and "equality" it calls for long-term deals in which foreign imperialists will provide China with complete plants or complete sets of equipment to be repaid with the materials produced with this equipment. If that is implemented—which it is now—it will mean that the basic socialist economic principle of planned and proportional development can not be carried out, that China will be vulnerable to imperialist political pressure and that the Chinese people will be forced once again into the position of working for the imperialists and their Chinese compradors. This is not a line on trade—certainly not Mao's line—but a line for capitulation and restoration of the old system. And again, while this particular policy jumps out as one of the clearest deviations from the line of Mao—who consistently fought against this kind of reliance on importing technology, especially when it is directly tied to repayment with the products produced with it—it is necessary to see this policy as part of the whole line running through the "20 Points," as summarized above, a line which enslaves the workers to production, enslaves the whole economy to the foreign and advanced and is bound to cause tremendous dislocation and ultimately stagnation in all spheres of the economy, including agriculture as well as industry.

There are many other parts to the "20 Points" which indicate its revisionist nature, a few of which I will touch on below. But as a general characterization of the "20 Points" we have not only the statement attributed to Chang Chun-chiao but the statement by Mao on Teng Hsiao-ping which clearly had the "20 Points" as well as other "poisonous weeds" in mind: "This person does not grasp class struggle; he has never referred to this key link. *Still his theme of 'white cat, black cat,' making no distinction between 'imperialism and Marxism.*" (see *PR* No. 23, 1976, p. 16, emphasis added) Again, Mao is no fool and no sectarian hot head, and with this shot, which he clearly allowed to be made public in the context of combatting the right deviationist wind, he was obviously blasting not just a statement—"white cat, black cat"—but a whole line, the line of the "20 Points" as well as the line of the right deviationists in general. Comrades should study over the "20 Points" and major statements of policy coming out in the *Peking Review* now, keeping in mind the above blast by Mao, as well as his other statements hitting back at Teng and the right deviationists, together with the summation attributed to Chang Chun-chiao on the "20 Points," to see if the "20 Points" as well as the whole line coming out now are not well summarized by these statements.

On Rules and Regulations

The line of the present rulers is to enforce rules and regulations that put production above all and reduce the workers from masters to slaves of production—and of those who control production, the capitalist-roaders. The Four fought to establish and transform rules and regulations so that the workers would be increasingly enabled to master production and develop it according to socialist principles and in accordance with the advance toward communism.

The current rulers even try to deny that rules and regulations have a class character and reflect production relations. In *PR* No. 14, 1977 they attack the article by Cheng Yueh (quoted before in this paper) for saying that " 'Rules and regulations reflect the relationships among people in production and are of a clear-cut class nature.' " To this the present rulers answer: "But the fact is that while some of the rules and regulations reflect the relationships among people engaged in production and have a class character, others reflect relations between the producers and nature and represent the laws of production technology and therefore have no class characteristics." (p. 25) This is the kind of sophistry that only a very naive person or a philistine would find convincing. Its method is well exposed by a statement in an article by Liang Hsiao (a pseudonymn for a writing group under the Four's direction): "Is it possible to say that the struggle for production and scientific experiment carried out by people can break away from certain relations of production and social relations? Can it be said that the struggle for production and scientific experiment are so 'particular' as to be free from the restraint of class struggle? The repudiation of the universality of contradiction by means of exaggerating the particularity of contradiction is precisely an important characteristic of revisionism."

The point is that rules and regulations as a whole, as any kind of system, exactly reflect production relations and in class society have a clear-cut class character, and all rules and regulations—even those which "reflect the relationships between the producers and nature and represent the laws of production technology"—have to be applied within the general framework of class relations in class society and the relations among people in production in all systems (this will even be true in classless communist society). Actually the present rulers let the cat out of the bag when they say (in both the "General Program" and the "20 Points") that "the system of responsibility forms the core of rules and regulations in an enterprise." If this forms the "core"—and here it should be said in passing that this "core" as presented is meant to replace the conscious activity of the producers themselves (read the "General Program" and "20 Points" again if you don't think so)—if this is the *core* then how can anyone argue that rules and regulations don't reflect production relations and have a clear-cut class nature?

And what kind of "rules and regulations" do the present rulers promote and implement, what principles guide them in formulating these rules and regulations? As pointed out in the last bulletin they are "only" those "required for the daily development of the production struggle" and those "in accordance with the objective laws of the developing production struggle." Contrast this with the following statement from the Shanghai textbook on political economy referred to earlier:

> "Any social production requires certain regulations and systems. But the type of regulations and systems instituted is determined by the production relations in a society. . . Participation of the masses in management primarily refers to the participation of the direct producers, the worker-peasant masses, in management. The masses who participate in enterprise management must not only direct production, technical know-how and accounting, but more importantly, they have to help and supervise the cadres in thoroughly implementing the Party line and general and specific policies. . . ."

Under socialism, the textbook continues, rules and regulations must be "favorable to the masses" and this "is the most fundamental difference between socialist regulations and systems and capitalist regulations and systems." And they go on to explain that "systems favorable to the masses" "means that such systems have to be favorable to the masses' role as masters, to the improvement and development of interpersonal relations in the enterprise [i.e., relations between people in production], to the exercise of socialist activism by the masses, and to the development of the Three Revolutionary Movements of class struggle, production struggle, and scientific experiment. Regulations and systems which are favorable to the masses will certainly be favorable to the development of production as they mobilize the activism of the masses. Under the influence of the revisionist line of Liu Shao-chi and Lin Piao, the regulations and systems of some enterprises often restricted the masses. The worker's criticism was that 'there are too many systems and regulations and they are either for the purpose of punishment or coercion.' Under good leadership, the masses should be mobilized to revise, phase by phase, the systems and regulations which are irrational, and alienating workers. Meanwhile, on the basis of the experience acquired in practice, a new set of healthy and rational systems and regulations which correspond to the need for socialist interrelations and the development of the productive forces should be established."

This same line was repeatedly stressed by the Four during the struggle against the right deviationist wind, and I would like to ask—which of these two totally opposed lines is a Marxist-Leninist line—which is in accordance with Mao's line and with the objective of transforming society to advance toward communism? And whose irrational, restrictive and coercive rules and regulations were abolished in the Cultural Revolution to be replaced by rules and regulations more "favorable to the masses" and socialism—none other than Teng Hsiao-ping, in particular, who in the early '60s concocted a "70 Points" similar to the recent "20 Points." It is these rules and regulations that Teng and the other right deviationists want to restore—and certainly are restoring. And this is why they raise a hue and cry about "anarchy," make clumsy attempts to deny the class character of rules and regulations and even talk about how it is necessary to learn from the "positive aspects" of the Taylor system—quoting Lenin's statements from the first few, desperate years of the Soviet Republic to cover their revisionist line (see *PR* No. 14, 1977—more on their use of Lenin from those years and similarities with the Soviet revisionists on this later).

(Someone may want to point out that in his speech to the

Taching Conference in 1977 Yu Chiu-li actually did call for "rules and regulations that reflect the new socialist relations of production and objective laws of production"—see *PR* No. 22, 1977, p. 15. But this is nothing more than a ruse, a concession in passing to the consciousness of the masses—raised by Mao and the Four—and it is in no way central to or consistent with Yu's whole speech. In fact, with its one-sided emphasis on the "responsibility" of the "chairman of the revolutionary committee" in an enterprise, on opposing "the phenomenon of having no one accepting the responsibility" and "Special attention must be paid to selecting and appointing the two top leaders in each enterprise" and so on, Yu's speech is in no way in conformity with developing *socialist* production relations which rely on the masses as masters. Significantly, in relation to this point, according to people recently visiting China there is serious talk in China now about eliminating or greatly reducing the role of revolutionary committees, which were another "new thing" achieved through struggle in the Cultural Revolution and which were institutionalized officially at the 4th People's Congress, where their strengthening was called for. Eliminating or seriously reducing their role follows the line of the "20 Points," where in discussing enterprise management, the call is made for setting up production "command systems," with no mention made at that point of the role of the revolutionary committees. This sheds light on what Yu Chiu-li actually means in stressing the role of the two top leading people, etc., despite reference to the role of revolutionary committees. And overall, like the "General Program" and the "20 Points," Yu's Taching speech is revisionist from top to bottom in its outlook and political line.)

Finally, to get a clearer view of the revisionist "theory of the productive forces" line of the current rulers, comrades should study over *PR* No. 39, 1977, where in a major policy statement by the State Council a number of totally wrong and outrageous statements are made, including this one: "Transformation in the relations of production and the superstructure is conditioned by the development of the productive forces and must help promote it and not vice versa." (p. 11) Even without adding the last phrase "and not vice versa" this would be metaphysical and mechanical materialist—but that last phrase is added just so no one misses the meaning, so the point is clear that production is the main task. Compare the statement above by the current rulers with the following statement from the Shanghai textbook:

> "Marxism holds that productive forces develop under the constraint and impetus of production relations. In class

> society, production is always carried on under certain class relations. Even though changes and developments in social production always start from changes and advances in the productive forces, big advances in productive forces always occur after big transformations in production relations."

Is it not very clear that, in opposition to the revisionism of the current rulers, the position of the Four as expressed above is the dialectical materialist one, which conforms to the principle of "grasp revolution, promote production"?

On Science and Technology

The position of the current rulers is to divorce science from the masses and from their experience in production in particular, to deny in fact the leading role of Marxism, to give free rein and the leading role to "experts" and promote the "white and expert" road and put "technique in command" of production. (Here comrades should study especially *PR* Nos. 40 and 44, 1977.)

The Four's line was that the principal aspect of scientific and technical work should be geared to serve China's developing production needs and be under the command of Marxism and proletarian politics and the leadership of the Party implementing Mao's line, and that theoretical research and study of the "basic sciences" while important should be secondary. They fought for the line of "red and expert" and for carrying out the principle of "open-door scientific research," a new thing emerging out of the Cultural Revolution, which means combining study and work in the laboratory with investigation and work in relation to productive labor and scientific experiment by the masses and combining the role of professional scientific and technical workers with movements of the masses in scientific experiment. The Four said the masses, organized on a broad scale to carry out scientific experiment, were the main force in this struggle, in opposition to the present rulers who say clearly it is the professionals who are the main force in scientific experiment. (For an idea of the Four's line comrades can study *PR* No. 18, 1976 and No. 47, 1975, p. 30 as well as Nos 8 and 11, 1976.)

A few comments on this. I have been able to find only part of the third "poisonous weed"—the "Outline Report" on science—but the part I have read puts forward the revisionist line summarized above. But we do not have to have the "Outline Report" to see the revisionist line of the current rulers. The statement by the Central Committee printed in *PR* No. 40, 1977 can serve very well for an exposure of this line. There we are told that "It is imperative to *install as Party committee secretaries those cadres who understand the Party's policies and have enthusiasm for science*, to select *experts or near-experts to lead professional work* and to find diligent and hard-working cadres to take charge of the supporting work." (p. 9, emphasis added) Note that Party secretaries are to be those who have an understanding of the Party's policies and have enthusiasm for science—here clearly the Party's "policies" referred to are the policies on science; there is nothing about an understanding of the Party's *basic line*. And this combined with what follows, about experts or near-experts leading professional work, makes clear that expertise, not politics, is to be put in command. In case, however, there is any doubt, comrades should continue reading this section of the CC statement in particular, where it is said that "Titles for technical personnel should be restored, the system to assess technical proficiency should be established and technical posts must entail specific responsibility." (p. 10)

This is then followed by the most revealing and most vicious statement of all: "*Just as* we ensure the time for the workers and peasants to engage in productive labor, *so* scientific research workers must be given no less than 5/6 of their work hours each week for professional work." (p. 10, emphasis added). One could hardly ask for a clearer statement that the division of labor—specifically between mental and manual workers—is to be made an absolute and everyone is to "keep in their place." This is exactly the Confucian doctrine of "restoring the rites" and completely in line with the Confucian—and generally the exploiting class—notion that those who work with their minds govern while those who work with their hands are governed. It is an out front declaration not only of expert over red but of experts in command over the masses; or as one comrade put it, with regard to the differences left over from capitalist society, the soil engendering capitalism and the bourgeoisie, it is a proclamation of "vive la difference!" (long live the difference!)

Mao was very emphatic in opposing exactly this line. As early as 1958 he insisted: "The non-professional leading the professional is a general rule... Last year the rightists brought up this question and created a lot of trouble. They claimed that the non-professional could not lead the professional... Politicians handle the mutual relations among men; they promote the mass line. We must study this issue carefully, because many engineers and scientists do not respect us, and many among us do not respect ourselves, arbitrarily insisting on the difficulty of non-professionals leading professionals. We must have the ways and means to refute them. I say that non-professionals leading the professionals is a general rule." (from the U.S. Government collection of Mao's post-1949 writings, speeches and talks) And we can see that once again, "Last year the rightists brought up this question and created a lot of trouble." Unfortunately, however, this time the rightists won out, reversing Mao's correct line.

What is the importance of this question of non-professionals leading professionals, what is the heart of it? It is the question of politics in command and the leading role of the Party's Marxist-Leninist line. As was pointed out by the Four, "Dialectical materialism holds that it is a universal law for non-professionals to lead professionals. Anyone who maintains that only those with scientific and technical knowledge can lead a certain branch of work is not only negating the leadership of politics over vocational work but is actually denying any possibility of giving unified leadership over various departments of vocational work. Of course, this does not mean that comrades engaged in Party work on the scientific and technical front should not learn scientific and technical knowledge at all. Our Party has always maintained that cadres should learn the vocational work they lead and strive to be both red and expert . . ." (*PR* No. 18, 1976, p. 9) In other words, without politics in command and the leadership of the Party's line, departmentalism and many different lines will be the inevitable result and there is no way revisionism can be prevented from taking hold. This is inevitably where the line of non-professionals cannot lead professionals and "experts or near-experts" must lead professional work will lead and is certainly leading in China today—all in the name of developing science and technology to "advanced world levels," of course.

Another note on this—the Central Committee statement claims that "The modernization of science and technology is the key to the realization of the four modernizations." (*PR* No. 40, 1977, p. 7) This view treats science as science and production as production and negates class struggle as the key link, whether in developing production or science. Further, this line is another way of putting forward the principal contradiction as between the the advanced socialist system and the backward productive forces. If we look at another major statement on science and technology by the current rulers, this will become even clearer. In *Peking Review* No. 30, 1977 there is an article whose title is a tip off that it takes this line—"We Must Catch Up With and Surpass World's Advanced Levels Within This Century." This article goes on to describe, with undisguised envy, the development of science and technology in the advanced capitalist countries and then says that on the other hand these advances are held back there because of the system of private ownership. China, by contrast, the article says, is in exactly the opposite position: it has the system of socialized ownership, the "superior" socialist system, but it lags far behind in scientific achievement and technology. In other words, the contradiction in China is, once again, between the advanced socialist system and the backwardness of technology, the backward productive forces.

The article goes on to say that this can be overcome because "Scientific and technical work in China is carried on under the leadership of the Party according to a unified plan. This makes it possible for us to organize the forces from all quarters to make energetic and concerted efforts, extensively unfold mass movements and bring into full play both the collective strength and individual talents and abilities." (*PR* No. 30, p. 11) What is missing here, characteristically, is the question of class struggle within the collective form, after the question of socialization of ownership has been settled (in the main).

In light of the above it is very interesting to look at a comment by Mao on the Soviet Political Economy Textbook (referred to before). Mao first quotes the Soviet textbook as follows: " 'In a socialist national economy, the latest achievements in science, technical inventions and advanced experiences all can be popularized in all enterprises without the least hindrance.' " This is indeed very similar to what was quoted just above from the *Peking Review* article (No. 30).

But note how Mao criticizes the Soviet statement: "This is not necessarily so. In a socialist society, there are still 'academic lords' who are in control of scientific and research institutions and suppress newborn forces. For this reason, the latest achievements in science cannot find popularization without the least hindrance. To say otherwise is not to recognize the contradictions in a socialist society." (from the U.S. Government collection of Mao's post-1949 speeches, writings and talks) Is not this statement by Mao in direct opposition to the article in *PR* No. 30 and is not the line of that article, representing those "academic lords," exactly the line of the Soviet revisionists Mao is taking to task? Of course, this *PR* article tries to put on a cover of talking about "class struggle" and "modernization . . . under the command of revolutionarization." (p. 11) But, again, comrades should carefully study this to get beyond the appearance to the essence and ask themselves whether this talk is more than just that and whether in fact this article really bases itself on the class struggle as the key link, in science as well as other spheres. In fact, a Marxist analysis of this article, and the whole line of the current rulers on science and technology, as well as other questions, will make clear that class struggle is not at all presented as the key link and the principal contradiction is not at all presented as between the proletariat and the bourgeoisie, but in terms of the revisionist notion of the "superior" socialist system vs. the backward productive forces.

Returning to the CC statement (*PR* No. 40, 1977) we find the two-into-one formulation that "Technological revolution is an important aspect of the continued revolution under the dictatorship of the proletariat." (p. 6) It is true that one of the main tasks of the proletariat in power is to develop production, including technological revolution as a key part of this. But this is not the same thing as continuing the revolution under the dictatorship of the proletariat, which refers to waging the class struggle. Look, for example, at the statement of the "General Programme" of the Party, as found in the Constitution of the 10th Congress of the Chinese Communist Party, where the existence of classes and class struggle and the danger of capitalist restoration throughout the socialist period are summarized, along with the threat of aggression by imperialism and social-imperialism; and then it is said that "These contradictions can be resolved only by depending on the theory of continued revolution under the dictatorship of the proletariat and on practice under its guidance." (p. 62 in documents from the 10th Congress)

In line with this Mao says in "On Contradiction" that qualitatively different contradictions are resolved by qualitatively different means, and that, for example, the contradiction between the proletariat and the bourgeoisie is resolved by the method of socialist revolution while the contradiction between society and nature is resolved by the method of developing the productive forces. Of course, these contradictions and the methods for resolving them are inter-related and this is especially important to grasp with regard to socialist society. But nonetheless they are separate contradictions resolved by different means, and between them the contradiction between the proletariat against the bourgeoisie is decisive for the question of developing the productive forces, including technological revolution as a crucial part of this, along socialist lines. To merge together the two contradictions and the methods for resolving them is another way of denying and attempting to obliterate the principal contradiction, the key link of class struggle and the commanding role of revolution over technological development.

But even leaving all this aside, the CC statement that the modernization of science and technology is the key to the "four modernizations" is still wrong. It is what the current rulers mean when they say science and technology must "precede production." They mean that "Only by learning what is advanced can we catch up with and surpass the advanced." (p. 9) In other words, they mean that it is necessary to rely on experts, studying foreign experience in isolation from the actual struggle for production in China and the actual masses who carry out that struggle, in order to develop "new techniques" that will bring about "great increase in labor productivity." (p. 7—if anyone thinks that is not what they mean, study over this CC statement again and see if the few stock phrases about combining with the masses or the emphasis on experts in command is the actual essence of this statement)

Is it wrong to study foreign experience and to be acquainted with and attempt to make use of the most advanced techniques? Of course not. But it is completely wrong to rely on this, because, in the main, scientific and technical breakthroughs have to come on the basis of advancing from the actual production base and production conditions in your own country—unless you want to sell out for foreign technology as the "20 Points" advocates, and even then you can only bring about lop-sided "development." And furthermore, as an article criticizing the "20 Points" stated very correctly, "foreign technology must be divided into two. Technical designs of capitalist countries serve the pursuit of the highest profits by the monopoly bourgeoisie and bear a clearcut class coat of arms. How can we use them without distinguishing the 'white cat and black cat'?" (from an article in *Study and Criticism*, April 14, 1976) The current rulers may talk about independence and self-reliance and "China's own road of developing science and technology," but their "own road" is the capitalist road and their real line is "crawling behind at a snail's pace," relying on experts and the bourgeoisie of other countries.

Their line is well criticized by the following statement from the Shanghai textbook:

> "Advances in science and technology and innovations in production tools play a big role in developing production and raising labor productivity. But . . . science and technology are discovered by people, and production tools are created by people . . . [the revisionist line] deals with

> production as production and opposes revolution under the pretext of developing production. It even attributes the development of production wholly to the development of science and technology and the improvement of production tools, to a reliance on bourgeois experts."

It would be possible to go on for several more pages just criticizing the line of the current rulers on science and technology and the Central Committee statement in PR No. 40, but that is not necessary here—this statement is a rich vein of revisionism and this should be obvious if comrades study it seriously and subject it to Marxist-Leninist analysis.

It is possible that on this question of science and technology, while overwhelmingly fighting for a correct line in the face of a genuine hurricane to reverse correct verdicts, the Four may have erred a little in the direction of not giving quite enough emphasis to "science in its own right," to basic research and the study of advanced experience. It cannot be said, however, that they did not give any weight to this—they certainly did—though perhaps not quite enough. Still, even on that aspect, their line was overall correct and certainly when weighed against the right deviationist wind they had to combat, their errors are relatively minor. There can be no comparison between their overall correct line and the revisionist line of the current rulers and there definitely cannot be any justification for the revisionism of the current rulers on the so-called basis that the Four made errors. The fact is that the Four were waging struggle to uphold new things, sprouts representing the advance to the future communist society, which had been developed through struggle and were under attack, while the current rulers were and are attacking and attempting to root out these new things in order to drag things back to the old society.

On Education

This question is obviously closely related to the question of science and technology. The line of the current rulers is that the Cultural Revolution and the transformations it brought in education have brought disaster and that the old educational system, which led in the direction of creating an intellectual aristocracy, must be revived—all, again, in the name of "modernization," especially modernization of science and technology. So now in a "major reform" of education (*PR* No. 46, 1977, p. 16) we see already that the practice of having educated youth go mainly to the countryside—and some into factories and the PLA—and having them selected for college mainly on the basis of recommendations from their fellow workers, peasants, soldiers—this system is now being "revised," so that instead of this at least a certain number of people on the basis of their high examination scores will be selected to go straight to college. Along with this we hear increasing emphasis on "promising youth" and "talented young people" (see *PR* No. 46, 1977, pp. 16-17) who are obviously to be relied on to change the situation where "education has failed to keep pace with the needs of the country"—that is, it has "failed" to be based on modernization above all. This is nothing but reversing the gains made during the Cultural Revolution and deliberately widening the gap between mental and manual labor, and picking such a "select" group in this way is bound to give rise to an intellectual aristocracy. Along with this, of course, changes are being made in the educational system to restore more emphasis on study divorced from productive labor and the masses, and regulations and examinations are being reinstituted of the kind that students in the bourgeois countries are all too familiar with.

In *Peking Review* No. 46, 1977 we are left with the impression that Mao had a few minor criticisms of the educational system before the Cultural Revolution—for example he was "against the kind of examinations which posed tricky questions or were sprung on students by surprise as if to deal with enemies." (p. 17) True, Mao did make such criticisms, but more than that he called attention to the fact that before the Cultural Revolution education was under the influence of a revisionist line and was turning out bourgeois intellectual aristocrats. He issued the call that "The length of schooling should be shortened, education should be revolutionized, and the domination of our schools and colleges by bourgeois intellectuals should not be tolerated any longer." It is exactly such domination by bourgeois intellectuals that is now being re-established and the bourgeoisie is once again seizing control of education, which is an extremely important part of the superstructure and has a tremendously important reaction on the economic base and society as a whole.

The struggle around this actually reached a high point in the fall of 1975, November in particular. Some officials at Tsinghua University wrote to Mao calling for the kind of changes that are now being instituted. Mao sent their written requests to the students and staff at the University and initiated in this way a big debate around the line on education. It was very clear that Mao was (correctly I believe) opposed to these proposed changes and wanted mass criticism of them. It was in small part in response to these proposals that Mao declared, "Reversing correct verdicts goes against the will of the people." And Mao recognized that these proposed retrogressions in education were part of the whole right deviationist wind being whipped up —"The question involved in Tsinghua," Mao said then, "is not an isolated question but a reflection of the current two-line struggle." (See *PR* No. 17, 1976, p. 12—I certainly hope that no one will try to claim that this statement by Mao meant anything other than that he opposed the line of the officials at Tsinghua, the line now being implemented; if anyone does want to say that, I can assure them that they would be most welcome as a guest lecturer at Tsinghua University now, specializing in twisting logic. In any case it should be pointed out that this statement by Mao has not been taken up by the current rulers, they have just stopped mentioning it, again like petty thieves staying away from the place where they have stolen.)

It should be emphasized once again that education is an extremely important part of the superstructure and plays a very crucial role in maintaining and re-enforcing one kind of class relations or another in society. Comrades should think about their own experience and how the educational system plays such a role in this country in the hands of the bourgeoisie. It is not by accident that the all-out battle against the right deviationist wind to reverse correct verdicts began with a great debate on the educational front. In launching this debate Mao was consciously initiating a big struggle against the whole right deviationist wind, and his comment that the struggle at Tsinghua around educational policy was a reflection of the current two-line struggle shows he was well aware of and was calling attention to the fact that how opposing forces lined up on this question was indicative of how they lined up on every major question in society—on all the different fronts where the two-line struggle was raging. And, again, it is clear that the current rulers lined up on the bourgeoisie's side, while the Four stood with Mao in the proletarian camp.

The Four, and Chang Chun-chiao in particular, threw themselves into the thick of this "farrago on the educational front" as it was called then, fighting for Mao's line. Chang made a speech at Tsinghua where, according to the present leaders, he said, " 'Bring up exploiters and intellectual aristocrats with bourgeois consciousness and culture, or bring up workers with consciousness but no culture: which do you want? I'd rather have workers without culture than exploiters and intellectual aristocrats with culture.' " (see *PR* No. 8, 1977, p. 11) According to the present rulers this showed that Chang didn't want the workers to learn anything, that his statements represented "an attempt to stop laboring people from acquiring cultural and scientific knowledge their predecessors had created, a futile scheme to keep the workers and poor and lower-middle peasants for ever in a state of ignorance and without culture." (p. 13)

Perhaps Mike Klonsky believes this but I certainly do not. The Four consistently fought for Mao's line that education should enable people to "become a worker with both socialist consciousness and culture." Innumerable articles written under the Four's direction not only state but give great emphasis to both aspects of this. That was not the issue. The issue was that the rightists were declaring that working class leadership in the universities and the great increase in workers and peasants who came to the universities as students as a result of the Cultural Revolution were ruining everything because the masses' cultural level was "too low." The charge that the Four wanted to keep the masses dumb, that they wanted to do away with all examinations, etc. is once again the method of attributing a stupid argument to your opponent and then refuting it in order to cover up your own opportunism. What the Four opposed were examinations in command and examinations that required cramming and rewarded rote memorization instead of encouraging the linking of theory with practice and the application of Marxist theory to the subject matter.

To get an idea of what the Four's line actually was, and what kind of educational policy they promoted, comrades should study over an article in *PR* No. 25, 1974, "No Mark Can Do Justice to This Examination Paper" (p. 14 and following), which presents the relationship between policies and vocational work according to the correct dialectical view—emphasizing both aspects but showing how politics is the principal aspect and must be in examinations; it does not call for the elimination of exams but their reform to serve proletarian politics and the training of working class intellectuals with culture but first of all with socialist consciousness. It is these transformations that the current rulers are reversing and their slander of the Four's (and Mao's) correct line is an important part of creating public opinion for this reversal.

Further, the current rulers, at the time of the debate on the educational front (as well as before and since) were opposing the general orientation set down by Mao during the Cultural Revolution and fought for by the Four. "It is essential to have working class leadership" in the colleges and universities, Mao said, adding that "The workers' propaganda teams should stay permanently in the schools and colleges, take part in all the tasks of struggle-criticism-transformation there and will always lead these institutions." And Mao and the Four stressed, of course, that working class leadership meant leadership by the Party relying on the workers—and the poor and lower-middle peasants in schools in the countryside. (see *PR* No. 11, 1976, pp. 6-10)

Once again, this issue was very closely related to the struggle in the scientific and technical circles, especially the question of non-professionals leading professionals. It is to this question—and to the slanders of the rightists that the workers' cultural level was too low and was ruining the universities—that Chang Chun-chiao was addressing himself.

Anyone who has ever been involved in a struggle of that kind knows very well why and in what spirit Chang Chun-chiao made the statement in question (assuming he did). And again, the statement sounds very much like the following: "Some people have high cultural and technical levels, but they are neither industrious nor positive. Other people have relatively low cultural and technical levels, but they are very industrious and very positive. The reason is that the former kind of people have a lower level of consciousness, while the latter kind of people have a higher level of consciousness." (Mao, "Reading Notes on the Soviet Union's 'Political Economics,'" cited earlier) Can it be said that here Mao is praising the virtues of ignorance and trying to discourage the workers and peasants from learning culture? I don't think so. Nor can the same be said of Chang Chun-chiao. What Chang was doing was debunking the arrogant bourgeois notion of "culture," which counts the workers' vast knowledge, including their knowledge of Marxism-Leninism, Mao Tsetung Thought, as nothing and worships the sterile "culture" of the exploiting classes. No more than Mao did Chang mean that workers should not acquire book knowledge, but the key question is still consciousness—line. This, as I said, was stressed over and over and handled dialectically in many, many articles by the Four and their followers.

In short, what Chang Chun-chiao and the Four were doing was fighting to uphold the gains of the Cultural Revolution and the correct line in opposition to the onslaughts of the revisionists. It is clear where Mao stood on this: and it is also very clear where the current leaders stood and stand as well—in opposition not just to the Four but to Mao and Mao's correct line, which the Four fought for. Should Chang Chun-chiao and the others be criticized or condemned for the way they threw themselves into this battle and the line they took in it—no, they should be cherished and praised by the proletariat and all who stand with and for it. It is possible that they made some errors in dealing with the very acute struggle on the educational front —which, as stressed several times, was a crucial front of the two-line class struggle—perhaps they came down too hard on particular intellectuals who took an essentially bourgeois stand and played a bad role but were not diehard rightists. But that does not change the fact that overall and overwhelmingly the Four's line on this whole question was correct and their role in this struggle was to uphold and fight for the interests of the working class against the attacks of the bourgeoisie and bourgeois intellectual aristocrats.

On Culture, Literature and Art

The current rulers' line is to "let a hundred poisonous weeds bloom," even to promote "art for art's sake" and other trash repudiated long ago in the Chinese Revolution—anything so long as it unleashes the social base of bourgeois intellectuals and contributes to their bourgeois line. The line of the Four was to create proletarian models of literature and art and to popularize these, transforming art to serve the class struggle of the proletariat against the bourgeoisie.

To get an indication of the kind of line pushed by the current rulers on this question it is only necessary in my opinion to read "A Big-Character Poster That Denounced the 'Gang of Four' " (*PR* No. 4, 1977, pp. 22-26). The current rulers make a big deal of this poster, calling it a "fine bombardment." I think it is nothing more nor less than the arrogant bellowing of an outraged bourgeois intellectual, bridling at proletarian leadership and declaring, for example, "A work can be good or bad, refined or crude artistically and so on and so forth. But what is right and wrong in art? Who can make this clear? What a splendid view of aesthetics, which has never been heard of before." (p. 26)

Here we have nothing but "art for art's sake," under the pretense that form cannot have "errors." This, again, is to metaphysically separate form from content, declaring that there is no such thing as "right and wrong in art." If an artistic work incorrectly portrays the masses or the class enemy, not only in the words spoken but in their actions, in the prominence it gives to each on the stage, etc.—is this not a question of "right and wrong," does not this inter-penetrate with the question of content? Of course it does. To argue otherwise, as this "fine bombardment" does, is simply to promote the line that "anything goes" in art and that the question of form is only such things as whether it is "refined or crude"—a classless concept, which actually is not classless at all but serves the bourgeoisie.

It is extremely difficult to develop models of proletarian art, and this sphere has long been the domain of the bourgeoisie and exploiting classes. It was not without reason that Mao blasted the Ministry of Culture before the Cultural Revolution as the Ministry of "foreign mummies" and of Emperors, Kings, Generals, Talents, Beauties, etc. It is not by accident that the Cultural Revolution was called that—though not limited to the question of culture, one of the sharpest battlefields was certainly in this sphere. And no matter what ridiculous lines the present rulers cook up there is no doubt that the Four, and Chiang Ching in particular, played a big, and overall very positive, role in transforming art. Nor is it any accident that the revolutionization of art was launched in 1964 in Shanghai, which at that time was under the leadership of Ko Ching-shih, a consistent supporter of Mao's line and the "mentor," so to speak, of Chang Chun-chiao in particular, who served as a deputy secretary of the Party committee under Ko (more on that later).

It is true I believe that in this field in particular the Four—and I presume Chiang Ching especially—did make errors. There was a certain tendency under their leadership to insist so strongly on correctness that to some degree initiative was stifled, along with a tendency not to make full use of everyone, including some people who had made errors, even serious errors, but were not counter-revolutionaries. Some people in this category were apparently sent off to the countryside and kept there after they probably should have been allowed to resume some work in literature and art. This, I believe is true to some extent, at least in regard to professional art workers.

On the other hand the Four, including Chiang Ching especially, pushed very hard for the correct policy of integrating art workers with the workers and peasants and developing their roles in art works on that basis. It should be remembered that bourgeois individualism and resistance to proletarian politics in command and integration with the workers and peasants is very pronounced among professional artists, performers, etc. I remember that after visiting China and giving talks after returning here it was almost always the case that artists in this country put up great resistance to the idea of subordinating "individual creativity" to proletarian politics and the needs of the masses and the three great revolutionary movements (class struggle, struggle for production and scientific experiment). Even after the Cultural Revolution the spontaneous tendencies of the professional artists in China were not that much different. And, given encouragement to their bourgeois aspect—which was definitely forthcoming from rightists in powerful positions in the Party—it is even more difficult to lead such professional artists in taking the socialist road.

Further, as Mao pointed out in his talks at the Yenan Forum on Literature and Art, the reactionaries pit quantity against quality in attacking proletarian art. That is, those who oppose the revolutionization of culture seize on the fact that it is very difficult to produce works that are both correct politically and popular and on the fact that in China in particular the relatively low level of development of the productive forces makes it difficult to turn out large quantities of works—such as film and large productions—and make them accessible to the masses of people. In China's conditions the reactionaries point to the works produced in the bourgeois countries—and the large quantity of them—and use this to attack the revolutionary art works produced in China. This is precisely what the rightists have done for years in China in opposing the revolutionization of culture, and they stepped up such attacks in recent years as part of their wind to reverse correct verdicts and the Chinese revolution as a whole.

All this makes the two-line struggle on the cultural front extremely intense. And despite errors which I believe the Four—and Chiang Ching most specifically—may have made, there is no doubt that she and the Four stood with Mao in representing the proletariat in this sharp struggle, while the current rulers stood and stand for the bourgeoisie. Any errors the Four made do not nearly outweigh the fact that under their leadership—Chiang Ching's in particular—literature and art were revolutionized, and in a way not true in any socialist country before, a proletarian line guided literature and art workers and brought concrete results in creating proletarian models and popularizing the line of combining revolutionary realism with revolutionary romanticism, Mao's line. Of course it was Mao who set the basic orientation for literature and art, but the Four—and Chiang Ching specifically—carried this out, produced some fine new works and correctly transformed some old ones, such as the "White Haired Girl" (where she eliminated the suicide of the heroine's father and replaced it with heroic struggle on his part, among other changes)—transformations which, I understand, are now being reversed. And all of this was accomplished, as stressed several times, only through protracted and acute class struggle in a sphere where the bourgeoisie has long held sway and is still very strong.

Can criticism be raised of the fact that not enough works were being produced and not enough "flowers" were blooming? Yes, in my opinion, it can; but here we have to ask who is raising this criticism and with what objective. Are they uniting with the revolutionary advances made and on that basis calling for adjustment or are they using the notion of adjustment to attack the revolutionary advances? Mao is supposed to have criticized lack of quantity and variety of cultural works and called for adjustment, but assuming he did so his aim, I am sure, was not negating the revolution in literature and art and saying "the present is not as good as the past" like the right deviationists, but building on, strengthening the advances made. (This method of raising "adjustment" to carry out *reversal* is one employed by the current rulers on many other fronts as well.)

On the other hand, the current rulers have not only criticized lack of "variety" and numbers of cultural works under Chiang Ching's leadership, but have attacked and suppressed good works—such as "Breaking with Old Ideas." It is clear that their criticism is exactly to negate the revolution in literature and art—to attack a weak spot in order to kill the whole revolution in culture. And why not, since they represent the forces who want to carry out a revisionist line and in many cases have carried it out for some time. When Teng Hsiao-ping complained that not enough "flowers were blooming" in culture—what do you think was his purpose, what was he trying to promote?

The restoration of Chou Yang—and along with him Hsia Yen—long-time peddlers of the revisionist line in culture, is further evidence of the current rulers' line on this question. Chou and Hsia were overthrown during the Cultural Revolution, after having promoted a bourgeois line in culture for over 30 years: Chou at least was resurrected in 1975 when the right deviationists were whipping up their wind, and he was knocked down again in the course of the struggle against that wind, only to be resurrected once again along with Hsia Yen in recent months. These resurrections are another signal that the old bourgeois lines, such as "art for art's sake" and other such crap are being revived and that the bourgeois intellectuals in this as well as other fields are being unleashed.

With all the emphasis on tailing after the foreign and advanced—i.e. capitalist countries—it is not surprising that this takes shape in the cultural field as well. So now it is reported in the capitalist press that such things as Shakespeare, Greek mythology, the piano compositions of Beethoven, Chopin and Bach, the drawings of Rembrandt, etc. are being allowed into China and disseminated among the intellectuals, who are, of course, the ones who have special interest in these things. Is it wrong to study and even learn from certain aspects of these works? No, but as the Four repeatedly stressed in the last several years in sharp struggle over this very question, such works must be subjected to Marxist analysis and *critically* assimilated—they cannot be accepted wholesale or used as they are, for they have a clear-cut class character and as such represent exploiting class ideology. But now, with the whole line of relying on intellectuals and urging them to catch up with the "advanced" to modernize China, it is inevitable that these intellectuals will also strive to "catch up" in appreciating and uncritically swallowing down bourgeois works of art like their counterparts in "advanced" countries. In short, if the policy is to develop bourgeois intellectual aristocrats with capitalist culture—which most definitely is the current rulers' policy—then bourgeois works of art, foreign as well as Chinese, must be made available to them and actually upheld as the "model." This is clearly the direction of things on the literature and art front under the current rulers.

Finally, it should be emphasized that with whatever problems and errors there might have been in dealing especially with professional art workers, there is no doubt that under Chiang Ching's leadership there was a tremendous proliferation of revolutionary cultural works produced by and spread among the broad masses in the cities and countryside. And this creates a powerful social base for genuine proletarian art. Now, however, in the name of not disrupting production (what else?) workers' and peasants' cultural groups are to be disbanded, along with theoretical and propaganda contingents, etc. or allowed only so long as those who take part in them are not "divorced from production," a policy set forth in the "20 Points" and reiterated by Yu Chiu-li at the Taching Conference. Meanwhile the "20 Points," that "fragrant flower," says that technicians should be counted as productive laborers—so naturally there is no need for them to take part in productive labor, they are already doing so by being technicians! The activities of the masses which develop political and cultural life—the class struggle—are to be suppressed in the name of not divorcing the masses from production (!), while technicians are to be divorced from production in the name of developing production. Isn't it very clear?—the line is to create the situation where technicians and managers are in command and the workers are to be "treated as pure labor power in the production process by the 'head.' The laboring masses will no longer have the right to question whether this production process serves the interests of the proletariat and the laboring people. This way, socialist enterprises will gradually slide into the mudhold of capitalism." (Shanghai political economy textbook)

Many of the reversals that have taken place in China already, including many of those focused on in this paper, are in this realm of the superstructure. These are, as noted, closely linked to changes in the economic base and have a tremendous reaction (and "reaction" is doubly correct here) on the economic base. In fact, it is impossible to carry out such reversals in the superstructure without this being part of a reversal in the economic base, in the relations of production and the nature of how the economy is run and according to what principles. Mao attached great importance to the role of the superstructure, recognizing that at times the struggle in this realm was decisive in determining the direction of the whole society. The current rulers have learned well from Mao—just as the revisionists in the Soviet Union learned well from Lenin, as we point out in *RP7*—in order to betray his revolutionary line and reverse the revolution.

The current revisionist rulers of China are in fact acting in exactly the way Yao Wen-yuan predicted in his pamphlet, written in early 1975:

> "Once in power, the new bourgeoisie will start with sanguinary suppression of the people and restoration of capitalism in the superstructure, including all spheres of ideology and culture; then they will conduct distribution to each according to how much or little capital and power he has, so that the principle of 'to each according to his work' will become an empty shell, and the handful of new bourgeois elements monopolizing the means of production will at the same time monopolize the power of distributing consumer goods and other products. Such is the process of restoration that has already occurred in the Soviet Union." (*On the Social Basis of the Lin Piao Anti-Party Clique* pp. 8-9)

And such is the process that is now being carried out in China. That Yao was able to predict this is not at all because he is a "genius," but because he was deeply involved in the class struggle in China, and the line and intentions of the capitalist-roaders were already very clear—the struggle between restoration and counter-restoration was then raging over essentially the same attempts of the same revisionist forces in power now to reverse correct verdicts and the Chinese revolution as a whole.

And along with such reversals goes and must go the tampering with Marxist theory and Mao's revolutionary line, which is a most important part of the superstructure. As noted several times, the ideological line of the current rulers is characterized especially by eclecticism, which was repeatedly exposed and criticized by the Four. And it is most significant that in attempting to answer this criticism the current rulers only expose their line, and its eclectics in particular, even more.

Take for example, the article in *PR* No. 48, 1977, "Criticizing Eclecticism or Attacking the Theory of Two Points?" This article is itself an example of rampant eclecticism. It starts off at great length to prove that it is all right to say "on the one hand and on the other hand," as if this is the heart of the matter. And then it gets around to the real heart of the matter—the Four's criticism of the "Outline Report" on science and technology, the one of the "Three Poisonous Weeds" which Hua Kuo-feng was most *directly* responsible for. It lists five contradictions, which it presents as on the one hand this and on the other hand "*equally*" that.

As we know, dialectics teaches us that in any contradiction there is a principal contradiction. But what does this article do after listing these five contradictions, how does it address the question of principal contradiction and principal aspect? Instead of providing an answer as to which is principal, it suddenly starts talking about how "to grasp the principal contradiction and the principal aspect of a contradiction is by no means easy; very often it can be achieved only through repeated practice and a long process of cognition. This is because the conditions involved are complex, the scientific knowledge so far acquired is limited and the investigations and study done are not adequate enough." Therefore, the article warns that "we should not jump to hasty conclusions but should make further studies so as to determine which is the principal and non-principal." (see p. 13)

The purpose of the current rulers here is immediately to obscure the specific question—which has to do with the relationship between politics and vocational work—and to raise vocational work above politics without openly saying so. At the same time the more general purpose is to create confusion around questions like principal contradiction, which is very useful to the current rulers since, as shown before, they are actually adhering to a revisionist line on the principal contradiction while covering this with empty words about the real principal contradiction between the proletariat and the bourgeoisie. Such distortion of Marxist theory goes hand in hand and is an important component part of creating public opinion for and carrying out a revisionist line and capitalist restoration.

The whole revisionist outlook of the current rulers, which comes through in all their documents and propaganda, takes form as a bourgeois-bureaucratic approach to every question, including the crucial question of developing the economy. Instead of the Marxist-Leninist line, developed and enriched by Mao and fought for by the Four, which relies on and scientifically sums up the experience of the masses and unleashes their conscious activism, the current rulers' whole approach, as stressed before, is top down—at most the masses' role is to carry out the plans set at the top by methods and people divorced from the opinions, demands and experience of the masses and from Marxism-Leninism. This line and method and where they will inevitably lead was summed up in *Red Papers 7* in analyzing the restoration of capitalism in the Soviet Union:

> "It is impossible for some classless group of 'bureaucrats' to rule society in the name of the proletariat, because in order to maintain such rule these 'bureaucrats' must organize the production and distribution of goods and services. If bureaucratic methods of doing this prevail and come to *politically characterize* the planning process under socialism; and if a group of bureaucrats, divorced from and not relying upon the masses, makes the decisions on how to carry out this process; then inevitably this will be done along capitalist lines.
>
> "In the final analysis, the revisionists can only fall back on the law of value as the 'lever' which organizes production. They must reduce the workers to propertyless proletarians, competing in the sale of their single commodity—their labor power—to live. They must appeal to the narrow self-interest of the worker in this competition, backing this up with the power of the state, as a force standing above and oppressing the workers, a weapon in the hands of the owners of the means of production. They must do this because they must find some way to organize production which they cannot do consciously in a planned way by themselves. *They have no choice but to become a new bourgeoisie.*" (pp. 55-56, emphasis in original)

All this is what is happening in China today with the revisionists, the new bourgeoisie, in power.

Just compare the Chinese press under the Four with what it's like today. Before it was full of the life of the masses, their conscious struggle and daring to transform society and nature, their determination to reach for the heights, shatter convention and conquer the "unconquerable." Now it is heavy with the stuffy air of bourgeois bureaucrats and intellectual aristocrats.

On the International Situation, War and Military Policy

This is the subject about which I know the least concerning the two-line struggle, mainly because it is, by definition, the area where the least will be put out for public view. But there are indications of real differences between the Four and the current rulers on this. For example, in *Peking Review* No. 45, 1977, in a major statement on the international situation, it is said that the Four "cursed" the "three worlds" analysis, that they "opposed China's support to the third world, opposed China's effort to unite with all forces that can be united, and opposed our dealing blows at the most dangerous enemy," the Soviet social-imperialists. (see p. 18)

I think it would be a mistake to simply dismiss this as a routine denunciation of the Four and the usual attempt to say that they were against everything you are supposed to be for. This article not only makes the above accusations but goes on to emphasize that "The 'gang of four' in no way represent the Chinese people. They are traitors disowned by the Chinese people." (p. 18) I take this to be a statement to the numerous political parties and whatever diplomatic personages the Four had contact with that these people should not take whatever the Four told them on international affairs as the line of the Chinese. This suggests that there were, in fact, some real differences over this.

It is not clear to me at this time exactly what all these differences may have been, but some things do provide an indication of some of these differences. One is the fact that since the Four have been knocked down the "three worlds" analysis has been really pushed out as "the correct strategic and tactical formulation for the world proletariat in the present era and its class line in its international struggle." (from Hua Kuo-feng's report to the 11th Congress, *PR* No. 35, 1977, p. 41, see also the major article in *PR* No. 45, 1977) Part of the reason that this has been pushed in this way over the past year especially are, of course, the recent attacks on the "three worlds" analysis by the Albanians. But it may well also be the case that the Four, while agreeing with the general analysis of the division of the world into "three worlds," did not go so far as the present rulers in calling it *the* "strategic concept" for the international proletarian struggle.

What is more clear is that the Four, while agreeing with the policy of "opening to the West" to make use of contradictions in the face of the threat of Soviet aggression against China, also fought against any "major policy" of importing and relying on Western technology as the basis for developing the economy and national defense and definitely fought against importing uncritically the culture and ideology of the Western bourgeoisie. These were key points of struggle between the Four and the current rulers, as noted already.

It is also clear that on the question of war and military policy there were significant differences between the position of the Four and the present rulers—which would only make sense, since they have fundamentally opposed lines on all other questions. The Four, from what I can tell, regarded the danger of war as being more or less imminent, that is, the danger of the outbreak of war, including presumably an attack on China as at least a real possibility, was seen by them in terms of a brief period of years—as opposed to, say, 25 years. From certain polemics they carried out in the form of the "Lin Piao and Confucius" campaign—and the Legalists vs. the Confucianists in particular (more on that later)—as well as in some other more direct ways, it seems that they felt that primary attention should be devoted to agriculture and preparation for war, as opposed to a policy of extensive trade—that is, presumably, major trade to get modern arms. This is in line with the concept of storing grain everywhere and being prepared against war—as well as natural disaster—that is, preparing to fight a people's war, on Chinese territory and in circumstances in which, like the War of Resistance Against Japan and the War of Liberation that followed, there would be the necessity for relatively self-sufficient base areas. This is one of the main reasons—besides the fact that they had a weak base in the regular army—that the Four put stress on building up the militia, which plays an important role in a people's war of this kind.

The Four were not opposed to modernizing China's armaments, but they were opposed to putting main emphasis on this. This, I believe, is both because they thought that such a line is in conflict with fighting a people's war—which *reliance* on modernization is—since such reliance dictates a different kind of strategy and different kind of army—and because they did not think that China could hope to achieve anything like parity in weaponry with the imperialists, most specifically the Soviets, in the time before war would break out—they were also correct on this in my opinion.

In a nutshell, the Four felt that to put the main stress on

modernization and to base military policy on this would actually lead to disaster for China and that in order to "buy time" and "modernize" the present rulers would capitulate to imperialism and/or social-imperialism and in a war would follow a military line that would bring tremendous defeats.

That the present rulers are taking the road of modernization first and actually abandoning Mao's line on people's war is very strongly indicated by the restoration of Lo Jui-ching as well as associates of Peng Teh-huai, whom Mao knocked down in struggles which centered in large part over this question. Recent reports from not totally unreliable bourgeois sources indicate that Lo and others who now play a key role in the Logistics Department of the PLA have been proposing plans for fighting a pretty large-scale battle on or very near the border with the Soviets. This is opposed to the line which Mao put forward and which he—in opposition to these revisionist military "experts" in power now—did not consider "outdated."

Mao stressed that if attacked or invaded on anything but a small scale, the correct and necessary thing would be to pull back and lure the enemy in—and he stressed that this would be possible. In 1969, in summing up the Ninth Party Congress—a time, it should be remembered, when there was not only massive U.S. presence in South Vietnam and continued aggression against the North but also great tension on the northern Chinese border caused by Soviet provocations—Mao argued with powerful forces in the Chinese Communist Party (perhaps including Chen Yi) that "Others may come and attack us but we shall not fight outside our borders. We do not fight outside our borders. I say we will not be provoked. Even if you invite us to come out we will not come out, but if you should come and attack us we will deal with you. It depends on whether you attack on a small scale or a large scale. If it is on a small scale we will fight on the border. If it is on a large scale then I am in favor of yielding some ground. China is no small country. If there is nothing in it for them I don't think they will come. We must make it clear to the whole world that we have both right and advantage on our side. If they invade our territory then I think it would be more to our advantage, and we would then have both right and advantage. They would be easy to fight since they would fall into the people's encirclement. As for things like airplanes, tanks and armored cars, everywhere experience proves that they can be dealt with." (from Stuart Schram's collection, *Chairman Mao Talks to the People*, pp. 285-6)

Abandoning this line as "outdated" and relying on modernization and fighting a "modern war," which is a "war of steel," as Teng Hsiao-ping said in recent years, this is to follow a course that will bring disaster to China. And this, from all I can tell, is the line of the present rulers.

From this it is clear that, as touched on earlier, the argument that, "never mind if the modernizations are being made everything, China has to modernize to defend itself"—an argument which, I believe, is a last refuge for pragmatists on events in China—such an argument is self-defeating. Far from China's salvation in the face of admittedly difficult conditions, this line, the line of writing off revolution and subordinating everything to modernization, can only lead to serious setbacks and—if it is not reversed—defeat for the proletariat at the hands of the bourgeoisie both within China and internationally. In 1974, at the UN, Teng Hsiao-ping said that "If capitalism is restored in a big socialist country, it will inevitably become a superpower." (see *Peking Review*, No. 15, 1974, special supplement). This, I believe, should actually be considered wishful thinking on Teng's part. The line of Teng and the others who now rule China will lead not to its becoming a superpower—and certainly not to its becoming a powerful *socialist* country—but in various ways will lead it to being reduced once again to a country subjugated by various means by imperialists.

Only upholding and implementing a revolutionary line, on military policy as well as other questions, will enable China to defeat the enemy at home and internationally and to continue on the socialist road. This overwhelmingly is the line that the Four fought for in opposition to those in power now.

I should say that as for the general line on the international situation, the "three worlds" analysis, the Soviet Union as the main danger, most dangerous source of war, etc. I do not and our Party has not agreed with what I understand to be the line of the Four—and Mao—on every aspect of this. However, it should be said also that it is not at all clear that Mao or the Four dealt with the "three worlds" analysis as the great "strategic concept" in the way it is being put forward now. In fact the statement by Mao, quoted in *Peking Review*, No. 45, 1977, where he describes the division into "three worlds" to a third world leader, does not present this as a strategic concept and in and of itself at least sounds more like the way our Party has treated the "three worlds analysis"—as a general description of the role of countries in the world today and one part of the line of developing the international united front against the two superpowers. (See p. 11; it is also interesting to note, in passing here, that another quote from Mao in that same article actually goes against the idea that Mao expected China to surpass the advanced countries economically in a relatively short period, even within the next 23 years—"China belongs to the third world," Mao is quoted, and he continues, "For China cannot compare with the rich or powerful countries politically, economically, etc. She can be grouped only with the relatively poor countries"—see *Peking Review*, No. 45, 1977, p. 28)

Our Party does have disagreement with what seems to have been the line of the Four and Mao over the role of the Soviet Union. It is correct, as our Party has consistently pointed out, for the Chinese to target the Soviets as the main danger to them and to make use of certain contradictions on that basis; but there does seem to have been a tendency on the part of the Four and Mao (as well as the line of the latest major articles from China) to take this as far as saying the Soviets are the most dangerous source of war, the main danger to the world's people, etc.

With this our Party does not agree—while we do agree with the fact that the Soviets are overall on the offensive in the contention between the two superpowers, we do not go along with the idea that this makes them the main danger, most dangerous source of war, etc. Still I must say that the policy of lining up all possible forces against the Soviets has more justification, even if it involves some erroneous formulations such as main danger, etc., if the danger of war is viewed as being rather immediate, as the Four apparently saw it—as compared to the present rulers who seem to cherish hopes at least of being able to forestall it for some time, perhaps even 25 years.

In sum on this specific point, the line of the Four on this question, which was essentially the line of Mao, while in my opinion not correct in certain aspects, was certainly not a revisionist line. It was not a line like that of the present rulers which will, unless it is reversed, lead to the destruction of socialism in China.

****

From all that has been said I believe it is very clear that the present rulers of China have betrayed Mao's line and are implementing a revisionist line. As for how to view the Four, on a certain level that should be very easy in light of what has been shown. The present rulers of China have proclaimed a thousand times over that only by knocking down the Four—and their many followers throughout the country—is it possible to carry out the current line.

Therefore, on that basis alone, we should uphold the Four as revolutionary heroes. However, I believe that it has been shown in a deeper, more thorough way, by examining the line of the Four themselves in opposition to that of the current rulers on a number of crucial questions, that the Four were carrying out a correct line and fighting for the interests of the proletariat. Having, I believe, established this on the basis of examining major questions of line, it is now possible, and no doubt necessary, to examine and refute certain other questions and other arguments which are raised to justify or apologize for the present rulers and discredit and attack the Four.

II. Refutation of Certain Erroneous Arguments in Defense of the *Status Quo* and Against the Four

Here I would like to mainly pose and answer some of the main arguments raised by those who can't help but agree that there are some bad lines being taken by the people now running China, but say that somehow these should be excused or at any rate are justified or unavoidable because of the worse line and role of the Four or because of the situation and problems in China and other such nonsense.

At the start it should be said that, in my opinion, most of these arguments are rooted in a thoroughly pragmatic method that proceeds from the assumption that since the Four lost in the latest struggle therefore they must be bad. Flowing from such an assumption the approach is to try to find fault with the Four and justify the *status quo*, even inventing arguments and twisting facts to make things fit and to avoid the obvious conclusion which has to be reached by analyzing the actual two-line struggle that went down over the past few years and the role of various forces in that struggle—the conclusion that the Four represented, along with Mao, the proletarian headquarters while the current rulers, including most definitely Hua Kuo-feng, represented and still represent the bourgeois headquarters. Having said that as a preface, let's turn to the arguments.

"The 'gang of four' would not unite with anyone else, they broadened instead of narrowing the target, and so they had to go down."

Wouldn't unite with anyone else? Then why did a quarter of the Central Committee, including most of the representatives of mass organizations and forces who came to the fore in the Cultural Revolution, have to be purged, as well as perhaps as many as half of the Provincial Secretaries and thousands of leading cadre throughout the country?

Who should they have united with that they failed to unite with? People like Hua Kuo-feng? But how could they unite with him when he was one of the leading people pushing the revisionist line and whipping up the right deviationist wind? Over the past month and more in the *Peking Review* it has been emphatically stated that Hua was very much involved in formulating the "Three Poisonous Weeds" (sorry, "fragrant flowers"). If it is true, which it is, that these are indeed "poisonous weeds" then how could the Four unite with someone playing a major role in pushing this line? To talk about "uniting" abstracted from line is exactly to raise unity above the class struggle and will end you up in unity with the bourgeoisie—on *its* terms!

Further, Hua's report to the 1975 Tachai Conference is, as I indicated at the beginning, another "poisonous weed." (I want to say here that my understanding of the revisionist nature of Hua's speech was deepened by a paper written by a comrade criticizing it, which was submitted to the Party center over a year ago, in accordance with the directives set by the center for approaching the China question.) This speech has all the right deviationist code words—"rectification," deal sternly with the "soft, lax and lazy" and resolutely with "bourgeois factionalism"—and it reads very much like the "General Program." First and foremost it is a plan not for developing agriculture, but for a *purge*.

But more importantly, it even goes so far as to cut off Mao's quote about how the country practices a commodity system, eight-grade wage scale, etc., deliberately omitting the conclusion Mao draws, the part that indicates the whole point and the life and death nature of the problem—"*Therefore if people like Lin Piao come to power, it will be quite easy for them to rig up the capitalist system. That* is why we should do more reading of Marxist-Leninist works." (emphasis added) Omitting this, as noted before, goes right along with the line of the current rulers which says, in essence, bourgeois right, the three great differences, etc., can only be restricted under socialism—*this* is Chairman Mao's "brilliant idea"—so why worry about them. But, as we've seen, they're not restricting them at all, but expanding them.

To give a speech during the very time of the campaign to study the theory of proletarian dictatorship (1975) and to cut off this part of Mao's quote, as Hua does, is, as already indicated, to deliberately fly in the face of Mao's most important instructions and tamper with the basic line of the Party. This makes the call in Hua's speech for "Deepening Education in Party's Basic Line" (section 3) a mockery and explains why Chang Chun-chiao is reported to have said that Hua's version of the Party's basic line is not really its basic line at all—since that basic line stresses exactly the danger of capitalist restoration.

Along with this, Hua's speech rather openly promotes the "dying out of class struggle" line, saying that only in a few rural areas is class struggle very acute and that the class enemy is essentially defined by those who commit sabotage and that the main form of the capitalist road to be combatted is small scale capitalist production. This, again, is a speech made at the very time that the right deviationist wind is being whipped up on a big scale, yet the spearhead is directed downward, away from the revisionists in top leadership and their line. This is why the Four were supposed to have said that it attacks corrupt officials only and not the emperor (a reference to Mao's instruction on the novel "Water Margin," which he put out in August, 1975, to help the masses identify right capitulationists like Teng Hsiao-ping) and why the Four said that it does no good to assail foxes (corrupt officials and others at the local level) when wolves are in power (revisionists at the top of the Party).

Beyond this, Hua's speech gives no serious attention to the question of restricting bourgeois right and to combatting the tendency to do more work for more profit, less work for less profit and no work for no profit—which are serious tendencies that must be identified and combatted, especially in issuing a call for all-out competition among counties, communes, etc. to win the rank of "Tachai-type county." Nor, with all its emphasis on farmland capital construction contingents and increasing the scope of activity of brigade, commune, and even county level projects, does it address the problem of basically *equalizing* the income of the *teams*, which is an essential part of moving from the team to the brigade as the basic accounting unit, the next step in advancing the ownership system in the countryside.

About the same time as Hua's speech (probably a little later), Mao made the very important statement that "With the socialist revolution they themselves come under fire. At the time of the co-operative transformation of agriculture there were people in the Party who opposed it, and when it comes to criticizing bourgeois right, they resent it." Among other things what Mao is stressing here is that previously, if agriculture had not undergone co-operative transformation, capitalist polarization would have gone on in the countryside on a great scale; and now, if bourgeois right is not criticized and restricted, within and between brigades, communes, teams, counties, etc., the same thing will happen. Comrades should ask themselves: is this the spirit of Hua's 1975 Tachai speech, in fact does his speech even deal seriously with this question at all?

As a general characterization of Hua's speech it can be said that it is boring—which is not merely a criticism of style but of political content and basic method. Mao's comment on the Soviet Political Economy Textbook (referred to several times before) is directly relevent here: "It lacks persuasiveness and makes dull reading. It does not start from making a specific analysis of the contradictions between productive forces and production relationship and the contradictions between the economic basis and the superstructure. . . ." (From the U.S. Government collection)

Hua's speech mentions the Cultural Revolution very little and then essentially in the past tense. The whole point is that with the Cultural Revolution and the movement to criticize Lin Piao and Confucius such "brilliant successes" have been achieved in the class struggle that really the class struggle is dying out and it is time to take up production as the main task so as to achieve the "four modernizations" by the end of the century. This is not said straight up, of course, but this is what really comes through. And according to Hua, anyone who doesn't agree with this view is a "bourgeois factionalist," is not uniting and being open and aboveboard and so should be smashed as a revisionist.

To get a clearer view of the revisionist line of Hua's speech comrades should compare it with especially the speech by Wang Chintzu, which was reprinted together with Hua's speech, and another by Kuo Feng-lien, in a (green) pamphlet in late 1975. I think it is clear that, whether subjectively (consciously) or not, this speech by Wang is objectively a polemic against Hua's and is in direct opposition to it. (I don't know at this time what has become of Wang, whether he supports the current rulers or has gone along with them, or has been dumped or demoted; Kuo Feng-lien has gone right along with Hua & Co., but that is not the point, anyway; the point is that Wang's speech in particular is, as stated, objectively the opposite line from Hua's and puts forward the line of the Four, and Mao—it even uses the phrase, "exercise all-around dictatorship over the bourgeoisie," which echoes the title of Chang Chunchiao's 1975 pamphlet, a phrase which is now condemned in China.) Comrades should study over Wang and Hua's speeches in particular and compare and contrast the two lines in them.

Here I will make only a few comments of comparison and contrast between the two speeches. Wang stresses that "We must be able to recognize capitalism under the signboard of 'for the collective,' as well as obvious capitalism. If we know only how to struggle against obvious capitalism and not against capitalism disguised as socialism, we shall suffer defeats and fail to realize socialism." (p. 55, pamphlet) This is the opposite emphasis from Hua's speech.

Wang stresses that learning from Tachai "does not mean merely levelling hills and harnessing rivers, nor just raising grain production, but that it is one of continuing the revolution and consolidating the dictatorship of the proletariat." (see p. 54) This is not the emphasis Hua gives to learning from Tachai, despite some stock phrases about politics in command, etc.

Wang points out that "To realize farm mechanization involves a great revolution replete with sharp struggle between the two roads, two lines and two ideologies." (p. 64) This emphasis is missing from Hua's speech.

Hua's whole program for "rectification" is basically all top down. Wang, on the other hand, stresses that "Revolutionizing the county Party committee depends mainly on open-door rectification, i.e., arousing the masses to help it in this task." Hua presents the question as though somehow building Tachai-type counties will ("automatically") revolutionize the county Party committees (with purge and top-down rectification where necessary), while Wang puts the emphasis the other way around—"without revolutionizing the county Party committee there cannot be any sustained movement to learn from Tachai." (see p. 70, 71-2) It is Wang, in opposition to Hua, who puts forward the line of "grasp revolution, promote production," while the line running through Hua's speech is in essence, "grasp revolution—that is, promote production."

I could go on at much greater length analyzing the revisionism of Hua's speech, but if comrades go into it deeply and use the telescope and microscope of Marxism-Leninism, Mao Tsetung Thought, and if they compare and contrast Hua's speech with Mao's line and directives, as well as with the speech by Wang Chin-tzu, it will become clear that Hua's speech at the 1975 Tachai Conference is yet another indication that he was part of the right deviationists then as he is now. Now, with Mao and the Four gone, Hua's revisionism is less disguised than before. But keeping in mind Mao's line and emphasis in late 1975, Hua's speech even at that time stands out as clearly opposed to Mao.

A note on the second Tachai Conference and Chen Yung-kuei's speech there in particular. Chen does include a number of statements that are missing from Hua's 1975 Tachai speech and he does go into such things as capitalism in the form of the collective, the need to restrict bourgeois right, to pay attention to equalizing the level of the teams, and other things which are not wrong at all in and of themselves. But the first point that must be grasped is that the main purpose of this speech by Chen is to attempt to justify and to uphold Hua Kuo-feng's 1975 Tachai speech. And second, Chen's speech itself contains the totally incorrect formulation that the dividing line between Marxism and the "theory of the productive forces" is "whether one *attaches* the development of the productive forces to socialism or to capitalism," which is how we know what road one is really taking. (See *Peking Review*, No. 2, 1977, p. 12, emphasis added.)

This actually treats production not as the unity of productive forces and productive relations but as a thing which can simply be attached to one kind of production relation or another. It is metaphysical and in fact covers for the "theory of the productive forces." Hence, in the final analysis, despite many nice words to the contrary, Chen's speech actually promotes the incorrect line and is an accomplice of revisionism.

Similarly, the book *Tachai, The Red Banner*, while it contains a number of good things, also has the line running through it that basically the peasants on their own (sort of "automatically") can figure out the correct line and along with this it even promotes the idea that if you want to tell friends from enemies, look to see who lived in caves in the old society and who has callouses on their hands to tell who the revolutionaries are and then the counter-revolutionaries can be easily identified as those who attack such people. From reading this book it is quite possible to see how at least some people in Tachai and those following the line of the book itself could be taken in by a bad line if it was put forward by hard-working people seemingly dedicated to the interests of the masses. (For a flagrant expression of the same empiricist/revenge line, see interview with Chen Yung-kuei, *New China* summer, 1977)

This raises another very important point. There are two ways, not just one, to pull down the red banner of Tachai. One is to openly pull down the banner, but the other is to paint the banner white. In other words, it is quite possible to pervert the real lesson of Tachai, as Hua Kuo-feng & Co. have indeed done. As Marxists we cannot look upon Tachai as some kind of holy symbol, but must examine it, too, from the Marxist stand, viewpoint and method, concentrating on line. If the Soviet Union can be turned into its opposite, so can Tachai; and today we do not say "learn from the

Soviet Union"—except by negative example. This is why, after Hua & Co. had moved to turn Tachai into its opposite, Chang Chun-chiao was supposed to have said that there is no use in learning from Tachai *now*. The same holds true for Taching, the red banner in industry which Hua & Co. have painted white, turning it into a "model" for applying the line they laid out in the "20 Points" and other revisionist documents and articles. Once again, in going beyond appearance to grasp the essence of this we have to apply materialist dialectics and be "ruthlessly scientific." If we do this we will be able to discern how Hua & Co. are turning not just models in China but China itself into its opposite.

"But Mao picked Hua Kuo-feng as his successor and said 'With you in charge, I'm at ease'." First, from what I have been able to find out, this statement attributed to Mao does not say in the Chinese "With you in charge," it says rather "with you carrying out your work"—this is a much more accurate translation from what I have been able to learn. This expression "carrying out your work" is one commonly used with subordinates in a unit, department, etc. and does not at all carry the weight that a completely different expression in Chinese, "With you in charge," would carry.

But more importantly this argument that "Mao picked Hua" and the view it expresses is completely idealist and metaphysical. "Mao picked"—as though Mao had complete freedom to do whatever he wanted at any time.

To understand how Hua came to be Premier and first Vice Chairman it is necessary to keep in mind and analyze the overall situation, the different forces involved and how things developed up to the point where this decision was made and to view it from the standpoint of what lines different people and forces represent. It seems so clear to me that I find it difficult to believe anyone seriously doubts it—that Hua's appointment was the product of very sharp struggle which was very far from resolved at the time that Hua was appointed acting Premier (January, 1976) or when he was appointed Premier and First Vice Chairman (April, 1976).

What was going on then? Chou En-lai (about whom more in a little while) had just died and Mao had launched the struggle against Teng and the right deviationist wind. "Mao had launched"—am I falling into the same metaphysics and idealism I just criticized? No, because it is clear that no one but Mao could have launched such a movement. Before it was launched, Teng was riding high and he had plenty of powerful support. Who else but Mao could have made him the target of such a struggle and knocked him down, kept him from becoming Premier? The Four alone? Hardly!

In fact there were, as subsequent events have made abundantly clear, powerful forces in the Chinese leadership who strongly opposed the campaign against Teng and the right deviationist wind—not the least of which were powerful military commanders. But exactly because Mao threw his weight behind this campaign, these forces had to beat a temporary and partial retreat and go along with knocking down Teng. But they certainly were not about to allow one of the Four to become acting head of the Central Committee and the country in effect. Therefore they backed Hua, someone who, as an analysis of his line and role has shown, was politically in their camp but was not such an easy target with long years of brazen revisionism to attack, like Teng.

Under these conditions, with the balance of forces being what they were, Mao had to go along with Hua's appointments. It has been stated in the bourgeois press that Yeh Chien-ying, in particular, insisted that Mao give personal authority to Hua's appointments, or else there would be no compromise at all. Whether these specific reports are true or not, it is obvious that powerful forces in the leadership insisted on Hua and that this was the necessity faced by Mao, which he tried to make the best of.

How did he do that? By continuing and giving guidance to the mass campaign against Teng and the right deviationist wind, which was politically a blow not only at Teng but at all those who had joined with him in whipping up this wind, Hua included. Teng was made the specific target for the same reason that the rightists had to agree to dumping him—he was someone well known for taking the capitalist road and it would be difficult, at least while Mao was still around, to make an all-out fight to back Teng. Mao knew that the deeper this struggle against the right deviationist wind went and the more thoroughly it was carried out, the harder the blows at the rightists and the more favorable the conditions for the left. But the right knew it too, which is why they seized on every possible basis to kill this struggle—including the earthquakes. And we have seen what happened to that struggle after Mao died—those who were actively leading it, the Four, were almost immediately smashed and the target of the struggle was shifted from the right to them, the (genuine) left. And as I said before the struggle against the right deviationist wind has not been just stopped but completely reversed.

The argument that appointing Hua as First Vice Chairman was unprecedented in the Chinese Party's history is not only ridiculous but revealing. It occurs to me that there is a historical precedent for this—Lin Piao's enshrinement as Mao's successor at the Ninth Party Congress. And as became clear later, already at that time Mao had launched struggle against Lin and his line. I believe this is the same with Hua—Mao was forced to go along with and "officially endorse" his appointments, but the political movement he launched and led was aimed at the very line Hua, as well as others, upheld.

Mao's tactics here were actually masterful. What he did in the face of the necessity presented to him was to put Hua in the position where he had to go against the right deviationist wind and denounce Teng as a counter-revolutionary (see Hua's speech at the memorial for Mao, *Peking Review* No. 39, 1976, for another reminder of what Hua was forced to say in those days and also how far he has departed from, and how far he has gone in betraying Mao's line and actual last "behests"). Mao's tactics here were a way of creating a split in the ranks of the rightists. At the same time, no doubt Mao tried to win Hua over—but he did not rely on it. Most fundamentally through the movement he launched against the right deviationists' attempt at reversing correct verdicts and the specific direction he gave in this struggle, Mao made the conditions the most favorable possible under the circumstances for the genuine left, the Four, and for the masses in fighting to carry forward the revolution. The fact that despite this the right won out in this battle shows just how strong the right had become at that point and what powerful forces the right had in its camp.

Further, as to the question of Hua being Mao's "chosen successor," it is significant to note that it is widely reported that in late May or early June, 1976 (sometime after Mao's famous statement about being "at ease"—which, by the way, has to be one of the most ironic statements in political history, since Mao clearly was not "at ease"), Mao is supposed to have had a last meeting with most of the Politburo, including Hua. At that meeting Mao apparently talked about the question of succession, and he must have said something other than "With Hua Kuo-feng in charge, I'm at ease," because this last meeting is never referred to by the current rulers.

Am I saying that Hua and Teng have an identical line and that, except for the Four, there was one solid bloc of rightists on the Politburo? No, but from every indication there was indeed a rightist bloc, certainly with some divisions within it, and on the opposite side there were the Four (leaving Mao out of the picture for the moment) and undoubtedly a number of "middle forces" not firmly wed to either side. But the point is that with whatever differences they may have had then and no doubt have now (more on this shortly) Hua, Teng and others, including at least Li Hsien-nien and Yeh Chien-ying, were united in reversing the verdicts of the Cultural Revolution, promoting production as the main task and whipping up a rightist wind to accomplish this. Even after Teng was nominally dumped, and right after Mao died, the rightists, with powerful military forces at their command, moved on the Four and confronted any "middle forces" with a *fait accompli.* Having done that, they moved to make a mummy of Mao's body (a Confucianist act the Four absolutely correctly opposed in my opinion) and did the same with his line and Thought.

As far as differences among these rightists, and Hua and Teng in particular, I do not pretend to know all of what they may be. But the Four themselves, before their arrest, made clear (by analogy) in a number of articles that these rightists were not all one solid bloc, but had formed an opportunist alliance in opposition to the continuation of the Chinese revolution. One thing seems evident to me—Teng would very likely want to openly, or at least much more clearly if indirectly, attack Mao, while Hua can by no means afford to do that; he must pretend to uphold Mao because his sole authority rests on his supposed annointment by Mao—other than that Teng has it all over him in terms of long-established contacts in key places, forces at his command, etc. Yes, there is no doubt opposition among them, based on both personal ambition and different notions of how to carry out the revisionist line—after all, while there is only one correct line, there are many different ways to carry out an incorrect line. But these differences among these revisionist leaders are, to borrow from Engels, opposite poles of the same stupidity.

This brings up another very important political point: far from creating stability and unity, the smashing of the Four and the victory of the revisionists means that there will be tremendous dissension and anarchy in China. This is not only because followers of the Four, who despite the current rulers' claims, number at least in the tens of millions, will find the ways to put up some form of resistance to the revisionist line—and indeed already are, as even the current rulers are forced to admit, at least indirectly. But it is also because it is only the correct line in command that can provide relative unity to the country. Once things are unhinged from the proletarian line, as they have been, all sorts of conflicting interests will greatly sharpen—differences between regional commanders, heads of different ministries, the army and the agricultural sector, etc., etc. This anarchy will not mainly show up as mass upheaval—though this will occur, the rightists will unite to suppress it in the short run—but it will make itself felt very strongly all the same.

But back to the arguments in defense of the *status quo* and against the Four. "The 'gang of four' didn't just start attacking certain leading people at the time of the campaign against the right deviationist wind, they began these attacks as early as 1974, for example in the Lin Piao and Confucius campaign. And they didn't just attack Teng, they attacked good people as well, even Chou En-lai."

Did they attack certain leading people, by clear analogy, through the Lin Piao and Confucius campaign and the Legalists vs. Confucianists analysis in particular? Yes, they did. In fact these attacks by analogy began around the time of the 10th Congress in August, 1973. Were those they attacked this way good people?—let's look and see.

To gain an understanding of this we have to look at the events that led up to the 10th Congress and, again, to analyze the overall situation in its development, the different forces involved and the lines different people and forces represented. Of great importance to grasp is the fact that the Lin Piao affair was a truly traumatic one in China and caused tremendous turmoil—and it was also a signal for all those forces who opposed the Cultural Revolution to jump out on the basis of opposing Lin Piao. Further, even after Lin Piao died and his closest co-conspirators alive were arrested, his followers and the problems his camp created were far from cleared up, especially, but not exclusively, in the armed forces. It should be remembered that the PLA played a huge role during the Cultural Revolution up to that point—army people were everywhere, in every major institution, in city and countryside—playing a leading role, and this Mao had only begun to seriously curb when the Lin Piao affair happened (September, 1971).

Therefore, after the struggle with Lin came to a complete rupture, resulting in Lin's flight and death, there remained a monumental task of trying to restore order and clean up the mess that was inherited. In response to this, I believe, Mao and Chou En-lai had significant differences, though like all contradictions these differences went through a process of development, which ended up with Mao and Chou in fundamental opposition to each other.

What were these differences? While both agreed that the immediate task was to clean up on the remaining problems left by the Lin Piao affair and that a certain amount of "uniting all who can be united" against Lin's forces and line was necessary, they disagreed over how much this should go on and how far to take it. In substance, Chou felt the only thing to do was to bring back many people who had been knocked down during the Cultural Revolution and were bound to be strong opponents of Lin Piao, while Mao, agreeing probably to bring back some, did not want to go as far with this as Chou did. And besides just bringing back people, Chou wanted to push policies that would reverse the momentum of the Cultural Revolution and the continuation of the revolution. In substance, he wanted to put stability and unity and pushing the national economy forward as the main things. In other words he took the position that everything should be subordinated to stabilizing things after the Lin Piao affair and the upheaval of the Cultural Revolution and that a great number of people, and of things, that had been attacked by Lin Piao should be restored. (If it is asked, "how can that be, look at Chou's report to the 10th Congress," my reply is, look at Lin Piao's report to the 9th Congress, and now we can look back and see with whom and what Chou was increasingly aligned since after Lin fell.)

With some of this, I believe, Mao agreed, because he agreed that it was a necessity in the short run. But not all of it, even in the short run, let alone the long run. After all, Lin Piao had attacked not only many good people but many bad ones as well, and not all of the lines and policies he opposed should have been upheld—many should have been opposed. In short, Mao did not agree that everything should be subordinated to stability and unity and pushing the national economy forward—and specifically not that *correct* verdicts of the Cultural Revolution should basically be reversed. Here I believe, are the seeds of the struggle which broke out fully in the year before Mao's death with the campaign to beat back the right deviationist wind.

Prominent in all this is the question of Teng Hsiao-ping. I believe that Mao and Chou agreed that it was necessary to bring back Teng at that time—his return began in 1972, very shortly after Lin Piao crashed. But within that agreement between Mao and Chou there were, from all I can tell, the seeds of sharp disagreement. Chou thought Teng was basically good but had made some mistakes; Mao, I am convinced, did not trust Teng and recognized that upon returning to office Teng was likely to resume his old ways. Mao agreed to his rehabilitation for the reason that

Teng would be a powerful—and at that time necessary—force in cleaning up on the remnants of the Lin Piao forces, especially in the PLA where Teng has long and many close ties with key commanders. Thus, while Mao had the necessity to go along with rehabilitating Teng he took steps from the start to combat the revisionist influence—"tide" describes it accurately—that would inevitably accompany Teng's resumption of high office and the steps that went with it (more on this shortly).

This, I am convinced, is the main reason why the 10th Congress made such a big point of going against the tide, which was written into the Constitution at the 10th Congress. It is clear that the tide that was gaining momentum then was that represented by people like Teng Hsiao-ping—and ultimately Chou En-lai—who were bound to gain from the whole campaign to clean up right after the Lin Piao affair (criticize Lin Piao and rectify the style of work). The fact that Lin Piao, a big leader in the Cultural Revolution, turned traitor gave those who wanted to reverse the verdicts of the Cultural Revolution great initiative and momentum, and it was this that the 10th Party Congress documents were warning against—and clearly on Mao's insistence, for who else would both want to and have the ability to get this into the 10th Congress documents? Such principles in Chinese Party documents, it should be stressed, are never just the summation of past struggle but always bear directly on current struggles as well.

Also a part of the struggle shaping up around the time of the 10th Congress was how to sum up Lin Piao—that is whether to stress his overall rightist character, his promoting of the "theory of the productive forces," etc. or to call him "ultra-left." From what we have seen in the "General Program," those who are responsible for it, themselves promoters of the "theory of the productive forces," have insisted on calling Lin "ultra-left"—and no doubt these forces insisted on it at the time of the 10th Congress. (The fact that in public print now the present rulers refer to Lin and to the Four as "ultra-right" while all but saying explicitly that they were "ultra-left" is a dodge to confuse people and cover for the real right—themselves.) The characterization of Lin as right instead of "ultra-left" was a victory for the left—especially the Four—and indicated that Mao wanted to direct the spearhead toward such lines as the "theory of the productive forces"—without Mao's powerful backing it is extremely doubtful that the Four, themselves under attack from the right as being in Lin Piao's camp, could have won in the struggle to lay emphasis on Lin's right opportunism. (This question of whether the right or "ultra-left" was the main danger from the time of the 10th Congress was, as stated, a very important and very sharp point of struggle for obvious reasons. In waging this struggle the Four, or some of their followers, did make some errors, stating in one article for example that the right is "invariably" the main danger in socialist society. This is an erroneous formulation—the right is overall and overwhelmingly the main danger in socialist society but not "invariably." It certainly, however, was the main danger then; other articles by the Four explained this more correctly and overall they handled this struggle in a quite correct way.)

It is obvious that by that time, 1974, the rightists in the Party, represented by the fast-rising Teng—backed ultimately by Chou En-lai—were beginning to make a big offensive. They were beginning to bring back many people who were justly and correctly knocked down as unrepentant capitalist roaders—Chen Pei-hsien, former number 2 capitalist roader in Shanghai who was overthrown during the Cultural Revolution, is just one glaring example—and they were launching attacks on the new things that had been won through the Cultural Revolution—many of the same things they have now swiftly reversed after seizing supreme power.

It was not at all accidental or incidental to what was going on then that key themes running through the Lin Piao and Confucius campaign were how Confucius wanted to follow the principle of "restrain oneself and restore the rites" (feign benevolence to cover the restoration of the old order), how Confucius' program was to "revive states that were extinct, restore families that had lost their positions, and call to office those who had fallen into obscurity" (bring back the old order and its upholders and rehabilitate unrepentant restorationists), and that a rallying cry of Confucius and his followers was that "the present is not as good as the past." These were exactly the program and exactly the rallying cry of the right deviationists.

Can it be said that the emphasis given within the Criticize Lin Piao and Confucius campaign to the struggle of the Legalists Vs. the Confucianists was only the doing of the Four? No, it cannot. It seems very clear to me that Mao also pushed this, because as we know at that time he was very concerned with the grave danger of retrogression and restoration and recognized that the period of struggle between the rising landlord class and the declining slave class in China would hold valuable lessons for the class struggle to prevent restoration now. It is worth noting in line with this that at the 4th National People's Congress in January, 1975, Chou

En-lai's report says the following: "Our primary task is to continue to broaden, deepen and perservere in the movement to criticize Lin Piao and Confucius," and that "We should go on deepening the criticism of Lin Piao's revisionist line and the doctrines of Confucius and Mencius, and in line with the principle of *making the past serve the present*, sum up the historical experience of the struggle between the Confucian and Legalist schools and of class struggle and use Marxism to occupy all spheres in the superstructure." (See *Peking Review*, No. 4, 1975, p. 22)

I believe it is indisputably clear that this was Mao's line and that Chou included it in his report not on his own initiative but on the insistence of Mao. It would be very difficult to argue, I think, given the whole character of the campaign to criticize Lin Piao and Confucius and the Legalists Vs. Confucianists in particular, that Chou En-lai would be a big backer—or a backer at all—of all this. It is said by the current rulers that Mao insisted that Chou give the main report to the 4th People's Congress. This is probably true and the reason I think so is that, especially given the nature of the class struggle then and how the different forces lined up, Mao wanted Chou to be on record in support of the revolutionary struggle, including such things as were quoted just above from the report Chou gave. It is also no accident, and not simply because of attacks on him by the Four, I think, that the current rulers have built up Chou En-lai to such heights—clearly, in my opinion, elevating him far above Mao—and have insisted on the close ties between Chou and those in power now, including Teng in particular. Perhaps this is just slander on their part—but I don't think so, and the evidence points to the opposite conclusion, to the conclusion that Chou was tied in with and the powerful backer behind those now in power and their right deviationism.

The current rulers have given many clear indications that Chou and people like Hua Kuo-feng as well as Teng Hsiao-ping were all tied in together. In *Peking Review*, No. 50, 1977, there is an unmistakable identification of both Hua and Teng with Chou En-lai, in an article attacking the Four's writing group in Shanghai. This article gives us the following succession: The writing group attacked Chou En-lai, then "When Comrade Teng Hsiao-ping was in charge of the day-to-day work of the Party Central Committee and the State Council during Premier Chou's grave illness and following his death, he was made the prime target of the group's virulent attack".

Then the article immediately follows this by saying, "In 1976, after Comrade Hua Kuo-feng was appointed Acting Premier and then Premier and First Vice-Chairman of the Party Central Committee, the group turned to attack Comrade Hua Kuo-feng'' (See pp. 16-17).

What is being said here is obvious, in both form and content: Teng Hsiao-ping was Chou En-lai's "worthy successor" and then when Teng fell,Hua replaced him in this role. Even the order of Hua's appointments in April, 1976, is reversed from the resolution at that time (which put his post as First Vice-Chairman first and then his role as Premier) in order to make stronger the identification of Hua with Chou, and Teng.

And it seems very clear to me that by the time of Chou's death, when Mao was already launching the struggle against Teng and the right deviationist wind, Mao and Chou had come into clear and sharp conflict. Just one indication of this is the nature of the mourning ceremonies around Chou. His body lay in state not in the Great Hall but in the hospital where he died. For a leader of the stature of Chou in China this is indeed very strange and not at all in keeping with his position. To attribute this to Chou's "modesty," or some such thing is ridiculous, because obviously the question of what kind of "honors" to pay Chou was then a tremendously sharp political question and would be decided as part of the struggle then going on (look how Mao's body was dealt with, clearly against his personal and political inclinations). And it is even more ridiculous to think that especially with the forces lined up as they clearly were, the Four alone could have kept these ceremonies as low key as they were for a man of Chou's stature. They could play down reports of mourning of his death in the press, and no doubt they did, but there was only one person around who could keep the actual mourning ceremonies themselves as low key as they were—and you know who that is.

Further it is striking that, with Chou En-lai clearly under attack by the Four and the question of how to evaluate him such a very sharp point of struggle in China then, Mao neither said nor did anything to make a point of indicating support for Chou (neither made a statement at the time of Chou's death nor a special visit to the hospital where his body lay in state, nor any other similar act to indicate support for Chou at a time when, as stated, Chou's role was the focus of great struggle). But beyond that it is *obvious* that Mao and Chou were on opposite sides for some time before Chou's death, if we stop and think about how things developed over that period.

If this were not the case, if Mao and Chou were in basic

agreement during the last couple of years, then it is unthinkable that the Four could be taking shots at Chou repeatedly through analogy during this period and not be cracked down on for it. Yet during this period none of them was even demoted, let alone removed from key positions in the Party. If Mao and Chou were in basic unity and Hua Kuo-feng represented their common choice for successor, then the struggle would have gone down completely differently. The Four would have been at least demoted and very probably at a minimum had their control over the press taken away. Yet this did not happen. How could this be unless Mao was protecting them, and why would he do so if they continued to attack his close comrade-in-arms Chou En-lai who had united with Mao around a common line and common choice for succession to top Party leadership! Again, everything points to the *obvious* fact that Mao and Chou En-lai were basically not in unity but on opposite sides for several years and increasingly so in the period right before Chou's death.

If anyone wants to uphold Chou En-lai and "Chou En-lai Thought" then let them do so, but they cannot do so in the name of Mao and Mao Tsetung Thought. They can only do so by repudiating Mao and Mao Tsetung Thought—which is something I am confident our Party will not do.

Looking back, then, on the events right after the 10th Congress and especially the campaign to Criticize Lin Piao and Confucius, and the Legalists Vs. Confucianists in particular, what was Mao's line on all this, was it the same as the Four's exactly and were they simply carrying out Mao's line and in complete agreement with him, including in attacking Teng, Chou and probably others by analogy?

First, I believe the evidence points to the fact that Mao was obviously behind the movement to criticize Lin Piao and Confucius, including the thrust of the Legalists Vs. Confucianists material, and that he regarded the right, including at least Teng and perhaps Chou En-lai in the background, as the general target of this movement. Mao pushed this campaign to hit back at the attempts of the right, already gaining considerable momentum, to reverse the gains of the Cultural Revolution and the development of the Chinese revolution as a whole. The issues raised in the Lin Piao and Confucius campaign were essentially the same as those battled out later in more open form in the struggle to beat back the right deviationist wind.

This campaign was carried out on two levels, especially by the Four. The first, and principal aspect, was the use of historical analogy and analogy with Lin Piao's rightism to arm the masses to fight against the right's current attempts to reverse verdicts. With this Mao was in full agreement, I am convinced. The second, and secondary, aspect, which the Four did get into pretty heavily, was to indicate, especially to their followers, through clear and sometimes rather blatant analogy, exactly how the forces were then lining up in the struggle and who was playing what role. With at least some of this Mao disagreed, I believe—at the beginning at least (i.e. in 1974 and early 1975). Mao felt, I think, that it was better to concentrate on the line of the right and not focus so directly on specific people, and he no doubt held out the hope that he could resolve the question through struggling it out with Chou, and encouraged Chou to do right, though, as with Hua later, Mao did not *rely* on this. When, later, it became clear to Mao that Chou would not get up off the line he held and the backing he was giving to people like Teng and their right deviationism, Mao launched a more direct struggle against the right deviationist wind, with Teng as the main and clear target.

But it should be clear that Mao had been warning of the danger of a coup by people like Lin Piao (rightists) for several years. And it also should be clear that Mao did not only target Teng when he launched the movement against the right deviationist wind—he made specific reference to Teng and general reference to capitalist roaders, especially veteran leading cadres, with the *same line.* This is evident in Mao's statement that, "With the socialist revolution *they themselves* [note—not *he himself*] come under fire. At the time of the co-operative transformation of agriculture there were *people* in the Party who opposed it, and when it comes to criticizing bourgeois right *they* resent it. You are making socialist revolution, and yet don't know where the bourgeoisie is. It is right in the Communist Party—*those* in power taking the capitalist road. The capitalist roaders are still on the capitalist road." (emphasis added—it should be pointed out that at least at one point, around 1956, Chou En-lai was one of those who at the least wavered and took a conservative stand with regard to agricultural co-operatization—this is referred to by Mao in his 1959 speech at the Lushan Conference, in Schram's book, p. 138).

Overall, in my opinion, Mao's approach to this whole struggle, during the period from around the time of the 10th Congress to the time of his death, was better than the Four's where they disagreed with him and did differently. And I think that it is these disagreements that caused Mao to make certain criticisms of the Four for forming a "gang," especially during 1974 and early

1975—though, again, it should be stressed that they were never even demoted, let alone removed from leadership in the Party. And, further, as for the statements attributed to Mao against the Four, it is important to point out several things.

First, if we are going to consider them authentic, then it is just as reasonable to take as authentic the statement, in the form of a poem, which Mao is supposed to have written to Chiang Ching shortly before he died. What, according to reports of this, did Mao say in that statement? "You have been wronged," it says, and goes on, "Today we are separating into two worlds. May each keep his peace. These few words may be my last message to you. Human life is limited, but revolution knows no bounds. In the struggle of the past ten years I have tried to reach the peak of revolution, but I was not successful. But you could reach the top. If you fail, you will plunge into a fathomless abyss. Your body will shatter. Your bones will break." And Mao went on to warn her of the danger of the army backing the right—and if that should happen of the necessity to wage people's war again—something Mao had threatened to do himself, including at the Lushan meeting in 1959 during the very sharp struggle against Peng Teh-huai. (This letter/poem attributed to Mao was cited in the *Manchester Guardian*, November 7, 1976, also in a column by Jack Anderson and elsewhere—Anderson said he considered it authentic, though he didn't say exactly why.) It seems to me that there is at least as much basis for taking as authentic this statement of Mao's as there is for taking as authentic the statements attributed to Mao criticizing the Four.

In fact, exactly if Mao did make criticisms, including some sharp ones, of the Four and Chiang Ching in particular, that would be all the more reason for him to write a letter to her at the end indicating support for her and those aligned with her—assuming, as I believe I have shown, that Mao was in fundamental unity with them. Mao certainly knew that as soon as he went an all-out attack would be launched on Chiang Ching in particular and the Four generally and that, as he said, some of his words, including especially criticism of her and the Four, would be used by the right to attack them and the left they represented. This would be all the more reason why Mao would want to make a last statement "setting the record straight" and indicating with whom he basically stood and had fundamental unity, so that *these* words of his could be used, together with his basic line and overall political direction, by the genuine left, represented by the Four, to fight against the right.

Further, these statements attributed to Mao criticizing the Four, even if taken as authentic, were just that—criticism, even sharp ones in some cases—but in no way indicating that Mao wanted the Four knocked down or considered them the enemy or target of the struggle. These criticisms were certainly not the kind of statements he made—in public at that—about the right deviationists. And more than that, given everything that was going on and the thrust of the leadership Mao was giving as summarized before, if these statements were made and if this criticism was levelled at the Four, I see no reason to believe that even at that time Mao made such criticisms only of the Four. In short, I do not for a minute believe that there was only one "gang"; and I am convinced that even on the question of factional activities Mao must have criticized more than the Four, which is implied in the statement to the Politburo in May, 1975, where Mao is supposed to have said that "all present" should discuss the "3 do's and don'ts."

(As a general point, I would also stress that we should keep in mind that people in power certainly can suppress evidence against themselves, frame charges against those they have purged and claim that such and such is in so and so's "own handwriting," etc. What we make of the "evidence" presented against those purged has to depend, in the last analysis, on what we think of their overall line as opposed to the line of those who have purged them. In other words, we have to weigh charges and "evidence" on both sides against what we can see to be people's line—especially though not exclusively, on what they themselves put out as their line—and we have to put it in the context of what was going on overall, how things were shaping up, what the alignment of forces was, etc. to make any sense out of it and sort things out. For example, the charges now being made against the Four and "evidence" accompanying such charges were apparently circulated in China by those now in power even before Mao died. The Four denounced these as rumors at that time. On the other hand, today the current rulers now tell us that the Four framed up Teng Hsiao-ping, fabricated charges against him and, against Mao's instructions, launched a campaign against him. How are we to sort all this out? Fundamentally, I believe, by the criteria summarized just above, putting emphasis on line.)

Finally, on this point, with whatever criticisms Mao may have made of the Four, it is clear, I am convinced, that there is no way that he wanted them knocked down. He certainly knew that with them gone there would be no leading people who would carry forth what had been accomplished through great struggle in the Cultural Revolution. After all, who are the people in power now and what was their role in the Cultural Revolution? The most prominent ones were either targets of, opposed to or wavering elements in the Cultural Revolution. Teng was a target. People like Li Hsien-nien and Yeh Chien-ying were part of the group of officials responsible for the "February Adverse Current," in 1967, where they tried to put a stop to the whole Cultural Revolution—of course, no doubt the verdict on this has been reversed too, and that "Adverse Current" is no longer considered adverse but fine. As for Hua Kuo-feng, at the start of the Cultural Revolution he was the Provincial Secretary in Hunan Province and he supported the wrong side—lined up with the "royalists" as they were called, with the people aligned with Liu Shao-chi. He was criticized and went down for this, though it is true that he made a self-criticism and was returned to office in the same year, 1966.

As to what the outlook of those in power now is toward the Cultural Revolution, even in its early stages, besides what we know of Teng's role as target, we have the following statement by Yeh Chien-ying: "The third comparatively major setback [in the Party's history] took place *immediately after* we had settled accounts with Liu Shao-chi's revisionist line." (*Peking Review*, No. 43, 1977, p. 12, emphasis added) This is the same line that led Yeh to play an important part in the "February Adverse Current"—that the Cultural Revolution once started should have been stopped as soon as Liu Shao-chi was exposed. At the very most Yeh is saying that by 1968 the Cultural Revolution had turned from a good thing into a bad thing—to say the least this was hardly Mao's line, it is a repudiation of the struggle-criticism-transformation that took place through the Cultural Revolution and brought, overall, very positive, tremendously positive, results.

It would not at all be exaggerating to say that people like Yeh actually *hate* the Cultural Revolution and hated it from the beginning. They regarded it as a horrible disruption, throwing the country into chaos and subjecting venerable veteran cadres to humiliation at the hands of upstarts (many being dragged through the street with dunce caps on, being forced to endure long criticism meetings in front of thousands, etc.). Such people regard and have for some time regarded Mao's ideas on the class struggle as out of keeping with the time and conditions and, more than that, extremely dangerous. According to a text reprinted as an appendix in a book about the Cultural Revolution by Jean Daubier, Mao is reported to have said about the top leaders around him at the start of the Cultural Revolution (that is, the veteran leaders in top Party positions, which includes Chou En-lai), "Most people thought at the time that my understanding was out of date, and at times I was the *only person* to agree with my own suggestions." (*A History of the Chinese Cultural Revolution*, pp. 307-308, emphasis added) Chou En-lai in particular did go along with the Cultural Revolution after Mao struggled with him at the start, and during the early stages of it—up to the time of the Lin Piao affair—he played a good and very important role, overall. But, after the Lin Piao affair, Chou's role turned into its opposite. Further, the notion of many of these people that it was time to cut out all this class struggle and get down to business—the business of modernizing, building modern defense, etc.—was increased not decreased through the course of the Cultural Revolution; and, as noted, especially after the betrayal by Lin Piao, they jumped out all the more with this line.

How could Mao think that he could rely on such people to continue the revolution? Obviously, he could not—and events both before and since his death have proved this many times over, as shown in this paper. With whatever mistakes they may have made, and whatever disagreements with and criticisms of them Mao may have had, it is clear that he knew that the Four were the forces in top leadership who could be counted on to fight to carry forward the revolution.

Finally, while I think that overall on the question of how to handle the struggle after the 10th Congress Mao was more correct than the Four, I do think that in a certain sense they "caught" the extreme seriousness of what was going on before Mao did. Mao certainly recognized the real attempts of the right to reverse the revolution and, as pointed out, took steps to combat this politically, but I think that the Four ran smack up against the intensifying moves of the rightists to carry off restoration before Mao himself came up against this in such a direct way.

In other words, the Four were in the thick of the battle, they were under direct attack for defending the gains of the Cultural Revolution, while for a time those launching these attacks no doubt pretended to Mao's face to accept the very things they were attacking and talked differently to him than they acted in actually mobilizing their forces to oppose all that Mao stood for. Sooner or later, however, they were forced to go beyond just attacking those in Mao's camp, the Four and their followers, and to come into open, more direct conflict with Mao himself. (I have some experience with how this works and know that it sometimes, even often, develops in this way in the course of two-line struggle. Often the Chairman even thinks at first that those who warn him about the development of another headquarters attempting to overturn his line, the line of the Party, are just stirring up trouble themselves, even though he is aware of real differences with one or more other leading people; it is only later in the development of things that such people go from indirect attack to direct attack on the Chairman and fully reveal their opposition headquarters, and does it then become clear that it is not possible for the Chairman to win them over just by arguing differences out with them.) So it was, I am convinced, with the developments of the differences between Mao and other top leaders, Chou En-lai in particular, in the last few years.

Still, on the whole, I think Mao's approach was more correct than the Four's and the criticisms he apparently had of the Four around this were, in the main—though not, in my opinion, entirely—correct. But these disagreements and criticisms were tactical—that is, they were among people in the same camp—and can in no way be compared to the fundamental differences between Mao (and the Four) on the one hand and the right deviationists on the other, and to the struggle that Mao (and the Four) waged against these capitalist roaders.

There is one other fact which makes very clear, indisputably clear in my opinion, that down to the end it was the Four that Mao had confidence in and fundamentally relied on. And that is the fact that for at least a year before and right up until his death Mao entrusted his nephew, Mao Yuan-hsin, to be in charge of his day-to-day affairs, including controlling access to Mao. Mao Yuan-hsin was the closest and most important "sworn follower" of the Four—he was, in effect, the fifth member of the "gang of five." And there is no doubt that at any time Mao could have removed Mao Yuan-hsin from the position of managing his day-to-day affairs with a mere flick of the wrist—after all, Hua Kuo-feng and Wang Tung-hsing (head of the PLA unit guarding the Chairman and the Central Committee and now a Vice-Chairman of the new Central Committee) would have been only too glad to get rid of Mao Yuan-hsin, if Mao had wanted it (apparently they have now quite literally gotten rid of Mao Yuan-hsin—he is reported to be yet another "suicide" in the custody of the current rulers). Yet, while signing treaties with Hua Kuo-feng ("With you carrying out your work, I'm at ease," etc.) Mao continued down to the end to entrust Mao Yuan-hsin with the crucial job of controlling access to him and continued to rely on the Four and their followers, including their "sworn follower," Mao Yuan-hsin, to carry forward the revolution.

"But why would Chou En-lai want to go revisionist at the end, he was dying, and why would other long-time leaders of the Party, veteran revolutionaries, go revisionist?" I find it incredible—but such arguments have actually been made. Such an outlook makes the question of revisionism not a matter of line but of intent. As opposed to dialectical materialism, it is idealism and metaphysics. People go revisionist because there is a material and ideological basis for this and because in response to the situation they are confronted with they take an incorrect line, an incorrect road, in attempting to resolve these contradictions, and because the bourgeois aspect wins out over the proletarian. Why this happens with particular individuals is impossible to say precisely, but that it will continually happen with people, especially leading people, in a communist party so long as there is a party (so long as there are classes)—this is an inevitable law.

As a general guide to understanding this, we should look not to intent but to what Engels said about this kind of thing—revolution, he pointed out, develops in stages and at each new stage some people get "stuck." In addition, in the specific situation of China, the question of making the transition from the democratic to the socialist revolution, both materially and ideologically, is an extremely difficult and complicated question. And the phenomenon of people who were revolutionaries in the democratic stage but turned into counter-revolutionaries with the advance of the revolution into the socialist stage—especially the deeper the socialist revolution goes and the more it hacks away at remaining bourgeois relations and ideas—this is a big phenomenon, as Mao himself insisted.

Were the Four correct in stressing this question and in targeting a number of veteran leaders? Yes, they were quite correct. Besides what he stressed on this point in 1976, already in 1967 Mao stated that at the start of the Cultural Revolution it was only through very sharp struggle that he got a slight majority of the Central Committee to go along with it, and he emphasized that the power-holders taking the capitalist road were the kind of people who:

> "during the time of the democratic revolution actively participated in opposing the three big mountains [imperialism, feudalism and bureaucrat-capitalism], but once the entire country was liberated, they were not so keen on

> opposing the bourgeoisie. Though they had actively participated in and endorsed the overthrow of local despots and the distribution of land, after the country's liberation when agricultural collectivization was to be implemented, they were not very keen on this either . . . Let's just say it is 'veteran cadres encountering new problems!' . . . There are those who have committed errors of orientation and line in the Great Proletarian Cultural Revolution, and this has been said to be a case of 'veteran cadres encountering new problems.' But the fact that you have erred tells us that you have not thoroughly remolded your bourgeois world outlook. *From now on, veteran cadres are bound to encounter even more new problems.* To insure that you will resolutely take the road of socialism, you will have to undergo a thorough proletarian revolutionization, ideologically." (from the U.S. Government collection cited earlier, emphasis added)

(It should be pointed out that in this speech Mao is a little too optimistic about how well the current Cultural Revolution will resolve things, saying that "this Great Cultural Revolution, should consolidate things for a decade at least," and he also says that to launch such a revolution is possible only two or three times in a century—I will return to this last point, especially, a little later). If such people do not go through such ideological revolutionization they can only become the targets of the revolution.

Of course, such people rarely consciously recognize that they are going revisionist. Almost always they think that they are continuing to fight for socialism and that is why they don't stop fighting for their line until they breathe their last. Keeping in mind, however, what was pointed out earlier about how most of the very top veteran leaders tended very strongly to regard Mao's ideas of continuing the class struggle to be "outdated," and the fact that this tendency grew in many such people through the course of the Cultural Revolution, it is not surprising that in this last round a number of them, while intending to fight for what they saw as socialism, were actually fighting for all they were worth against the further development of the socialist revolution. And so, despite their intentions, they were transformed into targets of the revolution. Again, this is not surprising, for as Mao warned as early as 1967 (as cited above), "From now on, veteran cadres are bound to encounter even more new problems."

"But the Four did not just attack the leading people, including veteran cadre, during the recent struggles, they attacked them at the early stages of the Cultural Revolution, including people like Chen Yi and even Chou En-lai at that time. They were tied in with

Lin Piao and really played a bad role in the Cultural Revolution, and anything positive they did was just because they were at the right place at the right time and took advantage of the situation for their own ends."

It is no doubt true that in the Cultural Revolution, specifically during the peak of mass upsurge (1966-69), the Four made mistakes. So what? Revolutionaries cannot avoid making mistakes if they want to be revolutionaries. Chiang Ching sometimes associated herself with wrong tendencies in a particular battle, etc., but again, so what? Does this characterize her overall role or that of the Four? Most definitely not.

As for being associated with Lin Piao, what genuine leftist wasn't so associated during the high tide of the Cultural Revolution? Mao was certainly closely associated then with the man who was named his official "successor" in 1969. In fact, as Mao wrote to Chiang Ching in 1966, to make public criticisms of Lin Piao then would be "like pouring cold water" on the genuine left and "thus helping the right wing," and "at the moment all the left speaks the same language." (See Han Suyin's *Wind in the Tower*, p. 279) By this Mao meant then both the genuine left and "ultra-leftists" were temporarily united in fighting the main enemy at that time—the right (during this period, many of Lin Piao's actions and much of his line was "left" in form; as he reached the pinnacle of his power, however, his line became more and more openly right in form as well as essence). Therefore, naturally the genuine left, including the Four as leaders of it—and certainly including Mao—were linked with Lin Piao at that time.

Could this have once again been the case in the struggle against the right deviationist wind—that is, could Mao have been temporarily united with the "ultra-left" "gang of four," while making preparations to knock them down after defeating the more immediate enemy, the right deviationists? The facts point to the opposite conclusion. As I believe I have shown convincingly, the Four and Mao had fundamental unity on line and it was exactly the Four that Mao relied on down to the end—as shown by his relationship with Mao Yuan-hsin among other things. After Lin Piao fell, in going back over the line he put out, it was possible rather quickly to see the basic differences between Mao and Lin on fundamental questions of line. But today it is clear that it is Hua Kuo-feng and the others in power now whose line is in fundamental disagreement with Mao's, while the Four's line still stands as that of Mao. And as stressed before, if the Four and Mao were not in basic agreement, while Mao, Chou En-lai and people like Hua Kuo-feng were, the struggle would have gone down completely differently in the last couple of years. And finally it should be emphasized that the political guidance Mao gave to the masses right down to and especially at the end was to arm them to deal with the danger from the *right*, the right and the right again—in every campaign after the 10th Congress, from Lin

Piao and Confucius to the dictatorship of the proletariat campaign, to the instructions on *Water Margin* and finally the anti-right deviationist struggle.

It does seem true that Chiang Ching and Yao Wen-yuan in particular did get drawn into some of the sectarianism promoted by Lin and Chen Po-ta in the early part of the Cultural Revolution, for which they later made self-criticisms. It is also true that at a certain point during the upsurge of the Cultural Revolution Chiang Ching, at least, raised the slogan "attack by reason, defend by force." But she did not raise this as a general slogan for the Cultural Revolution; it was raised in particular circumstances. The "ultra-left" group of "May 16" (or 516) was running wild, making armed attacks, carrying out looting, burning, etc. In response to *this*, as Han Suyin told it in her book *Wind in the Tower*, "on July 22 (1967) at a Red Guard rally, Chiang Ching again told the Red Guards that they should attack only by words, but since Red Guards were being attacked, she conceded they could defend themselves. The slogan, 'Attack by reason, defend by force,' would lead to the formation of vigilante groups and provosts among the workers, to enforce order and to protect state property against hooliganism by the 516." (p. 311) So it is not all exactly as the current rulers tell us. I do think that there is a danger in this slogan, because anyone can say they were attacked first and use that as a pretext to attack others. But still, it cannot be said that Chiang Ching raised this slogan to promote anarchy or oppose Mao's line nor that the effect of this was overall to encourage anarchy, hooliganism, terrorism, etc.

And any mistakes made by Chiang Ching and Yao Wen-yuan were clearly secondary to their overall very positive role. I have already mentioned the truly great achievements of Chiang Ching in the revolutionization of art, and her positive contributions to the Cultural Revolution were not limited to that, though they would be great even if they were. And it is a well known fact that, as Mao himself said, it was the article by Yao Wen-yuan attacking the rightists who were calling for the return of Peng Teh-huai to office, which was "the signal" for the start of the Cultural Revolution. Further, together with Chang Chun-chiao, Yao led the "January Storm" in Shanghai in 1967, the first upsurge in which the masses seized back power from the capitalist-roaders. Mao hailed this as a great event and called on the whole country to learn from it—and it is true that Chang and Yao played a tremendous role in this, fighting against both the right and the "ultra-left," and it will remain true no matter how many times the current rulers go through their farcical attempts to deny it. (Wang Hung-wen also played a big, heroic role in this upsurge and in consolidating proletarian power in Shanghai—more on Wang shortly).

And it is beyond doubt that once Lin Piao had clearly turned against Mao there was only antagonism between him and the Four. The "Outline of Project 571," drawn up as the Lin Piao clique's counter-revolutionary program, contains blasts obviously aimed at the Four, and Chang Chun-chiao is especially singled out for attack (by name). Wang Hung-wen in particular distinguished himself in the struggle against Lin Piao at the Central Committee meeting in 1970 where Lin's forces made their first big bid for power. And the Four in general played a strong role in the struggle against Lin's counter-revolutionary attempts to usurp power. Otherwise, why would they have been as high up in the Party as they were after Lin fell, especially given the fact that the rightists were unquestionably launching big attacks on them at that time trying as they are now to link the Four with Lin as counter-revolutionaries? It could only be because such charges could not get over—at least not while Mao was around—and clearly Mao wanted them in leading positions.

As for the question of Chen Yi and attacks on him, I believe the Four, or some of them at least, did make mistakes on this. From what I have been able to learn the Four, or some of them, at first at least, did join in some of these attacks. It is true that not only Chou En-lai but Mao himself defended Chen Yi, against attacks from the "ultra-left" (represented especially by Wang Li in the Cultural Revolution Committee), though it was never said that Chen Yi should not be criticized. And it is also a fact that especially when it became clear that attacks on Chen Yi were being made as part of an "ultra-left" counter-current, the Four, and Chiang Ching most prominent among them, opposed the attacks on Chen Yi.

Chen Yi was popular among the masses generally and had respect among leaders because he had a history of backing Mao at crucial junctures in the Chinese revolution, and he was well-known for his straightforward, even blunt character—he was open about his views and frank in struggling things out.

These are, in and of themselves, good qualities but they are not the essential question. For example, much of the same could also be said of Teng Hsiao-ping. And as far as I'm concerned the question of Chen Yi is not a simple one. While he did many good things in the Chinese revolution and had many good qualities as described above, he also made some serious errors, and overall in the Cultural Revolution he did not play a good role. For example, he, too, was part of the "February Adverse Current," and it can be fairly stated that he never really supported, and definitely did not promote, the Cultural Revolution. Not only was Chen Yi a part of the "February Adverse Current," but at that time he declared his support for Liu Shao-chi, and during the course of the Cultural Revolution he said things to the Red Guards like why didn't they go to Vietnam if they were such hot-shot revolutionaries (which is certainly not a justified statement, even granted that many of the Red Guards got into infantile left errors during the upsurge of the Cultural Revolution). He was certainly someone who should have been criticized, even sharply, in the Cultural Revolution.

From what I have learned the Four held that Chen Yi was a rightist—and that his remaining on the Central Committee at the 9th Congress in 1969 was as a representative of the right. (Mao is supposed to have said something like this in 1969, at the time of the 9th Party Congress, but supposedly as a joke to Chen Yi himself, after Chen jokingly complained that he could not be on the CC because people called him a rightist. Perhaps Mao was simply joking or perhaps his thinking was that Chen was someone who had made right errors but had also made contributions and could make them again, especially in the struggles then shaping up—against Lin Piao.) In any case, it is certainly true that Chen Yi made serious errors, especially during the mass upsurge of the Cultural Revolution, including at its earliest stages. And it is not surprising that the Four came into the conflict with him in the process of carrying out the acute and complicated struggle of the Cultural Revolution, especially at its high tide of upsurge. Nor is it surprising that, given his role in the Cultural Revolution, the Four, while opposing the "ultra-left's" attacks on Chen Yi, did not think of him as one who could be relied on to carry forward the revolution.

Much has been made of the fact that Mao attended Chen Yi's funeral, a rare thing for him to do in his later years. Yes, Mao did, but this too has to be viewed in context. Chen died (in 1972) very shortly after the struggle against Lin Piao came to a head. Chen had been a resolute fighter against Lin for some time—partly, in my opinion, for good reasons and partly for not so good reasons having to do with Chen's own errors during the Cultural Revolution. But in any case, Chen Yi was a big force in the military and had close ties with a number of key commanders who had to be united closely with to consolidate things against Lin's forces, even after Lin died. Further, from what I have learned, many of these commanders insisted very emphatically that Mao come to the funeral, and it was only after they made a big deal out of this that Mao came, at the last minute. This is not to say that politically

Mao did not want to come, but such events were even then very trying on him physically and he probably would not have come if it weren't for the insistence of these commanders. I do think that Mao at that time wanted to make clear that he was siding with the forces represented by Chen Yi—but again the main reason for that was the need for consolidation coming off the Lin Piao affair.

To return, then, to what I said earlier, the case of Chen Yi was not so simple. In my opinion Mao was more correct in his approach to this question than the Four and they did make errors on this. But it also has to be kept in mind that the present rulers, in rallying all opposition they could to the Cultural Revolution, have—for some time no doubt—made extensive use of Chen Yi's reputation and his mistakes for this purpose—not presenting them as mistakes but good things, of course.

Chen Yi opposed Lin Piao, the present rulers tell us. Yes, he did, but as I have said, that too must be divided into two. Chen Yi opposed the "gang of four" the present rulers also tell us. Yes, it is true that he and the Four came into conflict—but that was primarily as a result of the fact that Chen Yi's role in the Cultural Revolution was not on the whole good, and secondarily because the Four did make errors in dealing with the question of Chen Yi in the midst of complicated, on-going and acute struggle. Given all this, and especially the use the right deviationists were making of Chen Yi, it is not surprising and not altogether wrong I think, if the Four did not want to make positive mention of Chen in the press, etc.

"Well, that still proves that the 'gang of four' would not unite with people who made mistakes but were not counter-revolutionaries." It does not prove that at all. They united with a number of such people, not the least of whom was Ma Tien-shui, a veteran cadre in Shanghai, who at the start of the Cultural Revolution took the wrong stand and supported Liu Shao-chi's line. After Ma made a self-criticism, the Four united with him and in fact relied on him to keep things running in Shanghai on a day to day basis. Undoubtedly they made some mistakes in their evaluation of some people but in the main they did not and certainly they were overall correct—and I don't hesitate to say heroic—in the struggle against the right (and the "ultra-left" whom they were also locked in sharp battle with from the early stages of the Cultural Revolution, in Shanghai and elsewhere). And certainly they were correct in not uniting with die-hard capitalist-roaders such as those holding the reigns of power now.

One further note on this question of uniting with people who make serious mistakes but are not counter-revolutionaries. It is a good thing to unite with such people, provided it is on the basis of a correct line. But it is generally the case that precisely in order to be able to accomplish this, it is necessary to subject such people to sharp criticism and get them to make serious self-criticism. This was obviously one of the reasons why Mao launched the Cultural Revolution—first it was to overthrow the revisionist headquarters of Liu Shao-chi, but a major purpose was also to administer a "shock" to many high officials who were taking the wrong road. In other words it is not so simple a thing as saying, "well you have made mistakes and why don't you just correct them and unite and everything will be fine."

And it gets even more complicated if people who have made serious mistakes feel that the balance of forces is in their favor and they don't have to criticize themselves, or unite for that matter. This applies especially to the struggle in the last few years in China. A number of people who were knocked down in the Cultural Revolution were rehabilitated. This was not wrong in every case, though in my opinion in many cases it was most definitely wrong. But even where people should be rehabilitated, this has to be done on a correct basis, not by glossing over the question of their making serious self-criticism and certainly not by encouraging them to resume the wrong road. There is a certain dialectic in many cases between knocking such people down and uniting with them—in other words, sometimes it is even necessary in some cases to knock them down *in order* to be able to get them to reform and unite with the correct line.

This was true in the Cultural Revolution in more than a few cases. Again, so long as their rehabilitation is done on a correct and principled basis and so long as they have not shown themselves to be unrepentant, it is not wrong to bring such people back.

But if they are brought back not on the basis of serious self-criticism but instead on an essentially unrepentant basis, this is very dangerous—and also makes it extremely difficult, if not impossible, to unite with them. This was the situation the Four were faced with, especially after the Lin Piao affair and with the restoration of many people on this unrepentant basis, besides the restoration of certain people who should not have been brought back at all because there was no basis for thinking that they would take the revolutionary road, regardless of what they might say right then.

Again, it should be remembered that many of the top veteran leaders of the Party actually hated the Cultural Revolution and that this was especially true of many of those who were knocked down during it. Mao consistently encouraged such people not to bear a grudge but to learn from their experience in the Cultural Revolution and unite with the forward thrust of the continuing revolution, and a number did so. However, people like Teng Hsiao-ping, who was completely unrepentant, deliberately stirred up the resentment of veteran cadres while attacking new leading people who came to the fore in the Cultural Revolution, along with restoring other unrepentant capitalist-roaders like himself (the fact that people like Lo Jui-ching and Chou Yang could be brought back while Mao was still alive indicates how powerful the right had become even at that time).

As we wrote in the October 15, 1976 *Revolution*, Teng Hsiao-ping's policy was "driving out proletarian revolutionaries, including those who had come to the fore during the Cultural Revolution, and bringing back into the Party, and into leading posts, revisionists and degenerates of all kinds who had justly been cast down by the masses during the Cultural Revolution, who were still unrepentant and who wanted to 'settle scores' with the masses and their revolutionary leaders. In addition he tried to stir up people who had been criticized during the Cultural Revolution, but still had leading positions, to oppose and reverse the advances made through the Cultural Revolution. He also tried to sabotage Mao's line of training millions of successors to carry forward the revolution." (see p. 16) This is what Teng meant by "rectification"—and, as indicated before, what Hua also advocated and carried out and is carrying out now.

As for the statement that the Four attacked Chou En-lai as well during the early period of the Cultural Revolution, I do not think this is true. At that time Chou En-lai's role was overall a positive one, though in my opinion even then he went too far in protecting certain people who should not have been protected—Yu Chiu-li, who came under severe and for the most part correct criticism in the Cultural Revolution, is one of these. Further, it was exactly at the point that it became clear that the "ultra-left" attacks on various leaders, such as Chen Yi, were actually being aimed at Chou En-lai that the Four—and again, Chiang Ching most prominent among them—came out very strongly against such attacks. Undoubtedly the Four and Chou had differences even at that time but they were then not antagonistic and not dealt with as such by the Four.

Mao is supposed to have said that Chou En-lai was the "housekeeper" of China. This was true—in a major way he kept things together and running. But a housekeeper is only fine so long as he serves the master of the house—the proletariat in socialist China. If he ceases to do that and tries to replace the masses as master then he turns into his opposite and all his organizational and political skills become bad things not good things. This was not the case in the early period of the Cultural Revolution, but it became the case near the end, and it was then that the Four opened fire on Chou.

As for the statement that the Four never really did anything good in the Cultural Revolution and were just in the right place at the right time—if this weren't a criminal statement it would be laughable. Long before the Cultural Revolution, Yao Wen-yuan had distinguished himself in the struggle against the bourgeois rightists in 1957. And, as noted before, it was Yao who took up the task, under Mao's direction, of writing the article that served as the opening salvo in the Cultural Revolution. This was not a question of being in the right place at the right time—there was a big struggle even to get this article published, and in putting it out Yao was opening himself up to bitter attack from the right, which had a lot of power, and which definitely did attack Yao. Further, as touched on before, the struggle in Shanghai was very sharp and complicated and Yao and Chang Chun-chiao as leaders of the left were viciously attacked by both right and "ultra-left" forces. They did a tremendous job of uniting broad masses around a correct line in the face of all this—and the reactionaries had their mass base then, too, as they do now (there are still classes in China, we should not forget, and there are still advanced, intermediate and backward among the masses).

Chang Chun-chiao was, more than anyone else, the overall leader of this struggle in Shanghai. And he did not appear out of nowhere. As noted before, for a number of years he served as a deputy Party secretary in Shanghai under Ko Ching-shih, a very popular leader and strong supporter of Mao's, who, for example, went all out in favor of the Great Leap Forward and came under severe attack along with Mao for this. Ko died in early 1965 and after that the revisionists, with Liu Shao-chi's backing, took over in Shanghai, pushing Chang Chun-chiao aside for all practical purposes, because Chang had been closely associated with Ko and the revolutionary line he represented.

Once the Cultural Revolution broke out Chang came forward to support it and play a leading role in it, not only in Shanghai but in the country overall. And once again he was sharply attacked by the right—and the "ultra-left." During the high tide of this struggle, it is interesting and significant to note, all the charges now enshrined as truth about how Chang was a Kuomintang agent, etc., were brought up against him, were thoroughly gone into and refuted as the garbage they are. (It is true that over 40 years ago as a young man barely 20, and under the direction of bad leadership, Chang Chun-chiao did write an article under the name Ti Ke, attacking Lu Hsun and putting forward a bad line on literature. What of it? Does that make him an "out-and-out Old-time Capitulationist" as the current rulers say? Does it even compare to the important role he played in supporting the revolutionization of literature and art in China, beginning before the Cultural Revolution? Hardly, and if such are the criteria then there is not a single revolutionary in China today. And I find it extremely hypocritical and ridiculous to attack Chang Chun-chiao for this while resurrecting the man under whose leadership he wrote the article, Chou Yang!)

The attacks on Chang from the right and the "ultra left" were so sharp by the counter-revolutionaries that Mao emphatically stated at one point (in 1967), "If that meeting is held to bombard Chang Chun-chiao we will certainly take the necessary steps and arrest people." (see Schram's book, p. 278) No doubt if Mao had died and if the counter-revolutionaries had won out in China then, the various attacks like those on the Four now would have been printed as truth—and repeated as such by some people.

Yet through all this Chang played the leading role in Shanghai in advancing the Cultural Revolution and uniting the masses around the correct line. One particular action of his is most interesting and telling in light of current charges against the Four. At a certain point the counter-revolutionaries, especially those in "ultra-left" disguise, instigated the masses in Shanghai to "suspect all," insisting that only Chairman Mao was reliable. On that basis they mobilized large numbers of workers to leave the factories to go to Peking, under the pretext that they could deliver their complaints directly to Chairman Mao. At great personal risk to himself, Chang Chun-chiao intercepted the train and through long hours of struggle—in which counter-revolutionaries again instigated the masses, saying "don't listen to him, he's a counter-revolutionary"—he convinced the masses to send representatives to Peking while the bulk returned to the factories.

And what did Chang tell the workers, what line did he win them over with? He said—the counter-revolutionaries are luring you away from Shanghai so you can't make revolution there, and further, what kind of example would it set for the rest of the country if the workers of Shanghai (who led the first mass seizure of power from below in the Cultural Revolution) left their production posts and abandoned the task of production as the model for making revolution!

And once Chang assumed the leading role in Shanghai, production there boomed. You see, Chang Chun-chiao and the Four in general were concerned about production; that was not their difference with the right. But they did not raise it above revolution—*that* was their difference with the right, the difference between two opposing class stands and interests.

Wang Hung-wen also came to the fore in the struggle in Shanghai. At the early stages he led workers there in uniting to make revolution—and also came under heavy fire from the right, was branded a "counter-revolutionary" by Liu Shao-chi's forces, who still had considerable strength. This was no light matter—it meant putting your ass—and maybe literally your life—on the line. The same was true, by the way, of Mao Yuan-hsin, Mao's nephew and a "sworn accomplice" of the "gang of four." He was in Harbin at the outbreak of the Cultural Revolution and played a role similar to Wang Hung-wen and in the face of the same fierce attacks and the same risks.

I have already mentioned more than once Chiang Ching's great contributions in the field of literature and art, as well as contributions to the Cultural Revolution overall, despite certain mistakes. Here I would only stress again that this, too, was not accomplished without fierce struggle—she went right into a powerful lair of the bourgeoisie and overall did a hell of a job in making revolution. Chiang Ching, I believe, was capable of more than a little subjectivism, and no doubt she made enemies on this basis and gave her enemies a basis for attacking her. But, again, this is definitely secondary to her overall very positive role. And it should also be pointed out that, while she may have had certain "privileges" because of being the Chairman's wife, this was more than outweighed by the fact that she was a key target for all those who opposed Mao but could not attack the Chairman openly and so turned special fire on her as a way of getting at Mao—even as the current rulers are doing now. If it is said, as it is by the current rulers, that Chiang Ching wanted to be an "empress," I can only say that she is infinitely preferable to the Emperors now ruling from behind Tien An Men gate. (In any case I do not think that Chiang Ching was the political leader of the Four—that role was played by Chang Chun-chiao.)

"Well, if the 'gang of four' were all so great, then how do you explain the reports that the masses were jubilant at their smashing?" First, I would say that the reports of the Four's political death are greatly exaggerated. By this I do not mean that I expect them specifically to make a comeback—that is extremely unlikely. I mean that they have a good deal of support in China—support not only for them personally, of course, but for the line they fought for, Mao's line. This is true especially among the class conscious masses and the revolutionary forces who came to the fore during the Cultural Revolution—leading people in this category have been purged, of course, but there are undoubtedly millions of such people among the masses. That there is resistance to the campaign against the Four and the purge of all their followers and supporters, and that it is widespread, is something even the current rulers cannot hide—much as they want to deny it, they are forced to admit it indirectly and sometimes directly.

On the other hand the Four definitely do have a number of enemies in China—they certainly did at a time when there can be no question about their overall very positive role, for example at the high tide of the Cultural Revolution, as noted before. As I stressed earlier, we can never forget that there are classes in China and that there are advanced, intermediate and backward among the masses—this is not just some abstract formulation but has real meaning. The Four insisted on the "high road," and this was bound to run them up against not only counter-revolutionaries but the inclinations of many "middle strata" and the prejudices and backward ideas of many of the masses themselves. Then, too, they did make mistakes and this could only aid their enemies. But I will say it again—the essence of the matter is that they fought for a correct line and overall their role was revolutionary and very positive.

Further, we must not be taken in by superficial phenomena. The large demonstrations to "celebrate the smashing of the 'gang of four'" prove primarily one thing—the present rulers can organize a demonstration. So can most reactionaries, especially if they have power. We still have to base ourselves on the fundamental question—what is the class content, the line, of those demonstrations, which class do they serve? If masses of people could not be organized around a reactionary line, how much simpler our tasks would be!—and that they can is true not only in capitalist countries but in socialist ones as well, even China, *in the short run.* (And let's not forget that there were also massive demonstrations when Teng was overthrown—the masses can certainly be mobilized around a correct line, too.)

"But the Chinese people have been through the Cultural Revolution and are very class conscious." Things are not as simple as that. Many of them are very class-conscious—the bulk of these are opposed to what is going on now, of that I am sure—how could they be otherwise? But many are not that class conscious—this is a fact Mao was well aware of and repeatedly took measures to try to deal with, recognizing that even under socialism it remains a long-term problem.

In addition there are a large number of cadres, intellectuals and others who enjoy a relatively privileged position in the division of labor in society, and these can form a powerful potential social base for revisionism. Under the leadership of a correct line the great majority of these can certainly be united together with the broad masses in the forward motion of the revolution. But if those representing the proletarian line are smashed in a coup, as has happened, and if appeals are made to the negative, bourgeois aspect of these social forces, while fascist military discipline is imposed on the masses ("Obey the Central Committee! Obey the Central Committee!" repeatedly blares the press, especially the *army* press), then these strata mentioned above can be unleashed as a social base for revisionism and many of the masses can be drawn in and/or coerced to go along. This is no reason for us to go along with what is happening, no reason at all for us to support counter-revolution and counter-revolutionaries and oppose revolution and revolutionaries.

"Sure some bad lines are coming out now but that's not the point. The point is that the 'gang of four' just kept on causing disruption and there are lots of problems with China's economy, the threat of war and so on, and it is necessary to have an end to all the disruption and get things moving, so the 'gang of four' just had to be put down and we should support the people in there now and hope they can make things work. Sure the guys in there now don't say as much about class struggle and they put more stress on modernization, but that's what's needed; do you have to talk about class struggle all the time and if you don't does that make you a revisionist and if you do does that make you a revolutionary?"

On the last point first, yes, you do have to talk about class struggle all the time—Mao certainly said so; he said you had to talk about it "every year, every month, and every day," this was part of the Party's basic line he formulated. No, just talking about it doesn't make you a revolutionary, but correctly waging it does—and that's what the Four did, overwhelmingly. And not to talk about it—yes, all the time—is a guarantee that you're going to go off the track. The point is, as Mao stressed in his last few years especially, in many ways the new society is not much different than the old. And it is not a static thing, it has to be moved one way or the other—forward through revolution toward communism or backward through restoration to capitalism. The class struggle is not an abstract, it actually determines this life and death question; and the bourgeoisie is waging it all the time so you have to talk about—educate people about—and wage it all the time: if you don't, if you rely on spontaneity, you will inevitably lose out to the bourgeoisie. This is why making production—or modernization—the main emphasis is not just wrong in the abstract but will lead to revisionism and capitalist restoration.

Second, on the question of "disruption." As I indicated before, it is not correct to lay all the disruption that undeniably went on at the doorstep of the Four. There is no doubt that in struggling against the revisionist line they and their followers caused some "disruption"—how could that be avoided?—but as I pointed out before this does not cause nearly as much disruption to *socialism* as the carrying out of a revisionist line. Communists are for order under socialism but not any kind of order, not "order" which means capitalist restoration—in other words, they do not raise stability and unity above the class struggle.

I also have no doubt that in the turmoil that was going on not only did order break down in some instances but there were cases more than usual where socialist economic relations were disrupted, people went in for capitalist practices, some profiteering, black marketing, etc., went on, and so forth. And further I have no question that bad forces jumped into the fray, some of them siding with the Four, and perhaps some good people were wrongly attacked—as far as I know it is not possible to make revolution without this happening. Doesn't this kind of thing happen in every major struggle?

These things are not the essence of the matter and to make them such does not help us at all in understanding and evaluating what went on. The disruption and disorder that occurred were not due to the attempts of the "gang of four" to "create anarchy" but to the two-line struggle that was raging, to the fact that there was not unity at the top and that both sides—not just the Four—were making an all-out effort to mobilize their forces to topple their enemy. Both supported certain forces and opposed others, both encouraged one side to knock down the other—isn't the "General Program" exactly a call for "daring" to knock down the Four and their supporters, and does anyone seriously think that this call was issued only as late as Fall, 1975? In fact we know that this was not the case—the present rulers have repeatedly praised people who openly attacked the Four, going back many years. Who has ever heard of a serious struggle where such things do not happen, on both sides?

Our attitude toward such a struggle cannot be to wish it would go away or to say that whoever is calling for struggle and knocking down people is bad—both will call for struggle and for knocking down people, where they don't have the upper hand. As Marxists our approach has to be to examine what are the lines and class interests represented by the opposing forces and what is the balance of forces—and on that basis to evaluate matters. From all I have said, if we apply that standard there is no doubt that we should support the Four, and we could say that therefore the current rulers, the right deviationists, are really at fault for the disruption.

In fact in many cases at least the right was directly responsible for the disruption. This came down in two ways: (1) they instituted revisionist practices, including rules and regulations that did indeed control, check and suppress the workers, which brought forth resistance from the workers, especially the most class conscious; and (2) they instigated sections of the workers to strike for higher wages, promoting economism. According to the *China Quarterly*, Teng Hsiao-ping was responsible for a good part of the disruptions in Hangchow, especially in 1975, with policies like this, particularly the second, and it was in part in response to this that emphasis to the question of criticizing and restricting bourgoeis right was given by Mao—and the Four. (It is repeatedly charged by the current rulers that the Four pushed the line of "don't produce for the wrong line." Perhaps in some cases they did, but this does not necessarily mean that this was a call in every case for a strike; in fact in most cases it may well have meant resist and refuse to implement the rightists' reversals on the industrial front—restrictive and repressive rules and regulations, etc.—but continue to produce according to the principles and rules and regulations established through the Cultural Revolution. I don't know the particulars in most cases but it would be very foolish to accept at face value the charges of the current rulers, since an examination of their line has shown that they raise the specter of anarchy, etc., as a cover for propagating and implementing their revisionist line. And, on the other hand, as indicated before, an examination of the line of the Four—and their practice where they had leadership—shows that they didn't pose production against revolution but developed production under the command of revolution according to the correct dialectic, "grasp revolution, promote production." Again, of course, this is not to say that they didn't make mistakes in the course of extremely complicated struggle or to deny that in some cases bad elements jumped onto the bandwagon, from whom they were not able to distinguish themselves in the swirl of mass struggle; but as stressed before, this is not the essence of the question and to make it such does not aid us in getting to the heart of the matter.)

Overall, as stated before, we could say that the rightists, the current rulers, were responsible for the disruptions because of their line. But to put this forward as a general principle would be metaphysical—we might as well say that the bourgeoisie is at fault for being the bourgeoisie. Since it is, and since it will be around for quite a while, the only thing to do is to struggle against it and to support those everywhere who do the same—especially the proletariat and its leaders in a country where the working class is in power and is fighting to stay there and advance.

Mao never took the attitude, strategically at least, that disruptions, or disturbances, are bad things. Quite the opposite. And specifically, if Mao thought that there was so much anarchy that order was of primary importance, if he thought the disturbances at the factories were so terrible, etc., why was the right to strike included, on Mao's proposal, in the new Constitution of the People's Republic at the 4th People's Congress, in January, 1975, at a time when such disturbances were definitely going on? Was it included as window dressing with the intention that the masses would never be allowed to use it? —this was no doubt the intention of the current leaders but certainly it was not Mao's.

As for the economic situation, etc., it is true that there were problems in China's economy, including some poor harvests, a lack of at least some consumer goods, etc. The steel industry has had difficulty for a number of reasons, and there have been other problems—but there is nothing so new or startling about that. It is also true that whichever side won out, following this particular struggle there would have been increased emphasis on production. As I pointed out before, after Chang Chun-chiao assumed the leading position in Shanghai in 1967, production boomed ahead and he gave great emphasis to it. Revolutionary mass upsurges have repeatedly led to spurts ahead in production in the history of the People's Republic—that is, on the basis of transformations in the relations of production and superstructure achieved through revolutionary struggle, production has leapt ahead. If the Four had won out, this would have happened. What would not have happened is the raising of production above revolution; instead it would have been based on the commanding role of revolution. And everything would not have been hinged on "modernization" but on class struggle, so the country could *continue* to advance—on the *socialist* road.

Further, to use the problems in the economy as an excuse for a revisionist line is not worthy of a Marxist. Revisionism will not "solve the problems" of a socialist country—except that it will transform it into not being a socialist country, so there will be no socialist country to "have problems." As an article put out by the Four pointed out, "in opposing Marxism, all revisionists first make a fuss about the 'situation' " (from a collection of articles criticizing Teng Hsiao-ping's revisionist line). And while it is true that there were problems in the economy in recent years, in essence the current rulers are slandering the masses, saying that they have made a mess of the economy, which is a complete lie. A clear indication of the depth to which the current rulers will sink to slander the masses and the Cultural Revolution is seen by the fact that Han Suyin, who is nothing if not a mouthpiece for the people in power in China, is now going around saying that the economy in China has been stagnant and in a mess for 10 years! This, of course, is a great slander and was directly refuted at the 4th People's Congress where Chou En-lai found himself having to say, "Reactionaries at home and abroad asserted that the Great Proletarian Cultural Revolution would certainly disrupt the development of our national economy, but facts have now given them a strong rebuttal." (See *PR* #4, 1975, p. 22.)

Reversing the verdict on this shows exactly what the right deviationists were up to in making a fuss about the situation in the last few years—they were seizing on certain difficulties to attack the whole revolution. And this was not the first time Teng, in particular, had done so.

It was around 1961 that he first came out with his infamous "white cat, black cat" formulation. Wasn't the situation very serious then? Several years of natural disasters, dislocations caused by some problems arising in the Great Leap Forward, the pull-out of Soviet technicians and blue-prints, hostile powers surrounding China on all sides, the recent experience of the reactionary revolt in Tibet and Indian aggression against China backed by the U.S. and the Soviets, and so on. It is always at such times that the revisionists jump out most boldly and aggressively.

It is significant that the "70 Points" dished up by Teng and others in 1961 (reportedly Li Hsien-nien and Chou En-lai as well were also responsible for these revisionist regulations) make a point not only of seizing on the situation in general but specifically call for an end to "bitter battles" in the factories. Having read over a summary of the "70 Points," I can only agree with the Four that the "20 Points" was only a refurbished version under new conditions of the same revisionist trash. That we should go along now with the same rotten line, covered with the same "concern" about the situation, disruption, etc., as was repudiated more than a decade ago is something which I cannot comprehend and certainly cannot accept!

It is most significant that the current rulers, on the pretext of the "situation" and on the basis of totally distorting it, resort to Lenin's writings from the period of the first years of the Soviet Republic, including the period of the New Economic Policy. Such works as "The New Economic Policy and the Tasks of the Political Education Departments" (see Lenin Vol. 33, pp. 60 and following) and Lenin's speeches to the "The Eighth All-Russia Congress of Soviets" (Vol. 31, pp. 463 and following) where Lenin openly advocates allowance of some capitalist methods and concessions to foreign capitalists, are treated as the Bible by the current rulers and form the basis of their actual "general program."—almost 30 years after China has entered the socialist period! Here, what was said in *Red Papers 7* about the Soviet Union is of direct relevance:

> "Since 1956 revisionist economists had scrounged around for quotations from the Marxist-Leninist classics which, taken out of context, might seem to justify their attempts to reintroduce capitalist economic methods and relations in the Soviet economy. They hit pay dirt in Lenin's writings dating from the introduction of the New Economic Policy (NEP) in 1921." (p. 30.)

To argue that line does not matter now, things just have to get done—i.e., production, order, etc.—is precisely to promote revisionism. Mao fought Teng and others tooth and nail when they did this in 1961, and he fought them the same way, even more sharply, when they did it recently. That is exactly why Mao said, "Still his theme of 'white cat, black cat' "—and why he called for Teng's ouster. For the life of me I cannot see any reason why we should support revisionism, and I cannot see why any Marxist would wallow politically in the mire with Teng and the other right deviationists on the basis that this will "solve China's problems"!

Of course all of this revisionism will be carried out under the banner of "concern for the well-being of the masses." This is exactly what Khrushchev did with his "goulash communism." And in this light, Mao's poems, reissued on New Year's Day, 1976, have direct bearing, poems which repudiate this "goulash communism" and in answer to whining about how terrible things are, that " 'This is one hell of a mess!' " reply, " 'Stop your windy nonsense! Look you, the world is being turned upside down.' " We know where Khruschev's "goulash communism" led, and we should have no greater difficulty in understanding where the same line of those now in power in China will lead as well, unless the *present* situation is reversed.

"Yes, but you don't really take into account the 'gang of four's' errors, you just excuse them, but you won't allow for any errors by those in there now." As far as making excuses for the Four's errors, I do not make "excuses" for them. I have said what I think some of their errors were and at the same time tried to put them in context. The point is that their errors were exactly that—errors—the mistakes of revolutionaries, made in the process of carrying out complex and acute struggle and fighting in difficult circumstances for the correct line and the interests of the proletariat. For the Four their errors stand as the secondary aspect in relation to their overwhelmingly positive—and again I will say it, heroic—role.

As for the current rulers it is not a question of errors—their whole line is an error. Or, rather, it is not an error, but a line for restoring capitalism. Any errors they make we should be glad for, because it will aid the proletariat in struggling against them. Again, as in all matters, it is a question of line—assessing what is the overall line, what class it serves, and evaluating the question of errors from that standpoint. If we do that we can still only reach the by now oft-repeated conclusion—we should not support the current rulers and we should support the Four and those now fighting for the proletarian line and proletarian revolution, as the Four did.

"Well, it is true that the line of those now in power is no good, but neither was the 'gang of four's' line any good. Actually there were three lines: the correct line of Mao and Chou En-lai to put stress on modernization but to do it on the basis of revolution in command and class struggle as the key link, while the people now in power opposed this from the right and the 'gang of four' opposed it from the 'left.' "

What "three lines"? I believe that actually I have answered this from many different angles already, but I will briefly answer it straight on.

As I said earlier, there are certainly differences among the present rulers—opposite poles of the same stupidity—but what is principal is their unity in opposition to revolution and in agreement with a general line that will lead to capitalist restoration. And I think it is very clear that Chou En-lai stood with those in power now. His line, in essence, was their line, and he gave them backing with all he was worth—otherwise they would never have gotten as far as they did while Mao was still alive.

On the other side, as I have pointed out, there were some disagreements between Mao and the Four, but the principal aspect, the essence of the matter, was the unity between them. The Four's line was in essence Mao's line—otherwise they would have never been as high up as they were while Mao was still alive (can anyone doubt that if Mao had agreed they could have and would have been smashed or at least demoted long ago?!), and the struggle against the right deviationist wind would never have gotten as far as it did.

Mao's line was the line put forward in Chang Chun-chiao's article (pamphlet), quoted before—and I will quote it again,

> "Full of militancy, all our people are determined to build China into a powerful socialist country before the end of the century. In the course of this effort and in the entire historical period of socialism, whether we can persevere all the way in the dictatorship of the proletariat is a cardinal issue for China's future development. Current class struggles, too, require that we should get clear on the question of the dictatorship of the proletariat." (pp. 1-2, pamphlet)

This is how Mao, and the Four, saw the relationship between revolution and production, between the class struggle and the drive to build China into a "powerful socialist country."

And I would like to ask a question: if Mao and Chou En-lai, two extremely powerful and influential leaders, stood solid together, had fundamental unity, on the correct line, why is it that they could get none of the other top leaders to go along with them? This is a question that anyone putting forward this "three lines" argument must answer. And anyway it does not conform to facts—they each did have certain top leaders in the same basic camp with them—Mao had the Four (and for a time at least some wavering "middle forces") and Chou had those now in power, the right deviationists (who have also clearly put the "middle forces" in the position where they must go along, or be smashed, too). A further note of interest on this point—Teng Hsiao-ping is reported by the *Far Eastern Economic Review* to have told the CC meeting where he was officially restored, right before the 11th Congress, that in early 1975 he, Chou, Li Hsien-nien and Yeh Chien-ying took steps to bring forward people to make sure the Four did not "inherit" leadership later. This seems quite probably true—and who did *this* "gang of four" promote as *their* "successor"?

Chou, Teng and others, being astute politicians if not revolutionaries at the end, sized up the situation and recognized very well that, especially if Mao outlived Chou En-lai, the chances of Teng succeeding Chou were extremely thin. Therefore, going back several years Chou in particular brought forward new people to be a "second line" of succession. Hua Kuo-feng was one of the more significant of these—he was (and remains) Chou En-lai's "man," not Mao's. Then, when it became clear near the end that Mao would indeed block Teng's ascension to power, and specifically when the struggle sharpened up through the battle to beat back the right deviationist wind, the right deviationists brought forward and insisted on Hua, faced as they were with the necessity of going along—for the time being—with the dumping of Teng and the anti-rightist struggle with him as the target. This may sound like a "power struggle," and indeed in one basic sense it was—a struggle for power between *two classes*, the proletariat and the bourgeoisie, represented by two different headquarters within the Communist Party, with Mao, and the Four, leading one headquarters, and, at the end, Chou, Teng and others leading another, the bourgeois, headquarters.

Instead of inventing a "third line" that does not exist it is far more instructive to examine the two lines that did exist in direct opposition to each other. We have the "Three Poisonous Weeds" and the fact that Hua as well as Teng and the others in power now were responsible for them. We have Hua's 1975 Tachai speech which is in the same mold and puts forward the same basic line. And we have the material put out by the Four. Looking at all this, and especially in light of the revisionist nature of the documents with which Hua and the others are and have been associated, isn't it very clear that not only was the line put out by the Four correct, but that they obviously were not "inventing" a revisionist line to attack in order to "promote anarchy" and cover "ultra-leftism"?

Speaking of "inventing," and the whining of the current rulers that the Four took statements and documents by the current leaders, including drafts of the "Three Poisonous Weeds," and published them together with criticism of them—in relation to all this, what Lenin says in *What Is To Be Done?* concerning the *Credo* of the Economists is very enlightening. This *Credo*, Lenin said, provided such an excellent self-exposure of Economism

> "... that, had there been no *Credo*, it would have been worth inventing one. The *Credo* was not invented, but it was published without the consent and perhaps even against the will of its authors. At all events, the present writer [Lenin], who took part in dragging this new 'programme' into the light of day, has heard complaints and reproaches to the effect that copies of the resume of the speakers' views were distributed, dubbed the *Credo*, and even published in the press together with a protest! We refer to this episode because it reveals a very peculiar feature of our Economism, fear of publicity." (Lenin, Vol. 5, p.364)

"Well, the 'gang of four' may have served a useful purpose, while Mao was alive, in 'stirring things up,' and he may have wanted them around, as long as he was, for that purpose, but after Mao went the Four had to go, too."

First, this argument in essence admits that there were no other forces in the leadership who could be counted on to make revolution—at least not if it posed the danger of "stirring things up," which by definition it always does. If this argument is inverted it will have some aspect of truth—that is, actually *some* of those now in office could be kept in line as long as Mao was around, but after he went they went along with the hard-boned right.

Second, show me how the Four's line is essentially different than Mao's—we still get back to that. And third, who saw to it that the Four "went"? And what is their line?

As I have shown over and over the Four's line was Mao's line, while the line of the current rulers is completely opposed to Mao's line—and that was all clear well before Mao "went." So all this argument says is that it is right for the bourgeoisie to put down the proletariat because the latter can only "stir things up"—which in fact is the line of the current rulers. I do not think it is a Marxist line by any means, and I don't know why any Marxist would want to parrot it.

Finally, as I have also shown, the Four could not only "stir things up," they could and did lead in developing production under the command of revolution, in revolutionizing art and literature, and generally in transforming the material and ideological conditions to advance toward communism. That such people have to "go" is surely the line only of the bourgeoisie and most definitely not of the proletariat!

"The 'gang of four' wanted another Cultural Revolution and it wasn't time for one, so they had to be smashed and they were." Here we have a complete reversal of right and wrong.

Actually, the Four did not exactly want another Cultural Revolution—they wanted the *same* one—that is, they fought to prevent the reversal of the Cultural Revolution and of the Chinese revolution as a whole. Through the course of this struggle, had it been successful, new advances would have resulted, both in the economic base and the superstructure. Would that have been bad? Only to the bourgeoisie.

If this argument means that the Four were in favor of and did "stir up" mass struggle against the revisionists, then why is that bad? Do you want to say that they shouldn't have done everything possible to prevent a revisionist takeover?

Here I have to say that an extremely naive and idealist and metaphysical notion of class struggle, specifically in socialist society, is behind such an argument. It presents things as though the proletariat has complete freedom to choose when and how it will fight the bourgeoisie, and ignores the fact that the bourgeoisie is always waging struggle against the proletariat and that, as pointed out before, it will jump out even more ferociously when there are difficulties. This is proved by the whole history of class struggle in every socialist country, including the latest round in China which ended in the smashing of the proletarian headquarters led by the Four (after Mao died).

I should point out that to some degree the article in *The Communist,* Vol. 1, No. 2, "On the Relationship Between the Forces and Relations of Production and the Base and Superstructure," does feed this erroneous view to a certain extent—though it cannot be said to be the *cause* of this view or to present it as fully as the argument above does. That article was written the way it was because there has been struggle over the question of China, and the article reflects that and represents a certain compromise between opposing positions. Therefore, to a certain extent, it presents things as though the proletariat under socialism pushes production forward and then at a certain point it is time for a leap in the relations of production and the superstructure and so the proletariat carries that out, and so on. While the article does contain points which oppose this incorrect view, it does to a certain degree reflect and feed it as well—for the reasons just summarized.

From reading this article one could get the impression, for example, that at the time of the 9th Congress in China, in 1969, after three years of mass upsurge of class struggle, Lin Piao was correct in calling for production as the main task. Still, on the other hand, the article, despite its weaknesses flowing from its compromise character, does point to the fact that the bourgeoisie is continually attempting to reverse the gains of the revolution and the entire revolution itself, and does make clear that class struggle is the key link. And, in fact, even with all its weaknesses, if that article—which includes an emphasis on the fight against capitalism in the collective form and puts stress on how the class struggle goes on after the means of production have in the main been socialized and which does make class struggle the key link—if that article is used as a standard to judge the current rulers they still come off as revisionist traitors. (Incidentally, having "personally" written that article, I think it is fair to point out that something "personally" done by a leader does not necessarily indicate that such a thing represents his "personal choice": it is often the product of sharp struggle and some sort of compromise between conflicting views—*apropos* the "personal appointment" and endorsement of Hua by Mao.)

Finally, on this point, to condemn the Four for "wanting another Cultural Revolution," that is for waging all-out struggle against those in power now, is to beg the issue. If, in fact, as I believe I have shown many times over, you are faced with the real threat of a revisionist takeover, it is absolutely correct to wage all-out struggle against this and those attempting to bring it about. In fact, to do otherwise, to fail to do so as fully as possible, would be criminal.

I believe we should be good for our word. By that I mean we should apply to the Four what we said about those who opposed Khruschev at the time he made his coup. Specifically, in *Red Papers 7*, the following is stated, which I believe has amazing relation to and relevance for the situation in China and the struggle between the Four and the current rulers in the recent period:

> "In the spring of 1957, a showdown came. V.M. Molotov and L. Kaganovich were able to assemble a majority in the Politbureau against Khruschev. In fact, the majority may have been overwhelming. But Khruschev, as ever a wily fox, held a hidden card. This was the support of the notoriously self-seeking and individualistic Defense Minister, Marshal Zhukov. When Zhukov apparently indicated that he would oppose the Politbureau majority with armed force, the more vacillating allies began to reach for a compromise. Soon Khrushchev had the majority. Molotov, Kaganovich, Malenkov and Shepilov were expelled as the so-called 'anti-Party group.' Bulganin and Voroshilov were to follow in the not too

> distant future. As for Zhukov, Khrushchev, seeing in him a future rival, dumped him, too.
>
> The members of the 'anti-Party group' *failed to bring the struggle out of the Politbureau and to the masses*. . . We do not know all the circumstances which prevented the proletarian forces from bringing the struggle into the open, *developing mass action*. Nor are we clear on exactly who did represent the proletarian line. Nonetheless, it can be stated that *this failure was a major factor contributing to the revisionist takeover*." (p. 23, emphasis added).

Should we condemn the Four for *doing exactly* what we criticized the proletarian forces in the Soviet Union for *not* doing at that time? No, we should praise and cherish them for the struggle they put up.

Of course there are certain differences—a main one being that, exactly because the struggle was brought out into the open, we do know who the proletarian forces are and what the line struggle was. And that can be the basis for being a lot better prepared to deal with the setback than the international proletariat was after Khrushchev's revisionist takeover, providing we grasp the essence of what has happened and support revolutionaries while opposing revisionists.

One final point on this question of "wanting another Cultural Revolution." Mao said in late 1974 that it would be desirable after eight years of the Cultural Revoluiton to have stability and unity (this was the directive he gave on this question). But he said this, I believe, because he recognized that this would create the most favorable conditions for the left in struggling against the right. But he certainly recognized at the same time that the right had a lot to do with whether or not stability and unity could be achieved and to what degree it was not only desirable but possible to have stability and unity. And we know that Mao certainly did not raise stability and unity above the class struggle—he made that point abundantly clear.

Further, if Mao did not then "want another Cultural Revolution," he certainly did want a major struggle against the right. This is clear in the pamphlets by Yao Wen-yuan and by Chang Chun-chiao in particular, which openly declares that there is a major struggle going on and two lines within the Party leadership. I believe it is obvious that Mao not only agreed with but was behind these two pamphlets. Certainly I thought so at the time, and from what I know so did almost everyone I talked to in the RU at that time who followed events in China. But more than that, the

Chinese masses certainly must have thought so. Major articles signed by top leaders of the Chinese Party who had been closely associated with Mao, and specifically people whose articles before (at least Yao Wen-yuan's in late 1965) constituted a "signal" for big struggle—such articles were bound to be taken by the Chinese masses as an indication from Mao that a big struggle was necessary. And there is no evidence that Mao criticized Chang and Yao for these articles or for writing them under their own names, which suggests all the more that Mao was indeed behind them and the message they sent out that major struggle was called for.

It is true that Yao Wen-yuan's pamphlet emphasized the need to combat empiricism and that, in reference to some study material Yao had apparently prepared, Mao criticized one-sided emphasis on combatting empiricism. But two things should be said on this. First, as noted, Mao's criticism was not in reference to Yao's pamphlet itself but to study material produced a little later. And two, from all indications the Four did take up Mao's criticism and called for criticism of both dogmatism and empiricism. (See, for example, the article by Tien Chun in *PR* #20, 1975, p. 8, which is clearly an article written under the Four's direction and includes lines now condemned, such as the question "What are the new changes in class relations?" in China today. Further, it is my opinion that in calling for criticism of dogmatism as well as empiricism Mao was not denying that empiricism was the main problem then—he was warning against one-sidedness just as he avoided this one-sidedness in such works as "*On Practice*," where in laying stress on combatting dogmatism he also criticized empiricism).

Further, the Mao poems released on New Year's Day, 1976 unmistakably call for big struggle and oppose the line that everything should be or can be "smooth sailing." And, as pointed out earlier, it is also clear that Mao approved of and was behind the publication of these poems at that time. As we wrote about these poems in the October 15, 1976 *Revolution*, they were

> "a sharp attack on the revisionists and their 'theory of the productive forces'—what the people want and need is not revolution to liberate themselves and the productive forces but just production with the promise of 'plenty to eat'—in other words that the masses of people are backward, are only good to work as slaves, can only think about the most narrow and short-sighted personal interests and certainly cannot transform society through class struggle. The publication of these poems struck deep at Teng Hsiao-ping's attempt to rally reactionary forces, promote backward sentiments and play on contradictions

> among the masses; and it acted as a rallying call for the masses, summing up powerfully their own experience that through great struggle comes great advance and out of great turmoil and upheaval comes greater unity for the cause of revolution." (p. 17)

I believe this analysis in the *Revolution* article still stands and speaks directly to the question of "wanting another Cultural Revolution"—that is, how not only the Four but Mao as well saw both the necessity and desirability of waging "great struggle" against the class enemy, the right deviationists.

"The line adopted at the 8th Congress of the Chinese Party, in 1956, was a bad line and that didn't mean a revisionist takeover, so just because the line at the 11th Congress and in general is bad now, that doesn't mean there has been a revisionist takeover."

Any nonsense will do, apparently, to avoid drawing correct conclusions. The fact is that if the line of the 8th Congress had not been overturned, and if those whose revisionism was mainly behind it, Liu Shao-chi most especially, were not overthrown, then China would have been taken down the capitalist road. The 8th Congress did not lead to a revisionist takeover, but only because it did lead to a Cultural Revolution, which reversed its incorrect line and overthrew those—or at least the core of those at that time—who were bent on taking the capitalist road. I will be extremely happy to see a new revolution to overthrow those now in power and reverse their revisionist line, but such a revolution will not and cannot be led by those in power now (though they will undoubtedly continue to use certain forms of the Cultural Revolution, such as big-character posters, in their own bourgeois factional disputes). A genuine revolution now can only come from the "bottom," and frankly I don't expect to see such a revolution in the near future. These are bitter facts—but they are the facts. And that points to a key difference between the 8th Congress and now—after the 8th Congress Mao and other revolutionaries were still in key positions and overall the proletariat and its revolutionary leaders still held power, though the capitalist roaders were in a strong position and had usurped power in many places; today the capitalist roaders have usurped supreme power.

"The people in there now at least have a program for how to develop China, but the 'gang of four' had no program for this, so therefore the people in now should at least be given a chance."

All this amounts to is saying, "If you don't like the current rulers' plan for capitalist restoration, then what is your plan for capitalist restoration?" That's the first point—the current rulers' "program" is a program for "developing" China along the capitalist road.

On the other hand, as I have indicated many times, the Four did have a program, a line—Mao's line. And they had specific policies, as indicated in the Shanghai textbook, in articles in the *Peking Review* and elsewhere, and in practice where they were able to implement their line—policies which flowed from a correct line, were based on the principle "grasp revolution, promote production," and which followed the general line for building socialism and a whole set of specific policies formulated by Mao—such as agriculture as the foundation and industry as the leading factor, grain as the key link in agriculture, steel as the key link in industry, and so on. Not having a "program" only means that they didn't hinge everything on modernization and develop a whole set of principles and policies which are opposed to the correct line and would lead to capitalist restoration.

It is true that the Four put emphasis in the latest struggle on opposing the revisionism of those now in power and defending the gains of the Cultural Revolution. This was necessary and correct, and not to see that is to fall into the idealist and metaphysical view of the class struggle summarized earlier. There certainly have been times in the history of the communist movement in this country when it was necessary to take the same approach—for example the struggle against the Bundists, during which some people raised the same argument—well if you don't like our program for carrying out bourgeois nationalism, what is your program for doing so? We answered, and defeated, them not on that level, but by exposing and repudiating their incorrect line, and on *that basis* we have been able to make headway—if only beginning—in carrying out work among the oppressed nationalities guided by a correct line. (And certainly we made mistakes in that struggle, didn't we?)

So it was with the Four's struggle against the revisionist line and program of those now in power. And as I said before, had the Four won, production would have leapt ahead under their leadership, as it did, for example, in Shanghai and other places following mass upsurges and seizures of power in the Cultural Revolution. As also pointed out before, such leaps in the economy have generally followed such upsurges of mass struggle in China.

"The 'gang of four' were responsible for the earthquakes in China." So far this argument has not been raised, but it wouldn't surprise me if it were raised.

Again, when it is all said and done, we get back to the basic fact that the Four fought for, and implemented where they could, a revolutionary line in opposition to the revisionist line of the current rulers. This fact will not change no matter how many phony arguments are cooked up to try to divert things from this central question.

Of course if the Four had mustered the necessary forces to take the first necessary step—bust Hua and his cronies—rather than the other way around, everything would not have been "rosy." In fact, there no doubt would have been upheaval right away, maybe even for a brief period something approaching a kind of "civil war," as the current rulers have blustered. That "civil war," however, would not be a rebellion by the masses but a revolt by certain commanders in the military. To put this down the Four would have to rely mainly on the masses, including the militia and masses in the PLA, as well as certain other commanders who they could win over. By definition discussing this takes us into the area of at least a certain amount of conjecture, but I think this is a roughly accurate picture of what would have happened. And I do not hesitate to say again that this situation, especially assuming the Four were able to carry it through and put down any reactionary revolt, would be infinitely preferable to the quick rightist coup and "slow death" of revisionism that the Chinese people have to confront now. In any case, even as things turned out, it is far better that the Four dared to "scale the heights" than if they had quietly submitted to revisionist betrayal of the Chinese revolution and the Chinese people.

III. Why Did Revisionism Triumph in this Battle and What Lessons Should We Draw?

As to why the revisionists triumphed, that is obviously a big question to which a great deal of attention and study should be devoted. But certain things which contributed to this can be indicated now.

First, in general there is the truth that Mao stressed over and over again that socialism is a long period of transition from capitalism to communism and that all during this period there are classes and class struggle and the danger of capitalist restoration. More specifically there are the things Mao focused on in the last few years of his life as providing a powerful material base for capitalist restoration—the persistence of commodity relations, the three major differences (mental/manual, town/countryside, worker/peasant), of bourgeois right as well as other powerful remnants left over from previous society in the material and ideological sphere. The events of the last year, the success of a revisionist coup, is bringing home more and more sharply how incisive Mao's directives on this were. And the results of this coup will show just how correct Mao was in saying that it will be quite easy for them to rig up the capitalist system.

All of us, I think, have had something of an idealist and metaphysical tendency in regard to these things in the past—we took these statements by Mao as "heavy thoughts" and didn't really grasp the life and death character of what he was repeatedly raising and stressing. Now the reality of what formed the basis for those "heavy thoughts" is slapping us in the face.

Further, as Mao also called special attention to, in a country like China, a backward country economically, where it is necessary first to go through the democratic stage and then to make the immediate transition to socialism, the problems of making that transition and continuing to overcome spontaneous capitalist tendencies are enormous (this doesn't mean, I don't think, that it will somehow be "easier" to stay on the socialist road after seizing power in an economically advanced country—the problems there will be enormous, too, but they will in many respects take different forms, though some will be the same or similar). The point is that as Lenin said on this question, the force of habit of millions and tens of millions is a most terrible force, and in a country like China the tendency toward small production and the small producer mentality is very great.

Further, there is the whole deep-rooted Confucian tradition in China, which along with the still backward conditions economically, means that many people are still strongly weighed down by the old spiritual fetters—superstition, etc., as well as the tendency to meekly follow those in authority. And there is still the legacy of colonialism and the colonial mentality—or rather, colonized mentality—which promotes the idea that what is foreign is better and that it is necessary to rely on the foreign and the "advanced." At the same time there is a tendency to nationalism, which has a strong material base in the still largely peasant character of the country and in the fact that the Chinese revolution in its first stage was not just democratic but national. This, I believe, led revolutionaries in China to a certain extent, and even Mao to some degree, to view the revolutionary movements in other countries, especially in the advanced capitalist countries, "through the eyes of the Chinese revolution," so to speak—even though Mao was aware and pointed out that the Chinese revolution had different characteristics than those in the advanced capitalist countries. But much more important than any such tendency—which was most definitely a very secondary aspect in Mao and other revolutionaries in China, including the Four—was and is the tendency on the part of those who actually do get stuck at the democratic stage, or who degenerate ideologically, to take a bourgeois nationalist stand which, under China's present conditions, assumes the form of great power chauvinist views of China's relations with other countries and peoples and of China's need for "national development." (Again, in an imperialist country it can hardly be said that the problem of nationalism—specifically great nation chauvinism—will not be a tremendous problem, but it will take a somewhat different form.)

These then are some of the general problems, the general elements that provide the basis for a revisionist triumph and capitalist restoration in a socialist society and in China in particular. But beyond that there were some more specific and very immediate events which stand out. One is obviously Mao's death, an event long-awaited by the reactionary forces as the signal to make their big move. Another is the devastating earthquakes that struck China last year, causing tremendous damage and dislocation. And at the same time there were the deaths of several longtime leaders in China besides Mao, all in the space of a couple of years, and several within one year (which role these different people played in the most recent struggle is not the point here—the point is that such deaths were bound to cause uncertainty and anxiety among the Chinese people about the situation in the country, and this is magnified by the superstitious traditions referred to above, one of which links earthquakes with the end of an Emperor's reign, etc.).

And there is the fact that with all the twists and turns, back and forths, of the two-line struggle in China, and intensely so since the start of the Cultural Revolution, there was undoubtedly a section of the Chinese masses, and a larger percentage of cadres, intellectuals, etc.—though certainly not all and not the most class conscious—who were tired of it all and wanted an end to it. Here Lenin's words are of great significance:

> "The misfortune of previous revolutions was that the revolutionary enthusiasm of the people, which sustained them in their state of tension and gave them the strength to suppress ruthlessly the elements of disintegration, did not last long. The social, i.e., class, reason for this instability of the revolutionary enthusiasm of the people

> was the weakness of the proletariat, which *alone* is able (if it is sufficiently numerous, class-conscious and disciplined) to win over to its side the *majority* of the working and exploited people (the majority of the poor, to speak more simply and popularly) and retain power sufficiently long to suppress completely all the exploiters as well as all the elements of disintegration.
>
> It was this historical experience of all revolutions, it was this world-historical—economic and political—lesson that Marx summed up when he gave his short, sharp, concise and expressive formula: dictatorship of the proletariat." ("The Immediate Tasks of the Soviet Government," Lenin, Vol. 27, pp. 264-65, emphasis in original).

Of special relevance in these words of Lenin, as far as the recent developments in China are concerned, is the fact that to a certain degree the "revolutionary enthusiasm of the masses, which sustained them in their state of tension" was weakened in recent years. In short, some of them tired of the struggle. Does this mean it was wrong to wage the struggle, was it wrong to continually have campaigns aimed against opportunist lines—should we blame Mao and the left, especially the Four? No, we do not blame the proletariat for the existence and resistance of the bourgeoisie. There was no alternative but to wage this struggle, to carry forward these campaigns—the only alternative was to give in to the revisionists and allow capitalist restoration without a fight, to allow the bourgeoisie, the greatest force for the "disintegration" of socialism, to just take over.

The reactionaries, as Mao said, follow the law of make trouble, fail, make trouble again, fail again . . . until their doom. But they do not necessarily fail every time and their doom does not come about through a straight line process, but through long and protracted struggle, along the road of which there can be temporary setbacks, even serious ones. The revisionists in China were making trouble and being beaten back and then making trouble again, often in a new form. This made the struggle in China extremely complicated and frequently, no doubt, confusing to many of the masses, especially with the back and forth, up and down, character it assumed in recent years, when Mao's death and the question of succession was imminent.

In addition there is the very real threat of imperialist, especially Soviet, aggression against China and the international situation as a whole. While the internal class divisions in socialist society are the main basis for capitalist restoration, the existence of international capital is also part of the basis. And in recent years, with the growing danger of an attack on China by the Soviets in particular, and with the necessity to make certain agreements and compromises with reactionary and imperialist governments, with the whole "opening to the West," and all the bourgeois influences that inevitably accompany this, there was bound to be a powerful "pull" away from taking the socialist road and toward taking the seemingly "easy road" of relying on and tailing after the imperialists, for economic development and defense. And the cultural and ideological corrosion that is bound to accompany increased contact with bourgeois countries certainly had no small effect on the Chinese masses. A big part of this was the fact that as they learned more about the imperialist countries many of the Chinese people could be deceived by the secondary aspect of the masses' situation in those countries—that they had a higher standard of living than in China—and not grasp firmly the principal aspect—the exploitation and oppression of the masses in these "advanced" nations.

All these factors—the earthquakes, the death of a number of long-time leaders, including Mao, the complicated and tortuous nature of the struggle, plus certain real difficulties in the economy, the growing danger of war and the necessary "opening to the West," etc.—all these made the situation favorable to "order" as Hua Kuo-feng boasted in his report to the 11th Congress. In other words, there was a strong current among some of the masses—and many of the cadres—to have order above everything. Clearly this is favorable to the revisionists, who can promise and in the short run deliver "order"—the order of bourgeois dictatorship and capitalist restoration, which over any period of time can only bring disorder and misery to the masses. And closely linked with this the line of modernization as the main task and "goulash communism" found a favorable following among the same forces who wanted order above all, and for the same reasons. This, in my opinion, had much to do with why the revisionists were able to triumph in this battle.

This most recent battle, of course, was not a self-contained thing but was a continuation of the two-line struggle that had been waged throughout the history of the Chinese Communist Party and which became all the more intense after state power was captured. And more specifically, it was the continuation of the struggle that has been raging, in one form or another, since the late 1950s, from the time of the Great Leap Forward, the People's Communes, etc. This must be viewed dialectically, of course. On the one hand, the victories of the proletariat in those struggles led to great advances in socialist revolution and socialist construction. On the other hand, the more there were advances, the deeper the socialist revolution went, the more it dug away at the soil engendering the bourgeoisie, and the more it called forth desperate resistance from the bourgeoisie. Along with this, as noted before, at each stage in this process, some people get "stuck," including especially, as Mao pointed out, those who have become high officials and want to protect the interests of high officials, as against the interests of the masses.

This does not mean that all high officials by mere virtue of their position are bound to become revisionists—that would be mechanical and not dialectical materialism. But as Mao said, there really is a problem here—people who have a higher position than others do tend to feel themselves superior and to take advantage of that position for personal, narrow interests—which in socialist society will lead to capitalist restoration if it is not struggled against and defeated. It is a bitter truth, but a truth nonetheless, that in the history of socialist countries large numbers of top leaders have sooner or later turned traitor to the revolution—not all by any means, but not just a few either. This is why Mao put such stress, and explicitly so in recent years, on combatting and preventing revisionism and studying the theory of proletarian dictatorship to get clear on *why* it is necessary to exercise dictatorship over the bourgeoisie, what are the material and ideological conditions that continually give rise to bourgeois elements and pose the real danger of capitalist restoration and how to deal with this through the exercise of proletarian dictatorship and class struggle, continuing revolution, under the dictatorship of the proletariat.

Mao also paid special attention and gave great emphasis to the question of "bringing up revolutionary successors." I believe Mao approached this on two levels—one, bringing up large numbers of successors among the masses, that is, training large numbers of the masses, including basic level Party members, as class conscious revolutionaries through study combined with concrete struggles. And on the other hand, he fought to establish revolutionary successors at the top level—the Four and their supporters in top leadership. It is exactly because he relied on the Four strategically, I believe, that Mao was upset by some of their actions, their tactical errors—this is how I believe the criticisms he is supposed to have made of them have to be read, as Mao "chewing out" the people he knew had to be counted on to continue the revolution and the people who therefore, in a certain sense, he had to be very hard on—in a qualitatively different way, of course, than those with whom Mao had fundamental differences of principle, the capitalist-roaders.

(One last note on this question of Mao's criticisms of the Four and how such things can be taken completely out of context, which is a real possibility when Mao is no longer around. In his conversations with Mao Yuan-hsin in 1964 and '66, Mao rakes his nephew over the coals. He tells him such things as, "In [the] future, if you do not become a rightist, but rather a centrist, I shall be satisfied . . . Isn't it true that you don't understand a thing about society? Your father was dauntless and resolute in the face of the enemy, he never wavered in the slightest, because he served the majority of the people. If it had been you, wouldn't you have got down on both knees and begged for your life?" and so on. To anyone reading these comments out of context it might well seem that Mao regarded Mao Yuan-hsin as someone on the brink of becoming a counter-revolutionary, or even already one, already the kind of traitor who would get down on his knees before the enemy. But in context it is obvious that Mao had high regard for Mao Yuan-hsin and considered him a successor to the revolution—and for that very reason Mao is "letting him have it" to help him to become a better revolutionary. I am convinced that Mao's attitude toward Mao Yuan-hsin, and the Four with whom Yuan-hsin was firmly allied, remained the same down to the end, and that the quotes we are seeing now from Mao taking the Four to task, assuming they are authentic, fall exactly into the same category as those cited above from Mao to Mao Yuan-hsin and are being shamelessly distorted and perverted by the current rulers to suit their counter-revolutionary purposes. Comrades should find these discussions between Mao and Mao Yuan-hsin very instructive, not only on the question being addressed here, but also on the question of class struggle, the relationship between politics and vocational work, Mao's line on educational affairs, some aspects of his military thinking, etc.—they are found in Schram's book, *Chairman Mao Talks to the People*, pp. 242-52).

In the fundamental sense, training millions of revolutionary successors among the masses is the main thing, because if that is done, even if there are defeats for the revolution, there will still be class conscious masses, and new leaders will emerge to replace those who fall in battle. On the other hand, in any immediate sense, the existence of a leading group at the top levels is decisive—a point the Four correctly stressed in the Legalists Vs. Confucionists articles and elsewhere—for without such leaders at a given point, the resistance of the masses to revisionism cannot be successful—the current rulers know this very well and that is exactly why they smashed the Four as the first step in pulling off their restorationist moves.

What conclusion should we draw from all this? From the fact that the Four have been smashed in a revisionist coup and that those in power are taking the capitalist road, should we conclude then that "Mao failed?" Yes—and no. We must conclude that in the short run he did not succeed in the final battle of his life to prevent Soviet-style reversion. But he did certainly succeed in the policy of training millions of class conscious forces among the masses, and they are bound to wage struggle in very difficult circumstances against the capitalist-roaders and plant the seeds of their future overthrow.

Most of all we should not draw the conclusion that it is not possible to succeed in socialist revolution and not possible to achieve communism. Nor that it is impossible to build socialism and continue to advance toward communism in an economically backward country like China. Difficult to carry forward the revolution, even very difficult? Yes. Impossible?—not at all, in fact it is inevitable that socialism will eventually replace capitalism and communism will ultimately be achieved in every country, throughout the whole world. Nothing that has happened in China changes this.

We must keep in mind that the struggle of the proletariat is international and that this has real meaning. In particular, viewing things on a world scale, it is the case that in the contradiction between the proletariat and the bourgeoisie, the bourgeoisie is still the principal aspect—that is, taking the world as a whole the bourgeoisie still has the upper hand, though it is undeniably and irreversibly the proletariat that is strategically on the rise. The fact that the bourgeoisie still has the upper hand on a world scale does have real meaning and consequences and real effect on the class struggle in every country. This does not mean that until the proletariat has gained the upper hand on a world scale it is bound sooner or later to lose the upper hand in any particular country. But it does increase the danger of capitalist restoration in a socialist country, even though the main basis for this lies within that country itself.

Further we must not only view the class struggle in international but historic terms. The past 100 years, since the time of the Paris Commune, must be viewed as only the dawn of proletarian revolution and communism. It will indeed require a protracted struggle, no doubt for at least several hundred years, and a struggle, even more than in the past, full of twists and turns, reversals and setbacks, before the great goal of communism can be achieved worldwide. But, again, this struggle, too, is made up of stages and takes particular form in different countries and at different times. At each stage, under all circumstances, the proletariat worldwide must seek to defend the gains it has made while at the same time fighting to make new breakthroughs. And where it suffers setbacks it must sum these up, learn the causes and seek to avoid them in the future. And in fact this is exactly what the proletariat has done—its struggle has developed in an upward spiral with each advance higher than the peak before, and this will continue to be true until the proletariat wins final victory over the bourgeoisie on a world scale.

We should keep firmly in mind what we wrote at the end of the Party's *Programme*:

> "The proletariat in the United States and throughout the world faces a protracted and complicated task, for the objective of its struggle is nothing less than the complete transformation of all society and involves the complete break with all previous forms of society and all past traditions. But its triumph is inevitable, because the whole of human history and the development of society itself has prepared the conditions for it and only proletarian revolution can continue to move society forward in this era." (p. 163)

Naturally it is very painful to accept the fact that, after the experience of capitalist restoration in the Soviet Union, China is now being taken down the same road. And it is all the more painful because the Cultural Revolution in China provided such a powerful force for preventing the repetition in China of what happened in the USSR. And no doubt some will resist accepting it for that reason. But it is a truth, it is objective reality, and in order to change the world we must accept and analyse it as it is.

Further, it is wrong to look at the experience of the Soviet Union and China as the same. There are a number of differences, not the least of which is that at the time of Khrushchev's coup, denunciation of Stalin and repudiation of Marxism-Leninism, the masses in the Soviet Union and millions of revolutionary-minded people in other countries (though not all of them) were left confused, without an understanding of what was taking place, and this could only create large-scale demoralization. On the other hand, because of the Cultural Revolution in China, because of Mao's great leadership and because of the heroic struggle put up by the Four, millions of people in China are armed with an understanding of what is going on, and millions more are debating and struggling over the questions involved, while those of us in other countries also have the basis for understanding not only what has happened but what is the basis for it.

Nothing in Marxism-Leninism, Mao Tsetung Thought tells us that once the proletariat has seized power and socialized ownership of the means of production it is guaranteed against capitalist restoration. In fact, it tells us just the opposite—that for a long time, throughout the entire transition period of socialism, there will be classes, class struggle and the very real danger of capitalist restoration. And it tells us that there are the means to deal with this and advance—though not without twists and turns, setbacks and reversals, even serious ones.

And certainly nothing in Marxism-Leninism, Mao Tsetung Thought tells us that if the ruling proletariat loses power and if capitalism is restored in one or more of the socialist countries—even if it should happen in all of them for a time—then socialist revolution is a hopeless dream. In fact, all of Marxism-Leninism, Mao Tsetung Thought tells us the opposite of that, too. Fight, fail, fight again, fail again, fight again . . . until victory—that is the logic of the proletariat, as Mao put it.

As an article put out by the Four explained, even the revolutions in which one exploiting system replaced another were full of twists and turns, advances and setbacks, and "The proletarian revolution which aims at completely eliminating the bourgeoisie and all other exploiting classes and all exploiting systems will take much longer and will go through many more twists and turns and reverses," and that "The revolutionary optimism of the proletariat differs from blind optimism in that we understand the dialectics of historical development . . . Dialectical and historical materialism are the ideological foundations of revolutionary optimism . . ." ("Proletarians are Revolutionary Optimists," *PR* #36, 1976) Despite what has happened in China, the statement from Mao, quoted at the end of the pamphlet by Yao Wen-yuan, remains true—"The conclusion is still the two familiar comments: The future is bright; the road tortuous"—and the sentence with which Chang Chun-chiao ended his pamphlet still carries full force—"The extinction of the bourgeoisie and all other exploiting classes and the victory of communism are inevitable, certain and independent of man's will."

IV. What Do We Do Based on a Correct Understanding of What Has Happened

I have put forward in blunt terms what I believe to be the undeniable truth about events in China. A revisionist coup has taken place, a serious blow has been delivered to the proletariat and its revolutionary leaders. The capitalist-roaders are not only still on the capitalist road, they have now usurped supreme power and are taking China down the capitalist road. This is a severe setback to the proletariat in China and worldwide.

But does this mean that I am saying capitalism has already been restored in China, that it is no longer socialist? No. It is true, as Mao said, that the rise to power of revisionism means the rise to power of the bourgeoisie, that the seizure of supreme power by the revisionists will, if not reversed, lead to capitalist restoration. But this does not take place in the manner that Monday the revisionists seize power and Tuesday the country is capitalist. Seizure of power is the first, decisive step, it marks a qualitative leap—backwards. But there is still the task for the revisionists of actually transforming society according to their world outlook and line, of destroying the socialist relations, including the ownership system, and restoring capitalist relations. This takes time and is bound to meet with resistance—and indeed already is in China today. Still, it remains true that, unless this situation is reversed, within a certain period of time—no one can say exactly how long, but we are talking in terms of a relatively short period of time as opposed to some abstract remote future—capitalism will be restored.

The situation presents us and genuine Marxists everywhere with many difficult and complicated questions. Here I will touch on only a few, but I believe we should devote considerable and careful attention to this question right away and as things further develop.

Should we come out now and publicly support the Four and denounce the current rulers? No, but we must arm our own ranks and advanced, reliable forces we are working closely with as to which class the Four and the current rulers represent, what has happened, why, to the best of our understanding, and so on.

Should we continue to put forward China as a socialist country? Yes, for now we should, because it is still an objective fact. But we should, in discussing China, put stress on Mao's line, the Cultural Revolution and the fact that in socialist society classes exist, class struggle is acute and the danger of capitalist restoration is ever-present and great. At the same time we should use the achievements of the socialist revolution in China, especially those that have not yet been reversed, to illustrate the way socialism is actually superior to capitalism and how it eliminates many of the evils of capitalism. We should avoid as much as possible giving any support to the current rulers of China and certainly continue not to congratulate them on any posts any of them assume, and most definitely not on any of their victories over the proletariat—i.e., the smashing of the "gang of four."

As far as our public position on China we should take the following approach. With the "general public"—that is people not close to us, including opportunists—we should say that there are obviously reasons for concern about what is happening in China, there are some good things under attack—for example the transformations in education—but we should put this in the context that China is a socialist country and that the class struggle under socialism always goes on and at times becomes very acute. In short, we should uphold China as a socialist country while pointing to problems and areas of struggle and say that we are closely following and continuing to study events in China. On Teng Hsiao-ping, since our last public statements on him (correctly) labelled him a counter-revolutionary, but since he has since been restored to very high office, we should just say (to the "general public") that his return to office has to be viewed in the overall context of what is happening in China and that we are taking up the question of his return to office in that light and in the same spirit as we are following and studying events in China in general, as summarized just above. Comrades should keep in mind that what they say to workers and others whom we cannot count on as being completely reliable have to be put in the category of statements to the "general public," since they may very well become that (for example a worker may have contact with both us and the OL-CP(ML), and may not understand why he should not discuss with them what we tell him about our position on China).

At the same time, as stressed before, we must educate not only our own members but reliable advanced workers and others close to us (those who will understand why they should keep what we say to them about China confidential) about what is actually going on in China and give them the basis for grasping the real lessons of this. Otherwise there is no way we can carry out our duties as a Party or overcome demoralizaton that will inevitably set in as it becomes more and more clear what road China is taking. Further we should find the ways to do broader education on the crucial questions related to developments in China without commenting directly on the situation there—for example articles about the process and lessons of capitalist restoration in the Soviet Union, articles about the gains and lessons of the Cultural Revolution in China, etc.

Should we continue to work in U.S.-China? Yes, we should, but we must recognize the obvious fact that it will be an extremely difficult task to carry out. In particular it will be extremely difficult to balance building friendship for China as a socialist country, which is still correct at this time, with not contributing to building up the current rulers in opposition to the Four (not to go along with the Association's doing the latter will be impossible of course, and we should not put up struggle to try to prevent it from doing this, though we should try to keep it from being the main thing the Association does, and as much as possible we ourselves should not contribute to it—as I said this will be extremely difficult). Careful guidance must be given to comrades doing this work.

Similarly, our work among Chinese-Americans will be faced with many of the same kinds of problems and we must handle this case by case depending on the situation, the forces involved, etc. But, again, systematic attention must be paid to this and careful guidance given.

Does this change our analysis of the international situation? Since it is still objectively true that China is a socialist country our basic analysis should not change. We should continue, as we have in the past anyway, to put forward our own line on the international situation and to explain the actions of China to the best of our ability and in keeping with principle, and defend what can be defended while refraining from directly criticizing what we think is wrong.

There are obviously other important questions relating to this that should be taken up. These, as well as the ones I have briefly touched on, should be given considerable attention right away and as things further develop.

It is worth re-emphasizing that the most important thing is to come to and unite around a correct line on what has actually happened, as laid out in this paper. But having done that, and on the basis of being firm in principle, we should approach the question of what to do on this basis very carefully, keeping in mind always the interests of the working class, in this country and internationally. To sum this up, we should first unite around principle and remain firm in this principle, and adopt tactics flowing from this and in accordance with what will best serve the struggle of our class here and worldwide.

V. The Problem of Bad Tendencies in Our Own Party Connected With the Line Questions in the Struggle in China

In the past year and more since the arrest of the Four a number of erroneous tendencies in our Party have developed around and in relation to events in China. Bad lines coming out of China were picked up, repeated and used as the basis for actions and even a frame of reference for struggle within our own Party. "Gang of Four idealism," "that's the 'automatically' line," statements equivalent to that made by Teng Hsiao-ping at the 11th Congress—what we need is "less empty talk and more hard work"—and other such stuff were heard in many places.

Suddenly the "Ten Major Relationships" was the greatest thing since color TV—actually it is far better, it is a very important work, but it is not, as the current rulers have claimed, "The Basic Policy for Socialist Revolution and Construction," not Mao's last word on these questions and not nearly as important a guideline as many of his later works on the question of socialist revolution *or* construction. And, unfortunately, in some cases no account was made of how the current rulers have tried to use this work of Mao's against the further development of his line and ,in sum, against Mao's line itself.

The "Ten Major Relationships," written in early 1956, does not deal with the urgent questions to which Mao increasingly addressed himself in later years and intensely so in the last few years before his death. In particular, it does not deal with the class struggle and the danger of capitalist restoration after the socialization of ownership of the means of production has in the main been completed. This was obviously a big question and big point of struggle in China. As indicated in Chang Chun-chiao's 1975 pamphlet, there were then people in China who basically argued that after the socialization of ownership had in the main been completed, the danger of capitalist restoration and the regeneration of bourgeois elements was of no great consequence—in short people who under today's conditions in China promote the "dying out of class struggle" line. It is not difficult for me to understand why such people would want to raise the "Ten Major Relationships" up as the pinnacle and end point of Mao's Thought and works. That people in our own Party essentially did the same indicates that perhaps they share a common outlook with and agree with the line of the current rulers, or at least that they have been seriously influenced by the same line and outlook.

In some cases the more that the current rulers' line came out the more it was picked up on and became a basis for reversing and even opposing correct conclusions that had been drawn about China and basic principles that have been a part of our Party's stand from the beginning (and the RU before it). Pragmatism was given a big shot in the arm by the line that narrow and immediate "results" are everything, which has streamed out of China since the current rulers took over. Regrettably, such stuff was welcomed in some quarters and a fundamental principle enunciated by Mao more than 30 years ago, and re-emphasized by the Four in the struggle against the right deviationist wind, was forgotten or cast aside:

> "We are proletarian revolutionary utilitarians and take as our point of departure the unity of the present and future interests of the broadest masses, who constitute over 90 percent of the population; hence we are revolutionary utilitarians aiming for the broadest and the most long-range objectives, not narrow utilitarians concerned only with the partial and the immediate." (From "Talks at the Yenan Forum on Literature and Art.")

All this and more has had a very unhealthy effect within our Party. It has flown directly in the face of and hampered the grasping and implementing of the line adopted at the last Central Committee, with its correct and important emphasis on the "high road."

In our Party, too, we have been infected with the widespread influence of a "white cat, black cat" line. What counts most to some people, I am afraid, is not ideological and political line, but how many people came to this particular demonstration, how many leaflets were passed out, how many posters put up, etc. All of these things can be very important but they cannot be the standard for judging our work, and to make them such is to lose sight of what we are doing our work for, in other words, to lose sight of the final goal.

What is worse, there have been more than a few cases where particular successes in work are turned into capital, and this merges with pragmatism and empiricism so that more or less success, greater or fewer numbers, at any given time determine whether or not one has the right to speak or at least how much weight should be attached to what one says. And, along with this, where successes are in fact made, there is often the tendency to divorce this from the question of the Party's overall ideological and political line and to make it a question of the "organizing ability" of various "hotshots." Tactics is raised above, even substituted for, overall line.

All this has been coupled with metaphysics and eclecticism. Often line struggle is not promoted in a way that arms everyone with a deeper grasp of the correct line but in a way that builds up a few while keeping most in the dark. Theory is separated from practice in much the way the old CP did it even when it was basically revolutionary—rank and file Party members are often reduced to mere "implementers" of the line who hold no discussion of line and theory, while a handful of people study and discuss theory in a way that divorces it from the practice of the Party and the class struggle overall, so that the link between theory and practice and constant education in the Party's line are not maintained and in fact are interfered with. Or else Marxist theory and the experience of the international proletariat are presented as being embodied in so many scattered recipes for "how to do" this or that, with no unifying principles, so that, once again, the arming of the whole Party with theory and education in the Party's line are obstructed and interfered with.

These tendencies in our Party have a life of their own but they have grown in dialectical relationship with basically the same lines coming out of China since the current rulers have pulled their coup, smashed the proletarian headquarters and distorted Mao's line and Marxism-Leninism. And, in turn, the influence of such lines in our own Party has poisoned many people's ability to grasp the essence of what is going on in China and to correctly distinguish revolution from counter-revolution.

With the benefit of the line struggle put up by the Four and the whole legacy of Mao's thought and his revolutionary leadership, with the experience of the Soviet Union and Mao's summation of it, and with the line and history of our own Party (and the RU before it) and the two-line struggles involved in building it, we should have done much better than this as a whole in grasping the essence of what was going on in China and resisting the corrosion of tall tales and rotten lines coming out of China in the past year. And we will have to do much better to carry out our tasks and make revolution.

At the beginning of this paper I cited part of bulletin Vol. 2, No. 3 on China, including the statement that "the attitude and approach every Party takes in understanding and evaluating the events in China will have much to do with determining whether or not that Party remains a Marxist-Leninist Party or degenerates into one kind of opportunism or another." In other words there is a dialectical relationship between one's line on China and on all other major questions. I also stated that the "China Question" is the most important question of line now confronting the international communist movement, including our own Party. Therefore we should concentrate first on deepening our grasp of and uniting around the correct line on China, as set forth in this paper. And then, unfolding out of that, we should pay particular attention to rectifying the incorrect ideological, political and organizational lines that have had a corrosive effect within our Party to a serious degree, as also summarized in this paper.

In this way what has undeniably been a severe setback for the international proletariat—the triumph of the revisionists over the revolutionaries in China—will not be compounded by us in our own Party and the struggle we have to lead in this country. Instead, in the face of difficult circumstances, our whole Party will be strengthened, advance, and fulfill our responsibilities and make our contributions to the revolutionary movement of the working class here and worldwide.

China Advances Along The Socialist Road

The Gang of Four Were Counter-Revolutionaries and Revolutionaries Cannot Support Them

By the Jarvis-Bergman Headquarters

Comrades,

We with the help of many comrades have formed the Revolutionary Workers Headquarters in order to wage the struggle that must be fought in the Revolutionary Communist Party, USA, to reverse the counter-revolutionary line represented by the new CC report on China and the "Rectification" (read Sectification) Bulletin.

We as individuals and as a group have thought very seriously about the nature of our actions and our responsibility to our comrades, along with whom we have pledged to "put the interests of the working class and the revolution above everything else;" (Article 3, Section 1, Constitution of the RCP.) To be true to these principles as well as the principles on which our Party was founded, there is no other avenue except to lead our Party into open and determined rebellion against the line of the new CC report. We who have signed our names below readily accepted the responsibility to serve on the Central Committee of our Party; we feel very strongly that our actions are perfectly consistent with shouldering that responsibility.

It's Right To Rebel Against Reaction!

Members of the Central Committee and its Political Committee
Mickey Jarvis
Glenn Kirby
Mike McDermott
Mike Rosen
Ginny Jarvis

Members of the Central Committee
Rob Devigne
Lee Ornati
Dave Cline
Christine Boardman
Dave Clark
Nick Unger

The above comrades include:
Vice-chair of the Central Committee and its standing bodies
Chair of the East Coast Region
Vice-chair of the Mid-west Region
Chairs of the Milwaukee-Minnesota, Chicago-Gary, NY-NJ, and Phil-Balt Districts
Head of Party work in the RCYB
Head of Party work in the NUWO
Head of Party work in UWOC
Editor of The Steelworker

Introduction—Practice Marxism Not Revisionism; Drive Counter-Revolution Out Of The Party Of The US Working Class

- Working class rule smashed in China.
- The Gang of Four, target of the hatred of the Chinese masses, upheld as revolutionaries by the RCP Central Committee.
- The Chinese masses, steeped in Confucianism and tired of the high road, capitulate to counter-revolution. And here at home,
- A bourgeois-revisionist headquarters, with no actual revisionists in it, unearthed and exposed. The source of the

disorientation and floundering in our Party finally eliminated.

- ½ of the standing bodies of the Central Committee purged. Almost ½ of the Central Committee cast down, removed from responsibilities, reassigned.

The new CC report has arrived, and it is a barn burner on a scale few had expected. The Chairman has already summed up that its reception in the ranks of the Party has been both enthusiastic and liberating, a real breath of fresh air. But the opposite is the case, and none can deny it.

This Party, our Party, is in the beginning stages of open, militant and determined rebellion. Rebellion about the way this line came down. And even more rebellion against the line itself, against this attempt by a few to turn this Party into its opposite and change its political color. The rebellion is widespread and deep.

- The NY-NJ District Committee, as well as the sections and branches, overwhelmingly voted to rebel. A meeting called by The Chairman from which the district leadership was barred was boycotted by over 80% of the cadre. A "gentlemen's purge" where all Party members were required to "re-up" or be considered no longer members was even more strongly boycotted.

- The New England District Committee voted to rebel against the CC bulletin and the ram job. They voted to take this paper down to all cadre along with the CC bulletin, and not to recognize any leadership changes.

- The Milwaukee District Committee and all branches voted to rebel.

- The Philadelphia-Baltimore District Committee and the majority of cadre voted to rebel.

- The majority of cadre and branches in Chicago voted to rebel.

- The National Office of the RCYB branch [sic] voted to rebel.

- The Pittsburg District Committee voted to rebel.

- As of now, over 40% of the entire Party has been purged by the "re-up" attack.

Comrades, the rebellion is real. ½ of the old day to day leading body of the RCP, ½ of the old Political Committee, and almost ½ of the old Central Committee of our Party have united with many other comrades to form the "Revolutionary Workers Headquarters of the RCP" in order to: *hold up* this new line, *criticize it,* and *drive it the hell out of our Party.*

There can be no paper unity on the question of China. China is a watershed question, a fundamental question of what is revolution and what is counter-revolution. The task before all of us is to drive the line of Avakian and company out of our Party, or to drive out the line of the Revolutionary Workers Headquarters. They cannot both exist in our Party. There are two lines in our Party, and there are two Headquarters with many forces in the sharpest struggle. There can be no retreat from struggle around this question. Neither can there be a formalistic or organizational resolution in advance of a political and ideological one. Our line on China is our line on the political and ideological question of the highest importance to the international working class. The Chairman through a combination of idealism and outright deceit is trying to ignore this. But reality will assert itself, and it is doing it all through the Party.

Comrades, to rebel against reaction is justified. It is necessary. Let the rebellion spread. Let the fury of the working class against all oppression rage against the counter-revolutionary line of the new CC Report.

What Has Happened

The Chairman has said that the Revolutionary Workers Headquarters has presented the cadre with a "fait accompli" on the question of China. Nothing could be further from the truth. There has been a fait accompli. It has come from The Chairman, who is trying to organizationally (through using the form of democratic centralism against the working class) ram through this line and turn our Party into a defense group for the Gang of Four. Along with this, The Chairman has summed up that the Gang were a little slow in getting the jump on the bourgeoisie in China, and The Chairman will not make the same mistake over here.

Think about what has happened. If the gang-building campaign of The Chairman has not led us to a fait accompli, the word has no meaning.

- Bulletin 1 on China raised some questions.
- Bulletin 2 on China did not sum up the questions raised, but added three new questions and told all of us not to "draw conclusions."
- Bulletin 3 came out before most comrades had discussed Bulletin 2, did not discuss the Gang at all, and set artificial guidelines designed to create public opinion for their line.

Now, out of the blue, the CC embraces the Gang as revolutionary heroes and saints, denounces the CCP and Hua as revisionists, and condemns the masses to capitalist restoration.

Having set the comrades to struggle over points like the significance of "concentrate" and "reflect," the Chairman was setting up the Party for a coup. Our Party was to be the new home of the Gang. While The Chairman made sure that the rank and file would not draw any overall conclusions, he made sure that the CC meeting would do that and only that—both to win his point on the Gang and also to cut down the opposition to The Chairman's Gang of Four left idealist line for work in the U.S.

The manner in which this railroad job was conducted makes a mockery of the current CC's lip service to the chain of knowledge in our Party. Rather than concentrating the results of previous discussions and returning them in a higher form, each succeeding bulletin ignored the ones before it, switched, with no explanation, to a new set of issues to be discussed, and discouraged analysis of the real world. To crown it off, the CC meeting was held at a time when the overwhelming majority of branches and higher units had not completed their discussion of the third bulletin and many had not even begun. Avakian's paper was prepared weeks earlier. What clearer proof could there be that The Chair does not believe that the cadre could come up with *any* contributions to determining a line on the question of China—no analysis, no ideas, no facts, not even any questions worth considering! This is sheer petty bourgeois contempt for the rank and file communists of our Party and for the Marxist-Leninist concept of the chain of knowledge and command. It is the "genius" theory, pure and simple.

Was the Party of the U.S. working class led by The Chairman to determine truth from facts based on applying Marxism-Leninism, Mao Tsetung Thought to the situation in China? Was the initiative of the cadre released to make a step by step evaluation of the overall situation in China? Were the opinions and the understanding of the Party members systematized from the discussions that were held? Were the lines on the struggle in the

United States drawn out, based on the practice and theory of our Party? We have to answer NO, and in all four places.

Why did things go down this way? The answer is simple for The Chairman. No two line struggle could be permitted throughout the Party exactly because there were 2 lines. The way to deal with this is a shoot out at the top, where The Chairman would smash the other line and his position would go down as the line of the entire Party. *By his own admission, The Chairman would have split the Party if he did not win at the CC.*

Some of the authors of this paper were in a position to put real roadblocks in the path of The Chairman and his coup. But because of our own fear of splitting the Party and our desire for unity, and because of our fear of having to take on The Chairman in a big face to face battle, we incorrectly went along with the way he wanted to conduct the struggle. We made serious errors and should criticize ourselves and be criticized for doing this. But we will be damned if we are now going to go along with the decision on China, go along with the rectification bulletin which reverses our Party's line on the U.S., and most of all go along with the fact that the very orientation of our Party is being turned around just because we made the error of going along before.

Comrades, The Chairman has presented us with a real "fait accompli." Go along with calling the Communist Party of China revisionist without investigation and without seeking truth from facts. Renounce China on the basis of a 78 page paper short on fact, without concrete analysis, absent of proof, but long on conjecture, subjectivism, idealism and metaphysics. Accept an anti-Marxist, counter-revolutionary document as the line of the Party. And if you do not, you are going against the Party and will be disciplined. We cannot and we will not accept this. The Revolutionary Workers Headquarters will stand up and fight for our Party and for the working class.

Down With The Counter-Revolutionary CC Report

What is revolution, and what is counter-revolution? What is Marxism, and what is revisionism and Trotskyism? This is the central question under debate here. This paper from the Revolutionary Workers Headquarters is a beginning defense of the building of socialism and putting down of counter-revolution in China. On this question the paper has 2 parts: one, on the overall situation in China, and the other, a criticism of The Chairman's paper "Revolutionaries Are Revolutionaries. . . ." In addition, there is a paper on the development of a left idealist line to "lead" the work in the U.S.

The 78 page treatise from the CC would be a farce if it were not proposed as the line of our Party and if it were not the leading edge in turning our Party away from uniting with and leading the struggles of the working class in this country.

The method of this report is thoroughly bourgeois. Quotes out of context. No analysis of concrete conditions. No discussion of condition, time, place. No discussion of the role of the masses, the mood of the masses, anything about the masses—except how backward, superstitious and tired they became. Outright lies, and subtle distortions. And a slew of unsupported assumptions, personal opinions and "I believes" to fill the gaps.

For the method alone, this paper must be condemned by all comrades. But the crime of The Chairman is far worse than that. The method goes with the conclusion—supporting counter-revolution, and opposing socialist revolution and socialist revolutionaries abroad and at home. The depths of counter-revolution are reached in Section 3, where The Chairman blames the masses for the "defeat" of revolution, with not one word about bad lines, errors or anything else that led to this situation. Here, alone in the paper, do we find mention of the objective situation. But here, it is to put it as obstacles to socialism. What a shameless departure from the line and method of Mao, who saw in the history of exploitation and oppression and enforced backwardness the potential for great revolutionary enthusiasm and drive. There is a historical precedent for the analysis of The Chairman on why socialism failed in China. It comes from the Progressive Labor Party, who saw in these same conditions the failure of socialism 6 years ago. And both PL and The Chair owe a debt to the founder of this school of thought, Trotsky, who told us all that socialism cannot be built in one country, let alone a backward, superstitious peasant country. Comrades, after so many years of denouncing Trotskyism, why in hell should we embrace it now to accomodate The Chair.

The Rectification Bulletin

While The Chair can come up with a 78 page broadside on China, he can only get up 10 pages on the existence of a revisionist headquarters that has existed in one form or another since before our Party was even founded. This does not, however, mean that he has no line on the situation here and how to resolve the contradictions in the work we face. The problem is that he has the same smash and grab line as the Gang. First get rid of the opposition headquarters, then the work goes on. But the way to get rid of the headquarters is not through line struggle, but through an organizational coup, busting them all in one struggle.

The Chair had to call for sweeping rectification in our Party not only because he wants to consolidate his putsch with purges extending clear down to the basic levels, but because there have been real problems in the Party requiring rectification and the cadre recognize it. Increasingly the Party's chain of knowledge and command has been sabotaged by a left idealist line and the "genuis" theory. The rectification the bulletin promises, the current CC cannot deliver. They are turning their backs on what the Party needs—more summing up of both line and practice, more line struggle over real issues, more motion from practice to theory and back to practice. This campaign, on the contrary, can only impede real rectification, can only institutionalize the idealist line and bureaucratic centralist methods which have fueled the problems in the first place.

The rectification bulletin is a follow-up to the coup. It aims to "rectify" our Party by consolidating The Chair's incorrect line through the entire Party. If it succeeds, our Party will be reduced to a sect, guided by a firmly entrenched left idealist line in the Center and utterly incapable of uniting with the working class and masses, bringing scientific socialism home and leading them toward revolution.

Democratic Centralism, Factionalism, And Who Believes Line Is Decisive

In the early days of the rebellion, The Chair has repeatedly and strenuously made the main point the question of organization. This must be settled before there can be a struggle over the line. In or out, he asks us all, and then we can talk about China. On this basis he has refused to struggle over the lines in a way that reflects the actual situation and contradictions in our Party. There must be sharp 2 line struggle on all levels of the Party, including Congresses. This represents the best interest of the Party and the working class. Both lines and the headquarters that reflect them cannot both exist together in the Party, and the Party must decide on the basis of which line is the correct one. It is both correct and responsible to recognize this fact and have faith in the masses of cadre to rise to the challenge that this struggle poses for all of us.

The Chair is the principal roadblock to the struggle in our Party.

He has moved to split our Party under the banner of upholding democratic centralism and factionalism. We refuse to recognize the authority of him and his CC to kick us out of the Party or remove us from our posts. We refuse to accept that honest, responsible comrades have to re-apply to the new CC and its agents or be dropped from the membership rolls. As of this writing, the CC has thrown out over 40% of the membership of the Party in this manner. This is an outrage, and it will also not be recognized. Some people think that they own our Party! Just like our class brothers and sisters, we want no condescending saviors and will accept none either. The CC has some learning and remolding to do about what a communist is and what a communist is not.

The Revolutionary Workers Headquarters of the RCP asks all of our comrades to think about two points in relationship to the current struggle.

"Members of the Revolutionary Comunist Party must:

> **(1) Put the interests of the working class and of the revolution above everything else;"**
> **Constitution of the RCP, USA, Article 3, Section 1, p. 168.**

> **"Stability and unity do not mean writing off class struggle; class struggle is the key link and everything else hinges on it."**
>
> **Mao Tsetung, 1975**

Comrades!

Hold Up—Criticize—Drive Out the line of counter-revolution and retreat represented by the new CC report.

The death of Mao Tsetung presented new challenges for communists around the world and in the CPC in particular. Our Party, a young but vibrant Party, was shaken by the loss. We didn't choose these conditions, but our task is to deepen our understanding of Marxism and continue to struggle. The two lines in China produced two lines in our Party. Because of the ideological, political and organizational line pushed by The Chair, he and the CC have forced a crisis in our Party. It is a crisis that the masses of Party members neither desired nor were prepared for. But it is a crisis that we must stand up to and overcome, not by making the question of principle factionalism or violations of democratic centralism or the unity of the Party, but by making the question of line, in China and right here, the point of principle. Parties waver and degenerate, but the historical mission of our class stands above all. It Is Right To Rebel Against Reactionaries!

Support The Socialist Revolution In The People's Republic Of China Led By The Communist Party With Comrade Hua Kuo-feng Its Head!

The Gang Of Four Were Counter-revolutionaries And Should Not Be Supported! They Represent In Theory And Practice A Repudiation Of Marxism-Leninism Mao Tsetung Thought!

The U.S. Working Class Needs Its Party! Fight To Keep It Out Of The Hands Of Those Who Would Destroy It!

Uphold The Interests Of Our Class Above All!

RUSH TO JUDGEMENT

The RCP and its predecessor, the RU, has a proud history and devotion to the struggle of the US working class. It has led many important individual struggles and made important theoretical contributions to the development of the ultimate revolutionary victory. It has in the past period been dealt a number of severe self-inflicted blows which the Party must vigorously rebuff. What has distinguished the RCP from the many so-called Marxist-Leninist sects? Essentially, it has been its concentration in the major battles of the working class, the oppressed peoples and their allies, and its summing up of these struggles through applying the worldwide experience of the working class, Marxism-Leninism, Mao Tsetung Thought. In the ideological battle with these sects, it has distinguished itself by demolishing the right and left dogmatism and stressed the fundamental duty of Marxist-Leninists to link up with the masses in struggle. As the Party Programme puts it: "The central task of the Revolutionary Communist Party today, as the Party of the US working class, is to build the struggle, class consciousness and revolutionary unity of the working class and develop its leadership in a broad united front against the US imperialists, in the context of a worldwide united front against imperialism aimed at the rulers of the two superpowers." (bottom p. 101, top p. 102)

And further it maintains:

"In carrying out its central task today, the Revolutionary Communist Party takes part in, learns from and brings leadership to the struggles of the working class and its allies, unites all who can be united, consistently exposes the enemy and points to the final aim of overthrowing imperialism and building socialism. To do this it bends every effort to fulfill three main objectives in these struggles: to win as much as can be won in the immediate battle and weaken the enemy; to raise the general level of consciousness and sense of organization of the struggling masses and instill in them the revolutionary outlook of the proletariat; and to develop the most active and advanced in these struggles into communists, recruit them into the Party and train them as revolutionary leaders.

"Through this process the Party leads the masses of workers in fighting against the capitalists and in developing this into an all-around battle against the capitalist system." (Party Programme, p. 102)

Of course, there has been shortcomings and errors, and at least some of them have been summed up and corrected. We still have a long way to go, but shall we in silence reverse our correct stand? Shall we, who as the RU exposed PL as Trotskyite counter-revolutionaries follow their footsteps down the road to hell? Shall our comrades trained in toe-to-toe struggle with the bourgeoisie cave in to petty bourgeois degeneration and despair, throw up our hands and forsake the struggle? Shall we join the Trotskyite anti-China chorus, do the job of the bourgeoisie from the left, that the bourgeoisie needs to supplement its attack from the right? Our comrades are used to battle and will certainly resist and defeat this counter-revolutionary deviation.

While the battle to resist this trend away from working class concentration, towards a safe but harmful left idealism and Trotskyite interventionism has been going on for quite a while inside the Party, it has not been general knowledge among the cadre, although many cadre have resisted and protested. But it has come to a head over the China question, and as such has both concentrated a trend into a gallop, and has demanded that we make common cause with PL, WVO, Spartacists and other Trots. This rush to judgement forced on the Party by a willful and disruptive few stands to turn our honorable history around unless the cadre make it forcefully clear that they refuse to follow the Judas goat to the slaughter house. This carefully orchestrated rush to judgement developed under a barrage of pyramiding bulletins escalating the stakes at each turn.

Bulletin 1: Simply raised certain questions.
Bulletin 2: Did not sum up the questions raised in #1, discussed three other questions and said, "don't draw conclusions."
Bulletin 3: Came out before most had discussed #2, did not at all discuss the Gang of Four, except to practically make it impossible to oppose them. And then, this last CC report which enshrines the

Gang as revolutionary saints and condemns the Chinese masses to capitalist restoration.

This line, based on selected conjecture and flying in the face of a mountain of contrary evidence, needs to be reversed by the cadre if our record is to be upheld and if our future is to be fought for.

It is important to note that both the two highest standing bodies of the CC are evenly split on this matter. And on the basis of the correct stand of those who oppose the frantic head-over-heels rush to catch up with the Sparts, all opposing have been removed from their posts. This not inconsiderable purge (only the beginning) of those who proved themselves in past struggle and proved themselves anew in this battle consolidates the attempted sectification of the RCP.

The question of China is a question of principle, the question of Marxism-Leninism, Mao Tsetung Thought vs. Trotskyism, or one should say shame-faced Trotskyism because the ridiculous stand of maintaining it only internally and orally upholding China as a socialist country is both ridiculous and nothing but a creeping escalation to fullblown betrayal. We are told to lie to the masses, and tell close forces the truth only if they promise to lie to the masses.

This dubious tactic is already a public failure and bound to be even more thorough in the immediate future.

The China question needs to be reversed, and above all the central task of the RCP has to be reaffirmed. And the three main objectives have to be reaffirmed and stuck to. Otherwise how can the RCP be maintained as the Party of the working class? This reckless disregard of the needs of our Party and of the U.S. masses will certainly be denounced by the overwhelming bulk of the cadre and this counter-revolutionary line will surely be defeated.

Written by a veteran comrade
who has been through this kind of thing before.

THE CC REPORT ON CHINA IS A COUNTER—REVOLUTIONARY DOCUMENT AND MUST BE CRITICIZED

The report on China put out in the name of our Party by the Chair and his CC is counter-revolutionary and must be criticized and repudiated by all comrades. The line of the report is wrong—dead wrong. The Gang were not revolutionary heroes. They were counter-revolutionary traitors and enemies, and their fall is a workers' victory. To uphold them is to replace revolution with counter-revolution in our Party. The Chinese Communist Party headed by Comrade Hua Kuo-feng is not a revisionist Party. China is still on the socialist road, it is still a beacon light for the working class and all oppressed people around the world. To deny this is to set our Party against the revolutionary tide of history. This must be opposed on all fronts.

The CC bulletin marks a complete break with Marxism. The wrong line was arrived at and is set out with anti-Marxist methods. It is being pushed throughout our Party with equally anti-Marxist methods of inner-Party struggle. The unity of line, method of investigation, and method of inner-Party struggle shows how fully counter-revolution has been embraced by the Chair and his CC.

Uphold the Marxist Method

Seek truth from facts. The correct line develops in opposition to the incorrect line. These Marxist principles should guide all comrades in dealing with the situation we face. The incorrect line of the CC bulletin will be held up, criticized and defeated. The correct line and truth about the situation in China will be developed and deepened in this struggle and through consciously applying Marxism to the situation in China.

This paper by the Revolutionary Workers Headquarters of the RCP represents the beginning stages of both aspects of this process. Our approach has been to examine the general features and general conditions of China to determine if revisionism has in fact triumphed. And we have used Marxism to evaluate the CC paper. From the beginning, the burden of proof was on them. They had to show that revisionism had won. In this, they have failed miserably. On that basis alone the CC bulletin must be rejected. But more can be said. Though our investigation is only at the opening stages, it shows that China is clearly still socialist, that the working class still holds power. The exact part played by each and every Chinese leader and the exact nature of each current struggle is not yet known. But enough is known to say that Hua Kuo-feng deserves the support of all comrades as a follower and developer of the correct line of Mao Tsetung.

This introductory section on the counter-revolutionary methodology of the CC paper opens the criticism of that document. It is followed by sections on the class struggle, why the CC thinks revisionism triumphed, Chou En-lai, and the 11th Party Constitution. The criticism section is followed by an entire part on the gang's counter-revolutionary role in China and an analysis of the current situation, including a discussion of agricultural modernization and the development of socialist new things. Through the active participation of many comrades across the country, and through summing up with Marxism-Leninism, Mao Tsetung Thought, both the correct line and our understanding of the nature of the incorrect line will be deepened through struggle. Our Party will defeat the incorrect line of the CC. We will unite around proletarian revolution here and in China, and through this class struggle, move forward the cause of the working class.

Bourgeois Methods Only Serve the Bourgeoisie

The position paper offered by the Chair and accepted by his CC, called "Revolutionaries Are Revolutionaries And..." is a disgrace to Marxism and our Party. It is a qualitative leap—backwards. Comrades need only compare it to the past work of the RCP and the RU to see how shallow and empty of Marxism it is. There is precious little analysis, but instead subjectivism and egocentrism. This paper spits on the high level of polemic that our Party has struggled to develop within this country.

Why did this happen? There is only one reason. The CC paper was guided by an incorrect line. It is not true that material about China is so difficult to come by that all anyone could do is offer up superficialities. The class struggle in China, including the contending lines and roads, are not so hidden that one can only guess at them. If this was the case, why in hell was our Party forced to take a position right now? The class struggle in China, like any other process, is knowable. The RCP could have set itself the task of using Marxism to learn its laws and their actual development. Our Party, based on the science of the working class, is the best instrument to carry out this task. But the Chair and his CC would have none of it, and they still won't. This cannot stop us. The Revolutionary Workers Headquarters will not let the banner of Marxism be dropped. We have taken up this task as part of a righteous rebellion against counter-revolution and as part of fulfilling our duty to the international working class. It shall continue.

Starting at the End and Ending Where He Started

When comrades first heard about the arrest of the Gang in October, 1976, there was general and genuine confusion in our ranks.

Something momentous was happening in China, fast upon the death of Mao. But only one among us was certain as to what was happening. Only one knew the answer before the question was even fully asked. The Chair had it down from the first day. He was not entirely alone. As was to be expected, Mike Klonsky of the OL also knew it all from the start, continuing his record of consistent slavishness and opportunism. It is a bitter shame that the Chair chose to adopt his approach (regardless of the fact that their lines were opposites). But the ugly fact remains that the Chair *knew* "the truth." There was no question to investigate. Revisionism had won, capitalism would soon follow. His only task remained to prove it.

As a result of knowing the result before the investigation—apriorism pure and simple—the Chair could dispense with real Marxist analysis. He did not have to seek truth from facts. He already had truth, and the only thing he would call facts were things that helped show it. An open, deep, concrete analysis would just postpone the inevitable verdict in support of the Gang, so why bother?

Metaphysics, Idealism and a Legal Brief for the Gang

The approach of the Chair determined that the CC would adopt as the line of the RCP a 78 page paper that really doesn't teach or lead the comrades in understanding the class struggle and Marxism. The CC paper is divided into 3 main sections, and the very division itself exposes the anti-Marxist method of the Chair.

Section 1: This is supposed to prove the entire case. After it, we are told, "From all that has been said I believe it is very clear that the present rulers have betrayed Mao's line and are implementing a revisionist line. As for how to view the Four, on a certain level that should be very easy in light of what has been shown... However, I believe that it has been shown in a deeper, more thorough way, by examining the line of the Four themselves in opposition to that of the current rulers on a number of crucial questions, that the Four were carrying out a correct line and fighting for the interests of the proletariat." (CC Report, pp. 69-70)

Section 1 is the section of the paper most empty of facts, on analysis of the situation in China, however fanciful. And yet it is the one that proves the case. This is the section of lifting quotes, measuring them and throwing them away. Lifting them means taking them out of context, offering quotes without regard to time,place and conditions, and without these there is no Marxism.

Section 1 is a dozen different ways to restate the original conclusion. The Gang is always presumed correct. The quote from *Peking Review* is always presumed to be the line of a unified Party leadership. (The CC's general approach to *Peking Review* is, like the rest of their line, almost a carbon copy of PL's notorious *Road to Revolution III:* "Material incentives are reappearing as the emphasis shifts overwhelmingly in publications and propaganda to technical innovations (see any recent *Peking Review*)" This was in November, 1971.) The rest is easy. The quote from the Gang is stated to be the same as Mao, but then again, that was the starting point for this section. This section and the entire paper passively reflect the line and thought of the Gang. Nowhere is there an analysis of whether Gang thought, or Chang Chun-chiao Thought, really is the same as Mao Tsetung Thought. It is just assumed, and this assumption is used to prove itself.

Section 2: This has far more "facts" than Section 1. To the Chair, facts are things you need in arguments with people who don't agree with you, but they are not necessary to formulate your own line. Section 2 is the legal brief, cross examination, following the Section 1 opening argument. It is the debating tricks, hunt for the loopholes, and fast talk. Section 2 is where the major questions have to be decided with "I believe" and "In my opinion" not once, but literally dozens of times. Whether this is to substitute for facts or to conceal facts is immaterial. It is no wonder that one comrade commented, after reading this legal brief for the Gang, that the lawyers should plead insanity.

Section 3: This is in many ways the most disgusting of all. Here, for the first time, the full objective situation is brought into play. Here the Chinese masses make their first appearance. Only by now, they are too tired to resist revisionism and are fair game for whatever goulash Hua dishes up. Section 3 blames the objective situation and the masses for what the Chair thinks happened in China. The Trotskyism of this section will be dealt with later.

Section 4: This can be summed up in a few words. Lie to the masses, and tell the truth to our friends only if they promise to lie to the masses. It is a fitting conclusion to the entire method of the paper.

Mao Tsetung was confronted with similar arguments some 40 years ago. His response to them hits the mark today, and serves both to expose the CC bulletin and to guide communists in a correct approach.

> "The most ridiculous person in the world is the 'know all' who picks up a smattering of hearsay knowledge and

> proclaims himself the 'world's Number One authority'; this merely shows that he has not taken a proper measure of himself. Knowledge is a matter of science, and no dishonesty or conceit whatsoever is permissible. What is required is the reverse—honesty and modesty." (On Practice, *Selected Readings*, p. 71)
>
> "Only those who are subjective, superficial and one-sided in their approach to problems will smugly issue orders and directives the moment they arrive on the scene, without considering the circumstances, without viewing things in their totality (their history and present state as a whole) and without getting to the essence of things (their nature and the internal relations between one thing and another). Such people are bound to trip and fall." ("On Practice," *Selected Readings*, p. 73)

What the Chair Leaves Out is Marxism

The method of the CC paper stands exposed both for what is in it, and for what is missing. There is no real analysis of the objective situation in China and how it developed. There is no discussion of the role of the masses in making history, where they stood and why on the key questions. The mass line is never mentioned. How the line of the Party was grasped by the masses, or not grasped, and how on that basis the masses changed the objective conditions, none of this is present. The advances of the 76 CC Report are thrown away by its supposed defenders. The United Front strategy is never mentioned, even though it is a cornerstone of working class rule. (Again, all of this comes up from the other side of Section 3 to blame the masses for revisionism.) After 78 pages, we are as lacking in an all-around Marxist analysis of the struggle in China as we were on page 1. Comrades here are given the same treatment the Chair gives the Chinese masses. We too, are too undeveloped (they mean and often say stupid) to figure out which line is correct in a 2 line struggle. The masses, here and there, are reduced to passive onlookers to a battle of titans at the top levels of the Party. This is the real politics of the Chair. He saw his heroes fall in China, and redoubled his efforts to stage the coup here they could not stage there. Bourgeois power politics replaces proletarian politics, both in the CC bulletin and in the CC meeting.

In its place there is only supposition and bourgeois logic. This is why comrades cannot learn from the CC paper. Mao spoke to this point very sharply: "One cannot acquire much fresh knowledge through formal logic. Naturally one can draw inferences, but the conclusion is still enshrined in the major premise. At present some people confuse formal logic and dialectics. This is incorrect." (Speech at Hangchow, Dec. 1965, *Chairman Mao Talks to the People,* p. 241)

It would take a book to unravel every syllogism and twisted "If A is like B, then Hua is a revisionist" argument. One stark example serves to indict them all. "As a general characterization of Hua's speech it can be said that it is boring—which is not merely a criticism of style, but of political content and basic method. Mao's comment on the Soviet Political Economy Textbook . . . is directly relevant here: 'It lacks persuasiveness and makes dull reading. It does not start from a specific analysis of the contradictions between productive forces and productive relationship and the contradictions between the economic basis and the superstructure . . . '." (CC Report, p. 73) This powerful combination of the Chair and Mao could surely deduce anything. The rub is that Mao did one other thing that is even more "directly relevant here." He got the text of Hua's speech the day Hua gave it at the Tachai Conference. He read it, he approved it, and he had it distributed all across China to lead the Learn From Tachai movement. So much for the logic of the Chair. In this same Critique of Soviet Economics that the Chair refers to, recently published by Monthly Review Press, Mao talks about why it is wrong to make the major premise of an argument its conclusion and the danger of proceeding from definitions and abstractions. Chapters 33, 35, and 67 are directly relevant here. (One last point—those members of the current CC guiding the Party's propaganda work should think twice before they popularize the argument that boring means revisionist.)

Materialists Have Nothing to Fear from the Truth

The current CC and their Chair have resorted to the basest dishonesty in preparing and accepting the CC report. They cannot plead ignorance, since material showing the truth about the situation was sent to them well in advance of the CC meeting by comrades struggling for a correct line.

*They knew that Hua Kuo-feng played a significant and very positive role in the Cultural Revolution, that he led a province to unite around Mao's line in opposition to the right and the ultraleft. They knew he wrote reports about this struggle that were circulated nationwide for all to learn from. They knew he had played a similar role during the Great Leap Forward. Still, they sum him up in one distorted sentence. Again, a lawyer looking for a loophole instead of a Marxist looking for the truth.

*They knew that the workers cultural teams and many other such forms have not been abolished, and that the position of the Chinese leadership in the face of sharp class struggle is to adjust and develop them, to correct abuses and preserve the strengths. But the current CC does not stoop to analyze to actual class struggle[sic]. It is better to say that Hua forces are riding roughshod over the Socialist New Things and hope that the comrades get blind with fury at Hua. We are not blind, and our fury is at the deceit of the current CC.

*They knew that the foreign trade policy developed under Mao has not been changed, and that the class struggle over it continues to be sharp. They knew that at the recent Trade Fairs, the Party leadership said no to any major changes. Still they say that these wholesale changes are being implemented. Anything goes if it can help boost the Gang and tear down Hua.

*They knew that there were serious problems in the educational system in China. But to admit it would open the Gang's role up for questioning. So of course they refuse to admit the truth.

*They have said in private for the past year that China's foreign policy under Hua, is, if anything, a little better in its handling of the two superpowers. Now, when Peking Review 45 comes out with not one new and significant difference from the foreign policy for the past many years, they call it a marked departure from Mao, and so lay the basis for an attack on China's foreign policy without having to openly attack Mao.

The current CC will stop at nothing to uphold the Gang. They have to try and knock down real revolutionaries like Chou En-lai. If he was a revolutionary, the Gang could not have been heroes, not the way the Gang made him the main target of attack for years. So the apriorism of the CC sends them scurrying to find something Chou said or did to attack. It would have been naive to expect them to turn back when they could not find anything. Instead, they just make it up along with an entire made-up private history of Mao's relationship with Chou. To raise the Gang up to the heavens, the red flag has to be dragged in the mud.

It would have been impossible for the current CC and the Chair to uphold Marxism in the service of the Gang. Marxism-Leninism, Mao Tsetung Thought is a partisan science. It belongs to the working class, and only the working class can use it to change the world. The current CC repudiates the Marxist method, and the principles and line of our Party. They abandon all of this to make a home for the Gang here in the US. Our task is to stop this before the Gang moves in and settles down.

This paper by the Revolutionary Workers Headquarters starts to do this. In both the sections criticizing the CC bulletin and analyzing the situation in China, the reactionary line and method of the CC and their models, the Gang, will become clearer and more concrete. The masses in China are today enthusiastically criticizing the line of the Gang. We must do no less. The 2 line struggle and rebellion in our Party has released the initiative of comrades everywhere, who have started to carry through and deepen the criticism and repudiation of the counter-revolutionary line of the current CC.

CLASS STRUGGLE IS THE KEY LINK

"Never forget classes; never forget class struggle." "Class struggle is the key link, everything else hinges on it." These statements by Mao Tsetung reflect the historical and objective nature of socialism and give the outlook that the working class has to have to move forward. The general line of the Chinese Communist Party embodies this outlook:

> "Socialist society covers a considerably long historical period. In the historical period of socialism, there are still classes, class contradictions and class struggle, there is the struggle between the socialist road and the capitalist road, and there is the danger of capitalist restoration. We must recognize the protracted and complex nature of this struggle. We must heighten our vigilance. We must conduct socialist education. We must correctly understand and handle class contradictions and class struggle, distinguish the contradictions between ourselves and the enemy from those among the people and handle them correctly. Otherwise a socialist country like ours will turn into its opposite and degenerate, and a capitalist restoration will take place. From now on we must remind ourselves of this every year, every month and every day so that we can retain a relatively sober understanding of this problem and have a Marxist-Leninist line."

The fundamental contradiction under socialism is between the proletariat and the bourgeoisie, the same as under capitalism. However, there is a historic difference, in that the primary and secondary aspects of this contradiction are reversed. The proletariat is the principal aspect under socialism. It is the ruling class, and on that basis can-step by step consciously transform all of society through a long period and through this move forward to communism.

This advance takes place through the three great revolutionary movements—the class struggle, the struggle for production, and scientific experiment. Mao stressed that because of the class nature of socialism, the fundamental contradiction under socialism and the prime importance of proletarian rule, the class struggle is and must be grasped as the principal revolutionary movement. This will no longer be true under communism, when classes themselves cease to exist.

Mao's analysis of this problem did not end by saying what is principal. Only a pseudo-communist would smugly stop there. He said that everything else hinges on the class struggle, that the class struggle must be taken up within and guide everything in society. It runs through all the movements, and ultimately guides the development of all the contradictions in society. This is an objective fact, and communists must subjectively grasp it in order to lead the masses and move forward on all fronts—theoretical, political, and economic.

The line of the gang on the class struggle and how to grasp it and wage it was a counter-revolutionary, anti-Mao line. It resulted in abandoning the class struggle on all fronts, always of course under the banner of the class struggle. The gang metaphysically separated all the various fronts and tasks and pitted them against each other, they confused tasks and policies with principles, their view of the class struggle was idealist, and in doing all this they stood against the working class consciously ruling and transforming all of society.

The current CC upholds all of this, and would make this the guiding line and understanding of our Party. This puts them squarely against proletarian revolution in this country. The Gang's line on the class struggle is not Mao's line, it is not Marxism. It is counter-revolution dressed up in phrases about the class struggle. Adopting the line of the Gang as the line of our Party is base treachery against the working class.

The Three Directives

A wrong line on the class struggle runs through the entire line and practice of the gang. This question was brought into sharp focus in the struggle over Mao's directives, the three directives, of late 1974. And in their treatment of this struggle, the current CC stands exposed.

The three directives—calling for, in short, study the theory of the dictatorship of the proletariat, stability and unity, and pushing the national economy forward—were issued at different times that fall. Taken together, as they were intended to be, they serve as a programmatic outline of where China had to go in the period ahead, as a general formulation by Mao of the key tasks facing the Party and the masses. These directives did not come out of the blue, or come from a Mao detached and above the current struggles, as the current CC thinks. They are consistant with the thrust of the 10th Party Congress the year before, and were reinforced at the 4th NPC in January 1975.

Teng Hsiao-ping jumped on the three directives, raising the formulation "take the three directives as the key link," a serious error of principle which resulted in the Chinese masses being drawn away from grasping class struggle as the key link. Teng's jumping out served as a lightning rod, drawing fire from all quarters. And the many responses show how correct Mao's teachings on the necessity to watch out for a correct line covering another, incorrect line.

Mao was short and to the point. "What! 'Take the three directives as the key link'? Unity and stability do not mean writing off class struggle; class struggle is the key link and everything else hinges on it." Compare and contrast this with the response of the current CC, slavishly following once again the line of the gang. They "enrich" Mao's criticism and come up with a line that is the opposite pole of the stupidity of "take the three directives as the key link."

First, they say the problem is that there are too many directives to be the key link—you can't have three, you can only have one. This is meant to attack eclecticism, but only shows how idealist the current CC is. It is not a question of how many, but what is the key link. None of the directives was the key link; as Mao pointed out, the class struggle is the key link. The current CC disagrees with Mao on this.

"In fact in the three directives of Mao that came to be referred to as the 'three directives' the one on socialist construction was, as far as I can tell, limited to a general call for 'pushing the national economy forward', and was certainly not meant to be out on a par with his instructions on the class struggle, and the theory of the dictatorship of the proletariat and combatting and preventing revisionism in particular, which was the main and decisive directive." (CC Report, pp. 33-34)

The current CC would have us believe that 'pushing the national economy forward' was not really a directive, certainly not an important directive having much to do with any of Mao's instructions on the class struggle.

No, this is not what was going on. There were three directives—and not one big directive and a couple of minor afterthoughts. "Class struggle is the key link," is not one of the three. Everything has to hinge on this—including the carrying out of the three directives. Mao spoke about the second directive, saying "unity and stability don't mean writing off class struggle." He was saying that this directive hinges on the class struggle, that the class struggle has to run through and guide this one, and the first and the third. The gang wants to say, and the current CC would parrot, that the first directive is the class struggle one. Do they think that there will not be fierce class struggle between the proletariat and the bourgeoisie on the basis and the reason for unity and stability? Objectively, there certainly was, and Mao's comment cuts two ways: don't write off class struggle in the name of stability and unity, *and* fighting for stability and unity does not require that you write off class struggle. And as we can see, the gang and their friends think that it does.

Even their saying that the first directive was the "main and decisive" one is pure metaphysics. They oppose this to it being part of the three directives, which it of course was. The question is not "can the three directives be separated"? Just like the atom, they can be. The question was who was separating them and why? The gang was, and the reason was opportunism. Comrades should ask themselves, can our Party's three objectives be separated? Yes, and when they are, we have to stop it and strive to fulfill all three. Mao said that the working class and its Party has to formulate ideological tasks and policy tasks together to move forward. (See Smashing The Gang on this point.) Mao's point was that you needed both. The current CC ducks the main and decisive question with a lecture on atomic physics. (We anxiously await the CC criticism of Chang Chun-chiao's pamphlet for saying on page 16 "Here it should be noted that Marx divided the sentence on the dictatorship of the proletariat into three points, which are interrelated and *cannot be cut apart* (emphasis ours)." (Here is a case of outganging even the gang).

The gang separated out tasks, not once but all the time. They separated the Lin Piao-Confucius campaign from the tasks of the 10th Party Congress, they separated studying the theory of the dictatorship of the proletariat from studying and implementing the decisions of the 4th NPC. And, of course, they separated and opposed the three directives. This separation was undialectical and anti-materialist and damaged the socialist revolution in China.

The Four Modernizations Don't Mean Writing Off The Class Struggle Either

The defense of the Gang puts the current CC against the necessity of the modernization of socialist China. "In sum then, the Four were in favor of the four modernizations in accordance with Mao's line on revolution and production but they were against what the right deviationists tried to make the 'four modernizations' stand for. They were very aware of the danger that making a big push for the four modernizations would give the green light to 'production first' revisionist [sic] and they were very concerned that in the effort to fulfill the task of modernization the basic task—the class struggle—not be thrown overboard and that in the name of promoting production to achieve modernization the commanding role of revolution not be thrown out." (CC Report, p. 37)

That the Gang was not in favor of the four modernizations will be shown in other parts of this paper. But there is something else to note in this passage. Again, the CC plays fast and loose with tasks and tasks [sic]. They take the key link of socialism, persisting in the class struggle to step by step eliminate the bourgeoisie and all exploiting classes and all the bases for their existence, and oppose this to the tasks at each stage of development of socialism. And in doing so deny that the class struggle does in fact and must consciously run through and guide such tasks as the four modernizations.

Modernization, big jumps forward in the socialist economy and the material base of socialism, these are important tasks. They are necessary. The current CC says do it if you can, but it is not very important. This amounts to turning over the field of the economy and modernization to the bourgeoisie. The bourgeoisie will try to take the movement around modernization out of the hands of the working class. Only in that sense, are they getting a "green light." But that does not make the task any less important or necessary. Completing it is not a nice idea, as the gang and the CC put it. Precisely because it is a necessity, and because the conditions for it existed in China, the four modernizatins were a real opportunity for the proletariat to strengthen its rule over the bourgeoisie by conscously transforming society.

The working class can launch a big economic push or a Cultural Revolution because it has state power. This is not automatic. It requires the conscious summing up by the Party, practicing the mass line and using Marxism-Leninism, Mao Tsetung Thought to grasp the necessity and turn it into freedom. And this, always involves the sharpest class struggle—to formulate the correct line, to advance on the correct road, to keep the initiative firmly in the hands of the working class.

Without constant advances, in the base and the superstructure, socialism will fail. The gang portrays socialism as a purely defensive battle. The working class seizes power, and from then on in, it is downhill. The bourgeoisie keeps coming at you until they probably win out. And it is precisely this view that accompanies their failure to take class struggle as the key link in all spheres and lead an all round advance to constantly and consciously build socialism and restrict the three great differences and other birthmarks of capitalism. Both together, advance and defend.

The gang's line in practice was to turn over the spheres of unity and stability and the economy to the bourgeois rightists. The gang considered them bourgeois turf, full of dangers and green lights for the right. And, of course, the right was glad to accept the banner of unity and modernization. They always try to pose as the real champions of development and the well being of the masses. The 'General Program' reflects this, taking up the banner of modernization to hit at the gang and sacrificing the interest of the masses as it does.

The Class Struggle Takes Place In The Real World

The current CC is totally reversing the understanding and line of our Party. It is necessary to fight the bourgeoisie tooth and nail on every front, to concede no sphere to them. This is just as true under socialism. The gang reduces everything to a question of stand and ideology. This is the only class struggle they see. In the name of fighting the bourgeois line of "the dying out of class struggle," they offer the equally bourgeois line that the class struggle is just, or mainly, struggle over whether the class struggle is dying out or is it the key link.

All this takes place while the actual class struggle is raging on all fronts, not just in the superstructure and ideology. And the working class needs conscious leadership on all these fronts. The view of the gang and our CC is idealism—whether in a rightist form or an ultra-revolutionary leftist form. Either way it is poison for the working class.

This idealism leads the current CC to repudiate even those advances that they were part of in the past. Now they say "where a revisionist line leads and the leadership is not in the hands of Marxists and the masses, bourgeois relations of production will actually exist, even in the collective form." (CC Report, p. 9) And they have the nerve to call this the line of Mao.

This complete mixing up of the objective and subjective sets the current CC against Mao and our Party. We have studied this question in the past, and, agreeing with Mao's criticism of the Soviet Union and Stalin, we wrote in *Red Papers 7*:

> "Though Stalin never in fact abandoned the class struggle, his lack of clarity on the precise nature of the enemy weakened the proletariat. Further, though Stalin argued forcefully (and correctly) that the law of value continues to operate under socialism, he did not draw the correct conclusion from this—that capitalist production relations must then also exist in some (often) hidden forms." (*Red Papers 7,* p. 21)

These bourgeois relations do not exist because a revisionist line leads. They exist because of the nature of socialism itself—the continued operation of the law of value, commodity production, small scale production, the force of habit. In a word, socialism is a transitional system. It is a qualitatively higher social system than capitalism, but still has many of its features and is not yet classless society.

The CC gets this wrong on both sides. Most of the time, along with the gang, they downplay the advance of socialism, negating the key importance of proletarian rule, and so give the bourgeoisie damn near equality in the fundamental contradiction, and treat the socialist economy as if it is almost identical to capitalism.

Here, they go the other way. They imply that the question of the law of value, etc., has been solved, by saying that it is the revisionist line that recreates the bourgeois relations. They get quantity and quality wrong, and the only consistency is that they make the error that serves their immediate needs and immediate arguments.

The danger of having a revisionist line in command is that it does not expose and restrict bourgeois relations of production, but gives them free rein to operate and even uses them as a motor to try and increase production (or in the case of the gang, gives them free rein by promoting anarchy and weakening the Party's leadership). The contradictions within the socialist economy itself are pushed towards capitalism when the revisionist line strengthens the secondary, weaker aspect—and if representatives of that line seize and control the superstructure, the secondary aspect will become principal and capitalist relations will be restored in full. But to say that the revisionist line creates or causes the bourgeois relations denies the dialectical relationship between thinking and being, denies that the revisionist line and ideas have roots in the material world and have an effect on the real world precisely because people use them to deal with real contradictions. The CC report would have us believe that if you defeat the bourgeois line, you have defeated the bourgeois relations. No matter that the law of value, commodity production, etc., still operate. Ideas don't have to be made a material force. This is idealism as naked as any since Descartes proclaimed, "I think, therefore I am."

This same idealist confusion of quantity and quality leads the gang and their supporters in our Party to in essence date the Chinese Revolution as starting with the Cultural Revolution. They divide China's history into the 17 bad years and the 10 good years, throwing dialectics out the window, and preventing them from seeing the actual content of the class struggle in the superstructure over taking back power usurped by the bourgeoisie.

No matter how hard the gang tried, and no matter how much the current CC tries to carry on, they cannot paint Mao as an idealist to get him to line up with them.

The Gang's Line In China

The gang's idealism seriously weakened the campaign on studying the theory of the dictatorship of the proletariat, and did considerable damage to the Chinese Revolution. The campaign was intended to wage the class struggle against the bourgeoisie ideologically, to raise the understanding and consciousness of the Chinese masses about the contradictions and tasks of socialism as a transitional system, to arm them against revisionism. And it was intended to stress the necessity for the conscious transformation of all of society under the leadership of the working class, to provide a higher base of understanding and enthusiasm for building socialism. This is not "theory in its own right" but the opposite, theory to serve the overall and immediate class struggle. The entire country was about to launch into a big economic push, and the whole country was coming out of the Cultural Revolution. Conscious leadership and direction were decisive. Releasing the initiative of the masses around the correct line was decisive. To separate this campaign from the tasks ahead, both general and particular, is making a hollow phrase out of "Grasp Revolution, Promote Production." And that is just what the gang did. They could only see in the four modernizations a danger, and could only see the theory of the dictatorship of the proletariat campaign as a blocking of the immediate rightist forces. How narrow these idealists are, and how narrow their home-grown supporters have to be to defend them.

The leadership of the gang's idealist and metaphysical line was no idle philosophical problem. It was a matter of life and death. In one formica, furniture and plywood plant in Peking, the influence of the gang's attacks on rules and regulations under the guise of criticizing "control, check and suppression," led to the effective, if not official disbanding of the plant's safety committee. Even when a worker was seriously injured by a machine, nothing was done. This situation was made more serious by the fact that the Party leadership of this plant had grown increasingly isolated from the actual day to day struggle. They were infrequently on the shop floor, and instead spent a great deal of time studying, discussing and arguing over the campaigns like the theory of the dictatorship of the proletariat, together with a sizeable contingent of workers who were full-time worker theoretical group members at full pay. Because the campaign itself, as distorted by the gang, not only ignored but attacked such tasks as developing production, even as these leaders and workers tried to take up and spread the campaign, they became more divorced from the actual situation in the plant. In this leadership vacuum, bourgeois individualist tendencies of going for self and favoring short term advantage over long term interests or quantity over quality were strengthened among the workers, and struggle, class struggle, among the workers over these issues often went unresolved or even became antagonistic. This situation around rules and safety continued to deteriorate with the result that an accident identical to the earlier one killed a worker.

The current CC would uphold the gang's line. Didn't they stress the overall? Didn't they oppose narrow self interest, production first, immediate results? No, in fact, they fed it among the masses, by robbing them of leadership in *all* aspects of the class struggle. And they made the overall into something that had no relation to the present. The situation in this factory was not turned around until the gang went down, and the masses of workers began to repudiate and criticize the line of the gang. Mao is clear on this kind of error, and he is clearly against the gang and the CC:

> ". . . the particularity of contradiction is still not clearly understood by many comrades, and especially the dogmatists. They do not understand that it is precisely in the particularity of contradiction that the universality of contradiction resides. Nor do they understand how important is the study of the particularity of contradiction in the concrete things confronting us for guiding the course of revolutionary practice." (On Contradiction, Selected Readings, p. 91)

Mao goes on to say:

> "The truth concerning general and individual character, concerning absoluteness and relativity, is the quintessence of the problem of contradiction in things; failure to understand it is tantamount to abandoning dialectics." (On Contradiction, Selected Readings, p. 109)

The Gang's Line In The U.S.

This is precisely what is happening in our Party. The methods of the gang, their metaphysics and idealism, are being upheld and propagated. Like the workers in that Peking factory, we have suffered through revolutionary sounding general calls from a divorced leadership, and been left to our own devices to determine the dialectical relationship between the general problem and the concrete conditions of the class struggle. And like them, we are beginning to see the damage this kind of leading line can do. And we too have been called pragmatists for every effort at actually making revolution.

It has not taken long for the line of the gang to lead the CC into repudiating the line and program of our Party. The current CC has begun to sum up the U.S. through gang-colored glasses. An entire section of this paper is devoted to this question, but a few comments are in order here.

Page 5 of the rectification bulletin sets up another of the devil's choices and metaphysics that this line leads to. Are you for keeping the proletariat's consciousness tense, or are you for building big battles with small forces? The gang line in the U.S. reduces the class struggle to an ideological question, and in doing so sets the CC against the mass of cadre who are trying to build the struggle against the bourgeoisie with the small forces that are around. Just like in China, this is being done under the banner of fighting rightism. But you can't fight rightism with leftist, metaphysical idealism.

The working class does have to consciously seize power, and this requires a consciousness of the class as a class for itself. This is what Marx means when he says that the "growing union of the workers" is more important than any particular gain in any battle. This is why keeping the consciousness of the proletariat tense is decisive. But how can this be done outside of the class struggle, on all fronts? Putting it any other way is an appeal to retreat from the class struggle to somewhere else and get the consciousness and tenseness there. Reducing the class struggle to the ideological struggle, separating consciousness and tenseness from the class struggle on all fronts—this is a recipe to feed rightism and spontaneity among the masses of cadres, accompanied by and guided by a leadership locked into abstraction and sectarianism. This line was soundly rejected in China, and the same must happen here.

Unity and Class Struggle

The CC tries to answer the charge that the gang was sectarian, that they wouldn't unite with people. (Throughout this section of the bulletin, it is hard to distinguish between their views on China and their views on the U.S. The current CC paper reeks of this subjective transference, and shows how far the gang line has permeated.)

"Who should they have united with that they failed to unite with? People like Hua Kuo-feng?. . .To talk about 'uniting' abstracted from line is exactly to raise unity above the class struggle, and will end you up in unity with the bourgeoisie—on its terms." (CC, p. 71) (Again, it seems like they are talking about the U.S. For this is a perfect description of the line of the CC on the current struggle.)

How simple unity was for the gang. Unite with the folks who already agree with you, and the other folks are on the other side. Then the good guys move ahead. What garbage! Political unity is based on struggle. Unity, struggle, unity. That is the correct view. And that means that within unity at any point there will be differences, including basic ideological differences, both open and hidden. This cannot be made a bar to unity, or the working class can never advance and lead the entire masses in advancing. The view of the gang was in essence sectarianism—differences meant quality, period. And only if people changed could you unite with them. Mao's line is the opposite.

That is why in 1975 he told the gang, "Unite with the more than 200 members of the Central Committee." He surely knew that there were some among them who were not pure proletarians. He surely knew that there were even some plain revisionists. Still he called for unity, because the proletariat has to lead in making revolution. And there is a difference between the core and the front, among the masses and within the Party.

Unity and stability were the best basis for the proletariat to carry on struggle at that time. The gang opposed this, constantly seeking new ways to expand the attack, until the target was everybody in leadership but themselves. Now the current CC broadens it still further. The leadership was all either revisionists or cowards, and the masses were tired and backward.

The gang and the current CC treat uniting all who can be united to defeat the common enemy, and the instruction to narrow the target of attack, broaden the target of education, as fetters on their revolutionary purity. But in fact they are principles of the united front strategy, reflecting the fact that 95% of the masses are basically good, and the same holds for the cadres. The working class has to forge unity to achieve any tasks. This understanding is key to maintaining proletarian rule, and it is even more the case in China, where the working class itself, let alone its most advanced sections, are a small fraction of the masses. The banner of revolution must be a banner of unity, or revolution is doomed. Rather than writing off the class struggle, this reflects the fact that the interests of the working class are the interests of the vast majority of the people.

The Gang Goes from Very Big To Very Small Very Fast

The current CC is faced with the task of simultaneously denying that the gang was isolated and explaining why it was. The masses rejoiced at their fall? That's easy, remember that millions in China hated the Cultural Revolution, and anyway, the bourgeoisie can organize a demo. The stuck pig squeals. The outpouring of joy in China was not organized. The demonstrations were just the tip of the iceberg. There was a mass phenomenon—spontaneous marches and parties. The masses bought up all the wine and whiskey in the major cities on their own, the better to wet their whistles for more celebrating and anti-gang chanting. They stayed out in the streets all night without being organized. They did this because they wanted to, because they were glad to see the gang go.

Why does the current CC refuse to admit that the gang was isolated and unpopular with the masses? And why, to the extent that they have to admit it, do they try to blame the masses for it? It is because of their own view of the high hard road of revolution. They think nobody will take it, that the masses don't want it. Only the super-heroes will do it, the condescending saviors. The rest have to be dragged to socialism and communism, against their will with constant encouragements like better conditions and three squares a day. In this country, the gang line leads to retreat from the day to day struggle in the name of the revolutionary goal. In China, it means trying to usurp the Party and state power to use them against the working class.

The current CC is forced to resort to a shell game to deal with this point of support for the gang. Their number one advocate is "convinced that the followers of the Four . . . number at least in the tens of millions." His faith is touching, but it is no substitute for evidence on this question. Even if his fondest dreams are true, in China this is a mere handful. It takes 45 million just to give you 5% of the people. Resistance by the masses of gang's supporters to their fall was small—significant, but small. What is the reason for this? They were isolated from the masses. Without the masses, you cannot win.

In Chou En-lai's report to the 10th Party Congress, he stated:

> "Chairman Mao teaches us that the correctness or incorrectness of the ideological and political line decides everything. If one's line is incorrect, one's downfall is inevitable, even with the control of the central, local and army leadership. If one's line is correct, even if one has not a single soldier at first, there will be soldiers, and even if there is no political power, political power will be gained."

The current CC may think that Mao made Chou say all this. They would do better to inquire why Mao did not make the gang listen to it. For their sorry history reaffirms what Mao and Chou said. Their support was not static. The current CC would like to hide that point. The gang started out as part of the proletarian headquarters of China, which commanded the respect and allegiance of hundreds of millions—of the vast majority. Dialectics requires of us that we examine the motion of this process, its development.

Our Party has some experience in this. We have seen what happens when the force in the leadership of the masses fails to grasp the key link of the class struggle and concretely lead the struggle forward together with the masses. We have seen how an incorrect line opens the door for the bourgeoisie to counterattack and destroy temporary gains. All this, of course, takes place under capitalism, where the bourgeoisie is the principal aspect of the fundamental contradiction, where they rule.

We summed up this experience in the phrase, "you can go from very big to very small very fast." And when that happens, you have to look at the objective situation and the masses and the line of the Party. The situation in China is this phenomenon on a mass scale under socialism. The gang went from very big—part of the leadership of hundreds of millions—to very small, isolated and hated, very fast, in less than 4 years. The same hundreds of millions who supported them as a part of the collective Party leadership and of Chairman Mao's proletarian headquarters (in part because of their individual contributions) wound up opposing them. This is a question of line—of the wrong line of the gang playing itself out in front of the Chinese people, and the correct line of Mao and after him, Hua, raising the pole of revolution for the masses to rally around. In rejecting the gang the masses weren't rejecting class struggle, they were waging it!

Our Party is faced with the same task under our conditions. We have to throw out the wrong line, and uphold the class struggle on all fronts against the bourgeoisie. Grasping class struggle as the key link requires us to rebel. The current CC can follow the gang to hell, but they must not be allowed to drag our Party there with them.

WHY SOCIALISM FAILS TO EXCITE THE CHAIR, Or—Pulling the Ice Pick Out of Trotsky's Head

Part III of the new CC report written by the Chairman and enthusiastically endorsed by the current CC, is a particularly disgusting and counter-revolutionary piece of bourgeois propaganda in the guise of a "Marxist" analysis. In this section, the Chair has literally pulled the ice pick out of Trotsky's head, making it crystal clear to most how seriously the line of our Party is being turned over.

In Part III, the Chair and the new CC set for themselves an impossible task: to prove something that has not happened.

The Chairman thinks that revisionism has triumphed in China and that capitalist restoration is near. But when it comes time to lay down the proof and stop picking at this and that, the Chair's idea and the development of actual events in the real world pass like ships in the night.

Setting aside for one second the question of what these opportunist armchair correct-liners do know, we would have to agree with a part of the Chair's statement. That is, he sets the task of determining why the revisionists triumphed as a *future task* requiring a "great deal of attention and study." Certainly there is not a word in the first 69 pages of the paper (where this quote appears) on the question of *why* and as we will see, none after. To any honest Marxist this fact would be a real cause for pause and alarm. But not for our opportunists, the key question of the objective situation *and* an analysis of the political lines that were developed and put forward that led to the triumph of revisionism are not essential to determining *why* socialism failed. Again, the reason for this is simple, there are none because it never happened. But to be sure, this will be no obstacle for the Chair or anyone else. All he has to do is to depart from Marxism and the Marxist method and say the "reason" for the triumph of revisionism is because:

> "On the one hand, the victories of the proletariat in those struggles led to great advances in socialist revolution and socialist construction. On the other hand, the more there were advances, the deeper the socialist revolution went, the more it dug away at the soil engendering the bourgeoisie, and the more it called forth desperate resistance from the bourgeoisie. Along

> with this, as noted before, at each stage in this process, some people get 'stuck,' including especially, as Mao pointed out, those who have become high officials and want to protect the interests of high officials, as against the interests of the masses." (CC Report, pp. 126-127)

So in this particular spiral in the development of socialism, the proletariat fought hard (on the one hand), but the bourgeoisie fought harder—the people get tired and despite the correct lines of the Gang and Mao, the revisionists win out.

To our correct-liners, their guys went down, and *this* and not line is decisive. As to why their guys lost since they were 100% Marxists and can't be blamed, then the reason must lie somewhere else. The chair says . . . "certain things which contributed to this [why the revisionists triumphed—ed.] can be indicated now."

The things that can be indicated now are covered in the CC report under four general points: the general reasons why the revisionists triumphed, the particular reasons why they triumphed, some thoughts on the last great line struggles, and finally an exhortation to the cadre not to lose faith, because socialism will triumph somewhere, some day.

General Reasons Why Revisionism Is Alleged to Have Won

According to the Chair, there are 5 general reasons that indicate why the revisionists triumphed in China:

> 1) ". . . the persistance of commodity relations, the three major differences (mental/manual, town/countryside, worker/peasant), of bourgeois right as well as other powerful remnants left over from previous society in the material and ideological sphere."
> 2) ". . . in a country like China, a backward country economically, where it is first necessary to go through the democratic stage and then make the immediate transition to socialism, the problems of making that transition and continuing to overcome spontaneous tendencies are enormous . . .
> 3) ". . . there is a whole deep rooted Confucian tradition in China, which along with the still backward conditions economically means that many people are still strongly weighed down by the old spiritual fetters—superstition, etc., as well as the tendency to meekly follow those in authority."
> 4) "and there is still the legacy of colonialism and the colonial mentality . . . which promote the idea that what is foreign is better . . . "
> 5) "At the same time there is a tendency to nationalism, which has a strong material base in the still largely peasant character of the country . . . " (All quotes from CC Report, pp. 122-3)

There are two points that must be made about the Chair's "general reasons." The first reason that socialism failed is that socialism is socialism, and not communism. All he has done is list some features of socialism. And the second reason, points 2 thru 5, is that China and its people are backward. They get the full brunt of blame for the failure.

Socialism is a transitional social system. It has many birthmarks of the old society, and is not yet a communist, classless society. All the problems the Chair puts forward have existed since the day of liberation. In fact, all of them were stronger then than they are now. They are problems that every socialist country faces to one degree or another, certainly every backward country that advances to socialism. To list them without any discussion of how socialism dealt with them and what turns around [sic] is to say that the conditions of socialism and "human nature" together give rise to the fall of socialism.

The list of points is used to slander the Chinese people. Here we have a masterpiece of true eclecticism. "Legacy of colonial mentality," "spiritual fetters," "nationalism," "spontaneous tendencies." This is not Marxism. How much? To what degree did these things take hold of the Chinese people? What was their motion, were they increasing or decreasing over the past 28 years? What turned them around? How did these things come out? Why—or what—were the lines that turned them loose? There is nothing of this in the section.

Once more the Chairman plays us for fools. Perhaps after 70 pages he thought our guard would be down. But point 4 says the Chinese have the idea that "foreign is better." And point 5 says that the Chinese are nationalists, which is bound to make them think "Chinese is better." Just throwing out a list of factors cannot substitute for even an initial analysis.

Mao addressed all of these points many times in the course of the Chinese Revolution. He said that we live in "the historic epoch in which world capitalism and imperialism are going to their doom and world socialism and people's democracy are marching to victory." He further pointed out that "imperialism has pushed the great masses of people throughout the world into the historical epoch of the great struggle to abolish imperialism."

The line of communists until now has been that the revolutionary storm center of the world resided in the "weakest links"—in precisely those countries where the Chair's list applies. The history of the past 60 years bears this out. Now, the very materialist basis of the revolutionary anti-imperialist struggles as part of the socialist revolutionary movement is being discarded to build support for the Gang.

And together with this, the 5 points are together a strong repudiation of Mao's line on building socialism in a backward country; a country with a large peasantry, poor economy, superstitions, nationalism (even Mao gets hit with this one)—these are the general characteristics of the vast majority of the world's peoples and countries. And this is what Mao said about it:

> "In addition to the leadership of the Party, a decisive factor is our population of 600 million. More people mean a greater ferment of ideas, more enthusiasm and more energy. Never before have the masses of the people been so inspired, so militant and so daring as at the present. The former exploiting classes have been completely swamped in the boundless ocean of the working people and must change, even if unwillingly. Undoubtedly there are people who will never change, who would prefer to keep their thinking ossified down to the Day of Judgment, but that does not matter very much. All decadent ideology and other incongruous parts of the superstructure are crumbling as the days go by. To clear away the rubbish completely will still take some time, but there is no doubt of their inevitable and total collapse. Apart from their other characteristics, the outstanding thing about China's 600 million people is that they are 'poor and blank.' This may seem a bad thing, but in reality it is a good thing. Poverty gives rise to the desire for change, the desire for action and the desire for revolution. On a blank sheet of paper free from any mark, the freshest and most beautiful characters can be written, the freshest and most beautiful pictures can be painted." ("Introducing A Cooperative," 1958, *Selected Readings,* p. 499-500)

Poor, backward, even blank. Are these conditions good or bad for revolution and socialism? Mao said they provided a good basis to advance to socialism and communism if there was a Party that integrated the universal truth of Marxism-Leninism to the concrete conditions of the Chinese revolution. There were and still are two roads ahead for China and all poor countries like it. The capitalist road of spontaneity and smash and grabbism, of short cuts and neo-colonial bondage, and, the socialist road of consciously transforming these backward conditions through struggle of revolutionary drive and all-round development with the initiative in one's own hands. The correct line and leadership of the Party is decisive in deciding which road is taken. The Chair does not agree. For him, the conditions lead to taking the capitalist road, even when and in spite of taking the correct line. The Chair disagrees, for him in spite of a correct line and a Party these conditions provided the basis for the rise of revisionism and the fall of socialism.

Particular Reasons Why Revisionism Is Alleged to Have Triumphed

The Chair follows the general attack on Mao and socialism with a list of particular reasons for the supposed triumph of revisionism.

1) "Mao's death, an event long awaited by the reactionary forces as the signal to make their big move."
2) Another is the devasting earthquakes . . ."
3) "the deaths of several long-time Chinese leaders besides Mao, all in the space of a couple of years, and several within one year (which role these different people played in the most recent struggle is not the point here—the point is that such deaths were bound to cause uncertainty and anxiety among the Chinese people about the situation in the country and this is magnified by the superstitious traditions referred to above, one of which links earthquakes with the end of an Emperor's reign, etc.)"
4) " . . . there was undoubtedly a section of the Chinese masses, and a larger percentage of cadres, intellectuals etc.—though certainly not all and not the most class conscious—who were tired of it all and wanted an end to it."
5) " . . . the fact that to a certain degree 'the revolutionary enthusiasm of the masses, which sustained them in their state of tension . . . was weakened in recent years. In short, some of them tired of the struggle."
6) In addition there is very real threat of imperialist, especially Soviet, aggression against China and the international situation as a whole. . . . And in recent years, with the growing danger of an attack on China by the Soviets in particular, and with the necessity to make certain agreements and compromises with reactionary and imperialist governments, with the whole 'opening to the West,' and all the bourgeois influences that inevitably accompany this, there was bound to be a powerful 'pull' away from taking the socialist road . . . And the cultural and ideological corrosion that is bound to accompany increased contact with bourgeois countries certainly had no small effect on the Chinese masses."

(All of this from CC, pp. 124-126)

The striking thing about these particular reasons is that they are the same as the general reasons with slightly more detail. Again, no line is offered as to how these factors played their negative roles. What we learn over and over is that people get tired of the struggle for socialism. But how is it that the Chinese people did not get tired in the darkest days of the anti-Japanese War, or in the Civil War. Or the Great Leap, or the Cultural Revolution. How is it that they were full of enthusiasm just a short while ago? What changed? Not a word is offered to answer this question. The eclecticism of the previous section is re-doubled. How many got tired? How much were people corroded? How big was the loss of enthusiasm? And how did these continuing secondary aspects become primary? Again, not a word. The particular reasons boiled down to the Chair's view that only Mao could keep China red. When he died, the floodgates opened. Heroes make history, pure and simple.

The particulars are more slanders and more exposures of the Gang. The earthquake caused more than "tremendous damage and dislocation." They caused a sharp two-line struggle between Hua and the Gang. The Gang did not cause the earthquakes, but they sure used them to smash and grab. And the current CC upholds them and blames the Chinese masses. No sooner did the earthquakes hit than the Gang published an article entitled "When the Earth Turns it Signifies the Advent of A New Earth." Here in the guise of fighting Confucianism, they reminded whole new Chinese generations of an old superstition that was dying out. They pushed backwardness in the guise of attacking it, and raised the question of succession in the bargain. This is the same method of a pornographer saying that people think of women as sex objects.

Point 6 in particular re-writes the line of our Party. It is a wholesale reversal of verdicts in a short space. China's foreign policy is portrayed as a necessary but tragic compromise with the imperialists and reactionary governments. The "opening to the West" is presented as coming out of weakness. This is not the line of Mao or of our Party. The generally correct foreign policy of China in the 1970s has won real victories, not only for China but for the entire working class worldwide and for all oppressed peoples. Would the CC throw away the International United Front Against Imperialism Aimed At the Rulers of the 2 Superpowers in order to support the Gang? It appears so. This foreign policy put China more firmly at the core of this front by breaking the imperialists encirclement and blockade. This came from strength, not weakness.

In Point 6 the slander on the people of China continues: who the hell is supposed to believe that the pull of the good life in the West was a "powerful force" and "had no small effect" on the Chinese masses. How big was the effect? How corroded were the people? As much as 90% of the Chinese masses have never even seen a Westerner. The reports of every single visitor to China right through today go directly against the idealism and wishful thinking of the Chair. They all report on the high class consciousness of the people they meet. Far from lusting after our appliances and blue jeans, the Chinese suffer sincerely and deeply over our having to live under capitalist exploitation and oppression. Compare this to reports from the USSR or Cuba, including those in Red Papers 7. Working class rule makes a difference.

The Chair has finally discovered that China is a poor country. After 70 pages of downplaying the big need for economic development, mechanization and modernization, he puts economic backwardness as a big reason for why revisionism triumphed. Not only that but it makes the Chinese masses easy prey for revisionist and bourgeois Western lures.

On page 31 he hits the other side with the same idealism and arrogance. "I remember that after an acquaintance returned from a trip to China he was asked by a worker how it was, and he replied, 'It was like going through a time machine.' The worker, on the basis of bourgeois spontaneity and prejudices said, 'Yeah, they're still a long ways behind us, so it's really like going back in time.' 'No', the acquaintance replied, 'it's like going forward.'"

Opposing the economic backwardness to the socialist system, leads the Chair to blame Americans for seeing China is poor, blames the "opening to the West" for finally letting the Chinese see it, and then blames them for seeing it. Only the Chair can see the truth, that it all leads to revisionism.

The Chair sets out to show how revisionism has triumphed, and as we said before this is a very difficult task, especially if your method is seeking truth from facts. What we have seen from his presentation of the general and particular (read peculiar) reasons why the Gang lost is that *even though* the Gang had a correct line, the forces of capitalism were just too strong for them.

In Red Papers 7, when the RCP analyzed the restoration of capitalism, it was decisive to go into the line errors Stalin made that contributed to the rise of revisionism and the bourgeoisie. Without this, people would not be fully armed to understand how this reversal happened. But this is not possible here. The Chair himself says: "But with the Four it cannot be shown that their stand deviated from Marxism-Leninism, Mao Tsetung Thought and that they created public opinion for an opportunist line that they were attempting to carry out. The public opinion they created was for a correct line." (CC, p. 21)

This is the big contradiction the Chair finds himself caught in. The Gang was correct, they were the revolutionaries, but they lost. They were defeated by Hua, so Hua must be a counter-revolutionary revisionist. So how then could Hua get on top—how could he and the rest of the revisionists triumph?

The only way, if you prescribe to the opportunism of the Chair, is because of the conditions of socialism. Socialism is a transition between capitalism and communism, the masses have backward aspects to their consciousness, the imperialists exist worldwide, under socialism some leaders turn color and betray the revolution. It is not enough just to put these aspects forward, to support the Chair you have to distort them, to raise them from the secondary role (and often relatively small secondary at that) they play when the working class is in power into problems far bigger than they really are. This is why the CC report treats such questions of getting tired, superstition, and nationalism totally out of context and with no discussion of the struggle and the effect of Mao and other revolutionaries striving to root them out in the course of continuing the revolution under the dictatorship of the proletariat.

To support the Gang, who were counter-revolutionaries, you have to turn reality on its head. You have to turn the advance of the working class in fighting the class enemy and building socialism into its opposite. You have to take the leadership that Mao gave to the revolutionary struggle and say when asked if he failed, "yes and no" and really mean "yes" but be afraid to say it. All this is a despicable insult to our class and to the science of our class.

And when the Chair has laid out his reasons, after he has been ruthless in his science, then he lays a heavy rap on all the comrades to tell them not to lose heart and to understand that socialism will win out in the end. But what is this enthusiasm based on? Mao says that the masses of people have "inexhaustible enthusiasm for socialism." But the Chair reminds us that this was before they got too superstitious and tired. Mao says "the correctness or incorrectness of the ideological and political line decides everything." And that "if you have a correct line, you will win soldiers." But now we learn from the Chair that even if you have a 100% correct line not only will you not win soldiers, but you will lose them.

Trotskyism Is Still Counter-Revolution

While the Chair is caught up in the contradictions of his position, and therefore can't identify any line errors giving rise to revisionism, he none the less puts forward a line as to why revisionism did triumph.

The message is clear. The objective conditions were not ripe for socialism, but they were ripe for capitalism and revisionism. Poor backward countries have too many strikes against them. The material and cultural base for socialism is too low. The forces for capitalism are too strong. The working class is too small and weak, and the peasantry too large. The surrounding world is too hostile, and every effort to deal with them contaminates you. The leadership is too corruptible, and the Party cannot deal with these contradictions. Nationalism sooner or later drives out internationalism in peasant countries. And there is nothing that the subjective forces, the revolutionary communists, can do about it. Not even Mao could stem the tide of capitalism, and when he died, it was all over.

This analysis is not new. It is simple and classical Trotskyism applied to China. Listen to what Trotsky said, on page 280 of *Permanent Revolution*: "The world division of labor, the dependence of Soviet industry upon foreign technology, the dependence of the productive forces of the advanced countries of Europe upon Asiatic raw materials, etc., etc., make the construction of an independent socialist society in any single country of the world impossible." And in *Preface to 'The Year 1905'* he observed, "The contradictions in the position of a workers' government in a backward country with an overwhelmingly peasant population could be solved only on an international scale, in the arena of the world proletarian revolution."

Trotsky never finished one of these analyses without telling all his followers not to feel bad. He always said that there would be revolution and socialism some day, even as he attacked it each and every day.

Our Party has always stood with Comrade Stalin in his attacks on Trotsky and Trotskyism. We have always waged a determined battle against its followers in the US. We said of them in the Programme of the RCP, and we must uphold today that:

> "Historically these Trotskyites have alternated between 'left' and right opportunism—between 'revolutionary' slogan-shouting to oppose the actual stage of struggle, and outright tailing after the bourgeoisie. But in essence they have always been right-wing servants of the reactionary classes. They attach themselves as parasites to the revolutionary movement to promote their organizations at the expense of the masses. They act all-wise and

> try to lord it over the workers, but the working class in every country has learned to deal with them in the same manner as it deals with their imperialist masters." (Party Programme, p. 92)

Trotskyism says that you can't build socialism in a backward country. It says the masses, especially the peasants, will not go along. And that the workers are too few and will tire quickly. It says the Party cannot lead, that the ideological and political line do not decide everything. In short, it says the same damn thing that the Chair and his CC are now saying about China.

The current CC paper opens with the statement that " 'And the attitude and approach every Party takes in understanding and evaluating the events in China will have much to do with determining whether or not that Party remains a Marxist-Leninist Party or degenerates into one kind of opportunism or another." (CC, p. 2)

The line of the Central Committee of our Party on China is a counter-revolutionary, Trotskyite line. This must serve as an alarm, a call to drive this line out of our Party before it takes hold and leads it down the path of counter-revolution and betrayal of the working class.

CHOU EN-LAI WAS A REVOLUTIONARY COMMUNIST

The role of Chou En-lai is a central one in the arguments put forward by the current CC. In order to try and bestow the revolutionary mantle of Mao on the counter-revolutionary gang, they have to bend every effort to attack and discredit the reputation of Chou.

More than 5 full pages is devoted to this underhanded effort, starting with page 80 of the report. The treatment of Chou En-lai is one of the most glaring examples of the *apriori* and subjective method of the entire paper, and far from discrediting Chou, fully discredits the author.

The paper never ceases to whine about reversing verdicts. In the section on Chou En-lai, we are presented with a revisionist reversal of the correct verdict and line of the RCP, and a total abandonment of Marxism-Leninism, Mao Tsetung Thought.

The old CC of the RCP responded to the death of Chou with a sum-up of his life and role in the Chinese Revolution. Our Party said then, in January of 1976, that all communists should learn from Chou En-lai:

> To be a revolutionary Communist all of one's life. To maintain one's bearings in the face of difficulties and set-

> backs. To aim high and persevere in step-by-step struggle according to changing conditions. To be firm in principle and good at uniting with others. To stand, ever, with the surging masses; to learn and to lead. To be conscientious in preparation and bold in execution. To uphold the Red Flag against all enemies within and without.

But this correct summation of Chou does not fit in with the purposes of the current CC. In fact, it stands as a real roadblock that they must attempt to deal with.

What are they trying to prove? First, that the gang and Chou were on opposite sides. The gang went after Chou from at least 1972, and the CC says that this was correct. If the gang were revolutionary heroes, then they must have gone after Chou because he was not a revolutionary, and if they went after him hard, he must have been a revisionist. This is their formalistic, twisted logic. And to demonstrate this, they try to show that Mao and Chou were on "opposite sides" during this period.

The paper says that "In response to this [the task of cleaning up the Lin Piao mess—J-B], I believe Mao and Chou En-lai had significant differences, though like all contradictions these differences went through a process of development, which ended up with Mao and Chou in fundamental opposition to each other."

What pseudo-Marxism. All contradictions develop. But all contradictions do not develop with people winding up on opposite sides. Mao and Chou worked together for some 45 years, and their differences did not "develop" in the straight line way that the CC paper offers. This view of how line struggle takes place runs through the entire paper, and runs through the entire way that the current CC conducted the China struggle in our Party.

What happened to Mao and Chou to put them on "opposite sides?" All the bulletin can do is repeat the point, each time with more emphasis. "And it seems very clear to me that by the time of Chou's death . . . Mao and Chou had come into clear and sharp conflict." "But beyond that, it is *obvious* that Mao and Chou were on opposite sides for some time before Chou's death, if we stop and think about how things developed over that period." ". . . everything points to the *obvious* fact that Mao and Chou En-lai were basically not in unity but on opposite sides for several years and increasingly so in the period right before Chou's death." All this on one page (p. 86) and they emphasize the *obvious* lest we try to really look at the situation. And finally, on page 91, we are told when Chou En-lai went bad. "Chou En-lai in particular did go along with the Cultural Revolution after Mao struggled with him at the start, and during the early stages of it—up to the time of the Lin Piao affair—he played a good and very important role, overall. But, after the Lin Piao affair, Chou's role turned into its opposite."

The paper lays out its view not only of the issues around which there were differences between Mao and Chou, but also decides where each stands. But what we are really given is a re-writing of history to give Mao the gang's line.

> "In substance, Chou felt the only thing to do was to bring back many people who had been knocked down during the Cultural Revolution and were bound to be strong opponents of Lin Piao, while Mao, agreeing probably to bring back some, did not want to go as far with this as Chou did. And besides just bringing back people, Chou wanted to push policies that would reverse the momentum of the Cultural Revolution and the continuation of the revolution. In substance, he wanted to put stability and unity and pushing the national economy forward as the main things." (p. 81)

And Mao?

> "With some of this, I believe, Mao agreed, because he agreed that it was a necessity in the short run. But not all of it, even in the short run, let alone the long run. . . In short, Mao did not agree that everything should be subordinated to stability and unity and pushing the national economy forward—and specifically not that *correct* verdicts of the Cultural Revolution should basically be reversed." (p. 81)

And furthermore, "Chou thought Teng was basically good but had made some mistakes; Mao, I am convinced, did not trust Teng and recognized that upon returning to office Teng was likely to resume his old ways." And this right after we have been told that "I believe that Mao and Chou agreed that it was necessary to bring back Teng at this time—his return began in 1972, very shortly after Lin Piao crashed." (p. 81)

This is not a comparison between the lines of Chou and the lines [sic] of Mao. It is nothing but a single assumption, that Mao was closer and closer to the gang as time went on, stated and restated with "I believe" and "probably" to substitute for concrete analysis. And the assumption is not true.

Did Chou En-lai and Mao have differences over these points, key questions of how to build and develop socialism, including how to push the economy forward, on what basis to stabilize and unite, cadre policy and the direction of political campaigns? It is inconceivable to say that they did not, even often sharp ones. But there is not one shred of evidence to support the characterizations offered by the CC of what these differences were, and none at all to support a conclusion that they wound up on "opposite sides." This is only the wishful thinking of the current CC, aping the futile four year struggle of the gang to set Mao against Chou and knock down Chou.

But even more underhanded is the attempt to imply that Mao and the gang were in fundamental unity. On the very points mentioned, it was with the gang that Mao had very sharp differences. On the necessity of stability and unity and pushing the national economy forward, it was the gang who in fact stood in the way of these correct thrusts by metaphysically opposing them to "revolution" and "class struggle." Mao said "stability and unity don't mean writing off class struggle." Not that stability and unity can wait until we finish the class struggle. The policy of liberating cadre knocked down in the Cultural Revolution was Mao's policy, and it did not begin with the question of the Lin Piao affair, though that speeded up the process through the new necessity. This policy was a concrete application of Mao's view of how contradictions are resolved. And now we are even being told that the foreign policy of Mao and Chou over the past period was not really Mao's. A crack for worms to crawl in, so that soon they can attack the Chinese foreign policy and say that they are not attacking Mao. They can say what they like, but the truth is the opposite.

The paper of the CC advises us that the correct method to judge these questions is to compare and contrast the different lines. Even if they will not allow this to take place over China, it must be done.

Where are the incorrect lines from Chou En-lai that we are supposed to compare with the lines of Mao or the gang? Where is the statement from Chou that shows he is violating Mao Tsetung Thought, that he is standing against the Cultural Revolution? Where is Chou's revisionism?

There is none. Not one quote, or even a fragment. Not even a statement taken out of context like we find through the rest of the paper. The current CC does not even pause for a moment about not having found any bad lines from Chou. No, they plunge ahead to explain away all the good things he said.

The paper quotes Chou often, especially his reports to the 10th Party Congress and 4th National People's Congress. But both of these reports put out the correct line on the situation in China and the tasks coming out of this situation. Both represent Marxism, and both are Mao's line. The only explanation we are offered is that Chou was secretly against them and that Mao made him say all these good things. And the facts on this are clear. Chou agreed with the line of the 10th Party Congress and the 4th NPC, and the gang consistently went against it.

Raising the spectre of Lin Piao is a vain attempt to cloud the issue through innuendo and bourgeois analogy. The CC says "... look at Lin Piao's report to the 9th Congress, and now we can look back and see with whom and what Chou was increasingly aligned after Lin fell... (p.81) Yes, let's look. Lin Piao was forced to change his revisionist draft of the report to the 9th Congress and accept the Party's line that he did not agree with. And Lin Piao smuggled in as much of his garbage as he could get away with, such as the genius theory. Lin Piao had many rotten lines which have been thoroughly exposed and criticized by the Chinese people.

Chou's reports to the Party and Peoples Congresses have no such garbage smuggled in. The 10th Congress is a Marxist work, whose basic thrust has been confirmed by the events following it and by Mao's issuing of the 3 (yes 3) directives in response to the situation coming out of it and in preparation for the 4th NPC of January 1975. His line was correct, it was Mao's line, and the gang were the ones who diverted from it. It will not be long before the current CC finds themselves forced to repudiate the reports to both the 10th and 4th Congresses.

The paper tells us to check out how Mao forced Chou to put going against the tide into his report. If this is true, then Mao forced Chou to deal a heavy blow against the metaphysics of the gang and the current CC. What did Chou, (and Mao if you will "for who else would both want to and have the ability to get this into the 10th Congress documents?"—what a subjective view of line struggle again) really have to say about going against the tide?

> "Chairman Mao has constantly taught us: It is imperative to note that one tendency covers another. The opposition to Chen Tu-hsiu's Right opportunism which advocated 'all alliance, no struggle' covered Wang Ming's 'left' opportunism which advocated 'all struggle, no alliance.' The rectification of Wang Ming's 'Left' deviation covered Wang Ming's Right deviation. The struggle against Liu Shao-chi's revisionism covered Lin Piao's revisionism. There were many instances in the past where one tendency covered another and when a tide came, the majority went along with it, while only a few withstood it.

> Today, in both international and domestic struggles, tendencies may still occur similar to those of the past, namely, when there was an alliance with the bourgeoisie, necessary struggles were forgotten and when there was a split with the bourgeoisie, the possibility of an alliance under given conditions was forgotten. It is required of us to do our best to discern and rectify such tendencies in time. And when a wrong tendency surges towards us like a rising tide, we must not fear isolation and must dare to go against the tide and brave it through. Chairman Mao states, 'Going against the tide is a Marxist-Leninist principle.' In daring to go against the tide and adhere to the correct line in the ten struggles between the two lines within the Party, Chairman Mao is our example and teacher. Every one of our comrades should learn well from Chairman Mao and hold to this principle."

This was said in the 10th Congress Report. It is not just a point of Marxism in general, but directly related to the situation in China then, a thrust that is missing in the CC bulletin. The bulletin reduces this to a simplistic tactic, saying "It is clear that the tide that was gaining momentum then was that represented by people like Teng Hsiao-ping—and ultimately Chou En-lai—who were bound to gain from the whole campaign to clean up right after the Lin Piao affair (criticize Lin Piao and rectify the style of work)." And later we are told that Mao warned against ". . . the right, the right, the right again . . ." How easy it all is to the current CC idealists.

The truth is far more complex and very different. The 10th Congress begins to lay out the task of pushing the economy forward, and strengthening the Party. The stress on economic development and unity is growing, not against Mao's line, but as Mao's line. And the struggle to deepen the defeat, ideologically and politically, of the Lin Piao headquarters and its effect on the masses is continuing. All this means that there must indeed be a caution to watch out for right-errors and bourgeois rightists. But at the very same time, the Party center is launching campaigns against the right—Lin Piao-Confucius, and shortly thereafter the campaign around the study of the dictatorship of the proletariat. This struggle certainly could cover and did cover a "left" tendency. The strategic guidance given by Chou at the 10th Congress leading up to the smashing of the gang, "to discern and rectify such tendencies in time" was both correct and prophetic, much to the dismay of the gang and their supporters who tried to sneak into power behind "opposing" the right.

All of the quotations from Chou do not discredit him, but do in fact deal blows to the gang. So the paper has to come up with another method to smear Chou. The Chou section stands out as a model of subjectivity in a subjective paper.

"I believe." "Mao, probably agreeing." "With some of this, I believe, Mao agreed." "But not all of it." "Here, I believe, are the seeds." "I believe." "I am convinced." "I am convinced." "It is obvious." "It seems very clear to me." "I believe it is indisputably clear." "This is probably true and the reason I think so is." "Clearly in my opinion." "But I don't think so."

All of this is from just 3 of the Chou pages. Phrases like this are the heart and soul of the entire Chou argument. It is obvious and clear that the CC "believes" all this trash. This is what the struggle is all about. Unlike them, communists demand proof.

Still further the CC is forced to retreat. How could Mao and Chou have been in basic unity? If they were, the gang would have gone down and the struggle would have been very different. This reduces class struggle to simple power politics at the very top. Nowhere is there a serious discussion of class forces and the conditions, including the mood and understanding of the masses, that shape the necessity and freedom of the proletariat. Nowhere is there an analysis of the actual contradictions that different class forces were lining up around.

A brief look at the Cultural Revolution or the struggle in China at any period shows that things never develop or go down in this simplistic and easy a manner, precisely because many contradictions are at work and conditions have to be created, within the Party and among the masses, for ideological and political and organizational struggle. In fact this simplistic and idealist notion of the class struggle and the 2 line struggle has led the current CC to seek a scapegoat within the Party rather than engaging in the far more difficult and principled task of answering the actual questions and contradictions we confront. And so they tried to deal with the question of China, all questions within the US and the supposed "revisionist headquarters" in one organizational coup. This is the opposite of Mao's line, methods of struggle and outlook, which enabled the Chinese Party to successfully wage 11 major line struggles without degenerating into either revisionism or Trotskyism.

Once more rewriting history is used to say that the Lin Piao-Confucius Campaign was led by Mao and aimed at Chou. The truth is quite otherwise. The gang distorted the Lin Piao-Confucius campaign to try and aim it at Chou and their veteran cadres and at the masses. They did this through innuendo, and they did this through adding such contradictions among the people as "going through the back door" to the struggle against class enemies Lin Piao and Confucius. The gang may have wanted to aim at Chou, but what they did aim at Mao and the CCP [sic]. Mao told them to stop it, to stop weakening the campaign. The gang separated the conduct of the Lin Piao-Confucius campaign from the tasks of the 10th Congress. This was another attack on Mao and the Party. Far from supporting them, Mao replied "Metaphysics is rampant" and directed the gang to criticize themselves before the Party center. The current CC says that the gang's line was Mao's line. Mao and the Chinese CC said it was not.

Much has been made of the nature of Chou En-lai's funeral services. They took place in the context of sharp struggle over the question of succession, over who would take over the post of Premier of the State Council and inherit at least much of the mantle of Chou. The question of blocking the bourgeois rightists from using the death of Chou En-lai to advance their position was a real one confronting Mao, and must be taken into account in evaluating the form of the services.

Other facts are known and must be considered. Mao did in fact visit Chou in the hospital before his death, not once but several times, even to the point of spending entire days and nights by the bedside of his old comrade. This even though Mao himself was quite sick and weak at the time. The current CC might want to believe that he went there to struggle with Chou to "get up off his line." But this only shows how far from human reality they have traveled.

The funeral services at the center were not the only ones in China. The entire Chinese people mourned Chou as a revolutionary leader and hero. This was an *obvious* fact. This was not just because the Chinese are backward and Confucian and anti-Mao, but just the opposite. The outpouring of grief at the death of Chou was a reflection of the masses' commitment and determination to continue on the road to socialism.

This situation caused the gang to jump out. Right after Chou's death, the gang-controlled press played down reports about memorial meetings and played up advances on the ideological front in the struggle in education. This setting the two in opposition to each other served to weaken the ideological campaigns of the Party.

The right was trying to use the masses' feelings for Chou to divert and hide from criticism of the right deviationist wind. The gang response to this was to step up the attacks on Chou, and by implication the masses who mourned him. They set themselves above the masses as condescending saviours protecting China from the right. This of course created many new hiding places for the rightists in the anger of the masses for the gang.

This situation led the anti-right deviationist wind campaign and anti-Teng efforts of the Party to flounder from the start. The right was an unceasing obstacle and the gang led their resistance with pseudo-revolutionary phrase-mongering and increasingly open attacks on Chou. Right before the April day of mourning, the gang openly attacked Chou in the Shanghai press for several days running, prompting the masses in Shanghai to poster an entire Peking bound train in protest. The gang was helping set the conditions for serious disturbances on the day of mourning.

The situation reached a critical point with the Tien An Men incident. The anti-socialist right was out in full force, emboldened by the mass outrage at the gang's attacks on Chou. They tried to hide among the masses and set them against socialism and the Party. The response of the gang was to take advantage of the need to suppress counter-revolutionaries to press their own case, again at least by implication calling mourning for Chou a backward action by the masses. This again strengthened the right and seriously weakened the efforts of the Party to conduct struggle against the right. Rather than leading the struggle against the right, as the current CC would have us believe, the gang was an obstacle, a real fetter on the Party and the masses.

The gang tried to paint Chou as a revisionist before and after his death to show the masses that they were the only real followers of Mao. Instead, they showed the masses that they were against Mao and the Party. Now, two years later, the current CC does the same, setting themselves against the line of Mao, the CCP and the Chinese people.

The portrait of line struggle that comes out clearest in the Chou section of the bulletin is idealist and recreates the genius theory that Lin Piao failed to put over. Chou and all other Chinese leaders are painted reluctant revolutionaries who sooner or later go bad unless Mao personally stops them.

"Chou En-lai in particular did go along with the Cultural Revolution after Mao struggled with him at the start." Chou "wavered" on the Great Leap. Mao tried to get Chou to "get up off his line."

Mao is portrayed not as a Marxist-Leninist but as someone who has it all together then has to get all the other waverers to line up behind him. The paragraph in parentheses on the bottom on page 91, where the Chairman finally tells all about the hard times of being a Chairman is a masterpiece of a distorted ego and a subjective idealist line.

Condescending saviors and geniuses do not make revolution. The current CC has thrown away analysis of class forces, thrown away the concepts of advanced, intermediate and backward. They have abandoned the method of dialectics with its interpenetration and relations between things. The paper has not one word on how the line develops in constant struggle, on the mass line within the Party and among the masses, on the movement from confusion to clarity and from one-sidedness to all-sidedness. All this is missing. You get the impression that they think Mao didn't need it, so why should they. That is how they interpret Mao's statement that often he was in a minority, even a minority of one. This is a rank attack on Mao and Mao Tsetung Thought, and represents a consolidation of opportunism in our Party.

What are the facts. The paper distorts the role of Chou in the Cultural Revolution to further this view of line struggle. Chou first plays a leading role in the Cultural Revolution just 20 days after the publication of Yao Wen-yuan's "signal" article. He gets it published in Peking, the very headquarters of Liu Shao-chi and Peng Chen. And this was even before the Cultural Revolution had even become one. This same distortion of lines and role extends to Hua Kuo-feng, who did not disappear late in 1966 as the bulletin suggests, but in fact played a leading role in his province in consolidating the Cultural Revolution against attacks from the Right and ultra "left." His reports on the struggle there were circulated by the Central Committee throughout the country.

And as for Yeh Chien-ying hating the Cultural Revolution, all we have to do is read the very next sentence of the *Peking Review* article quoted, *PR* 43, 1977 to see how the CC has tampered with the facts. The report quotes Yeh as saying "The third comparatively major setback (in the Party's history) took place immediately after settling accounts with Liu Shao-chi's revisionist line." Yeh said that, and in the very next sentence he said, "Our Party suffered from sabotage by a bunch of anti-Marxist swindlers—Lin Piao and the 'gang of four.' This resulted in the greatest damage and the most harmful influence in the history of our Party. Wielding that portion of power they had usurped, they wantonly tampered with Marxism, sabotaged the Great Cultural Revolution and deceived many of our comrades." This is not hatred for the Cultural Revolution after [it] knocked down Liu

Shao-chi at all, but saying what is true, that it did not end there and in fact other counter-revolutionary headquarters jumped out, caused damage and had to be dealt with.

All of these facts are and were readily available to the CC. They were presented to them. But they are ignored. Why? There is only one explanation. The facts don't fit the conclusion, so the facts have to go. This is not the Marxist method, and it should not be the method of the RCP.

Comrade Chou En-lai died on January 8, 1976. The current CC says that by that time it was obvious that he was not a revolutionary but a revisionist. They say it is obvious that the Lin Piao-Confucius campaign had been directed at Chou. They say that it is obvious that Teng and other rightists were supported by Chou and riding high. They say that it is obvious that Chou was heading one camp and Mao heading another. None of these charges are new. The bourgeois press was filled with them all through 1974 and 1975. They saw China as a shaky alliance between the "moderates" and the "radicals." It was all obvious to veteran China-watchers stationed in Hong Kong and Taiwan.

But the RCP did not stoop to follow the bourgeoisie in January of 1976. We made an analysis of the situation in China, and we made it based on Marxism-Leninism, Mao Tsetung Thought. On that basis we put forward the truth and organized meetings of workers around the country to do so and draw out lessons about socialism and revolution.

The RCP then said about Chou En-lai, in the January 15th, 1976 issue of *Revolution*:

> "Yet today, even as they are forced to make reference to Chou, they try to present him as a 'moderate' or a 'pragmatist' as if his accomplishments were due to the fact that he was not really a communist when, in fact, the opposite is the truth."

Who is the "they" that distorted the life of Chou. It was the bourgeoisie, then and now. The article goes on to say:

> "What the bourgeoisie slanders as 'pragmatism' is precisely the step by step application of Marxism-Leninism to advancing the cause of the working class in China and throughout the world. For Chou and all communists, 'Marxism is not a dogma, but a guide to action,' a tool in the hands of the oppressed to make revolution and build a new world."

This verdict on Chou En-lai and on Marxism-Leninism, is correct. It must be upheld. The CC report must be overthrown.

Uphold the 11th Party Constitution

A glaring example of how far off the idealism, metaphysics and apriorism of the current CC will take you is in their analysis of the Constitution that was adopted at the 11th Party Congress in August of 1977.

There are many changes between the 11th Constitution and the one adopted by the 10th Congress some 4 years earlier. On the basis of these changes, with nary a word about the conditions of the class struggle that gave rise to them, the current CC has decided that this new Constitution is "fascist."

The 11th Constitution comes out of the struggle against the gang. That is their only point of reference, and that is what they don't like about it. Calling it a "fascist" and dictatorial Constitution is nothing but a vain effort to add weight to their case. Their method shows how far into rank emotionalism they are willing to sink in this effort. After these very same forces have vacillated and postponed a scientific discussion of fascism within our Party starting even before the Founding Congress, they seize on the word to apply it in a backward and even socialist country. Cut the crap and deal with reality before it is too late.

The goals and method of the current paper prevent it from dealing in a materialist manner with the current Consitution, including the changes. First they offer a long section on "overthrow" vs "eliminate." The 10th Constitution says that the basic program is "the complete overthrow of the bourgeoisie and all other exploiting classes, the establishment of the dictatorship of the proletariat in place of the dictatorship of the bourgeoisie and the triumph of socialism over capitalism." The 11th Constitution says that the basic program "for the entire historical period of socialism is to persist in continuing the revolution under the dictatorship of the proletariat, eliminate the bourgeoisie and all other exploiting classes step by step and bring about the triumph of socialism over capitalism."

The formulation of the 10th Congress reflects the general tasks of establishing socialism, and the formulation at the 11th Congress reflects the tasks of continuing the revolution under the conditions of socialism. Compare this with the Constitution of the RCP:

"The basic program of the Revolutionary Communist Party is the complete overthrow of the bourgeoisie, the establishment of the dictatorship of the proletariat in place of the dictatorship of the bourgeoisie and the triumph of socialism over capitalism. The ultimate aim of the Party is the realization of communism.

"In order to accomplish this historical mission the working class, led by its Party, must establish under its leadership the broadest united front, uniting all who can be united against the main enemy, and must carry the struggle through to the complete elimination of the bourgeoisie and all exploiting classes." *Programme and Constitution*, p. 167.

We are offered as an argument that "overthrow" means "bottom up" struggle and "eliminate step by step" means "top down" struggle. This is nonsense. The appeal to the cadre to sign up for "top down" or "bottom up" is nothing more than an anti-communist appeal. Is the dictatorship of the proletariat top down? Is the leading role of a Communist Party top down? This argument has been offered before, by petty bourgeois revolutionaries in the 60's as a reason not to move towards Marxism-Leninism and the working class. The Cultural Revolution with its mass character and rebellion against reactionary authority made Marxism acceptable to large numbers of petty bourgeois revolutionaries. But these same forces summed up the Cultural Revolution without regard to condition, time and place, and many within our Party, as well as in China, have raised the forms and methods of the Cultural Revolution as an idealist "best" method of carrying on the class struggle. In any and all circumstances. They have in a word, gotten stuck. Not that there is no such thing as "top down and dictatorial" methods. We have only to look at the way the current CC is trying to conduct the struggle over China to see it.

The argument that the 11th Constitution denies the necessity for another Cultural Revoltuion is equally laughable. Who would not agree that "China's Great Proletarian Cultural Revolution was a political revolution carried out under socialism by the proletariat against the bourgeoisie and all other exploiting classes to consolidate the dictatorship of the proletariat and prevent the restoration of capitalism." And who would not agree that "Political revolutions of this nature will be carried out many times in the future." This is the line of Mao Tsetung. And it is the line of the current Chinese leadership headed by Hua Kuo-feng. The quotes are from the 11th Constitution, coming just 2 pages after the statement on the step by step elimination of the bourgeoisie and all other exploiting classes. Again, would the current CC cut the crap.

Well, they say, maybe overthrow and eliminate are not the

point. The real proof that the 11th Constitution is "fascist" is:

> "...the fact that in the tasks of the primary organizations of the Party, the Constitution is specifically changed from the 10th Party Congress to *take out* '...wage an active ideological struggle so as to keep Party life vigorous,' which is replaced with the instruction to report the opinions and demands of the masses to higher Party organizations and to be concerned about the masses' political, economic and cultural life... This is dialectically related to other changes in the Constitution, such as instituting 'commissions for inspecting discipline' at various levels of the Party, re-instituting one-year probationary requirements for new members—something previously dropped from the Constitution as a result of the Cultural Revolution—and the direct tying of going against the tide to upholding the 'three do's and don'ts' which really means that the last two are the basis for defining the first—that is, anyone who goes against the tide is splitting and conspiring and is therefore a revisionist."

This is another eclectic mixture of fact and fancy, petty bourgeois hysteria over discipline with idealist abstracting of the Cultural Revolution, all to prevent a real analysis of the 11th Constitution and thereby hopefully win support for the gang. The current CC will do anything before a concrete analysis of concrete conditions, because after one, they will have to abandon their position.

The 11th Constitution did drop the section on "wage an active ideological struggle so as to keep Party life vigorous." The fact of the situation in China was that ideological struggle in particular was distorted by the gang, especially through their running of the major ideological campaigns like Lin Piao-Confucius and study the Dictatorship of the Proletariat, and through their control of ideological education. But active ideological struggle is important to the life of the Party. And it is primarily because of the damage done in this sphere by the gang that the conditions were created that allowed elements within the Party to force the removal of that phrase from the new Constitution. The revolutionaries within the Party on all levels are waging struggle to keep it in the Party.

The new Constitution contains a greater stress on inner-Party democracy than even the 10th Constitution did. "Promote inner-Party democracy." "The whole Party must prevent Party members, especially leading Party cadres, from exploiting their privileges, and wage a resolute struggle against bourgeois ideology and the bourgeois style of work." "The correctness or incorrectness of the ideological and political line decides everything." "The Party persists in combating revisionism, and dogmatism and empiricism." The Party "must give full scope to inner-Party democracy and encourage the initiative and creativeness of all Party members and Party organizations at all levels, and combat bureaucracy, commandism and warlordism." "It is absolutely impermissible for anyone to suppress criticism or retaliate. Those guilty of doing so should be investigated and punished."

All of these formulations are either new to the 11th Constitution or are strengthened over the 10th Constitution. All of these clearly come out of sharp class struggle within the highest levels of the Chinese Communist Party, and it is precisely by following the class struggle in China that we will be able to sort things out.

And even the thing that is substituted for "wage an active ideological struggle..." is derided as reporting the masses opinions up, or in other words spying and finking. Reporting up is no substitution for ideological struggle, but neither is it a thing to deride. It is absolutely indispensable to the practicing of the mass line, and for the chain of knowledge to function based on dialectical materialism rather than idealism. Only the idealist, genuis theory of the current CC prevents them from seeing this. Our Party has stressed this point many times as a basic point of Marxism and a basic point for the functioning of the Party and the Party branches.

The question of the discipline, probation and the like can only be viewed through examining the class struggle, not by linking things metaphysically to a missing phrase.

The 10th Party Congress called for strengthening the Party. This was a key task for moving socialist revolution and socialist construction forward, coming out of the Cultural Revolution and consolidating its gains. But what was the result. There was a crash admissions program led by the gang, with 7 million new members entering, 20% of the Party, in less than 4 years. Fully one half of the Party Membership is now new, joining since the Cultural Revolution. The gang pushed ahead with educating Party members, especially new ones, in metaphysics. They pushed going against the tide means blindly rebelling against authority. They pushed don't produce for the incorrect line. All this was criticized and repudiated by the Central Committee as early as 1974, but it happened and had its effect none the less. The situation in China was changed over the years, and a materialist analyzes this and brings his thinking and actions into conformity and reality.

So where the 10th Congress dropped the probationary period

because of the Cultural Revolution the way that Liu Shao-chi tried to make the Party a base for revisionism and reversion, (Lin Piao had and used a different base primarily), reinstituting a probationary period at the 11th Constitution can enable the Party to strengthen its leading role and train a new generation of successors, train them in Marxism, not revisionism.

The current CC is afraid that the rightists will use this probationary period to keep out proletarian fighters. But this is nothing more than fear of the actual class struggle that comes down in every sphere of life. The rightists and revisionists will try to use probation to their advantage. And there will be struggle over it. How can this be an argument against taking necessary steps to enable the proletariat to strengthen its Party. This is nothing but a call for an idealist purity, for something that only the working class can use and that the bourgeoisie cannot. There is no such thing, and to look for one is to retreat from the class struggle.

The argument over discipline is the same. "Commissions for inspecting discipline" precisely grew out of the recent class struggle, especially the struggle against the gang and their constant eroding of the leading role of the Party and the Party leadership. They were set up to "strengthen Party members education in discipline, be responsible for checking up on the observance of discipline by Party members and Party cadres and struggle against all breaches of discipline." The actual imposition of discipline remains in the units on all levels, as do all the rights of Party members to disagree, reserve their opinion, and appeal.

The Party in China had in fact, admitted by all, been hit by factionalism, disruption and sabotage of Party unity, forming of gangs on many levels. This requires attention to discipline. And this is an area of class struggle. The discipline commissions are necessary tools for the Party, and both classes, the proletariat and the bourgeoisie, will try to grab this tool and use it against the other. (A comparison with the current struggle in our Party is enlightening. The current CC is trying to grab onto the rules of democratic centralism to use them against the cadres and the working class overall. And this is in fact and right now, an area of sharp class struggle.)

The current CC says that all of this is nothing but a document calling for "absolute obedience to higher levels and unquestioning compliance with orders." We have all seen one recently, the "Rectification Bulletin" and can compare it with the 11th Constitution.

The 11th Constitution provides a real basis for the continuation of the class struggle in China on favorable terms for the proletariat. All of the changes, and the entire document are to be used by the proletariat to help strengthen the dictatorship of the proletariat, and advance the socialist revolution and socialist construction. And that is the basis on which communists should uphold it.

Raising the 10th Constitution in an idealist manner to oppose the 11th Constitution is nothing but opportunism. There is no basis for such a document to stay the same after intense class struggle. The 11th Constitution comes out of the struggle against the gang and their counter-revolutionary headquarters. For it to stay the same as the 10th would be for the Chinese leadership to lie to the Chinese people about the current situation. They did not do so.

Any attempt to flee from the class struggle around the 11th Constitution would be dangerous, either here or in China. The proletariat in China will not stand by idly while the bourgeoisie tries to use the Constitution against them. We will not stand by idly while the current CC tries to use it to support the gang. Their only argument is that anyone who would want to put the gang down must have been fascist, so off they go in a futile search for fascist evidence. All they could find was petty bourgeois hysteria and two pages of anti-Marxist and even anti-communist arguments.

(All quotes from the current CC paper are from pp. 18-19. All quotes from the 11th Constitution are from *Documents of the 11th Congress,* pp. 121-142.)

SMASHING THE GANG OF FOUR WAS A GREAT VICTORY FOR THE WORKING CLASS AND SOCIALISM

The line on China adopted at the recent Central Committee meeting of our Party is dead wrong, opportunist and must be smashed. If this position is consolidated, it will place our Party, the Party of the U.S. working class, in opposition to the actual development of the worldwide proletarian revolution. The crushing of the Gang of Four was a necessary step and a great victory for socialism in China. Far from representing Chairman Mao's revolutionary line, the Gang had become new bourgeois elements who would have led China down the road to capitalist restoration, had they succeeded in seizing power.

Both their line and practice made this clear. Ignoring the actual tasks which the development of the revolution had placed before the Chinese Communist Party and the Chinese people, they pursued a policy of divorcing class struggle from those tasks. In particular, this took the form of making the overthrow of bourgeois elements in the Party a prerequisite for taking up anything else. In doing this their philosophic outlook was idealist in that they made the main battle over ideas in men's minds that were but a reflection of the material world, rather than uniting all who can be united against the main enemy to resolve the actual contradictions that face the proletariat to move society forward. By doing this they reversed the correct relationship between thinking and being, made thinking always the primary aspect and then drew out the class struggle as a battle between revolutionary and counter revolutionary ideas divorced from the actual state of the class struggle, time, place and conditions. For the Gang their idealism developed in a left political form: that they were the revolutionaries, the sole repositories of the correct line. But increasing their super revolutionary cover became nothing but a hammer to pound down any opposition to them and to their drive for more and more power. This "left" idealist and metaphysical line led to sabotage of socialist construction, splitting the Communist Party, strengthening the very capitalist tendencies and rightist forces the Gang claimed to oppose—in short, to undermining the dictatorship of the proletariat. Holding fast to this line, the Gang could only end up as they did, capitalist roaders whose increasing isolation from the leadership of the Party and the masses alike left them only one path to try and win victory for their incorrect line—a coup attempt.

It was because the Gang of Four had come to be an objective fetter on the development of socialism and, in fact, the gravest danger to the working class dictatorship in China, that the Central Committee headed by Hua Kuo Feng had to crush them. This bold and timely victory is the reason that China remains a socialist country today and can continue along the difficult road of working to build communism. Both socialist China and the Chinese Communist Party and its Central Committee deserve the support of all Marxist-Leninists, and their gratitude.

At the same time, it will not do to pretend, as careerists like the OL do, that there is no more class struggle in China. It is raging right now between real class forces in every field over what road the revolution will take. Waging and consolidating the battle against the Gang has made necessary not only aiming the blow away from the right, but close unity with rightist and revisionist forces in the Party. (In much the same way, Mao during the Cultural Revolution had to unite with Lin Piao, "against my will," to be able to build the mass movement and defeat Liu Shao-chi & Co.) With their freedom increased by this alliance and by such factors as the tarnish the Gang put on the weapons of Mao Tsetung Thought and the Cultural Revolution, these forces are testing and seeking to expand their strength.

Reports coming out of China, including articles in *Peking Review*, show both that the different forces making up the current leadership are making compromises to maintain their alliance (the report to the 11th Party Congress itself is a good example) and that a sharp two line struggle is going on (over cadre participating in manual labor, agricultural mechanization, socialist new things, and many other issues). This situation obviously calls for close attention and careful evaluation on the part of revolutionaries outside China. On the other hand, to use the present twists and turns of the class struggle to justify support for the Gang, who are to blame for many of the difficult conditions in China today, and not supporting the proletarian line in the current leadership, is nothing but opportunism.

A Matter of Principle

What line we take on China is a question of principle. As Mao pointed out, "Who are our friends? Who are our enemies? This is a question of the first importance for the revolution." The socialist countries are beacon lights of our class, the international working class. China helps communists everywhere understand and explain to the advanced and the masses the great leap in human history represented by socialism. The complex class struggle to preserve and build socialism, and will also make the road easier to travel in the socialist revolution in this country. [sic] Proletarian internationalism requires we do what we can to defend socialist China from its enemies, especially those in our own country. Principally this means the ruling class, but it includes as well those who wave the red flag as they echo the capitalists' slanders of China to the masses!

Secondly, the adoption of this line means the betrayal and degeneration of the ideology, policies and organization of our own Party. Support for the Gang of Four means replacing Marxism-Leninism, Mao Tsetung Thought with what their followers hailed as "Chang Chun-chiao Thought": Trotskyite-style left idealism, contempt for the masses and sectarianism. This is already a clear trend not only in the documents upholding the Four, but in other areas of our Party's work. This trend must be smashed along with the pro-Gang line that nurtures it.

For these reasons the entire Party must reject the 3 propositions made by Avakian in his paper:

(1) That China has gone revisionist and is fully on the road to capitalist restoration. This is untrue and upholding this as the truth, based especially on the "reasons" developed in Avakian's paper is the height of irresponsibility. In particular at this time where the class struggle between the bourgeoisie in China [sic] is very sharp, to say all the leaders represent opposite poles of the same stupidity is traitorous. (2) That the Gang were revolutionaries and should be supported. Since 1974 the Gang pushed an opportunist line, that undermined the unity of the Party, the dictatorship of the proletariat, caused the broad masses to doubt the leadership of the Communist Party, and objectively gave a big opening to the right. The Gang developed into capitalist roaders and pushed a counter-revolutionary line. It was a victory for the proletariat in China and throughout the world when they met their political deaths. (3) That the political thought of the Gang is consistent with and a development of Mao Tsetung Thought, that the Gang of Four was really a gang of five and that the Gang, with whatever errors they had made, fought for and represented the line of Mao as applied to the concrete practice of the Chinese revolution. This is utterly false and ridiculous and flies in the face of the content of the contribution of Mao to the world proletariat. In our own Party Gang of Four thought is being substituted for Mao Tsetung Thought as well as Marxism-Leninism and must be held up—criticized and driven out.

The Gang Was The Bourgeoisie in The Party

The Gang of Four by the time of their fall, had become capitalist roaders, representatives and commanders of bourgeois elements inside the Communist Party and in Chinese society as a whole, deadly enemies of the proletariat. They unleashed tremendous forces for the restoration of capitalism and proved unable to lead the masses in combatting either such forces or other bourgeois enemies. Precisely because they claimed to be the leading members of the proletarian headquarters, while they had become by seeking capitalists on the capitalist road, [sic] leaving the masses of the people without a genuine proletarian headquarters. In a complicated period of class struggle the Gang went their own way once more, stabbing the people in the back all the while struggling to keep the mantle of the left. For these reasons the Gang had put themselves directly and immediately in the path of the revolution with their attempted coup. Their coup, far from the act of proletarian heroism that some would have us take inspiration from, was a direct continuation of their theoretical, political and organizational line as it had developed over several years. Out of desperation not valor, out of the desire to have a grab and not to serve the interest of the people, their coup fortunately had no chance at success but represented the last gasp of a small clique of counter-revolutionary scum.

The Gang were bourgeois elements because, irrespective of their motives (which were piss poor and will be dealt with as well), their line would have put China onto the capitalist road and to the extent they succeeded in implementing it, it would have caused certain civil war and certain capitalist restoration if their ideological and political line held sway. Their line and policies caused splits and factions among the working class that led to disunity and great disruption in the industries. In agriculture their left line led back to private farming and the promotion of degenerates and bad eggs.

The Gang not only unleashed forces for capitalist restoration, they represented and were themselves capitalist roaders. Like the poverty pimps in the U.S. they seized on and rigidified for their own gain and power base positions from the period of the Cultural Revolution, that is in the mass organizations, the trade unions, the women's federation and the people's militia. In the same way they turned many of the socialist new things into positions of patronage and graft. As they became more isolated from the masses of the people, the only forces they could rely on became more and more the bad eggs in society, and who because of their political line the Gang was forced to unite with and promote.

The Gang of Four for sure are not the only bourgeois elements in society, nor will all capitalist roaders take the same "left" in form and right in essence form that they did—as pointed out above, the principal danger in China at this point is from "traditional" Liu Shao-chi style revisionism.

They did not grasp the nature or demands of the whole period of socialism at all. They did not understand or apply Mao's theory of the continuing revolution under the dictatorship of the proletariat or the Marxist-Leninist approach of resolving different contradictions with different methods. Instead, as some veteran cadres became stuck in the stage of the new democratic revolution and were unable to make the leap to socialism, the Gang got stuck in the social relations of upheaval and rebellion which characterized the Cultural Revolution and were unable to advance with the revolution. This became crystal clear during the campaign to criticize Lin Piao and Confucious which got going in early 1974 and in the Study the Theory of the Dictatorship of the Proletariat Campaign the next year. Before looking at these, however, it is necessary to lay out some background on determining key tasks in the period of socialism and on the situation in China as the first of these campaigns began.

A Few Points On The Socialist Period

In the period of socialism at every point and around every question the proletariat and its allies are faced with the emergence of contradictions whose existence reflect the two classes and whose resolution reflects the 2 lines and the 2 roads. In socialism 2 roads present themselves to the working class and its allies. Only one road will lead forward toward the proletariat's final goal; the other, no matter what guise it takes, leads back to exploitation and capitalism.

In the historical period of socialism classes and class struggle exist and as Mao always stressed—class struggle is the key link, everything hinges on it. In socialism the proletariat is constantly battling to strengthen its dictatorship over the old exploiters, restrict the soil from which the bourgeoisie emerges and eliminate the bourgeoisie step by step. The bourgeois elements for their part attempt to undermine the dictatorship of the proletariat, create the ideological and political conditions from which they can enrich themselves, seize control of parts, gain influence in others, usurp party and state leadership and establish their dictatorship and gain control of society.

This class struggle fought out in the period of socialism under the dictatorship of the proletariat is a battle on three general fronts. As Mao puts forward in his criticism of the Soviet textbook, "A thoroughgoing socialist revolution must advance along the 3 fronts of politics, economics and ideology." (Page 48 M.R.)

This is the first point that we must grasp firmly to evaluate the practice and lines of the Gang of Four. How did they grasp the principle that class struggle is the key link, that everything hinges on it and how did they take up the battle against the bourgeoisie on the three fronts: the economic, the ideological and political, i.e. on this front how did they deal with the task of strengthening and consolidating the D of the P.

The second major point that we must grasp to evaluate the line and policy of the Gang is how they analyzed the key task and the relationship between this task and other tasks confronting the proletariat. Lenin in "Immediate Tasks of the Soviet Government" written just before May Day in 1918, had the following to say on this general point:

> "The real interest of the epoch of great leaps lies in the fact that the abundance of fragments of the old, which sometimes accumulate more rapidly than the rudiments (not always immediately discernible) of the new, calls for the ability to discern what is most important in the line or chain of development. History knows moments when the most important thing for the success of the revolution is to heap up as large a quantity of the fragments as possible, i.e., to blow up as many of the old institutions as possible; moments arise when enough has been blown up and the next task is to perform the 'prosaic' (for the petty bourgeois revolutionary, the 'boring') task of cleaning away the fragments; moments arise when the careful nursing of the rudiments of the new system, which are growing amidst the wreckage on a soil which as yet has been badly cleared of rubble, is the most important thing.
>
> "It is not enough to be a revolutionary and an adherent of socialism or a Communist in general. You must be able at each particular moment to find the particular link in the chain which you must grasp with all your might in order to hold the chain and prepare firmly for the transition to the next link . . ." (Lenin, *Collected Works*, V. 27, pp. 273-4)

The point made here, and it is a crucial one, is that in the course of the revolution a concrete analysis must be made to determine the key task, no matter how "boring," and that on the basis of this, the people have to be united to grasp the main task.

Finally, that based on grasping the key task(s) at any particular time and the key link of class struggle, the Party must pay attention to the proper method of work. Mao again in his criticism of the Soviet textbook quotes Lenin in saying:

> "On page 375 is a quotation from Lenin. It is aptly spoken and can be used in defense of our work method. Lenin said: 'The level of consciousness of the inhabitants and their attempts to realize this or that kind of program will certainly be reflected in the salient points of stepping onto the road of socialism.' Our putting politics in command was precisely to raise the level of consciousness of the inhabitants and our Great Leap Forward was precisely an attempt to realize this or that kind of program."

The correct method that Mao is stressing here is in taking up any task to pay attention to the ideological and policy tasks. Both reflect and raise questions about the other and both must be grasped in order to move forward correctly. The Gang, however, was the master of not grasping this correct work method. For example, in the period of the 3 directives they separated the primary ideological task of study, the theory of the D of the P, from the policy task of move the national economy forward. As opposed to this the *Tachai the Red Banner* book and the whole experience in Tachai is an example of paying attention to and uniting the ideological and policy tasks. In this way the correct Marxist method is adopted and implemented.

The work of all communists in any struggle must take into consideration the handling of the ideological and policy tasks. This must go on to *develop* the actual struggle against the enemy and in order to *sum* the development of the struggle up. In analyzing the current line struggle in China and in particular the lines and practice of the Gang, the question of how *they* handled these tasks in the course of the work they were responsible for is a key political question.

To sum up there are three fundamental political questions that we must grasp and apply to the line and practice of the Gang in order to make a Marxist-Leninist evaluation.

(1) Class struggle is the key link, everything hinges on it and class struggle and this principle must be grasped in order to fight the bourgeoisie on all three fronts.

(2) At any one time, many tasks present themselves to the proletariat, among these tasks there is one, that is key, that must be identified and grasped to move all the contradictions forward.

(3) That the correct Marxist method is at any time to determine the key ideological and policy tasks so that concrete plans for the taking up of both can be made.

The Situation And The Tasks At The Point Of The Tenth Party Congress, 1973

The Gang of Four proved unable or unwilling to grasp the tasks confronting the Chinese revolution after the fall of the Lin Piao clique. The line and policies they put forward did not represent a socialist road for China, and could only steer it onto the capitalist road.

What *was* the situation in China? What were the tasks? China was just emerging from the furnace of the Great Proletarian

Cultural Revolution (GPCR) a great historic upheaval which had left no part of China untouched. Initiated and led by Mao the GPCR was a struggle from the bottom up aimed at overthrowing the bourgeoisie where it had stolen power, critizing capitalism and the capitalist road and replacing leaders who had degenerated with fresh proletarian revolutionaries. The GPCR was a world historical event for the fight of the working class and the advance in the period of socialism, it was an answer in both theory and practice to the problem raised by the experience of the USSR how to prevent the restoration of capitalism.

The task of the GPCR was to criticize and overthrow those in authority who were on the capitalist road, but this task was not the overall goal of the struggle. Mao in a speech to an Albanian military delegation described it like this: "To struggle against power holders who take the capitalist road is the main task but it is by no means the goal. The goal is to solve the problem of world outlook; it is a question of eradicating the roots of revisionism." Mao in saying this is very consistent with his prior statement on the importance of paying attention to the question of ideological and policy tasks. And based on handling these tasks well the GPCR won victories in mobilizing the broad masses of the people to seize power from the bourgeoisie, to knock out the bourgeois headquarters of Liu Shao-chi and then Lin Piao, and in raising the revolutionary consciousness of the masses, which found expression in a whole range of changes in society.

The Cultural Revolution could not, however, win final victory in its task or fully accomplish its goal. Both will require continuous struggle, including more cultural revolutions, and cannot be achieved until the dawn of communist society. At the same time, as an outburst of intense rebellion, the GPCR could not continue indefinitely without turning into its opposite—anarchy and attacks on the masses—as events like the "100 Days War" at Tsinghua University showed.

To consolidate the gains of the GPCR and to keep the revolution advancing on the socialist road, the stage of intense ideological struggle from the bottom up had to be summed up, the advance consolidated and the whole Party and people united behind the task of making a leap into the new period—the period of the tasks set forward at the 10th Party Congress, the 4th NPC and Mao's three directives. The GPCR was in response to the bourgeoisie jumping out in the period of the Great Leap Forward, a period where economic construction was given stress, the bourgeoisie had been pushed back, and the consciousness of the people raised. The task of socialist construction had not fallen away during the GPCR, but there was a two line struggle over how this construction would go on, on the capitalist or the socialist road. In fact, the GPCR led to a rapid growth of production from 1967 to a tapering off in 1971-72. This leveling off further called for creating conditions for a new leap.

Only under such conditions could in-depth mass political education help the masses scientifically sum up the lessons of the GPCR—and replace such phenomena as the Lin Piao-sponsored substitution of Red Book memorization for political study. Only under such conditions could new things, born in the Cultural Revolution, be developed and tested in practice to determine which were genuinely socialist. Only under such conditions could the well-shaken up and revolutionized Party reassert its role as the leading force in all sections of Chinese life and reestablish its authority among the masses. Only under such conditions could the rate of economic development be stepped up. Only under such conditions could new forms of struggle with capitalist tendencies and with capitalist roaders, be developed out of the summation of the Cultural Revolution. Only under such conditions could China play its role as an organizing center for forces in the world opposed to the two superpowers.

The leadership of the Chinese Communist Party set about to establish such conditions. In the aftermath of the Lin Piao shock, massive transfers of top PLA officers helped weed out Lin's clique and subordinate the Army to the Party. With Mao's approval a great number of cadres who had been knocked down in the Cultural Revolution were liberated, in most cases after having made self-criticisms for real errors, to strengthen the Party and state apparatus. Among them was Teng Hsiao-ping. This large social force and the fact that Lin Piao's crimes tended to cast a shadow on the Cultural Revolution with which he had closely associated himself, meant that the danger of right deviations was very real.

But at the 10th Party Congress, held in August of 1973, the Party leadership made it clear that they felt the situation did not call for a revival of the Cultural Revolution. The Congress was designed as a transition out of the period of the Cultural Revolution. Chou En-lai gave the main report to the Congress. He showed the leadership had not forgotten the danger of capitalist restoration, calling on the delegates and the Party as a whole to "continue to do a good job of criticizing Lin Piao and rectifying the style of work," to study Marxism-Leninism and to "pay attention to the revolution in the superstructure," emphasizing the importance of differentiating between antagonistic and non-antagonistic contradictions.

He also pointed to two other main tasks in his speech, both of which addressed the question of the country entering a period of greater stability—not reverting to the status quo before the Cultural Revolution, but consolidating forward out of it. One dealt with the need to strengthen both the Party's leadership in all sectors of Chinese society and its training of revolutionary successors. Chou also called for building up the economy, saying "ours is still a poor and developing country."

Taken together, the tasks which Chou En-lai laid out in his speech, studying Marxism-Leninism and combatting revisionism, strengthening the Party's leading role and developing the economy, made up a program. In it are summarized the view of the Chinese leadership of the situation and the direction in which they intended to move.

The Lin Piao-Confucius Campaign Begins

The Lin Piao-Confucius Campaign started in the fall of 1973 and became a national study campaign by January of 1974. The campaign took Lin Piao's advocacy of Confucian ideas like the theory of "genius" and "restoring the rites," restoring the old society as a starting point. Based on this, the campaign was developed to lay bare the ideological roots of Lin Piao's treachery and to hit at feudal, capitalistic and revisionist outlooks with the goal of arming the masses against future attempts at restoration. As such it was a timely blow to hinder a rightist wind from blowing up as has been pointed out above.

In preparing to lead the Party forward in these tasks, Mao assigned a key role in the proletarian headquarters to the Gang of Four. For example, Wang Hung-wen was elevated to the position of second Vice Chairman and when the Gang started a new theoretical journal, *Study and Criticism* in Shanghai, it bore its title in Mao's distinctive calligraphy.

But with the beginning of the campaign the back stabbing began: the Gang straight away betrayed Mao's trust and the interest of the working class. In the campaign the Gang used their control of the media to distort the campaign in three big ways: (1) they separated the campaign from the other tasks set out in the 10th Party Congress, (2) they added "going in the back door" to the targets of the campaign to aim the arrow down at the people and (3) they used the campaign to attempt to launch a new or the same Cultural Revolution. In doing this they set up a pattern that would flow through all their "work": that is, in each campaign the Gang would become increasingly more isolated from the masses of the people and Mao Tsetung and the forces on the right would grow.

Although the 10th Party Congress documents and the campaign to criticize Lin Piao and Confucius were supposed to be studied together and the tasks set forward taken up as fronts in the class struggle, the Gang separated the Lin Piao campaign off from the other tasks. As will be pointed out later Wang Hung-wen criticized himself for separating these tasks off in the campaign, but a look at any of the Gang material in this period clearly shows how the Gang downplayed the task of the 10th Party Congress and blew up their distorted view of the content of the campaign.

In late January the Gang tried to tack a third target (in addition to Lin and Confucius) on to the campaign, that is "going in the back door." The actual practice of "going in the back door" is a widespread system of exchange among the people based on past favors or friendship. It refers to a whole host of transactions, from getting scarce goods, more food, admitted to a good hospital, auto transport, or school admission or even military posts. By attacking the practice of the "back door" the Gang argued by analogy at Chou's (and Mao's) policy of bringing back cadre who had gone down in the GPCR and who had been liberated, and at the same time they raised a real contradiction in the socialist society "the back door" which is non-antagonistic on a par with the Lin Piao contradiction which is certainly antagonistic. When Mao read a report on this, he was furious and wrote on it, "Metaphysics, one-sidedness, is rampant. To bring in criticism of going by the back door during the movement to criticize Lin Piao and Confucius would weaken the movement to criticize Lin Piao and Confucius." (Chang-fa No. 24, 1976 in *Issues and Studies* Sept. 1977, pp. 89-91).

But the Gang didn't mend their ways. They dropped "going in the back door" but raised the same point by criticizing Confucius' wish to "*call to office those who have fallen into obscurity.*" Again through the use of historical analogy they shifted their emphasis more and more toward a campaign of slander with Chou En-lai as the main target (in the form of Confucius, the "duke of Chou" and a whole array of villainous prime ministers). Despite the obvious fact that this was not Mao's line the Gang even went further to continue to attack in a one sided way the bringing back of liberated cadres.

The Gang criticized Lin and Confucius for wishing to "call to office those who have fallen into obscurity," whether Lin made this error is doubtful, but even if he did, the target of attack was not Lin but Chou (and Mao) for bringing back many liberated cadre.

They did great damage to an important ideological and political campaign among the masses—and why? Because they used it to put forward their arrogant left-idealist line: our faction, though a minority, has better, more historically advanced ideas. The majority of Party leaders, led by Chou En-lai, want to restore capitalism. The masses can be saved from the threat of restoration, only if *we* are Mao's (the Emperor's) successors.

The Bid For A New Cultural Revolution

Along with the line they were putting out in the Criticize Lin Piao-Criticize Confucius campaign, the Gang had a plan of action. It, too, became clear fairly quickly. The erroneous and short-lived "going by the back door" slogan was initiated at two quickly called mass rallies in Peking. Newspaper articles began featuring slogans the Red Guards had popularized, like "without destruction, there can be no construction." There was a wave of attacks on Western music, denouncing those who brought it to China as "class enemies." An article written under Chiang Ching's guidance and published under the name Chu Lan explicitly compared itself with "On the New Historical Play 'Hai Jui Dismissed from Office' " article by Yao Wen Yuan, which triggered the Cultural Revolution (*Peking Review*, #11, 1974). As the Gang's Lin Piao and Confucius articles increasingly targeted Chou, daily newspapers under Gang control like *Renmin Ribao* escalated to calls for "revolutionary violence," "revolutionary rebellion," and "attacking reactionaries." Wall posters appeared in Peking attacking Party leaders like Hua Kuo-feng and Wu Teh, for "repressing rebels."

Although the masses did not rally to this orchestrated effort to kick off a new cultural revolution, grasping that it was not in their interests, factional "fighting teams" were formed around the Gang's line and a wave of factional battles broke out in hundreds of factories throughout the country. This caused the disruption of production not only in plants immediately effected, but by a ripple effect, in those they supplied and so on. Compounded by troubles on the railroads, the disruption in China's industry was greater than it had been since the late '60s.

Two points must be made about this attempt by the Gang to whip up a new cultural revolution. First, it flowed out of a very wrong analysis of the situation. No evidence exists that Chou En-lai was bent on restoring capitalism in China and plenty does that the thrust of the tasks laid out at the 10th Party Congress was one which would move the revolution ahead on the socialist road.

Second, it showed the Gang's thoroughgoing idealism—they did not consider either whether the material conditions for such an upheaval existed or what its results would be in the real world.

Speaking at the height of the Cultural Revolution, Mao said that "Ghosts and monsters will jump out every 7 or 8 years." Yet in the same period he said "We can have Cultural Revolutions only three times a century . . ." The important point here is not the particular time estimates, but the implication that every time bourgeois forces jump out under socialism, it won't be possible or correct to have a full blown cultural revolution. They must be knocked down, and different forms have to be developed to deal with the situation, whether it be purge, education movement, rectification campaign or some new form. But the Gang is ready to have ten consecutive cultural revolutions (or one long continuous one), regardless of the effects on the masses of people and on the maintenance of the proletarian dictatorship itself.

The effects of the line and practice of the Gang were the exact opposite of what the Lin Piao and Confucius campaign were aimed to bring about. The tasks laid out at the 10th Party Congress were not only purposefully ignored by the Gang, but sabotaged. The study campaign itself was metaphysically separated from other tasks, and it distorted both history and the criticism of Lin Piao to push an erroneous line. Instead of strengthening the Party, it promoted factionalism and disunity in the Party and society as a whole, instead of developing the economy seriously undermined it.

The Gang was not, however, able to run this line out unchallenged. There was sharp class struggle within the Criticize Lin Piao-Criticize Confucius campaign. The Party center also put articles in the press, taking particular advantage of holidays like May Day, articles which upheld the original line and aims of the campaign, linking it with study of the 10th Congress and stressing the 3 do's and the 3 don'ts, a theme which seldom appeared in the articles the Gang was responsible for. In many areas where the correct line won out and the campaign was taken up in a correct way, it did deepen political understanding among the masses, mobilize them to defend the fruits of the Cultural Revolution from attacks from the right and make big strides against feudal remnants, like the Confucian line of women's inferiority. It also showed the battle lines that were being drawn in the Party.

This correct trend in the campaign was greatly strengthened after July by a document in the internal bulletin of the Central Committee, *Chang-fa.* This summed up things so far, leveled criticism both at the Gang-promoted anarchy and resistance to the campaign from the right and called for rectification of the campaign. In dealing with problems in production, this document criticizes two calls the Gang would use again and again during the next two years, "rebelling against leadership is going against the tide," and "don't produce for the incorrect line."

The main form the *right* errors took was many leading cadres refusing to take up the campaign and especially to bare their heads to criticism from the masses. Instead cadres even fled their posts and where they stayed would not take up leadership tasks, fearful of criticism. (*Issues and Studies,* January, 1975). Here one further effect of the Gang's incorrect line and practice can be seen—letting the right off the hook. Their distortions of the campaign and raising it to the level of antagonism could only feed hesitancy to take it up and provide excuses for those who really wanted to sabotage it. Hua's later criticism of "soft, lax and lazy" was directed at this kind of problem.

The question of Mao's line on all this has been left until last on purpose. The main thing is to investigate the Gang's line and practice in its own right and see how they stood with relation to the actual situation and tasks of the time. But Mao's views, while not inherently correct just because they're his, certainly warrant our attention and study. And Mao made it very clear where he stood with regard to the Gang of Four.

After Mao's criticism of the Gang's metaphysics, an even sharper development took place. In late February, *Issues and Studies,* in which many of the Gang's articles first saw light of day, was pulled off the newsstands. When it reappeared, it no longer carried the title in Mao's handwriting! There are only two ways to explain this—either Mao disapproved of what the Gang had been doing, or they disapproved of what he had been doing. The next month he made Chiang Ching move out of his house, telling her, "It's better if we don't see each other. You haven't done many of the things I talked to you about over the years. What's the use of seeing each other more often? The works of Marx, Engels, Lenin and Stalin are there, my works are there, but you simply refuse to study." (*Peking Review* #3, 1977, p. 28)

Even these steps did not pull the Gang up short, and at a politburo meeting in July, Mao for the first of many times openly criticized them for acting as a Gang of Four.

Not only Mao's criticisms, but the open manner in which he made them, indicated the depths of his disagreement with the Gang. In the early stages of the Cultural Revolution, a great social upheaval in which the main task was to expose and overthrow Party people in power taking the capitalist road, Mao expressed serious reservations about Lin Piao in a private letter to Chiang Ching. But, he continued, to open fire on Lin and similar forces would destroy the united front needed to smash the capitalist roaders: "At present what I have just said cannot be made public (because) at the moment all the left speaks the same language. If one divulged what I have just written, it is like pouring cold water on them, and thus helping the right wing." (Han Suyin, *Wind in the Tower,* p. 279). In 1974, however, Mao was actively working to pour cold water on the Gang in the Party Center, and in the case of *Study and Criticism,* right out in public.

The Three Directives And The Fourth National People's Congress

With the publication of the 3 directives at the end of 1974, the past practice of the Gang came under attack, on the basis of emphasizing the three general tasks for the period. Again as was the case in the Lin Piao campaign the Gang made the same errors and in practice defined themselves in opposition to the line of Mao and the interests of the people.

The first of the 3 directives which came out in the fall of 1974 was a statement by Mao "to push the national economy forward." In saying this is Mao stressing just that people should work harder at their posts? No, what Mao is saying, and he is being consistent with his line in the 10th Party Congress and the 4th NPC, is that a *leap* in the economy needs to be made. Also this directive was a sharp blow against the Gang-caused severe disruptions in the economy resulting from the factionalism of the Lin Piao and Confucius campaign.

The second directive first appeared around December 14th on wall posters that said: "Eight years have passed since the GPCR started. It is preferable to have stability now. The whole Party and whole army should unite." This call is directly aimed at the Gang for their disruptive and factional activities. Mao clearly does not put stability and unity above the class struggle as the right would have it, but the main thrust of the directive is clear and consistent with the tasks being developed for the general period.

The third directive came right after two significant events. The first and most important was after Mao and Chou had reviewed the preparations and speeches planned for the 4th NPC. Mao spent a sleepless night as the present leadership has told us and came out with the directive on the dictatorship of the proletariat. Mao said: "Why did Lenin speak of exercising dictatorship over the bourgeoisie? It is essential to get this question clear. Lack of clarity on this question will lead to revisionism. This should be made known to the whole nation." Mao then followed this quote with three other points on the same subject. More to come on this campaign a little later.

The thrust of the 3 directives is both clear and consistent with Mao's line for the period and both in ideological and political tasks that face the working class. Despite the ravings of the Gang, the 3 directives uphold what Chou put forward at the 10th Party Congress and raise it to a new level. The three directives represented concrete direction as to how to consolidate the gains of the Cultural Revolution to enable the Party to lead the broad masses down the socialist and not the capitalist road of economic development and modernization of industry and agriculture.

The development of the actual contradictions in the class struggle demanded the resolution of the struggle in the Cultural Revolution over the 2 lines and the 2 classes on the basis of which actual way or road production and economic construction and other tasks would take place on.

Why did Mao say that 8 years have passed, it is preferable to have stability now; the whole Party and the whole army should get united? Was this just a general call for unity or had Mao gone soft in his old age and capitulated over to the bourgeoisie. Neither is the case, the call is a big deal and rather than getting soft Mao in his three directives is preparing the basis for the working class to struggle against the bourgeoisie in new conditions and in the face of new contradictions. Independent of anyone's will the CR had gone on for 8 years and the people want to move forward, to develop a plan for the economy to overcome some of the backwardness of the country. The question at hand is not whether this should be done, the question is what kind of politics are going to be in command.

To separate off the actual task of modernization and economic construction from the class struggle will not end class struggle, but will only insure that the capitalist roaders hold sway and that the proletarian headquarters will be further isolated from the masses. If this continued the three major contradictions would bloom full flower and the basis of the rule of the working class the D of the P would be undermined. This is why Mao held a sleepless night, he recognized that the task of building stability and unity and pushing the national economy forward would unleash the right who would wage class struggle all over the place against the proletariat. At the same time Mao was also worried about the continued factionalism and disruptions in the cities caused by the Gang and their followers. In the face of all this the cardinal political question is the strengthening of the form of its rule of the working class—the D of the P. With the theoretical campaign on the D of the P Mao wanted to draw the attention of the masses to just this question.

Mao, as some would have us believe, put forward the D of the P campaign because this is where the sharp class struggle would be found, as opposed to the carrying out of the other directives. This is nonsense, no one will deny that there will be sharp struggle in this campaign, but when Mao says that class struggle is the key link, everything hinges on it, he means *everything*, every question in every front of struggle against the bourgeoisie. The D of the P campaign would be an important arena of class struggle, but so would the implementation of the other directives.

Although the Gang was to leap on Mao's new quotations about the dictatorship of the proletariat, it is evident that they are aimed at the Gang as well as the right. "Lack of clarity on this question will lead to revisionism," points exactly to the dangers inherent in the Gang's line and activities, as the previous year had shown. (For that matter, the emphasis on the need to read Marxist-Leninist works surely included Chiang Ching—as Mao had pointed out in March.)

1975 began auspiciously with the 4th National People's Congress, attended mainly by delegates who had not been at the 3rd in 1964. Many had come forward in the Cultural Revolution and many were liberated cadres. As at the 10th Party Congress, Chou En-lai made the main report, on the work of the government. He summed up the favorable developments on the national [sic] and since the previous People's Congress, he laid out a number of tasks. First he put forward the class struggle on the ideological front, calling for deepening the movement to criticize Lin Piao and Confucius and the cadre and masses to study and "arm themselves with the basic theories of Marxism." Calls followed for strengthening the revolutionary committees, distinguishing between contradictions among the people and with the enemy and strengthen the great unity of the masses of people. The task of developing the national economy was laid out in somewhat more detail than the others: "The first stage is to build an independent and relatively comprehensive industrial economy in 15 years, that is, before 1980; the second stage is to accomplish the comprehensive modernization of agriculture, industry, national defense and science and technology before the end of the century, so that our national economy will be advancing in the front ranks of the world." Chou then talked about the political principles which guide the development of the economy and stressed the importance of revolution in the superstructure and paying attention to class struggle "while tackling economic tasks." He closed this point with a call for a basic policy of self-reliance, "while making external assistance subsidiary," quoting Mao.

The 4th National Peole's Congress, like the directives from Mao, which preceded it, laid out a path for the Chinese Revolution in the period to come. The fact that both called for unity, stability and particular attention to be paid to economic development did not negate the class struggle. These tasks were necessary for the strengthening of the dictatorship of the proletariat and, as Chou implied, were the terms around which two roads would present themselves and the two line struggle break out. The ideological and political tasks of arming the masses to struggle against revisionism and restoration were also necessary and aimed at making sure the proletarian line won and the socialist road was followed as the different tasks were implemented.

The Campaign to Study the Dictatorship of the Proletariat

A month after the 4th NPC, the campaign to study the theory of the Dictatorship of the Proletariat began. This was to be taken up in connection with the study of the documents from the National People's Congress. This campaign marked a qualitative step in the Gang's degeneration into a roadblock in the socialist road of China's development. Their basic approach to the Criticize Lin Piao and Confucius campaign was repeated—the same stand, the same line, the same method, even if altered somewhat to fit the situation. If it could be considered a serious error, perhaps of overenthusiasm or ignorance, the year before, now it moved toward becoming an antagonistic contradiction.

In response to criticism by Mao and other Party leaders directed at the incorrect approach around criticizing Lin Piao and Confucius, Wang Hung-wen had written a self-criticism the previous year which said in part, "In the early stages of the movement to criticize Lin Piao and Confucius, I divided the criticism of Lin Piao and Confucius with the implementation of policies decided at the Tenth Congress," (*Chang-fa* #24, 1976, in *Issues and Studies*, Sept. 1977, p. 92). But the first thing the Gang did in this new campaign was to try and split it off from the study of the documents of the 4th NPC! In fact, here was a general effort to black the NPC out of the media altogether. *Peking Review,* for example, ran an article greeting the event, and four short pieces in #5, then silence for months.

Once again the study of theory was separated metaphysically from the other tasks of the Chinese Revolution. In practice it was upheld as the *real* form of class struggle and, therefore, as the only real task of the moment, completely negating the others—and dialectics. Where were the articles showing how at certain periods, including the immediate one, stability and unity are necessary for strengthening the dictatorship of the proletariat and, far from requiring writing off the class struggle, create the best conditions for it? Where were the articles on how the drive to build a modern socialist China would strengthen the proletarian dictatorship and provide both opportunities to restrict right [sic], as small production in the countryside fell for example, and new problems along these lines to be resolved, like the vast numbers of new skilled technicians China will need before the end of the century?

What the Chinese people got instead were more distortions, as the Gang looked for handles to push their line. The same thing they were doing to historical materialism around Confucianism and Legalism, their articles in this new campaign did to Marxist-Leninist theory and classics. The method was to select quotes, often out of context, and articles, and write "explanations" of them, twisted to reinforce the Gang's positions. In particular, they would metaphysically separate one point or one aspect from an article, reducing dialectics, the motion of the unity and struggle of opposites, to their own static metaphysics. Comrades should contrast their article on "studying Lenin's *A Great Beginning*" with the original work, which deals with many important questions on building socialism and communism. In it Lenin dealt with such questions as nurturing "shoots of communism" in the precise context of the situation and tasks of the Russian Revolution. But the Gang's piece, one of their better ones, at that, omits Lenin's emphasis on the importance of raising labor productivity in building communism; omits his call for trying hundreds of new methods to vanquish the remnants of capitalism and his criterion for determining real communist shoots from false ones—results in practice; and omits his call for fewer pompous phases and more plain, everyday hard work on behalf of society as a whole. It's not surprising they didn't like this last point, since it could have been easily updated to "less Gang and more Tachai and Taching."

In March and April, Yao Wen-yuan and Chang Chun-chiao published their articles "On the Social Basis of the Lin Piao Anti-Party Clique" and "On Exercising All-Round Dictatorship Over the Bourgeoisie." The publication and wide distribution of these signed pieces was aimed at establishing the Gang as the theoreticians and leaders of the campaign. In keeping with their clique's general thrust, the questions of promoting stability and unity and developing the national economy are ignored, as if they have no relationship to the dictatorship of the proletariat or were not tasks of the moment. (Chang Chun-chiao does tip his hat—once—to the need "to build China into a modern socialist country by the end of the century.")

Although these are major theoretical works on the question of the bourgeoisie in the Party, neither mentions the scientific summation made by Mao in the Cultural Revolution that the main enemy is Party persons in power taking the capitalist road. Yet it is precisely this formulation that best describes the commanders of the bourgeois elements inside and outside the Party and enables the masses to identify and struggle against them and to deliver their blows with both force and accuracy.

Yao Wen-yuan also sounded the theme that, "At present, the main danger is empiricism," a Mao quote from the 1959 struggle against Pen Teh-huai. This phrase became a catchword for attacks on veteran cadres, including Chou En-lai, who were said to raise their long experience (in making revolution) to oppose Marxist-Leninist theory. Chiang Ching and Chang Chun-chiao also began pushing the danger of empiricism in speeches and articles. Like the "going by the back door" business the year before, this drew an angry response from Mao. On April 23, he refused to approve a New China News Agency (NCNA) report calling for opposition to empiricism, directing, "It seems the formulation should be oppose revisionism which includes empiricism and dogmatism. Both revise Marxism-Leninism. Don't just mention the one while omitting the other . . . Not many people in our Party really know Marxism-Leninism. Some think they know, but in fact know very little about it. They consider themselves always in the right and are ready at all times to lecture others." This blast was first and foremost a comment on the situation in China—contrary to the

Gang's line, the right danger, represented by empiricism, was not so overwhelming as to justify making it the exclusive target at this point. It also pointed out that the Gang's theoretical pretenses were shallow and self-serving. Further, Mao commented "Those who criticize empiricism are themselves empiricists." This was certainly true of the way the Gang regarded their experience in the Cultural Revolution as universally applicable in the different conditions prevailing at the time. This time the Gang did not even go through the motions of self-criticism. To the contrary, when the head of NCNA wanted to spread Mao's instruction on the rejected article inside the agency, Yao Wen-yuan ordered him to keep it to himself!

The Gang also took up in this period the difficult question of restricting bourgeois right in socialist society. In many ways they treated the concept as a portable spearhead which could be aimed at first one, then another section of the masses to condemn them as hotbeds of restoration: "red experts" (Chang Chun-chiao's article), peasants (numerous articles on spontaneous capitalist tendencies in the countryside), highly paid and skilled workers ("Worker Aristocrats Are Termites Inside the Workers Movement"). This last may have been aimed particularly at Taching, where pay rates are well above the Chinese average, although this point has never been emphasized by Mao or the Party in calling for Learning from Taching in Industry. Overall, after being forced to tone down "empiricism as the main danger," the Gang was never able to focus their efforts within the campaign until the right deviationist wind blew up late in the year.

The movement to study the dictatorship of the proletariat deepened and consolidated the erroneous tendencies displayed the year before. The Gang's line was idealist in the extreme—it separated the studying of theory from society as a whole and dealt with it primarily as an ideological question. This is contrary to taking the class struggle as the key link and to the Marxist-Leninist understanding that "a thoroughgoing socialist revolution must advance along the three fronts of politics, economics and ideology." (Mao Tsetung, *A Critique of Soviet Economics,* Monthly Review, p. 48) The emphasis on this task and the attempted burial of others which dealt primarily with the political or economic fronts meant that this idealist approach to study also became, by default, the main political (and economic) task the Gang was putting forward openly. There was still, however another task the Gang saw although their articles only hinted at it, particularly the continuing Legalist and Confucius articles. This was the overthrow of any Party leaders, first of all Chou En-lai, who stood between them and their goal—control of the commanding heights of the Party and then of Chinese society as a whole. This view that they and only they could keep the Chinese Revolution red, by force of their superior ideas, was consistent with their overall idealism, although it also represented the most despicable form of careerism.

Hang Chow

Once again, the Gang's line had a sharp reflection in practice which made it easier to judge. Although disruptions were not as widespread as they had been in 1974, in some places the situation had deteriorated. Most serious of all was Chekiang Province and its capital Hangchow. The lives of many hundreds of workers had been lost in faction fighting there. Production had collapsed in many plants due to fighting, strikes and absenteeism, and the national rail transport system, of which Chekiang is an important hub, had been severely disrupted. Behind the fighting and much of the rest of the trouble was a close sidekick of Wang Hung-wen named Weng Sen-ho. An activist in the Cultural Revolution, Weng was vice-chairman of the Chekiang track unions and a member of the standing committee of the Province's revolutionary committee, but only an alternate on the Provincial Party Committee.

Weng ran out the Gang's line without most of their refinements and cover, saying for example, that criticizing Lin Piao and Confucius was "flogging dead tigers" and "not worthwhile" and that the point was to attack a "living tiger," namely Chou En-lai. The factional set-up he established indicates something about the social base the Gang was trying to cultivate. He drew in Party members who were cadres in non-Party organizations, the trade unionism, women's associations, revolutionary committees, and so on, and by pitting these organizations against the Party committees enhanced their importance and power. Promotions and official posts were used to reward and consolidate his followers. He appealed to young people by playing on their revolutionary spirit and desire to change the world with slogans like "going against the tide," and he established a factional armed force, a "militia headquarters," and made sure its core was tough lumpen elements who would do his bidding.

Weng Sen-ho followed the policy, which the Gang would use even more extensively in 1976, of creating large scale disruption as a basis for extending control and seizing power. With the militia as enforcers he set out to paralyze Party committees, which strengthened the position of mass organizations under his influence. In the plants he used dual tactics to disrupt production. Economism was stirred up and wage demands aimed at the local Party Committee. At the same time, workers who rejected this and the factional fighting and continued to work were criticized for holding the theory of productive forces and denounced as belonging to Command 8315—work 8 hours a day, eat 3 meals a day and get paid on the 15th.

Over the first half of 1975, discussion of the Party Center returned repeatedly to the worsening situation in Chekiang. The Politburo heard reports on the Hangchow situation from Ten Chi-lung, the province's first Party secretary, Teng Hsiao-ping, Wang Hung-wen and Chi Ten-kuei. Chi's case is particularly interesting. Previously he had tended to line up with the Gang on a number of issues, but his investigation of Hangchow as early as January 1975 led him to blame the Gang's line and followers for the situation. It took the Party Center some time to even begin to restore order. In the spring, after a personal investigation visit to Hangchow, Mao condemned Wen and said he should not be allowed on any three in one organ. In June, the head of the militia, the head of the Hangchow Revolutionary Committee, and a military commander were purged and an entire division of the First Army sent in from outside. In July, the Central Committee and the State Council issued a resolution which supported the provincial Party leadership, demanded the dissolution of all factions and demanded a big list of crimes committed by counter-revolutionaries "who plot to seize the leadership power." Even these steps only stabilized the situation in Hangchow somewhat and the Gang continued their interference until they fell. At the Hangchow Iron and Steel Works, for example, output for 1974, 1975 and 1976 combined was lower than what had been in '73 alone.

The Gang Gets Rescued By the Wind—Temporarily

The Gang's line was in contradiction with the line of Mao Tsetung and the Party Center, was in contradiction with the course of action the objective situation required. Because they persisted in their errors, they were weakening the Party, undermining the dictatorship of the proletariat and causing havoc. The Gang was increasingly isolated from the masses of people to whom they had nothing to offer but exhortations to study their articles, one-sided praise for everything related to the Cultural Revolution, severely limited cultural fare and evident contempt for people's desire for a better life. The Gang was increasingly isolated from the rest of the leadership of the Party. Even other "leftists" and those who had come forward in the Cultural Revolution could not unite with their incorrect line and destructive practice. Nor could they go along with the Gang in essentially giving over the very important questions of stability and unity and developing the national economy to the right which would pose as sole upholders of these goals among the masses.

Criticism of the Gang in the Center had become general and intense. On May 3, Mao stepped up the attack at a Politboro meeting. He named all those present against factionalism, [sic] repeating again the three do's and don'ts, "Practice Marxism and not revisionism, unite and don't split, be open and above-board and don't intrigue and conspire." Then he turned his attention specifically to the Gang: "Don't function as a Gang of Four. Don't do it anymore. Why do you keep doing it? Why don't you unite with the more than 200 members of the Party Central Committee? It is no good to keep a small circle of a few. It has always been no good to do so." Once again this is not just a case of Mao chiding the Gang for sectarianism or inept tactics. It is a political criticism which indicates that the Gang lacks clarity on the need for proletarian dictatorship. Mao has always followed the policy of maintaining a united front inside the Party as well as in society as a whole—uniting the maximum possible forces to tackle the main task and oppose the main enemy at any given point. Had Mao not always been willing and able to unite with people who disagreed with him or did not have his grasp of the situation, he never would have been able to lead the revolution through the twists and turns that faced it. The approach of the Gang he was criticizing was exactly the opposite—refusing to mobilize all positive factors for struggle. Calling on them to unite with the more than 200 CC members was a basic criticism of the Gang's line that the commanding heights of Chinese society were in the hands of the class enemy.

After this meeting Mao opened up the Gang to general criticism by the Politburo, various forces took this up in various ways. Among them were Mao himself. During the summer he called for a major adjustment to be made on the cultural front, criticizing the fascist constraints Chiang Ching had kept on her area of work. In particular he defended the film *Pioneers,* about the building of the Taching oil fields, from her unprincipled censorship. (See Hua's report to the 11th Party Congress). Wang Tung-hsing, for instance, speaking to high level cadres at a conference in Canton, raked the Gang's line, strategy, and tactics over the coals as revisionist. Among the charges he made were trying to establish a second center and putting forward the theory of political parties alternating in power (promoting the mass organizations over the Party), confusing contradictions among the people and with the enemy, promoting anarchism, and practicing capitualism [sic] to class enemies at home and abroad.

The criticism of the Gang was led and spearheaded, however, by Teng Hsiao-ping, who was by this time the leading active figure on the Politburo. This set up the stage for developments at the end of 1975 and in early 1976, when contradictions sharpened up and opportunists began jumping out left and right. At the same time in the course of this class struggle, the road forward for the Chinese Revolution became clearer and a new leadership core began to develop with Hua Kuo-fung at the core.

When Teng moved to take on the Gang of Four, he wound up giving himself a new lease on life. Unlike the Gang, Teng recognized the importance of the tasks of promoting stability and unity and developing the national economy, and saw them and their line as the main obstacle to doing so. He was ready to engage in class struggle against the Gang, but in doing so showed that he downplayed the importance of class struggle in socialist society as a whole. This came out most clearly in "On the General Program of Work for the Whole Party and the Whole Nation," completed under Teng's personal direction in October. This was a big broadside against the Gang, who are compared to Lin Piao and accused them of waving the red flag to oppose the red flag, and promoting bourgeois factionalism. "Rebellion" and "going against the tide," must be subjected to class analysis—who is rebelling against whom, what tide is being resisted, and deeds not words must be the main criteria in judging people. There is a lengthy criticism of the practice of counterposing revolution to production and labelling economic construction the "theory of productive forces." The "General Program" focused sharply on a number of the ways in which the Gang was hampering the development of the Chinese revolution.

On the other hand, it is in no way a correct, or adequate General Program which could be used to guide the work of the CP and the Chinese people over the next 25 years *and* it contained serious errors of principle, revisionist errors. The most important of these is the tendency to negate the class struggle which was symbolized by the formulation "Take the 3 directives as the key link." The document basically takes the position that the only danger of capitalist restoration will come from those who are "left in form, right in essence," and conspiratorial like the Gang and from capitalist roaders of the Liu Shao-chi type. The question of studying the dictatorship of the proletariat was not dealt with as a campaign to increase the consciousness of the masses and address the problems of building socialism and keeping China red but merely as an excuse to wail on the Gang. The "General Program" lacked clarity on the need for the dictatorship of the proletariat. Therefore, it treated the tasks of stability and unity and developing the economy basically as goals in themselves not as necessary tasks for strengthening the proletarian dictatorship and advancing toward communism. This, too, leaves the door wide open for revisionism.

Teng's activities were not limited to the drawing up of anti-Gang documents. He set up to resolve serious problems which were impediments to carrying out the program for modernization laid out at the 4th National Party Congress. His approach to the problems, however, reflected the same outlook as the "General Program." In taking up shortcomings in fields like science and technology or education, his concern was primarily that things function better than they had been, without concern for questions like remolding the outlook of intellectuals and avoiding the reproduction of bourgeois social relations (see, for example, Teng's comments on science, reprinted at the end of Chi Hsin, *The Case of the Gang of Four*).

Thus Teng, in his attack on the Gang finally succeeded in bringing their political line into sync with the real world. He had stirred up a right deviationist wind, which posed a danger of capitalist restoration and had to be opposed. Talk about opposite poles of the same stupidity! The Gang and Teng each pointed to the other as the justification for their line!

Chairman Mao became extremely concerned at Teng's failure to uphold the Marxist-Leninist line. He criticized the line of the General Program in the famous remark, "What! Take the three directives as the key link? Stability and unity do not mean writing off class struggle. Class struggle is the key link and everything else hinges on it." He also criticized Teng for failing to grasp class struggle and retaining his "black cat, white cat" pragmatism and posing the danger of restoration. In summing up he said, "With the socialist revolution, they themselves come under fire. At the time of the cooperative transformation of agriculture there were people in the Party who opposed it, and when it comes to criticizing bourgeois right they resent it. You are making the socialist revolution and yet don't know where the bourgeoisie is. It is right in the Communist Party—those in power taking the capitalist road." There was no question that Mao was calling for struggle against Teng and the right deviationist wind. In this struggle, which developed in 1976, the Gang once again proved incapable of leading China down the socialist road and new forces came forward which did have that ability.

THE ROAD AHEAD FOR CHINA

Hua Kuo-feng Comes To The Fore

Even as the right deviationist winds were warming up, the first major practical step toward implementing the 4th NPC was being carried out. This was the National Conference on Learning from Tachai in Agriculture, held in September and October, led by Hua Kuo-feng. Hua was a member of a new generation of leaders who had come forward during the period of the socialist revolution (although his Party work began in 1946). He rendered valuable services to the Revolution at key points in its development. As a local cadre in Hunan, he not only pushed forward agricultural communization and the Great Leap Forward, but provided Mao with important summations of this for use in the struggle against Peng Teh-huai's revisionist line. During the Great Proletarian Cultural Revolution he played a leading role in the province and his report on the successful struggle against one of the best organized "ultra left" rebel groups, Sheng Wei Hieu (PL's favorite) was distributed nationally. He was called to Peking to take much of the responsibility for investigating the case of Lin Piao and brought into national leadership by Chairman Mao, who knew him from when he had responsiblity for Shaoshan, Mao's Hunan birthplace. Hua was elected a member of the Politburo at the 10th Party Congress and after the 4th NPC served as Vice-Premier and in the key post of Minister of Security.

The Tachai Conference, which lasted a month, set forward a revolutionary plan for the transformation of Chinese agriculture. As laid out by Hua Kuo-feng in his speech in summation, the major call of the conference was to transform, in several waves, all the rural counties of China into Tachai type counties, characterized by good Party leadership, class struggle, to stay on the socialist road, and all around economic development. In this context, the goal of the basic mechanization of agriculture by 1980 was put forward.

The movement to build Tachai type counties on this basis would weaken the force of small production, develop and show the superiority of more public forms of ownership like the people's communes and narrow the three great differences. At this conference, the Gang's line also had a representative. Chiang Ching called Hua's report "revisionist," and made her own speech. From what we can tell she didn't mention the question of agricultural development and mechanization but dealt largely with her own and incorrect interpretation of the novel, *Water Margin*.

Mao's response to the conference was very clear. He immediately approved Hua's report for distribution, dismissed Chiang Ching's speech as "wide of the mark" and forbade its circulation in any form. Despite the Gang's employment of their typical media blackout tactics, the movement to implement the conference decision began to be implemented across the country, with Party workteams totalling 1.6 million people mobilized to go into the rural areas and get things rolling.

The situation took another leap with the death of Chou En-lai on January 6, 1976. Chairman Mao had spent several days and nights with his old comrade on his death bed. Amidst widespread mourning among the masses, Teng Hsiao-ping delivered the Party center's memorial speech and was clearly hoping to drape himself in the mantle of the dead leader, many of whose tasks he had assumed since 1974. The Gang meanwhile treated Chou as an enemy, earning the bitter hatred of the masses. News of the mourning for Chou was perfunctory and on inside pages of the papers, while the lead articles featured the struggle against the right deviations on the educational front.

After his speech, the criticism of Teng on the Politburo increased, and he stopped appearing in public or the media. The Gang cherished hopes of replacing him, but Mao chose Hua Kuo-feng to serve as Acting Premier. When the decision was announced Feburary 3, Chang Chun-chiao bitterly predicted Hua's rapid downfall.

Hua, however, began handling his leading responsibilities well. In late February, Hua delivered a report endorsed by the Politburo and approved by Mao to a leadership meeting (and to which the later famous statement, act in line with past principles referred) and in it called for narrowing the target to Teng to get maximum clarity in the struggle. This was hardly the approach the Gang was taking. Using Mao's remarks on Teng as a jumping off point, they were actively broadening the scope of the struggle, by targeting the bourgeoisie's agents inside the CP, "those bourgeois democrats who were reluctant to go forward and pass the test of socialism," (Chuang Lan, *Study and Criticism,* May 14, 1976, in "The Struggle Against the Revisionist Line"). This simultaneously presented a one-sided picture of where the social base of the capitalist roaders lies, and misdirected fire at a whole layer of veteran Party fighters. It was accompanied again, by the call for the Cultural Revolution (see the same article), which was not the line of Mao or the Party Center. The Gang even disagreed with Mao over how Teng's case should be treated, with Chiang Ching complaining to a meeting she was called[sic] to run the Gang's line, "In China there is an international capitalist agent named Teng Hsiao-ping. It might be correct to call him a traitor. Nevertheless, our Chairman has been protecting him. What I have said is my personal opinion." (Chang-fa #24, 1976, *Issues and Studies*, Oct. 1977, p. 92)

The Tien An Men incident in April is a nodal point in the development of the class struggle. The masses took advantage of the spring festival to honor Chou En-lai and protest the suppression of his memory. Counter-revolutionaries also took advantage of the situation, as the anti Mao poem "To hell with Chin Hsi-huai" publicized at the time showed. But the method of dealing with the situation, the removal of all the memorial wreaths, was sure to provoke an antagonistic response among sections of the people. It did and a protest flared up and was suppressed.

The incident showed that for many people, Teng had, in fact, inherited Chou's mantle. The Gang had only reinforced this by their backhanded attacks on Chou in similar terms to the criticisms of Teng. Likewise, by publishing and denouncing the poisonous weeds without seriously acknowledging the importance of the tasks of promoting stability and unity and developing the national economy, they deserted the banner of "concern for the well-being of the masses" in the hands of Teng, further tightening his identification with Chou who had been famous for his concern for the masses.

Because of this, the incident forced quick action on the question of Teng so the campaign against the right deviationist wind would not be turned into its opposite. The Politburo met and removed Teng from all his positions and announced that the contradiction with him had become antagonistic. There was clearly line struggle over this point as the statement also said that Teng would retain his Party membership while people saw how he acted. (Where Mao stood in this discussion is unclear, the only evidence, besides his opposition to Teng during the GPCR, is the fact that as soon as he died Chiang Ching put forward at a meeting of the center he demanded that Teng be expelled.)

Mao's stand on another question is not in doubt and that is the matter of succession. After Teng was removed from his posts, the Gang was passed over. Hua Kuo-feng was confirmed as Premier and First Vice Chairman of the CCP. Mao seconded this on April meeting with Hua [sic] and writing him out three messages "Take your time, do not be anxious," "Act according to past principles," and "With you in charge, I am at ease." This was a most important vote of confidence in Hua and those he was working with closely in the center, like Yeh Chieu-Ying and Wang Tung-Hsing.

Any argument that Mao supported the Gang of Four must explain not only the consistent differences of line and principle between them and Hua over the preceding two years, but his firm rejection of them as potential successors. While Mao did not want to see them broken out of the Party leadership at this point, he could not rely on them to uphold Marxism-Leninism and move China ahead. Instead he chose Hua Kuo-feng. Any theory which suggests some undetailed "necessity," perhaps in the form of threats from military commanders, forced Mao to choose a man he knew or suspected to be a capitalist roader as a successor with his death rapidly approaching, is arguing that Mao had lost either his bearings or his revolutionary will. There is no evidence to suggest either is true.

The Gang Goes For Broke

After this point, the next six months in China were a big political battlefield. The Gang shifted the gears of their dictatorship of the proletariat articles. The main target now was Hua and he could not be attacked as a veteran communist who had gotten stuck at the stage of a new democratic revolution. Instead, the Gang turned out articles like the Kang Li piece, distributed in an earlier bulletin, which argued for the first time, that the bourgeoisie in the Party is primarily made up of "newly engendered bourgeois elements." Their opportunist efforts on the theoretical front were a reflection of the difficult situation in which they found themselves. Isolated, bypassed by history, their hopes of achieving supreme power beginning to vanish, the Gang took the position that, as one of their followers put it in a government forum on planning, "Do genuine Marxists hold the leadership of the state apparatus in their grip? My answer is no." (Chang-fa, #24, 1976, *Issues and Studies,* October 1977, p. 99.) Since Mao was not about to replace these "non-Marxists" with the Gang and their supporters, the Gang decided they would have to go for broke.

During the summer they stirred up factionalism and interfered with production and transport on a scale even broader than in 1974. "Fighting groups" were formed and established networks between cities and provinces. Their idea was to create conditions of turmoil both to discredit the Party leadership and to gain opportunities to establish their supporters in power. Slogans like "Don't produce for the incorrect line" and "Confucians produce, legalists rebel" were circulated. Whole plants turned out working for months at a time[sic] and workers showed up only on pay day.

Hua fought to keep the economy functioning and to keep the criticism of Teng Hsiao-ping on the track. In the midst of this battle, he was confronted with a massive national disaster, the Tangshan earthquake, which killed 600,000 people, destroyed whole industrial centers and forced evacuations of apartment buildings in large cities as distant as Peking. Hua quickly mobilized the whole country to provide relief to the stricken area, and visited it himself to provide leadership and inspiration. The Gang for their part played a most despicable role, saying that people were using "anti-quake and relief work to suppress revolution and brush aside the criticism of Teng Hsiao-ping," and making light of the disaster. They even went so far as to play on superstitions regarding earthquakes the Chinese government had been working for over 26 years to eradicate—with considerable success. *Study and Criticism #9* published in September 14, carried an article which praised a leader of the Taiping Rebellion who said an earthquake was a sign from heaven that his cause would be victorious for his "sparkling revolutionary optimism." The article was entitled "When the Earth Turns, It Actually Signifies the Advent of New Earth!" From distorting history and twisting Marxist theory to peddling feudal mysticism to support their cause—this was the route the Gang had travelled!

Hua Smashes The Gang

The final act in the drama began with the death of Mao Tsetung, Chairman of the Communist Party of China, on September 9, 1976. It is a story which can be told briefly, for the actions of the people involved flow out of their political lines as they had developed over a long period of time.

From the start the Gang moved toward a seizure of power. Among their supporters they prepared opinion for their coup with talk ominously asserting the power of revisionism at the Center, and issued calls to prepare for struggle. To circumvent the Central Committee and its general office, run by Wang Tung-hsin, they sent out orders that all Party organs should report directly to Wang Hung-wen. They acted to get from Chairman Mao when he was dead what he would not give them alive, his official support.

Chiang Ching tried repeatedly to lay claim to the files of Mao's documents and materials to make herself the source of his posthumous writings, but she was stopped by Hua Kuo-feng and Wang Tung-hsin, who forbade anyone to take any of Mao's documents from where they were stored. Even without the documents, the Gang tried to pass themselves off as the executors of Mao's great theoretical heritage, as the true Marxist-Leninists by palming off on the Chinese people a phoney bequest—"Act according to the principles laid down." Publicized throughout the media, this was a distortion of Mao's words to Hua, "Act according to past principles," designed to mystify things and make it appear that there existed some special principles which were not public knowledge at the time. This was the same theme as their lauding of the legalists, over two years before—proclaiming themselves condescending saviours with special knowledge who will look out for the interests of the masses.

Hua, meanwhile, undertook to lead the nation through this most difficult period, working collectively as much as possible with the rest of the Politburo. He refused to be buffaloed by the Gang, either into turning over Mao's files to Chiang Ching or into going along with "Act according to the principles laid down." He timely instructed that this false formulation should not be used.

Hua's competence, decisiveness and grasp of the situation left the Gang no choice. They had to move fast because conditions could only get less favorable for them. On October 4, their writing group, Liang Hsiao, published an article which basically called for rebellion against Hua, proclaiming, "Any revisionist chieftain who dares to alter 'the principles laid down' by Chairman Mao will not come to a good end." Simultaneously with this, they initiated attempts at "power seizures" in a number of localities, armed and mobilized the Shanghai militia and put their followers there and elsewhere on red alert and tried to order military units under their command or influence into the Peking area.

On October 6, based on information about these activities and after consultation with other Party leaders, Hua had the four arrested. Within the next few days he broke up their strongholds like the propaganda centers and the Shanghai Municipal Party leadership, without having to resort to fighting. There was only sporadic attempts at an uprising by the Gang's followers and for the masses of the Chinese people, who had learned to hate the four deeply, from their own experience, there was jubilation.

For Hua Kuo-feng, there remained the job he has been working to tackle ever since: not only undoing the harm done by the Gang, but helping the masses sum up the experience so that their understanding of the class struggle under socialism, and the need for the dictatorship of the proletariat is deepened and their enthusiasm for the tasks ahead is given free rein.

The Current Situation

What has the smashing of the Gang of Four meant for the class struggle in China today? First and foremost, it means the class struggle is still taking place under socialism, which is to say on the working class' turf, with its forces occupying the commanding heights. This would hardly have been the case had the Gang usurped state power and established a bourgeois dictatorship, or, more likely, plunged the country into bloody civil war in their attempt. The continued existence of the dictatorship of the proletariat is the single most important factor determining how the struggle in China is going on now and will take place in the future. At the same time, within this overall favorable situation, the Chinese proletariat today faces certain difficult conditions in the class struggle resulting directly from the degeneration into capitalist roaders and bourgeois elements of the Gang of Four. Again, however, the fall of the Gang has removed a major roadblock to transformation of adverse conditions by the masses and the great majority of Communist Party members and leaders who genuinely want to make revolution. No longer are they being undercut and stabbed in the back at every turn by enemies claiming to be the leading force in the proletarian camp, and the only real upholders of Mao Tsetung Thought and the cultural revolution.

Hua Kuo-feng and the forces close to him, including Chen Yung-kuei, Chen Hsi-lien, Ni Chih-fu, Wang Tung-hsin, Li Teh-sheng, Chi Teng-kuei, and Wu Teh, all leading members of the Party who have long been associated with the "left"—make up and are working to strengthen the proletarian headquarters. They are in a position which requires both unity and struggle with rightist and revisionist forces in the Party leadership. (Nor does everyone in the Party leadership fall either 100% in the proletarian headquarters or 100% set himself against it; this is never the case and it certainly is not at present.) The right is currently very powerful, strengthened in no small degree by the aims of the Gang, as pointed out before. The anarchism and economic disruption they spawned in the name of rebellion, "don't produce for the incorrect line," "going against the tide" and "fighting the theory of productive forces," has spontaneously helped discredit the idea of "class struggle" itself, which they so distorted. Their undialectical and anti-materialist approach to the socialist new things they posed as defenders of, caused some of those things to stagnate and turn into their opposites (more on this later in the paper). And by refusing to uphold the tasks of promoting stability and unity in the country and the Party and pushing the national economy forward, and attacking those who did for revisionism (including Hua Kuo-feng, Chen Yung-kuei, and countless revolutionaries among the Party's ranks, as well as Teng and others with his line), they built the prestige of the right as those who were truly concerned with building socialism and insuring the well being of the masses. Even without the Gang's "help," tasks like those of the present period have always provided certain opportunities for the right to jump out with lines and programs which do negate grasping the class struggle in the name of accomplishing other tasks.

But contrary to the Gang's line, these tasks do not belong to the right. Just like the ideological tasks to which they are tied in the real world by a thousand threads, the political and economic tasks of building socialism belong to the masses of the people and to the genuine Marxist-Leninists who can best accomplish them and who seek to accomplish them precisely in order to strengthen the dictatorship of the proletariat and to move toward communist society. The two models, Tachai in agriculture and Taching in industry, show concretely how such tasks can be tackled in a revolutionary way, how the masses can put politics in command and develop socialist consciousness precisely in the process of carrying out the kind of "prosaic," "boring" tasks Lenin referred to in the quote from *The Immediate Tasks of the Soviet Government* above. In doing so, moreover, they are laying the *material base* for further advances in the social relations and in socialist consciousness by breaking down small production, by cutting away at the three great differences, etc.

In the course of taking up the actual tasks of building socialism, two roads continually present themselves. This is all the more true when the right is strong and "black cat, white cat" pragmatism is an influential tendency, even if it is not necessarily advocated openly. The two roads can be perceived arising around numerous issues in China today. A few examples follow which are mainly taken from such readily available bourgeois publications as the *New York Times, The Weekly Manchester Guardian,* and the *Far Eastern Economic Review.* (All such sources must be taken with a considerable dose of salt, naturally, and confirmation sought from other, including Chinese sources; many are issues over which struggle has taken place many times in the past—although in studying them, it is important to remember that the context of current struggles can't be judged by this alone.) One Chinese publication is reported as carrying articles on the importance of implementing the plan to build Tachai type counties and mechanize agriculture while an editorial in another emphasizes higher immediate productivity on the communes at the expense of side-line industry and farmland capital construction projects. Articles appear referring to the Gang (and Lin Piao) as "left in form, right in essence," while others refer to them exclusively as "ultra-rightist." Some articles and speeches argue for rapid military modernization to prepare for war, while others emphasize this can be accomplished only on the basis of strengthening agriculture and industry as a whole. And so on.

Such struggles over particulars reflect and at the same time come to clarify and deepen the general struggle between two lines. This is going to be more true with the campaign to criticize the Gang of Four now focusing on the theoretical plane. (*PR* #1, 1978, p. 10) Already a sharp conflict can be seen between Hua Kuo-feng's emphasis in his speeches and writings on upholding the class struggle as the principal aspect in the contradiction with the struggle for production under socialism and a number of articles in the Chinese press arguing, in different guises, the opposite (and revisionist) view, that production should, and does, take precedence over class struggle. Note for example, Hua's use at the 11th Party Congress of Mao's quote, "Stability and unity don't mean writing off the class struggle," which is a pointed reference to the 1976 struggle against the right deviationist wind.

An additional point to which the bourgeois media pays a good deal of attention in Kremlinological speculation on leadership, portraying everything as a "power struggle at the top." This is the same approach, it should be remembered, they used in dealing with the Cultural Revolution. Nevertheless, there is a point here. People do hold lines and represent tendencies and developments in the Party and State apparatus—who holds what positions—are important. For instance, the Ministry of Propaganda, which was the

Gang's big stronghold for so long, and Liu Shao-chi before them, is now dominated by the right, although many "compromise" and left articles find their way into print. (See, for instance, the fine material on Taching in Sept. 1977 *China Reconstructs*.) Hua, for his part, has succeeded in placing leftists with whom he has worked in the past in charge of a number of key provincial Party committees, and so on.

Nor is this question limited to one of particular individuals and posts. There are important struggles over policy questions involved. Take liberated cadres—who should be brought back, how fast should they be given major posts, are the criticisms of them raised in the Cultural Revolution correct, or should they be ignored outright? The liberated cadres are not a homogeneous group; although most were overthrown in the struggle against Liu Shao-chi, some fell for ultra-leftism, and some in the battle against Lin Piao. The other side of this is the question of those associated with the Gang of Four. Some of the main leaders attacked in the campaign against the right deviationist wind in 1976 have tended to demand harsh treatment, while Hua, who was himself targeted by the Gang, and others have argued strongly for narrowing the target and not pushing aside any of those taken in by the Gang who can be won by education. It is also clear that for Hua and those around him, while questions of cadre policy and assignment are important, they are not decisive. Their main orientation is toward mobilizing the masses around the proletarian line. This is manifested particularly in their emphasis on the building mass study and action campaigns, like those around learning from Tachai and Taching, which aim at revolutionizing consciousness and practice.

These, then are the outlines of the class struggle in China now—two roads arising continuously as the Party and the masses undertake the tasks before them in every sphere, a powerful right, and increasing line struggle within the united front in the Party's leadership. There will be plenty of setbacks as well as victories as the class struggle develops, and its development will not follow a straight line or be easy to discern. Eventually, a bourgeois headquarters will consolidate around a revisionist line and jump out in opposition to the proletarian headquarters and there will be a new test of strength between the two classes. In every such sharp class struggle—and there will be many more in the long period of building socialism—the danger of restoration becomes very sharp, but every victory by the proletariat creates new conditions which make it that much harder to drag China back down the road to hell.

In evaluating what is happening in China, now and in the future, both the objective situation and the lines being put forward must be taken into consideration. Mao prophetically pointed out that after his death the right would use certain of his words to try and turn China back and the left would use others of his words to combat and overthrow them.

Despite all the damage the Gang did, the masses of the Chinese people still retain their basic enthusiasm for socialism and the great majority of Communist Party members and cadres want to continue the revolution under the dictatorship of the proletariat. The defeat of these opportunists has kept the socialist road open. The Chinese working class and masses have a great deal of experience in waging the class struggle under socialism. They are hard to fool—look how little success the Gang of Four actually had—and whatever the real difficulties which confront them, we are confident they will continue to struggle to grasp the proletarian line and through their practice make it a mighty force for changing the world.

Two Particulars

To provide a deeper understanding of the Gang's counter-revolutionary line and practice and to flesh out the picture of the situation and tasks facing Hua, the Communist Party and the masses of people, the next section of this paper will focus on two particular questions—agricultural mechanization and socialist new things.

These were not chosen at random. Right now millions of Chinese peasants are mobilized in a vast mass campaign to create conditions for and carry out the basic mechanization of agriculture over the next few years. This undertaking will thrust Chinese farming from the general level of U.S. agriculture at the turn of the century to its level in the 1940's. Furthermore, the question of mechanization may appear to be solely one of economic development, but a closer look shows that it is in fact a political question as well, a dividing line as to whether China will continue to advance on the socialist road or not. Socialist new things are an important aspect of the forward motion of socialist society. Many have been the subject of re-evaluation and struggle since the fall of the Gang and this has become the source of glee in the bourgeois media and concern, controversy and opportunist slander among the ranks of communists and other friends of China.

At the same time, these are only two among many subjects

which have to be investigated in depth—bourgeois right, foreign trade, the *Water Margin* campaign and dozens more must be better understood if we are to draw out all the lessons of the class struggle in China and deepen our grasp of Marxism-Leninism, Mao Tsetung Thought. Even the points on agricultural mechanization and socialist new things, like the general analysis that opened this paper, are far from definitive. In each case, however, a concrete and scientific analysis of the information that is available leads irrevocably to the conclusion that the smashing of the Gang was an absolute necessity for the preservation of socialism in China. The deeper the investigation, the clearer this becomes.

Learn From Tachai Or Down With Tachai—2 Different Roads

In the fall of 1975, the Party leadership initiated a National Conference to Learn From Tachai. It marked the beginning of open struggle between Hua and the Gang, with Hua upholding and developing the revolutionary line of Mao against the direct opposition of the Gang.

Hua delivered the major speech at the Tachai Conference, summing up the importance of learning from Tachai in agriculture. His speech is reprinted in a pamphlet, "Let The Whole Party Mobilize For A Vast Effort To Develop Agriculture And Build Tachai-Type Counties Throughout The Country." Comrades should read all three speeches in this pamphlet for a deeper understanding of the struggle in agriculture.

Hua's speech on the learn from Tachai movement upheld Tachai as a red banner on the agricultural front. Hua laid out the task of building Tachai type counties, of carrying out Chairman Mao's revolutionary line in agriculture. He touches on the need for ideological education, the leading role of the Party, combatting the bourgeoisie inside and outside the Party. The speech deals with raising the level of ownership, and the key importance of farmland capital construction and mechanization. Learning from Tachai means learning to walk on two legs down the socialist road, putting proletarian politics in command. Hua lays out the role of leadership bodies on various levels to the movement to learn from Tachai. And he gives 6 criteria for becoming Tachai-type counties, clearly laying out the fighting tasks ahead. These criteria are remarkably similar to those laid out by Mao some 11 years earlier to serve as a yardstick for judging success in the Socialist Education Movement.

The entire conference and Hua's speech upholds and promotes

Tachai as a red banner. This in itself was a victory, a consolidation around a line and a plan to transform society along the socialist road. Because of this, the other two speeches, which concretely laid out the Tachai experience in grasping revolution and promoting production were able to become part of a mass movement. Coming out of the conference was a revolutionary call to action to all the peasants from the Party. It unleashed an enthusiastic response. Within 24 hours of the end of the conference, Mao approved Hua's speech for nationwide distribution. Work teams were set up to go all over China to spur the mass movement. The number of cadres assigned to these work teams was a staggering 1.6 million.

Based on this, the movement to learn from Tachai grew, though not without opponents. The conference took place at a time when the right was beginning to whip up the right deviationist wind to reverse correct verdicts, and they did not support any mass movement to revolutionize the peasantry and mechanize agriculture. And the self proclaimed "left," the Gang, was actively working to sabotage the movement before it could pick up steam.

Hua has remained a champion of the banner of Tachai, continuing with the second Tachai Conference, where Chen Yung-Kuei also gave a major speech which was distributed, and the publication in 1977 of "Tachai The Red Banner" which upholds and deepens the experience of Tachai. Learning from Tachai remains a focal point in the struggle to mobilize the masses around Mao's line and a sharp weapon to oppose the right. (More on the current situation later.)

The unity of the masses around Learning From Tachai is deep. The writers of the two other speeches in the Hua pamphlet are often set against Hua in an effort to deride the movement. Kuo Feng-lien is an ardent supporter and ally of Hua in this battle. Wang Chin-tzu is a provincial secretary in Shansi. Reports of the split among them are only wishful thinking.

Two Line Struggle on Mechanization of Agriculture

The Gang's line on the question of mechanization of agriculture was a counter-revolutionary line. Where it was implemented, it severely weakened socialism and encouraged capitalism. Where it was propagated, it stood directly opposed to the line of Mao which was continued by Hua. It was an actual fetter on the development of China along the socialist road that had to be smashed for that advancement to continue.

Struggles around agriculture and mechanization are key in

China. Over 80% of the people are peasants. Conditions for the peasantry are far poorer than in the cities. All three great differences—mental/manual, town/country, worker/peasant—are centered in great part on this question. And while there have been great advances in China over the past 28 years, the mass of agriculture is still not mechanized, and the peasantry spends the vast majority of its time on basic and difficult production. The worker-peasant alliance is the foundation of proletarian rule in China. Without it, the working class cannot play its leading role in the struggle to consciously transform all of society.

In 1957, Mao spoke on the importance of mechanization. "Gradual implementation of agricultural mechanization . . . can greatly raise labor productivity, progressively solve the problem of linking the development of agriculture with the development of industry, and *progressively consolidate the worker-peasant alliance.*" (emphasis added)

By 1962, Mao said "Our worker-peasant alliance has already passed through two stages. The first was based on the land revolution, the second on the cooperative movement . . . At the present time our worker-peasant alliance has to take the next step and establish itself on the basis of mechanization." And furthermore, "When state ownership and mechanization are integrated we will be able to begin truly to consolidate the worker-peasant alliance, and the differences between workers and peasants will surely be eliminated step by step." (Mao, *A Critique of Soviet Economics*, p. 46, 47.)

Mechanization of agriculture was then a key to developing socialism, not just for the boost in agricultural production, but also for the political rule of the working class, for the development of side line industries and the proportional development of society, for the principle of self reliance, preparedness for war and preparedness for natural disasters.

As early as 1970, Chen Yung-Kwei, the leader of Tachai, spoke of the opposition of the right and the "ultras" to mechanization. The right regarded mechanization as an ordinary measure to save labor and increase production, failing to see the political significance of it to the worker-peasant alliance. And the "ultras" "seem to stress revolutionization, but actually they neither understand revolutionization nor want mechanization." In 1971, Yao Wen-yuan opposed the publication of an article on mechanization of agriculture by a provincial secretary named Hua Kuo-feng.

The struggle over mechanization was of the first importance in China, and reached a high pitch in 1975 that has carried through to today. The conditions were present coming out of the Cultural Revolution for a leap in this area, and the question of which road to take came to the fore.

The Gang Attacks Tachai

The gang did not wait for the conference to attack it. They had already played down the buildup for this historic conference in the media under their control. Once the conference started, they tried to take it over. Chiang Ching spoke at the opening of the conference. She gave the assembled delegates a lecture on the novel *Water Margin*, using the opportunity to attack the conference and by implication Hua. Her media was geared up to give her speech a big spread. *Hsinhua* reported that she made an important speech. But the text did not appear, and the speech was not mentioned after that.

The gang had run up against a very powerful and angry opponent, Mao Tsetung. When he heard about her speech he could not conceal his disgust. "Shit! Wide of the mark." He gave specific instructions—don't print the text, don't play the tapes, don't distribute the speech.

Prevented from playing up Chiang Ching, the gang responded by playing down the conference and movement to learn from Tachai. Reports shrank, and at the conclusion of the conference Hua's speech was buried in the middle of *Renmin Ribao*. *Hsinhua* did write some articles about the conference, but generally they ignored it, and they even started a short series about agriculture without even a mention of the Learn From Tachai movement that was taking roote throughout the country.

Instead, the gang searched around for some other model to put up against Tachai, some commune they had control over, or a village where everyone wrote poetry. All this was just so much sabotage of a major effort of the Party under the leadership of Mao.

The Gang's Line for Weakening the Worker-Peasant Alliance

The gang and their line worked at weakening the worker-peasant alliance from three different directions. First, they opposed and stood in the way of the Tachai movement. Second, their policies in the cities weakened it, and third, their agricultural policies weakened it. All added up to a serious undermining and threat to proletarian rule in China.

The gang-led disruptions in the cities were not without effect in the countryside. For all their talk about restricting bourgeois right and the three great differences, their policies magnified them. The peasantry, and especially in the collective form of organization, depend on the cities for agricultural implements, supplies, fertilizer, etc. as well as consumer goods. And they are faced with strict "laws" of production, like the necessity of planting during the planting season.

The peasantry was frequently unable to obtain these needed goods because of disruptions in basic industry and transport that the gang pushed with such calls as don't produce for the incorrect line. Workers on strike in China receive full pay, while peasants get paid only on the basis of what they produce. Disruption in production that cut agricultural production therefore magnify the differences between workers and peasants and town and country whether they are done in the name of "revolution" or not. That is why there has to be an overall view and plan for the economy. Spontaneity means nothing less than capitalism. The results of the most serious disruptions was to break down the collective economy and push the peasants to private small scale farming in order to survive. The black market also flourishes in these conditions. This is capitalism, and is pointed out in Hua's Tachai speech. The gang attacked him for "going after foxes while wolves are in power." The truth is that the gang were the wolves who turned loose the foxes.

The gang had relatively little influence in the countryside, it mostly centered around the bigger cities like Peking and Shanghai and Hangchow. In these areas, they took Mao's line of taking grain as the foundation of agriculture and get prepared for war and used them to destroy Mao's line of planned proportional development of the economy.

Grain as the key link reflects the overall need of the masses and the economy. The peasantry must strive to fulfill the state plan in grain, and supply the state with the required amount, in order to ensure proportional development, and therefore other crops must be planned for with this in mind.

In the areas the gang controlled, they threw the overall plan out the window and metaphysically raised grain to oppose it. They converted vegetable growing communes around major cities and turned them into grain producers. But this was done without regard to where the vegetables were to be used. They were for the workers in the nearby cities, a small example of local self reliance. The quantity and quality of vegetables dropped off, with resulting resentment by the workers at the peasantry, and with new fertile soil for black market vegetables. Of course the most advanced did not blame the peasants or the plan, but rather blamed the bad communists who were messing things up—the gang and their henchmen.

Mechanization of agriculture was never an actual part of the gang's efforts in agriculture. They focused instead in developing the economy by "restricting bourgeois right." And in doing so they showed how a correct Marxist concept can become a weapon against the masses when used to promote an incorrect line.

The gang launched a movement to restrict bourgeois right in the countryside by attacking rural fairs and open markets. These exist throughout China, and are legal and generally even state regulated. Through them, the peasants supplement their income by trading the produce from the remaining private plots. And these fairs and markets also serve to enable communes, brigades and work teams to make small adjustments to fill needs not accounted for in the overall plan, like a draft animal or a tool.

These markets certainly contain soil for capitalism to grow and for capitalist ideology to expand. But this is very secondary, both in relation to total agricultural production and distribution and to their positive roles.

The gang attacked, without any investigation of conditions, any practice of the mass line, and without using the method of persuasion and education to deal with contradictions among the people. Under the signboard of restricting bourgeois right, they simply closed down the fairs and markets in at least two provinces.

In Chekiang, the Hangchow disturbances and riots had dealt heavy blows to the worker-peasant alliance. Distribution of goods to the countryside was heavily curtailed, with the resulting push to private plot farming. This process was speeded up when the gang's supporter in the area, the infamous Wen Sen-ho, closed down the local market by force. In one prefecture, Wanchow, the cumulative effect of the gang's leadership was the almost total breakdown of the communes and redivision of land among the peasants for private farming.

In Liaoning Province, the home base of Mao Yuan-hsin, Mao's nephew and a close ally of the gang, the local rural fairs were closed down under his leadership. This was done under the signboard of restricting bourgeois right and capitalism. The result here was not as serious as in Chekiang. The communes did not break down, but a flourishing black market did spring up. Bourgeois right was not restricted, and instead a new strata of very rich speculators was created through the leadership of the line of Mao Yuan-hsin and the gang.

These are not simply "rash advances" by well meaning revolutionaries. These were cases of socialist relations degenerating and actual capitalist relations openly growing. The gang followers would not pull back and say that the conditions were not ripe. They lashed out at the masses again, this time blaming them for being too backward to restrict bourgeois right.

This three pronged attack on the worker-peasant alliance—from the cities, in the countryside, and in opposing Tachai and the Party's line for developing agriculture—placed the gang in direct opposition to Mao and the Chinese masses. They had become a real fetter on the development of the socialist revolution that had to be smashed. But smashing the gang is no guarantee of smooth sailing ahead for mechanization and revolution in agriculture or in any other sphere. In fact, agriculture remains a key focus for the class struggle in China today as it has been for the past 28 years and more.

The Struggle To Learn From Tachai Continues Under Hua

"Only socialism can save China." This was Mao Tsetung's statement on which road was the road forward. And for agriculture, Mao said, "the fundamental way out for agriculture lies in mechanization." Mechanization of agriculture is a key step along this road. This will provide the basis for still further leaps in socialist ownership, consolidation of the worker-peasant alliance, and restricting the three great differences. But these gains will only be realized by putting ideological and political work based on Marxism-Leninism, Mao Tsetung Thought in command. This is the fundamental lesson of Tachai.

Now that the gang is gone, the struggle over mechanization is still raging. Capitalist roaders of all stripes, either those like the gang or those like Liu Shao-chi all oppose the mass movement to mechanize agriculture.

The Right is all for the four modernizations on paper, but not in an all round, proportional way to build socialism stronger. They historically stress heavy industry over agriculture, because it is the most profitable sector of the economy. On a capitalist basis, mechanization of agriculture is hardly profitable on a nationwide scale. On this basis, it could wait until industry has moved much further ahead. And in fact this has been proposed time and again, both in the history of the Soviet Union and in China right up until today.

But as Hua points out, "We should see to it that the mechanization of agriculture will more effectively push forward and guarantee the modernization of industry, national defense and science and technology so as to greatly strengthen the material base of our great socialist motherland . . ." (Let the Whole Party Mobilize, p. 3)

The gang opposed mechanization and the Tachai movement as a key point of their counter-revolutionary line. Smashing them maintained working class rule in China, and laid the basis for further struggle.

The debate over agriculture is relatively open. Different articles in different publications put the stress on different sides of the question, and so the lines become clear. The right is stressing grain production and fulfilling and exceeding the plan. The revolutionaries under Hua, and including Chen Yung-kuei, are stressing the need for both immediate production while providing the peasantry with sufficient time to energetically take up farm land capital construction and mechanization.

Hua put forward in his May Day speech this year that "Under socialism, too, the growth of the productive forces is bound to expose flaws in the economic and political systems and rouse people to make changes."

Hua continued by stressing the importance of learning from Tachai: "Chairman Mao long ago pointed out: 'The social and technical transformation of the rural areas will proceed simultaneously.' The growth of agricultural cooperatives into people's communes opened a broad road for mechanizing farming. Agriculture is of vital importance in our country's economic construction. The development of our agriculture calls for carrying out the mass movement to learn from Tachai in agriculture and popularize Tachai-type counties throughout the country, for carrying out education in the Party's basic line among the peasant masses, for criticizing revisionism and capitalism in a big way and for persisting in the socialist road while energetically to mechanize farm work. The present three-level system of ownership of the means of production in the people's commune, with ownership by the production team as the basic form, will in the future gradually be raised to fully collective ownership by the people's commune and eventually ownership by the whole people. This is a process of constant transformation in the superstructure and in the relations of production, a process of achieving farm mechanization and industrializing the communes and the country, and a process of constantly raising the level of mechanization and industrialization." (*Peking Review* No. 19, 1977, p. 24, 25)

Hua Kuo-feng is carrying out Mao's line in agriculture, understanding the conditions and continuing the revolution under the dictatorship of the proletariat, waging class struggle to build socialism. This is shown in his opposition to the gang and in his leadership of the Tachai movement and persevering in the task of socialist mechanization together with the masses against all enemies and obstacles.

Socialist New Things

During the past several years a major focal point of the sharpening struggle in China has been over the direction of the socialist new things. In recent months the bourgeois press, now joined by Avakian, has proclaimed that the socialist new things which arose during the Cultural Revolution have been essentially eliminated and that the bourgeoisie completely holds sway in these areas, reversing every correct verdict, while bending every effort to institute "capitalist" new things in their place. But those who wildly make these charges of reversal only peer through bourgeois tinted glasses, substituting the facts with their fantasies and desires. Presently, in China there is sharp struggle over the direction and adjustment of several of these new things. Much of this two line struggle is centered on how to rectify the damage the Gang heaped on these new things, while claiming to be their upholder. Already enough is known to characterize some of the main points of struggle in China over the current and future status of socialist new things. This struggle helps to clarify the nature of these new things. The first new things arose almost 60 years ago.

Lenin referred to socialist new things as "shoots of communism." They are developments within socialist society which show the road ahead and which, themselves, are a step down that road. Their origin is of particular importance. Socialist new things arise out of mass surges of enthusiasm for socialism to both build and defend it against the class enemy. They are based on a heightened level of ideological and political consciousness among the masses who, coming to grips with the actual problems immediately confronting socialism, are struggling to transform those conditions, a new shoot may be born. These shoots potentially represent a particular qualitative leap forward in social relations.

Arising from mass surges of enthusiasm, these new things

serve as a source for future enthusiasm. Although they are not the only source of enthusiasm, socialism itself is the main source of mass enthusiasm, for example, by wiping out unemployment and inflation, by step by step eliminating national oppression and women's oppression, by providing a decent standard of living for 900 million people who were the world's poorest, etc.

In *A Great Beginning*, Lenin summed up the spontaneous development of "communist Saturdays," "subbotniks," as "communist shoots." This referred to the achievements of the Moscow-Kagan railroad workers who voluntarily worked on Saturdays. Guided by their own class consciousness and enthusiasm they took the initiative to work and increase the social productivity of their own labor in order to build socialism without any regard to pay. In this article Lenin described another "communist shoot," the development of free public child care which freed women to enter the labor force to fully participate in the building of socialism.

Such things, of course, have also developed in China. At one time, the development of the mutual aid teams and then later, the people's communes were socialist new things in agriculture; they were leaps forward in man's social organization which in a concentrated way pointed the road forward. And of course there was sharp struggle over them. A handful of capitalist roaders jumped out to oppose and destroy these things. Some came straight out as rightists and others decked themselves out as super revolutionaries. Some of the masses resisted them because of conservative attitudes and habits. Others among the masses wanted to abandon them because of early difficulties. In spite of the bourgeois opposition and the difficulties in the work, the overwhelming majority of the peasants were won to them in the course of building and adjusting these new things. Eventually, they became integral parts of socialist agriculture and socialist society as a whole, and ceased to be identified as new things.

During the Great Proletarian Cultural Revolution—itself a great leap forward for socialism in China—a great number of socialist new things were initiated, nourished, and developed, such as: the mass movements to study Marxism-Leninism, Mao Tsetung Thought, genuine cadre participation in manual labor, the formation of contingents of theoreticians from workers and peasants, sending educated youth to the countryside, the creation and popularization of revolutionary model operas, May 7th Cadre Schools, the strengthening of the Party's centralized leadership, revolutionary committees, three-in-one combinations, barefoot doctors, educational reforms, mass participation in scientific and technical renovations, etc. (This list is taken from a list of socialist new things published in *Hongqi* 12, 1974. At the time the Gang was in control of this publication. The list they present is far from complete. Any number of new things were not included, for example, the worker-peasant villages, pioneered at Taching, an important concrete development in reducing the differences between workers and peasants.)

Socialist New Things: Objects of Fierce Class Struggle

The initiation and development of socialist new things are often targets of fierce class struggle. Lenin lays this point out clearly back in 1919. "When the new has just been born the old always remains stronger than it for some time; this is always the case in nature and in social life. Jeering at the feebleness of the young shoots of the new order, cheap scepticism of the intellectuals and the like—these are, essentially, methods of bourgeois class struggle against the proletariat . . ." *(A Great Beginning,* Vol. 29, p. 425)

Those attempting to hold back the further genuine revolutionizing of social relations, often make the weakness and fragility of the socialist new things a major focus of their attacks. The history of socialist China verifies Lenin's summation. From the early days of agricultural cooperation, through the Great Leap Forward, through the Cultural Revolution, and through the present day, those who oppose continuing the revolution often target the socialist new things for jeering attack. Some of this resistance arises from the conservative thinking of the more backward masses, while the organized attacks on the new things are a method of political struggle of rightists who step out onto the capitalist road. In recent years the rightists once again stepped up their attacks on the socialist new things in an attempt, as Mao stated, "reversing correct verdicts." But their efforts were greatly aided by another kind of error that Lenin referred to as well, an error which the Gang of Four turned into a reactionary principle.

Lenin, in criticizing cadre who were freely calling their enterprises "communes," wrongly representing them as shoots of communism, identifies the serious consequences of this error:

"Any kind of enterprise started by Communists or with their participation is very often at once declared to be a 'commune,' it being not infrequently forgotten that this *very honorable title* must be *won* by prolonged and persistent effort, by *practical* achievement in genuine communist development.

"...Let the title be simpler—and incidentally, the defects and shortcomings of the *initial* stages of the new organizational work will not be blamed on the 'communes,' but (as in all fairness, they should be), on *bad* Communists. It would be a good thing to eliminate the word 'commune' from common use, to prohibit every Tom, Dick and Harry from grabbing at it, or to *allow this title to be borne only* by genuine communes, which have really demonstrated in practice (and have proved by the unanimous recognition of the whole of the population) that they are capable of organizing their work in a communist manner." (*A Great Beginning,* p. 431)

The Gang of Four were bad communists. They cloaked themselves in the banner of the Cultural Revolution and posed as the staunchest defenders of the socialist new things. Those "things" under their leadership and control (in such fields as culture, education, etc.) were stifled and rigidified. Hard work was replaced by hot air. They opposed adjustments necessary to aid the growth of these socialist new things, and to meet the needs of the class struggle; they rejected proposals and failed to implement instructions. All of this under the pretense of upholding the socialist new things, and claiming that all proposed changes were "revisionist" attacks that had to be repelled. The Gang's bad leadership crushed and misdirected the masses enthusiasm for socialism, draining the lifeblood out of these genuine socialist new things, as a result they stagnated.

The Gang's role as bad communists, becomes immediately apparent by examining Chiang Ching's leadership in culture. The revolutionizing of culture was a central part of the GPCR and represented a tremendous advance for the working class in exercising all round dictatorship over the bourgeoisie in this sphere of the superstructure. In particular, the development of proletarian model operas was a major step forward in driving out decadent bourgeois culture that glorifies rulers, exploiting classes, etc. However, the rigid development of these model operas—under the signboard of not tampering with socialist new things—completely stagnated the development of revolutionary culture in China. In a 9-year period, a grand total of 8 model operas were developed to serve China's 800 million people. Literature, movies, poetry, etc. stagnated. The film "Pioneers" under the supervision of Chiang Ching Art was essentially suppressed.

In July, 1975, recognizing the deteriorating situation in culture, Mao called for an "adjustment" in policy, while criticizing

Chiang Ching. Mao was not very pleased with this self-proclaimed "great" communist. "Model operas alone are not enough. What is worse, one comes under fire for the slightest fault. No longer are 100 flowers blossoming. Others are not allowed to offer any opinion, that's not good." "People are afraid to write articles or produce plays. There is nothing in the way of novels and poetry." He added, "There should be some adjustments in the Party's policy on literature and art, and the performing arts should gradually enlarge their repertories in a year or in 2 or in 3 years." "Enliven the atmosphere in a year or 2, if it takes 3, 4 or even 5 years, that will be all right too." And of course there's the famous criticism of her suppression of *Pioneers*: "There is nothing seriously wrong with this film. I suggest it be approved for release. We shouldn't demand perfection. And to bring as many as 10 charges against it is really going too far. This hampers the readjustment of the Party's policy on literature and art."

Mao's criticisms of Chiang Ching clearly indicate how her bad leadership had become a major fetter in cultural work. In the first statement of criticism Mao is hitting at the failure of cultural work to accomplish its basic political task to serve the workers, peasants and soldiers. Even though quality is important, it is dialectically related to quantity: quality cannot be developed in a vacuum. Also, how many times can 800 million people sit through 8 operas, as the main form of socialist culture, before they get bored and disgusted?

What is worse, in the hands of Chiang Ching revolutionary model operas, a socialist new thing, were transformed into the absolute measuring stick and used to bludgeon down initiative and the masses' enthusiasm for socialist culture. This method of work was a sure guarantee that 100 flowers couldn't blossom. Chiang Ching was an extremely bad communist or, more correctly, an extremely good fascist. She had faithfully violated all of Mao's instructions on developing cultural new things, as she continued right along proclaiming herself to be the arch-defender of socialist new things. While rightists at this point could only aspire to reverse correct verdicts, Chiang Ching was doing so on a daily basis, by negating all the guidelines necessary for advancing the new things and at the same time claiming to uphold them. Mao instructed Chiang Ching to readjust the policy on culture and put some life back into it before culture once again degenerated into its former "mummy-like" character as he, during the last couple years of his life, called on the Gang to alter their general direction.

They failed to heed Mao's advice. The Gang's bad leadership

provided the right with a mountain of ammunition to launch an attack. As the right deviationist wind began to blow, the Gang stepped up their counter-revolutionary activity, portraying themselves as the defenders of socialism against the right. Trying to cover themselves by the opposite pole of the same stupidity, they laid plans, until the only way to deal with their counter-revolution was to smash the Gang down.

Chiang Ching's leadership in culture provides a general indication of the kind of damage the Gang inflicted on the socialist new things under their control. As a result a number of these new things require major adjustments to get them moving again in the correct direction. Already there has been sharp struggle within the present leadership in evaluating and developing policy for making adjustments. And possibly depending on the viability of these "shoots" in relation to the necessary political tasks, it could be correct to let some die. On the other hand, given the intensity of struggle, it is conceivable that the right could kill off some viable socialist new things. Through a number of methods they could employ to choke the life out of these new things, such as, continuing the Gang's method of rigidifying, which prevents them to grow and causes them to degenerate, or gut the heart out of them while preserving the name, or finally just straight up abolishing them. Currently, there are possiblities for the right and not actualities. The methods of destruction and the methods for advance look similar, and basically the only way to make a distinction requires an analysis of concrete conditions.

Most socialist new things are actively being supported and promoted by the present leadership. These include, among others, sending educated youth to the countryside, three-in-one combinations, revolutionary committees, barefoot doctors, mass campaigns to study Marxism-Leninism, Mao Tse-tung Thought and the formation of worker-peasant theoretical groups, strengthening Party leadership, May 7th Cadre Schools, etc. But even though these socialist things are being supported, it is important to grasp class struggle runs through everything, which always implies the possibility that these things could be reversed. Also by recognizing class struggle through everything it is clear that there can be no external static socialist new things. They must continually be adjusted in the heat of the class struggle and must advance with society which means they will inevitably be negated to a higher level.

Currently, a major struggle over educational reforms produced a program for next year. The development of this struggle will be dealt with in the next section. A major struggle has been emerging over the direction of scientific and technical work; a national science conference has been announced for this spring. The developments in the struggle over the direction of science and technology, will be thoroughly presented in the future. Also, quite recently a struggle has developed over genuine cadre participation in manual labor.

In December, Hua Kuo-feng and a group of leading supporters went to the countryside to participate in genuine manual labor. They worked on the construction of a reservoir. By doing, Hua made a clear statement in supporting genuine manual labor for cadres. He was also providing standard to judge cadre and unleashed the initiative of the masses to struggle with cadre to fulfill these responsibilities. Genuine participation of cadre in manual labor has been, historically, a sharp point of struggle within the Party. The growing intensity of this struggle is reflected in the fact that reports of Hua's participation in manual labor appeared in the press, only after an unexplained delay. Hua clearly stands for upholding this socialist new thing, and while there has not been public opposition, there is resistance nonetheless.

The Question of Education

The best publicized struggle over socialist new things in today's China has been that concerning what the 1974 *Hongqi* official list called, "the reform in education," which actually included a number of socialist new things. Both the controversy and the information it has made available make this a good subject to look at in detail. In trying to evaluate what is going on, it is necessary to investigate the history, the damage done by the Four and the line struggle now, and to apply a yardstick Lenin suggested, "practical success in prolonged efforts," to determine what actually serves the interests of the working class and where adjustments are required.

Education was the first mass battlefield during the Cultural Revolution. Under Liu Shao-chi, capitalist roaders had increasingly tightened their grip on the educational system. Politics was divorced from education, and book knowledge held superior to manual labor—before the GPCR only one middle school in all Peking had a policy of part-time productive labor for its students. Teaching methods and course content were not designed to arm students to change the world. Higher education tended to reproduce capitalist class relations by turning out experts and intellectuals with bourgeois and feudal values and by "objective" admissions criteria which favored the children of cadres, the urban petty bourgeoisie and national bourgeoisie and kept the working class and peasantry greatly underrepresented.

The masses of students rose up to criticize and overturn the leadership taking this road and repudiate their line and methods, and in doing so closed down the schools for several years. Mao was generally very enthusiastic about the revolution on the educational front and in his directive of May 7, 1966 provided a general orientation for it: "While their (students) main task is to study, they should in addition to their studies learn other things, that is, industrial work, farming and military affairs. They should also criticize the bourgeoisie. The period of schooling should be shortened, education should be revolutionized, and the domination of our schools by bourgeois intellectuals should by no means be allowed to continue." (*Peking Review* 47, 1967, p. 9). As time passed and classes continued to remain in limbo while many campuses experienced small civil wars between Red Guard factions, workers' propaganda teams were sent into the campuses to restore order and help reorganize and provide working class leadership to education. The lessons of this period could be summed up in a comment Mao had made in the late '50s, "Education must serve proletarian politics and be combined with productive labor."

The struggle over how to consolidate the advances of the Cultural Revolution in education and how to make the educational system strengthen the dictatorship of the proletariat ("serve proletarian politics") has been going on since at least 1971. It has been so intense because the problems have been very great. Year after year visitors and articles have reported that university enrollment remained well below the pre-Cultural Revolution level and many graduates and advanced technical training facilities had never reopened. Wuhan University, for instance, had 5,000 students in 1965. Today it is finally moving to rectify the criminal decadent luxury of having only 3,000 enrolled and a 1 to 3 teacher to student ratio! Severe problems existed in the quality of education as well. Since the fall of the Gang this can be quantified to some extent. Shanghai recently gave college graduates in science working in local scientific and technical departments a *middle school* test in their specialities—68% failed basic math, 70% physics and 76% chemistry! (*The Economist,* December 31, 1977, p. 29-30)

Mao was extremely concerned about the state of China's education, in 1974 telling a meeting of liberated cadres, "Education needs to be revolutionized, pedagogy needs to be reformed; but that doesn't equal to abandonment of professors, quality and quantity of pedagogy, and going to universities without examinations, but a change of methods. Henceforth, it will be necessary to continuously elevate the quality and quantity of teaching, to include theory, practice, politics and administrative functionings." He also pointed out, "If education can't catch up, there will be no scientists in the coming years." (*Issues and Studies,* February, 1975, p. 92)

As the struggle over this problem developed, the Gang took their characteristic stand of upholding "socialist new things" to oppose socialism. Chang Chun-chiao's famous remark, "Bring up exploiters and intellectual aristocrats with bourgeois consciousness and culture or bring up workers with consciousness but no culture: what do you want? I'd rather have workers without culture than exploiters and intellectual aristocrats with culture." (*Peking Review* 8, 1977, p. 11) was not some abstract debating point. It was his answer to the problem that the universities were turning out workers without culture (a term which refers to learning and education in general, not poetry appreciation). As such it was no answer at all, only bluster in defense of the status quo, Gang control over much of the educational system. This went right along with the Gang's general line, which in education came out as the position that colleges should only teach the "specialty of struggling against capitalist roaders." (*Peking Review* 46, 1977). This was the same division of "class struggle" from the many tasks of revolution and socialism they pushed everywhere. It narrowed and distorted Mao's point about education *serving* politics, went against the May 7 directives' call that students' "main task is study" and flew in the face of the objective need of socialist China for ever greater numbers of educated and trained people. What it did do was try and stake out the schools as areas for training (to the extent they controlled the selection of students by "political criteria") and recruiting Gang supporters and as centers from which to disseminate the "theory" they covered their line with.

Although the Gang's semi-anarchist line was the main one crippling the education system, the right posed a serious danger, too. Mao's remarks (quoted above) were clearly aimed mainly at the need for rectification in education but they also cautioned against negating revolution in the process. Advocates of the bourgeois line on education did jump up as the right deviationist wind began blowing up in the second half of 1975. Taking advantage of the difficult situation and the Gang's perversion of many of the gains of the GPCR, they proposed "reforming" education back to its pre-cultural revolution state. Mao's response was to turn a couple of letters to him to this effect over to the students at Tsinghau to kick off debate on the questions they raised. Instead of a real debate on what had to be done in the educational field, Gang backers who were dominant at Tsinghua and other schools set up an orchestrated campaign which defended the existing situation in education and soon shifted into an equally distorted version of the anti-right deviationist wind campaign. The result was that stagnation continued and problems deepened until the Gang's fall.

Current Problems in Education

China's need for a functioning, expanding and socialist educational system is critical. Right now, there is a great shortage of every kind of trained scientist, expert and technician. There are two criticially needed steel mills at Wuhan, imported with Mao's approval, which are way behind construction schedule because the engineers and other trained personnel required just aren't there. And the demand will grow as China undertakes the big push to complete the four modernizations and other tasks. Taking the long view, the need is even greater—as China approaches 100% literacy, the goal for the minimum level of education everyone reaches must be raised and as that level is approached, raised again. This is key to eliminating the differences between mental and manual labor, which can only be done by raising the cultural level and capabilities of the masses as a whole.

The wreckage the Gang leaves behind in the educational field is massive. Much of it consists of "socialist new things," some of which proved bogus in practice, and more often, real "sprouts" which became petrified under the Gang's metaphysics and were turning into fetters on the development of socialism.

An example of this is the question of textbooks. Most of those used before the Cultural Revolution were permeated through and through with bourgeois ideology and methodology and when the GPCR broke out they were dumped. Instead, teachers were encouraged to compile their own, revolutionized teaching material, working with their students and workers or peasants attached to the leadership of their institutions. At the time, this was an excellent development. But the gang *kept* textbook production more or less at the local level ever since. Instead of taking the initial advance to a higher level by summing up and consolidating the most advanced experiences and texts and using the collectively acquired knowledge to produce good national or regional texts, which could serve as the main leg or perhaps a strong secondary one, they turned this advance into its opposite. Elevating local produced texts to a principle removed the most effective way to maintain national standards in education. Many locally produced texts students and teachers had to rely on could not help but be inadequate or downright bad, reflecting problems their authors had, the lack of models, and the general breakdown of the chain of knowledge on this question.

The potential for a similar problem developing arose in the case of the workers assigned to revolutionary committees in the schools. In many instances, the same workers have been doing this for ten years now, without ever having returned to their jobs. As some lose their ties with their class brothers and sisters, the danger of degeneration becomes severe. Proletarian guidance can over time turn into "class stand" bogarting, and maneuvering to keep a relatively privileged job. (The Gang tried to foster this situation and recruit these new-born "hacks" to their cause.) At Peking University it has been summed up that the most valuable contributions in recent years have been made by campus workers who have continued on their jobs while taking part in guiding the school.

There is sure to be plenty of struggle around how to sum up the overall role of the representatives of the worker propaganda teams and how to move ahead. The very idea of special forms of working class leadership in the schools will be opposed by conscious rightists, by academic overlords and some whose positions will be enhanced if they're dropped. But others, in the schools, in the Party, and in the class, will fight and devise the best ways of making that idea a material force.

Is the Verdict on Education Being Reversed?

One of the issues the Gang sowed the most confusion about was tests. Like textbooks, these had tended to have a particular character before the Cultural Revolution—bourgeois. They were frequent and used by the teachers to punish and cow their students, and as pointed out before, tended to re-produce capitalist class relations in school admissions. Like textbooks, they were dumped in the GPCR and like textbooks the Gang tried to keep it that way. Tests in general are not inherently bourgeois in character. They are extremely useful as a means for evaluating how much a student has learned, how well a teacher has taught, where a graduate should be placed to make best use of his or her capabilities or to further develop them, etc. In the absence of tests as an objective gauge of such things, the use of "political line" as the single decisive criterion encouraged abuses both by individuals trying to "go by the back door" and on a broad scope by opportunists like the Gang. The Gang's anti-test line had wide effects. Two Canadian teachers recently returned from working at Canton Foreign Languages Institute report that when a final test to evaluate graduating seniors was proposed this spring many of the students rebelled because they had not taken an exam since junior middle school—before the Cultural Revolution. (The struggle was resolved by setting up a similar test a month and a half in advance to help students detect and work on their weak points.) The Gang desperately fought off moves to resume testing. Their most successful tactic was the promotion of a petty opportunist named Chang Tieh-sheng. When he did poorly on a just established college entrance exam in 1973, Chang appended a whiney note to it about how he was a hardworking production team leader and all the other communes had chosen "bookworms" and careerists to take the test, so the test wasn't fair and please let him go to college anyway. The Gang prettified this incident—editing Chang's note and claiming he turned it in with a blank test—and splashed him all over the national media as a model of rebelling against the incorrect line of using exams in college enrollment. Chang took to his new role like a hog to slops and became a key mouthpiece for the Gang. (For more on Chang Tieh-Sheng see *Peking Review* 8, 1977). Meanwhile, the wide publicity given his model led not only to a new wave of anti-test sentiment but to many middle school students summing up that there was no point to studying because they could always bogart their way into college.

With the Gang gone (and "Blank Test" Chang with them) the current leadership opened general college entrance exams this fall to the great majority of the country's young adults as part of a general move to step up enrollment and recruit the most qualified candidates, including some directly from middle school, without the recent standard minimum of 2 years in a plant, commune or army unit. This was a sweeping move to rectify the overall stagnation the educational system had been in for so long. While it would be wrong to attempt all-around evaluation of this without more information on the test and on the general situation in education than is available now, a few points can and must be made. Use of tests as one standard for choosing who goes to college is not wrong but desirable, although it must be in conjunction with taking into account such questions as whether candidates "have given a good account of themselves politically" and "are determined to study for the revolution," standards required for taking this fall's exam. At the same time, there are dangers in the resumption of entrance tests which must be recognized and adjusted for—first and foremost that of reverting to the pre-GPCR situation with those from "higher" class backgrounds squeezing out workers and peasants. Class struggle over the 2 roads and the 2 lines on this question is sure to continue as "efforts will be continued to improve and perfect the proletarian enrollment system on the basis of summing up the experience, both positive and negative in enrolling college students." (*Peking Review* 46, 1977)

Even though cleaning up after the Gang and rectifying the situation in education are monumental tasks, a number of the most important socialist new things in education from the period of the Cultural Revolution are being made an integral part of this process. Perhaps the most important is the combining of productive labor with study, a principle which is now universally applied from elementary schools on up. At the university level such labor, without pay, takes up about 20% of a student's school time, either regularly at a nearby plant or commune, or in long "vacation" stretches at a commune or both.

Another is political education, which includes not only a minimum of a half day a week of study and discussion of Marxist-Leninist theory but the integration of politics into every field of study whether it be the subject matter in foreign language classes or science classes taking up "open door" research projects to aid local plants, communes or municipalities.

In addition, other forms of educational institutions developed both before and during the Cultural Revolution to provide education for workers and peasants, such as the Kiangsi Communist Labor University (see *Peking Review* 33, 1977) and the part-time schools attached to factories, are being maintained and their enrollment increased. Still other forms are being developed and expanded, like correspondence courses in various technical skills for people in the countryside.

The Future of Socialist New Things

In education and in every field, the class struggle continues over socialist new things, going on in open and hidden forms with the proletarian forces attempting to defend them, to adjust them and to incorporate them fully into socialist society. But especially at this time it is wrong to fall into the Gang of Four's static view that the question is just one of defending those which grew up during the Cultural Revolution.

The enthusiasm of the masses for socialism brings forward new things all the time. (Various reports, for instance, suggest that Tachai has moved to commune level accounting, a big step closer to transforming agriculture from collective ownership to ownership by the whole people. This is a splendid thing even if at present it would be incorrect to announce it and in doing so change the content of the slogan Learn From Tachai to a call for a rash advance for which the material and ideological conditions have not yet been prepared on a broad enough scale.) With mass movements stirring and big tasks to be tackled in China in the coming period, socialist new things will be born in great numbers.

". . . We must carefully study the feeble new shoots, we must devote the greatest attention to them, do everything to promote their growth and 'nurse' them. Some of them will inevitably perish. We cannot vouch that precisely the 'communist subbotniks' will play a particularly important role. But that is not the point. The point is to foster each and every shoot of the new; and life will select the most viable. If the Japanese scientist, in order to help mankind vanquish syphilis, had the patience to test six hundred and five preparations before he developed a six hundred and sixth which met definite requirements, than those who want to solve a more difficult problem, namely, to vanquish capitalism, must have the perseverence to try hundreds and thousands of new methods, means and weapons of struggle in order to elaborate the most suitable of them." ("A Great Beginning," Lenin, *Selected Works,* Vol. 3, p. 235)

CONCLUSION

To sum up:

● The Gang of Four was a cancer in the Chinese Communist Party and the Chinese Revolution, a tumor which had grown and become malignant through stages. Because their activities undermined the dictatorship of the proletariat, because their plans would directly lead to the restoration of capitalism, and because they had begun as part of Mao Tsetung's proletarian headquarters, as they turned into their opposites, subverted and usurped that headquarters, the Gang had come to pose the greatest and most immediate danger to the survival of socialism.

This cancer was removed by the decisive and timely action of the Party Center headed by Hua Kuo-feng, forestalling the crisis which would have arisen from a reactionary coup attempt planned by these capitalist roaders and bourgeois elements.

● The Gang's general line posed an idealist view of "Class struggle" against the actual tasks of moving the Chinese revolution ahead in the spheres of ideology, politics and economics. They had "gotten stuck" in and seized upon particular social relations which characterized the first Great Proletarian Cultural Revolution, when they were flying high. This line manifested itself principally in calls for the constant overthrow of capitalist roaders, real and imagined, and their replacement by genuine revolutionaries, meaning themselves and their followers. This they made a prerequisite for doing anything else. In seizing hold of the real task of fighting to overthrow Party people in power taking the capitalist road in order to advance their own ends, the Gang divorced it from the actual class struggle. This task is neither the extent of the class struggle, nor is it at all times the main form that the class struggle takes. As the masses and the party take up the tasks of building socialism, the struggle between the two roads, the two lines and the two classes develops and must be consciously tackled at each juncture, using different methods to resolve different contradictions under different conditions. If the various tasks faced by the revolution are not taken up it does not stop the struggle, it merely insures that it takes place on terrain more favorable to the bourgeoisie.

● The Gang's line was at the service of a very definite goal—getting themselves into power. They demonstrated this by their repeated and futile demands that Mao place them in charge and by their consistent refusal to unite with others in the top leadership of the Party. Instead, always widening the target of attack, they aimed at those who stood in their way, like Chou En-lai. These were not tactical slip-ups but errors in principle flowing from a growing "smash and grab" style opportunism, errors which weakened both the proletariat's dictatorship and the Party it needs to maintain its rule. They also showed their colors as would be "New Mandarins" in their lust for privilege as well as power, engaging in degenerate "hobbies" and squandering the collective wealth produced by the laboring masses.

● The Gang got farther from the correct line and more isolated from the masses and the Party leadership as they failed to carry out, and in fact actively sabotaged the ideological, political and economic tasks of the period. They divorced class struggle from these tasks, distorting to serve their own purposes the task of studying theory to raise the socialist consciousness of the masses and arm them to fight against revisionism and restoration, thus negating the other tasks. Stability in the country and unity in Army and Party were called for precisely because they provided the most favorable terrain for the proletariat and its allies to *wage* the class struggle; in general and around immediate particulars. Among these were making the transition to a new generation of leadership, moving forward on the basis of consolidating the gains of the Cultural Revolution, among them many socialist new things; the need to spur the national economy forward; the need to further develop in practice Mao's revolutionary line on foreign affairs, etc.

The liberation and unleashing of the productive forces is an indispensible and fundamental part of the process by which the working class emancipates itself and all mankind. Big strides in developing the national economy were necessary for many reasons—to strengthen the economic base of socialism and provide the material base without which certain advances in the relations of production, including the strengthening of socialist ownership and the continuing restriction of bourgeois right, cannot be made; to deal big blows to the three great differences; to put the country in a better position to deal with war and natural disaster; to keep the masses enthusiasm for socialism high by constantly improving their conditions of labor and standard of living; to provide the world's people with a living example of the superiority of socialism; and through increasing foreign trade give China a bigger role in world political affairs.

Tasks like this call for acute class struggle, for the two roads will present themselves again and again in the course of the battle to implement them. The Gang, however, tried to stand reality on its head and push the idea that to carry out these tasks *was* to take the capitalist road, as they did with their attacks on learning from Tachai and the plan for agricultural mechanization.

Even when changes in the objective situation brought the Gang's line closer to expressing the tasks of the moment (somewhat as a broken clock still tells the right time twice a day), as happened when the right deviationist wind blew up late in 1975, the Gang failed to provide the masses with correct leadership. Instead they contrived to broaden the scope of attack, to sow theoretical confusion, to split the Party and to push themselves forward by any means possible. Their attacks wound up strengthening the rightists, who were downright eager to wear the "hat" of advocating stability and unity and building a modern and powerful socialist country.

● The Gang's degeneration, and dishonesty, created all sorts of other favorable soil for capitalist tendences and restoration. They were the Chinese version of the petty bourgeois "left" communists of 1918 at whom Lenin's remark, "As for those who look at the victory over the capitalists in the way the petty proprietors look at it—'they grabbed, let me have a go, too'—indeed every one is the source of a new generation of bourgeois," (*Report On The Immediate Tasks Of the Soviet Government*) was aimed. In other words, in their efforts to exploit the revolution these "revolutionary leaders" pushed a semi-anarchist line which unleashed the forces of petty capitalism.

The Gang's various methods of advancing their cause demonstrate how richly they merit the description "smash and grabbers": forming fighting groups and promoting factional fighting, stirring up economism, interfering with production, raising contradictions among the people to the level of antagonisms, all to create a situation in which they and their followers could "have a go, too," and particularly extend their web of political control.

Their "contributions" to important political campaigns hurt the masses' ability to grasp Marxism-Leninism, Mao Tsetung Thought. The Legalist/Confucianist articles which made a mockery of historical materialism and those on studying the theory of the dictatorship of the proletariat (including ones from the period of the anti-right deviationist wind movement) with their target of the month approach—now red experts, now peasants, now higher paid workers, now bourgeois democrats, now new-born bourgeois elements, and so forth—both showed that the Gang's "theory" was based on expediency and opportunism.

They consciously built up a base among certain sections of the people and pitted them against the Party and the masses. Revolutionary sounding slogans, including many with reactionary content—"Confucianists produce, legalists rebel," "Don't produce for the incorrect line," "Rebelling against leadership is going against the tide," and the like—were used to win supporters. (Even advanced workers can sometimes by lured by appeals to their revolutionary aspirations away from the real struggle into this kind of trap—like dual unionism in the US.) They used plenty of sugar-coated bullets to corrupt their followers too: official posts; long-term, full-time, full-pay reassignments of workers, peasants and youth sent down to the countryside from manual labor to study and cultural groups under their direction; college admissions based on political line, that is upholding the line of the Gang. In doing so they stifled many socialist new things by turning them into "capital" and using them to breed loyal "poverty pimps." And the Gang's overall approach attracted others of their stripe—the Weng Sen-ho's and the "Blank Paper" Chang's who served them as lieutenants.

- The logic of the Gang's line and method led them invariably to organize a coup attempt. Their incorrect line, far from winning a large conscious following, had earned them the hostility of the masses of people and isolated them from the active revolutionary forces in the leadership of the Communist Party. Mao himself, to whose coattails they tried to cling even as they more and more opposed his line, repeatedly poured the cold water of criticism on them. When they came under heavy attack from the Summer of 1975 on, he did not speak out boldly in support of them, as he had of the left during the Cultural Revolution every time it came under fire. Instead, he let the struggle develop, taking a hand only in initiating and in tempering the campaign against the right deviationist wind. Bitterly disappointed by both the Gang and Teng Hsiao-ping and fully aware that his death was near, Mao chose Hua Kuo-geng, a leader of the anti-Gang left forces on the Politburo, to serve as acting-Premier, then as First Vice-Chairman and Premier, and worked actively to build public opinion in support of Hua.

With no other route remaining to the power they craved and claimed they alone could be trusted to exercise on behalf of the masses, the Gang stepped up their disruption of society and the economy and prepared for an armed coup. Desperate, they were upping the ante to the limit in a last effort to force on the masses and the Party members and cadres the same bogus choice they had offered all along: it's us or restoration.

In fact, the two options were the same. Had they not been forestalled, the Gang's coup might well have pushed China into a bloody civil war, with such results as the spontaneous eruption of capitalist tendencies and relations in many places, the fragmenting of the central government into separate kingdoms, widespread combat, destruction and famine—in short a tailor-made situation for capitalist restoration, or Soviet invasion to "restore order." Even granting for a moment the most unlikely prospect of a successful Gang seizure of power, their line and the training they had given their supporters would have led them soon enough to turn on one another, cannibal fashion, in continual "class struggle against capitalist roaders," consolidating in the meantime the restoration of capitalism and accelerating the disintegration of the country. Who can deny that the Gang had become full blown capitalist roaders, bourgeois elements hell bent on destroying socialism.

● In sparing socialist China and the international working class the very real setback a coup attempt would have meant at the absolute minimum, by nipping it in the bud, Hua Kuo-feng showed that he deserved the faith that Mao had placed in him. He greatly reinforced the respect from the masses that he had earned from the time he led the first Learn From Tachai conference and through his handling of such problems as the Tangshan earthquake after he became Mao's chosen successor.

The necessity of smashing the Gang and the immediate threat of capitalist restoration they posed and of consolidating the victory over them required Hua and the proletarian headquarters in the Party he leads to conclude a common front with rightist and revisionist forces. Their strength in the first place was in no small part a legacy of the Gang's idealist and sectarian line which had made the rightist positions seem rational, credible and deserving of sympathy. This same poisonous line had to an extent discredited the very idea of class struggle under socialism and to a great extent confused people as to what it means to wage it.

But recognizing and acting on the necessity of smashing the Gang made it possible for Hua Kuo-feng and the proletarian headquarters as a whole to lead the Communist Party in preserving the proletarian dictatorship and breaking a major fetter barring the masses and the Party from taking up *all* the tasks of building socialism. As the masses are mobilized to carry out these tasks, they will also be taking on in concrete practice the question of which road to follow. With help and guidance from the Party, they will be able to apply Marxism-Leninism, Mao Tsetung Thought to sum up and carry on the line struggle, understanding what class forces and interests lie behind the different lines, and to deal with the class enemies when they do jump out.

Today the Chinese Communist Party, the Chinese proletariat and the masses of the Chinese people are carrying out a great historic mission—they are building socialism on all fronts and defending the dictatorship of the proletariat from the spontaneous drag of the old society and from conscious capitalist roaders, whatever form they may take. They are in the vanguard of our class' worldwide struggle to achieve its final goal—communism.

Some Final Points

As we said in the beginning the question of China is a watershed question, a question of principle of the utmost important to the class we are a part of and strive to serve and for the political color of our Party. The new CC report has posed the question of revolution and counterrevolution in our Party, the events since its publication and the actions of the Chairman have clearly demonstrated how deep and fundamental the questions are.

We call on our comrades to hold up the new CC report, to analyze it, based on its content and its method with the microscope and the telescope of our class, of Marxism-Leninism, Mao Tsetung Thought. We think that what we have written can be a help in making this basic initial analysis, we think it can be a weapon in our hands to evaluate the new CC report, to criticize it and powered by the determination of our comrades, to drive this anti-working-class shit out of our Party.

Fundamentally what we face right now is a basic difference of line. We have two headquarters in our Party, each one determined to drive the other out. This is not struggle over democratic centralism or organizational affairs, this is no struggle to be brushed aside under cover of factionalism or emotional calls to evaluate our Party on any other criteria except for its ideological and political line. Those who do so should check out and obviously think about the reasons behind their motivation.

In spite of the wishes of a few who would love to stem the tide of this struggle, to cut it off and to stop it—the struggle continues and develops momentum. This is because our Party was the Party of the U.S. working class, whose line and practice reflected the day to day aspirations of our class not to be crushed and to break through—to have revolution and move on to communism. But of late problems and mistakes have been consolidated into a line that is and will increasingly lead us away from the orientation that had characterized our earlier days. With the line on China a cancer has developed, real and with a terrible appetite. We can not let it terminate the working class line of our Party, and replace it with a low-road retreat from the class struggle.

Comrades do you think this is untrue? We think the facts, represented by the line of the new CC report speak for themselves. Comrades should take heed of the words spoken by Mao in "Rectify the Party's Style of Work":

"... We should boycott all the wares of subjectivism,

sectarianism and sterotyped Party writing, make their sale difficult, and not allow their purveyors to ply their trade by exploiting the low theoretical level in the Party. Our comrades must develop a good nose for this purpose; they should take a sniff at everything and distinguish the good from the bad before they decide whether to welcome it or boycott it. Communists must always go into the whys and wherefores of anything, use their own heads and carefully think over whether or not it corresponds to reality and is really well-founded; on no account should they follow blindly and encourage slavishness." (Mao Tsetung, *Selected Works*, Vol. 3, p. 49)

Who is it that has encouraged subjectivism and slavishness? Who has it been that has fought to make this a battle over principles and over line? Who is for cutting the cancer out and who wants the cancer to spread?

This Party is in a state of rebellion, every comrade, every branch, every area will be touched. Already the Chairman has purged over 40% of the membership of the Party. This has stopped nothing, this has turned no one around, this has shut no one up. The exact opposite has been the case. Comrades must decide. Join the rebellion. Hold up the current CC report, criticize it and drive it out of our Party.

In many areas mass meetings have been held, branches have continued to be an arena and special mass cadre forms like China struggle-study groups have been formed, to debate and struggle the issue out. These forms and additional ones must be developed to bring the full play and enthusiasm for revolution to the question of driving the Gang of 4 out of our Party.

Bibliography

As these groups develop the Revolutionary Workers Headquarters will work to give them guidance, in, among other things, developing methods the groups and individual comrades can use in going deeper into the issues raised in this paper and the CC report. A number of comrades have already raised the question of sources. The following bibliography indicates the main theoretical and factual sources on which this paper drew.

A wide range of Marxist classics, among those with particular application are Engels on the force theory in *Anti-Duhring*; Lenin on the struggle against such Gang predecessors as the "left communists" of 1918 and the "workers opposition" and Trotsky in the early '20s, including "A Great Beginning," "Immediate Tasks of the Soviet Union," and the debates on the trade unions, etc.; and Mao on the theory of knowledge, in particular *On Practice, On Contradiction* and "Where Do Correct Ideas Come From."

We also made considerable use of the works reliably attributed to Mao published by non-Chinese sources, Stuart Schram, *Chairman Mao Talks to the People,* a U.S. government collection, *Miscellany of Mao Tsetung Thought, Parts I and II,* key articles from which appear in the *Monthly Review* book, *Critique of Soviet Political Economy.*

Many of the Chinese Party internal documents printed were from the Taiwan publication *Issues and Studies* (which also carries biographies of Chinese leaders and articles of analysis from which much information can be gleaned, although it must be double-checked with care.)

Peking Review, China Reconstructs and *Hsinhua News Service* can be supplemented by the regular collections of translations from Chinese newspapers, magazines and radio broadcasts the U.S. government publishes. Xeroxes of documents quoted in this paper can be provided to areas on request.

The bourgeois periodicals with the most extensive coverage of China have been the *New York Times* and the English weeklies, the *Manchester Guardian* airmail edition and the *Far East Economic Review.* A more scholarly publication, also published in England, *China Quarterly,* is also very helpful.

Few books cover the recent period in China, but three paperbacks on slightly earlier periods are particularly useful for background: Jean Daubier, *A History of the Chinese Cultural Revolution,* Vintage, Jean Esmein, *The Chinese Cultural Revolution,* Anchor, and Jaap von Ginnekin, *The Rise and Fall of Lin Piao,* Avon.

Finally discussion with visitors to and especially long-term residents in China have provided much information on conditions now and in the past.

There are other sources available which must be sought out. The authors of this paper have not yet been able to survey and go into even the ones cited above as fully and carefully as they deserve. The task of study and analysis is continuing, using the method of seeking truth from facts and applying Marxism-Leninism, Mao Tsetung Thought to make a concrete analysis of concrete conditions, as opposed to the method of divine revelation employed by Avakian and for that matter by Mike Klonsky of the OL.

(The restoration of capitalism in China is still a possibility and a danger as it has been since 1949 and will continue to be throughout the socialist period. If such a restoration were to take place and a chihuahua were to be chosen to take the post once held by proletarian fighters like Mao Tsetung and Hua Kuo-feng, Klonsky would still do just about anything to get his picture in Renmin Ribao.)

The results of our continuing study will be gotten to comrades as soon as possible and a much longer and more thorough analysis is being started now. All comrades studying the present paper can help this by raising questions, formulating criticisms and passing along the results of any investigation they take up on their own.

Internal Journal

The most important thing now is to continue, to deepen and to spread the rebellion. This means first and foremost holding up, criticizing and repudiating the line of both sections of the current CC report. To aid and guide this process and keep cadres informed, the Revolutionary Workers Headquarters will be publishing an internal journal. It will include bulletins from the leading core of the Headquarters and will consist mainly of articles submitted by the individual comrades and branches around the country criticizing the CC report, the development of the left idealist line in the U.S. and the CC's methods of conducting, or to be more precise, sabotaging, the line struggle and contributing to the development of a Marxist-Leninist understanding of China.

Deepen the study and repudiation of the Gang of Four in the interest of proletarian internationalism and working class revolution!

How the Mensheviks Take Revisionism as the Key Link

RCP Reply to Mensheviks on China, Adopted By the 2nd Congress of the RCP, 1978

A Method to the Madness

The Menshevik opposition has produced a document which purports to answer the CC report on China. The ramblings and whinings of the authors are palmed off as new and persuasive evidence of the incorrect line of our Party. The only problem is that most of their arguments of substance—if one can be so generous—have already been answered; in fact, the bulk of what they raise was rebuffed and repudiated at the CC meeting and the substance of it was refuted in the CC Report.

But maybe—just maybe, they hope—by repeating the same arguments, like a sorcerer repeating an incantation, they can perform magic and convince someone that there's an ounce of Marxism in their argument. Maybe their confused and uncertain followers, worried by the prospect of joining up with the CP(ML) and a little sickened by the thought of embracing Teng Hsiao-ping will be temporarily distracted by these pages of muck. Maybe they can make the question seem so confusing that they can force these people to conclude that you have to be a genius to understand it.

Answering their preposterous claims puts the Party in a curious position: what's called for is almost a *Red Papers* with the CC Report, their attempted response, and the CC Report again, since nothing much new has been said by them. But there is development—more accurately, degeneration—as well as repetition here. Freed from the constraints of the Party's line, our Mensheviks have beat a hasty retreat from Marxism and the basic revolutionary positions of our Party.

In many ways their paper is similar to the BWC's first response to National Bulletin 13. On the one hand, it's very flabby. Their case against the Four is very weak and their arguments not at all compelling, especially if one adopts even a critical attitude toward what's appearing now in the *Peking Review* rather than swallowing it wholesale without questioning as our Mensheviks do. Further, it's not clear what their evaluation of Teng is and it's even less clear who the revisionists in China are, etc. On the other hand, the paper is definitely transitional and it's only a matter of time before they adopt even more outrageous positions as they free themselves totally of any influence of the Party and plunge fully into the embrace of revisionism here and in China.

Let's look more closely at their method. To begin with, the Mensheviks have never ceased yammering about facts, facts, facts. "Empty speculation," "opinions," "we want hard and fast facts," they chirp. One would have expected a richly detailed and lavishly documented case from them, but one searches in vain for such analysis. What we get instead is the pablum and distortions of the current rulers. For instance, the Four are said to have been unconcerned about production and opposed to modernization. The proof? *Peking Review* articles that say so. Never mind the fact that in literally thousands of pages, experience and struggle around these questions were summed up in the *Peking Review* and elsewhere under the Four's leadership or that the Shanghai textbook deals systematically and fully with basic problems of socialist construction. No attempt is made to analyze the line of the Four, but only to regurgitate horror stories from the *Peking Review*.

The Mensheviks have extreme difficulty dealing with certain obvious facts. Where articles in the *Peking Review* have put forward the view of experts and professionals in command, and done this consistently over the past year, the Mensheviks can only reserve comment and promise us future discussion on these developments. Is it or is it not a fact that the three poisonous weeds are being upheld in the *Peking Review*? What do the Mensheviks have to say about them? Very little, except for some token criticism to cover up their support for the content of the three weeds. What do the Mensheviks have to say about the fact that Hua was, at the very least, associated with the "Outline Report on Science and Technology," something that the *Peking Review* has pointed out on numerous occasions? The pro-Hua book *The Case of the Gang of Four* links Hua with Teng and Li Hsien-nien in the formulation of the three weeds. Again, the significance of this is ignored, the line of the three weeds and the line of the Four in opposing them is put to no analysis.

The point of all this is not to say that facts speak for themselves, because they don't. Truth and facts are not the same thing. Facts represent perceptual knowledge. Truth is higher than facts—it involves rationally grasping the interrelations between facts, this is what it means to seek truth from facts. It is possible to agree on certain facts and reach quite different conclusions. Certainly there were disruptions and difficulties in the Chinese economy over the past three years—these facts are undeniable, but is this to be blamed on revisionists and a revisionist line or the genuine revolutionaries? Does the fact that socialist new things are struggling to survive indicate that they are basically flawed or that they are coming under attack?

In other words truth has a class character and there are certain universal truths of Marxism-Leninism. There is no condition, time, or place that justifies replacing dialectics with eclectics as our Mensheviks and their revisionist mentors in China do. There is no condition, time or place that makes pragmatism ("black cat, white cat") somehow acceptable to Marxist-Leninists. And there is no condition, time, or place that warrants replacing the theory of continuing revolution under the dictatorship of the proletariat with the "theory of the productive forces" and the dying out of class struggle.

The method of the CC Report is not to start from a conglomeration of scattered facts, but to compare and contrast the different lines that have been contending in China over the past period and on that basis to examine and evaluate facts. The Chinese do not, for example, publish data on absolute output in the economy for every sector. Does this mean that it is not possible to understand questions involving the direction of the economy? No, not at all, because very clear and definite lines on the development of the economy and the relationship of that to other questions emerged at the very start of the Cultural Revolution and have been fought out ever since.

The method of the Mensheviks is not to proceed from the high plane of two-line struggle. The method to their madness is to start with the assumption that the Four were rotten, self-seeking disrupters, to provide for proof of this the absurd slanders and lies of the *Peking Review* and other material put out by the current rulers, and then to reach the surprising conclusion that the Four were rotten, self-seeking disrupters. Their method is the real *apriorist* one and not because they, too, had an opinion on the events in China shortly after the Four were arrested. Hua, according to their view, represents the truth. This becomes the principle with which they examine and evaluate the situation in China. Why does he represent the truth? Here their pragmatism shines brilliantly. Hua is in office; he won, therefore whatever he says must be true. The Four lost and therefore whatever they said must be false. But how else is a *Marxist* to judge the "facts" that appear in the *Peking Review* except by analyzing what line they are in the service of and what line is being attacked with these "facts"?

In a sense our "fact"-obsessed authors hang themselves. They nonchalantly inform us that the Propaganda Ministry is controlled by the right. (By the way, with this we do agree—the Propaganda Ministry is indeed controlled by the right, and this is true regardless of which specific faction in the current regime has control—it's still the right.) This would cast doubt, it would appear, on the facts they glean from the *Peking Review* and other current Chinese sources to back up their case. But our authors, we're sure, would dismiss these sorts of observations as nit-picking; after all, of what significance is it that the right is the source of the Mensheviks' most precious information? When push comes to shove, it matters very little for them because their arguments about chaos and disruption in society and stagnation in production are the familiar and standard arguments of the bourgeoisie in China and abroad—arguments reaching a fever pitch since the Great Leap Forward. As if to impress the point on unwary readers, they gleefully report test scores—showing just what an unmitigated disaster the Cultural Revolution was. "This is one hell of a mess. I want to flit and fly away." That's how Mao described such people. Birds of a feather, these goulash communists.

What Defines the "Actual Situation"?

Reading through this garbled document it is possible to sift out two major assertions. The first is that the Four were unable to link and carry out work simultaneously around the three directives. We are told that they posed one against the other, confined themselves to the question of ideology apart from concrete tasks and failed to recognize that class struggle "runs through" all three directives, that is, "runs through everything." The second and related point concerns the "actual situation" that our Mensheviks are so fond of. According to their twisted logic, the period of sharp and intense class struggle characteristic of the Cultural Revolution, what they somewhat disdainfully refer to as social relations of upheaval and rebellion, had subsided and new tasks and opportunities presented themselves—notably the development of the economy. The "Gang of Four" got stuck in an earlier period, that of the Cultural Revolution, and that was their doom. Their stubbornness and self-righteousness, their wanting to wage the class struggle from the mountaintops, strengthened the right, hastened their fall, and necessitated new alliances between the genuine revolutionaries, as represented by Hua, and the right (who the right is at this point remains unclear). (See pp. 201-214.)

What about the actual situation? Mao seems to have maintained his lucidity during this period so one would expect a fairly credible analysis from him. In 1969, following years of tumultuous struggle in factories, universities and major convulsions in the Party, in this same period that the Russians are attacking on the northern borders and the U.S. is heavily engaged, still, in Vietnam, Lin Piao comes forward and says enough is enough, it's time to settle down and push the economy forward. The argument had a certain appeal; after all there had been major disruptions and external aggression was a growing danger. But Mao emphatically rejects Lin's report, casts it aside as the "theory of the productive forces" and counter-revolutionary rubbish. Now all our Mensheviks can say about this episode is that Chou En-lai never used the blatantly revisionist language that Lin does. But they have nothing to say about why Mao rejects this orientation. They have nothing to say about what is so different about the current situation that makes Lin Piao's line correct today where it was wrong in 1969.

This is crucial because Mao saw no justification then and certainly no justification in 1976 when he initiated the struggle against Teng (a "fact" which even our authors concede—for now) for making the development of the economy the central task for the working class, which is what Teng was advocating. If Mao believed all of this he could have said it. If, as some would have us believe, the Four blocked his access to the media, he could have told Chou En-lai that the main task was modernization with a socialist orientation, he could have gotten the word out.

In fact as we indicated in the CC Report, Chou's description of four modernizations is taken from a statement Mao made in 1964. In delivering his speech to the 4th National People's Congress in 1975, Chou En-lai is not able to say that Mao recently reissued his call for the four modernizations in two stages by the year 2000. This is not to say that Mao disagreed with trying to build China into a modern socialist country, even with the general goal of modernization by 2000. But it would indicate differences over the interpretations that were being placed on the four modernizations at the time of the 4th National People's Congress. Moreover, the four modernizations by the year 2000 were not incorporated into the new State Constitution that was adopted at the 4th Congress as they were into the Constitution adopted at the 11th Party Congress, after Mao had died. In other words they were not then, as they are now, made the "historical mission" for the next period.

What sort of things was Mao emphasizing in the last few years? In 1973 a Party Constitution is approved that emphasizes that going against the tide is a Marxist principle. This doesn't sound like a call for cooling out the class struggle, nor does a Lin Piao-Confucius campaign which not only hits at blind obedience but which actually takes time away from production. Is this the sage advice of someone who thinks it's time for everyone to put his nose to the grindstone—get back to your posts, maybe study a little if it doesn't interfere with production, and cut out all this time-consuming struggle?

Mao spends a sleepless night just prior to the opening of the 4th National Peoples Congress, and it wasn't because he couldn't find his sleeping pills. He was worried—even Hua and Company acknowledge this—and issued his directive on studying the theory of the dictatorship of the proletariat and combatting and preventing revisionism. Why? Might it have something to do with the dangers associated with the implementation of the four modernizations? Mao did not attend the Congress. He could have, at least, made a symbolic appearance at the Congress to show his approval, but he did not, even though his health permitted it. His absence might well have implied that he did not go along with the political thrust of the push for modernization and the general line (or "general program") that this particular push represented.

And, at Mao's personal insistence, the right to strike is written into the new State Constitution. Again, it doesn't sound like Mao is exactly in the frame of mind of cooling things out. What does Mao say about the danger posed by people like Lin Piao? That they are few and far between and would have an awfully difficult time turning things around? No, he makes it clear, the capitalist roaders are still on the capitalist road and bitterly resent attempts to restrict bourgeois right. If they come to power it will be quite easy for them to rig up the capitalist system. Mao continually emphasized not the dying out, but the intensification of class struggle and the pervasive danger of restoration. Not that he is hysterical—quite the contrary—he is quite sober in this regard: "Everything reactionary is the same: if you don't hit it, it won't fall."

Whether to continue making revolution or not, this is the key question, and whether one fails to, makes serious mistakes in the process or achieves great victories, as with the Cultural Revolution, the bourgeoisie is bound to react and at certain points jump out. It happened in the period following the Great Leap Forward, it happened three times since Liu Shao-chi, with Lin Piao and Teng and Hua. When Mao spoke of the desirability of stability and unity (apparently in late 1974) this did not mean, as he so vigorously pointed out when Teng and others tried to make it mean, that stability and unity could be raised above the class struggle or that the class struggle would die out—or even die down. As the CC Report points out, Mao felt that striving for stability and unity on the basis of a proletarian line would be advantageous to the proletariat at that time; but he certainly recognized that such a policy could in no way guarantee that the bourgeoisie would not jump out and try to disrupt the achievement of stability and unity on this revolutionary basis—which is exactly what the bourgeoisie, commanded by people like Teng, and backed by Chou, did during that very period.

The danger of capitalist restoration is no less the danger 25, as opposed to 10, years after the seizure of power. The deepening of the revolution in all spheres of society, the radical transformations that take place through class struggle and the more conscious grasp and application of the science of revolution by the masses in the course of these battles heightens their vigilance and capacity to carry forward. But socialism is a society in transition, it is in motion and new contradictions arise which present new difficulties and new tasks, especially as the working class grows more conscious of the need to effect radical ruptures with traditional property relations and ideas. Those, especially leading people, who cease making revolution become its target and the relations of socialist society even as they undergo transformations contain capitalist elements which constantly engender new bourgeois forces. The movement of socialist society to a higher level moves the class struggle to a higher level and it grows more complex, complicated and intense. This applies particularly to the struggle within the Party.

This is what Mao was drawing people's attention to, especially through the campaign to study the theory of the dictatorship of the proletariat and the struggle to restrict bourgeois right. And as we shall see these instructions and warnings of Mao were not simply general admonitions, but very much related to the "actual situation." But our Menshevik scholars bleat, you can't have a Cultural Revolution all the time, new tasks and policies are called for. The Gang of Four, they inform us, got stuck in the Cultural Revolution. This, incidentally, is the main way the Mensheviks discuss the Cultural Revolution, along with pointing out that socialist new things aren't working out too well in some places.

The Cultural Revolution was, in fact, a watershed. As the Shanghai text points out, "It was a great revolution in the superstructure, a great political revolution under the conditions of the proletarian dictatorship. It could also be called the second revolution of China." This escapes the attention of the Mensheviks—in fact they vigorously disagree with it. Rather it is over with, not much different from a five-year plan superseded by another.

Of what importance is the Cultural Revolution—which, rather than being an interlude in the history of the class struggle, thrust the struggle on to an entirely different level? It is all important because how to evaluate the gains of the Cultural Revolution, which really represent an orientation for building socialism and moving towards communism, was at the heart of the struggles in the '70s. That the Four got "stuck" in the Cultural Revolution is very much to their credit because what our Mensheviks really mean to say is that they fought in it and fought to defend it and the gains and transformations achieved through it. The Mensheviks couldn't possibly have gotten stuck in an event like the Cultural Revolution because like their mentors in power they hate and despise it. It was a nuisance at best, a disaster at worst.

Most of the social base and many of the leading forces of the revisionist faction came into the struggle towards the culmination of the first phase of the Cultural Revolution in 1968-70. Jarvis of course was waving his CP program madly at the time so it's not surprising that he never quite grasped the historic importance of the Cultural Revolution. The point is that many of these people became aware of the Cultural Revolution when it was already in high gear and when many of the detested practices and methods of the revisionist headquarters had been swept away. As for the people newly involved in the revolutionary movement who have been sucked into the Menshevik madness, many have little sense of what was actually involved and at stake. Therefore it is not surprising that the faction can casually gloss over the Cultural Revolution and, ironic as it may seem, win many of the youth to the view that it was a holy mess and it's high time to pick up the pieces. Listening to the Mensheviks, you would have no idea that before the Cultural Revolution in many factories workers had to have passes to go to the bathroom or that the operas performed on the Peking stage were often feudal romances. (Our Mensheviks also suffer a lapse in memory when it comes to the role of their heroes in China, the present rulers, many of whom opposed the Cultural Revolution or, like Teng, were a target of it. They insist that Hua was not knocked down in late 1966. This is true—he was knocked down in early 1966—though returned to office the same year. Comrades should read over *Peking Review* articles over the last 15 months which chronicle the illustrious career of our mensheviks' knight in shining armor—for some reason his brilliant achievements during the year 1966 are inexplicably missing.)

The Cultural Revolution was a necessity. Had it not occurred, had those persons in power taking the capitalist road not been overthrown, the rule of the working class would have been overthrown. Mao never minced words in getting at its timeliness. He spoke of ministries of culture and education dominated by the bourgeoisie, of factories—not a few, but many, even the majority—in the hands of people following a revisionist line—not all of whom were bad, but many of whom were. There was an encrusted Party bureaucracy and a good part of the state apparatus weighing on the masses. The capitalist roaders pushed a revisionist line and, the protestations of the Mensheviks notwithstanding, it had very tangible, very concrete effects in the real world, it led to oppression and resistance. These people had to be and were in significant numbers overthrown. It must be borne in mind that this revolution—yes, revolution—occurred after socialist transformation in the realm of ownership in the main had been completed in industry and at a lower stage in agriculture. And it must also be remembered that this revolution was intense and sharp, and provoked bitterness and hatred not only among those who were overthrown but also among many who were sharply criticized.

Mao recognized that more Cultural Revolutions would be required, that it was not enough to settle the question of ownership at a certain level, that the existence of collective forms was not a guarantee against restoration, and that, in fact, uninterrupted revolution had to take place within a given stage of ownership, especially as concerns relations among people. Furthermore there would be those who would inevitably resist the continuing advance of the revolution and organize against it. The Cultural Revolution was not a holding action, it involved very real transformations in society which laid the basis for the consolidation of the dictatorship of the proletariat. This revolution which overthrew many capitalist roaders gave birth through this struggle to new things: worker-propaganda teams at the universities, barefoot doctors, revolutionary committees, open door scientific research, the revolution in art and literature, and many others.

Our Mensheviks don't have this kind of appreciation of the Cultural Revolution. Nowhere do they mention that the Cultural Revolution constitutes the forward spiral in the development of the international working class movement, that it represented the highest development of working class rule and contributed greatly—though not finally as Mao would point out—to solving the question of how to maintain working class rule. What the Mensheviks do is to slip in criticisms of the Cultural Revolution through "the back door"; they use Lenin's study on the Subbotniks to make the point that not every shoot of communism is durable or worthy of the name communist, that it is necessary to sort out the good from the bad in these new things. Here we find the essence of their stand, that the Cultural Revolution and the new things emerging out of it were at best fashionable means, good for a while, but necessarily subject to review and at this point up for grabs. (See pp. 242-255) They even tell us that some of these new things should die off, to which we could only reply in their fashion when they criticize our treatment of objective conditions "how many, which ones, where and when?"

The Socialist new things were the products of the Cultural Revolution, the fruits of its victory; a correct attitude toward them had all to do with a correct attitude toward the Cultural Revolution. The Mensheviks act as though they are raising a new question and a new problem. They call for dividing one into two on these new things, of critically assimilating them. But Mao dealt with this. He said reversing correct verdicts goes against the will of the people. There were many in China, like our Mensheviks, who seized upon the difficulties encountered by these new things and actively sabotaged them in order to overturn these verdicts. But these new things were not comparable to the Subbotnik movement, which while very significant was not a widespread phenomenon and was not the product of the titanic sort of struggle that was the Cultural Revolution. These things had been tested and proved their worth. In Party documents up to and through the Fourth National People's Congress Report they were upheld and calls were issued to defend and further develop them. The Four sought to preserve, strengthen and popularize these new things.

Any adjustments and changes in these new things were being carried out by proletarian revolutionaries on the basis of building on these achievements in the context of this new spiral. What was at issue between the Four with Mao behind them and the capitalist roaders was exactly this question of whether the Cultural Revolution marked a new spiral. The leaders in China with whom the Mensheviks are in bed are just the people who in the words of Wang Hung-wen, "instead of seeing the development as a spiral ascent, they look upon it as a turning movement within a circle... they urge the resumption of old rules and systems which have been discarded by the masses." That strengthening new things is the last thing our Mensheviks have in mind is attested to by their fascination with reliance on tests and technical expertise and even bonuses, which has been whispered by several of their stalwarts. These are (capitalist) old things under today's "actual conditions" in China. And they are not enthusiastically welcomed by the masses.

Because of the experience summed up by Mao and the crucial lessons and gains of the Cultural Revolution there can be no excuse for this sort of retreat. One could find situations in the history of the Bolshevik revolution and misread them. Lenin after all introduced the Taylor system. But nowhere in Mao's writings can you find a defense for this at this stage of the Chinese revolution. History does not simply repeat itself, if that were the case there would have been no Cultural Revolution. Raising productivity does not and should not depend on such methods as the Taylor system which represent the domination of dead labor (machines) over living labor, not after years of struggle to make workers masters of their factories and successful efforts to raise productivity through socialist activism and enthusiasm. Workers who in plants fought against bonuses and eventually eliminated them during the Cultural Revolution are now being told that they are useful instruments—if applied "fairly"—to step up production. Stalin cannot be condemned for not having a cultural revolution, but Hua Kuo-feng is to be condemned for reversing it in the name of adjusting to new conditions.

Our Mensheviks retort, "but you can't have a cultural revolution all the time." There's some truth to this, though coming from them it means something quite wrong. The class struggle does not remain at a constant level of intensity; it develops in waves. Mao recognized this in 1966 when he said, "Great disorder across the land leads to great order. And so once again every seven or eight years. Monsters and demons will jump out themselves. Determined by their own class nature, they are bound to jump out." Mao was not making the point that an exact timetable was at work, but that there is a general law involved. (It should also be noted that Hua conveniently cuts out the sentences following the first one in order to distort the continuing dialectic between disorder and order and to fit into his call for permanent "great order"—i.e., the dying out of class struggle.) The Four also spoke to this point in the Shanghai Text, "Class struggle in the socialist society develops in wavelike motions with peaks and troughs. This is due to a difference in the conditions of class struggle and not to whether there is class struggle or not. The history of the socialist society tells us that class enemies and all monsters and freaks will show themselves... The law of class struggle requires that there be a big struggle every few years."

In 1969 Mao recognized that the Cultural Revolution had entered a new stage. It was necessary to consolidate advances and, yes, even to put somewhat more emphasis on order—stability and unity. But this did not prevent the objective laws of class struggle from asserting themselves—Lin Piao jumped out. He jumped out because the moves to consolidate the gains of the Cultural Revolution, in particular to reassert and reestablish Party leadership based on the transformations of the previous years, challenged the vested interests he had built up—the fact that he and his men had through the stormy years of the Cultural Revolution seized hold of important positions of authority through the tactic of "overthrowing all." Small wonder that he had proclaimed that revisionism was no longer a problem.

Independent of the will of individuals, class struggle goes on and every few years big struggles break out. While it was not possible to wage the class struggle in the same way as during the early stages of the Cultural Revolution when mass rebellions and seizures of power throughout society were the order of the day, it was necessary to continue to defend the Cultural Revolution and to overthrow new bourgeois elements who actively opposed it. And the sharpening and accumulating contradictions of these years did, in wavelike fashion, lead to a big struggle, the campaign to beat back the right deviationist wind. This confrontation in 1975-76 represented the most significant trial of strength between the working class and the bourgeoisie since the Lin Piao affair.

The Mensheviks, needless to say, have a fundamentally different view. The bourgeoisie, or the right as they seem to prefer to call it, does not really figure as an independent force in society, acting according to its own class interests. This right is not launching attacks on the new things, it is not trying to seize portions of power and unleashing its social forces, be it plant managers or lower Party officials. The left is messing up and the right is kind of waiting in the wings ready to take advantage of the mistakes and excesses of the left. Is this not the argument of these people? Isn't this their view of the right deviationist wind, that it was precipitated by the errors of the Four? Comrades should read their paper over carefully. One hardly hears about the danger of capitalist restoration. The continuing exposure of the political line of these new bourgeois elements and the mobilization of the masses to hit back at their influence and pockets of strength scarcely forces the right to jump out, according to our authors. What does is the mistakes of "bad eggs" like the Four.

The picture we get from the Mensheviks is that the "Gang of 4"ruined a good thing. Conditions were ripe for bold economic initiatives what with the fury of the Cultural Revolution long past, but the "gang" insisted on broadening the target and got too dogmatic about socialist new things. What a pity! The slumbering right might have dozed off to sleep for good had the "gang" not been so dogged about ideology and all that bunk. Our authors present very little evidence to support the view that things had settled down: there is hardly any analysis of the period from the Lin Piao affair onward. We get the usual horror stories of how the Four distorted the Lin Piao/Confucius campaign and a new interpretation—and wrong of course—of the Tenth Party Congress that suggests that the development of the economy was coming to the fore as the main task. But, again, there is nothing but errors by the Four which embolden the right—and no sense of the bourgeoisie as a class striving for power. The bourgeoisie wouldn't dare attack if you did everything correctly according to this idealist logic.

Actually, as the CC Report goes into, the shock waves of the Lin Piao affair and the necessity of cleaning up in the army and reorganizing the Party called forth certain compromises. The rehabilitation of Teng makes it more possible to reshuffle a substantial number of regional military commanders and strip them of certain Party posts. The international situation makes it necessary to seek new alliances and engage in diplomatic activities which the bourbeoisie at home and abroad will try to use to its advantage. In the years following the Lin Piao affair, 1972-73, the right does gain strength. Many jumped into the fray opposing Lin Piao to really get at the Cultural Revolution and socialist new things. Others harboring profound hatred for having been criticized and pulled out sought revenge. This explains the sharp struggle over how to sum up Lin Piao and the criticism campaign of '73-'74. Should the Four have united with these elements who in growing numbers and influence were clamoring for a return to "normalcy," that is, who on the basis of the increasing danger of war and the existence of real difficulties in the economy and society generally, wanted to reverse the verdicts and momentum of the Cultural Revolution?

Mao was clear on what the correct orientation was and this was why he relied on the Four. Lin Piao would be criticized, but the Cultural Revolution which had brought the struggle of the working class to a higher level would be upheld and the transformations in the base and superstructure must and would continue. The Four were perfectly correct in describing the Cultural Revolution as opening up a new era—the aristocratic educational system was changing, genuine worker management in the factories was developing and spreading and so on. The right perceived it in the same way and many people who had originally gone along with the Cultural Revolution joined their camp. The terms of the struggle were sharpening: in educational circles the new policies were coming under attack and in many plants management practices were reverting to the ways of the pre-Cultural Revolution etc. The arguments of the right very often assumed the same form as that of the Mensheviks: let's not be one-sided about the Cultural Revolution and let's not forget that we can't afford big upheavals now, not with all these problems we have.

The Mensheviks ignore all of this and would have us believe that the working class has the freedom to fight the bourgeoisie when and how it wants or to shunt aside the class struggle or redefine it and go in for something else, like a new leap in the economy in which the class struggle is reduced to the question of who—the bourgeoisie or the proletariat—has a better plan for developing the economy. The big changes which the Cultural Revolution wrought don't particularly inspire our Mensheviks, which is why fighting the bourgeoisie to defend these things smacks of "petty bourgeois fanaticism." We hear of some surprise test (see p. 249) administered to students which tells us about as much about the real condition of education and the real capability of students as would a test given to a practicing doctor who had not studied for it. Of course, *some* doctors are not qualified for anything but just a test would not necessarily be the best gauge. Why don't we hear about the fact that in 1973 in Shanghai alone over 2800 of the more than 3000 enterprises had some kind of technical education programs which involved over 200,000 workers. Or that in 1975 over 260 factory-run worker colleges were in operation in Shanghai. Perhaps our Menshevik technicians agree with the current educational "reform" which will bring the talented few of technical and scientific students directly into the universities. This we suppose is a better way of breaking down the division of labor.

The Mensheviks have even given theoretical justification to the new emphasis on tests and expertise in command. They tell us that the "key to eliminating the differences between mental and manual labor [is]. . .raising the cultural level and capabilities of the masses as a whole." This is the revisionist line that turns things upside down. In fact, it is by carrying on struggle to transform the relations of production—specifically here to restrict the division of labor—and preventing class polarization, it is only on this basis that the general cultural and political level of the masses can be raised step by step in tempo with the development of the economy.

Attempts to overturn the achievements of the Cultural Revolution were very real, indeed. The Four were not paranoid. They understood what was happening in society and if they should be damned for fighting revisionists then damn the dictatorship of the proletariat. The slogan "Be the Master of the Wharf, Not the Slave of Tonnage" was raised in Shanghai in 1974 to oppose attempts to pressure workers to quickly fulfill their quota with the promise that they could go home early if they did. Struggles intensified—particularly as the demands of production grew—over the degree to which cadres would participate in labor, whether or not worker suggestions for technical innovation would be heeded and how much of a role workers would have in formulating rational rules and regulations. The Four played a major role in these struggles—a positive one—and who but the bourgeoisie and their lackeys would fault them for challenging the revisionist world outlook and practices.

In sum, the Four were not "stuck" but rooted in and steeled by the experiences and lessons of the Cultural Revolution. The Cultural Revolution was not simply an event, but an "unprecedented event," raising the consciousness of the masses and indicating and representing a fundamental breakthrough on the road to communism. In bringing the revolution to a higher stage, the Cultural Revolution also increased the resistance from the forces representing the old order, and the transformations fought for came under continual attack. Mao did not conclude that the difficulties and setbacks encountered by many of these new things meant that there was something wrong with them or that they ought to be abandoned. He upheld them and called for their strengthening.

It was true that the class struggle did not proceed in a straight line from the early stages of the Cultural Revolution, and the Four recognized the zig-zag nature of the class struggle. The struggle to defend these new things would not and did not take the same form as the struggle during the earlier period of the Cultural Revolution which brought them forward. There is a difference between an uprising in Shanghai against a municipal Party committee and a campaign to criticize and reject Lin Piao and Confucius. But this is the same class struggle and eventually, as Mao says, the class nature of the enemy determines that they will show themselves. Such is what happened as these contradictions boiled over with the right deviationist wind and the subsequent defeat of the Four. To accuse the Four of sectarianism for not uniting with this wind is not just absurd, but the height of hypocrisy coming from those who would not unite with the majority of our Party's Central Committee—which holds a correct line. Freaks and monsters must jump out, this is a law of class struggle.

To get an idea of just how far things have regressed comrades should look at the article in *Peking Review* #1 which upholds the work of a mathematician who has been studying the so-called Goldbach conjecture. This theorem has little practical value. What's more we learn that this mathematician "more often than not, spends all day long in the library or his office"—and this was held up as a moving example of the spirit of self-sacrifice. This should be contrasted with an article from the *Peking Review* #50, 1972, entitled "Mathematicians Among Workers." The article says, "while paying attention to the study of basic mathematical theories, mathematicians are making energetic efforts to let mathematics directly serve production and the working people." It describes how a leading mathematician who had written a popular study on planning methods which employs an approach to determine through the least number of experiments satisfactory ratios for, let's say, the amount of an element to be added to a heat of steel, had gone out with other mathematicians to workers to teach this method and conduct further studies. The 1978 article highlights how this Goldbach research has produced theoretical results approaching advanced world levels. The 1972 article emphasizes mathematics in the service of the Chinese revolution. (The Goldbach conjecture, if proven, will enable one to understand that 8=3+5. We hope our earnest researcher will continue to diligently carry out Hua Kuo-feng's line, remain steadfastly in his study and make still greater contributions.)

Class Struggle Runs Through Everything— Once Again, Taking the Three Directives As the Key Link

The section of the Menshevik document entitled "Class Struggle is the Key Link" sets a new standard for eclecticism. (pp. 158-62) It resurrects Teng's formulation that the three directives concerning study of the theory of proletarian dictatorship and combatting and preventing revisionism, promoting unity and stability and pushing the national economy forward are an inseparable whole. But they pull off an intellectual coup by saying that the class struggle to which Mao refers is not the study of the dicatatorship of the proletariat to combat and prevent revisionism; this is an ideological directive, they maintain, and taking class struggle as the key link means recognizing that class struggle runs through all three revolutionary movements of class struggle, the struggle for production and scientific experiment.

In a way their formulation sounds quite revolutionary—class struggle runs through everything. But upon closer inspection we find that they water down what is meant by the class struggle exactly by denying that the directive pertaining to the theory of the dictatorship of the proletariat and combatting and preventing revisionism is the key one, is the directive which speaks to what the heart of the class struggle is. Our authors tell us "The gang wants to say, and the current CC would parrot, that the first directive is the class struggle one. Do they think that there will not be fierce class struggle between the proletariat and the bourgeoisie on the basis and the reason for stability and unity?" But what these Mensheviks won't accept is that it is precisely and only by grasping the theory of the dictatorship of the proletariat and the fight against revisionism that one can make a correct determination of what kind of stability and unity is in the interests of the working class.

This attempt to render Mao more profound would be laughable were our Mensheviks not making it so central to their argument. What's the point of Mao attacking the formulation that the three directives must be taken as the key link if not to criticize putting them on a par with each other? Mao does not say, "What! Taking the three directives as the key link! Class struggle runs through the three directives and runs through everything!" He says class struggle is the key link. Stability and unity and pushing the national economy forward are not in themselves class struggle. Class struggle will determine the nature of this stability and unity and what road to take with regard to the national economy, but to make them class struggle is classical two-into-one logic. But what is studying the theory of the dictatorship of the proletariat and combatting and preventing revisionism if not class struggle? Of course, if Mao had issued a directive that simply said "read some books" then our Mensheviks might have a point that class struggle is something else, but again we ask our Mensheviks—Mao says study what in order to do what?

To say that class struggle runs through the directive on the dictatorship of the proletariat is absurd—it's like saying one pound weighs one pound and palming this off as a weighty statement. The point is that the first directive focused the key questions of the class struggle and the two lines at that time. Taking up this directive and putting it in first place is the basis for the proletariat to wage struggle on all fronts. Putting the three directives on a par, as the revisionists in China and their sycophants here do, can only prevent the proletariat from successfully waging the class struggle on any front.

The Mensheviks object to the CC Report's comment that the Four were "concerned that in the effort to fulfill the task of modernization the basic task—the class struggle—not be thrown overboard..." By raising this point we are accused of denying that the "class struggle does in fact and must consciously run through and guide such tasks as the four modernizations." But the point is not that the struggle for production is unimportant (more on this later) nor, for that matter, that the class struggle doesn't interpenetrate with the struggle for production or the four modernizations.

The most important question that has to be dealt with is whether or not the four modernizations are the main task of the working class. The Four were very clear about this as indicated in the CC Report. The four modernizations were a task in connection with the development of the national economy but they could not be made the historic or lofty goal to which the working class aspires as the current rulers present it. For these people the class struggle essentially boils down to whether you go fast or slow in production. For Leibel Bergman the Four sinned by criticizing and attacking the revisionist line behind the "four modernizations" scheme. According to the paper Bergman presented to the CC, the Four, instead of publishing and attacking the three "weeds", should have followed the policy of "contributing to their improvement." Failing to do this was, according to Bergman, the Four's "Final nonsense." Here we have the Mensheviks' two-into-one method nakedly advertised by their leading exponent of it—"improve" revisionism instead of exposing it—perhaps Bergman would like to rewrite Mao's directive to say study the theory of proletarian dictatorship and improve and strengthen revisionism.

Our Mensheviks are so "into" the revisionist line in China that they accept without blinking the notion that the four modernizations should be the main task and "historical mission" for the next 20 plus years.

This is very important because two possibilities face the working class in power: to advance toward the realization of communism or to go back to capitalism. To identify and smash the restorationist activities of the bourgeoisie the working class must be able to distinguish Marxism from revisionism, socialism from imperialism, restoration from counter-restoration. It's not enough to proclaim that class struggle runs through everything, what must be grasped is what question the class struggle centers on and this is the restriction of bourgeois right in the economic base and struggling against bourgeois ideology, in particular the ideology of bourgeois right. So it is not us or the Four who are up-in-the-cloud class strugglers but our Mensheviks, with their mealy-mouthed "class struggle runs through everything" thinking, who really negate the class struggle.

We are accused of "turning over the field of economic development to the bourgeoisie" and not seeing that the "actual class struggle is raging on all fronts, not just in the superstructure and ideology." In effect our Mensheviks are denying the decisive role of ideological and political struggle and liquidating struggle in the superstructure over the big issues in society. Unless struggle is carried on in the realm of ideology and politics, it will not be possible to deal with questions pertaining to "economic development."

It was Mao who attached tremendous importance to the superstructure and the struggle over line. In his criticism of Stalin's *Economic Problems of Socialism* Mao says, "This book by Stalin has not a word on the superstructure from the beginning to the end. It never touches upon man. We read of things but not man." The struggle in the superstructure is dialectically related to the struggle in the economic base. The Four consistently paid attention to production but did this by putting revolution in command. Production developed in a socialist direction under their leadership because they armed the workers with an understanding of what was going on in society broadly and because they mobilized the workers to revolutionize the relations of production through such measures as the transformation of rules and regulations and training worker technicians.

In the supplementary reading material distributed for the China discussion, Chang Ch'un-ch'iao criticizes the slogan "conscientiously embodying into the tasks of production the class struggle in the sphere of production." What is wrong with it is that the consciousness of the masses, their understanding of overall line can only be raised through "the practice of concerning oneself with the revolution in the superstructure." Moreover, and very much linked with this, capitalist tendencies in other spheres of society will go unchecked and the bourgeoisie will be able to wreak havoc in the superstructure and the base if the masses are organized around a line of concentrating on carrying on the struggle for production.

Only by starting from the overall line of the Party and by paying attention to "affairs of state" is it possible to grasp how to lead the struggle for production and to wage class struggle on this front. Our Mensheviks speak of the *microscope and telescope* of Marxism-Leninism. It is quite fitting and telling that they reverse the order of the two as spelled out by Mao, who speaks of the *telescope and microscope.* Because you need the telescope first to get a picture of the whole situation and to get a long-range view of the larger questions in society before you can use the microscope to analyze particulars.

This outlook fits in perfectly with our Mensheviks' notion of class struggle in this country. Out of each particular battle—which would be the equivalent of out of each production unit in China—it is possible to draw the whole class struggle. It also explains their enthusiasm for the "prosaic tasks" of socialist construction (this appears in their criticism of socialist new things and the Cultural Revolution). Good hard work will be quite enough, and Jimmy Higgins or Chen Yung-kuei serve as excellent models for these Mensheviks. Take up political questions as they arise in the course of production or a particular battle, this is the kind of spontaneity and pragmatism for which they have enduring fondness. Don't raise a stink about two-line struggle at the commanding heights of the Party and society, line questions will be settled in due time in connection with "concrete" tasks.

The class struggle cannot be limited to individual production units—either in the handling of production questions which require, yes, that politics be put in command, or in the struggle against bourgeois methods of leadership of leading cadre. This is why the Mensheviks fall head over heels over the Tachai example which *for them* means solely working in the spirit of self-sacrifice and self-reliance. This is all very good, but it opens the possibility of a Tachai surrounded by a sea of capitalism. How different is it fundamentally from a kibbutz in Israel if workers and peasants are not concerned with and acting on questions that go beyond their immediate experiences. The bourgeoisie in China can make excellent use of a Tachai brigade—practicing all the virtues of hard work, thrift and self-reliance—just as it does in this country with industrious farmers. The Four correctly emphasized that the peasants at Tachai and every other brigade must lift their heads and deal blows against the biggest capitalist roaders and their revisionist outlook and practices on every front, and in particular in the superstructure.

Two articles in the *Peking Review* written under the guidance of the Four present the correct view of what class struggle means in the period of socialist revolution. The first from #18, 1976, describes what it means for workers to be masters of the country and the factories. (We should point out in this connection that the slogan referred to earlier, "Be the Masters of the Wharf, Not Slaves to Tonnage," is being criticized currently.) This article says, "They [the workers] pay attention *first* [our emphasis] of all to 'cardinal affairs' which means taking an active part in the political movements led by the Party, carrying out class struggle, combatting and preventing revisionism and consolidating the dictatorship of the proletariat. Meanwhile, *they also* [our emphasis] keep any eye on whether their factories are advancing along the correct line and in the correct direction and whether the Party's principles and policies are correctly implemented." The key point here is that workers must be principally concerned with "cardinal affairs" and on that basis supervise the orientation of their factories. These "cardinal affairs" first and foremost involved the movement to criticize Lin Piao and Confucius and to take hold of educational and cultural positions long dominated by the bourgeoisie. 700 shipbuilders from this plant lectured on Legalist works at the Talien Polytechnic Institute. One wonders whether a test of competence and academic excellence has been designed for these workers by now. One wonders whether their in-plant study classes even exist any more since they get in the way of production, no doubt.

Another article from #2, 1975, describes how at an oilfield a sharp struggle developed over whether to introduce a new hoisting method. Several workers felt it would be too risky to test it out given the demands of production. The article then goes on to say, "They did not argue over the actual work of whether to adopt the new technology or to use the old method. They first criticized Lin Piao and Confucius' crime in plotting restoration and retrogression." This is not to separate or divorce theory from practice, but to grasp questions in the ideological realm in the most sweeping way exactly in order to activate the enthusiasm and deepen the understanding of the masses and to bring to play the active role of the superstructure.

For our Mensheviks this approach would obviously be labelled idealist. Wasn't this after all their objection to the Party Branches article (*Revolution*, September 1977)—too much "line in its own right"—and wasn't this their view of the RCYB, that we should just get it on in the struggle and that it wasn't very important to wage ideological struggle, much less win students and youth to the historic cause of the working class. The "gang of 4," we are constantly reminded, separated the ideology task from the policy task. But, again, how can you be in a position to analyze these so-called policy tasks, which from Hua & Co. are nothing but revisionist calls to boost production and heal the wounds of class conflict, anyway, unless they are approached from the high plane of two-line struggle. The most important thing is to combat and prevent revisionism, that is waging the class struggle and making revolution against the bourgeoisie. The first directive was the key link. Teng put the three directives on the same par: so do the Mensheviks. Teng raised economics over politics by separating politics completely from economics. Our Mensheviks reduce politics to modernization, to the fulfillment and struggle over production tasks. Herein lies their unity with Teng.

Revisionists Revise Red Papers 7

Line counts for even less with our authors in their rewrite of *Red Papers 7.* (See p. 164) They chafe at the CC Report's point that "when a revisionist line leads and the leadership is not in the hands of the masses, bourgeois relations of production will actually exist." Idealism, they shout. These "bourgeois relations do not exist because a revisionist line leads. They exist because of the nature of socialism itself." It is truly amazing how quickly these people repudiate the basic line of our Party and tip-toe into the garden of revisionism—and Trotskyism, for that matter. Their attack exactly echoes the Trotskyites.

They take as their authority on this point a passage from *Red Papers 7* that although "Stalin argued forcefully (and correctly) that the law of value continues to operate under socialism, he did not draw the correct conclusion from this—that capitalist production relations must then also exist in some (often) hidden forms." But the point of this statement is not that where the law of value operates you of necessity have bourgeois production relations, but that the existence of this law lays the basis for capitalist relations to emerge and is bound to engender new bourgeois elements. If there is any confusion on this point the Mensheviks ought to read further into *Red Papers.* On page 55 we find an elaboration and deepening of this point, "Even under socialism, the dictatorship of the proletariat, commodity production continues and there is some scope for the law of value. As Lenin pointed out, this provides the material basis for capitalist relations, even in socialism, and provides the material basis for capitalist restoration."

The law of value and commodity production are residues and defects left over from the capitalist system. Under the dictatorship of the proletariat the commodity system is *not* aimed at the production of surplus value and its harmful political and ideological influences are strenuously struggled against. The working class uses the law of value and commodity production to promote socialism while at the same time restricting and working to eliminate them. The bourgeoisie will try to use them to promote capitalism. If a revisionist line prevails in a particular unit, the social relations will degenerate, they will not be the same as before, they will be relations of profit in command and oppression. This is because line will transform reality—whether the Mensheviks are conscious of this or not—and it will transform reality one way or another exactly because these relations contain the seeds of capitalism. But whether they are transformed into capitalist relations or advance to a higher level of socialist relations depends on the line in command.

Perhaps our Mensheviks can't accept this view that the persistence of commodity relations implies the possiblity of capitalism because that would place "ideology tasks" too far above "policy tasks". Almost in anticipation of the Menshevik argument, *Red Papers* has more to say in the above quoted section: "This is why it is not idealist to stress the importance of proletarian ideology as the leading blow against capitalism, and why it was essential that Stalin's and Lenin's proletarian line be smashed first." But the real irony of their position is that here they are grumbling about our defeatist view of socialism and now they tell us that bourgeois relations exist irrespective of the line and the transformations attempted by the working class. Socialism has become capitalism.

It is not the case that a revisionist line "creates" or "causes" bourgeois relations but that it transforms socialist relations—based on their contradictory character—into their opposite. It's curious that the Menshevik argument could have been lifted from

CL's critique:

> "We are to believe that a new bourgeoisie and proletariat emerge or do not emerge based on whether revisionism does or does not predominate in a given mine, or factory...it reduces itself to a giant checkerboard of 'units' which are now capitalist, now socialist, depending on which line the management carries out."

But isn't this the point that Mao draws attention to in his 1969 statement that many factories were in the hands of revisionists and that China would have changed colors had the Cultural Revolution not taken place? If certain social relations, for instance the division of labor, are everywhere bourgeois then every plant manager, every Party official, even Mao are bourgeois. But what makes a member of the CC a capitalist roader or a plant manager a bourgeois is not simply his position, but the line he pushes; this is what is decisive and what transforms his position from one of relative privilege into absolute tyranny, this on account of his relationship to the control and distribution of the means of production and to the instruments of the proletarian dictatorship.

Socialist Production Relations: Seeds of Communism, Vestiges of Capitalism

This point must be gone into further. Capitalist production relations are first and foremost *exploitative* relations. The working class does not own the means of production and must therefore sell its labor power in order to live. The labor of the worker is a source of enrichment to the capitalist and, bound by the laws of capitalist accumulation, the capitalist must continually step up the exploitation of the workers. This of necessity gives rise to profound inequalities in the material conditions of life of the proletariat and the bourgeoisie.

Under socialism, production relations cease being relations of exploitation. This becomes possible on account of the revolution that takes place in the ownership of the means of production. The means of production belong to the working class and workers therefore are no longer forced to sell their labor power to another class that controls the means of production.

But while the means of production have ceased to be a means of sucking surplus value out of workers, inequality is not eliminated under socialism. In particular, inequality still predominates in the field of distribution—some people receive more than others. Here bourgeois right still exists in large measure. On the basis of an equal standard—the amount of labor supplied by a worker—products will be distributed. Workers are paid according to the contribution they make. But since the contribution of different workers will vary depending on experience, skill and strength, some will receive more than others, even though others may be in greater need of a larger quantity of the articles of consumption. At the same time, while it is illegal to employ the labor of others under socialism, some people in society in comparison to others possess more responsiblity and control over the means of production such as factory managers and government planners. This is also a form of social inequality that must be restricted under socialism.

Communist production relations represent a further negation. These relations are neither exploitative nor involve inequality. The means of production are common property and distribution of products takes place according to need so that relative advantage of strength, skill, etc. no longer determines differences in distribution—such differences are solely on the basis of need. Moreover with the extensive development of the productive forces it becomes possible to eliminate the subordination of the individual worker to the division of labor and the inequalities stemming from the different positions occupied by different workers in the social process of production.

So what we have are three different types of production relations: capitalist relations which are characterized by exploitation and inequality; socialist relations which are no longer exploitative but which still contain elements of inequality; and communist production relations which have abolished both exploitation and inequality. The contradictory quality of socialist production relations derives from the transitional nature of socialist society, between capitalism and communism.

The bourgeoisie will try to seize upon the bourgeois aspects of these relations in order to restore capitalism. The proletariat will try to restrict and eventually eliminate the vestiges and remnants of inequality that persist in these relations in order to push forward to communism. The point to grasp here is that both the proletariat and the bourgeoisie will attempt to transform these same relations in directions opposite to each other.

In China the 8-grade wage system is not a capitalist production relation. The wages paid out are not in exchange for the labor power of propertyless laborers. Yet the inequality inherent in this wage system, if not restricted and handled correctly, can lead to such a situation. How can this be? Let's take a fairly representative example from China. In the Anshan Steel Works in the early 1970's the highest paid production worker received a wage that was three times greater than that of the lowest paid worker. The highest paid engineer or technician salary was about six times that of the lowest paid worker. With the extension of bonuses and rewards as seems to be the rising trend in China today, these gaps will widen and the highest paid personnel will derive large shares of the social product. If this develops unchecked the result will be polarization. Workers organized around a line of working to make money and tantalized with all kinds of material incentives will increasingly be looking out only for themselves and this will corrode the unity of the workers' ranks. This distribution relation will react on the relations among workers and create a situation more favorable to manipulating workers and creating privileged sections that will seek to preserve and extend that privilege.

Here we can see how this distribution relation can react on the system of ownership. If we look at the manager or technician whose salary is six times that of the lowest paid worker's and this grows wider, though private ownership does not exist formally, these higher incomes will increasingly take on the character of exploiting the labor of others. This is because the mass of workers will be paid just enough to survive while a privileged stratum will be in effect accumulating surplus which will represent the unpaid labor of the mass of workers. Hence, the basis for *initial* accumulation can be bourgeois right and these people will treat the means of production as means to enrich themselves. They will be pushing the workers harder under the signboard that this is the way to get ahead—more output means more money for all of us. The extension of bourgeois right can lead to instances of exploitation, and distribution will be based on the power that some have over the productive process. This is not to say that all inequality is the same as exploitation but that at a certain point quantity will turn into quality—expanding differences, giving free rein to bourgeois right, will transform inequality into exploitation.

What must be stressed again is that such polarization and degeneration of ownership will arise out of the existing production relations. This is linked very closely to the question of the bourgeoisie in the Party. (On this very important question, the Mensheviks have almost nothing to say.) The leadership of the Party is in an objective position where the power of management and distribution of the means of production and control over consumer goods is concentrated in their hands. For those leading people who take the capitalist road this position becomes the material basis for their role as the bourgeoisie in the Party and the core of the bourgeoisie in society as a whole. The planning commissions and ministries which are headed up by Party personnel are in a position to set wage policy, enact work rules, make investment decisions, decide on pricing policy for agriculture and so forth, which when guided by a revisionist line can lead to the separation of the workers from the means of production and the destruction of the socialist economy in the countryside. This bourgeoisie inside the Party is not just the agent of those who fight for and carry out a line of expanding inequalities and other policies favorable to the growth of capitalism. The bourgeoisie in the Party is the commander of all social forces in society who stand for the restoration of capitalism. It is able to mobilize and unleash these social forces by promoting a revisionist ideological and political line which concentrates their interests.

The proletariat represents socialist relations of production, the capitalist roaders represent capitalist production relations. The static view of social relations of the Mensheviks makes it impossible for them to draw this line of demarcation, and it also makes it that much clearer as to why they downgrade the tasks of revolutionizing the relations of production and carrying the struggle into the superstructure. If social relations are everywhere the same and if commodity relations are tantamount to bourgeois production relations then they'll be around for a long time. Social relations neither move backward to capitalist nor forward to more perfect socialist relations. Hence our Mensheviks' one-sided emphasis on fortifying the level of productive forces.

Basic Contradictions of Socialist Society

The socialist economic base consists of the socialist relations of production.* There is no prescribed level of the productive forces

*In the original "Reply," where this sentence now appears, the text read: "The socialist economic base is a unity of the productive forces and relations." This is incorrect; the economic base consists of the relations of production and does not include the productive forces as such. On the other hand, as the "Reply" explained, citing an article in Volume 1, Number 2 of *The Communist* (theoretical journal of the Central Committee of the RCP), "while the relations of production are what essentially define the economic base at any time, these relations of production are ultimately determined by the stage of development of the productive forces . . ." (The article in *The Communist* goes on immediately to say, "such is the dialectical relationship between the forces and relations of production." But that article, as well as the "Reply," did contain some confusion on this point in particular, which should be cleared up.)

Overall, and overwhelmingly, the original "Reply" dealt quite correctly with the dialectical relationship between the forces and relations of production, as well which, once and for all, acts as a barrier to capitalist restoration. Highly developed industry in the transitional period is no more a guarantee against such a regression—is no more a guarantee against yes, bourgeois social relations—than a less developed industrial base. Wasn't this the experience of the Soviet Union? The CC Report points out that there is no specific quantity in the development of the productive forces which can be associated with communism. For all we know, Marx might have considered a society that could send spaceprobes to Mars and duplicate forms of life as possessing an adequate material basis for communism. But we do know that Mao saw the transitional period as an extended one, perhaps lasting for centuries.

The development of the productive forces must be understood dialectically both with respect to the relations of production and more broadly as a back and forth interaction between the base and superstructure. It will not do to say, with our Mensheviks, that "Without constant advances in the base and superstructure socialism will fail." Of course, as a general statement about the need for the two to be developed it is unassailable, but it misses the point of the dialectical relationship between the two. The essentially static view they take of social relations and the struggle to transform them and their consistent underestimation of the importance of creating the political and ideological conditions for the advance toward communism makes it important to examine this question more closely.

How are we to understand Mao's statement that "The Great Proletarian Cultural Revolution is a strong motive force for the development of the social productive forces in our country"? Mao, of course, had defined what revolution is decades earlier, "A revolution is an insurrection, an act of violence by which one class overthrows another." Our Mensheviks probably view this statement, like the Cultural Revolution, as irrelevant to today's "actual condi-

---

as that between the base and the superstructure. And it is correct in particular in noting the ultimate dependence of the relations of production—the economic base—on the productive forces. But to include the productive forces as an aspect of the economic base is to confuse, and incorrectly combine, two different contradictions—between the forces and relations of production and between the relations of production (economic base) and the superstructure. In fact, this error is not only misleading in general, but specifically tends to underrate the importance of both the relations of production and the superstructure—and of the contradiction between them—and could weaken criticism of the "theory of the productive forces," the very opportunist line that is being exposed in this section of the "Reply" and is repudiated throughout the "Reply" as a whole. Some other slight changes were made from the original text to reflect the correct understanding of this point more clearly.

tions." How, on the other hand, are we to interpret the statement in *PR* #4 (1978) which castigates the notion that " 'revolution' is always a political concept in a society where there are classes and class struggle"? Continuing further, the author writes, "can we ultimately defeat and eliminate the bourgeoisie and ensure the transition from socialism to communism simply by carrying on the struggle in the superstructure and not rapidly developing the productive forces?" The difference between Mao's statement and that of the Hua cabal is not one of degree or emphasis, they are fundamentally opposed. Mao is saying that the Cultural Revolution was exactly that, a revolution in the superstructure, and revolution is indeed political, involving as it does the struggle between classes. The eclecticism of this second statement defies belief.

First off, this statement—and the whole article of which it is a part—does not express the actual dialectical relationship between revolution and production but in effect sets them against each other; it opposes Mao's revolutionary formulation of "grasp revolution, promote production." Second, it poses the contradiction—which, as noted, it treats as essentially an antagonism—as that between "carrying on the struggle in the *superstructure*" and "rapidly developing the productive forces" (emphasis added here). Thus, while downgrading the importance of struggle in the superstructure and in fact pitting it against developing the productive forces, this statement leaves out the question of revolutionizing the economic base, constantly transforming the relations of production. And insofar as this article deals with the question of transforming production relations it treats this as a by-product of the development of the productive forces under socialism. This article even resurrects the position that attention should be paid "first and foremost" to developing the productive forces, in order to promote the revisionist line of the current rulers. (See *PR* 4, 1978, p. 8.)*

---

*In the original text of this "Reply," instead of this paragraph the following appeared: "To be sure, "simply" to struggle in the superstructure is not everything, but it is, in fact, the decisive thing. And Mao's statement is that such a struggle gave great impetus to the development of the productive forces." This formulation was criticized at the Second Congress of the RCP because it did not give sufficient emphasis to the question of revolutionizing the economic base and tended to run counter to the correct thrust of this whole section of the "Reply," which explains how overall the economic base is principal over the superstructure. What was correct and crucial in the original text, especially in opposition to the revisionism expressed in the *Peking Review* article, was the emphasis given to waging struggle in the superstructure and the dialectical relationship between this and developing the productive forces. As the "Reply" puts it somewhat earlier, "Unless struggle is carried on in the realm of ideology and politics, it will not be possible to deal with questions of 'economic development.' "

PR #4 also raises a new "automatically" line. We are told that "the realization of farm mechanization in particular, will bring about the revolutionization of relations among all the small collectives which will in turn revolutionize the peasants' minds." Here the revisionists miss two points. One, perhaps not so salient from their standpoint, is that large-scale and more technologically advanced production will not have this effect unless there is conscious struggle in the realm of the superstructure. Two, that within a given level of ownership it is necessary and possible to constantly revolutionize relations which in turn will promote the further development of the productive forces.

Changes in the forces of production do lead to changes in the relations of production, but big changes in the relations of production lead to *big* changes in the productive forces. This is what happened in the period of the Great Leap Forward when peasants organized communes—raised the level of ownership by bringing together land and implements and establishing communal facilities—and gave tremendous drive to the productive forces. Mao summed this phenomenon up by saying that "collectivization precedes mechanization." But it is also the case that there will always be the need to improve these relations exactly because the productive forces are active and constantly developing.

In *The Communist* (Vol. 1, No. 2), we point out "while the relations of production are what essentially define the economic base at any time, these relations of production are ultimately determined by the stage of development of the productive forces . . ." (As pointed out in the CC Report this article was written as a compromise. But even as is, it stands as an indictment of the Men-

In other words, at all times it is of great importance to pay attention to waging the class struggle in the superstructure will indeed be decisive in determining the nature of the economic base—and at such times therefore the superstructure is principal over the base, reversing the overall relationship between the two.

It should be noted here that the "Reply," including in the section in which the above change has been made, does place emphasis on the importance of revolutionizing both the economic base and the superstructure, as for example in the following statement, which appears shortly after the one changed: "Hence, the working class must carry out revolution in all spheres of the superstructure as well as in the economic base."

It should also be noted here that the Four, while attaching great importance to revolution in the realm of the superstructure, also strongly stressed the need for continuous revolution in the economic base—a point which is also made several times in the "Reply." In fact, the revisionist rulers now reigning in China have repeatedly attacked the Four for laying great stress on revolutionizing the economic base and in fact for leading the proletariat and masses in class struggle in this realm.

Some other minor changes have also been made in the text to reflect the correct understanding of these points more clearly.

sheviks and their mentors.) In this sense, the productive forces remain principal in the socialist period. The productive forces establish certain boundaries and limits to what can be achieved at any given point in history. But the relations of production exert a tremendous reaction on the productive forces. The working class can exercise great freedom within any stage in revolutionizing and transforming the relations of production, further liberating the productive forces and propelling advances toward the next stage. And at certain points in this process the relations of production will play the principal and decisive role. For instance, it is not possible given the level of development of the productive forces to eliminate the individual enterprise as a unit of production and calculation. But it is possible to bring to a higher level relations of socialist cooperation between enterprises, for instance campaigns to spread technical innovation or check up on quality of goods. For some time to come in China, the work team will remain the basic accounting unit in the countryside, but it is possible to reduce and narrow differences between them, which not only prevents polarization but which in dialectical relation with the development of the economy helps lay the basis for the advance to a higher level of ownership.

The working class does not passively wait on the further development of the productive forces in order for changes to take place, but actively seeks to transform social relations. There is, then, a continual interaction between the forces and relations of production, now one, now the other, pushing the other forward.

As pointed out before, the economic base of any given society consists of the relations of production, while these are ultimately determined by the level of development of the productive forces. The socialist economic base cannot grow spontaneously out of the old system of capitalism nor can it advance under socialism without decisive interventions by the working class itself. What is required in the first place is a revolution in the superstructure which is the seizure of state power by the working class. This constitutes only the first step of its historic mission, which is to wipe out all class distinctions and achieve communism. In order for this to happen the working class must subject production to conscious control, and this requires grasping the economic laws of society and acting in accordance with them. This, however, is possible only by sweeping away ideological influences, the force of habit and other remnants of capitalism which stand as obstacles to understanding and transforming the world on the basis of the proletariat's interests. Hence, the working class must carry out revolution in all spheres of the superstructure as well as in the economic base.

How in light of this are we to assess the role of the superstructure in the period of socialist transition? Clearly, when the proletariat seizes power, the superstructure is principal. Without first establishing the proletarian dictatorship the new forms of ownership cannot be developed. Once established, the state power of the working class, its ideology, and its cultural and educational institutions promote the growth of the economic base. It is the economic relations of society that call forth a particular superstructure. It is not just any superstructure that can be grafted at will onto the economic base. The institutions and ideas of society are ultimately rooted in the material conditions of society.

On the other hand, socialist production relations cannot develop without the support and influence of the superstructure. To give one example: to make a leap forward in the wage system, for instance in going from piece-rates to time-rates, as occurred in many places in China in 1958, required intense ideological preparation and struggle. But, though this ideological struggle was decisive for this particular leap, what was possible under these circumstances was in the end determined by the economic base. No amount of ideological struggle could eliminate the wage system.

In sum, the economic base of society—that is, the relations of production—is principal over the superstructure. It is principal in so far as (a) it determines for the transitional period as a whole the character of the superstructure, and (b) at each stage of development of the revolution it sets the limits or terms in which the superstructure can exercise its influence. Yet, at all times the superstructure reacts upon the base and influences it enormously. This can be seen in the very powerful role that the Party of the working class and its line plays. The relationship between the base and superstructure can be seen as one in which the base is the principal or *determining* factor and the superstructure is the *initiating* one.

Under socialism there is both harmony and contradiction between the base and superstructure. It is a general law of historical materialism that the superstructure will sooner or later become an obstacle to the further development of the economic base. This is because the productive forces are the most active factor in social development and their development continually requires transformations in the relations of production. But there will come a point at which the superstructure no longer can facilitate these transformations. At such a point, changes in the superstructure become decisive. When the superstructure more impedes than fosters the further development of the base, it becomes principal. This does not mean that only when it is principal are changes required in the superstructure; it only means that when changes in the superstructure are decisive in determining the nature of the economic base then the superstructure becomes principal.

The contradiction between the superstructure as a progressive force promoting the development of the base and as a reactionary influence assumes the form of class struggle. Every few years in a socialist society a major struggle will break out and find its concentrated expression in the superstructure. The outcome of this struggle will determine whether the working class continues to rule. Therefore at such times, the superstructure becomes principal since the socialist base will be destroyed if the working class loses power.

Such struggles will occur often under socialism since the bourgeoisie reemerges out of the productive relations of socialist society and will continually jump out under new conditions. For this reason, the transformation of the relation between the base and superstructure, with now the one, now the other principal, will go on in a way not found in preceding societies. The superstructure was principal at the start of the Cultural Revolution. Contradictions had emerged in the management of enterprises, the system of education, the relationship of the Party to the masses, etc. A fierce struggle raged between the bourgeoisie and proletariat, which initially resulted in a great victory by the proletariat. The transformations carried out in the superstructure did not simply bring it into mechanical conformity with the base but spurred further transformations in the productive relations. In fact it is a general rule that through winning victories in these major struggles concentrated in the superstructure the proletariat is able to make new leaps in transforming society as a whole.

Even when big struggles like these do not take place, class struggle is the key link. Chang Chun-chiao explains in his pamphlet: "In the various spheres of the superstructure, some areas are in fact still controlled by the bourgeoisie which has the upper hand there; some are being transformed but the results are not yet consolidated, and old ideas and the old force of habit are still stubbornly obstructing the growth of socialist new things." The bourgeoisie will try continually to regain positions it has lost and to prevent the working class from winning new ones. Out of this necessity, the working class must wage active class struggle. This is the decisive condition for carrying out any other task.

That class struggle is the key link is not in opposition to the fact that the base is overall principal in the socialist period. Classes do, after all, arise out of the material conditions of the base, and the questions fought out by contending classes have their ultimate point of determination in the base. This can be seen in the case of a correct or incorrect line. The correctness or incorrectness of ideological and political line is decisive. Line must guide the forward advance of the working class. But any old line won't do—it is not line, but *correct* line that moves things forward. Whether or not a line is correct is determined by whether it conforms to and promotes the needs of the development of the base. This is not to say that every line struggle turns on economic questions. On the contrary, sharp line struggles also take place over cultural, educational and other questions in the superstructure. But here, too, in the final analysis what is progressive and advanced in these fields is that which contributes to the development of the economic base—to changes in the production relations which further liberate the productive forces.

The bourgeoisie will, as mentionied above, try to win back its lost positions and throw up barriers to every new advance by the proletariat. The development of the productive forces in and of itself cannot defeat the class enemy. Only resolute class struggle by the working class can and there are no circumstances under which the development of the productive forces can take precedence over class struggle. Otherwise the bourgeoisie will win out no matter what the level of development of the productive forces.

What the working class strives to do is to *liberate the productive forces* from the shackles of capitalist production relations and the remnants of bourgeois relations still existing under socialism. This is not the same thing as *developing* the productive forces, though in the long run it will have this effect. Liberating the productive forces is fundamentally a qualitative question of removing the fetters that prevent the working class from consciously using and developing these productive forces. For example, a rule that stipulates that only certain people can perform repair work in a plant stifles worker initiative and is a fetter on the productive forces. If the question is approached, as the current leadership in China does, as one of developing the productive forces, then rules which chain workers to routine and convention and uphold one-man management are justifiable if in the short run they raise production. Achieving the abundance necessary for communism can only take place through the continuous interaction of the forces and relations of production and the base and superstructure such that the working class gains increasing mastery over society and nature.

Mao's all-important formulation "Grasp Revolution, Promote Production" expresses the dialectical relationship between waging the class struggle and developing the productive forces. Fundamentally, the fetters on the productive forces represent the influence of the bourgeoisie and the vestiges of capitalist society. Attacking and striking down these fetters to the greatest degree possible, in the superstructure and the base, on the basis of consciously grasping the laws of society will lead to the further development of the productive forces. This is the only way that the economy can continue to advance in great strides along the socialist road.

Two, Lines, Two Roads on the Economy

The Four were not opposed to modernization. They were not opposed to the mechanization of agriculture. Maybe Mickey Jarvis believes that Chang Chun-chiao went into plants and told people to let production take care of itself and preached against economic development. But, then again, Mickey Jarvis probably believes that the Minister of Culture, a "sworn accomplice of the Gang of Four," swallowed detergent and killed himself. It's the Mensheviks, it seems, who will swallow anything.

In fact, the suburban communes under the leadership of the Four had been making strides in the direction of mechanization. Shanghai was not exactly what you would call an industrial backwater. Major innovations in ship building, machine-tool manufacture, and textile production were pioneered in the city. Moreover, significant renovations of industrial facilities were made with little or no assistance from the state. We'll have more to say on this later.

What the Four were opposed to was modernization with a capital M. This was not a moral injunction that small is beautiful or to be backward is sublime. Rather their objections were twofold. First, the four modernizations as they were conceived and programmatically implemented by the Teng/Hua headquarters were guided by a revisionist line. In essence it was a line that held that nothing should interfere with production and anything that gave it a boost was perfectly acceptable. Look at the "20 Points." It says that all this non-productive activity like cultural and political work in the plants that detracts from production must cease and desist. But the same document redefines the work of technicians as productive labor. Hua does this one better and restores their titles in the CC circular. If this isn't the outlook of these people—which is to say, get rid of anything that stands in the way of production—comrades should look twice at *PR* #4 (1978) which says "since we are dedicated to the cause of communism, we must, *first and foremost,* be enthusiastic about developing our productive forces." (our emphasis).

But the second objection of the Four, and very much related, was that the economic plans of the revisionists were just plain wrong, they did not reflect the realities of the world situation, the Chinese economy and the Chinese road to socialism. These plans could not utilize the real strengths of the Chinese economy since they did not flow from its actual material base. They would lead to failure and demoralization, lopsided and unbalanced development, increasing dependency on foreign powers and would have disastrous consequences militarily, when war broke out. It is to these points that we turn.

The current leadership in China paints a picture of stagnation and disappointment in the performance of the Chinese economy. We have to ask ourselves, then, why is it that in 1975 Chou En-lai presents a report to the 4th National People's Congress which upholds socialist new things and declares that "Reactionaries at home and abroad asserted that the Great Proletarian Cultural Revolution would certainly disrupt the development of our national economy, but facts have now given them a strong rebuttal." To whom is he referring and what might they be saying?

Chou's report indicates that the total value of agricultural output for 1974 was 51% higher than that of 1964 and that gross industrial output increased by 190% over the same period. These are impressive gains. The Four are arrested some 20 months later. Had they in that period so botched things up that it was no longer possible to say that the Cultural Revolution was a good thing for the economy or that the assessment of the overall performance of the economy could no longer be upheld? Facts are interesting in this regard. In 1974, industry grew by only 4% and growth overall was below the 10 year average. Does this call into question Chou's report, is he running from the truth? No, it does not. Not because there were not problems, but because, overall, the Chinese road to socialism was the correct one and reactionaries at home and abroad were on the one hand trying to seize on these difficulties to justify a detour from that road and, on the other, trying to stir up further problems to add strength to their argument. The solution to these problems lay in persevering on the Chinese road to socialism. There was certainly nothing that occurred during the years '74-'76 which justifies the new turn of the current rulers in economic practices and priorities.

Mao makes the statement in 1974 that "China cannot compare with the rich or powerful countries politically, economically, etc. She can be grouped only with the relatively poor countries."(See *PR* #45, 1977.) This is an important point to keep in mind in deciding what kind of standards to apply to the development of the Chinese economy and how such development will proceed. It also focuses attention on the current leadership's insistence that "advanced world levels" be the measuring rod for future economic growth.

The Chinese Road

Based on the fact of its underdevelopment and summing up the lessons of socialist construction in the Soviet Union as well as China's own experiences, the CPC under Mao was able to develop a model for growth which took shape with the rising struggles of the masses following liberation. This was to rapidly promote the productive forces by making maximum use of the initiative of the workers and peasants—that is fundamentally through the practice of revolution—and by practicing independence and self-reliance. Intense two-line struggle occurred within the Party over whether this was the correct path forward.

This struggle turned first and foremost on the question of whether the struggle for production had superceded the class struggle. Liu held that it did and fell back on every rotten scheme and capitalist method around to promote production, even going so far as to say that exploitation had its good points. The major problem facing the Chinese people in the development of their economy in the '50s and at the bottom of controversies over the direction of the economy is agriculture. How to boost its growth rate? This isn't simply a matter of feeding people, which is obviously of great concern given the historic condition of agriculture in China, but something upon which hinges the entire development of the economy. Marx explained about capitalist societies and those that preceded them that "an agricultural labor productivity exceeding the basic requirements of the laborer is the basis of all societies . . ." He also said in connection with socialist society that it "creates a material prerequisite for the new synthesis of a higher level, the combination of agriculture with industry." The working class must arrange these relations on the basis of objective laws.

The growth of agricultural production will be an important

determinant of the rate of industrial growth both in terms of the resources that can be set aside for such growth after allocations to agriculture and, more decisively, because industry depends on agriculture for raw materials, markets, accumulation funds, and labor. The revisionists, headed by Liu, had a position on this and it came to a head with the Great Leap Forward. They claimed that agriculture could not advance without first undergoing mechanization. This depended on large-scale industry supplying implements and equipment. In the main, the Chinese industrial base was not sufficient for this and, therefore, China ought to look abroad for this machinery, even if it meant going deep into debt.

Mao said that the key link was to raise the activism and enthusiasm of the peasants and on that basis to bring about collectivization. This would then provide the basis for mechanization. Moreover, the development of small-scale rural industry would make use of local raw materials and know-how, thereby contributing to the national economy, diffuse skills and technique among the peasants and help to break down differences between peasants and workers. It would serve the immediate needs of agriculture while developing into a major force for mechanization. All this related to another big question, an extremely important strategic principle, "Be prepared for war." With its population concentrated in the countryside, its transport system relatively backward, and its defense capabilities dependent on mobilizing her people, agricultural self-sufficiency and local self-reliance in industry would be key to fighting the kind of war favorable to the Chinese.

The Great Leap saw millions of peasants joining together into communes, practicing new agricultural techniques, breaking with tradition and superstition in family and social life, and carrying on political education. It saw peasants smelting steel in their back yards and manufacturing fertilizer in villages, besides the further advances in the ownership system. All this was narrowing the differences between town and country and between worker and peasant.

In industry the Great Leap Forward gave rise to new industries and technologies in the cities, the elimination of bonuses and piece rates in many plants and new management practices. The bourgeoisie never ceased to sabotage this movement. The specter of peasants making iron and steel was held up to ridicule. Small plants in the countryside were ordered shut as were many health and recreation centers in the communes. Within the communes individual plots were restored and encouraged, private markets were promoted—in a word the two most significant achievements of the

Great Leap, the communes and the "walking on two legs" principle of combining small and medium industry with large industry were systematically attacked.

It's interesting because you can look at the rural construction index for the Great Leap period and see that farm buildings, small scale irrigation and water conservancy works and small industrial facilities grew immensely. And you can see the same in cities where plants were renovated and capacity expanded. But industrial output fell and grain production which soared initially also fell on account of natural disasters. The dislocations in industry were caused in large part by the exodus of the Soviet technicians, but also a movement of this scope and magnitude was bound to cause problems, such as bottlenecks in transport and certain breakdowns in plan fulfillment.

The reins had to be pulled in, the revisionists shouted. Things were a total mess. Mao, who saw the great social and political consequences the Leap was having, even though certain adjustments would have to be made, replied "this is chaos on a grand scale"—and he regarded this as mainly good and not bad. He pointed out that this upheaval taught millions what they could not have learned in years. Nevertheless, the revisionists headed up by Liu, Teng, Po I-Po, Li Hsien-nien (and it seems, for a time, they had the backing of Chou) had the upper hand. The 70 Articles (the forerunner of today's "20 Points") represented their program of reassertion of central control over enterprises which had been run with local initiative, close monitoring of their finances, the reaffirmation of the role of specialists and the reduction of study time.

These revisionists slandered the achievements of the masses. They told them that they ran the factories badly, did not produce up to high standards. The "irregular" methods of the masses were said to be the source of countless disruptions and bottlenecks. And they cracked down (not always successfully as many peasants resisted the orders to shut the rural plants) in the name of economic efficiency. They could produce mounds of statistics to make their case and they even could show how production picked up under their regime. But what happened is that many of the projects and creations of the masses came on strong—new strains of rice, cultivation methods, dams and canals, improvements in technique—that is, they paid off and these creeps took credit for it.

The 70 Articles were introduced on an experimental basis in Shanghai in 1961. Control over workers was increased ("too much anarchy during the Leap") through the imposition of new rules and regulations, and full-time supervisors were brought in to enforce them. Some plants had manuals with as many as 800 pages of rules (if you need this part, make out a request and put it on this form, and give it to this person and so on). *Peking Review* defends the Taylor system. This is nothing new. Around this time, in a steel works in Peking some 100 job analysts were assigned to watch over workers and make time/motion studies to be used for calculating piece rates and bonuses. Quality control became one of the main ways to control the workers and slander their defying convention. Workers would be penalized and some plants even shut because they did not meet the standards imposed on them.

There was a trust system experimented with in 1963. Each industry was to be vertically integrated, which means brought into a central command structure. Decisions regarding material and finished products would be made at the very top and the performance of these enterprises would be judged according to their profitability. This was an obvious attempt to pour cold water on a situation which had grown up during the Leap, when enterprises practicing local initiative would make use of local raw materials and waste material, help set up and assist small local industry, spread technical knowledge, and aid agriculture locally. Teng, Hua and others in '75-'76 were advocating something very similar in discussions of the roles of central ministries.

Many of the same people involved in the reversal of the Leap are now in the cockpit. They are making the same arguments about disorder and inefficiency wrought by the mass movements coming off the Cultural Revolution. Like the Great Leap, the Cultural Revolution did not solve all problems, it even created some new difficulties, but its enduring legacy was that it set a new orientation. Today, it is that orientation of mass initiative that is under attack, of putting politics in command that is under attack, of being bold and critical that is under attack. We hear nothing of the creations and achievements of Shanghai shipbuilders who broke with international norms and challenged accepted designs in constructing vessels.

The Chinese road to socialism under Mao's leadership was summed up in the phrase "take agriculture as the foundation and industry as the leading factor." It meant making grain the key link and promoting locally-run industry. Industry was to direct its efforts first toward agriculture and those branches serving it. Industry was to combine small and medium size enterprises with large ones and to rationally distribute and locate them. It was a road that saw all of this as a question of political line, of breaking down the gaps between industry/agriculture, worker/peasant, and town/country. It was based on the principle of combining local initiative and administration with central planning and predicating all of this on independence and self-reliance. This was a road which took socialist enthusiasm and activism as the main stimulus to production.

Performance of the Economy and the Four Modernizations

Was the economy stagnant or even shipwrecked in the last few years? This is the conclusion one is forced to reach if we accept certain propositions of the Hua cabal and their domestic lackeys. There are strange indications here that the very phenomenal changes that have taken place in China over the past 27 years are being slighted. Clearly what must be grasped is the long-run trend of development of the economy. The last two years, for instance, have seen poorer harvests than anticipated, largely because of natural difficulties. Particular sectors of the economy may lag behind or spurt ahead of others; in fact as Mao points out in his discussion of the Soviet texts it is through the unity of balance and imbalance that the economy develops. It is also the case that certain sectors such as transport will for some time to come remain relatively backward. But, overall, the development of the economy has been very positive.

Growth has proceeded at a pace that exceeds that of many other less developed countries with a similar per capita income. It is also the case that if we were to compare China's growth rate with that of major industrialized countries today such as the U.S., France, Germany, or Great Britain during earlier and more recent periods, China's rate of increase of per capita income has been extremely high. These measures by themselves don't tell us much since they really don't take into account the question of the real *quality* of growth: the elimination of poverty, the raising of skills level, the extension of social services, the equalization of income, and, most of all, the consolidation of the proletarian dictatorship.

The chart reproduced here reveals some interesting trends. It is taken from a congressional study. First it shows a rate of growth of GNP on an annual basis from 1953-1974 of 5.6%.[2] The makeup of this GNP shows that agricultural production has been advancing over population; industrial production starting from a small base has made rapid increases in capacity and output of industrial materials, machinery and military equipment, and very advanced technologies in nuclear weapons and satellites have been developed.

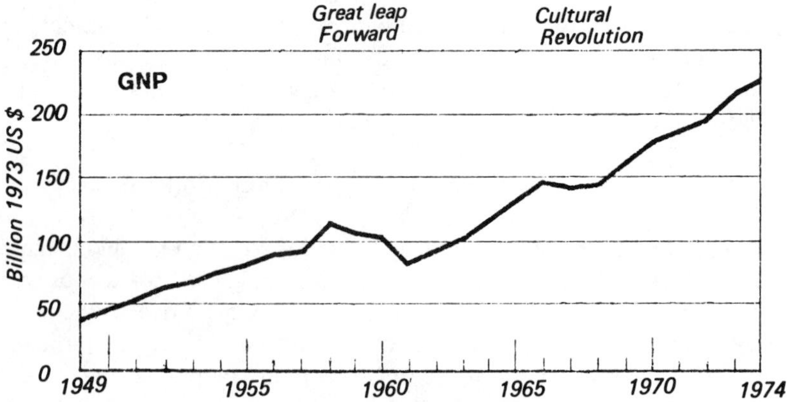

Another point which can be seen from the chart is that substantial increases in output followed the Great Leap and the mass upsurge of the Cultural Revolution. Industrial production grew at an astounding rate of 18% in 1970. What is very important to understand here is that growth has not been confined to certain sectors—although the producer goods industries have advanced impressively—but has been gradually and intentionally spread from the old and newer industrial bases to the rest of the country. This point will be gone into later, but what should be underscored here is that development has taken place according to the socialist principle of planned and proportionate development even if this has meant in the short run a slower rate of growth. What's more, as the Great Leap and Cultural Revolution indicate, on the basis of limited productive forces production relations have been radically altered. The rural industrial networks born out of these movements have played a major role in the economy providing over 50% of the nation's output of cement and 20% of its iron.

Steel has been a weak link in the economy. The Four have been blamed for its shortcomings. This weakness expresses itself in the falling off in growth in the production of steel and a shortage of special steels. The Mensheviks seize upon this to buttress their case that things were not going too well. That there were problems in steel was undeniable, but to suggest, as did a wall-poster that went up in Canton[3] in early January '77 (clearly reflecting the views of Hua, Teng, *et al.*) that China ought to be where Japan is at in total tonnage (in the range of 110 million tons) is absurd.

The Chinese steel industry was built on the foundations of the old, and massively expanded with Soviet technology and technical assistance. The sudden withdrawal of that aid and the ensuing disruptions resulted in a decline in output of just about 10 million tons and it would not be until the years of the Cultural Revolution that production would reach these levels again. The rural plants which the revisionists like Teng tried to shut down played a big part in helping to get the steel industry back on its feet. The Mensheviks we suppose would have argued in the period of the Soviet withdrawal that the polemics against the Soviets and the disagreements over the terms of this assistance incited strife and retaliation. Nothing could be worse than for industrial output to suffer and, if it took begging and concessions to keep it going, then that's what would be necessary.

The Mensheviks tell us that two new steel complexes can't get going because of the lack of trained personnel. We don't know the exact details involved here. We do know that at least one of these facilities was imported, that foreign technical personnel have been associated with some of these projects and that there has been continuing controversy over the place and exact terms of these imported plants. We also know that China has made great advances in continuous casting technology—about which we hear very little from our Mensheviks—and that a caster was built in Shanghai by the workers in 18 days during the Cultural Revolution which served as a prototype for others.

The wall poster in Canton says that if Japan and China were roughly producing the same amount of steel in 1957 (about 10 million tons) then by now why aren't things equal? This analogy with Japan is hardly a valid one. The Japanese industry was rebuilding from war devastation through the '50s. Much of this involved a massive flow of investment capital from the state and foreign capital. Japan's pre-war steel output was so much in excess of China's (which hadn't even attained one million tons of output) that comparisons serve no useful purpose. The Japanese industry had as its backbone large plants with extensive application of modern technology. Taking 1957 as a common point of departure for the growth of the steel industry in Japan and China is especially misleading when we compare the productive bases of the two countries. Japan was fully industrialized at the time whereas China was and still is in the early stages of industrialization.

Fifteen per cent of the steel produced in China comes from small rural plants. These plants which continuously grow in number will add to total steelmaking capacity, while serving local needs more effectively. On the other hand, China is not going to be able to depend on the construction of big, new complexes to boost output, given their enormous cost. Production of *finished* steel increased from 13.4 million metric tons in 1970 to 19.5 in 1975. It was in the years of '74-'76 that it hovered around the same levels. This was a source of concern to the leadership of the Party, but two things must be said in this connection. The difference between that performance and something approaching a more optimal level is not between 20 million tons and 60 million tons or even 40 for that matter, though there was room for significant improvement. Second, how to assess and deal with these difficulties is of major importance. Part of the difficulties of the industry stem from low grade ores and inadequate finishing facilities. These are problems which have been tackled in a variety of ways, from importing equipment to improve the quality of iron ore and coke to importing special steel. Nevertheless the quality of steel produced in China has continued to improve and local enterprises have grown by developing their own raw materials sources.

Though these technical questions loom as important ones, the vitality of the industry depends on the political and ideological line in command. The Mensheviks who see the Four behind any slowdown in production making no attempt to really analyze the struggles that took place in let's say the Anshan Works, the largest in the country, over management practices, will go right in with the "20 Points" and call for firm management and raising the status of technicians. The Four approached production difficulties differently. An article in *Peking Review* #50, 1975 describes some of the advances made during the Lin Piao/Confucius campaign. It tells how workers struggled over rules which called for the phasing out of certain equipment and departments after a set period of time. The workers felt this equipment could still be utilized. It tells of struggles over whether workers should receive extra pay for making use of leftover molten steel at their own initiative. It asks how can we best spur the enthusiasm of the workers? It describes how workers struggled against a system of material punishment which would deduct from the production quota of workers who did not leave machinery and accessories in a proper way for the next shift. It was concluded that such a system intensified contradictions among workers. Replacing such coercive measures with political measures to solve the problem led to increases in production.

It has been reported in the Western press that Mao issued a document on China's steel and iron industry in June of '75. The campaign to criticize Lin Piao/Confucius summarized above would seem to fit right in line with what Mao said needed to be examined in the enterprises: "whether or not the ideological and political line is correct; whether or not the movement to study the theory of the dictatorship of the proletariat has really been developed; whether or not the masses are fully mobilized; whether or not a strong leadership core has been established; whether or not the bourgeois characteristics in the management of the enterprise had been overcome; whether or not the Party's policies have been implemented; and whether or not an effective blow has been struck against the disruptive activities of the class enemy. In sum, whether or not the tasks of consolidating the dictatorship of the proletariat has been implemented at the basic level."[4]

How are our Mensheviks going to explain away this directive by Mao? Here we are in 1975 during the height of the so-called "factional activities" of the Four and at a time when the steel industry is encountering difficulties. Look at what Mao puts in first place: Whether or not the ideological and political line is correct and whether or not the campaign to study the theory of the dictatorship of the proletariat has really been developed. Now if this isn't "gang of four idealism" we don't know what is. Mao doesn't ask if these mills are making up for production time lost to political discussion and study and class struggle in general. He doesn't ask if these mills are approaching world levels in efficiency. He doesn't even make a point about the four modernizations. Mao's statement is obviously a rebuke to revisionists then and today for whom the problems of the steel industry can be solved only by phasing out politics and worker management in the mills. In fact Mao knew that such problems can only be solved—in a socialist way—by putting the class struggle in command as indicated in the questions he does pose.

While the steel industry has encountered difficulties in the last few years, the oil industry has grown impressively. The line of those in power is to increasingly build the economy around it, notably as a source of foreign exchange, and therefore aggravate differences between sectors. The "20 Points" says that oil can be used as payment for drilling equipment. This was criticized in the CC Report correctly as a form of enslavement. Suppose, for instance, oil is required in greater quantities in one sector and yet this same oil is earmarked for repayment to a foreign country. Such a policy, beyond tying China's development to that of other countries, tends to undermine a unified policy of making the entire economy serve the needs of the people. One account that appeared in the *Economic and Political Weekly*, told of how in 1976 transport systems were being used to move oil for export at the expense of the movement of grains and foodstuffs to the cities and machinery and fertilizers to the countryside. The Four called for a reduction in oil export and are now hounded for their interference.

The real interference of the Four was interference against the revisionism of Teng, Hua, et. al. Their opposition to the "four modernizations" was not an objection to pushing the national economy forward; in fact, they themselves held that in the early '70s a "new leap" situation appeared. The great advances during the Cultural Revolution did provide favorable ground for a forward thrust in the economy. But by 1974-75 the right, which had been attacking continually since the Cultural Revolution, was gathering force and it had to be dealt with by mass campaigns to defeat them politically and ideologically. This in turn would spur the whole of society forward.

The issue that divided the Four from Chou, Hua, Teng, et. al. was not whether to develop the economy or not, but how. It is necessary to set long-term goals against which 5- and 10-year plans can be evaluated. But the four modernizations as it was defended and elaborated by the capitalist roaders was on the one hand a grand blue-print, i.e. by the year 2000 going through two phases, the one to be completed by 1980, the second by the end of the century, China will have reached the front ranks of the world. It brooked no interference. The possibility of war which would surely set such an ambitious program back, which more accurately would ravage it, is not considered in these calculations. And if this "four modernizations" is the surest defense in the event of war, then it has to be completed in less than 25 years. Wasn't Mao thinking about war as somewhat more imminent than 25 years off?

On the other hand, this "four modernizations" doesn't contain much substance. The changes in planning policy and orientation were not spelled out other than to achieve agricultural mechanization by 1980. The only real attempt to put some meat on it, that is to show more exactly what was intended was the "20 Points" and it's obvious enough what's wrong with them, to any Marxist at least. The Mensheviks act like the issue was simply one of going in for growth or not. This betrays their ignorance of Marxism and the actual conditions in China, yes the *actual conditions* in which transformations in the relations of production would lead to the development of the productive forces.

While presented as a grand blueprint, the "four modernizations" could be used to justify just about anything and its vagueness could permit the most elastic definitions of its goals. The front ranks by 2000. Which front ranks? Japan, France, the Soviet Union, the U.S.? A comprehensive industrial and economic system by 1980? What does it mean? A steel industry with an output of maybe 30 million metric tons? It seems unlikely. Even the mechanization of agriculture is somewhat fluid in meaning. And this may well have been adjusted downward from what it meant five years ago just like the bourgeoisie in this country toys with unemployment statistics. Mechanization presently means that 70% of agriculture is to be semi-or fully mechanized by the mid '80s. *Peking Review* #7 (1978) does put forward more specific targets for necessary increases in output from different sectors in order to meet the 70% goal. But this still doesn't change the fact that what is meant by mechanization remains vague and subject to redefinition as the circumstances dictate. For instance, at the end of the article it is pointed out that even when the 1980 targets are fulfilled "agricultural mechanization will still not be at a high level." According to this logic it could be said that agriculture in China is already mechanized but still at a low level. This emphasizes again that the call to mechanize by 1980 smacks of a big hype job.

The Four were the realists, they had the sensible and sober-minded approach to the economy. Not that they didn't think that the Chinese people could scale the heights, but that they knew it would have to be through their own efforts and by mobilizing the truly positive factors in society. It was more, not less realistic, to base hopes for increased productivity on moral incentives, political movements and campaigns in the enterprises rather than on material incentives. Any other method will mean speed-up and demoralization. Given that China is poor it is realistic to suppose that small and medium size industry can be the backbone of industrial advance. No doubt the Four opposed some of the ambitious targets that were being floated about in the discussions for a 1980 plan. No doubt they felt that it was not possible to expect China to be at the level of the U.S. by the turn of the century. But understanding this made it realistically possible to promote the most vigorous development exactly by staying on the course that had been set through the Great Leap Forward and the Cultural Revolution. The fulfillment of the "four modernizations"as they were conceived by Teng and Chou would lead to lopsided development—for instance, an oil industry receiving a growing disproportion of the state's funds—and, in the end, to dependency on abroad.

"The Four were opposed to growth and Shanghai was a mess." This we are told in current issues of *Peking Review*. This question of disruptions, incidentally, is very complicated. (The Mensheviks tell us that Comrade Avakian's "left idealist" line leads to rightism and ruined the NUWO. Meanwhile, they actively set out to sabotage work with their right line around the miners and bring confusion and dishonor to the NUWO.) Through 1974 and 1975 disruptions took place in China. Black markets increased in the countryside, there were reports of embezzling in some plants, factional disputes in many factories. But these things were the consequences of sharpening class struggle. The right would step in to sow confusion and division; they had experience with this dating back to the Cultural Revolution.

In 1975, at the height of many of these disturbances, the right pressed hard for a wage conference. The Four opposed it as we learn in the *Peking Review*. But what they opposed was the incorrect precedent that was being set—resolving grievances and unrest through wage increases. And, again, they were the realists. Worker morale could be raised only through raising consciousness and beating back the right. They were the realists because wage differentials that widened would not only lead to further divisions but, given the output of the economy, to inflationary pressures.

The line of the Four on wages was predicated on understanding that the wage system which undergoes a fundamental change with socialism—no longer the exchange of labor power as a commodity—still contains contradictory elements. From each according to his ability stands in opposition to payment according to work, and it was first and foremost necessary to rely on the communist spirit of work and not the promise of immediate reward to raise production. The Four advocated that workers' living standards be gradually improved according to the development of the national economy. This meant, especially, upgrading the lower paid workers, extending collective and state provision of social services like health, education and recreation which were not dependent on wage levels, and the maintenance of stable and declining price levels. The Four opposed piece-rates, bonuses and other material rewards which tended to promote the ideology of individual gain. They stood for the narrowing of differences between workers and peasants and, in particular, the reduction of differentials between administrative and state workers and staff and production workers.

This is a view that is not shared by the current rulers. Their latest wage increase starts simply from the premise that distribution according to work is a socialist principle. It denies what Mao stressed in the last two years of his life, that the wage system, especially as it existed in its eight grades, was a defect of socialist society. This wage increase earmarks technical workers for special consideration by rapidly promoting technical personnel.

The promotion of the lower paid technical workers is obviously a deliberate move to restore the rites, that is to upgrade technical workers whose pay and position had been restricted over the years as a consequence of efforts to narrow gaps and break down the division of labor. Most important, this is part and parcel of unleashing the revisionists' social base. The Nov. 11, 1977 *Workers Daily* advocates bonuses paid proportionally, that is higher-wage workers should receive higher bonuses out of "fairness." This is the sort of extension of bourgeois right that the "four modernizations" is bringing with it. And it even comes in political wrapping. Wage increases will be awarded with due consideration to political attitude. It will be this combination of bribery and force (the new and improved brand of rules and regulations) that is counted on to achieve speed-up.

Peking Review #6 (1978), in taking on Yao's pamphlet provides some theoretical justification for the bold new wage initiatives. The article hails the distribution principle of to each according to his work as "a newborn socialist thing" which "enables workers to be concerned about the fruits of their labor and brings their enthusiasm for socialism into full play." This should be compared with Mao's statement (which Mao entitles "An Opinion"!) about the free supply system in 1960: "We must eradicate bourgeois jurisdiction and ideology. For example, contesting for position, contesting for rank, wanting to increase wages, and giving higher wages to the intellectual worker and lower wages to the physical laborer are all remnants of bourgeois ideology. To each according to his work [contribution] is prescribed by law, and it is also a bourgeois thing."

Things certainly do turn into their opposites. Suddenly this "bourgeois thing", this birthmark, has become "a newborn socialist thing." It's no longer so surprising that our Mensheviks would have qualms with the real socialist new things that came out of the Cultural Revolution. It should also be noted that the Four were concerned about the effect wage increases of the sort enacted at the end of 1977 might have on widening the gap between peasants and workers. These are not the kind of considerations the revisionists seem interested in entertaining.

The Four's Line on Agriculture

The Mensheviks try to throw more sand in people's eyes by making a series of outrageous accusations about the Four's line on agriculture. (See their section on Tachai and Worker-Peasant Alliance.) They state pure and simple that the Four opposed mechanization of agriculture. This charge is so absurd that they couldn't even find a bourgeois periodical or professor upon whom they could base the claim. We are led to believe that the Four arbitrarily converted vegetable growing communes into grain producers at great pain to urban dwellers. (pp. 238-9) Where this information comes from is anybody's guess—we don't even recall seeing it in the *Peking Review,* by now. This charge, by the way is all the more interesting because it was none other than the clown prince himself, Mickey Jarvis (we assume it is fair to call him that since it was the CP(ML) which originated the phrase), who presented in his characteristically incoherent and slobbering way at the CC the view that the Four had turned the suburbs into green-belts, producing only to meet the immediate needs of the cities. Well, consistency should never be expected from a pragmatist.

By examining this question from the vantage point of line—a method which our Mensheviks shun like the plague—there is something to be said about this vegetable question. The role of agriculture in the Chinese economy has already been discussed, but a few things more can be said. Agricultural production includes food grains, silk, tea, sugar, fruits, herbs, vegetable oils, and other foodstuffs. Of all these crops, food grain is the most important and is considered the key link. Why? Because feeding her people is the first task that must be fulfilled in China; this must be done in a planned and expanded way to improve quantity and quality, to satisfy the needs of a growing population, to reduce the impact of natural disasters, and also for feeding and raising animals. But it is also the key link because of the ever-present and growing danger of war. Mao said, "dig tunnels deep, store grain everywhere, and never seek hegemony."

As an article in *Peking Review* #35,1975 explained, "with adequate reserves of grain we shall be able to guarantee food for our army and people when war breaks out and win victory in the war against aggression." The principle of "self-reliance and self-sufficiency" which guided the revolutionary wars in the period of the new democratic revolution was, according to Mao, and the Four, no less applicable in the present period. The importance of grain is reflected in the fact that unlike other foodstuffs it is directly purchased from the producers by the state and sold directly to consumers in fixed quotas. Moreover, grain reserves—that left over after purchases, collective distribution, and that set aside for new seed—have increased continually. Reserves have been built up by the state, the collective and the individual in keeping with the principle of storing grain everywhere. It is not unusual for some teams to have grain stored away to feed their members for 30 months.

Some regions in the country are more suited to growing some crops than others or engaging in livestock raising and so forth. On the basis of taking grain as the key link, these considerations are taken into account, and these communes will be assured necessary supplies of grain. But it must be remembered that China's grain production must rise by at least five million tons a year just to stay even with its population growth, and the country has ½ the cultivated acreage of the U.S. or the Soviet Union. China has over the last 14 years continually reaped bumper harvests.

Vegetable production has expanded in China. *Peking Review* #51, 1975 carries a story which explains that "ensuring an ample supply of vegetables and non-staple food in cities is a matter of great importance." And it goes on to point out that "following the principle of serving the cities, cadres and commune members in suburban Chingchun have concentrated manpower, machinery and funds on vegetable production, water conservancy, and soil amelioration." These may sound just like fine words, but the point of the story was that the city had achieved self-sufficiency in vegetables by 1975.

It is true, though, that the priority in agriculture is in grain and the Four fought vigorously for this. This has real consequences; for instance, not much land is given over to forage crops for livestock, and agricultural technology and research is far more advanced with respect to grains than for vegetables. Chinese rice yields approach the highest in the world. The goal has been to make as many provinces self-sufficient in grain as possible, both to reduce costs of transportation borne by the state and to build up these strategic grain reserves in the event of war.

It is quite possible that land under cultivation for vegetables might have had to be cut back, we don't know, but the kind of analysis given by the Mensheviks illuminates nothing. There are facts readily available which indicate more cities became self-sufficient in vegetables in recent years, but the important thing to see is that the proportions of food grain production to other agricultural activities must be correctly handled by putting politics in command. This involves not only the strategic principle of storing grain everywhere, but the question of putting the interests of the whole, of the state, above all else. For instance, some communes under bourgeois influence might go in for cash crops rather than grain with an eye towards increasing their income at any expense. Also a line which puts undue emphasis on exports—like textiles or processed foods—as a means of acquiring foreign exchange for machine purchases would lead to more acreage given over to cotton cultivation.

As for this question of closing rural trade fairs and alienating peasants in the process (p. 239), this requires some discussion. The situation in Liaoning Province to which our Mensheviks refer is not quite what they would have us believe. We are told that the provincial Party Committee shut the fairs down and as a result black markets flourished. Actually something else happened. What really happened was gone into in depth in an article in the *People's Daily,* May 9, 1976.

These trade fairs are places where peasants can sell farm produce grown on private plots, household side-line products and handicrafts. Their scope has been a point of continuing controversy since the Great Leap Forward, when they were extensively criticized.

In one commune in the province, the trade fair became a center of profiteering and swindling. What's more, it attracted significant numbers of peasants and this increasingly came to interfere with production tasks, especially farmland capital construction. The problem that faced the commune leadership was how to struggle with the force of habit that drew many people to the fair while, at the same time, fulfilling the functions the fair served in providing products not normally available through existing supply channels and making it possible for peasants to supplement their incomes.

What was summed up was that the old methods of containing the negative aspects of these fairs were not sufficient. It was not enough to restrict them nor to simply shut them down. Instead the commune leadership set up a "socialist big fair" in which peasants who still held private plots and engaged in side-line activities would buy and sell their private goods through the collective commercial channels, the supply and marketing cooperatives. This on the one hand put a brake on the speculation that had gotten out of hand at the trade fairs and, on the other, continued to provide peasants with an outlet for private output still necessary and useful at this stage. Overall, it had the effect of establishing new exchange relations in the countryside whereby individual bartering and bargaining was replaced by the planned acquisition and sale of these side-line goods. The principle of free trade, which is a carry-over from the old society and a continuing source of capitalism in the countryside, was being struggled with.

This was not, as our Menshevik authors would have us think, a mindless act of "ultra-leftism." Careful preparation, both ideological and organizational, went into the establishment of this new kind of fair. Extensive study and public discussions went on and the supply and marketing cooperatives expanded the scope of their purchases and kept in close contact with peasants growing or manufacturing these products so that they became more tied into the overall production plan of the commune. While continuing to encourage some individual side-line activities, the Party Committee also mobilized peasants to take up collective side-line production in place of some private side-line production. In the period since this new kind of fair was set up, which was in early 1975, grain output rose considerably and the amount of terraced land soared over previous years' figures.

Clearly this was an ambitious attempt to restrict capitalist influences in the countryside. The example was popularized throughout the province, as it was summed up that this was a major contribution toward strengthening the collective economy and changing the world outlook of the peasants. Might there have been opposition to this from some peasants? Undoubtedly, yes, but in and of itself this means nothing. Undoubtedly some rich peasants would put up such opposition, but does this mean that the new fair should be shut down and a reversion made to the old one? Might illegal markets crop up in the face of this new exchange relation? This, too, is a distinct possibility but it is not surprising that such things will happen just as the issuance of rationing coupons for cotton might result in a temporary increase in illegal transactions by those seeking to get around the rations. Certainly the fact that there might be resistance and problems is not a basis for abolishing and condemning further advances in strengthening the positions of socialism—at least no basis for a Marxist.

This fair was a socialist new thing which, judging from the experience in this commune, was worthy of study and emulation where the conditions permitted. Our Mensheviks, for all their whining about "actual conditions," make no attempt to analyze the kind of difficulties posed by the old trade fairs nor to evaluate attempts to transform them. Rather we get an hysterical accounting whose facts are untrue (the trade fair was not simply shut down—a new kind of fair was established in its place) and whose premise is that bourgeois right is just fine.

"In the areas the gang controlled, they threw the overall plan out the window..." This is what we are told about those communes outside of Shanghai and Peking. But as of 1975 the peasants in the communes under the city's jurisdiction were producing and supplying the whole population of Shanghai with edible oil and vegetables, as well as other farm and side-line products. What's more these communes achieved self-sufficiency in grain and even provided the state with a surplus. Total output of grain, cotton and oil-bearing crops doubled their 1962 levels in 1974.

And then we get the clincher, "mechanization of agriculture was never an actual part of the gang's efforts in agriculture." (See p. 239) On the face of it this charge is absurd. By 1974, communes in the rural areas of Shanghai had 82.8% of the cultivated land tractor-ploughed, a fourfold increase over 1965, and 97.4% of the land power drained and irrigated.[5] Usually the argument the revisionists throw at us is that in the areas they controlled the Four wanted to make things look good. Now they tell us the opposite, but the opposite of what they say is actually the truth. It was local industry in these counties and communes that gave the biggest spurt to mechanization since the Cultural Revolution, and all of this was vigorously defended.

The view of the Four was that agriculture had made great progress since liberation and especially since the Cultural Revoltuion, but that it still remained at a low level in terms of agricultural labor productivity and its level of mechanization. In the *Shanghai Textbook* they explain, "China's agricultural production is still in a relatively backward condition. This condition is not in line with the develoment of China's industry and other sectors of the national economy. Therefore, it is necessary to further realize agricultural mechanization and promote a rapid development of agricultural production on the basis of continuously consolidating and developing socialist production relations in the rural areas." Earlier the text quotes Mao about mechanization being the fundamental way out for agriculture and adds, "When the stimulative role of socialist production relations with respect to the productive forces is fully exploited and with the support of socialist industry, especially heavy industry, the pace of achieving agricultural mechanization will be quickened."

There is nothing the Four wrote and there is nothing that occurred in the Shanghai suburbs that indicates they opposed mechanization. Yao, it is said, would not have Hua's article on mechanization published in 1971. Well, so be it if it contains the same revisionist palaver of his Tachai speech. That speech was already analyzed in the CC Report where it pointed out that it says nothing about narrowing the difference between work teams as a crucial step in moving forward to both mechanization and higher levels of ownership. Since the Mensheviks chose not to reply to the criticisms of the speech, we'll let those criticisms stand on their own merit.

The Four opposed any mechanization plan that was not under

the command of revolution. If going all out for mechanization meant that anything goes, then they were not for it. Their differences with Hua in 1971 may have concerned this timetable that agriculture would be mechanized by 1980, which is now only two years away. The country's steel output, not then and not now yet 30 million tons, was reason to doubt some of these targets. Not that the Four wanted to slow things down; on the contrary, they wanted to push ahead but on the basis of utilizing the economy's real strength and capabilities, rather than undermining them.

Slandering Workers' Achievements

The method of the revisionists is to denigrate those things which obstruct their revisionist path to the four modernizations. Hence we find wholesale attacks on the people of Shanghai and their revolutionary activities. Whether or not there were setbacks in one particular sector or city is quite secondary to the real aim of these people which is to establish a new reactionary order whose long-run effect will be real economic disorder, i.e. capitalism.

Peking Review #4 (1978) carries an article on Shanghai which is revealing for what it omits about the development of socialist industry and how it sums up some of the weaknesses of the last few years. The article cannot deny the very impressive technical achievements of the city. Shanghai has contributed enormously to the national economy with machinery and equipment, accumulation funds, and a pool of skilled workers for other parts of the country. But then the article goes on to report industrial output value fell in 1976 and the city did not fulfill its revenue plans three years in a row. In addition, we are told the city opposed the unified leadership of central authorities.

While all the pertinent statistical data is not available, by looking at *Peking Review* #9 (1976) we can get a different picture of what was actually happening in Shanghai. First off, the technical transformations which are simply enumerated in the '78 article are analyzed as the product of "socialist cooperation" in the earlier article. This kind of cooperation within and between enterprises went so far as to break down barriers between different trades and involved over 300 factories, hospitals, and scientific research institutes in the transformation of the medical appliances industry. By 1976 it was capable of producing high precision tools. On its own, one trade, it is summed up, could not have possibly done it. It gives another example of a whole new industry coming into being—TV manufacture—thanks to joint efforts of enterprises to set aside manpower and materials. To what does this article attribute the great surge in socialist cooperation? The Cultural Revolution, of which there is *no* mention in the 1978 article.

This point of "opposing unified leadership of central authorities," the attack on low output value, and the concluding part of the article which simply lists what output tasks lie ahead for different sectors, takes on wider significance when we look at another example of socialist cooperation from the 1976 article. This concerns an engineering equipment plant that manufactures two major products. One is a certain machine that uses much material, but little labor, and is high in output value. The other is a toothpaste filling machine which has a low output value.

Workers from this plant visited a nearby toothpaste plant and found that nine toothpaste filling machines were urgently needed in order to achieve automation. But the problem these workers faced was that if they went ahead with the project their output target of 300,000 yuan might not be met. The question put to discussion and debate was whether to help the toothpaste factory boost production even if it put an additional burden on them. They launched a criticism of the revisionist line of management which held that it was better to do light work and shirk the heavy and decided to do what they had to, to assist this plant despite the possible consequences to their output. In the end, it just so happened that they met their output plan, but the point should be fairly obvious. They went in for what was in the long-run interests of the working class—to help this plant achieve automation, which would ultimately raise output—even though there may have been some short-run loss in their output value.

This is how the Four ran Shanghai. This is how they combined unified leadership with enthusiasm from all quarters. This is how they integrated lofty line struggle with the actual process of production. That output value may have fallen in 1976 as the recent *Peking Review* article indicates may or may not be true. But, clearly, what is under attack is this principle of socialist cooperation and the role of mass campaigns. These relations between enterprises represent the kind of local initiative that is vital to the success of central planning and which can hasten the spread of technologies and the establishment of more advanced socialist relations. This was a focal point of the struggle with Teng during the right deviationist wind, when he strongly advocated bringing industries under the stricter control of the respective ministries, something which has the effect of cutting off these local relations between enterprises and removing local and central party control.

The 1978 *Peking Review* article also calls for special attention being paid to developing Shanghai into a scientific base "ranking among the world's advanced." The socialist cooperation described above gave rise in the city to thousands of meetings, exhibitions, and centers with workers and technicians taking part in activities to exchange these experiences. Why Shanghai should all of a sudden have to "become" an internationally renowned scientific center is understandable only by recognizing the revisionist world outlook of those running China today for whom all this cooperation and technical exchange is just so much "sabotage" and "interference." Small wonder they ooze with delight over the 10% increase in profits since the Four fell.

Line on Technology

Leibel Bergman made the point in his paper presented at the CC that the Soviet Union under Stalin imported about 50% of its machine tools. He cites that in connection with China's increasing desire to acquire advanced technology from abroad. Teng and Hua in the "Twenty Points" explicitly refer to a policy of exchanging oil for advanced equipment. The growing stress on technical study reflecting international standards points in a certain direction as well. Technical innovation is made to increase production. The question is, is any technical innovation going to boost production as well as another, and how should the process of technological advance be expected to develop?

While paying attention to building up a modern industrial sector, the technological policy that Mao advocated was to avoid concentration of investment in big facilities and to promote the development of small and medium enterprises which could marshall local resources and know-how in both meeting local needs and contributing to the growth of the national economy. As far as possible, plants should be capable of supplying as much of their required parts and accessories, and in the case of some plants producing final goods, even machinery.

Moreover, the question of increasing output cannot be seen as a one-to-one relation between more equipment and more production, for two reasons. First, under the relatively poor conditions of China a good part of technical innovation has to take place by "digging out of potential capacity," that is making better use of and renovating existing capacity so as not to put a drain on the state's accumulation funds. Second, even with the addition of capacity, production will not necessarily rise where the masses are not guided by a revolutionary line.

Mao's is an approach which yields quick returns and thereby accelerates development and which, again, makes it possible to fight a people's war to victorious conclusion. It is an approach that limits dependence on foreign countries. Foreign technology must be used in such a way as to promote this general development. In short, the most favorable conditions must be created so that the workers can constantly improve and revolutionize the methods of production and this struggle in production must be seen as the principal source of technical progress. This is what guarantees also that technical innovations can be extensively applied and learned from.

The process of technological change is one that develops from a lower level to a higher level, from quantitative to qualitative change. In other words simple methods will progress to more complex ones and the simple methods of change will be the ones that initially will have the widest applicability and which will be most easily mastered by others. The Four's line on this appears in an article from *Red Flag:* "Two young electricians in a sweater factory, taking the practical needs of production as their starting point, set out to create an innovation by simple methods. At a cost of only $72 they created a light and electricity control box that automated four working processes. Due to its low cost and effectiveness, it was warmly received by the workers. In half a year's time, the device was popularized sufficiently to be found on some 1500 knitting machines and raised efficiency by 15%. *This device has been further popularized and is employed in twenty factories including steel rolling...*" [our emphasis].

This sheds light on what it means to achieve greater, faster, better, and more economical results. It is not simply the introduction of an advanced piece of equipment. The technical innovations that will have the most sweeping consequences are those that start from the current and actual conditions of production. Foreign methods can be integrated with indigenous methods on this basis. This same article points out, "we must absorb what is useful, reject what is useless, and add what is peculiar to us making foreign things serve our purposes." And, at the same time, it is on this basis of *breaking through the barriers of the given level of production and technique,* through unleashing the inventiveness and creativity of workers, that advanced world levels can be reached.

Study and scientific experimentation must go on to sum these kinds of experiences up and to learn from international experience. But this must reflect the laws of development of the productive forces and class struggle to promote all-round development. This is where Bergman goes wrong on two counts. First, while not correct altogether, the Soviet Union could import the machine tools it did and employ them because it had a more developed productive base relative to China. Second, China in the 1950's did, in fact, import roughly 50% of its industrial equipment from the Soviet Union and Eastern Europe and its industrial output grew on an annual basis at a faster rate than at any time since.

But while this might initially have led to rapid growth, in the long run it would operate to the detriment of the balanced development of the economy. This experience was summed up negatively because this dependency on Soviet technique became self-perpetuating as more sophisticated parts and equipment were constantly required and this widened the gap with other sectors. This technology was not suited to the existing conditions in China since it could not be integrated throughout the economy, but was rather grafted onto a portion of it.

The current push to learn advanced technology in China does not reflect Mao's thinking on the development of technology and the economy. It represents a shift away from the indigenous experiences and technologies in Chinese society and basic scientific research on them. It is not enough to study and understand a given technology, to grasp its laws. It must be introduced into the productive base and if this technology does not reflect its actual conditions, dependency and distortions in the economy will result. In rural industry, in particular, what must be paid attention to is just what kind of advanced experiences can be learned from. The simple fact that some technicians (no doubt those who will now under the new educational policy go directly to school without intervening work experience) have mastered advanced design and development will not make it any more feasible than if they knew nothing about it.

What accounts for China's advances in technology is the process of fully utilizing its industrial base in connection with mass movements and mobilizing all trades and professions into a big socialist cooperation. This has led to continuous advances from a lower to a higher level of technological proficiency and to major innovations which can be popularized and diffused. Technical innovation groups consisting of workers, cadres and technicians had been formed in factories and breakthroughs like automatic production lines, high efficiency equipment, many of which were unorthodox and irregular as far as international standards go, were common. Nevertheless, and exactly because these innovations came out of the experiences of the masses, they proved to be durable. The city of Tientsin before it was hit by the earthquake had between 1972 and 1975 adopted 82,000 technical innovation and transformation items, produced or renovated 23,000 pieces of special purpose equipment and introduced over 600 automatic or continuous production lines, all of which contributed to large increases in output.

The view of the Hua leadership comes down to this as summarized in *Peking Review* #30 (1977): "Only when we admit in a down-to-earth manner that there is a gap between the level of our science and technology and the world's advanced levels can we realize how compelling is the need to quickly catch up with and surpass them." This is based on the observation that "while...there are things in our country that are approaching or have surpassed the world's advanced levels...this is only a part of the picture and a rather small part at that..."

These people have not been in power long, but the direction is unmistakeable. In 1973 the Kwangtung *Southern Daily* editorialized against too many small hydroelectric projects, reflecting the influence of Teng. This was an attack on a development that had brought electricity to more than half of the production brigades in the country. Teng had later gone around the country complaining about "too many bright local ideas." On the other hand, when in 1973 and 1974 attempts were made to construct generators and turbines with large capacities, Teng had said that China was not in a position to build this kind of electrical power equipment and that foreign imports should be increased. Workers in Shanghai breaking with convention successfully built it.

This, of course, is based on information from the nefarious "gang of 4"[7]. But there is every reason to believe that it is accurate. The Four in articles on electric power used Kwangtung as a model and pointed out that while big and small and medium stations should be built simultaneously, the medium sized and small hydroelectric stations which already supply about ⅓ of the country's electricity should receive the main emphasis. The revisionist line they criticized was that big networks built by the state were the way to solve local power needs. They also upheld the emergence of peasant-technician teams, numbering some 26,000 in Kwangtung in 1975, who could oversee the construction and maintenance of these stations.

What about the standards of these small and medium stations. Did they approach world standards? Well, yes and no. They did not compare in their sophistication of design and obviously in their capacity with the mammoth stations that have been built in other parts of the world—which employ extremely advanced technology. On the other hand, these small stations have been exported and are considered of high quality by foreign engineers. The engineering work involved in these small stations is relatively easy and within the grasp of rural areas which build them to serve their local needs. But these rich experiences and mass initiative have made them of "high quality."

On the other hand, if we look at *Peking Review* #3 (1978) we find, again, the point that "a big gap still exists between China and the developed industrialized countries in the power industry." And what flows from this is a changed emphasis on the relationship of big to small and medium-sized stations. The article states that *big* ones "are the mainstay." But worse, the article puts forward the rankest expression of the "theory of the productive forces" yet, declaring that "electricity would eventually destroy capitalism."

The Two Lines Summed Up

In sum, what can be said about the economy, its performance and direction under the Four? To begin with, it was not the case, as some would have us believe, that it was foundering. By all estimates, granted that no official data base is available, the economy was growing at a clip of anywhere from five to six percent a year in GNP terms; industrial output was rising perhaps at an average annual rate of ten percent since the Great Proletarian Cultural Revolution. Small, but gradual, improvements in the people's living standards occurred in this period as reflected in food consumption, clothing allowances, improved education and health services, particularly in the countryside, and consumer goods like bicycles and radios. There was progress and it rested on internal momentum. Some sectors, like steel, coal and transport suffered from erratic output, comparatively lower growth rates, or long-term structural problems. But, this was not a one-sided thing either. Technical innovations had been made in these sectors, like steel, and new ports had been opened, some highly mechanized. The Four were not complacent about China's growth. The last three years of *Peking Review* under their editorship shows what kind of efforts were being bent to raise output.

In talking about how well China was doing, like the song says, "compared to what?" To throw up the standard of Japan or the U.S. is misleading and downright stupid—to say nothing of reactionary. This is a country that had only 13,750 miles of railroad track in 1949, a country that was producing 5.5 million tons of oil in 1960, and which in 1976 was still overwhelmingly poor. Yet, it has, for the most part, achieved agricultural self-sufficiency and greatly expanded its industrial capabilities based on a rational investment program which begins with the needs of agriculture. The kind of breakthrough that had taken place in China coming off the Great Leap or the Cultural Revolution were not the sort that would take her from being poor to rich right away, but which would thrust her economy forward in the context of her still being a less developed nation.This would be a path that would lead to communism not by attempting to go through the same forms of development of advanced capitalist countries where industries are centralized and populations concentrated in the cities. It would be based on uniting agriculture and industry and town and country in new social forms.

1976 was a bad year. Farming was hit by unprecedented disasters; the earthquake ravaged several industrial installations; and the right jumped out. It was to be expected that the economy would suffer, but even this was not without its bright spots: the early rice crop set an all-time record in per unit and gross output.[8] If we want to be technical about these sorts of things, then blame Hua Kuo-feng for last year's disappointing harvest and the fact that 12 million tons of grain were imported from Australia and Canada. If the Four in some places "made things worse" by politically mobilizing people in such a way that temporarily disrupted production in some places, it would have in the long run, had they won, been to the benefit of economic growth.

The Four actually understood the needs and capabilities of the economy better than these bureaucrats and administrators who palm their wares off as economic wisdom. They understood, with Mao, that China was a poor country and would stay that way for some time to come. They did not make a principle of this. They saw it as something that was necessary to overcome, but in a way that would allow China to develop into a powerful *socialist* country. They also recognized the awesome revolutionary potential of its people and the distinctively Chinese path forward: walking on two legs, the use of simple technologies, giving a practical orientation to education, linking research closely with production, squeezing the most out of existing capacity, local raw materials and waste, practicing economy and frugality.

The transfer of resources—technical, financial, and manpower—to the countryside and the stress on despecialization will in the long run promote economic growth, even at the expense of short-run gains. This kind of development will make maximum use of resources and reduce transportation costs. If old and obsolete equipment rather than being discarded can be used in small and medium plants this will be a boon, a plus, to accumulating funds. Industries can assist each other, spread skills and through this raise the level of the economy as a whole, avoid lopsided development and bring into being an engineering industry which can serve the needs of the whole economy. Yes, there were lags in China's technical work force, but Mao's line was not to produce the same kind of technical work force that existed in the capitalist countries, but one which would help China develop in a socialist way. The starting point for this kind of technical work force is that the main source of new technology is both on-the-job experimentation and self-reliance and the conscious and organized spread of knowledge and technical know-how.

The point is that the Four were not operating with idealist notions that the only thing that matters is a correct idea, to hell with the economy. The fact is that they understood it. Reports have circulated that they might have opposed the 1976-80 plan of doubling average annual GNP to 16%. It might very well be true. These were get-rich-quick schemes which would only lead to defeat. The current leadership, complaining of dismal economic performance, goes ahead with a wage increase involving maybe 60% of the workforce. They're calling for massive investments in research and development, doubling the size of universities, the installation of new equipment and technology. Where will the finances for this come from? What kind of development will this lead to?

What may sound ambitious on their part is actually ambition for restoring capitalism. It is guided by revisionist thinking and does not reflect the realities of China. It is a short-cut that will keep China poor and dependent, whatever they say. These changes in university policy are going to create a technological elite, not raise technical standards generally. The program they advocate can only be based on bribes, (Taylor system) speed-up, and foreign dependency.

These revisionists have only been in power for 18 months. But let's watch how they act. The Mensheviks tell us the Chinese haven't changed their commercial policies with respect to foreign trade. But changes are being discussed and they know it, because they read the *Far Eastern Economic Review* and read of delegations visiting Germany and Great Britain exploring new ways of doing business. It's also a fact as reported in the *U.S. China Business Review* that China is now pressing companies like Mitsui to deposit savings in the Bank of China. These deposits, quite substantial already, are not really different from loans to finance trade. Some of these things have been advocated for some time by the likes of Teng and even practiced before the Four went down. But they opposed it. The current leadership lets us know how much the Four hated Chou's foreign trade policies.

The military purchases these revisionists are negotiating abroad—let's see how they are financed. Let's see what happens to petroleum exports. Let's see what happens to petroleum derivatives, like fertilizers, synthetic fibers—if they even get manufactured in China under this new regime—and whether or not they are used to finance heavy technology purchases—at the expense of planned and proportional development. The example cited earlier of the transport problems caused by oil exports in 1976 shows how an incorrect exports policy can undermine the domestic economy.

That this is the direction things are going in can be seen from a commentary in *Red Flag* last year:

> "We have the superior system of socialism in our country, and our people are diligent, intelligent, and courageous. What foreigners can create and invent in science and technology we Chinese people can achieve likewise, and in certain cases we may even do better. However, we face the problem of how to race against time and contend for speed."

The article then goes on to quote Lenin:

> "Our present objective is to sign a trade agreement with Great Britain so that trade can be regularized and the machinery needed for the tremendous plan of restoring our national economy can be purchased as soon as possible. The quicker this job is done, the larger will be the basis on which we can free ourselves from economic dependence on foreign countries."[9]

What is the point behind all of this?

Lessons of Soviet Union and the Fight Against Capitulationism

The bottom line for the revisionist axis in China is the notion that unless China becomes an economic power it will lose a war. The Mensheviks, for their part, say that "big strides in developing the national economy were necessary for many reasons..." and they list as one "to put the country in a better position to deal with war." They don't elaborate too much on this which would seem to indicate some cultural lag with their Chinese counterparts. But this theme runs through major statements from the Chinese leaders. For instance, in the previously mentioned article "We Must Catch Up With and Surpass World's Advanced Levels Within This Century," it says that "catching up with and surpassing the world's advanced levels in science and technology is urgently required if we are to defend and build up the motherland..." Yu Chiu-li, the planning minister, makes the point more strongly, "A world war is bound to break out some day...Lenin sharply pointed out: 'Either perish or overtake and outstrip the advanced countries economically as well.' " Hua takes up the theme at Taching when he sets the four modernizations in the context of imperialist war preparations, "We cannot afford to let time slip through our fingers..."

(Of course, if the revisionists don't succeed in "catching up and surpassing" on the technical front, they can always fall back on some other front—like sports. The March 1978 issue of *China Reconstructs* contains a Howard Cossell-like description of international meets the women's volleyball team has recently competed in. Complete with scores and graphic accounts of the thrill of victory and agony of defeat, it ends on a somber note. The women must, the author points out, improve their game because "they have a long way to go to catch-up with the world's strong teams." Actually what might seem at first to be a grotesque parody of the "outstrip or perish" line is part of the calculated effort to pervert and destroy the socialist superstructure by promoting competitiveness and the "championship mentality." Nowhere in this article is friendship first mentioned. The situation in China where amateur and mass participation in sports has flourished is sure to take a back seat to this push to attain world levels. All this is dialectically related to putting a bourgeois line in command of the economy.)

The presumption that the Chinese can overtake the U.S. by the end of the century is highly dubious at best and it represents, as we have indicated, a departure from Mao's views on the development of the economy. To suggest as the current leaders do that the Chinese can beat the Americans or Russians at their own game, that is in economic and military superiority, flies in the face of reality even more. The hope for China militarily lies in its ability to wage a people's war, to establish self-sustaining base areas, to lure the enemy in deep, surround it and destroy it. It is not likely and not really to China's advantage to expect its borders to be defensible. But the strategy of the current leaders seems to turn on extensive modernization of the armed forces meaning, in particular, modern arms and equipment along with a sophisticated back-up force of technicians.

Mao was extremely concerned over the effect that the growing war danger and the necessary measures taken by the proletariat in power to put it off and protect its flanks would have on the revolution. It is a law that imperialist countries will always try to subjugate and vanquish socialist countries and it is also a law that even where open war has not broken out, international class struggle will be reflected in the socialist countries and react upon the internal class contradiction. The crucial problem in this regard was not whether people were acting quickly enough to confront the danger of war, but whether in the name of that forces would jump out to reverse the revolution and undermine it—which would lead, in the end, to capitulation. The CC Report speaks to this where it points out:

> "with the growing danger of an attack on China by the Soviets, in particular, and with the necessity to make certain agreements and compromises with reactionary and imperialist governments, with the whole 'opening to the West,' and all the bourgeois influences that inevitably accompany this, there was bound to be a powerful pull away from taking the socialist road."

In the early '70's, there arose a need to shift policy internally and externally. The Lin Piao affair made it urgent to reestablish and strengthen party leadership. Many cadre who had gone down were returned to their old or new posts and the sharp and scorching criticisms characteristic of the early years of the Cultural Revolution tapered off. This was a policy that the right would seize upon to settle old scores. At the same time, the growing war danger called for new initiatives on the diplomatic front; for China to seek and forge new alliances. The Mensheviks deny that there was compromise involved here. They say this came from strength, not weakness. The point, however, is that it came out of *necessity.* That China could pull it off—for instance, that Nixon came to them and that they held other talks with lesser imperialist powers—was a product of its strength, the strength of China and the people of the world. But this doesn't alter the fact that these moves arose out of real *necessity*—the need to fend off and delay an attack on China.

If there wasn't compromise to all this—and no one is going to say that supporting the Shah's military build-up doesn't involve compromise—then why does Chou in the Tenth Congress Report make a point of distinguishing necessary compromises between revolutionary countries and the imperialists from betrayal? And if there wasn't real danger connected with these sorts of policies, why in the same speech does it point out that "in both international and domestic struggles, tendencies may still occur similar to those of the past, namely when there was an alliance with the bourgeoisie, necessary struggles were forgotten..." Chou goes on to mention the opposite danger of all struggle and no alliance, but it is rather obvious from the context of the speech and the overall situation what is being pinpointed.

There was a precedent for this concern. Lin Piao on the basis of the growing war danger held that the productive forces had to be developed at the expense of class struggle and, ultimately, that China had to seek the protection of a stronger power, notably the Soviet Union. The right, though they attacked him mercilessly, actually had a similar perspective. Not in the sense that they necessarily agreed that falling under the wing of the Soviet Union as opposed to the U.S. was the correct strategic choice right then, but that China could not stand up on its own. It was objectively necessary to reach some agreements and tactically maneuver for position with the bourgeoisie internationally which called for compromise. But would the working class continue to make socialist revolution and uphold and strengthen the dictatorship of the proletariat under these circumstances or have it whittled away in this united front?

Mao's line was to take full account of the interational situation and make use of every contradiction, but not to give up the class struggle on the basis of the real necessity to build the international united front. The war danger aggravated the pull toward revisionism and Mao was determined that China go into the war situation on a revolutionary basis. The shifts that were called for and the bourgeois influences that would accompany them made it necessary to wage struggle and while it might be possible to do it without the form of the mass upheavals of the Cultural Revolution, it was no less important to combat revisionism, to fight capitulationism.

The campaigns of the last few years of Mao's life must be seen in this context. Mao was not only summing up the experiences of the Chinese revolution, but the lessons of history. China was not the first socialist country to be faced with the prospect of war and the need to make rapid preparations for it. The Soviet Union had gone through this experience and Mao, clearly, saw its two aspects—the Nazis were defeated, but ten years later the revisionists won out.

The Mensheviks remind us that China is poor and blank. Is this a good basis to build socialism, they ask? They answer, yes it is. But while it is primarily a good thing, it has two aspects. The imperialists on the basis of a less developed country's backwardness will try to blockade and strangle it. They will try to bully it militarily. They will try to penetrate and corrode it ideologically and culturally in attempts to reinforce notions of inferiority. Being poor and blank is something that is not seen as a source of strength by petty-bourgeois and bourgeois forces in a poor country. In fact, nothing rankles them more than such economic and cultural backwardness—it inhibits their ability to flower into a big self-confident bourgeoisie.

But being poor and backward takes on added meaning in the context of inter-imperialist war preparations. The likelihood of an attack and with it the possibility of devastation and ruin causes alarm among the bourgeois and petty-bourgeois forces; war is seen as a complete and total disaster. Something must be done and done quick. The external situation interpenetrates with the internal one and the demand for order and for stability to cope with the threat of attack grows and influences other strata. Powerful pressures are generated to put a lid on the class struggle.

In China, historically, the bourgeoisie in the face of backwardness and the threat of foreign invasion raised the slogan "only industrialization can save China." Mao raised the slogan, "only socialism can save China," in opposition to this. But as pointed out in the CC Report, many elements who rallied behind this banner did so on the basis that socialism is the best way to catch up with the rest of the world and the best way for them to get ahead.

Stalin in 1931 made the prediction, "We are fifty or a hundred years behind the advanced countries. We must make good this distance in ten years. Either we do it, or they crush us." Was this Mao's strategy? Did Mao anywhere suggest that only under certain material conditions could China defeat the social imperialists? He did say "dig tunnels deep, store grain everywhere and never seek hegemony," and put forward the directive to push the national economy ahead, but nowhere did he put forward a comparable strategy to Stalin's for industrialization and link it with the war danger.

Was Stalin wrong in what he said? The experience of the patriotic war shows the very important part that the massive industrialization of the preceding years played in supporting the front lines and holding the economy together. The Soviet Union's industrial base was at a higher level than China's is today and they were in some ways able to "make good this distance." Nevertheless, it must be recognized that this "forced march" industrialization was linked with putting technique and technicians in command in economic affairs. It led to some lopsided development in the economy, particularly the emphasis on heavy industry, and went together with the denial in theory of the existence of antagonistic classes in the Soviet Union, which weakened the proletariat. In sum this process must be seen from two sides: it materially contributed to the defeat over the Nazis, but gave vent to bourgeois forces and influences which Stalin began to attack only after the war. Mao felt that China could not fight a war of "steel" and, moreover, that unless the political and ideological forces unleashed by this changing international situation, which reacted upon the internal class contradictions, were dealt with before and not after the war, the whole thing would go down the drain, as happened in the Soviet Union.

In *Red Papers 7* we describe some of Stalin's efforts at the end of the war to deal with some of these problems. There were attempts to rectify the party's recruitment policies and to counter bourgeois influences which had entered from the West during the war. This was the campaign against what was called cosmopolitanism. But Stalin was not able to successfully mobilize the masses to correct these problems inside and outside the party and following his death the revisionists took over.

The Dictatorship of the Proletariat campaign that Mao launched in 1975 came at a time when powerful forces inside China were clamoring for less class struggle and more hard work. These people who are presently in power were saying then as they are saying today that only industrialization can save China. Mao was reaffirming that only socialism can save China and this campaign was designed both to raise people's understanding of the nature of the socialist transition and to combat the bourgeoisie and its influence right then, in particular the ideological and material manifestations of bourgeois right. If China were to successfully stave off a military attack and continue down the road to communism, then socialism had to be strengthened; modernization was part of this, but by no means the major part. By the same token, when the Four launched struggle against bourgeois art and music it was not to deny the need or to undercut making use of contradictions and the "opening to the West," but to resist corrosive influences which would weaken the proletariat in the class struggle.

The line "outstrip or perish" precisely because it was not realizable would lead to capitulation. In the name of catching up, in the name of being strong and modern, in response to the "unsatisfactory pace" of industrial development in China, the bourgeoisie would cave in and barter away China's national interests. Why does it have to go that way? Because, once the assessment is made that the country cannot go up against an aggressor given its economic and military capabilities and that these must be radically improved, certain things follow. Lacking the internal ability to produce this kind of equipment and technology the revisionists look abroad for the needed technology and this opens the floodgates to the "advanced" techniques of the West along with its cultural influences. Because of the great gap between China and her potential adversaries, catching up with them can only mean relying on them and eventually selling out to them since it becomes clear this gap cannot be bridged. Mao was keenly aware of the pressure and temptation of this path. What came to be called the comprador philosophy outlook was an important element of the Lin Piao campaign and the fight against the right deviationist wind. But it was especially prominent in the *Water Margin* campaign.

Our Mensheviks have very little to say about this campaign. At the CC meeting the "herky-jerky theoretician" included a speech by Wang Tung-hsing as part of his argument that the *Water Margin* campaign was aimed at the Four. This argument has since been dropped from their arsenal (though comments from this so-called speech still appear, the fact that this speech was supposedly about the *Water Margin* campaign has been curiously omitted) since as was pointed out at the CC meeting the speech is at best incoherent and at worst a fraud perpetrated by Taiwan (as investigation seems to suggest)—it doesn't fit in at all with the themes Mao was raising around the *Water Margin*.

In August of 1975 Mao issues an instruction to study the novel, *Water Margin*. The merit of the book, he points out, "lies precisely in the portrayal of capitulation." What happens in this novel—which kind of has a Robin Hood flavor to it—is that a lower ranking member of the landlord class penetrates the ranks of the peasant movement at a time when it is engaged in fierce struggles against the landlords. He maneuvers for leadership and pushes a capitulationist line. But this is not a line of going out and prostrating himself before the enemy. Rather he fights corrupt officials—another faction of his class—and then surrenders to the emperor whom he never challenged. Having built up his bargaining strength he accepts an amnesty and then proceeds to turn on the genuine peasant rebels, swearing his eternal allegiance to the emperor. The lesson of the novel according to the *Red Flag* article which carried Mao's instruction was "whoever practices revisionism practices capitulationism."

Why is Mao stressing this theme of surrender and national betrayal toward the end of 1975? Why does he earmark a character who fights, but only to a degree, and who will not persevere in struggle to the end? Why is the theme of the dying out of class struggle (revisionism) linked to national betrayal (capitulationism)? This was not a literary exercise; it had all to do with those within the party who were bent on toadying up to imperialism, particularly social imperialism. The criticism of the novel argued by analogy that there was a struggle in the party over whether to fight resolutely against imperialism or to kow-tow and give up. Previous capitulationists like Liu and Lin did not start that way, but their revisionism dictated ultimately that they would betray their country. As an article linking Lin Piao with Confucius explained in the same month that Mao's instruction was published, "Because he wanted to practice revisionism in China, he was extremely isolated among the people. Awed by the strong might of the dictatorship of the proletariat, he felt that his own strength was inadequate and had necessarily to form an alliance with international revisionism."

While the exact parallels and analogies are quite complex, it is possible to extract from what Mao says about the novel certain major questions and points. To begin, the main danger to the revolution comes from within, from among the ranks of the rebels; in particular, from those who for a while put up a fight but never carry it on in a thoroughgoing kind of way. That the protagonist in the novel is from the landlord class would indicate that this danger of subversion comes from the more venerable elements of the party, i.e. some veteran cadre or bourgeois democrats who fought the "corrupt officials," but never the emperor. This would signify that these people were willing to fight the abuses of the old society but never to make a complete break with systems of exploitation and oppression, that is to say, never became thoroughgoing revolutionaries. Second, is the notion that there is a direct relationship between wavering on the class struggle at home and capitulating to the foreign enemy, or as LBJ used to say, one's foreign policy is a reflection of one's domestic policy.

The comment by Mao then would seem to indicate two lines on how to deal with the current situation. There are those who hold that "social peace"—minimal disturbances in the country, i.e. "great order"—is the best defense against aggression since sharp class struggles make the country more vulnerable to attack. This leads to a line of peace at all costs in order that China can prepare for the war danger. But the greatest threat to this kind of peace comes from those who persevere in making revolution. Sung Chiang, the main figure in the novel, doesn't simply come to terms with the emperor; he attacks the genuine rebels. Mao has pointed out that those who preach the dying out of class struggle always attack the revolutionary forces. In sum the program of these revisionists is to appease, coddle up to and eventually sell out to imperialism, and to go after the real revolutionaries.

In opposition to this, and obviously representing Mao's line, is the view represented by the genuine rebels who persist in struggle, aiming their blows at the emperor and the whole landlord class. This is the idea that the unity of China can only be forged through sharp class struggle—through opposing revisionism—and that concessions to the enemy, i.e. attempts to get amnesties from them, will get you nowhere but into capitulationism. Again this makes the question of the capability and will to resist foreign aggression conditional on waging the class struggle which will strike hard blows against those who would betray their country.

In China at the time there were many issues related to foreign policy that this campaign was evidently opening up to discussion and evaluation. There was the question of border negotiations with the Soviets, the capture and subsequent release of several Soviet helicopter pilots, the negotiation of trade protocols with the Soviets, the extent to which foreign military technology could be depended upon. The fact that Chou was from an aristocratic background and the fact that he was generally associated with the policies of putting stress on modernization in the context of a peaceful atmosphere, led many bourgeois scholars,among whom was Leibel Bergman, to conclude that Mao was directing this campaign against Chou. When Bergman was reminded of this at the CC he whined, "yeah, I thought that, but I didn't like it, did I?"

Teng, who was linked with the release of the helicopter pilots, which was accompanied by a virtual apology to the Soviets, was also a likely target of this campaign. But the general theme of this campaign is that whoever liquidates the class struggle at home is going to sell the country out. These people may challenge and threaten the enemy abroad, and even militarily resist an attack for a time, but only to get a better deal.

These themes became more explicit with the campaign against

the right deviationist wind in which Teng's liquidation of class struggle is directly linked with bartering away to foreign interests China's resources and eventually bringing China under the wing of an imperialist power. The message is that these people have to be ferreted out before they betray us. Right now, just because the current leaders are banging away at the Soviet Union doesn't mean they won't eventually capitulate to it. There are compelling reasons to see this as a likely possibility. For one thing, the Soviet Union is a powerful enemy that is right there on the border with over a million troops massed and missiles targeted for Chinese industrial and population concentrations. For another, the more the current leaders practice their Soviet-style line internally the more likely it is for them to come to terms with the social imperialists and patch up their differences.

That revisionism could triumph in China is very much related to the international situation, and the program of these revisionists reflects it. What they see in the enemy is its military and economic superiority, and they take that as their point of departure for policy. "We must catch up." It becomes essential to build up the economy, and the military. In order for this to happen, a modern technological base is required. And this requires that directors take their rightful place at the head of research institutes instead of revolutionary committees running them. It means increased imports. Old cadre must be brought back, regardless of politics, the wasteful political activities of the Cultural Revolution must not stand in the way of production and the workers must be motivated—paid more—to set this machine in motion while being whipped into line with oppressive rules and regulations. Since everything turns on technological and military superiority, the outstanding characteristic of China is its *weakness*. The Mensheviks, for all their yammering about the strengths behind China's foreign policy and the unlikelihood of capitalist restoration, basically operate within this framework.

This is a perspective that will have disastrous military consequences. It will lead, step by step, to making weapons the decisive question and the means to get them the central economic issue, and to putting professionalism ahead of politics in the armed forces. It is a recipe that will lead to concessions to foreign powers, dependency and, finally, defeat. China cannot, as the CC Report went into, fight this kind of war of steel. Mao stuck to that conclusion and we'll stick with him and his facts. Mao did place stress on upgrading the quality and technology of China's weapons—the nuclear weapons and missles programs he obviously approved of.

But this was not the basis for China's defense; what was, was the infantry and militia and the strategy of people's war. Any attempt to manufacture and equip the Chinese army with the kind of weapons that measure up to Western standards would require a massive redirection of the Chinese economy. This shift of investment priorities would bankrupt it outside of foreign assistance. The alternative is to export needed goods to get foreign exchange, which would have the same negative effects on planned and proportionate development of the economy.

By their own standards, these revisionists could be no match for the imperialists and that's why they'll put up a little resistance, like the character from *Water Margin,* and then, when the moment is ripe, capitulate. Mao knew two things: China couldn't fight the kind of war these revisionists are whooping it up about (with their hometown cheerleaders) and the class struggle would be lost anyway if they got the upper hand.

The Chair is accused of Trotskyism for making a Marxist-Leninist analysis of the situation in China and showing that its backwardness is an important factor to grasp in assessing the reasons that revisionism triumphed. Nowhere did he say that it was impossible to build socialism, only that there were formidable difficulties which the bourgeoisie in China and abroad would seize upon and which the working class would have to overcome through revolutionary struggle. But who, we have to ask, are the real Trotskyites? Who is saying that a certain material level is required for socialism to survive in China? Who is really saying that if China doesn't become "modern" soon, it's all over with?

We are told that the Four didn't promote the development of the productive forces. But, as we have said repeatedly, this is a question of what line would guide that development. Indonesia today has a faster growth rate than China. So what? Had the revolutionaries stayed in power, China would have continued to develop in a self-reliant and *socialist* fashion. If it's a question of going fast with capitalist roaders at the helm or going slow with proletarian revolutionaries in leadership, we'll take the latter, even if Chang Chun-chiao said it first. Hua said the question of speed is a political question. Indeed it is—how fast he and his revisionist wrecking crew can drag China down to capitalism and dependency.

Where is the Defense of Chou En-lai?

Frankly, we were disappointed by the Mensheviks' defense of Chou En-lai. (p. 180) We expected some real fighting words, some real exaltation of "beloved Comrade Chou." Instead we get complaints about too many "obviouses" and too much argument by "logic." Actually, this section contains some rather curious logic, itself. First, the authors concede that, "All contradictions develop. But all contradictions do not develop with people winding up on opposite sides." If that's true then why can't it also be the case that some contradictions *do* develop that way—which is "obviously" true? Mao and Chou worked together for 45 years, they tell us, and their differences did not develop in the straight line way we say. Well, we don't say that. It was exactly the new spiral coming off the Cultural Revolution and the Lin Piao affair that brought them into conflict, not 45 years of gestating contradictions. And isn't it to be expected that high party leaders will come into fundamental opposition over key questions, because line struggle is concentrated at those levels? Hasn't that been the history of the Chinese Communist Party?

Our Mensheviks, who liken the CC Report to a legal brief, find that it falls short on the incriminating evidence: "Where is the statement from Chou that shows he is violating Mao Tsetung Thought?" If only class struggle were that easy. We can't help it if Chou and Mickey Jarvis play their cards close to their vest and refuse to put much down on paper. It is revealing though to look at Chou's interview with Hinton in *New China* from the Spring of 1975. The whole thrust of this interview makes it understandable and compelling that Chang Chun-chiao would raise questions about Mao's analysis of classes back in the period of the new democratic revolution as it applies today. Chou basically operates in that mold. He discusses landlords, workers, peasants, urban capitalists and the like but doesn't get around to the question of the new bourgeoisie until Hinton prods him. And even in this regard the existence of capitalist roaders in the Party is downplayed. Earlier in the interview he states, "in the countryside, under socialism, classes still exist. There are, of course, some special places where old exploiters are few in number or even absent," the point being that this is who to look for as far as the class enemy goes.

There are other written materials which have been attributed to Chou. They may or may not be authentic and so must be treated with some caution. However they are consistent with the outlook and policies of those associated with Chou. For instance, in a report[10] that Chou was supposed to have delivered to the party on the international situation in 1973 he says, "The most important kind of strategic deployment is to have a great leap forward in all areas, such as industry, agriculture and technology *by adopting the advanced techniques of other countries*" [our emphasis]. (The original source is an excerpted speech that appeared in *Issues and Studies*, the source of the two speeches by Chang and Wang and much of the other material which our Mensheviks used as exhibits at the CC, so it is not entirely unjustified that we throw some of their own sources back at them.)

The line of modernizing by adopting advanced techniques from abroad was officially associated with Teng during the campaign to beat back the right deviationist wind—which went on while Mao was alive. The Four in attacks on certain foreign trade policies were, according to the current rulers, railing at Chou for his part in formulating them. Chou's statement quoted above would appear quite in line with his overall approach to modernization which the Four saw as tying China's development to the coattails of imperialism.

(There is another document[11] purporting to be the will and testament of Chou that was originally broadcast on Japanese radio. According to the radio commentary it was circulated to the CCP Central Committee by his wife. Its authenticity is even more difficult to ascertain than the above quoted speech, but again the points it makes are quite in keeping with the character of the two-line struggle that was raging in the period just prior to his death. According to reported quotes from this "will" Chou lays major stress on the development of heavy industry which fits in with an emphasis on advanced foreign technology. Also, according to the same report, Chou describes the Cultural Revolution as a "mistake" that should not be repeated, a position which was actually held by quite a few members of the CCP and which is essentially echoed by our Mensheviks. Finally, according to these sources, Chou does not mention in his assessment of the international situation the Soviet Union—which would give credence to the idea that Chou was angling for 'reconciliation' with the Soviets.)

If these documents are forgeries we have to ask why do certain themes—such as reliance on advanced technology—consistently appear in these documents? Were there or were there not powerful currents in China promoting these views? And aren't there strong indications, including the words of these forces themselves, that Chou was associated with them?

The Mensheviks make no effort to answer the arguments of the CC Report. Why doesn't Mao issue a statement following Chou's death—when the air was full of tension—and settle his case once and for all? Mao did not do that. Everybody from the Four to the current leadership agrees that Chou and Teng were closely allied. Is this a good or a bad thing? The editors of the *Peking Review* inform us that Chou was instrumental in pushing for changes in the educational system that were "hampered by the gang of 4." But, Mao gave his support to the students at Tsinghua in 1975 when the rose up against the backsliding ways of the administration. The Mensheviks make a principle of ignoring what the current leaders want no one to forget, namely that Chou and Teng were like lips to teeth.

Another point they wish to be oblivious to is the infatuation of the right with Chou. Why, we have to ask, is it the right that always "exploits the masses' feelings towards Chou?" At Tien An Men it is Chou who is venerated, his four modernizations that are consecrated, and Mao that is excoriated. Why? The Mensheviks criticize the CC Report for failing to indicate the class forces. But Chou and Teng were closely associated since Teng's rehabilitation and it is more than coincidence that Teng can only be brought down after Chou dies, which would indicate something about how the class forces line up. Mao could have stopped it, the only problem being that he ordered it! We suppose this is unfair because the Mensheviks haven't passed the final verdict on Teng yet. But, really, these people almost put their feet in their mouths: "The question of blocking the bourgeois rightists from using the death of Chou to advance their position was a real one confronting Mao . . ." One of the few true statements in this compendium of garbage.

Since we're on the subject of the right, we ought to remember that the Mensheviks regard the propaganda ministry as a stronghold of the right, in fact controlled by them. Yet, this same propaganda ministry is building up Chou En-lai as though he were the new Confucius. If Chou were such a staunch revolutionary these rightists would be making at least some veiled attacks on him. They've certainly found ways of rubbing Mao into the dirt by upholding the three poisonous weeds which he obviously disapproved of and so forth.

The Mensheviks claim that Chou steadfastly agreed with the line of the Tenth Party Congress. This Report upheld socialist new things, but Chou did not play a positive role in defending them—he initiated and fought for many "adjustments" which amounted to reversals, especially as regards education. Of course, one way they can avoid unhinging Chou from the Tenth Congress Report is to tell us that it was laying out the task of economic development, which in the sense that the Mensheviks mean it, is simply not the case.

Speaking of that Congress, what followed was the Lin Piao/Confucius campaign. The "herky-jerky theoretician" presented a paper at the CC which had this to say about the campaign: "Who exactly this was directed at is a major question, whether against some rightist *or even Chou En-lai* is significant, but whichever, these points were the essence of the movement" [emphasis added.] This is conveniently dropped from the new improved version. The Mensheviks deleated this point not simply because it would more closely associate Mao with the Four. More than this, if the campaign were at least, in part, aimed at Chou it would throw to the winds the charge of the Mensheviks that the Four were hell-bent on broadening the target just out of spite or fancy. Chou En-lai was a powerful force, he commanded tremendous loyalty among large sections of the party and he was respected by many of the masses. This would on the one hand point to the difficulties inherent in prosecuting the campaign and, on the other, to the fact that, as it deepened, it would force many cadre and social forces to jump out in defense of Chou's policies. In other words, the target would objectively have to be broadened—it would broaden itself. And by the way, this would certainly lead to many instances of disruption and so on. These kinds of questions the Mensheviks refuse to entertain.

To ignore the arguments made by the CC Report about Chou, the Mensheviks must out of desperation and ideological bankruptcy seek refuge in emotionalism in order to cover over the line questions involved. Basically, the Menshevik argument, shorn of all its quibbling over detail, comes down to this: how could such a great revolutionary go bad? How could someone who was so loved and cherished by the Chinese people sell out? It's not possible. But many, if not most, of the revisionist chieftains in the Chinese Party were "heroes" of one sort or another. Peng Teh-huai was a veritable folk hero, a veteran of the liberation war and a hero of the Korean campaign. He was extremely popular, but he betrayed the revolution. This came as a shock to many cadre and the broad masses, but it was a fact and Mao fought it out with him. Liu Shao-chi was, like Chou a venerable party and state leader. Lin Piao's picture hung in the homes of millions of peasants. But the class struggle can't be fought with sentimentality. Our Mensheviks chafe at the CC Report for being so callous as to think that Mao would actually struggle with his old comrade Chou on his deathbed. Our Mensheviks tell us it defies "human reality." So now Marxism is to be replaced with humanism!

Similarly, and you can almost see the tears streaming down their cheeks, how could we disagree with what we said in the CC statement at the time of his death? We loved him then and why don't we love him today? In fact, it was not clear at the time to our Party what Chou's role was. To the extent we understood the situation we knew that Chou was identified with Mao and if Chou stood with the forward march of the revolution for a lifetime it was certainly worthy of commemoration. It was also known at the time that there had been differences between Chou and Mao on different occasions and that there may have been differences more recently. The fact that Mao did not issue a statement to clarify Chou's role (a point which our Mensheviks will not address) raised more questions. But on the basis of our knowledge at the time it was correct to have gone ahead with the memorial meetings. Not to have done so would have been to pass a negative verdict on Chou in fact. Our knowledge has grown since then and we militantly repudiate the statement issued upon his death. If the Mensheviks want to enshrine it, fine. In that case it would be far better if they would break with their tradition and habit and be honest enough to openly repudiate Mao Tsetung and Mao Tsetung Thought.

Our Mensheviks cannot resign themselves to the most obvious facts. Mao Tsetung initiates a campaign against Teng Hsiao-ping and the right deviationist wind in the last half of 1975. If Teng, and the substance of this wind, including the three poisonous weeds, are being upheld today while they were being criticized in 1975-76 as counter-revolutionary, Mao was obviously, with the Four, arrayed against some powerful forces. We have to ask our Mensheviks what line was Chou giving support to, what line is Chou associated with by *both* those in power and those who have been overthrown? And, as the CC Report asks, if Mao and Chou were so tight why does the struggle fall out the way it does, with Teng, in line to be Chou's successor, going down only after Chou dies and the Four going down only after Mao dies? The CC Report analyzes the lines that would explain these important facts. Our Mensheviks can only fall back on sentimentalism and Confucian idol worship.

We have analyzed actual statements by Chou such as the Hinton interview, along with others that seem quite credible like the foreign policy speech, and still others that may be more questionable as with the "will." But the key issue is not the words that he uttered or put down on paper, but the forces to whom he gave his support and was allied with and the lines and forces he opposed. This is, in fact, the most important evidence to examine and the evidence which quite clearly reveals Chou to be a revisionist.

Why does the question of Chou loom as such an important one to the right in China and to our Mensheviks? Why is his reputation and standing such a cutting edge of struggle between the Four and the right and why is it necessary that we take a position on his role? It is because of the particular function he served to these forces.

In the last years of his life Chou's policies and lines on key questions promoted the interests of the right. But more than this, he had the allegiance of powerful forces in society, including large numbers of cadres, intellectuals, etc. At the same time Chou became a shield for the right. He had a distinguished record as a veteran revolutionary and his name was associated with that of Mao, and a large section of the masses had respect—or at least reverence—for him, for both good and not so good reasons (yes, Mensheviks, the masses *can* be influenced by non-proletarian ideology, including Confucian traditions, as well as the idea of the dying out of class struggle, etc.)

In all this Chou conferred respectability on the designs of the right as well as giving them protection. In China the right, in the face of resistance and opposition, could raise the specter of Chou being attacked to whip up an emotional appeal to cover over their policies. By the same token our homegrown Mensheviks raise the Chou En-lai question—the fact that he was coming under attack—to shield their support for revisionism and their utter bankruptcy.

How The Mensheviks Make Revisionism Serve Revolution

If revisionism has any meaning to these Mensheviks, it beats us because their defense of the Eleventh Party Congress is so shameful that it's laughable. (See p. 191) They have an easy explanation for the very significant change in the Eleventh Constitution which replaces the word 'overthrow' with the word 'eliminate' in talking about the bourgeoisie in the socialist period. It doesn't affect them one iota that the formulation "the complete overthrow of the bourgeoisie and all other exploiting classes" appears in both the Ninth and Tenth Constitutions, written when Mao was alive. Oh, no, Mao didn't understand what they do; namely, that overthrow refers to the period in which the proletariat *comes to power*—from there on out it's a process of eliminating the bourgeoisie.

In other words, the overthrow of the bourgeoisie is a task of the past according to the Mensheviks and the revisionists in China, on whose ideological authority they speak. But Mao didn't think so and that's why the formulation was written into the Constitution at the Ninth Congress and retained at the Tenth. As the Chair points out in his paper, "eliminating the bourgeoisie, Mao stressed, meant repeatedly *overthrowing* it..." The Mensheviks would have us believe that it just so happened at this Congress that a new and better formulation appeared. No way. Mao deliberately changed the wording when he was alive because the word "overthrow" expressed the reality of how the struggle would develop. The revisionists have deliberately changed this wording—taken "overthrow" out—because it expresses the reality of their class interests. If eliminate is so much better, then why didn't Mao have the foresight to make the change? It certainly wasn't the first time the question came up.

The Mensheviks rationalize other changes in the Constitution with their stock-in-trade argument that the excesses of the "left" strengthened the right and made it necessary for the center to unite with them. The provision for "active ideological struggle" has been removed because the Four abused it in the Lin Piao and Dictatorship of the Proletariat campaigns. The addition of new disciplinary measures was occasioned by the Four's vigorous recruitment of new, and mostly working class, members who fell under "their spell." The Mensheviks, in their own perverted way, have given new meaning to negation of the negation: first there is the Eighth Party Congress Constitution which was summed up as revisionist. It is changed in the wake of the Cultural Revolution. Now it is negated—revisionism is brought to a higher level.

For these Mensheviks everything is condition, time, and place. Yes, they would say, active ideological struggle was good but some people went too far or went their own way with it and it's gotta be toned down. Sure, they would concur, the Cultural Revolution was important but times have changed. In short, for these Mensheviks everything from active ideological struggle to the Cultural Revolution is a task or tactic to be replaced by another. There are no universal principles for them, only the particular needs of the moment. What the Chair says hits the mark exactly, "There is no justification on any basis for this [removing ideological struggle as a requirement of basic units]..." But the Mensheviks tell us that "there is no basis for such a document [the Eleventh Party Constitution] to stay the same after intense class struggle." This is the kind of statement that is aimed at a social base that has not been trained in Marxism. These people have been fed revisionism and are getting another dose of it.

The fact of the matter is that the Cultural Revolution is of universal significance to the international working class because it brought the struggle of our class to a whole new level. As for active ideological struggle, Lin Piao certainly banged people over the head with "active ideological struggle" setting off "atomic explosions of the soul" and so on, but this didn't convince Mao that it ought to be taken out, because it is a general principle under all conditions. But if the Cultural Revolution and the new—born things are tactics and if ideological struggle is a negotiable issue with the right, then even revisionism can be a tactic, a useful weapon in the hands of the genuine revolutionaries.

That's where all this leaves them. They say it right at the outset of the section "Smashing the Gang...": "Waging and consolidating the battle against the Gang has made necessary not only aiming the blow away from the right, but close unity with rightist and revisionist forces in the Party." This is the double-edged sword of the Mensheviks. They can blame some of the obviously bad things going on in China on the right who were given a new lease on life by the Four. Hence some of the defects and errors of the three poisonous weeds. But because of the "4's crimes," these weeds are not so poisonous after all and will help straighten the situation up.

At times, it is necessary for Marxist-Leninists to make concessions and compromises, but never with basic principle. We can even conceive situations in which it is necessary to have some temporary united front with revisionists, but never on the terms of revisionism. What we have here is not a united front of opposed class forces, but unity in opposition to socialism and revolution, with differences over just how to carry out counter-revolution—opposite poles of the same stupidity. By the way, it is the height of hypocrisy for our Mensheviks to accuse us of calling Mao a coward for having to make some *temporary concessions* to the right, with the appointment of Hua, etc. These Mensheviks have no compunctions about excusing what's going on in China today by telling us repeatedly that Hua has all this necessity to forge "*close unity* with rightist and revisionist forces [our emphasis]."

But let's for a moment accept the brutal logic of the Mensheviks and see how it can't possibly explain certain "facts." O.K., the Four were smash and grabbers and were on the verge of usurping supreme power. Mao saw through them, criticized them and threw his weight behind a new headquarters. The Four grew more desperate and dangerous. So why didn't Mao—with the prestige and authority that is distinctively his—settle the issue, while he was alive? Why didn't he unite with the right and put them down? The Mensheviks don't speak to this. They don't tell us why Hua Kuo-feng did what Mao couldn't or wouldn't do—unite with the likes of Teng to smash the Four. Oddly enough, they themselves have to admit in discussing the fire the Four were coming under (ostensibly from Mao) that "he [Mao] did not speak out boldly in support of them, as he had of the left during the Cultural Revolution every time it came under fire. Instead he let the struggle develop *taking a hand only in initiating and in tempering* the campaign against the right deviationist wind [our emphasis]." This is all that Mao did, to launch a campaign against the right rather than slap the Four on the shoulders and say I'm with you 100%! But who were Teng's biggest antagonists, if not the Four? Mao knew full well how to give timely support to proletarian revolutionaries, even if he didn't put them on reviewing stands right then.

Hua, all of a sudden, has so much necessity that he has to unite with the right. More than this he has to unite with their program, the three poisonous weeds (which isn't all that odd when you get down to it since he assisted in drafting them, but never mind that), and there you have it, revisionism in the service of revolution. It's a heady brew. But, comrades take heart, they bellow. The class struggle is still raging. This is their last refuge from reality. It sounds just like the old refrain from apologists for social-imperialism confronted with certain distasteful lines and practices: "Oh, but there's heavy struggle going on in the Soviet party." Which, by the way, is not really much different than what Jarvis thought back in 1968-69.

To sum up this point on the 11th Congress Constitution, let the Menshevik paper speak for itself: "For it to stay the same as the 10th would be for the Chinese leadership to lie to the Chinese people about the current situation." How true! The proletariat is no longer in power . . . and the Constitution reflects it.

More On Their Method

By now it should be obvious, yes, obvious, that the Menshevik paper is nothing more than a feeble attempt to promote more eclecticism and revisionism. It's a conscious effort, on their part, to wipe out the last traces of Marxism in their thinking and to keep their followers as ignorant and stupefied of the science as is possible. It would take a long time to respond to every point they make, which is why we have concentrated on the major ones, though, again, there isn't much they have raised that isn't already answered in the CC Report. And, as past experience has shown, fairly soon their paper will be superseded by another one. But we should take a cue from history. Late in 1976 and early 1977 the right deviationist wind became Comrade Teng's "revisionist line errors" and soon after he became the Four's fall guy and victim. He got his reward at the Eleventh Party Congress for his meritorious revisionism and it won't be long before our Mensheviks at home who are presently at the stage of criticizing his "line errors" will make the leap. Barring the unlikely prospect of Hua muscling out Teng in the near future in a bourgeois factional struggle, our Mensheviks will soon be fully and openly embracing Teng (as some of them have already done).

The method of the Mensheviks is so bankrupt that even where they wander past the *Peking Review* and sources based on the revisionist propaganda mill they pick up boulders only to drop them on their own feet. It was the Mensheviks who produced those two speeches by Wang and Chang apparently to show just how two-faced and out of touch with reality the Four were. But these speeches have shown just the opposite and we thank the Mensheviks for locating them for us. The "herky-jerky theoretician" took up the theme that the Four were criticized for not identifying both empiricism and dogmatism as being elements of revisionism and refused to mend their ways; in fact, suppressed the criticism. In his rambling discourse he makes a big point of the fact that Mao had to go to someone else, other than the Four or their followers, to write an article criticizing their error. He cited an article in *Peking Review* #20 (1975), "The Sole Purpose of Mastering Theory is to Apply It" by Tien Chun to prove his point. At the CC meeting this article was analyzed and it was shown to be an article written with the themes the Four had been stressing all along like the emergence of new class relations. So this stunning evidence he produces to show just how unrepentant the Four are establishes that they accepted the criticism and summed it up. The new version of their paper simply says that the head of the New China News Agency was forced by Yao to deep-six Mao's criticism.

The Central Committee Report is a Revolutionary Document And That's Why the Mensheviks Must Criticize It

In sum, the method, the stand and outlook, and the conclusions of the Mensheviks smack of the most twisted logic and naked revisionism. At one point we thought it was enough to point out to some of these people the flagrant reversals of the Cultural Revolution that could be found in the *Peking Review* and the repudiation of the themes that Mao had stressed these last few years. It has now become abundantly clear that the reason the Mensheviks were so stubborn at the CC and so unconvinced by the Chairman's paper that revisionism has won out in China was that they saw nothing wrong with revisionism. They see nothing wrong with experts and profit in command. They see nothing wrong with top-down methods of management. They see nothing wrong with making the fulfillment of production quotas the highest goal to which the working class can aspire. These Mensheviks would neither recognize nor repudiate revisionism in China since it is precisely what their approach to the class struggle in this country is.

The Mensheviks find it impossible to accept the fact that the revisionists have triumphed in China. That such a thing could happen defies their most fundamental assumption of the class struggle—that if you plug away and work hard, you've got to win. Theirs is a view of socialism that minimizes the danger of capitalist restoration and the forces operating against the working class. They come straight out and say it: if you have a correct line things will everywhere and all the time go your way. The Four went down, they lost and therefore they could not have had a correct line. Hua, he's in power, so he must have the correct line. Nothing succeeds like success.

You see, if socialism turns out to be a struggle of great difficulty and endurance then maybe the struggle to overthrow capitalism won't be as easy as the Mensheviks want to believe. Maybe it'll take more than telling the workers that "we've got the power" and all we have to do is to get things "spinning" and we'll spin our way to communism. Because, in fact, there are bigger things involved. There are laws of society which more than any leaflet we can distribute now or 20 years from now will propel millions into motion and, just the same, laws which if we don't grasp them and help the masses to grasp will continually smack us in the face.

The class struggle as we have emphasized does not develop in a straight line. It goes through twists and turns and the working class is bound to suffer setbacks. But in spite of these difficulties, history is moving in the direction of the working class emancipating itself, which the old and new bourgeoisies cannot alter. For the Mensheviks the law of class struggle comes down to this: if you do everything right, if you have it all together and luck out a little here and there, you can't go wrong. If the bourgeoisie beats you back, it's because you messed up. This is why they hated the miners article ("Miners' Struggle At a Crossroads," *Revolution*, December 1977) with such venom. They couldn't reconcile themselves to the fact that while we have to fight like hell in the day-to-day struggles, we can only go so far in these struggles. Unless we begin to help the workers to realize the limitations of these struggles and take up bigger questions, the gains we make will turn into their opposite.

The Mensheviks regard the struggle for communism not in terms of the working class grasping the laws of society and its historical mission, but rather as a question of strategy and tactics in the most vulgar and pragmatic sense. "The Four couldn't unite with people," they chant. Around what and for what, that doesn't matter; what does is the fact that they didn't master the politics of compromise. They couldn't finesse their way to communism. They didn't know how to maneuver for position. They were not the "tough cookie" that Teng Hsiao-ping is.

The Mensheviks do not understand that socialism is a transitional period and that it involves making a radical rupture with all traditional property relations and ideas. They do not understand that the socialist period is one of making continuous revolution in stages in order to dig out the soil that breeds capitalist relations and gives rise to the bourgeoisie. Nor, for that matter, that it involves big clashes with the bourgoisie precisely because socialism aims at wiping out the very conditions of its existence. This is why our Mensheviks find it impossible to accept that 27 years after the seizure of power the working class in China would be confronted with and temporarily defeated by the most serious challenge from the bourgeoisie. The Mensheviks gasp in amazement: how could it be that bourgeois influences could be so powerful in China, they've been struggled with for all these years. The working class could not possibly lose it all, not after this much time. This is how our Mensheviks look at history, not as one of spirals in which the working class and bourgeoisie are engaged in repeated trials of strength over whether society will move forward or backward,but as a straight line where the working class gets stronger and the bourgeoisie dies out.

This is why our Mensheviks are so enamored of the "hard-nosed" and "realistic" rulers in China. All that one has to do to get to communism is carry out the economic tasks of the day and sprinkle them with a little socialist propaganda. It's really the Chinese version of their program for the U.S. working class—"fuse" Marxism with the day-to-day struggles, never mind any qualitative developments in society or the need to raise the overall level of struggle of the working class.

The bourgeoisie does have many advantages in the socialist period—the force of habit and the pull of spontaneity, the strength of international capital, etc. And it must be frankly admitted that the working class has not been able to hold onto power for an extended period of time. But the international working class is not at point-0. It is not as though history simply repeats itself. The working class movement has advanced to a higher level through the experience of making revolution, learning from past experiences, summing up new conditions and charting out a clearer path forward. It was only a little more than 100 years ago that the working class first rose up in an organized way and established the first workers government, the Paris Commune. It was short-lived, but it put the question of workers' rule on the front burner. The problem of seizing power and consolidating the rule of the working class was resolved through the experience of the Bolshevik revolution. And with the Chinese revolution, the problem posed by the Soviet experience, how to mobilize the masses to prevent restoration, was theoretically and practically resolved through the Cultural Revolution.

But each of these resolutions brought forth new contradictions and difficulties which will be resolved through the world-wide experience of the proletarian revolution. For this reason, though the working class held power in China for a shorter time than in the Soviet Union, its ability to push past the contradictions posed by the Bolshevik revolution has brought the working class movement to a higher level. Mao Tsetung Thought concentrates these experiences and lessons of class struggle and will make it possible for the working class to advance even further. For the Mensheviks, there is no spiral development and so if the Chinese working class was defeated all is lost. Things go straight forward or straight backwards.

Our Party regards the CC Report and our stand on China as a great victory. It is a great victory not because we are happy to see dogs like Hua and Teng trampling on the achievements of the Chinese working class and restoring the bloody rule of capital, but because we did not follow in the wake of the rulers of China and sink into the swamp of revisionism, could distinguish genuine from sham Marxism, and remain the vanguard of the U.S. working class and stay on the high road. Our defeat of the Mensheviks, who would have turned our Party into a revisionist party and failing that tried to wreck it, is a concentrated expression of that victory.

The Four persevered on the high road. This was not a road of bribing workers or speeding them up or lulling them to sleep with the sort of "I'm OK, you're OK" pablum of Hua Kuo-feng. The Four set out to arm the masses with line, to arm them with an understanding of the decisive and crucial questions of socialist society so that the masses could transform it and more consciously battle the bourgeoisie's attempts to stage a comeback. And, always, they approached these problems and difficulties from the standpoint of the final goal of achieving communism, which the Four correctly understood to mean the abolition of classes. If this is what our Menshevik authors disparagingly refer to as "Gang of Four Thought," and if the *Peking Review* under their leadership is what "Gang of Four Thought" is all about, then we'll stand with it over the goulash and drivel of "Chou En-lai and Hua Kuo-feng Thought." We'll stand with it because it is the application of Mao Tsetung Thought.

The Mensheviks have thrown up a lot of sand in people's eyes because they know their arguments could not get over in the Party—after all, they were defeated at the CC—and this is why they split. Had their followers stayed within the Party, the large part of them would have been won over to the correct position, which explains why the leaders bolted and took what they could with them. Their paper is so light-weight and flimsy, so eclectic, that it tends to depress people's ideological and cultural standards. Nevertheless, it does give us the opportunity to deepen our grasp of the CC Report. And we can see why truth is higher than facts, why the truth of the CC Report synthesizes the most important facts—what lines and class forces were contending in China. The CC Report stands as our answer to the Mensheviks: **Revisionists Are Revisionists and Must Not Be Supported, Revolutionaries Are Revolutionaries and Must Be Supported.**

Footnotes

1. Data based on Chinese sources cited in Andors, Steven, *China's Industrial Revolution* (New York: Pantheon Books, 1977).
2. Joint Economic Committee, *China: A Reassessment of the Economy* (Washington: U.S. Government Printing Office, 1975).
3. Cited in *Far Eastern Economic Review,* February, 1977.
4. *Hua-chiao jih-pao* (New York), February 28,1977. Cited in *China Quarterly*, September, 1977.
5. *Economic and Political Weekly* (Bombay), December 3, 1977.

6. *Peking Review* #40 (1975).
7. *Far Eastern Economic Review,* October 1, 1976.
8. *People's Daily,* August 25, 1976.
9. *Red Flag* #4, April 1, 1977.
10. *Chinese Law and Government,* M.E. Sharpe, Spring, 1977.
11. *Foreign Broadcast Information Service,* January 29, 1976 (*Tass* broadcast of article appearing in Japanese newspaper *Sankei Shimbun*).
Other sources cited in text.

Appendix I: Verdicts May Be Reversed in Literature and Art—But Not the Will of the People

The present rulers in China are step by step transforming culture according to their bourgeois outlook as a key part of promoting and implementing their revisionist line. In the last round of struggle they mounted an intense attack in this sphere beginning in 1974. Since seizing power, they have begun to carry out their line fully. They are on the one hand systematically taking culture out of the hands of the masses and putting it in the hands of "experts." At the same time, they are unleashing a social base among professional literature and art workers which views art as above the class struggle (art for art's sake), as a creation of "geniuses" and "experts" and which resents ideological remolding and going among the masses into the midst of struggle to create socialist art. The revisionists can not do any of this without reversing correct verdicts, particularly on the leadership of Chiang Ching in revolutionizing literature and art, and the model works. Furthermore, they must attack Marxist theory. This shapes up presently around the question of "Let a hundred flowers blossom, let a hundred schools of thought contend." The revisionists reduce its meaning simply to a question of "quantity." It was put forward by Mao Tsetung in *On the Correct Handling of Contradictions Among the People* as a question of forms and styles in art and a question of method (letting them develop freely) and settling questions on the basis of discussion and struggle and not coercion.

They use certain relatively minor errors on Chiang Ching's part in this respect and comradely criticisms Mao Tsetung probably made of her to go against Mao's correct line and attack Chiang Ching's overall very correct work and real contributions, and thereby attack the proletariat.

In this our Mensheviks entirely agree and cheer. As is the case on other questions, the Menshevik indictment of the leadership of the Four, Chiang Ching in particular, concerning culture turns out to be an unintended confession of their own revisionism.

They give Chiang Ching no credit for leading the struggle to revolutionize Peking Opera, while hypocritically paying lip service to upholding that struggle and its results. Like their counterparts in China, they know that to uphold the struggle is inseparable from upholding Chiang Ching's leadership of it. For the model operas were not just the product of "hard work" though there certainly was hard work, but were principally the product of a correct line, something our pragmatic revisionists regard as "hot air." Yes, a correct line which developed in opposition to and in fierce struggle against a revisionist line and which united cultural workers to sweep the bourgeoisie off the stage of Peking Opera.

For as soon as the words of praise are out of our Mensheviks' mouths, they immediately call what they have praised ". . . the rigid development of these model operas—under the signboard of not tampering with socialist new things—that completely stagnated the development of revolutionary culture in China."

In fact, Chiang Ching led the struggle to actually implement Mao's revolutionary line and in opposition to the revisionist line of Liu Shao-chi and Chou Yang (head of the Ministry of Culture at that time, now rehabilitated by the revisionists.) She personally participated in and led the struggle to create the first five model Peking operas, *Taking Tiger Mountain by Strategy, The Red Lantern, Shachiapang, On the Docks* and *Raid on the White Tiger Regiment;* the model dance dramas, *Red Detachment of Women* and *The White Haired Girl;* the model symphony *Shachiapang.* In the early 1970s, added to the list were the Peking Operas *Song of the Dragon River, Red Detachment of Women, Fighting on the Plain* and *Azalea Mountain;* the piano composition *The Red Lantern;* the piano concerto *The Yellow River;* the symphony *Taking Tiger Mountain by Strategy.* Several other dance dramas, operas, etc. were being experimentally performed (i.e. the performances were for criticism and not yet broadly popularized) as of 1974.

That adds up to nine model operas and six other model productions (another was added in 1974.) Our opportunists claim only eight operas. They are either lying or they think that doing a symphony of an opera or vice versa is to do the same thing. If they had ever *investigated* Chinese culture they would know better. Peking Opera (and other forms of Chinese opera, like Hopei Clapper Opera) is completely different than western symphonic music and western opera. It is sort of sing-song regular lines whereas the symphonic forms are a fuller musical interpretation of the story. To make an analogy, the one is like doing a sing-song play on the civil war, the other is like a choir singing "The Battle Hymn of the

Republic." Both are obviously needed. Our revisionists neither investigate the facts nor interpret them correctly.

The struggle to revolutionize Peking Opera was taken up by art and literature workers at great risk to their freedom and for some even their lives in the beginning of the Cultural Revolution. Through this struggle many lessons were learned about how to actually apply Mao's line. For example, the question of how to portray proletarian heroes and how to portray reactionaries was consciously taken up and resolved on a whole new basis. This did not occur before in the history of the international communist movement, including in the Soviet Union when it was socialist. These lessons learned by our class in struggle have been taken up by revolutionary fighters on the cultural front in this country and others and they will not be so easily forgotten as our Menshevik butchers would like!

With what line did Chiang Ching lead? What did this lead to in practice? In the pamphlet, *On the Revolution of Peking Opera*, Chiang Ching's speech in 1964 affirmed Mao's line on culture and gave concrete guidance to the struggle then beginning to mount. Her line is by no means dogmatic or "ultra left." She sums up several points:

1.) The orientation should be to serve the majority, the workers, peasants and soldiers and to serve and develop the socialist economic base.

> "It is inconceivable that, in our socialist country led by the Communist Party, the dominant position on the stage is not occupied by the workers, peasants and soldiers, who are the real creators of history and the true masters of our country. We should create literature and art which protect our socialist economic base. When we are not clear about our orientation, we should try our best to become so."

2.) She sums up the present situation concretely, listing all the various professional companies and what they produce, exposing the fact that the bourgeois line is dominant in Peking Opera.

> "Theaters are places in which to educate the people, but at present the stage is dominated by emperors, princes, generals, ministers, scholars and beauties—by feudal and bourgeois stuff."

3.) She calls for putting stress on contemporary themes "which reflect real life in the fifteen years since the founding of the Chinese People's Republic and which create images of contemporary revolutionary heroes on our operatic stage" and gives guidelines for how to evaluate historical works.

4.) She calls for the development of pace-setters or models.

5.) She identifies the main problem in carrying out the task as producing scripts, and as the method of solution calls for writers to go among the workers, peasants and soldiers in three-way combinations of the leadership, the playwrights and the masses;

6.) She sums up experience where the artists on that basis have been willing to revise and develop their work and therefore created good works welcomed by the masses.

7.) At the same time she warns against lightly knocking down what has been accomplished and gives examples of how works some wanted to knock down were revised on the above basis and were excellent works.

These are only the major points. What did her line lead to? To go deeply into just one example: *The White Haired Girl*, originally written during the Yenan Period, was revised.

1. The love theme between the heroine and the hero was downplayed so that the class struggle was the motive force, not love between two individuals.

2. The father of the heroine fought the landlord's troops when they came for the daughter instead of killing himself.

3. The heroine fought off the attempted rape by the landlord instead of being debased.

4. The hero was told about the Red Army by an underground Communist and went to find it as opposed to running off and being found by the Red Army.

5. Many other revisions in choreography and music were made in line with showing the peasants as strong and not downtrodden.

Now the present rulers, led by Hua Kuo-feng, are "restaging" *The White Haired Girl* as it was before the Cultural Revolution (see *China Reconstructs*, May, 1977). The changes that were made under the leadership of Chiang Ching were correct and warmly welcomed by the masses. They were not "rigid" or "stifling" to anyone but the bourgeoisie. "Proposed changes" have been put into effect by the revisionists. Chiang Ching and others tried to "repel" these "proposed changes" and they acted in the interests of the proletariat.

Our Menshevik scoundrels stand entirely with the bourgeoisie in jeering at the creations of the proletariat, at the successes of the proletariat won through the bitterest, most soul-stirring struggle. They say, "In a 9 year period, a grand total of 8 model operas [sic] were developed to serve China's 800 million people."

It is exactly a tremendous inspiration and victory that in *only* a 10 year period so many truly revolutionary works were created, the like of which was never before seen! The ugly features of the bourgeoisie, the class stand and world outlook of the bourgeoisie, are fully reflected in the shameless attack of these revisionists on the victories of our class.

Chu Lan (a pseudonym used in some articles written under Chiang Ching's leadership) in *Chinese Literature*, September, 1974, page 93, answered this same revisionist attack:

> "If we review the history of the literature and art of mankind, we see how many years the exploiting classes took to create a literature and art of their own. Under feudalism it took thousands of years and under the bourgeoisie hundreds, yet only a limited number of works have been handed down. By the time it reached the stage of imperialism, capitalism was in its decadence and decline. The stage became a platform for the 'modernist school,' fauvism, strip-tease and other degenerate rubbish. The works are numerous and varied but share the common characteristic of poisoning or lulling the minds of the people . . . Contrasting our decade with the thousands of years and hundreds of years of the landlord class and bourgeoisie, we find that 'The landscape here is beyond compare,' as Chairman Mao's line runs."

That so-called "dogmatist" Chiang Ching is entirely correct. Her method is to view things from the high plane of the class struggle.

Persisting in the revisionist road they have taken, our Mensheviks hasten to clamor, "Also, how many times can 800 million people sit through 8 operas, as the main form of socialist culture, before they get bored and disgusted?" Come now! Really! All 800 million Chinese people, *unfortunately* have *not* seen all or most of the model works. Former comrades, China really *is* an underdeveloped country! Furthermore, the three great differences *actually* exist and this has real meaning as regards the difference in cultural levels between the city and countryside. In this context by 1974 the task of popularizing the model works was only *initially* completed.

Shanghai's Peking Opera Company and others have undertaken tours in the countryside, with bicycles pulling carts of equipment and artists walking with back packs to both perform for the peasants, especially in remote areas, and to assist the spare-time groups in performing all or parts of the model works, while at the same time viewing local works and learning from them and popularizing them. The PLA has done this too.

In China the record, radio and TV industries are not very developed. Broadcasting for TV is several hours a night and not every night of the week in normal times. Almost no masses own TV's and not all neighborhood committees or communes or brigades have them. Many commune brigades have loudspeaker systems over which they play radio broadcasts and records but many do not. In the cities large numbers of masses have radios, but there is a big difference in the countryside.

Besides, there is a political question involved in how much emphasis you give to such media forms as opposed to the masses themselves in social and production units throughout society actively taking up and taking part in culture.

As for films, first off China's film industry is not all that developed. The movie industry did not develop in America until after World War I, when the U.S. became a major world power. What makes our revisionists think that China's film industry should be so advanced? Still, steps like developing movie projectors light enough for transport on one bicycle were undertaken under the "evil influence" of the Four (or the Five including Mao Tsetung) so that films could be taken to even remote areas. This is actually dealing with the difference between town and country. Without taking such measures, and putting them in the forefront, the level of culture in the cities would advance while the countryside would be left to "rural idiocy." Moreover, in the national minority areas steps were taken to adapt the model works to the local forms and language.

Once again, the main problem still was that the majority of the population had not even seen all or most of the model works, that popularization of the model works remained an important task. This is clear from reading the *Chronicle* sections of *Chinese Literature* over the past years. To cite just one example, from *CL*, August, 1974:

> "The model revolutionary theatrical works have also greatly helped the transformation of many of China's local opera forms, and experiments were made to transplant the model works. *The Red Lantern* has been transplanted into the form of Hopei clapper opera, *Taking Tiger Mountain by Strategy* into pingchu opera" . . . etc . . . "People of the minority nationalities in Sinkiang, Inner Mongolia, Kwangsi and elsewhere are also staging them in their own languages and art forms. The Uighur opera, *The Red Lantern* has won wide acclaim among the many nationalities of the vast Sinkiang Uighur

Autonomous Region."

In the same quote referred to earlier, our revisionists (out of stupidity or more likely in a vain attempt to cover their ass) maintain that the model operas are "the main form of socialist culture."

Lie if you like, but don't be ridiculous! Neither in theory nor in practice have the model productions ever been the "main form of socialist culture" for the masses. The model works are exactly models, meant to act as pace-setters, as Chiang Ching laid out in 1964. They have played the role of setting a political and artistic standard and at the same time of inspiring the masses of people and literature and art workers to create new works of socialist art. This has actually happened. For example, *Chinese Literature,* November, 1975, page 110, reported:

> "In recent years, the broad masses in Huimin Prefecture, Shantung Province, have done a great deal of literary and art work which reflects our socialist revolution and socialist construction, thus effectively occupying the ideological and cultural front in urban and rural areas.
>
> "Huimin Prefecture, situated by the lower reaches of the Yellow River near Pohai Bay, consists of twelve counties. Before Liberation, the labouring people there lived too hard a life to give any time to art and literature. Before the Great Proletarian Cultural Revolution, owing to the revisionist line in the cultural field, mass literary and art activities were discouraged and their development was hampered. During the Great Proletarian Cultural Revolution the people and cadres in this district criticized the counter-revolutionary revisionist line. They organized and trained a contingent of literary and art workers, so that socialist literature and art began to flourish. Now many communes, production brigades, factories and schools have set up spare-time groups of writers and artists, most of whom are workers and peasants. Since 1973, the whole district has already produced 55 plays, more than 180 short stories, more than 300 revolutionary tales, more than 2000 poems, over 180 new songs, more than 200 ballads, 12 serial-picture books and more than 300 art works."

Even a casual glance at *Chinese Literature* for the past three or four years, not to mention the past ten years, will prove to anyone interested in investigation that this is typical of most provinces, not at all the exception but the rule!

The most important point is that communists applying a correct line must lead so that socialist culture is more and more created by the masses themselves and used in the social and production units throughout society as a weapon in the struggle against the bourgeoisie—and against nature—as well as being popularized throughout society along with works produced by revolutionary professional literature and art workers.

The masses of workers, peasants, etc. have not only performed all or parts of the model works but have created new works, and these have been popularized. This our Mensheviks spit on and ignore. This the revisionists in China are abolishing, starting with the spare-time teams in the factories, which are "divorced from production"—see the "20 Points" and Yu Chiu-li's speech at Taching (*PR* #22, 1977).

They are working to stop the initiative of the masses in cultural and political affairs in the social and production units, as an important part of destroying the political life in these units, and to transfer all the initiative to the top, by relying on that section of the artists who go in for "art for art's sake" and think of themselves as stars and geniuses who are above the masses. To do this they must destroy the model works and along with them and as a prerequisite for doing so the political lessons that were learned in their creation.

True to their Confucian mentors, our revisionists here reveal in their statements their notion that the masses themselves cannot create socialist culture but that this is the sole province of "talented" big shots. Their mentors in China cannot take this step without going even farther and separating the professional literature and art workers from the masses. Overcoming such separation was a major part of the creation of every model work and it was a tremendous struggle to unite people who considered themselves "stars" to go and learn from the workers and peasants.

Our Mensheviks are great defenders of the proletariat . . . so long as there is no bourgeoisie, and no bourgeois offensive against the proletariat. This is utter metaphysics. They state: "While rightists at this point could only aspire to reverse correct verdicts, Chiang Ching was doing so on a daily basis . . ." (p. 246)

What is their proof? They "quote" Mao Tsetung, as reported in recent issues of *Peking Review.* When did these quotes appear? After Mao died and the Four went down, which 1) makes their legitimacy highly questionable and 2) certainly leaves doubt as to whether the target of these criticisms were the Four or not. And what do our Mensheviks say about *Peking Review*? They say, don't pay any attention to *PR* because the right controls it. You can't have it both ways, former comrades. At any rate, assuming the quotes are legitimate and they were directed at the Four, Chiang Ching in particular, SO WHAT!!!

One thing is certain. The criticisms have to be taken in the context of Chiang Ching's handling of a right wing offensive against the advances of the Cultural Revolution starting in the cultural sphere with the production in 1973 of the opera *Going Up to Peach Peak Three Times,* a dirty mummy originally produced by Liu Shao-chi's wife, and slightly revised in name, and which *in practice* overthrew and reversed most of the verdicts on what constituted proletarian art, both in form and content, and in essence called for reversing the verdict on Liu Shao-chi. (See *Chinese Literature,* July, 1974, page 79.)

These criticisms Mao supposedly made of the Four around culture are all to do with method. Never once is Chiang Ching's basic orientation or line criticized. There is certainly nothing that says the way forward is to reverse the verdicts on art of the Cultural Revolution, which is *exactly* what the current rulers are doing, even widely promoting bourgeois music, literature and other such art from the West, as well as old reactionary stuff from China itself (as reported, for example, in an article on Chinese culture in *Eastern Horizons*, November, 1977).

To our Mensheviks all these things the revisionists are doing are either just fine or "justifiable" because, "The methods of destruction and the methods for advance look similar, and basically the only way to make a distinction requires an analysis of concrete conditions." In typical agnostic fashion, they say that in actuality the left looks like the right and it's impossible to tell the difference between the two, and they cover this shameful agnosticism by calling for a concrete analysis of concrete conditions which they do not attempt to do!

They are as eclectic as they are agnostic. They say, "But even though these socialist things are being supported [sic] it is important to grasp class struggle runs through everything, which always implies the possibility that these things could be reversed." One might as well say that the dictatorship of the proletariat is being "supported" but since class struggle exists it might be reversed. This is indeed true, but there is no way in hell you can support it and reverse it at the same time! There is likewise no way you can support genuine socialist new things and reverse them at the same time.

Mao Tsetung said, "The right is more arrogant, but the left is more tenacious." These revisionists, in China and our own, will be laid to rest in the sewer of history where they belong.

Appendix II: Two Lines On Learning from Tachai and Taching

With sweeping profundity our Mensheviks have announced to the world that (in addition to many other "crimes") the Party has repudiated Mao's two red banners of Tachai and Taching. But as the CC Report states:

> "There are two ways, not just one, to pull down the red banner of Tachai. One is to openly pull down the banner, but the other is to paint the banner white. In other words, it is quite possible to pervert the real lesson of Tachai, as Hua Kuo-feng and Co. have indeed done."

As an example of this process, let's first look at the example of Taching. Before and during the Great Proletarian Cultural Revolution at least three industrial institutions were upheld by Mao as examples: The Anshan Iron and Steel Company in 1960, the Taching oil field in 1964, and the Shanghai Machine Tools Plant in 1968. Each was upheld in the course of particular struggles against revisionism, and not on the basis of production statistics, although each had outstanding accomplishments in production as a result of victorious struggles in the realms of ideology and the relations of production.

For example, Mao praised the Constitution of the Anshan Iron and Steel Company in the thick of the struggle against the revisionist line of rationalizing the work process through bourgeois rules and regulations (as opposed to placing reliance on heightening the consciousness of the workers and mass movements) and the revisionists' insistence on single manager responsibility in socialist enterprises. Referring to the line of Liu Shao-chi, Teng Hsiao-ping and others, Mao wrote:

> "They were opposed to launching vigorous mass movements, to the principle of cadre participation in productive labor and worker participation in management, of reform of irrational and outdated rules and regulations and of close cooperation among cadres; they relied on just a few people working in seclusion. Many favored the system of placing responsibility solely on the factory director and were against the system of the factory director designated to undertake responsibility under the leadership of the Party Committee. They held that the 'Charter of the Magnitogorsk Iron and Steel Combine' (a set of authoritative rules practiced in a big steel plant in the Soviet Union) was sacred."

This was Mao's stand in the struggle against the "70 points" of Teng and others.

In 1964 Mao raised the slogan "In industry learn from Taching" after a protracted struggle against the revisionist line in the construction of the Taching oil field. Taching was a product of the Great Leap Forward. Its initial work force consisted of demobilized PLA men and veteran oil workers from the Yumen oil field, many of whom were accompanied onto the great Manchurian plain by their families. The exploration of this area, the former bed of an inland lake, was in defiance of the advice of Soviet geologists who said that such formations would never yield oil. One aspect of Taching was this break with slavishness to things foreign. The first oil was struck in 1959, but in 1960 the Soviet Union abruptly withdrew all technical assistance and placed an oil embargo on China. (The U.S. had already established such an embargo.)

It was at this point that Liu Shao-chi vigorously opposed continuing the Taching effort—without the Soviet aid he held it impossible. Yet the workers of Taching refused to give in, they engaged in a mass study of Mao's philosophical works, heightened their consciousness, and created new and favorable conditions through their own efforts. It is interesting to note here that one major criticism by the Four of the film "Pioneers" is that it completely leaves out this aspect and thus white-washes Liu Shao-chi.

Beyond their perseverance and ideological study, the workers of Taching and their families began to create new and revolutionary social relations. While in the cities, Liu was pushing the practice of bringing women into the workforce as low-paid helpers to skilled men in state-owned industries, the family dependents in Taching responded to Mao's call to develop industry in an all-round way, bringing closer together the different sectors of the economy, striking a blow at the three great differences, and bringing women into the productive work force without dependence on state capital investment. Starting with "three shovels" the families of the oil workers took up the reclamation of the wasteland in which the oil field was located and pioneered the development of "worker-peasant villages" in which industrial and agricultural workers lived side by side. It was as a result of this intense struggle that Mao held up Taching as a red banner, and again pointed to it in his famous "May 7 directive" (actually a letter to Lin Piao, after which the May 7 cadre schools are named):

> "Likewise, workers should, in addition to their main industrial work, learn military affairs, politics, and culture,

> and take part in the socialist educational movement and in criticizing the capitalist class. Under adequate conditions, they should also engage in agricultural production, following the example of the Taching Oilfield."

The Shanghai Machine Tools Plant was upheld by Mao as a result of the struggle of the workers there to break open the doors of technological education to the workers and to unleash the initiative and skill of the working class in technical innovation. Mao's comments on this question were released in a famous report on July 21, 1968, after which the July 21 universities in the factories are named. In this struggle Mao forcefully upheld the leading role, not just of proletarian ideology, but of the workers themselves in the sphere of technology. Slashing at the Liu-Teng line on science and technology, the same line which is now being implemented, Mao wrote:

> "It is still necessary to have universities; here I refer mainly to colleges of science and engineering. However, it is essential to shorten the length of schooling, revolutionize education, put proletarian politics in command and take the road of the Shanghai Machine Tools Plant in training technicians from among the workers. Students should be selected from among workers and peasants with practical experience, and they should return to production after a few years' study."

The point which our Mensheviks try so hard to evade is that Mao consistently held up as examples those units which were exemplary in the struggle against revisionism (and in fact against the same lines that are now being implemented by Hua & Co.). The significance of Taching was not that it excelled in the production of oil (which it certainly did—as a result of grasping revolution), but in the fact that it was a stronghold of proletarian politics in the intense class struggle in China in the early sixties.

In this light then, let us see who it is that is really upholding the red banner of Taching and who is casting it down. At the National Conference on Learning from Taching in Industry, Hua Kuo-feng delivered a speech which contained, scattered throughout it, many correct statements and assessments, e.g. "Taching vigorously stimulates the growth of production by making revolution in the superstructure and in the relations of production," or:

> "...Taching also undertakes agriculture, forestry, animal husbandry, side-occupations and fisheries, increasing collective welfare step by step and building up an

> oilfield of a new type which combines industry with agriculture and town with country. All this contributes to narrowing the three major differences between workers and peasants, between town and country and between manual and mental labor, restricting bourgeois right and preventing the emergence of a class of bureaucrats."

Yet read as a whole, Hua's speech elevates the tasks of production to equality with the tasks of class struggle (and equates class struggle with rooting out the influence of the Four), upholds the "historical mission" of the working class as making China a "great and powerful modern socialist country," by the year 2000 and most importantly serves as the introduction and seal of approval on the main report by Yu Chiu-li wherein the concrete programmatic goals of the conference are laid out.

If indeed Mao's red banner of Taching were being upheld, one might expect a concrete program placing the contradiction between the proletariat and the bourgeoisie up-front (the film "Pioneers" tended to present the principal contradiction as between China and the encircling imperialists and social-imperialists), and calling for continuing revolutionization in the superstructure and the relations of production, strengthening of the socialist new things, continued restriction of bourgeois right, etc. Instead Yu offers a ten point program as follows, summarized by key quotations. (*The National Conference on Learning From Taching In Industry, Selected Documents,* Foreign Language Press, Peking 1977.)

> 1) "What we mean by rectification is carrying out a widespread Marxist education movement, carrying out education in political line, and settling one by one those issues over which the 'gang of four' created confusion."
>
> 2) "Special attention must be paid to selecting and appointing the two top leaders in each enterprise."
>
> 3) "The leading bodies concerned should strengthen management, institute strict discipline in financial and economic affairs, and take appropriate measures to solve the actual problems in mapping out plans for the enterprises, in linking production with supply and marketing and in co-ordinating the work of various enterprises."
>
> 4) "All enterprises should take Taching as the example,... establish and improve their organizations, systems and rules of political work, and take effective steps to strengthen political and ideological education."... "They should launch large-scale mass campaigns to comment on the ideology and outlook of the comrades, compete with one another in making contribu-

tions, elect model workers and select pace-setters . . ."

5) ". . . work out ways and means to reverse the situation of certain enterprises running at a loss, improve quality, lower consumption of materials, overhaul and repair equipment and installations, and ensure safety in operations."

6) "The number of non-productive personnel in general should not exceed 18% of the total payroll in an enterprise."

7) "We must strictly carry out the Party's policy of uniting with, educating and remoulding the intellectuals and bring into full play the role of technical personnel."

8) "A special conference will be held to study and tackle the problems involving employment and wage rates."

9) "Enterprises should strengthen centralized Party leadership and institute the system of division of labor and responsibility under the leadership of the Party Committee. Responsibility for the daily work in production, construction and management in an enterprise rests with the chairman of the revolutionary committee."

10) "Work by city authorities must be done in line with the principle of serving production and the masses of workers, with great efforts being made to run educational and public health institutions, public utilities and commerce and the service trades well."

This isn't learning from Taching—it's learning from Khrushchev!

"Learning from Tachai"

The treatment of Tachai by our Mensheviks is no less gruesome. Sure that they have a winner this time, they devote six pages of their "Smashing" paper to Tachai and the question of mechanization of agriculture. In studying this point people should again re-read pages 40-42 of the CC Report on China which covers the basic issues of Hua's and Chen Yung-kuei's line on agriculture. But a bit of background on Tachai itself and why Mao upheld it as a red banner is in order.

Mao issued his call "in agriculture, learn from Tachai" in 1964 after several protracted struggles with revisionism in the field of agriculture. Immediately following the victory of the New Democratic Revolution in 1949, a fierce struggle broke out between the line of Mao which insisted on moving at once into the socialist transformation of society and Liu Shao-chi's line of extending the period of "new democracy" during which time a "synthesized economic base" of both capitalist and socialist sectors would build up China's productive forces.

In the agricultural field, Liu opposed the cooperative movement after land reform as being "utopian agrarian socialism" and maintained that mechanization must precede cooperation. On June 14, 1950, Liu wrote: "Only when conditions are mature for the extensive application of mechanized farming, for the organization of collective farms and for the socialist reform of the rural areas, will the need for a rich peasant economy cease, and this will take a somewhat long time to achieve." Liu further advocated a policy of "four freedoms": freedom to buy and sell land, to hire tenants, to select crops to plant, and free markets and pricing. He sought to justify this policy by saying it was necessary to preserve the united front of the four classes in the New Democratic Revolution and to unleash the "natural" productive forces in the countryside.

In contrast Mao called for a mass movement of the peasants against the re-emergence of exploitation in the countryside, saying, "The greatest efforts must be made to organize various mutual assistance cooperatives and for the improvement of agricultural techniques." "In no way can the spontaneous forces of the countryside be allowed full play."

It was in this setting that Chen Yung-kuei repeatedly sought permission from county authorities to set up a cooperative, which was granted in 1953 with the provision that it be limited to 30 households!

Even after the establishment of a people's commune in 1958 the class struggle in no way let up. Following the three bad years of natural disasters, in 1961 Liu Shao-chi proposed his infamous *sanzi yibao* solution: extend the private plots and free markets, set agricultural output quotas by the household and not by the collective, and promote small enterprises with private responsibility for profit and loss. County representatives who came to Tachai to preach this rightist wind were sternly rebuffed, but at the national level Liu was distributing his revisionist Sixty Regulations on agriculture.

At the Tenth plenum of the eighth Central Committee in 1962 Mao again called attention to the centrality of class struggle in preventing China from "changing color." One can just imagine Teng sitting in the corner grimacing as Mao declared: "Class struggle must be talked about every year, every month, every day."

In 1963, Mao issued guidelines for a Socialist Education Movement. But Liu Shao-chi, by issuing further guidelines to "clarify" Mao's original instructions tried to pervert the Socialist Education Movement in the countryside by transforming the "four cleanups" campaign into a "knock down the many to protect the few" affair—a technique frequently employed by the rightists in the Cultural Revolution. Rather than unleasing the masses through their mass organizations (Poor Peasants Associations, Women's Associations, etc.), Liu said "the problem lies with the leadership" and dispatched work teams to the countryside to "rectify" the situation.

One such work team, headed by Liu's wife, Wang Kuang-mei, was dispatched to a relatively well-off brigade at Taoyuan. After secretly interrogating most of the local cadre, a bureaucratic "rectification" was carried out, and a report of the Taoyuan experience was circulated by Liu as a model for how to carry out the campaign. Chou Yang, Minster of Culture, ordered his staff to work producing plays and movies about Taoyuan.

In the meantime, the little brigade of Tachai in the Taihang mountains had been perservering on the socialist road, had refused to accept state aid when natural disasters struck, had accomplished wonders in land capital construction, and had posted impressive gains in agricultural output. Revisionist officials immediately dispatched a workteam to investigate the "exaggerated claims" of tiny Tachai. After weeks of struggle the workteam withdrew after the Tachai Party committee refused to knuckle under. Summing up the experience of the Socialist Education Movement in January 1965, Mao wrote: "The main target of the present movement is those Party persons in power taking the capitalist road."

Mao upheld Tachai as a model of *class struggle* (which had in turn resulted in phenomenal growth in Tachai's productive forces). Hua & Co.'s perversion of this can be found even in our Menshevik's Bible "Tachai—The Red Banner." As the CC Report notes, this book is generally eclectic. Along with statements about politics in command, etc., it lays out the same line as *PR* #1, 1978, whose revisionist purpose is clear: "Why do we say the socialist system is superior? In the final analysis, it is because the socialist system can create higher labour productivity and make the national economy develop faster than capitalism." This is the real line of Hua, *et al.*, on Tachai. Contrast the "Red Banner" book with a 1972 pamphlet "Tachai—Standard Bearer in China's Agriculture," whose line is based on this theme: "The fundamental experience of Tachai . . . is that the poor and lower-middle peasants and other commune members are ever better grasping Mao Tsetung Thought and that the peasants in their millions are consciously farming for the revolution." Unlike the "Red Banner" book, this pamphlet does not combine such statements with the "theory of productive forces," the "revenge line" and empiricism.

Leery, and rightly so, of Hua's open support of the theory of productive forces in agriculture, our Mensheviks have developed their own "original" analysis to support the same conclusions. In a nutshell, their argument is that mechanization of agriculture is the key to socialism because the workers supplying the peasants with tractors is the material basis for the worker-peasant alliance, and hence the continued rule of the proletariat. Opposition to primary emphasis on mechanization is thus tantamount to attempting to break up the worker-peasant alliance. Further, in the whole question of mechanization, our Mensheviks discern an important line difference between Hua and the "rightists."

In the first place our Mensheviks are quite wrong in their analysis of the importance of mechanization. For them the only point is a "you scratch my back and I'll scratch yours" relation between workers and peasants for the purpose of keeping the alliance in state power. They even take this so far as to oppose any kind of disruptive class struggles in the cities which might interfere with production and hence upset the worker-peasant alliance. It's truly a wonder that China made it through the Cultural Revolution what with all the worker-peasant disruption that must have caused!

The introduction of mechanization into agriculture, the creation of sideline industries in the brigades, the building of chemical fertilizer plants in each county, the introduction of scientific farming and technology in general to the peasants provides the material basis for *the transformation of the peasants as a class into agricultural proletarians.* This smashes down the distinctions between city and countryside (note however our Mensheviks: "The peasantry, and especially in the collective form of organization, *depend on the cities* for agricultural implements, supplies, fertilizer, etc. as well as consumer goods."—emphasis added). In short, this is crucial in narrowing and eventually eliminating the differences between city and countryside and workers and peasants.

None of this however occurs spontaneously as a result of the mechanization of agriculture. What happens if spontaneity holds sway in the mechanization of agriculture is rural capitalism. Mechanization must be led by the conscious dictatorship of the working class and accomplished through class struggle carried out by the masses of peasants.

A decisive question in this is restricting bourgeois right. Given the fact that bourgeois right has not been completely eliminated even in the sphere of ownership—that is, ownership is collective and not by the whole people—and that there still exist commodity relations in the accumulation of means of production, especially in the countryside—that is, accounting units sell part of their output and buy machinery, etc.—the spontaneous tendency will be for the rich to get richer and the poor, poorer, for the more well-off units to be able to acquire more advanced technology and go further ahead with mechanization, while the less well-off ones fall further behind in this. Unrestricted, this will lead to a vicious cycle and to tremendous polarization.

To overcome this and make further strides along the socialist road in agriculture requires conscious policy to restrict bourgeois right, to assist the poorer teams, brigades, communes, etc. to catch up with the more advanced, in the context of making overall strides forward in agricultural mechanization and production. It requires constant education in line and sharp class struggle over questions relating to the superstructure and the economic base in order to overcome spontaneous capitalist tendencies and defeat the forces of capitalism in the countryside (and throughout society). It is very significant in light of all this that the current rulers are more and more openly attempting to deny the importance of such questions, even, for example, downplaying the significance of the fact that ownership in the collective form has many defects that can provide an important basis for the reversion to capitalism—this stands out sharply, for example, in the article "Why Did Chang Chun-chiao Kick Up a Fuss Over the Question of Ownership" (*PR*#1,1978), whose title is a hint of the revisionist line of the article.

For the revisionists in power in China revolutionizing the relations of production is now a mechanical result of raising the productive forces. A most instructive article (by negative example) on this subject is "Is It Necessary to Develop the Productive Forces in Continuing Revolution" (Peking Review #4, 1978. Note also this article demotes *Chairman* Mao to *Comrade* Mao.):

> "With regard to the social change in agriculture, the switch-over (sic) from the small-scale peasant economy to collective ownership with a low level of public ownership merely (sic) frees the productive forces from the trammels of outdated relations of production. Even in the absence of technical revolution, this change can be effected on the basis of hand tools and draught animals already in use.
>
> "But the switch-over or transition from collective ownership to ownership by the whole people in agriculture

> is quite a different matter. It can be achieved only through a large-scale technical revolution for accomplishing the mechanization and electrification of agriculture and creating a new kind of agricultural productive forces based on modern techniques."

Lest anyone get the mistaken idea that class struggle will be the key link in this process, the revisionist line of the Sixth Plenary of the Eighth CC is brought alive like Frankenstein's monster: "Since we are dedicated to the cause of communism, we must, *first and foremost*, be enthusiastic about developing our productive forces" (emphasis added).

Revolution, of course, follows automatically on the heels of increased production. The article goes on: "...doesn't it follow that under socialism the development of large-scale industry, and the growth of industry in the rural areas and the realization of farm mechanization in particular, will bring about the revolutionization of relations among all the small collectives which will in turn revolutionize the peasants' minds?" No, it doesn't follow. It only follows when the working class and its party heeds Mao's call in 1962: "Never forget classes and class struggle!"

Most pathetic is the attempt of our Mensheviks to breathe life into their theory of "three lines" in China, a theory which can serve only to blind people to what is actually happening in China and play upon people's subjective desires that it somehow isn't so that revisionists are in command. After asserting again and again with no substantiation that the Four opposed mechanization of agriculture they proceed to describe the other *two* lines:

> "The debate over agriculture is relatively open. Different articles in different publications put the stress on different sides of the question, and so the lines become clear. The right is stressing grain production and fullfilling and exceeding the plan. The revolutionaries under Hua, and including Chen Yung-kuei, are stressing the need for both immediate production while providing the peasantry with sufficient time to energetically take up farm land capital construction and mechanization." (see p. 241)

Here once again we have an effective demonstration of two poles of the same stupidity. The "rightists" we are told stress only production, while the "revolutionaries" on the other hand stress not only production but *also* farm land capital construction and mechanization! For our Mensheviks, the touchstone of proletarian ideology on the agricultural front is the question of mechanization. They assure us that: "Capitalist roaders of all stripes, either those like the gang [of four] or those like Liu Shao-chi all oppose the mass movement to mechanize agriculture." Now this is demonstrably false. The Soviet revisionists for example sought to make quick gains in agricultural output by selling off the assets of the socialist Machine Tractor Stations to the more profitable collective farms. The result of course was to unleash the spontaneous forces of capitalism in the countryside, leading to direct competition between units for accumulation, the conversion of collective property into private plot farming, and increased polarization in the countryside. Making the general point that mechanization if not carried out correctly will not strengthen but weaken socialism, Mao in his note on agricultural mechanization (March 12, 1966) rhetorically asks: "Wasn't agriculture in the Soviet Union basically mechanized?"

Here once again it is valuable to review the critique of Hua's speech to the first learning from Tachai conference contained in the CC Report (pp. 71-2) and to compare Hua's speech with that of Wang Chin-tzu (here the point is not to see if one can find lip service to class struggle in Hua's speech or to determine whether Wang today does or does not support the current rulers—the point is to compare the obvious differences in the overall emphasis, the different political lines, which the two reports reflect). As the CC report points out, Hua sees the danger of capitalism in the countryside primarily in the form of corruption and grafters on the local level with the material basis being small production. And the spearhead is to be directed at the local cadre. The solution proposed is strikingly like that employed by Liu Shao-chi in the Socialist Education Movement; Hua says, "The provincial, prefectural and county Party committess must send large numbers of cadres to the basic levels and carry this education to success in one-third of the units at a time. As for those communes and brigades which have very grave problems, the county Party committee leadership should personally go into the primary units and mobilize the masses to 'lift the lid' on class struggle and solve the question of leadership."

What is so strikingly missing is an understanding of the dangers of capitalist relations in the large scale socialist collective and thus the primacy of promoting proletarian ideology and consolidating the all-round dictatorship of the working class. This is a problem which can never be solved simply by mechanization and land capital construction (although both are necessary to China's socialist development). That mechanization does not in and of itself equal socialist development is dramatically demonstrated by such countries as India, Iran and others where various forms of bourgeois agrarian "revolution" have led to mechanization, all right—with a handful of well-to-do farmers able to purchase and utilize advanced technology, while large masses of the peasantry are driven into complete destitution. This is why such great attention must be paid to restricting bourgeois right in agricultural development. To inscribe in stone the bourgeois right of "to each according to his contributions" and to each work team according to its marketed commodities, is to make a mockery of socialism as transition to a classless society. Instead it sanctifies the basis of polarization in the countryside.

Hua's six criteria for a Tachai-type county, while each in and of itself has merit, are singularly lacking in promoting socialist new things, the transformation of the world outlook of the peasants, fighting the spirit of individual unit accumulation and promoting the outlook of "farming for the revolution" of which Mao spoke. Taken as they are the criteria and the campaign for Tachai-type counties basically calls for all-out competition in land capital construction, productivity, in marketing to the state and in improving the living standard of commune members. Nowhere is there any serious attention paid to the question of equalizing the severe disparities of economic levels between units as a crucial part of moving to higher levels of collectivity and social ownership. There are no criteria promoting unpaid labor donated to state or collective projects, or giving aid to poorer units, or cultural achievements, or the restriction of private farming and marketing. Ultimately what this leads to is the picture in *Peking Review* #1, 1978, p. 10 of the "happy peasant" counting his money—the kind of picture which, while Mao was alive and the Four were around, would have been justly condemned as disgusting revisionist poison.

This, despite some empty words about politics and class struggle, is where the line of Hua & Co. leads on the question of agriculture—put money not politics in command, put output above outlook and production above revolution. To say that this is upholding the *red* banner of Tachai is the grossest perversion. That the Four fought vehemently against *such* "learning from Tachai" and the same kind of line of the current rulers on "learning from Taching" is entirely to the Four's credit and completely consistent with their stand of fighting with and for the proletariat and masses of people in taking the socialist road.

Appendices

Report on Rectification From the 3rd Plenary of the 1st Central Committee Of the RCP

Recently a very important meeting of the Central Committee of our Party was held, which was marked by very intense struggle between two lines. At that meeting, an attempt to split the Party was defeated and repudiated.

Summing up the situation in China, the Central Committee debated at length over and adopted the position presented by the Chairman in a paper "Revisionists are Revisionists and Must Not Be Supported; Revolutionaries are Revolutionaries and Must Be Supported." This paper, now the line of our Party, which has been enriched and developed from its original text on the basis of the points brought out in the debate, is enclosed as the major part of this report. It was approved by a vote of more than 2 to 1—more than three to one counting alternate members.

Following this, the Central Committee discussed and repudiated what it summed up to be a revisionist line and headquarters in our Party, which had been increasingly intriguing, conspiring and working for a split. This headquarters was headed up by Comrade Mickey Jarvis. The Central Committee, however, does not regard Comrade Jarvis himself as a revisionist, an enemy, but as someone who is, despite serious errors, still a comrade. It has made arrangements for him to undertake work to make contributions to the Party, has assigned him some leading responsibility in the Party, and, while struggling with him, has expressed every hope that he'll change in the course of work and study. At the same time it is necessary to arm the whole Party with the knowledge of this line, this factional set-up, this attempt to split the Party and who was behind it. This has badly influenced our whole Party in regard to political and ideological line, theory of knowledge and organizational line—including methods of leadership and the practice of the mass line within the Party and among the masses. It has to be rooted out.

Through criticism and self-criticism and summing up this situation, the Central Committee took some political and organizational steps to begin dealing with this revisionist line and headquarters and decided the entire Party must take up a rectification campaign to deal with the influence of this headquarters, whose ideological, political and organizational line is eclecticism, pragmatism and factionalism. (More on this rectification campaign later.) These steps and this campaign were adopted by a unanimous vote of all members (and alternate members) of the Central Committee, including Comrade Jarvis. This sets an excellent basis for the Party to push ahead, develop its work, and deepen its study and grasp of Marxism in the course of criticizing revisionism.

Quantity To Quality

This revisionist line and headquarters has had its process of development, leading up to a qualitative leap around this meeting. Due in large part to the history of the development of the Party, in the main out of the old Revolutionary Union in various parts of the country, a second center has in fact existed for a number of years, including back before the Party was founded. It has developed, especially in the past year or more, into a separate headquarters organized around a different line from the Party's line—a revisionist line.

There has been a process of development of this headquarters and its factional behavior in relation to our Party's line on events in China since the "Gang of Four" were put down by Hua Kuofeng in October, 1976. Here, what is being condemned is not Comrade Jarvis' line on China, or even his vacillation over the question, but the way in which a factional headquarters in fact developed and went from quantity to quality in the last period. In this light it is useful to go into a little history around this.

Originally, Comrade Jarvis united with the position of a number of other comrades at the Party center that while further investigation of developments was important, this looked like a very bad thing. As a result, the center put out the October 15, 1976, article in *Revolution*, which, while upholding socialist China, had a clear "tilt" in the direction of the line of the Four. But within a very few weeks, Comrade Jarvis did a turnabout and began denouncing the Four as counter-revolutionaries, influencing some other leading comrades, even privately branding certain lines in our own Party as "Gang of Four idealism," sharpening the divisions at the center. As a result, the "tilt" had to be abandoned and a compromise, "even-handed" position was put forward as we continued to study and struggle over events in China. Then, in recent months, with certain lines coming out of China, the rehabilitation of Teng Hsiao-ping and the 11th Party Congress, Comrade Jarvis, while not changing his support for Hua and opposition to the Four, voiced opposition to at least some of the lines coming out of China. In this period the last bulletin (Vol. 2, No. 4) was put out.

Finally, in the weeks before the Central Committee meeting, particularly after further study and long conversations with the Chair, he stated to other comrades at the center that he felt his position had been wrong, that he would present a paper making self-criticism, and that the Four were basically correct, although he had some questions on some points. The Chairman offered to assist him in preparing his paper, arranged to set up a meeting to go over questions, etc., in the interest of uniting the Party and going ahead to have good and useful struggle at the Central Committee meeting. Approximately a week passed, with Comrade Jarvis failing to carry through with this meeting, evading phone calls, failing to return calls when messages were left. On the very eve of the meeting, in a conversation on China with a comrade at the center he gave no indication that he had changed his position. Then, without warning, without even an attempt to notify the Chair or the center of his position, he showed up at the Central Committee with a short and empty paper proclaiming his opposition to the Four as counter-revolutionaries and his support for Hua Kuo-feng. This paper contained little in the way of substance, but was a simple rallying cry, a tattered flag to appeal to those he regarded as his social base to rally and stand firm around him and a whole program.

He presented the Central Committee with an ultimatum, a threat to split the Party, which was taken up by others in his camp and around which an open faction solidified at the meeting. This had been foreshadowed several months earlier when Comrade Jarvis had stated he wouldn't change his position, so no Central Committee meeting should be held to discuss this. Again, what is being condemned here is not the position on China he presented, but his way of maneuvering and doubledealing. This in fact obstructed sharp and principled struggle around China at the meeting, and for a time and to a serious degree undermined struggle and solidified a faction that was stubborn, cliquish and arrogant.

This second center, as said before, had a process of development; it already expressed itself in the period leading up to and at the Party's Founding Congress. In part this came up in that period in the form of economist tendencies—the center of gravity and industrial concentration are everything—to which Comrade Jarvis had given some leadership, particularly in opposition to the Chairman. While he later changed and struggled against this economism, in the meantime a lot of forces had gotten into it and also apparently the ideological roots which gave rise to this tendency were not thoroughly eradicated, so the outlook and method of pragmatism which underlay this economism came out later with Comrade Jarvis in other forms, even in relation to political struggle. But still more stark at the Founding Congress was the tendency to federationism.

The criticism of federationism which was made in the Central Committee report immediately after The Founding Congress spoke to real material difficulties in forging the Party out of the pre-Party period. It spoke to the regional development of the RU, and to political tendencies that existed everywhere. But it was especially directed at the behavior at the Congress, and the line and outlook behind it, of a number of leading and middle-level comrades who had been "trained" under the leadership of Comrade Jarvis. This behavior, which amounted to using the work of an area as capital, showed itself in an extremely sectarian and arrogant approach to the rest of the Party. It was empiricist, in that it took particular and limited experience as everything and set it against broader experience of the entire Party and against overall summation embodied in Marxist-Leninist line. It promoted pragmatism in the form of the very harmful approach that "if you have more workers you have the right to speak; if you have fewer, then you really don't." At this time Comrade Jarvis directly and indirectly engaged in bargaining for and even offering up leading positions to others in "his camp." (Some of this has come out only recently as comrades have made self-criticism.)

All of this was sharply felt by many comrades at the Congress and it was sharply criticized, mainly among leading comrades, by the Chairman at that time. This method creates the tendency to turn modest but potentially important advances in the work into their opposite, to turn everything into capital within the Party.

All of this was very harmful, but it did not mean that at that time there was a bourgeois headquarters in the Party. Things had not taken that kind of qualitative leap. On the basis of some self-criticism and building off what was clearly the main aspect—the advances of the Founding Congress—Comrade Jarvis generally participated in the collective leadership of the Party and made some significant contributions to the Party's work.

But even in this period the other, second center, aspect continued. And in the last year or more this developed further into an objective factional set-up based on a line opposed to that of the Party center. This factional set-up had many contradictions within it; sometimes it was more, sometimes less, conscious in its opposition to the Party's line, but in many ways the Party as a whole has been effectively split for a year or more. This has come out around various issues, including the questions involved in forming a young communist league. This went so far that some comrades took a factional attitude toward the Party as a whole, and a hostile attitude toward the Chair. This was objectively encouraged by Comrade Jarvis who at one point told the Chair he had no right to speak on this question because he hadn't investigated (in fact, the Chair had done some investigation), and who, while upholding the line in some ways, also "floated" ideas to these comrades that encouraged them in their wrong thinking and their tendency to oppose the Party politically and organizationally.

Lately, as a means of hitting back at this tendency opposed to the Party's line a number of things have been written at the center, including the Party Branches articles (especially the second one), the *Worker* bulletin, and the reply to the youth appeal which were issued as blows against this line and in varying ways against this headquarters.

How did this faction form and operate? Why in fact were some people so stubborn, cliquish and arrogant instead of listening, studying and struggling in a comradely way in the period leading up to and at the Central Committee meeting? These questions were gone into at some length at the meeting, based to a great degree on the self-criticism and struggle against this revisionist line and headquarters by the comrades who themselves had been part of this factional set-up.

In this report these questions, and the crucial points of line involved, can only be characterized. Discussion in the Party and further guidance in the course of carrying out the rectification campaign will be required and developed to flesh these points out.

People in Comrade Jarvis' own camp, who had "owed allegiance" to him went into how this factional set-up operated on various questions, including the young communist league. This needs to be gone into more by the whole Party as a part of rectifying our work in the spirit of curing the sickness to save the patient.

Did the fact there has been a factional set-up and a bourgeois headquarters mean there have been formal meetings or that Comrade Jarvis has openly expressed disagreement with the Party's line on all these major questions? Not at all. The faction was based on a line and ideological outlook opposed to that of the Party. It operated while Comrade Jarvis generally upheld the Party's line in meetings of bodies, etc., and even vigorously upheld it on various bodies. But people who, in one way or another, were part of his factional set-up often did oppose it. He unleashed these forces, this social base, often by agreeing in words with Party documents, but then floating a scheme, raising a question or pushing a concept whose whole thrust ran counter to the line of the document in question. In effect, this comes down to saying one thing and doing another.

Philosophically it amounts to eclecticism, attempting to combine and reconcile two opposing points, or raising a secondary aspect of a contradiction to defeat the principal aspect. Such a method objectively increasingly "gave the green light" to people and tendencies more openly and vigorously opposed to the Party's line on the basis of their own outlook and mistakes.

Such people then thought they had Comrade Jarvis' support, at least relative to the Party center as a whole, for their lines. This whipped them up, flamed tendencies toward innuendo and departmentalism, and made struggle through regular Party bodies very difficult. In this way a line opposed to the Party's line was pushed, a social base was formed, a factional set-up and a bourgeois headquarters developed—all under the banner of carrying out the Party's line.

It often happened that when things then "got out of hand" and the Party center stepped in to struggle with these lines and forces that Comrade Jarvis would then take part, even vigorously take part, in the struggle along with the center. But the effect of this was usually to produce in those forces he had unleashed a feeling that he had "punked out" to the center and had, in fact, "set them up." This both perpetuated the faction and produced confusion and demoralization, not principled struggle and clarity.

Last CC Report

The period since the last Central Committee meeting has been a period of increasing factional spirit and struggle between Marxism and revisionism. A revisionist line and a headquarters increasingly developed in opposition to the basic point of the last CC Report, in the form of "raising the CC Report to defeat the CC Report." At that last CC meeting, there was sharp struggle against a rightist current which opposed the original report written by the Chairman and, after some discussion and struggle, submitted to the Central Committee by the standing bodies ("Some Points . . ."). This counter-current argued that "Some Points" distracted the Party from the main questions of how to build the struggle, and that it was "left" idealist and defeatist. Although other points were added (see other sections of the last CC Report) the body decided after sharp struggle that the original paper was correct "as is." This upheld the line and major principles of the report and beat back opposition to it from the right.

At that CC meeting Comrade Jarvis struggled for the line of the CC Report. But immediately after the report came out, as the whole Party was supposed to be studying that report, he and others close to him launched their own campaign in many places, outside of regular Party channels, around "the general resides in the particular." The effect of this was to seriously obstruct in many places grasping the essence of the CC Report, to unleash again around a wrong line those forces who had opposed the original report, and in effect to reverse the struggle over "as is" that had been decisive at the Central Committee.

The point about the particularity of contradiction is in fact raised in the CC Report (points 1 and 2), not in the narrow way it came to be taken up, but as a blow against idealism, particularly right idealism. It is clear from reading it in context that it is against the idea of just "plugging along straight ahead to revolution," it is a call to make an analysis *in a sweeping way* of the objective situation, including the state of the crisis and the mood of the masses, and on that basis develop the understanding and application of our general line. Distorting this, the "general resides in the particular" became a call to narrowness and tactics as everything—trying to make the *entire* general (laws of capitalism and the need for revolution) reside in one or a few particulars.

This is a violation of Marxist philosophy and distorts the correct understanding of the relation between the universality and particularity of contradiction. The purpose should be to fully make use of people's experience in any particular struggle and to help them raise their heads and see a picture far bigger than what can be seen in any particular struggle—the big picture of the laws of class society and the need for revolution and communism. This is quite the opposite of trying to reduce down the universal—to make the entire general reside in any one or a few particular struggles or exposures. This latter approach promotes narrowness and departmentalism, a downplaying of ideological work, losing sight of the united front strategy and historic mission of the working class. Where this "campaign" was conducted in the Party, it sabotaged the Central Committee discussion in the eclectic way of raising a secondary point to defeat the main point.

It tended to reinforce the opposition to the main point of the CC Report. Though both points are important, the essential and basic point is not that small forces can lead big battles in this period, but that we can and must take the high, hard road, make use of every opportunity in this period to fulfill all three objectives in our work and prepare for the big qualitative leap in the revolutionary situation ahead. Overemphasizing the first point, as the "general resides in the particular" campaign did, amounts to a reversion to the theory of stages—to stagism—which was key to the struggle at the last Central Committee. While periods or stages objectively exist, the point to emphasize, which runs through all this, is well put in Lenin's words: "The task is to keep the revolutionary consciousness of the proletariat tense and train its best elements, not only in a general way, but concretely, so that when the popular ferment reaches the highest pitch, they will put themselves at the head of the revolutionary army . . ." (*Collected Works,* Vol. 23, p. 246). Guided by this principle we can work to carry through the real fusion of Marxism-Leninism with the working class movement.

The concept of high road, which lays out not a moral injunction, but a political and ideological task, has been distorted, and become practically a dirty word in some quarters in the past period. Innuendo and rumors circulated that there were "two lines in the CC Report"—a correct line and a "left" idealist line. In fact what has been increasingly true is that there has been a Marxist line and a revisionist, essentially right opportunist, line existing in our Party.

Theory And Practice

On the question of the relation of theory to practice, this line and headquarters promoted both—theory over here and practice over there. The separation of theory and practice, the breaking of the chain of the Marxist theory of knowledge, is one of its hallmarks. This line downplays the "lifeline of the Party branch," education in the Party's general line. Instead of training people in the Marxist line and method, the most you get is "cook book theory," a book or a quote on how somebody else did something similar to what you're doing back in this or that year. With this method, ideological line and the Marxist method are thrown out. Even when the second Party branches article came out, even though it was in large part directed at his line and headquarters, Comrade Jarvis became a vigorous defender of it—in relation to cadre on lower levels—without really grasping its essence and changing his basic approach to the relation of theory and practice and line to tactics.

In politics and organization, pragmatism is promoted. Comrade Jarvis advocated, especially at the time of and after the Founding Congress, the idea that "it is easier to steer a truck once it's moving." It is correct to say that it is necessary to let practice develop and experience accumulate in order to sort out and convince people of correct and incorrect lines—as opposed to having a "two line struggle" every week. But to spread around this notion about "motion" can only feed the theory of spontaneity and undermine the guiding role of ideological and political line. This, in fact, is what happened. With pragmatism in the driver's seat, there tends to be an exaggeration of the importance of tactics, the promotion of the "tactics as process, not tactics as plan" (as Lenin says in *What Is To Be Done?*), a tendency to reduce political line to questions of tactics, exaggeration of stages and the adoption of stagism, and the throwing out of ideological tasks and the guiding role of ideology. All these tendencies have in fact existed in our Party's work, due not only to spontaneous tendencies but also the interference of this revisionist line.

There has also been in our Party a strong tendency to exaggerate and narrow down what should be meant by "results." Because our only purpose in knowing the world is to change it, results are in fact the goal and the test. But by results we do not mean only, or even mainly, immediate results, but results in carrying out the class struggle on all fronts, according to the three objectives. To fail to see results in this way will even turn immediate successes into their opposite by promoting a line of stagism in the class struggle, by promoting an attitude of careerism and sectarianism within the Party on the basis of getting dizzy with successes in the work.

Line On Organization and Leadership

This revisionist line and headquarters is also characterized by a strong tendency toward departmentalism, "hot-shotism" and making absolutes out of the division of labor within the Party. As a result, much damage has been done to the political role and initiative of leading bodies, along with much damage to the method and style of leadership within the Party, which has been spelled out in a number of places, including in the section on leadership in "Discussion/Decisions" of the last CC Report.

One example of the method and style of leadership of this headquarters, which was criticized sharply by people who had been in this camp, was seeing the overall role of leadership as one of putting out fires and thereby taking initiative out of people's hands, particularly out of the hands of the Party bodies with overall responsibility. With this line, the role of a leader, instead of applying the mass line and promoting genuine struggle over line, begins with an often preconceived idea of what you want out of a situation. Then you promote this one to take a line this way, and that one to take a line that way; you become the "synthesis" in the middle, while still basically promoting one side and "your people" who are putting it forward. This amounts to apriorism and eclectics. It means always setting it up so you come out of a situation with what you wanted in the first place, leaving you smelling like a rose and others confused and unarmed to lead themselves—only to "implement." (Of course implementing requires applying and developing line.) Such a method often ends up with the wrong result.

This is opposed to the correct method of leadership which is to lead in summing up a situation on the basis of Marxism and the Party's general line, promoting investigation and struggle over line, leading in synthesizing this "raw material" and in this way arming people not only with policies but with a heightened understanding of the general line and method.

Right along with this wrong method go the tendencies to put everything in the hands of a few people and to run the Party out of an office. This, of course, doesn't mean we don't need offices, but they cannot become another center that replaces or stands above the regular channels of the Party.

This line makes an absolute out of the necessary division of labor in the Party. It usually proceeds from taking the general line as "given" or "settled" and then proceeds to "get down to the business" of implementation. For this purpose, people's overall political understanding is not developed; instead their skills in this or that aspect—"organization man," "mass leader," "speech maker," "writer," and even "theoretician"—are regarded as the key thing to develop. Theory remains locked in the realm of abstraction and practice mired in pragmatism.

In this way the collectivity of leading bodies is undermined, self- and mutual-criticism comes to be based only on implementation, departmentalism runs rampant, and leading people develop a big-shot, or hot-shot "heavy" mentality in "their own field." Cadre on the lower levels either get appealed to on the basis of careerism or bludgeoned, and are left unarmed and demoralized.

The hot-shot mentality—which often takes the form of just plain old "macho"—also leads to a downgrading of the role of women inside and outside the Party and to downplaying the important task of politically and theoretically developing women to be communists and communist leaders. This does not mean we should apply "New Left" standards to the question of leadership or political training and promote feminism, but can we say there is nothing to the woman question inside our Party?

The hot-shot mentality stems from the line that those directly putting the line into practice are the real heroes, not the masses and the Party as a whole. It stems from the exaggeration of tactics as the basis of success (and of political line) and, in sum, leads to putting mass leaders in opposition to the Party as a whole. And there is the tendency to turn everything into capital. This is a clear example of the point made in the second Party Branches article, that pragmatism leads to a breakdown in discipline and factionalism whether anyone desires it or not. To get dizzy with success considering the relatively minor character of the successes we have so far achieved would be funny if it weren't so serious. It is obviously high time to sum this up and clear it out.

Pointing to and moving to correct all this does not mean weakening, but strengthening, democratic centralism. It means strengthening the lines of the Party as both chains of knowledge and chains of command. All this should strengthen the ability of comrades to take initiative on the basis of and under the leadership of a unified line.

All these wrong methods of leadership, this departmentalism and factionalism, stem from the fundamental question of line. There is an analogy between all this and what we say on page 55 of *Red Papers 7* about revisionist rule in the Soviet Union:

> "It is impossible for some classless group of 'bureaucrats' to rule society in the name of the proletariat, because in order to maintain such rule these 'bureaucrats' must organize the production and distribution of goods and services. If bureaucratic methods of doing this prevail and come to *politically characterize* the planning process under socialism, and if a group of bureaucrats, divorced from and not relying upon the masses, makes the decisions on how to carry out this process; then inevitably this will be done along capitalist lines.
>
> "In the final analysis, the revisionists can only fall

back on the law of value as the 'lever' which organizes production."

If leadership is not principally based on overall line, if "running a Party" does not principally mean arming its members with a constantly increasing understanding of the Party's line and the Marxist-Leninist method so they can act to lead the struggle in an increasingly conscious way, then every sort of lousy method will be resorted to.

In all this it is clear we have much to learn from the negative experience of the old Communist Party, even in its better days, and much remains to be done to struggle against the influence of CP-type revisionism in our own Party. Much of this is spoken to in the section of the *Programme* that begins on page 63. We should sum up our own experience and that of the old CP and more consciously fight pragmatism, departmentalism and bureaucratism. We must struggle against the concept of division of labor that reduces basic level Party members to "Jimmy Higgins"—good for loyal and hard work and little more. A division of labor that makes hot-shot heavies out of the heads of mass organizations and negates the role of the masses and the Party. A division of labor that produces big-time Party bureaucrats who dominate it all behind the scenes by leading organizationally, not on the basis of developing the overall line of the Party, using its channels and chain of knowledge, assisting comrades in grasping and applying the line and Marxism generally, and personally going into work principally in order to serve the further development of all this.

If the whole Party struggles to sum all this up and carry out this kind of rectification, then we can build on what has been the principal aspect of our Party's line all along—its Marxist-Leninist line—and for the other part we can turn a bad thing into a good thing. The key thing in this rectification is for comrades to deepen their understanding of line and the fact that two lines, Marxism and revisionism, have existed in our Party. We must build up Marxism-Leninism, Mao Tsetung Thought in struggle against, in the course of repudiating, revisionism.

In doing this we should not be liberal in regard to line, but neither should we seek retribution on comrades or emphasize organizational changes on every level. The sickness can be cured. There has been a bourgeois headquarters and a proletarian headquarters, a revisionist line and a Marxist line, but even at the top of this headquarters, which itself is full of contradictions, the contradiction is not one between us and the enemy. The key link is line, including in solving organizational problems. If this is grasped, then we can conduct a sharp and thorough rectification that helps unite the Party. If we grasp more clearly what Mao said about ideological and political line determining everything, then the whole Party, including comrades who have made serious errors, can make a big advance.

Some Questions Concerning Organizing Our Work, Including Rectification

Over the next half year we will have to give extra emphasis to study, to line questions internally, including rectification. This does not mean this should become our main emphasis however. Mass work remains our main emphasis, unlike in the period of forming the Party. However, adjustments will have to be made and we are obviously calling for something more intense than, for example, the mass line campaign. In the immediate period we should continue with and work hard to build various mass campaigns that have already been launched, including support for the miners' strike and the fight against Carter's unemployment offensive. Because of necessary adjustments at the center, including the need for more forces, the publication of the first bi-weekly news service has had to be put off a couple of months. The goal of May Day for many papers remains, and should even be more possible if these political questions are gone into well. The first three papers will come out bi-weekly before that, with a date to be set soon.

Immediately upon receiving this report, all bodies (with the area leadership having one initial discussion) should immediately begin discussion and study of it. This should go on in a regular way, only through Party channels, unless the area leadership, in consultation with the center, decides other steps would be helpful. This report, on China as well as on the revisionist line and headquarters, of course represents the line of our Party. Leadership of all units has the task of leading their units in study and struggle to grasp and apply this line. If there are any disagreements, they should be raised for struggle only in the highest body one belongs to.

For six weeks, beginning the first of the year, the discussion should center on the line on China in the accompanying report. One or at most two initial discussions of the part of the report dealing with rectification should be held during this period.

The discussion on China should focus on the basic point of *line*—that the revisionist line on major questions coming out of China now is the same revisionist line that was fought since around the 10th Party Congress by Mao, and the Four before they were put down; it is the line pushed by Teng, Hua and Chou En-lai and others. This is clear, among other things, by studying the "3 poisonous weeds," which Hua together with Teng claims credit for and upholds, as well as by studying the basic line of Hua's speech on Tachai, given in the fall of 1975. To assist in this study, we are sending out, in addition to the "General Program" which came with the last bulletin, another of the "poisonous weeds"—"Some Problems in Speeding up Industrial Development" ("20 Points")—together with three articles with the Four's line criticizing it ("Criticism of Selected Passages of. . ."; "Teng Hsiao-ping and the '20 Articles' "; "What Is the Essence of the '20 Articles'?").

Another major focus for discussion should be on the line on science and technology. (The "Outline Report," which is not available in full, was the third poisonous weed.) The reason for this focus is that unleashing bourgeois forces and tendencies in scientific and technical circles is an important part of the social base of the top capitalist roaders in China for wrecking the dictatorship of the proletariat. Even more, it is important to study this because the current leadership has put forward "improving" science and technology as the key link in their goal of "modernization." Obviously the line on this is not a minor question. In addition to studying the report, comrades should read the two major articles of the current leadership (*Peking Review* 30 and 40, 1977) and compare them to the line of the Four on this question (*PR* 18, 1976, and 47, 1975). The article defending the science report entitled "Criticizing Eclecticism or Attacking the Theory of Two Points?" (*PR* 48, 1977) is good teaching material by negative example on eclectic philosophy.

Finally there should be focus on the destruction of the Communist Party as the Party of the proletariat which is underway. Comrades should refer to the new Constitution adopted at the 11th Party Congress and Yeh Chien-ying's Report on the Constitution (*PR* 35, 36, 1977) and compare it closely to the Constitution adopted at the 10th Party Congress and Wang Hung-wen's report on the Constitution at the 10th Congress.

The last bulletin on China should be referred to for further points and explanation. For additional reference, comrades should study the Chinese Central Committee statement after Mao's death (*PR* 38, 1976) and our article in the October 15, 1976 issue of *Revolution*. People are encouraged to read over the "Breakthrough. . ." article on the Cultural Revolution in the October 1, 1976 issue of *Revolution*. These all should remind us exactly how far things have gone away from Mao's line since his death. Yao Wen-yuan and Chang Chun-chiao's two pamphlets should be restudied, and studied together, as they were written to go together. Hua Kuo-feng's 1975 speech at Tachai, and the third speech in the "green pamphlet" on the 1975 Tachai Conference should also be studied and contrasted. Finally, in *Red Papers 7*, people should study our definition of socialism (in italics on page 9) and our summary of leadership and the law of value (second column on page 55, first column on page 56). For those who have the opportunity, restudy of all of *Red Papers 7* (particularly the first three chapters) and the article on Nicolaus and Soviet social-imperialism in *The Communist*, Vol. 1, No. 1, would be very helpful.

In the second phase, after these first six weeks, focus should shift to rectification in our own Party. In light of the line of this report, all bodies should organize restudy of the last CC Report. Especially since they have come under some attack, the *Revolution* article on the "High Road" of the Bolshevik Revolution (November 1977) and the major article in the December 1977 issue on the miners' struggle, should be referred to as representing a correct line. In addition, study and discussion should be organized again around the mass line pamphlet and around the Party Branches pamphlet. These documents should be discussed principally in relation to the ideological, political and organizational line questions of rectification. On that basis, in separate discussions of the work of the unit, comrades can and should bring in points from the rectification campaign to assist in solving political questions in the work. In this period more emphasis must be given to the general line questions of rectification, using examples from the work to shed light on this, than to using rectification to give "new direction" to the branches' work (though this, of course, is very important). Further material and guidance will be developed nationally both internally and in *Revolution* to help develop this phase as it progresses.

As another part of this rectification, study of Marxist-Leninist works centering on Marxism-Leninism, Mao Tsetung Thought versus Eclecticism, Pragmatism and Factionalism will be organized in the branches. Guidelines for this will be prepared. Comrades are encouraged to continue their study of political economy on their own, but organized study of this will not continue.

Public Stand on China

We should carry out the line indicated in the part of this report on China. In short this means upholding China as a socialist country, while making clear there is very acute class struggle and the danger of restoration of capitalism in the socialist transition period. This is the correct and responsible position for a number of reasons. While a qualitative leap in the situation in China has occurred with the revisionist coup and unless this is reversed by revolutionary struggle of the masses socialism will be destroyed, it has not yet been destroyed. This is not a meaningless abstraction because, as the rather open statements in the *Peking Review* and elsewhere make clear, resistance is far from crushed in China. While the struggle to reverse this situation cannot be led from the top, while the conflicts between those in top power now are simply opposite poles of the same stupidity, revolutionary struggle from below cannot be ruled out. We should learn from the Chinese attitude to the Soviets in the late '50s, be prudent, and let things play themselves out.

There are many other complicated questions which cannot be settled in a minute. For example, if China in the near future were to be attacked by the Soviets, it would still be the case of a socialist country being attacked by imperialists and this would have to influence our actions (as well as having a significant effect on the class struggle inside China) and perhaps might even develop in a way favorable to revolutionaries in China.

It is also important to grasp that, having taken this line internally, our purpose and task is not to undertake an anti-China crusade but to arm ourselves and others as broadly as we can with a correct Marxist-Leninist line.

This means we will write articles in our press on such questions as studying the restoration of capitalism in the USSR and on the gains of the working class under socialism—focusing on gains of the Cultural Revolution, which now (though we won't go into this) are under attack. These articles will stress political line, without being open attacks on the Chinese leadership.

In talking to people outside the Party, we must draw distinctions. We can speak about our whole line on this only to people who are very close to the Party and who can be trusted to grasp not only the line, but the reasons we are not expounding it publicly (this should be explained to them). (For the line on Teng Hsiao-ping, see the end of the resolution on China.) To others we work with, we should explain we uphold China as socialist, answer their questions by saying that many of the gains of the working class there are under attack now, use this to arm people with an understanding that the class struggle is sharp under socialism and restoration can occur and why that is, and then go on to explain even if restoration were to occur, this would not mean you cannot win, but only that the historic mission of the working class—a radical rupture with the past to wipe out all vestiges of exploitation and oppression—can only be accomplished through twists and turns, temporary reversals, and hard struggle, but that it will inevitably be achieved. (Comrades may want to refer to an article by the Four, "Proletarians Are Revolutionary Optimists" in *Peking Review* 36, 1976.)

The RCYB, because of its nature, should not have a line on this question (though, obviously, Party members within it have a line). Only those closest to the Party within the RCYB should be told our full position, as outlined above. Within the RCYB generally, our line on China should be the same as our broad public position. Articles from our Party's press which touch on relevant line questions can be used for RCYB educationals on the victories of and the class struggle under socialism, but in these discussions all-around conclusions about China should not be drawn.

A related footnote: The Central Committee briefly discussed the 1977 appointment calendar which was recently produced in Philadelphia. This calendar is a factional calendar, particularly because of how it handled the Chou En-lai question when it was well-known to some that this was a very controversial question which would soon be summed up. It has *two* pictures of Chou—one of the type reserved only for the "Big 5"—Marx, Engels, Lenin, Stalin, and Mao. It printed the Central Committee statement on his death, praising him for "upholding the red flag against all enemies within and without," which in today's context of Chou being praised in China for fighting the Four is a back-door way of taking a position on this struggle. While we have not officially repudiated that CC statement, neither have we been repeating it, any more than we have been repeating the *Revolution* article of October 15, 1976. Still, the Central Committee felt the calendar should be sold. Many comrades who were not aware of the Chou question and how it was being used put a lot of hard work (and money) into this calendar and produced a number of worthy results. This should not be negated, even while being clearly aware of the factionalist character of the calendar around Chou En-lai. The calendar has some other errors, too (for instance, portraying the Civil Rights struggle by a picture of Rosa Parks) but, under the circumstances, there is not enough wrong with it to hold it up. It should be actively distributed.

In summation, by going deeply into line on China, by uniting around it and by carrying through deeply on the rectification campaign, the influence in our Party of the revisionist ideological, political and organizational line can be overcome and the Party of the U.S. working class which we declared had been founded for the second and the *last* time, can further consolidate and advance. ■

The Class Struggle In the U.S.

By the Jarvis-Bergman Headquarters

INTRODUCTION

Just as is claimed for the China paper, the recent rectification bulletin is called a major advance for our Party. It is in fact a most serious and dangerous step onto the road to hell. It stands as a qualitative leap backwards for the RCP and its development as the political party to lead our class in the war to smash its chains.

While it will certainly take a different form for the RCP, the ideological and political line of the Gang now being embraced ("Give the Gang a home," as it is being said) cannot help but lead to political degeneration and isolation from the working class. For the Gang it meant becoming the target of the hatred of the Chinese working class and peasants and the hatred of millions of genuine communists of the CCP. For our Party it will certainly cause less emotion from the U.S. working class but in some ways it can be more tragic—stripping the U.S. working class of its Communist Party—if it is not theoretically, politically and organizationally defeated by a genuine proletarian line that will continue to forge ahead and lead our class to victory—as was done in China.

The High Road

Chairman Mao states throughout his five volumes, and stresses particularly in his later years, that there is the ceaseless emergence and resolution of contradictions. The question is which road one will take in resolving these contradictions. There is a road to the accomplishment of the historic mission of the proletariat.

This is not the road of retreat from contradictions. The road of retreat from the battles of our class under the banner of general socialist ideals with the hope that the battles will be easier in the future. The road of rationalizing further isolation from our fellow workers than conditions demand with guarantees they will follow us when conditions leap and change. This is the recent vulgarization of the high road. And while this retreat may seem easier or sweeter for some—it is only so in the short run, while fundamentally aiding the bourgeoisie.

The high road is the road of grasping the key battles of our class at every point of the class war. It is the road of standing with our class in those battles on all 3 fronts (theoretical, political and economic) fighting with them and leading them forward to the revolutionary goal. It is the road of making every link with struggle and really carrying out the 3 objectives. It is the road of making the maximum advances for our class given the objective conditions—doing all we can to prepare our Party and the ranks of the proletariat, so that when the time is right we will not lose the opportunity. This is the high road. This is the road we must grasp firmly and continue on.

Two Lines—Two Roads

Despite the tone the rectification bulletin tries to set, we are indeed faced with a major contradiction in our Party right now. A contradiction that absolutely demands resolution along the correct path. Our Party has reached a major crisis point and the question of which road we take has come to the fore.

The rectification bulletin has claimed a major victory over revisionism. A removal of the fetters on the development of our Party and a smashing of forces that opposed our Party's line. It is based on anti-Marxist theoretical and political points, distortions, misleading statements and half truths. It is fundamentally anti-materialist. It is an attempt to theoretically, politically and organizationally cripple and destroy our Party.

The current report consciously mystifies the two line struggle in our Party. It reduces the struggle to questions of who liked "as is" and who didn't and other similar gems. For most comrades who knew little about the developing struggle, the report leaves us scratching our heads over what the actual lines were. Mostly, we have to take it on faith.

Faith is not the method of Marxist-Leninists. The struggle and two lines now burst upon our Party are not mysteries. They can be seen, grasped, and the incorrect line repudiated and defeated on the basis of Marxism and the interests of our class.

Necessity demands that we do this. Necessity demands that we be ruthlessly scientific. While no one can be cheered over the recent developments in our Party, we can turn this necessity, the bursting out of major line struggle in our Party, into our freedom to grasp, deepen and resolve many of the major line questions that have continued to exist in our Party. In the recent period, there has been an increasing struggle between clarity and confusion, right and wrong at the different levels. Many of the contradictions correctly identified at the '76 CC meeting have not been resolved: the right idealism, our work at the center of gravity, the relationship of the three fronts of struggle of our class, the theoretical development of our Party, etc.

Many comrades are presently shocked over the recent quick decision over China as well as reports that there was a major two-line struggle brewing. This is because the struggle was being conducted overwhelmingly through the regular channels of the Party, despite the ravings of the rectification paper that a major bourgeois headquarters and faction was set up. Before the leap on the "China question", the 2 lines in our Party were still in the quantitative stage of development and could still have been resolved non-antagonistically.

But increasingly a tendency in the line of the Party Center showed the basis of the eventual leap of a section of the Center to support for the Gang of Four. This came out most clearly in the campaign to found the NUWO, which was based on an idealist line from start to finish and left the Party more confused than ever when it was over. It also came out in a broad range of other questions from the elections campaign to having 4-5 internal campaigns running simultaneously, to the way political education has been carried out in the Party, and more. The line has been increasingly a "left" idealist line, failing to grasp and deal with the actual contradictions that exist in the working class and the Party. A retreat from the actual contradictions in the working class and Party and thus a retreat from the class struggle as it exists in the real world. A line that rests complacent at the stage of rational knowledge but is incapable of transforming this knowledge into revolutionary practice, incapable of developing political line to lead the Party and the masses to transform these ideas into a force to change the world.

This "left" idealist tendency of the leadership has actually promoted narrowness and empiricism in the branches and lower levels of the Party. It forces those who seek to develop political line to change the world to do so based only on their immediate experience, whether this is over *political* questions such as the relationship of center of gravity and building the UWO, developing internal Party campaigns, political education and on and on.

As has already been said, these tendencies, while increasingly serious, were still in their stage of quantitative development—but they begin to show the outlook that the leap to the Gang was based on. And it can show the direction the Party center's line will go once the world outlook of the Gang is consolidated in our Party. This paper will serve as a guide to understanding the development of this tendency and the development of the two lines and two roads in our Party.

It is a beginning analysis. It will put this major line struggle in our Party in the historical context of line struggles that often develop in the initial years of a party's development. It will focus on how the two lines developed in the struggle to transform and change the world. It will focus on the two major campaigns of our Party—July 4th and the founding of the NUWO—in which almost every Party member participated. It will also sum up how those who wore the "banner of theory and politics" in our Party were becoming a dead weight on its theoretical and political development. In the course of this it will refute many of the flimsy distortions of the rectification bulletin.

Now, given the objective development of the situation, we must seize the time and use our understanding of Marxist theory; our practical experience in the class war over the last two years and more on all three fronts; and the revolutionary drive that has characterized much of the spirit of the old RU and the RCP in its refusal to back off in the face of contradictions and difficulties, so that we can forge ahead and create new conditions that in whatever way is necessary our class will not be robbed of Marxist-Leninist line and leadership.

FUSION OF SOCIALISM AND WORKING CLASS MOVEMENT

A critical question faced our Party at its birth: would the RCP continue the difficult process of merging the socialist and working class movements, or would it fail in this task, as had so many other revolutionary and M-L organizations in the history of the U.S. class struggle, especially the recent history? For a Party which mainly grew out of non-proletarian struggles and which was made up mainly of communists drawn from non-proletarian classes and strata, this question means in the final analysis the difference between making revolution—going forward on the road to communism, and giving up on the historic mission of the working class.

Lenin's writing at the turn of the century immediately after the formation of the Social Democratic Party explains a phenomenon that is a crucial point for us to understand some of the ideological, political and social roots of the major errors of the center: the fact that the socialist movement in capitalist countries, in its early stages, and at different times during its development, develops "outside the working class movement." Lenin notes this creates the worst of both worlds, ". . . In every country there has been a period in which the working class movement existed apart from socialism, each going its own way; and in every country this isolation has weakened both socialism and the working class movement." (Urgent Tasks of Our Movement, see *Party Work in the Masses.*)

Certainly what Lenin says here is true of the U.S. in the past period. The working class movement of this country has not been combined with the socialist movement for over 20 years. U.S. imperialism had become the major imperialist power after WWII, and this helped provide the material basis for driving the socialist movement out of the working class. McCarthyism, the revisionist takeover of the CPUSA, the restoration of capitalism in the Soviet Union—all were part of the development of a long period of separation of the socialist and working class movements.

Genuine communist forces developed in the late '60s and early '70s mainly on the campuses and out of the various struggles of the oppressed nationalities. At the same time the material situation of the working class had deteriorated in relation to the '50s. Bourgeoisification is starting to break down. Vietnam, Watergate, the anti-war movement and minority battles for liberation all further developed the political consciousness of the working class. Still, today the struggles of our class are mainly scattered and largely economic, and politically the bourgeoisie can still rule, though with increasing difficulty. It is on this stage that the communist forces—led by the RU and eventually by the RCP have the task of beginning to break down the independence of the working class movement and socialist movements.

The MPR speaks clearly to this point in the section on orientation: "at the beginning of the past period communist forces arose mainly outside the working class and had at that time little connection with the working class. The task at that time was to begin the process of merging communism with the actual struggle of the working class, linking Communists with the working class, and building communist organization with ties with the working class—in the course of battle." (*MPR*, p. 2) The MPR stresses that this task had to continue, further deepen and develop off the formation of the Party, if the working class movement was to ultimately rise to "smash all social chains enslaving the producers and shackling production itself," and if we were to become a communist party that truly reflected and concentrated the advanced interests of the class and be capable of leading it on this mission.

The key question, the MPR notes, is one of line—and that this is a life and death question. The proletarian line will either transform the social base of our Party, or the social base (mainly from non-proletarian classes and strata) will transform the line.

Fusion Often Coupled with "Vacillation and Doubt"

But as Lenin runs down in "Urgent Tasks," as history has proven dozens of times over; and as we have seen in our own brief history—the road of fusing socialism with the working class movement is not always smooth. Particularly in its early period of merger this is a major contradiction to resolve and the underlying source of a great deal of struggle.

> "In Russia, the necessity for combining socialism and the working class movement was in theory long ago proclaimed, but is only now being carried into practice. It is a very difficult process and there is, therefore, nothing surprising in the fact that it is accompanied by vacillations and doubts."

As Lenin explains throughout his writings in that period, there are two ways you can go if you fail to resolve this contradiction correctly. You can step backward on the question of socialism, bow to the spontaneous struggle, only take up economic struggle, leave the theoretical and political battlefield to the students and bourgeoisie—thus disarm the working class and condemn it to continued wage slavery. Lenin writes much about this error at the turn of the century in his major battles with the economists, and the article, "Urgent Tasks" is mainly aimed at this tendency.

The opposite error he speaks to is giving up on the working class, making a principle of the separation of the socialist movement and the working class movement in the name of socialist purity. Lenin wrote his major articles on this deviation in the post WWI period, with the formation of the 3rd International and many new parties in Europe. He targeted a number of these new parties who failed to deal with the changing conditions and the new character of the class struggle. This new character was not as thrilling or "political" as the previous period of upsurge. Lenin particularly hit these parties for their failure to be based in the socialized industries and the everyday struggle of our class, failure to work in the bourgeois trade unions and failure to use bourgeois elections as a political platform to expose the bourgeois political parties and their role.

The question of continuing to fuse the socialist and workers movement and provide a durable basis for both is the heart of the present two-line struggle in our Party. A demoralized section of the CC has raised the banner of retreat and ultimately, surrender. Give up on basing ourselves on the actual contradictions and conditions of the working class—that is much too difficult. This question does not pose itself as an open struggle "to fuse or not." Rather it is reflected in a number of political questions, contradictions which must be resolved to keep on the high road of bending every effort to carry out the three objectives and make every possible advance in preparing our Party and the ranks of the proletariat ideologically, politically, and organizationally for the development of a revolutionary situation. A wrong line on any particular question has a quantitative effect on the overall line of the Party if not correctly handled through the process of criticism and self-criticism. But a wrong line on a major question in which an entire ideological and political outlook is taken up will inevitably lead to the situation Lenin states occurs at various points of the revolutionary struggle, "the separation of the socialist movement and the working class movement." This is what has developed at the recent Central Committee meeting off the adoption of the outlook of the Gang of Four.

It is in the face of this difficult situation that we must deepen our determination to refuse to be separated off from our class and to base ourselves in the actual contradictions and conditions of our class. We must deepen our theoretical and political understanding of how to continue to take this task on and build off the real advances that have been made. And we must continue to be guided by words of Marx and Engels in the *Communist Manifesto*:

> "In what relation do the Communists stand to the proletarians as a whole?
>
> "The Communists do not form a separate party opposed to other working class parties.
>
> "They have no interests separate and apart from those

of the proletariat as a whole.

"They do not set up any sectarian principles of their own, by which to shape and mold the proletarian movement.

"The Communists are distinguished from the other working-class parties by this only: 1. In the national struggles of the proletarians of the different countries, they point out and bring to the fore the common interests of the entire proletariat, independent of all nationality. 2. In the various stages of development through which the struggle of the working class against the bourgeoisie has to pass, they always and everywhere represent the interests of the movement as a whole.

"The Communists, therefore, are on the one hand, in the sphere of practice, the most advanced and resolute section of the working-class parties of every country, that section which pushes forward all others; and on the other hand, in the realm of theory, they have over the great mass of the proletariat the advantage of clearly understanding the line of march, the conditions, and the ultimate general results of the proletarian movement."

THE STRUGGLE AGAINST ECONOMISM

The rectification bulletin tries to claim that economism and overemphasis on industrial concentration was developed by Comrade Jarvis and his trained crew of pragmatists (who then, we are told, moved on to political pragmatism). The struggle against economist tendencies was certainly a sharp one in our Party. This was summed up after the July 4th campaign and further deepened at the '76 CC meeting. It was a struggle in which the overwhelming majority of Party members took part. It was a struggle in which members of leading bodies took clear positions. In this section of the paper we'll trace how economism developed, whether an economist line was promoted at the Founding Congress, the actual source of the economist tendency after the founding of our Party, and how the Party broke through in identifying and struggling against this tendency.

The rectification paper tells us nothing about the political and ideological basis and the history of economism in our Party. Instead it merely points the finger at Comrade Mickey Jarvis as the early leader of the economist tendency. We would rather not get into a "who shot John" and will do so only as it relates to the major lines called into question, before we move on to speak to the actual source of economism and how the Party as a whole waged struggle against it.

Founding Congress

Approaching the Founding Congress there were a number of major line questions being struggled out in all sections of the Party. In the leading bodies some were sharp, some were not and they were certainly not "Jarvis-Avakian" superpower exclusives, a confrontation of "geniuses." People lined up on this or that question, lined up again differently on another question, and so on.

On the question of concentrating the work of our Party at the center of gravity, Comrade Avakian held no opinion for quite a while, finally agreeing to it. Comrade Jarvis initiated the MPR's line on this question and struggled for it. As to whether he and others set out to shift everything into the center of gravity and industrial concentration we can only use one criterion—practice (sorry, Bob). Here we call on comrades to sum up the resolutions coming out of the working class committee headed by Comrade Jarvis at the Founding Congress and united on at the Plenary. (These are contained in the CC report on the Founding Congress, released to the cadre immediately after the Party was formed.) One resolution united around the present center of gravity of the workers struggle, while calling for clarity in distinguishing this from the central task of the Party.

Were there some who were leaning or even developing a line towards "everything through the center of gravity," confusing this with the Party's central task? Yes, there were. This line was especially coming from someone who is presently skyrocketing to the top of the Party, who held the most stubborn position on this question in the entire workers movement committee.

Another major question which came up at the Congress was over the relation of the intermediate workers organizations to the struggles of the workers in the shops. The draft said, "While these organizations must be based mainly in the plants and other workplaces their overall role is to apply the single spark method . . . etc." This tended to pit the "overall role" of the IWOs against their role in leading struggle at the center of gravity and sounded almost apologetic that the IWOs "must be based in the shops". The final program was changed at the initiative of Comrade Jarvis, and with some opposition from Avakian once again, to read, "These organizations must be based in the plants and other workplaces, must take an active part in building the fight there and play a leading role in the struggles of the rank and file workers. Their overall role is to apply the single spark method . . ." (RCP *Programme*, p. 109.) This reaffirmed the importance of the

Party linking up with and leading these day to day struggles and building organization among the workers which would play a big role in helping to lead them rather than "creating fashionable means" whereby to raise the workers consciousness.

In addition there was struggle around the formulation in the draft program over whether organization is built first to build struggle, or to raise the consciousness of the advanced. The changes in the Party Program from the Draft Program (for example, p. 109 *Programme*, p. 31, Draft) reflect this struggle and emphasize that it is key to analyze all questions in terms of how they serve the proletariat in the class war. Comrade Avakian at first opposed these changes (which were fought for by Comrade Jarvis) and it's clear he never learned the political lesson well. Check out his leadership of the campaign to found the NUWO, which in classic Gang of 4 fashion isolated the question of founding the NUWO from conditions, time and place, and very much fell into building an organization to raise the consciousness of the advanced. (More on this later.)

Something Smells

One last point. Comrade Avakian has now claimed (at the recent CC meeting) that he saw all kinds of rightism at the Founding Congress and resulted in his lack of open political participation. This rightism was caused by Comrade Jarvis and was the cause of major problems in our Party the first year. Something fishy has to be going on here. In the two times he spoke during all the plenary sessions of the Congress, we don't get one word about economism, syndicalism, or over-emphasis on industrial concentration. We are not talking about a major attack on rightism. But wouldn't some political points and guidance from the Chairman—such as watch out for the confusion of center of gravity and central task—have been well taken by those at the plenary sessions. Other comrades did so at the Congress (so it was not a vicious struggle of going against the tide). And certainly Comrade A was overwhelmingly looked to for political leadership at the Congress by the plenary members. Maybe he thinks Comrade Jarvis had an army waiting for him if he dared to speak against rightism like he claims Mao must have (and capitulated to) when he appointed Hua.

More seriously, we must ask ourselves why Comrade A is starting to launch an attack on the Founding Congress and whitewash his name for being responsible for the errors he claims it has. Why are the facts leading up to the Congress distorted? What verdicts of the Founding Congress are to be reversed? The MPR and *Programme* adopted at the Founding Congress were tremendous advances in the application of Marxism-Leninism, Mao Tsetung Thought in the conditions of this country and must be upheld.

New Idealism to Solve Old Problems

It is certainly true in the period following the founding of the Party that an economist strain rose to the fore. In the working class, there was a tendency to collapse the central task into the center of gravity and negate political struggle. The philosophical basis of this was the idealism spoken to in the '76 CC report, in a section of "Some Points" which was added at the initiative of Comrade Jarvis, although it came out in Comrade Avakian's name. This idealism mainly took a right form in that it isolated the immediate struggle from all other contradictions in society. Workers could learn all about society through day to day struggles. Students could learn all about society by fighting cutbacks, veterans by fighting the G.I. Bill, etc.

The struggle over how to resolve these and a number of other problems has been at the heart of a great deal of struggle and the development of two lines in our Party. Suddenly, here in this rectification bulletin we get a new idealist solution as to what brought it all on. Comrade Jarvis, we are told, is the one who has been behind it all. And at the CC meeting he was called the main reason for the early rightism in our Party because he trained people in rightism and more fundamentally pragmatism, though it is not explained how he managed this. This is nothing but more idealist solutions to the very real contradictions that developed in the early period of the Party, nothing but a gimmick, and it can't help but fail to resolve continuing problems and hold back all those cadre who are attempting to resolve them.

What is the truth? A number of these problems that developed during this period came from a rightist drift in applying the line of the newly formed RCP.

There was the opening sentence in the Workers Movement section of the *Programme* that blasted all Trotskyite idealism and metaphysics: "The working class learns through its day to day struggle." There was the push in the MPR to unite with the concrete battles of our class, and there was the call in the orientation section of the MPR to rely on, learn from and bring forward our class brothers and sisters, about which there is too little talk today. There was our determination not to be condescending saviours and lecturers, because we saw our class had far too many of those. All these things marked our distinction from every political organization which has existed over the last 20 and more years. It reflected the determination of the RCP to do what had not been done during that period: fuse socialism with the working class movement.

Isolating this contradiction from all other contradictions led to certain problems. It led to people negating the role of political struggle of our class. It led to not grasping what Mao calls the necessity to "create new conditions through struggle," a tendency not to move unless the workers are already moving. It led us to take up the center of gravity in a narrow way, not as part of our work toward the revolutionary goal of the proletariat. And we tended to downgrade the role of theory.

On top of this, there were straight-out idealist lines on a number of key questions, such as the formation of the Party and a "straight down" view of the crisis. And there were pragmatic errors when we were able to unite with the struggle of the masses, negating the 2nd and 3rd objectives. All of this was always secondary to the principal Marxist-Leninist aspect of our work.

There was also the fact that the MPR—an overwhelmingly excellent contribution to the development of Marxism-Leninism, Mao Tsetung Thought in the U.S.—failed to explicitly distinguish between economic and political struggle, although that is done without using these particular terms.

Was there struggle in the leading bodies during this early period over the tendencies towards economism and idealism of the spontaneous level of the working class? There certainly was developing struggle around these questions. Was the struggle aimed at Comrade Jarvis—not whatsoever. The struggle which did develop, and the lines were still in their early quantitative stage, was mainly directed at those who are now rallying around Comrade A's "left" idealist line. The main struggle with these forces would wait until the July 4th campaign and be further deepened and summed up at the 2nd plenary session of the CC.

These contradictions and problems could have led, in time, to major line deviations in our Party, if they were not identified and correctly resolved. Through political struggle in our Party in its first year, and especially during the July 4 campaign, these tendencies were to a large degree identified and struggled against. But Avakian's developing "left" idealist line has interfered with solving these problems over the last year; in fact it has set this process back, and caused greater confusion between right and wrong (we'll go into this later in the UWO section.) The current leadership has a new idealist scheme—Jarvis and the trained crew of pragmatists caused all those problems back then, when we root them out we will finally have overcome the rightist problems in our Party.

New Formulation Bound to Fail

The formation of the RCP was a major advance of our class, a product of the class struggle and a vehicle to serve the class struggle. It was also the result of the collective struggle of many communists who had gone to the working class, learned from the working class, and applied MLM to that experience to help provide the basis for developing a party that could lead the way to the future. The role of certain individuals was necessary and important in this process, and this certainly includes the contributions of Comrades Jarvis and Avakian. It's outrageous that the current leadership is going to start naming Comrade Jarvis as the source of all problems because he "trained pragmatists." This will only promote genius theory and an idealist solution of real contradictions that did exist, and still exist.

Correctly handling a number of key line questions that developed during the Party's first year and up to this day, many of which were first identified during the July 4 campaign and the '76 CC meeting, is certainly not an easy task. We could only have done this using Marxism-Leninism, Mao Tsetung Thought as our guide, with the Party's chain of knowledge/chain of command upheld through the use of the mass line both in the Party and among the masses, and by constantly developing political line to fight the bourgeoisie and change the world. This is not the way Comrade Avakian's increasingly idealist line developed the Party to function. And the new idealist line that Jarvis was the source of economism all the way back to the start of the Party is a glimpse of the present leadership's attempts to distort reality and turn right and wrong upside down (necessary to get over with the removal of so many leading comrades)—and stands as testament to Avakian's continuing inability to solve the major line questions facing our Party and the U.S. working class.

The July 4 Campaign

Most comrades would agree that the July 4th campaign was the most significant and successful campaign our Party has ever launched and developed. This is true in terms of our work in the working class and other sections of the population. We took up the battle against the capitalists' Bicentennial with a revolutionary line and united with and released the initiative of the advanced to take this major political fight into their shops, neighborhoods, unemployment centers, etc. We fought the bourgeoisie toe-to-toe in Philly and DC and stood as a militant and proletarian pole to our fellow workers in areas all around the country. It was the first major political demonstration by the working class led by a working class line in over 20 years.

In addition to this the campaign was a major advance for our functioning as a Marxist-Leninist Party. The mass line was developed well both within the Party and among the masses leading the Party to function as a chain of knowledge/chain of command in the course of changing the world. This enabled the Party to deepen its knowledge of many particular questions. More important, it enabled us to deepen our overall line on the task of leading the working class and struck a major blow at economist tendencies in our Party.

The proposal for the demonstration was out in Dec. '75, 2 months after the formation of the Party. The proposal came from that same one who's the evil behind all the economist winds—Comrade Jarvis.

As the campaign developed, there were tremendous battles between clarity and confusion, right and wrong in one branch after another and higher levels of Party leadership. The political tasks involved in building the demonstration were coming into contradiction with economist tendencies in our line.

Learn by Changing the World

The Marxist theory of knowlege was being applied—through the application of the mass line. To develop the line for the July 4th campaign, the Party analyzed society as a whole: increased economic problems of the bourgeoisie, their necessity to paint over people's cynicism and distrust in government, their calls for patriotism and necessity of steps towards war, particularly given the experience with the Vietnam war, etc.—and used Marxism to uncover the laws governing the development of the Bicentennial '76 and how it was part of the overall class struggle in the U.S. As the Party took this general line and developed particular policies to move forward the class struggle in the shops, cities, neighborhoods and schools, our overall line on July 4 was deepened as well as our overall line on leading the working class and masses toward revolution. Taking this out to our fellow workers we could see the errors of building a "jobs demo" on July 4th, or a "build our movement" demo as they were in contradiction to the political character of the day and the bourgeoisie's plans.

We gathered more experience which, in turn, deepened and developed our knowledge of the nature of July 4th and the working class movement as a whole. This is not to say that there were no problems in the campaign or every contradiction was resolved without a hitch. But weren't these times characterized by constant "up and down" discussions, struggle and deepening of line—which ultimately led to an important breakthrough in our overall understanding? Was this an accident? You might think so if you compare it to how the chain of knowledge/chain of command was used in carrying out the NUWO campaign. Or was it the result of carrying out part of the call in the first July 4th bulletin, and carrying out general principles of communist leadership—which must be from the masses to the masses:

> "Comrades must discuss thoroughly this bulletin and ways of implementing it, based on the preliminary ideas below. It is key that we root this discussion in summation of the sentiments and ideas of the masses and that this process of discussion, implementation, and summation be reported up through regular channels so that we can avoid being off the wall (idealism) and effectively apply the mass line." (1st July 4th bulletin)

At different stages in the campaign there were struggles in our Party over its nature and character. The leading body of our Party that called for the demonstration had a major struggle, with a number of people calling the demonstration a distraction to the work in the shops—our work at the center of gravity.

As the initial bulletin came out, it brought to the fore a number of problems in our work spoken to earlier—isolating the "economic" contradiction from all others in society, fear of being weird by taking an issue like this into the plants, unions, etc. This came out in dozens of ways from the units in building for regional conferences, in the extent of widespread agitation and propaganda, to the making of the campaign into a battle in our shops, neighborhoods, etc. In one way or another, the tendency was always to render the campaign into a campaign for palpable results, whether this was by making it into a "jobs" demonstration or a "build our movement" demonstration (see July 4th sum-up bulletin) which mainly had an economic form but which also had a political form.

In addition to this there was the question of how to turn our understanding of objective necessity—the bourgeoisie's necessity to use the Bicentennial to paint over the 1001 abuses and sores of capitalism into our freedom to expose the underlying class relations and point the finger at their rule as the source of everything rotten in society. This required not bowing to spontaneity. The working class' main form of resistance to the Bicentennial was cynicism or just ignoring it, but developing a line and tactics to unite advanced forces to create new conditions through struggle in our shops, unemployment centers, etc. so we could start to bring the issue home to our class. The struggles around July 4 also included whether it was to be just built among "other classes and strata" or whether workers would take it up.

It was these very real contradictions that the Party was taking up which could have a major bearing on our Party's ability to fuse the socialist movement with the working class movement. A retreat and failure to resolve them correctly would mean a big step backwards in the overall line of the Party, falling deeper into economism, as well as a step backwards for our class, which would be unable to stand up and put forward its political interests on this day. Here the two lines and the two roads were before us, with many of the incorrect tendencies in our Party hanging right out there on this question. The high road was the task of using Marxism-Leninism to sum up the development of the contradictions and develop political line to resolve the contradictions so the Party could continue leading the class forward. The overall sum up of the campaign clearly brings out how the correct resolution of the contradictions developed and deepened the overall line of the Party and moved it along the socialist road:

> "Politically what we can learn from all this is that if we restrict the building of actual struggle of our class to only economic struggle or substitute things such as build-our-movement for taking up the political attacks on our class, we will inevitably fall into the economist line criticized by Lenin many years ago: 'Economic struggle (around wages and working conditions) for the workers, political struggle (around broad social questions pointing to which class rules) for the intellectuals.' This comes up again and again when we fail to see in the struggles the workers are waging today against the *effects* of capitalism, the seeds of all-around battle waged by the workers on all fronts against capitalist rule. To develop the working class movement, *as it exists today,* in this direction, we have to bring the light of Marxism to the economic battles (center of gravity); *and* we have to seize every opportunity to build off of

> and advance the understanding and organization of the working class by taking on broader social questions, not as we decide the workers should face them, but as these questions actually present themselves to the workers and provide a basis to draw the workers into activity.
>
> "Building a workers movement to overthrow capitalism can come only as we seize on every opportunity to do this, based on the actual contradictions, and in doing this strive to fulfill *all three* major objectives set out in our *Programme*: 'to win as much as can be won in the immediate battle and weaken the enemy; to raise the general level of consciousness and sense of organization of the struggling masses and instill in them the revolutionary outlook of the proletariat; and to develop the most active and advanced in these struggles into communists, recruit them into the Party and train them as revolutionary leaders.' " (July 4th sum up bulletin)

One last point. It was also during the July 4th campaign we developed our line around waging "big battles with small forces". (By the way, the story that the so-called revisionist headquarters made this the heart of the CC report is a bare-faced lie, and comrades who worked with those now being attacked should use this as one more reference point as to who truly seeks truth from facts—who are fearless materialists and who aren't.) Their contempt for this concept shows their contempt for the mass line—which can be your only basis for developing it and carrying it out. Grasping the key issues of concern for the masses, the vulnerable points that the bourgeoisie is trying to cover up (moves to war, unemployment, housing in Philly, etc.) and concentrating these particular phenomena into a general line that concentrates the felt needs of the masses and exposes the class relations of capitalism. This enables relatively small forces to have far greater political impact and influence than their numbers. This question, which is always important is particularly critical in doing revolutionary work in this period, given the relatively small number of advanced forces and the present level of struggle among the masses. This ran throughout the campaign and the 4 days of fighting the bourgeoisie itself in D.C. and Philly.

July 4th was an excellent living example of the use of the mass line and revolutionary theory. Comrades learned from it throughout the Party and it mainly had a good effect in our work both in terms of immediate advances off the demonstration and in terms of what the Party learned overall.

Slaves of Necessity

Because we are under attack for giving leadership to

economism, because the J4 campaign was a source of rich lessons in the Party's political line, and because of the absurdities in the rectification bulletin around the source of economism in the Party's line and practice it is important to point out the role of different forces in the Party during this campaign. As already said, this was the first major line struggle in the RCP and so it is not difficult to point out the role different forces played in it.

Those who held the strongest and most stubborn line of economism are now those who are the chief supporters of Comrade Avakian's left idealist line in our Party. It was also at this time a number of these forces had one excuse or another why not to go ahead with May Day demonstrations. In addition to their overall economist bent there was also a very serious tendency to fail to leap beyond our general line of J4, to fail to develop policies and plans based on this line and rooted in the particular contradictions that would lead the advanced forces to create new conditions through struggle, raise the proletarian pole, and make the campaign a battle in our shops and neighborhoods.

Instead they became slaves of necessity. As the class spontaneously was not fighting against July 4th and there was no ongoing social movement to unite with, the campaigns were caught in a state of paralysis. This point is well spoken to in the J4 bulletin (sum up). The consistent inability of these forces to lead people to deal with the actual contradictions, and develop political line to move the class struggle forward has been a basic reason why these forces have flipped from economism (leaving the class struggle to spontaneity) to left idealism that stays in the realm of general line, refusing to return this overall line to policies and revolutionary practice given the actual conditions, time and place.

The 5 CC members who were in the Party's positions of responsibility for this demonstration to politically develop the campaign, lead the 4 days of activities and provide political summation have all been removed from full positions in the CC and from their leadership posts. Comrade Jarvis was in charge of the campaign as a whole. (As we'll point out in a second, this is also in the context of the Party center barely functioning in this period.)

We are sure that Comrade Avakian and Co. are going to start screaming "using July 4th as capital." We are equally sure that comrades will understand the seriousness of the situation, study the bulletins, especially the summation bulletin, and sum up with the science of Marxism the campaign which they had direct experience in over the question of lines. Was economism promoted or opposed? Was pragmatism promoted or opposed? Didn't the line and practice during the July 4th campaign make a major contribution to the development of the Party's line in a number of key questions?

As the struggle against economism started Avakian played a good role. He supported the call for the July 4th demonstration and he also wrote the mass line articles. However, for the major part of the campaign in which the major line struggles around economism developed, Avakian was in a state of severe demoralization and disorientation. He basically withdrew from any active functioning as chair.

We would not make a point about this except for 3 reasons. First, the absurd argument that he played a major role in the struggle against economism. He did make certain contributions—the already mentioned mass line articles and the article "Day to Day Struggle and the Revolutionary Goal" in the June *Revolution*, (although the lifelessness of the article reflects his inactivity for 4-5 months). But this was after the Party had already broken through on the major line questions.

Second, the fact that his withdrawal as any type of functioning chair was brought on very much by demoralization and doubts about the objective situation of the US working class and his ability to play a leading role given the situation—the situation and struggle not being "political" enough.

Third, and key—the fact that he came out of his demoralization with a line that more and more retreated from the actual contradictions in the working class, from the objective conditions. He has more and more stayed at only the idealist rational level of knowledge, and failed to root this in the actual conditions of the class struggle. This would provide him with the "political" role he sought, but it would also give leadership to the tendency in the Party center to develop line independent of concrete conditions.

The second plenum of the CC, held shortly after the July 4th demonstration, represented a crossroads for the Party. The meeting and the report issued from it consolidated and raised the struggle against idealism, further developed our understanding of the nature of the qualitative leap involved in the change to a revolutionary situation, reaffirmed and deepened the Party's understanding of the UFAI as the strategy for proletarian revolution in this country, identified certain features of the present period (downward spiral and some general points about the consciousness of the masses), identified certain tasks for the period in general and specifically (NUWO, YCL, elections campaign, etc.).

Comrade Avakian made many important contributions at this

meeting. At the same time, he also showed a tendency towards vacillation and doubt, a tendency which found some support in a section of the CC. At a meeting of the standing body of the CC before the full CC meeting and at the CC meeting itself, certain strains of defeatism and retreat in the face of difficulties were struggled out, resulting in a few changes in the "as is" original version of the final drafts eventually adopted and distributed by the CC ("Some Points"). At a certain point one CC member jumped up and said, "I think we should accept this report *as is.*" This point was not voted on, although the rectification bulletin tries to deny that *anything* was done to improve Comrade Avakian's paper and states basically that certain forces were routed over "as is." Actually, certain changes *were* made, and of course "Further Remarks" was written off the discussion and struggle in the standing bodies and distributed along with "Some Points".

In point 3 of the report, the original version read, "But it is the BEGINNING of the new spiral—and so the fact that it is an advance is not immediately evident." This was changed to "not *always* immediately *so* evident."

A small point? No. Failing to see that this period is an advance over the last one ("it is not always immediately so evident" but it *can* and *must* be seen) is to have closed ones eyes to the beginning stirrings of the workers in this country. Not only in their struggles at the center of gravity such as the Meatcutters strike, the rank and file movement to oust Abel, the struggles of the miners, but also we had just come from the streets of Philadelphia where we had summed up that the working class had taken the political stage for the first time in over 20 years! The original "as is" version tended to be an appeal to the nostalgia of the petit-bourgeois radicals who continually want to return to the high tide of the revolutionary movements of the 60s, and reflected to some degree the demoralization of the petit-bourgeois radicals in the early and mid-70s as that high tide ebbed.

About 3½ paragraphs were added to point 4 of the original "as is" draft before it was circulated to the cadre. The paragraphs deepened the line on the idealist basis of the rightism and secondarily some left lines in the Party, and added the criticism of the line that "it is enough to wage the economic struggle in an economist way, not linking it with other struggles throughout society against the ruling class and with the long-range goal of proletarian revolution," and criticisms of confusing the central task of the Party with the center of gravity, and of the line that the economic struggles of the workers are "potentially revolutionary."

In other words, this obviously strengthens the paper against rightism; the rectification paper tries to say all criticism of the original draft was from the right.

The demoralization came out even stronger in the draft of point 4. The distributed report reads, "While, *overall, advances including some very important ones—have been made in concentrating its forces in the key industries and major struggles of the workers,* this idealist view and its rightist essence (and generally rightist form) have run counter to these advances and could, if not checked, turn these advances into their opposite. *While generally the morale of the Party members is high, based on grasping and applying the Party's correct line,* this idealism has led to some demoralization—and will lead to still more, unless we get down on it and begin to root it out." (emphasis added) Of all this, only the last half sentence, "this idealism has led to some demoralization in the Party and will lead to still more, unless we get down on it and begin to root it out" was in the original "as is" version. This speaks for itself. Nothing on the important advances that had been made, nothing on the obvious fact a month and a half after July 4th that Party morale was overall high based on grasping and applying the Party's line. A one-sided and demoralized view. Comrade Jarvis made the suggestions for the changes in both points 3 and 4.

The fifth paragraph was part of the additions, too, with the statement that the "left" and right idealist tendencies "are based on a refusal to take the world—including the level of struggle, consciousness and unity of the working class—as it is—and *on that basis* develop the lines and policies to *change* it, in accordance with the laws governing its development." The tendency spoken to here is exactly what Comrade Avakian and the former rightists have consolidated on today.

The point is that the rectification paper distorts the struggle at the CC meeting. While there were criticisms from the right, there was also some correct criticism of the original "Some Points" which helped to oppose rightism and correct a demoralized view of the working class struggle and the work of the Party.

Who Is Making "High Road" A Dirty Word?

The question is not whether there were "two lines in the CC Report," as the rectification paper puts it, but how two lines developed in the Party over the last year and more. They did in fact develop and one way they came out was in how people took the

CC Report down, what they emphasized, how they interpreted it and applied it. This couldn't be more clear than in the rectification bulletin itself where they have re-defined the "high road" in idealist and even Trotskyite fashion: "Though both points are important, the essential and basic point is not that small forces can lead big battles in this period, but that we can and must take the high, hard road, make use of every opportunity in this period to fulfill all three objectives in our work and prepare for the big qualitative leap in the revolutionary situation ahead." (page 5)

When the "high road" is introduced on page 7 of "Some Points" (point 8), it is described as follows: "And that (the danger) is abandoning the hard road—and the high road—of perservering in the class struggle, *and making every possible link with all struggles against the enemy,* striving to fulfill the 3 objectives and preparing our own ranks and the masses for revolution when conditions are ripe." (emphasis added)

At the end of "Concluding Remarks," the "high road" is put this way: "What the high road means is striving to make qualitative advances step by step—without falling into any 'theory of stages'—*waging big battles, together with the masses, and through every battle* strengthening not only the masses but our own ranks, ideologically, politically, and organizationally." (emphasis added)

The CC Report *always* has "making every possible link with all struggles against the enemy" or "waging big battles, together with the masses" as part of the high road. The rectification paper takes this *out* of the "high road" formulation and poses it *against* the high road. This is metaphysical and idealist, turns the high road into a call for retreat from the actual struggles the workers are waging and merging this with the socialist movement, and can only lead to all kinds of problems.

Just how fast the left idealists went down this road and what kind of problems they would lead us to we would see when we started our next major campaign in the working class after the July 4 campaign.

Correction: The quote from Concluding Remarks in the 3rd paragraph this section should read: "What sticking to the high road means is striving at every point to fulfill all 3 objectives, and striving to make qualitative advances in building toward the revolutionary goal, advancing step by step—without, etc.

NUWO

The other major campaign in the working class our Party took up in its first two years was the campaign to found the NUWO, a campaign which involved to one degree or another all cadre in working class work for nearly a year. An analysis of the leading line and method in the Party during this campaign can only lead to one conclusion: that this line and method marked a major quantitative step in the development of left idealist line in a section of the Party leadership, a retreat from the political task of merging socialism with the workers' movement and a total breakdown of the chain of knowledge/chain of command which in the Party is a reflection of the Marxist theory of knowledge.

Due to the desire of the working class to fight being crushed, to take up political questions and lead the fight for freedom—and the hard work of many, many Party members, some real advances were made in the campaign—but because of the leading "left" idealist line what was built was not an organization but a big meeting. Whether compared to the J-4 campaign or not, one can say the Party's overall line was not deepened, and the cadre learned little, and ended the campaign as confused about what was going on as when the order came down to take it up. The fight against right idealism in our work, identified as a major problem in the second CC report, was not carried out—in fact right idealism was *fed* by the left idealist leading line.

We think because of the left idealist line the campaign should be re-named "The Campaign of the Four No's." That is:

1) No line on why form the organization at this time
2) No line developed to build it
3) No line and leadership at the convention
4) No reason why the cadre should be criticized for the way the convention came out

And in doing this we especially want to aim the arrow at the appropriate target, this is Comrade A who led the national Party work team formed to head the campaign and who was responsible for the floor leadership and political content of the convention. We say "especially" because Comrade A and his close followers swear that his leadership in the campaign was a "model of communist leadership." This opinion, for good reason, is not held generally by those comrades who attended the convention or helped to build the campaign.

No Line on Why Form the Organization at This Time

When this campaign was put forward at the 2nd Plenary CC Meeting, certain political questions and tasks were laid out that were essential to the building of the NUWO. In Discussions/Decisions the fact that 3 area-wide IWOs exist is laid out and questions are developed out of the experience of these and other IWOs: Why does the *Programme* say what it does about the overall role and the slogan that best sums it up "Workers Unite to Lead the Fight Against All Oppression" is crucial to winning workers to understand concretely the powerful role these organizations can play. Finally, understanding the overall role and slogan is crucial to avoid both left and right errors in our work. On top of all this is a call to sum up the J4 campaign and the work in building the IWOs so far (including the tendency to put their formation off into the future) as key tasks to get the ball rolling.

But at the same time, we find the formulation in the CC on building the NUWO (and repeated in later places) that one can see the potential idealist trip that Comrade A was about to send the Party on:

> "The key to it we feel is a political question, not the question of do we have the ties and contacts, but the political question of can we bring home to workers who would be the base of this organization and consolidate in their understanding the question of what it means for the working class to take up and lead the fight against all oppression, to infuse its strength, discipline and outlook into every battle and to develop key struggles into campaigns of the class? Because if we can politically solve that question we can develop such an organization."(Further Remarks, 23)

Is the question laid out above a political question? It certainly is. But in building organization such as the National United Workers Organization we must go beyond our deepened general understanding of "bringing home the question" and root this in conditions, time, and place that exist in the class struggle. The question of the objective situation of the working class 1976-77, must be taken up in developing a call for building such an organization in 1977. It is here that the question of developments in different industry, society, etc. and the response of different sections of our class (miners, steel, etc.) must be summed up. And it is on this stage of objective conditions that we must sum up the political developments and strength of the subjective forces, what role they can play on the stage—both to sum up the potential base of the NUWO and how we could build the NUWO based on the actual struggles of our class. Attempts to take up these questions at the CC meeting were written off as pragmatic. Attempts by cadre to take up this question—in one way or another—were also written off as pragmatic in many parts of the Party. This was in spite of the opening section of the CC report that stresses the necessity of grasping the relationship of objective and subjective conditions.

This is not to say it was wrong to go ahead and build the NUWO. A powerful campaign could have possibly led to decent advances for our class and Party. But already one could see the beginning separation from the real world—basing the NUWO solely on the idea in an idealist and metaphysical way—apart from conditions, time and place.

The Chickens Come Home to Roost

This "good idea" had some real difficulties taking hold. In Bulletin Vol. 2 #3, which came out in early summer 1977, almost a year after the original call was put out in the CC report, it says: "Not surprisingly, some of the difficulty comrades are having in grasping the role of this organization is similar to that of many workers outside the Party, it is seen as a 'good idea' but just that—an idea, remote from the actual struggles and problems people face." And then, just in case you forgot, the bulletin lays out the objective reasons for the formation this year of the NUWO. This was the first time such an analysis was to appear in a bulletin on the NUWO. The single paragraph is an empty defense, saying the NUWO call was based on an analysis of such and such factors—an analysis of conditions, time and place which had actually never been made, or if it had it has been kept secret to this day from all the cadre, including those on leading bodies of the Party.

It certainly was "not surprising" that many Party and non-Party members saw the NUWO as just a good idea because that is exactly how it was developed under Comrade A's "model leadership," never leaping beyond the level of general rational abstraction to revolutionary practice. And it is also not surprising that cadre and non-cadre *shared* the confusion, because both were operating under the same conditions in that neither were getting any leadership that was based on the real contradictions facing the working class. The way this bulletin reads you would assume there had been a deep analysis made that went into the present economic crisis, our ability to develop program and stand for the organization and how to conduct the struggle against right idealism especially in work at the center of gravity. And off of this assumption you would think that those who saw the NUWO as only a "good idea" had somehow missed the boat and needed *even more* summation to be able to continue with the majority on the march forward to build the NUWO.

But the real situation was the exact opposite of the above. Most of the great majority of comrades and advanced saw the NUWO as a "good idea" that never moved beyond the level of general abstraction—because the line never was deepened in the course of rooting it in the particular conditions and contradictions in the working class. This was certainly the experience of the Cleveland meeting where the cadre and the advanced left correctly feeling that all discussiòn was "up in the air," and not much sense of what we were building other than an organization with an idea. We failed to take on a very real contradiction employed cadre and advanced face—the contradiction between winning people to the idea of fighting all oppression and the fact that our work is concentrated at the center of gravity.

While the center had initially posed some of the correct questions, called for summation and said they intended to keep on top of the campaign, none of this got much farther than putting the words down on paper. There was no organized discussion like that called for in the CC report, no organized summation of the J4 campaign, no organized discussion on "overall role" or "based in the shops," not even any on the tendency to postpone the building of the local IWOs. The Party chain of knowledge/chain of command did not function so that political line could be *developed* based on "concrete analysis of concrete conditions," then *deepened* as it was tested in practice in the struggle to implement that line. The Marxist theory of knowledge (perceptual to conceptual, and then a leap from rational knowledge to revolutionary practice) was not grasped and applied in our Party.

Was this because Comrade A was lazy, or a liar, maybe? It was because he had a wrong line, a line that says ideas themselves are a material force. Actually, it's the Gang of 4 line that if you grasp revolution, production will automatically follow. All you have to do is put out the idea of summation and it will be summed up.

Ideas are not a material force, they become a material force when they are grasped by the masses and put into practice in the struggle to change the world. Mao spoke to this point in "Concerning Methods of Leadership":

> "In all the practical work of our Party, all correct leadership is necessarily 'from the masses, to the masses.' This means: take the ideas of the masses (scattered and unsystematic ideas) and concentrate them (through study turn them into concentrated and systematic ideas) then go to the masses and propagate and explain these ideas until the masses embrace them as their own, hold fast to them and translate them into action, and test the correctness of these ideas in such action. Then once again concentrate ideas from the masses and once again go to the masses so that the ideas are persevered in and carried through. And so on, over and over again in an endless spiral, with the ideas becoming more correct, more vital and richer each time. Such is the Marxist theory of knowledge." (*Selected Works*, Vol. 3, p. 236)

From the very beginning, the idealist notion that ideas themselves are a material force took a left form in the leading line in the campaign. The campaign became in fact an ideological struggle to win the minds of the workers away from trade unionism and the minds of cadre away from economism in favor of "fighting all oppression"—apart from the actual class struggle. Supposedly if this was done then the organization would be formed on a correct basis.

The Two "Breakthrough Tools"

Suddenly, however, in Bulletin Vol. 2, #3, we get a main switch in gears in the campaign as we are now given the formulation of two "very dialectically" related tasks. That is—build the NUWO "through the course of struggle," and "in its own right." These "breakthrough tools" are to help us resolve that old problem—the continuing failure for the Party to continue to "understand the role of the NUWO." It was summed up in NB Vol. 2, #3, that the "basis for this (problem) is that the role of this national workers organization is still not firmly grasped in many cases, and there is still considerable confusion around this question of how to build it—especially around the relationship between building it 'in its own right,' and building it in relation to struggle, and generally the relationship between building struggle now and building the N-IWO." (page 1)

On page 2, the bulletin goes deeper into the problems in grasping this relationship, where it makes the summation: "So far there has been a significant weakness in this regard, a tendency to wall off struggle from the task of building the N-IWO, instead of finding the ways to link the task of building it with ongoing struggle." Then the bulletin lays out the solution to this problem:

> "In order to overcome this weakness, comrades working in plants in general must pay attention to the question of bringing out the N-IWO-and the fact that they, along with other workers, are active in building it—when they are involved in building struggle. This not only means basic things, like wearing the T-shirt and button regularly, and especially when involved in struggle, but also finding other ways to bring up the N-IWO in the course of struggles, as well as consistently bringing it out in the work, the publications, etc. of existing organizations in plants, industries, unions, areas. If done correctly, workers who see the role comrades—and other workers—involved in building the N-IWO are playing in building struggle will want to know more about the N-IWO, because they will begin to see that there is some connection between it and the struggles they are involved in."

What happened to the big idea about the struggle against all oppression and how politically we were going to bring home this question to the working class? It has disappeared without ever being summed up. Now all of a sudden here's Comrade A—who's failed to lead the Party in developing any political line to actively build the NUWO in accordance with resolving the actual contradictions in the working class—falling into tactics as process. Now the new heart of our line is "in its own right," and "in the course of struggle." Even two "very dialectical" tactics still cannot be substituted for political line. Now, the simple battle was on to bring the most workers possible to the convention—through these tactics—all political line was thrown out the window and confusion reigned.

Chain of Knowledge Broken

The chain of knowledge/chain of command in the Party broke down throughout this campaign. There was no up and down summation and development of line—basically comrades were told all along that the only problem was that they weren't grasping the line of winning the workers to the understanding of "fight all oppression." In fact, since there was no overall political line ever developed on how to do this (making the leap back to revolutionary practice) and no summation or deepening of the line in the course of the campaign, branches were inevitably left with only their own immediate experience and so there was a tendency toward "tactics as process," gimmicks—encouraged by the gimmick line from the center—"wear a T-shirt about the NUWO when you're fighting at the center of gravity, that'll get 'em."

This breach of the mass line in the Party and breach of Marxist theory of knowledge, based on Comrade A's "left" idealist line—will inevitably breed problems in our Party. For the leadership it will deepen and further develop their separation from the masses and increase the basis for idealism—whether in "left" or right form. For those local cadres, branches and comrades who are actively seeking to apply political line to concrete conditions to change the world, it will only breed tendencies toward empiricism and "tactics as process." As they can only base their political line on their own experience as a branch, city body, etc. as the leading center of the Party is not leaping beyond the task of raising knowledge to the rational level and returning to revolutionary practice, and not deepening the Party's general overall line off summation of the knowledge gained in the process of the class and Party actively changing the world. This was why both our overall general line on leading the working class movement in this country and line on various political questions concerning the NUWO, center of gravity, etc. never deepened or developed.

Other Important Points

At this time a couple of basic points need to be made. Number 1—In the campaign for the NUWO the struggle at the center of gravity is always spoken to in relationship to other broader struggles, like a stepping stone to the "real battles" or as a given—"build the struggle, build more struggle," etc. Concentrate in the struggles of the workers at the center of gravity has come more and more to mean only a physical concentration, "get jobs in the big plants," rather than a political line and ideological question. Rather than a battle we took up shoulder-to-shoulder with our fellow workers with all our hearts and minds, it was mentioned only as a grudging concession to the backwardness of the workers, and largely ignored altogether in bulletins and sum-ups.

Number 2—Just like we did not break through the middle on the all oppression question, we are not breaking through on the fusion of Marxism with the workers movement. Comrade A thinks that the comrades having general ideological line divorced from political analysis of the actual concrete conditions operating will be able to break through. When they don't Comrade A talks about "pragmatism" and "economist" tendencies and retreats more and more from the class struggle generally.

Now, of course, the cadre can't retreat as far as Comrade A can, they are trying to uphold the Party's line on the center of gravity for our work, so for the cadre the retreat is a political and ideological one—the separation between the day to day struggle and building a class conscious workers movement gets more and more pronounced, as does the head dancing by leadership for "rightism." All this causes is demoralization, the feeling that not much can be done and continued disorientation from the task of uniting with and leading the actual struggle of the working class against the bourgeoisie on all fronts.

Learn By Changing the World

Comrades should ask themselves, in a one-year campaign to build a workers organization what did they learn about applying Marxism to the day-to-day struggles of the working class? What did we learn about developing the struggle of the working class, the sense of organization and the training and recruitment of communist revolutionaries.

Or what was deepened about the mood of the masses, the nature and main forms of the class struggle at this time, how to fight in a revolutionary way in the unions, how to unite Black and white and other nationalities in and out of the shops.

Or, in fact, what was developed off of the general stand of the organization, what does it stand for in relationship to the big questions like the imports, the illegals, the right to strike, the question of jobs or income and the Carter offensive. What advances were made on how the NUWO can be a weapon in the class war? How much of an organization was actually developed?

On all these questions we failed to move beyond the general knowledge and line of the Party—because we never deepened it—in the course of applying it to concrete conditions and changing the world. None of the original political questions spoken to at the CC meeting—around building of the NUWO, were deepened at all. Comrade A can't lead the Party to deepen and develop its line because his line no longer leaps beyond rational knowledge back into revolutionary practice of changing the world. We raise this because the line of Comrade A is to retreat from the struggle in the face of difficulties, a retreat to idealism.

The Real Promoter of Rightism

But we can hear the response now—How can you talk about

these struggles when a right-wing pragmatic line holds sway in the work. Nothing can really be done until "you pragmatists" get off your line or get the hell out of the Party and then we will be able to really fight all oppression and not be rightists.

Well, we ask who's line leads fundamentally to rightism in practice. Despite various forces wearing the mantle of "fighters of empiricism and pragmatism," their line inevitably leads those who are dealing with the actual contradictions in the working class to fall into pragmatism and empiricism.

Is the way to break through the separation of the day to day struggle from the task of building a class conscious workers movement to fight hard and wear a button or a T-shirt? Will the determination of the two tasks of "in the course of struggle" and "in its own right", which is nothing but raising a tactic to a "political line" with absolutely no political content, will this put politics in command to either lead the struggle or to overcome the problems of right idealism in the Party? The answer is clear. Comrade A does not look at these questions as political questions—they are drab mundane work of the cadre and they will automatically be taken up if they grasp his general idea. This leads the comrades alone to develop political line to move forward the actual contradictions—inevitably breeding politics based on narrow and immediate experience. Or else, if they take up Comrade A's line—they are only tactical questions and not really political.

With this outlook you not only do not develop line, but you don't deepen the line that is developed. Because the spiral of knowledge is broken the same problems keep rolling right back in with no motion forward, while comrades get more confused over what is right and wrong.

In the NUWO campaign where very little line was developed, you also had very little deepening of line. This was made more than clear by the founding convention in September.

No Leadership at the Convention

The convention was a true reflection of the strengths and weaknesses of the entire campaign. The desire of the working class to get organized and fight to build a new world and the hard work of the cadre brought out a good crowd. But despite the high turnout, most people left the convention with a lot of questions about what exactly had been accomplished.

The organization had been formed and that was a big step, but the political questions, who came, of how much people were united, and how much could be consolidated back in the local areas were big in peoples minds. The plenary meetings were inspiring and some of the struggle was good but the question of how this organization could be a powerful weapon larger than its numbers, what its program would be both in an overall sense and in the industrial sections, were still very unclear. In fact, for a workers organization based in the shops and industries, the industrial workshops in the great majority of cases were disorganized and at a low level, a combination of denunciation of the bosses and shop experience which would have been okay if it had been unfolded around some political line to build the struggle in the industries. And that demanded political leadership.

But as has been pointed out before, the leader of the work (Comrade A) thought that the cadre had been well armed to lead with line at the convention. In fact, in the bulletin sent out right before the convention Comrade A lays out that the problem will not be too little line but too much. On page 2 he says, "Comrades will obviously exert significant influence on the discussion at the convention and they should actively take part. But we do not want this to be on the basis that the Party has a comprehensive position, worked out in every detail, on every question that will come up at the convention, and every comrade memorizes those positions and rigidly adheres to them throughout. The Party does have basic policies on the questions that will be focused on at the convention and all comrades should study Party documents and publications relating to the main questions to be discussed at the convention, especially in the "social question" workshops, and should strive to put the content of the Party's policies forward in a living way and struggle concretely from that standpoint."

We think from our view of the convention that A's wish not to have a detailed line on every question was certainly granted. The difference between what he thought was the problem and what in fact happened is so stark that it is amazing. No political goals were set on what exactly we expected to be able to accomplish at the convention. In auto some of the leaders met for the first time when they walked into the workshop. In electrical some of the major line questions came as a surprise to most cadre. We had a workshop and even launched a campaign around fascist groups, and the Party has hardly held a discussion of fascism. We even held a demonstration that had something to do with busing which to this day hardly anybody understands. Many key questions on the agenda were never discussed at all. No leading fraction ever met throughout the convention. Compare the line developed for this convention—the general call to "study Party documents and publications relating to the main questions to be discussed at the convention"—with the preparation for the Detroit UWOC national meeting. A general political goal for the meeting was set, line was developed and short papers written by chapters on different questions facing the organization, these were circulated before the meeting to rely on and involve the advanced in the political struggles, a leadership core was set up which met throughout the two days of the meeting to guide the work of Party cadre during the meeting. And UWOC was actually more consolidated, politically stronger, when we came out of it.

The entire pre-convention bulletin which is supposed to form the basic guidelines and objectives is filled with generally what should happen and what the cadre must do. But nowhere is there any breakdown on how all this is going to be accomplished. Again, for an idealist the 'should do's' and the 'must watch out fors' is concrete leadership, but for changing the world and dealing with the actual contradiction all these wishes fall far short. This much reality has forced us to accept. The only question left is who is to be blamed for it.

No Reason Why the Comrades Should Be Blamed for theWeakness of A's Line

Finally we get this big sum up on the campaign. But no, since the effort was one to build a meeting and not an organization, there was not much to sum up except the convention. So we have the sum up of the convention. We don't know what A is going to do about summing up the campaign for the whole Party. He, of course, has a summation—he did a model job and all the weaknesses belong to the revisionist headquarters and the cadre's [sic] rightism.

The summation of the convention can be described in one word—disgusting. It is a clumsy job of changing wrong into right and turning the world upside down. The comrades who made something out of a poor situation and almost no leadership get criticized for the tendency to replace substance with enthusiasm. What a crock of shit, the cadre made no such decision because there was very little substance to start with to replace with anything. The point is that the lack of substance was certainly nothing to be enthusiastic about, but the size of the crowd and the fact that we were founding the organization was something to be enthusiastic about.

A, who is primarily responsible for the lack of substance and the role of the Party at the convention (unless this too was a task of the NUWO leadership) comes out smelling like a rose. The whole bulletin is nothing but an attack on those who tried to deal with the contradiction under A's line while A's last bulletin is "proven" (once again) to be correct on every point (in fact its main weakness was that it didn't make the points strong enough).

A, we are sure, will deny the charge that he is an idealist and that his grasp of what went on at the convention, as reflected in his bulletin, is the correct interpretation. Was the problem at the convention the substitution of enthusiasm for substance? No it wasn't. But even if it was, where's the substance of the criticism, where's the line errors, where is the attempt of the center to educate the cadres based on Marxism of why mistakes were made. There is no attempt to do this, instead what the cadre get is a dressing down for their lack of substance. Maybe we read the wrong documents and publications in our preparations for this convention.

And anyway where is the materialism that led A to pick upon this point in a campaign marked by unclarity and confusion and its separation of the day-to-day struggles and the task of building the NUWO from the very beginning. Comrade A had an idealist line in initiating the campaign, in leading the campaign, and in summing it up. What consistency! Maybe *this* is what is meant by model communist leadership. Again we ask our comrades, what was learned with this sum up? After reading it do we have a better grasp of how to unite with the struggles of the workers, to bend every effort to fulfill the three goals of the struggle? Have we learned anything about leading the struggle on the job and off from Comrade A's thought? Anything about building the NUWO as a weapon in the class struggle?

SOME OTHER POINTS ON THE DEVELOPMENT OF THE PARTY OVER THE LAST YEAR

The internal development of the Party has also been affected by the developing idealist tendency of the Party Center to leave line at the rational level, fail to return it to revolutionary practice, apply it to the concrete conditions we face, and sum things up. Internal campaigns are launched, run for a while, and are called off—and cadre are often unsure about what came and went.

Does anybody know if the "War and Revolution" campaign is

over? The mass line campaign came and went—how was it summed up? Suddenly page 3 of *Revolution* became issues to have campaigns around. The Banner Book was thrown at the cadre. District level political education courses with a monstrous set of readings were set up—and dropped immediately in almost every district, because it was never based on a concrete summation of the necessities of the class struggle in the US today, including the theoretical level of the District bodies. The Party branches articles were printed and studied—again, what was summed up? And of course there's the mountain of bulletins sent out over the last several months as Comrade Avakian sought to line up his forces to smash the so-called "revisionist headquarters", especially the China bulletins, with each one seemingly unrelated to the last.

Many of these campaigns (and at one time there were 4 or 5 internal campaigns going on at once) were developed isolated from conditions, time and place. There was no relationship either developed *between* different campaigns which meant that anarchy reigned. Nor was there any relationship developed between the internal campaigns of the Party and its mass work. And there were no political tasks and goals set, no ongoing guidance and deepening of line to further initiative, and no overall summation based on Marxism-Leninism to deepen the line of the Party on these questions, as well as its line overall. Once again, the chain of knowledge is completely broken.

What can be more clear? The Party Center sends one idea after another down through the Party. The Party members try the best they can to get their bearings and take it up. Once again, cadre have to grasp the very real *political* questions, such as the tasks and goals of these campaigns, their relationship to each other, and their relationship to the mass work, with only their own experience to guide them. Apparently these questions are not "political" enough for the left idealists who hate to root line in the actual contradictions in the Party, in the working class and throughout society as a whole. And of course, because the Party center has failed to make the leap from general line to revolutionary practice they cannot learn from the process of changing the world and so are unable to sum up this experience with Marxism-Leninism, and move the overall knowledge of the Party forward. This is what has marked many of the internal Party campaigns in the last year.

Self-Study: The Rich Get Richer and the Poor Get Poorer

The low theoretical level of the Party was identified as a major problem at the '76 CC meeting. However, we have failed to make breakthroughs on this question, largely because of a decision at the '75 CC meeting over which there had been a good deal of struggle. That decision was that the main form of the Party's theoretical development should be self-study. This has only served to widen the gap in theoretical development between those who are skilled at studying and have a relatively high level of theoretical development to start with and those who are not skilled at studying and are newer to the Party. This latter includes many of the workers in the Party who the MPR says we are to rely on as a social force in the Party.

Once again, its simply "the idea" which is supposed to make everything flow automatically. The logic is simple. Comrades are pragmatic and only interested in what works. If they could only struggle to see the importance of theory, they would take it up on their own.

The struggle to raise the theoretical level of our Party is extremely important and must be taken up as a conscious battle. It must go beyond general pronouncements on the role of theory and then directives to read *Revolution, The Communist,* and the Banner Book. What is the actual level of theoretical development in the Party, around political economy, philosophy, etc.? How can we develop the theoretical struggle in our Party so that the workers come forward as a social force around it? How does it relate to major questions in our Party such as right and left idealism? How does it link up to the major overall questions of political line facing the Party right now? But as usual these types of questions are barely touched on, if they are addressed at all, and so spontaneity reigns. Also there has developed such a strong petit-bourgeois style of writing, particularly in theoretical articles, that many comrades have felt "when they get into the theoretical stuff they don't even *try* to make it understandable."

All this does is promote confusion and even resentment among the cadre towards theory. When comrades got the Banner Book thrown at them like it was a drugstore novel and were told to read it in self-study, everyone asked how? Not because they were stubbornly opposed to study, but because they got no help *to* study. The center's only guidance was generally, grasp the role of theory and stop being a pragmatist. Some comrades developed an anti-theory attitude that certain questions such as political economy and philosophy are for intellectuals only. Thus the rich get richer and the poor get poorer.

ASSORTED GEMS & QUIPS OF RECTIFICATION BULLETIN

The rectification bulletin constantly refers to "Jimmy Higgins," "results," "the entire general resides in the partiuclar," and other gems to keep the initiative out of the hands of the comrades so they're running around trying to find the real lines behind all this. Here's a few points around some of these gems to help clarify the issues and rectify the distortions in the rectification bulletin.

Jimmie Higgins Goes the Way of Chou En-lai and Chen Yung-kuei Or,—Reversing the Correct Verdict on Jimmy Higgins

While the rectification paper is taking the "Revisionist Headquarters" to task for its methods of leadership, a blow is also aimed in the direction of Jimmie Higgins. Now up to this point in history, before the present CC of our Party got their hands on him, Jimmie Higgins has always been a heroic figure in the workers' movement. He is mentioned here as though everybody should already know all about him, but the Center must be hoping that no-one will read William Z. Foster's description of Jimmie Higgins in *Pages From a Worker's Life:*

> "Jimmie Higgins is that active rank and file element which the French call the militant. He is the type of tireless, devoted, disciplined, self-sacrificing and brave worker—the very salt of the working class. Wherever there is hard, slogging work to be done, Jimmie Higgins is on hand. When the going gets tough and dangerous he is always in the front line inspiring the masses to struggle. He is the rank and file builder of every union, party and other working class body. And his reward is simply the feeling of his proletarian duty well done. Usually he is quite unknown to fame or glory, except in the esteem of his circle of contacts, who admire and love him.
>
> The Jimmie Higgins' are the natural heads of the toilers. All dynamic working-class leaders have been of this category. It is especially among them that the Communist Party recruits its members. In making a Communist of Jimmie Higgins, the Party enormously increases his efficiency by infusing him with class consciousness, by transforming his primitive proletarian militancy into burning revolutionary zeal.
>
> I have always been inspired by the Jimmie Higgins' militants. Their modesty, sincerity, selflessness, courage and invincibility are the qualities of the great heart of the

> proletariat itself. My experience in the trade union and revolutionary movement has been lighted up by innumerable devoted actions of these unknown but heroic working class fighters.
>
> . . .It was such valiant proletarian fighters who carried. . . . through the Russian Revolution, who are holding back the fascist legions in Spain and China and who will finally, by their unconquerable spirit, put an end to capitalism everywhere." (pp. 280-282)

But to the present CC all this means only that Jimmie Higgins is just a dumb mule of a worker, "good for loyal and hard work, and little more." Their idealism can only lead them to this: the heroic struggle of the cadre and the masses, who are stuck down there in the actual contradictions facing our class (also known as "real life"), are nothing; the ideas of the Center, everything. How the world has been turned upside down! How right and wrong have been reversed in the heady idealism of these geniuses! For they have forgotten even that most basic of Marxist truths:

> ". . . .the masses are the real heroes, while we ourselves are often childish and ignorant, and without this understanding it is impossible to acquire even the most rudimentary knowledge."
>
> (Mao, *Selected Works,* Vol. III, p. 12)

We call on the great theoreticians behind this "sectification" paper to learn from the spirit of Jimmie Higgins, to learn from the cadre, to learn from the masses.

Attack on Results—Cover to Attack Direct Experience

It is good to hear these comrades at least mention "results", even if it is only to oppose summing up work. It's true that results must be measured according to the 3 objectives and on all 3 fronts of the class struggle, not just by counting heads at a meeting or at a march—this has been hammered home a dozen times in *Revolution* articles and bulletins. And it's true that a successful meeting or action can make comrades "dizzy with success" and blur their Marxist-Leninist analysis, although anyone who thinks this "dizzy with success" is a major current in the Party today is very out of touch with the cadre.

But comrades should ask themselves, does the Party spend *too much* time summing up results, or too little? Did the *Worker* bulletin sum up too much? The leading comrade in that area never left his city or called a meeting of responsible cadres until the line on local bi-weeklies was already out. Did we correctly sum up the objective situation including our subjective forces and our work in building IWOs up to this point before and during the NUWO campaign? Have we summed up the results of the Banner Book self-study program? As a matter of fact, over the last year what campaign of the Party—either in mass work or internal to the Party has been summed up. Is not the summation of direct experience our application of Marxism to concrete conditions and the results of this important to sum up?

Since the MPR and certainly since the last CC Report it is generally understood that results means 3 objectives/3 fronts. So what's the purpose of pitting the 3 objectives *against* immediate results?

The effect of this line is to make "results" taboo. Don't feel that through raising to rational form your experiences in the Party's work that you have anything special to say in Party meetings. If you do it would more than likely be from careerism or sectarianism than from a desire to fight the bourgeoisie. Direct experience in particular becomes inadmissable in Party discussion—anything that might go against the rationalist line of the Center is downgraded as merely "immediate results" or "work-as-capital". The present leadership of the Party has fallen into exactly the error warned against in *On Practice:*

> Hence a man's knowledge consists only of two parts, that which comes from direct experience and that which comes from indirect experience. Moreover, what is indirect experience for me is direct experience for other people. Consequently, considered as a whole, knowledge of any kind is inseparable from direct experience. All knowledge originates in perception of the objective external world through man's physical sense organs. Anyone who denies such perception, denies direct experience, or denies personal participation in the practice that changes reality, is not a materialist.
> (Mao Tse-tung, Selected Readings, p. 59)

An idealist line *must* oppose summing up results to get over because its line does not coincide with reality, and summing up the results of that line or of a materialist line opposed to theirs, is a threat and can only prove them wrong.

General and Particular

As Mao points out in "On Contradiction," understanding the relationship of general and particular is a critical part of understanding materialist dialectics and the Marxist theory of knowledge. It is a major philosophical question, critical for a party to have a correct understanding of, if it is to stay on the road of proletarian revolution. Mao's writings on this subject, particularly "On Contradiction" and the related "On Practice" are crucial for comrades to read so that we can all develop a clear understanding of this question particularly now when right and wrong are being revised. As Mao was "strictly Marxist" he was able to struggle with those who were not proceeding from objective conditions—the actual contradictions and class relations in society—without opening the door to empiricism and negating the importance of rational knowledge and theoretical concepts in making revolution. A quote from Mao points out the role of the particular and general in the theory of knowledge and also warns us of dogmatists who always must launch an attack on the particularity of contradiction to back up their reactionary political line.

> These are the two processes of cognition: one, from the particular to the general, and the other, from the general to the particular. Thus cognition always moves in cycles and (so long as scientific method is strictly adhered to) each cycle advances human knowledge a step higher and so makes it more and more profound. Where our dogmatists err on this question is that, on the one hand, they do not understand that we have to study the particularity of contradiction and know the particular essence of individual things before we can adequately know the universality of contradiction and the common essence of things, and that, on the other hand, they do not understand that after knowing the common essence of things, we must go further and study the concrete things that have not yet been thoroughly studied or have only just emerged. Our dogmatists are lazy bones. They refuse to undertake the painstaking study of concrete things, they regard general truths as emerging out of the void, they turn them into purely abstract unfathomable formulas, and thereby completely deny and reverse the normal sequence by which man comes to know truth. Nor do they understand the interconnection of the two processes of cognition—from the particular to the general and then from the general to the particular. They understand nothing of the Marxist theory of knowledge.
> (On Contradiction)

Straw Man Argument to Promote Dogma

One way to get over with an absurd point is to set up and then knock down another absurd point. Have everyone concentrate on a stupid argument, and point out what's wrong with it while you slip in your madness as to the way to look at things.

The song and dance about the "entire general resides in the particular" is an attack on the importance of the particularity of contradiction. Of course the entire general laws of capitalism cannot reside within any one particular contradiction capitalism creates (exploitation, war, etc.). The entire general laws of capitalism only fully reside in capitalist society as a whole.

So what's going on here? The bulletin uses the fact that general laws of society as a whole do not reside within any particular contradiction—to lead us away from the fact that general laws do reside within every particular contradiction and to attack the concept the general resides in the particular.

Doesn't the struggle for African Liberation boldly feature laws of class society—the necessity for imperialists to export capital, the contention of the two superpowers and steps to war, the role of the state when its rule and authority are threatened, the source of discrimination and repression. Aren't certain laws of capitalism seen in the particular phenomenon of police repression? The role of the police as watchdogs to maintain order, the role of the courts, the source of discrimination, etc.

And here is where all these characters fall down—the particular contradictions are too difficult to deal with, so let's just deal with the universal. They don't take up analyzing particular contradictions (whether this be around layoffs in industry, the Bicentennial, Kent State, etc.) and using Marxist theory and our overall understanding of class society to grasp the laws governing the development of these particular phenomena and contradictions the masses are increasingly entering into struggle around and placing them in the light of the overall class war. And then returning to the concrete conditions, developing policies so the Party can build these struggles and carry out all 3 objectives.

It is true that sometimes comrades limit the amount of exposures, ideological work, etc. to only the questions that exist within a particular phenomena. And this will inevitably lead to rightism. Because every law and lesson of capitalist society does not reside within every particular contradiction. But the answer is not to lead people away from analyzing and summing up the actual contradictions our class face on the economic, political and theoretical front. We should get better at this "concrete analysis of concrete conditions—the living soul of Marxism" as Lenin said.

Our new task is to "fully *make use of people's experiences* in any particular struggle" to raise them up to our rational view of the world. "Fully use people's experiences in any struggle" becomes the fighting slogan of those who once stood behind the slogan that correctly laid out the relationship of struggle and consciousness: "Build the struggle, consciousness and unity of the working class. . ."

This view is bound to failure as it fails to see the correct relation between the objective and subjective world. At no time are our ideas fully in accordance with objective reality. As Mao often points out, even when communists are doing their best work their ideas still lag behind objective reality. And the objective world is constantly changing, contradictions move on, new ones develop, etc. As Mao points out, the "rationalist's" theory ("the big picture") is divorced from the experiences of the objective world and the struggle to change it, and they inevitably have their theory "petrify and wither away." And that's exactly what's going down at the Party center right now. The words of Mao ring out true where he calls out the doom of the rationalists who divorce themselves from the real world:

> Anyone who thinks that rational knowledge need not be derived from perceptual knowledge is an idealist. In the history of philosophy there is the 'rationalist' school that admits the reality only of reason and not of experience, believing that reason alone is reliable while perceptual experience is not; this school errs by turning things upside down. The rational is reliable precisely because it has its source in sense perceptions, otherwise it would be like water without a source, a tree without roots, subjective, self-engendered and unreliable. (Mao, *On Practice*)

Steering the Truck *Is* Easier When It's Moving

Comrade Jarvis is criticized for advocating the idea that "it's easier to steer a truck once it's moving." It's true that he did promote this—to oppose the idealist and metaphysical line and method of "develop the line in full (apriori), then all that remains is to call on the cadre to 'grasp' it so they in turn can call on the workers to 'grasp' it." Never mind the conditions, time and place on the basis of which a line has to be both *initially developed* and *deepened.* The left idealist line on the Banner book and building the NUWO are only a couple of examples of this. The phrase about the truck emphasized deepening line in the course of practice and opposed apriorist idealism, the line that Mao criticizes in "The

Important Thing is to Be Good at Learning."

> The process of knowing a situation goes on not only before the formulation of a military plan but also after. In carrying out the plan from the moment it is put into effect to the end of the operation, there is another process of knowing the situation, namely, the process of practice. In the course of this process, it is necessary to examine anew whether the plan worked out in the preceding process corresponds with reality, or if it does not fully do so, then in the light of our new knowledge, it becomes necessary to form new judgements, make new decisions and change the original plan so as to meet the new situation. The plan is partially changed in almost every operation, and sometimes it is even changed completely. A rash man who does not understand the need for such alterations or is unwilling to make them, but who acts blindly, will inevitably run his head against a brick wall.
>
> Reading is learning, but applying is also learning and the more important kind of learning at that...
> (Mao, Selected Readings, p. 50-51)

Compare this with the apriorist idealist line which comes out again right in the bulletin when it states "It is correct to say that it is necessary to let practice develop and experience accumulate in order to sort out and convince people of correct and incorrect lines—as opposed to having a '2-line struggle' every week." What about *learning* and *developing* line in the process of practice. Before this bulletin, most comrades were under the impression that we engaged in social practice to change the world, to fight the bourgeoisie and move closer to revolution and communism. We stand corrected. We have now learned that we engage in practice so we have a better basis to be won to the Center's correct ideas.

This is why Comrade Jarvis pushed the so-called "theory of spontaneity" in the phrase about the truck.

ORGANIZATIONAL ANSWERS TO POLITICAL QUESTIONS

In looking over the rectification bulletin one can say that the lack of theoretical and political line is astounding. One-half of the standing committee is removed, one-half of the political committee removed, almost one-half of the voting Central Committee members removed, suppressed or surrounded, and not a word of explanation on how the line of the so-called revisionist clique came out in relation to changing the world. All we get is a few quick quips of "economism," "industrial concentration," "AS IS," "Jimmy Higgins," and "workers as capital." What can be behind this—those who wrap themselves in the banner of theory putting out anti-Marxist trash? Let's try and go through some of the possible reasons for the bulletin's shallowness.

1. They decided to be nice to Micky—after all they make a great deal out of calling him "Comrade Jarvis." But no, this would be a violation of their principles laid out in their "China paper"where they talk about the need to criticize heavily all those who have erred—both to provide the basis for a comrade to rectify and to actually win the comrade over. One cannot believe that we would get one line on the theory of criticism and self-criticism in one paper and another line in practice. (It's those guys who hurry out with Jarvis who acted that way.)

2. Lack of time—and they wanted to get the rectification campaign rolling. It can't be that—this would be a violation of a principle that they have in the rectification bulletin itself. Their vulgarization of the concept "get the truck rolling" says you should not simply get something started when it's not based on a firm political line.

3. No, with this bulletin what you can really see is the rough position that the Central Committee is in. They want to avoid serious political struggle around the line they are promoting—until later on. First they want to create public opinion for their line, popularize the fact that a revisionist coup has been stopped, and get people to think now major line question has developed and to organizationally move what they hope are those with the center's line (or at least confused or ignorant of it) into the positions of authority that many people were removed from—which includes a large number of districts and departments. Then, once public opinion is created, people are more set in their ways and their people are in the organizational spots—then we get the rectification campaign. That's why for now comrades are getting an appetizer for the big meal to come. And party members are left chasing around over "as is," "workers as capital," "Jimmy Higgins"—but no development of ideological and political line (not counting the distortions).

This might seem far-fetched to say they are creating public opinion, setting themselves up organizationally, and then coming up with the political line. But was not this also the way the "China Question" was developed? What did the China bulletins do other than create public opinion that we were slowly but surely going to take a position supporting the Gang of 4—only to have it rammed right down at the proper time. Each bulletin, rather than arming people with an understanding of the tools to analyze and study China—led you down one road or down another road, only to find out the road was a dead end. In a number of areas the major battles that were going on in branches and bodies were over the profound "strictly Marxist" point "concentrate or reflect"—only to find out from the chair who once created this damn point that "it doesn't really matter." So the party members keep getting told of the seriousness of the question, and told to go chasing after phony anti-Marxist arguments ("Don't read the Marxist classics," Bob told one district committee about discussing China, "You'll just get confused.") and then one day—you get an entire line rammed down.

QUANTITY TO QUALITY

Given all these developments—the idealist strain in the Party's Center line that was coming out over the NUWO campaign, the internal party campaigns, self study and a number of other questions, the overall line of the RCP still was in the ball park and a number of different areas of work bear this out. The rising tendency was still in its quantitative stage of development and it was also being fought strongly on many of the leading bodies of the Party. Certainly open rebellion against the Party Center for these different lines would have been wrong and premature. They still were to be struggled out in the channels of the Party. *And the fact that almost all cadre were shocked that this line struggle was going on is proof that this struggle was going on in the regular channels,* with a very few exceptions.

Mostly at this point the "left" strain was helping to create a great deal of confusion throughout the Party over what is right and wrong and how to resolve problems that were sometimes correctly identified. For instance, certain articles from the Center would identify empiricism as a major problem in our Party and this would be correct. But the line of the Center would increasingly feed that empiricism as it would leave the development of political line to change the world to spontaneity.

But if you stay stuck at the rational level—at general knowledge or general line—and do not deepen and develop that general knowledge and line in the course of changing the world—corrosion will set in on the general line itself and it will become more and more isolated from objective reality. As Mao notes it will inevitably petrify and wither away. This is at the heart of a great deal of the Party's Center's increasing errors, due to its retreat from dealing with the actual contradictions of the class struggle.

It is this corrosion which can be seen when one traces the line of the Party in the last year which formed the internal basis for the leap to the ideological and political outlook of the Gang of 4. It's a clear lesson to all of us that no matter how good you talk, no matter how logical your arguments may sound, no one can isolate themselves from the actual contradictions of society and the masses and not have their line "petrify and wither away." Let this be a critical lesson to all of us.

To help comrades deepen their understanding of these points we would suggest that comrades read articles by Lenin—"Urgent Tasks of Our Movement," "Retrograde Trend in Social Democracy" and "Left Wing Communism, An Infantile Disorder." This is to take up the question of fusion of socialist movement with the working class movement on a desirable basis—and how under different conditions different tendencies arose.

The other critical question to take up is the Marxist theory of knowledge and the relationship of theory and practice. We would suggest comrades read "On Practice," "On Contradiction," "The Important Thing is to Be Good at Learning," and "Where Do Correct Ideas Come From."

Over a given period there is only so long one can stay at the rational level and not have the overall rational line corrode. And while Comrade Avakian's line was quantitatively on the road to the leap to the outlook of the Gang of 4, it had not happened until the line on China, and the rectification paper.

Today things have changed. The leap has been made. The present CC is hell-bent on turning the proud red banner of our Party, the Revolutionary Communist Party, into a miserable white flag of reaction and surrender. We cannot deny this, though some will try. We can't avoid this, though some will seek a way. We must not fear this, though this Party has been our home and our hope. We must fight, for that is the duty of all revolutionary Marxist-Leninists. We have not come this far to fall back in the face of difficulties.

Let us take as our model the stand of Mao Tse-tung and the Chinese Communist Party in the face of a far greater setback to the struggle of our class, the rise to power of revisionism in the Soviet Union:

> . . . our attitude as Marxist-Leninists is the same as our

> attitude towards any "disturbance"—first, we are against it; second, we are not afraid of it.
>
> We did not wish it and are opposed to it, but since the revisionist Khrushchov clique have already emerged, there is nothing terrifying about them, and there is no need for alarm. The earth will continue to revolve, history will continue to move forward, the people of the world will, as always, make revolutions, and the imperialists and their lackeys will inevitably meet their doom. . . .
>
> The proletariat is sure to win the whole world and communism is sure to achieve complete and final victory on earth. (*On Khrushchov's Phoney Communism and its Historical Lessons,* p. 74)

Our job is to sharpen our line in criticism of this new idealism in our Party. Our job is to toughen our spirits in rebellion against these new opportunists who would drive Marxism-Leninism and Marxist-Leninists from our Party.

Revolutionary Marxist-Leninist militants of the RCP unite! Unite so that by whatsoever means necessary our class will not be robbed of its Marxist-Leninist vanguard!

Rectification is Fine; The Mensheviks' Answer is Terrible

RCP Reply to Mensheviks on Rectification Adopted by the 2nd Congress of the RCP, 1978

With their piece on "The class struggle in the U.S." our Mensheviks undertake a systematic and vicious (if petty and disjointed) assault on the revolutionary line of our Party. As with all they do, it begins with a theatrical hype ("Comrades the rebellion is real.") and inflated accounts of their "rebellion" ("reaction" is more to the point). Of course there is a method to their madness—as well as a madness to their method. Hand in hand with their method of engineering a split (split first, study the line later), this paper seeks to divert its audience's attention away from its painfully obvious lack of substance and whip it up with numbers, desperate appeals ("Comrades Hold Firm!") and silly promises that if they do, they will be the Revolutionary Communist Party, USA.

Of course the essence of the question is line, not numbers. But despite these wild claims and this orchestrated hype, dear Mensheviks, we can count, too. As usual, your results don't measure up to your appetite, not to mention your claims. Despite all your factionalizing, you've fallen short. Even Bruce Franklin did better, both according to percentage of the organization and in terms of advancing and struggling for a clear political line.

This is testament not only to your bankruptcy but to the fact that in spite of all your efforts, Marxism is not so easily pushed aside by pragmatism in the ranks of this Party. In sum, as the Soviet anti-Trotsky caption (reprinted in the February 1978 *Revolution)* put it "The opportunists' show is unsuccessful." The RCP is indeed the Party of the proletariat—you, Mensheviks, who tried to wreck it, have learned this truth the hard way.

Today the situation in our Party is indeed excellent. An atmosphere is growing in which comrades are engaged in vigorous and healthy study, discussion and struggle over the question of China and, in a beginning way, over the class struggle here. And even now comrades are beginning to apply this understanding to practice, in our work, including support of the miners strike. A revolutionary spirit is growing, a spirit in which, as Comrade Gert Alexander put it, people want to make revolution so much they're willing to be scientific about it. More and more comrades are approaching all these questions from the high plane of the struggle between two lines.

Into this situation comes the paper by our Mensheviks. One would hope it would help us seize the opportunity to deepen our grasp of the struggle between two lines. But unfortunately in substance it's a bit more like grasping a handful of slime. In its very pettiness, in its whole approach, in the questions it chooses to address and the way it addresses them, it stands in sharp contrast to the situation where people are trying to grapple with the questions of linking our daily work with the revolutionary goal. It is most definitely living proof of what Stalin said—paper will, indeed, put up with whatever is written on it. The fact that such a paper could be a convincing argument for a relatively sizable number of people to split from our Party certainly shows the degenerative influence of this line in our Party, the depth to which this clique and its line has kept people in ignorance and promoted pragmatism, to the extent that many were not even aspiring to any heights.

Still this paper shows some things. Even its whole approach shows how thoroughly reformist this clique is in essence. We ask comrades to consider if overwhelmingly even the questions it poses are the ones which are posing themselves as obstacles to the Party doing revolutionary work. Their whole approach shows they have no concern at all for the crucial question of how to maintain and develop a revolutionary Party and revolutionary work in our situation.

They claim there is a major retreat from the "actual struggle." Where is this big retreat? Can it be seen in our efforts in the struggle of the miners—work which increasingly has been under the leadership of the proletarian line in our Party? Can it be seen in the years' long struggle which has been carried out at the I-Hotel? Can it be seen in the struggle we waged to even get their student headquarters to take up the battle at Kent State, or in the fight to get them to even take up vets work? Do we find it evidenced in smaller struggles like that over the fired workers at Chrysler Trenton

Engine or in many struggles in steel, despite interference from their narrow revisionist line?

It is apparent that there is no such retreat, that they are raising a quite transparent smokescreen and that by raising this now these Mensheviks are doing exactly what Lenin described in *What Is To Be Done?*—"wishing mourners at a funeral many happy returns of the day"—the problem in the Party in fact is not that we are retreating from involvement in struggle, but that we have not made enough advances in doing strictly Marxist work in all such struggles.

On the face of it their charge is both ludicrous and criminal. Here our Party, for some time now, has been correcting right errors, waging a struggle against the right—an effort to nurture and develop those revolutionary qualities which, along with the spontaneous pull of imperialist society, these Mensheviks had almost drummed out of our ranks. Here we are trying to correct something, bring back politics, and ideological work (even while making clear ideological work is not the main thing). And in doing this have we been saying that our Party should give up on the economic struggle, that nothing can be accomplished there, that this is just bowing to spontaneity? Obviously not.

But to take on rightist lines *at all*, to correct some things that obviously need correcting, is described as going from quantity to quality into Trotskyite interventionism! What a vivid self-exposure! These people have the same response as a common reformer to communist politics—"what are you bringing that around here for? You'll mess everything up!"

In light of all this, the pettiness and whole approach of this paper, it is in a way unfortunate to introduce it into the struggle. In contrast to the situation developing among the comrades, it tends to degrade the Party and its level. In answering this paper it will be necessary to descend for a time into the mud it inhabits in order to give it a few necessary bangs on the head. Through the further development of this whole process, we should soon get beyond this particular task. We hope comrades will be tolerant and try to keep their sights high—not limited to our Mensheviks' petty efforts.

Still there is much to learn by the negative example of our Mensheviks. Their line, or more to the point its pragmatist, rightist essence, represents a tendency that will occur again many times in the future. As both our *Programme* and first Main Political Report make clear, such rightism and pragmatism have historically been and will continue to be overall the main danger facing the revolutionary movement in an imperialist superpower like this.

The fact that such a struggle has broken out in our Party reflects some very real things about the class struggle, and in fact is in some ways a by-product and a measure of the progress we have made in integrating with the struggles of the working class. Before the Party was formed most—though not all—of the struggles were against "leftist" deviations, pulling away from the working class into adventurist or dogmatic isolation and sectarianism. But now, exactly as a reflection of having defeated such tendencies and deepened our ties with the actual struggles of the workers, the kind of lines which can find some following among sections of our Party, which can "fuse" to a certain degree with spontaneous errors, are more likely to be from the right.

While struggles against such a pragmatist, rightist line will inevitably occur in the future, this particular variant has features of its own which are largely determined by the period we are in. Because it is the *beginning* of a new spiral, and the working class struggle is at a relatively low level overall, a pragmatic reformist line in this period will tend to be less political (in a reformist sense) and more puny and petty than at a time of bigger upsurge. Overall the rightist essence of this Menshevik line determines its apolitical form. By its very nature it is so glued to whatever is going on at a given moment that its horizons are incredibly limited. There is no sense at all of the laws that underlie the objective situation that will give rise to big things and bring many into motion, and no sense of the danger of revisionism. Our Mensheviks prove utterly incapable of giving any real revolutionary meaning to the high road and have no sense at all of the sweeping, anti-revisionist world view poetically summed up by Mao Tsetung "Look, the world is being turned upside down."

For all these reasons the Mensheviks' paper, despite its apolitical pettiness, does raise some important things. We should welcome it. It represents an opportunity to join a struggle with a rightist line and to smash a revisionist headquarters. Fine. Both events are worth celebrating.

The Madness that is the Mensheviks' Method

Even the form of this Menshevik paper hints at its content. It is a paper that is a disjointed jumble of points, picking (and distorting) some from our Party's history while leaving out most.

This sort of method, compared with that of previous major opportunists, including Franklin and the Bundists, is disappointing and uninspiring. Both Franklin and the Bundists (especially as the latter got into dogmatism) put out and struggled over a clear, if opportunist, line. Answering this immediately required study of Marxism. If our answer to the Franklins was titled "Proletarian Revolution vs. Revolutionary Adventurism" and to the Bundists "Marxism vs. Bundism" we might be tempted to title this paper "Marxism vs. Marshmellowism."

But our Mensheviks' paper does, after all, have a line and a method. In its approach—even its form—this Menshevik paper has provided us yet another worthy, herky-jerky example of eclecticism. Lenin's words on eclecticism from "Once Again on the Trade Unions, the Current Situation and the Mistakes of Trotsky and Bukharin" (Vol. 32) are apt: "Dialectics requires an all-round consideration of relationships in their concrete development but not a patchwork of bits and pieces." and "When two or more different definitions are taken and combined at random . . . the result is an eclectic definition which is indicative of different facets of the object, and nothing more. Dialectical logic demands that we go further."

The definition of eclecticism given in Selsam's *Handbook of Philosophy* is worth reprinting and comparing to the Menshevik paper:

> "*Eclecticism* (Gr., eklegein—to pick out, to choose), the tendency to combine, in mechanical fashion, ideas, theories and conceptions which have originated in different schools and movements. At its best, eclecticism is an impossible attempt to create unity among disparate and irreconcilable philosophies, such as, for example, to combine 'the best features' of materialism and idealism, or of Marx and Freud. At its worst it is a deliberate effort to confuse issues by indiscriminate borrowing which results in a hodge-podge of nonsense."

Daring to descend the depths, our Mensheviks have produced eclectics at its worst.

Still, in this patchwork of pettiness, there is an even more specific method. It is the same one they employ in their "analysis" of China. First, while claiming to "seek truth from facts," in reality they twist facts to fit falsehood. Second, as on China, when they analyze the situation they wipe out of consideration any active role of the bourgeoisie—in this case their *own* role in this "history."

Their theme is clear—there is a "left idealist" line and headquarters leading our Party which has gone from quantity to quality with the latest CC Report. We have already begun to speak to this some earlier, but here it is useful to analyze how they try to put over this summation.

They attempt some overt appeals to rightism (such as their case on the "center of gravity"—more on this later). But they also seem to realize that it would be hard (if not laughable) to get over saying "ultra-leftism" is the main tendency in the work of our Party. So—just as they do in reference to China—they set out to blame the (genuine) left for the existence of the right: "Leftism" at the top is responsible for rightism at the bottom. A cute trick, but it won't stand.

The clear fact is, as any serious examination of the facts and the development of our Party will show, that rightism, especially economism, has been the main danger and that this has been due both to spontaneous tendencies and increasingly the influence of this Menshevik headquarters.

One obvious fact that exposes both their method and the conclusions they seek to draw is that, despite its modest claim to "serve as a guide to understanding the development of this ["left idealist"] tendency and the development of two lines and two roads in our Party" (see "Introduction"—p. 396), this paper attempts to write out of history the great majority of the key questions which have been the focus of the two line struggle in our Party. And when they do venture to speak of struggle waged against the right (as in the summation bulletin of the NUWO convention), they conveniently picture it as "attacks on the cadre" when they know damn well and acted on the understanding that these were criticisms of their line and headquarters.

Their "guide" to the two line struggle never mentions: the Party Branches articles (*Revolution,* August and September, 1977); the struggle over the YCL; vets work; and other key things they opposed such as, the "Theoretical Struggle" article (*Revolution,* January, 1977), the "High Road" article on the October Revolution (*Revolution,* November, 1977), the miners "Crossroads" article (*Revolution,* December, 1977), the question of building an independent union in one industry. It never mentions the War Conference. (Could this be not only because under the label of criticizing "idealism" they undermined building for this in such areas as the Midwest but also because the strong line our Party took against social chauvinism is looking embarrassing to them now?) They deal powerfully with the *Worker* bulletin in two potent sentences on supposed "lack of investigation." They deal in a phrase with the 1976 election campaign (apparently our Party's line was no good because it didn't center on promising palpable results to the masses).

They fail to mention in the history of the development of the "left idealist" tendency the articles in *Revolution* (April, 1977) and *The Communist,* (May, 1977) against the dogmatism of Workers Viewpoint Organization (WVO). Perhaps this is because, since the Chair of the Party wrote the article "Undaunted Dogma from Puffed Up Charlatans" in the midst of his supposed "left idealist" tailspin, this "strange" fact wouldn't fit their little story. And perhaps it is also because this article exposes WVO from the high plane of ideological and political line, and exposes the rightist essence that underlies WVO's dogmatism, including on the question of theory. Perhaps this hits too close to home since they, too, in their new student paper (*The Young Communist*) for example, have taken to attacking what WVO was attacking—the concept of "theory in its own right" (not "for its own sake") being of special importance now in our Party.

How else can we tell that their method of twisting facts to suit their conclusion that "the left produced the right" in our Party is indeed phony? Our Mensheviks themselves say it well in their paper: "we can only use one criterion—practice (sorry, Bob)." Yes, Mensheviks, it is *you* who are indeed sorry—a sorry bunch of rightists. Already, only a month after being free of our Party's "left idealism" your consistently rightist practice is coming out even more crudely. You have already dropped "Communist" from the name of your student organization (while, significantly, putting it into the name of your student newspaper, which now has the same name as the paper of the CP(ML)'s youth group—quite a coincidence!) You call in leaflets and speeches for "support" for the miners in the form of *you scratch their back, they'll scratch yours,* saying, for example, that postal workers and steel workers should support the miners not because the miners are waging a key battle of the working class against the capitalists, but because postal workers and steel workers need the right to strike, too. These Mensheviks have even advocated capitulation in the miners strike, saying, weakly, when the pressure was on that they, too, wanted the miners to go back to work, but only when "enough" of the miners' demands were met so they could call it a "victory"—and this when the Miners Right to Strike Committee was calling for no compromises in the face of Miller's backstabbing and the government's threats.

No, Mensheviks, your line and practice are clear enough proof that, far from the "left" creating the right, it is the influence of your rightist line which has nurtured rightist tendencies, your rightist line that has correctly been fought in our Party and needs to be fought still more.

The whole attempt of their paper to sum up a two line struggle out of what they can draw and distort out of a few events, above all July 4 and the NUWO campaign, is itself an exposure. It is a perfect example of what they later describe as a "straw man argument"—"the song and dance about the 'entire general resides in the particular' " (p. 433). It is exactly an attempt to evade the essence of the matter, to evade seeking out the interrelations of things in an all around way, concentrating especially on the differences in ideological and political line. Instead it seeks to substitute its eclectic method of drawing the entire general—the two line struggle—out of a handful of facts it picks and chooses. And, the facts it does present, as we will get into later, are perverted. It all amounts to an attempt to pickpocket the advances made through the line and work of the Party as a whole, to turn them into their own personal capital and to sum them up in such a way as to turn real gains into their opposite—into opportunism.

In studying the method of this paper, it is also interesting and revealing to note that its "history" begins at the Founding Congress. For our Mensheviks, apparently, only a void existed before. This is to serve two purposes. First is to present the Founding Congress itself undialectically. The Congress didn't come from nowhere. It was itself the product of a process, and in turn gave rise to a process which, like all things, divided into two. This paper attempts to deny this. In particular, to puff up their "big role" in founding the Party, they dwell at ridiculous length on small points they added to documents, thereby glorifying their role in making more of the economic struggle than should have been made.

The second reason for wiping out history before the Congress is that they thus are able to ignore the previous history of the Revolutionary Union, in particular its major contributions to developing Marxism-Leninism, Mao Tsetung Thought in the U.S. This further downplays what they seek to downplay in general—the key role of ideological and political line and of two line struggle—especially as it came out in the struggles with Franklin and the Bundists. These are lessons these pragmatists are indeed best advised to steer clear of. While dealing thoroughly with the history of the Party and the Revolutionary Union before it is beyond the scope of this reply, it is clear that this is a necessary task, one which would add to the understanding of our Party and one which should be undertaken soon.

But, again, while our Mensheviks have given us a most disappointing and empty "polemic" it is important to see that in it there is a line, even though it is less clear and consistent in principle than that of Franklin or the Bundists. It is a line for non-revolutionary work in any situation. Lenin's remark from *What Is To Be Done?* applies here, "Once again Parvus' apt observation that it was difficult to catch an opportunist with a formula was proved correct. An opportunist will put his name to *any* formula and as readily abandon it, because opportunism is precisely a lack of definite and firm principles."

This Menshevik clique has been characterized by *philistinism*—smug in its narrowness and contemptuous of real revolutionary theory guiding consistent revolutionary work. It has downgraded political line and practically wiped out the role of ideological line with pragmatism, and as we have pointed out in our *Programme* as well as other places, pragmatism is far more than a spontaneous tendency expressing ignorance of Marxism. It is bourgeois ideology which leads to revisionism—"the movement is everything, the final aim nothing."

This clique has promoted economism in our Party and, as we shall soon go into, their paper promotes it still more. But this has been determined less by any firm economist principles than by a general narrowing, bowing to, and attempt to capitalize on whatever seems to be going this morning or can be led by you this afternoon. Today, for this kind of petty bourgeois tendency, cashing in on the still low level of the working class movement appears to be where it's at—just as the national question was cashed in on when it was more of an icon. (In fact some of the leading Mensheviks were late seeing the crucial nature of that struggle, others never did see it and wavered, while still others continue today to bow to this particular pole of spontaneity as well—arguing for instance that liquidating the national question was the main tendency in our ranks as soon as the first sharp blows were delivered to the Bundists, a conscious distortion of the correct summation of this at the 1976 CC. Some have argued that a major reason for taking up Africa work among students is "to get Blacks.")

There is a close analogy between the line and behavior of this clique, particularly the behavior of M. Jarvis, and that of Trotskyites. The form of the opportunists' line is constantly changing, but its rightist essence remains. Its only consistent principle is lack of principle. But this "tactics are everything" is nonetheless a line. In *One Step Forward, Two Steps Back* Lenin said:

> "When we speak of fighting opportunism, we must never forget a feature that is characteristic of present-day opportunism in every sphere, namely, its vagueness, diffuseness, elusiveness. An opportunist, by his very nature, will

> always evade formulating an issue clearly and decisively, he will always seek a middle course, he will always wriggle like a snake between two mutually exclusive points of view and try to 'agree' with both and to reduce his differences of opinion to petty amendments, doubts, good and pious suggestions, and so on and so forth."

What underlies this behavior is not only careerism and eclectics, but the particular method of trimming your sails to the wind. This characteristic is one reason this line was not so easy to expose for some time. It is also why its line on democratic centralism—factionalism—was for a time its sharpest manifestation.

But such a line cannot co-exist forever with a proletarian line and sooner or later it had to jump out fully in opposition. And so it did. In "Marxism and Revisionism" (Vol. 15) Lenin sums up the character and behavior of such a revisionist line:

> "A natural complement to the economic and political tendencies of revisionism was its attitude to the final aim of the socialist movement. 'The movement is everything, the final aim is nothing'—this catchphrase of Bernstein's expresses the substance of revisionism better than many long arguments. To determine its conduct from case to case, to adapt itself to the events of the day and to the chops and changes of petty politics, to forget the basic interests of the proletariat, the main features of the capitalist system as a whole and of capitalist evolution as a whole; to sacrifice these basic interests for the real or assumed advantages of the moment—such is the policy of revisionism. And it patently follows from the very nature of this policy that it may assume an infinite variety of forms, and that every more or less 'new' question, every more or less unexpected and unforeseen turn of events, even though it may change the basic line of development only to an insignificant degree and only for the shortest period of time, will always inevitably give rise to one or another variety of revisionism."

Or as he put it in "The Russian Radical Is Wise After the Event" (Vol. 11): "Opportunism is the sacrificing of the long-term and vital interests of the Party to its momentary, passing, secondary interests."

Fusion or Confusion?

The Menshevik paper starts with a whole section on "fusion of socialism and the working class movement" and lays out the murky theme which runs throughout the paper that the "left idealist" headquarters has approached this task with "vacillation and doubt" and is now running head long to abandon this task. Well, the task *as they pose it* is a task no revolutionary party should ever take up, since their whole idea of fusion amounts to confusion of socialism with the spontaneous level of the working class struggle.

It has nothing in common with the actual task of fusion which is a political task of organizing and raising the level of the class struggle of the proletariat so that, as Lenin put it,

> "When this fusion takes place the class struggle of the workers becomes *the conscious struggle of the proletariat* to emancipate itself from exploitation by the propertied classes, it is evolved into a higher form of the socialist workers' movement—*the independent working-class Social-Democratic party.*" ("A Retrograde Trend in Russian Social Democracy," Vol. 4, p. 257).

To take up this task means building the working class struggle so that, in the words of our *Programme,*

> "Fighting blow for blow on all fronts, and led by its Party, the working class will develop its movement of today into a revolutionary workers' movement that fights exploitation and all oppression in order to end wage-slavery. To do this the working class must take up and infuse its strength, discipline and revolutionary outlook into every major social movement." (pp. 102-3)

Our Mensheviks appear very proud and seem to fancy themselves (together with Lenin we would presume) the defenders and developers of this line on fusion—both in their paper and, we are told in the next section, at the Founding Congress. However, what they are really responsible for is the political narrowing of this task. The RU long ago struggled for a correct understanding of this question. The "left" adventurism of the Franklins was opposed with the deepening of the understanding of the need to go to and mobilize the working class. This task was not, however, proposed in the narrow way our Mensheviks are arguing for it. "Left" adventurism was not countered by economism, but by putting out the task of politically organizing the workers (in fact the unity between economism and terrorism was demonstrated). *What Is To Be Done?* was studied and out of this struggle May Day was revived. So, too, in struggling against the Bundists, the need to organize the actual struggles of the working class was stressed. Again, overall this was not done narrowly. For example in one of Comrade Avakian's speeches on Party-building printed at the time (1974) it says "And we raised the slogan ['Workers Unite to Lead the Fight Against All Oppression'] to begin to develop in the working class its understanding that it wasn't its fight just in the plants, it isn't just around a particular strike or economic question though those are important, but that its fight is the broad political struggle uniting all that can be united in firm struggle against the imperialist enemy."

But where would our Mensheviks lead us with their idea of "fusion"? Where else but to the right? While they give one passing mention to the fact that Lenin was criticizing bowing to the spontaneous struggle when he talked about fusion, in the very essay they quote, this is immediately dropped. Nowhere is it developed or applied to today's conditions. Instead we get treated (and twice inside of three paragraphs in case we missed the point) to their idea of fusion—"basing ourselves on the actual contradictions and conditions of the working class." There can be no doubt from the whole context—from the stress they proceed to put on the "center of gravity," to "fighting big battles" etc.—that by this formulation they do not refer to the basic, fundamental and long term conditions of wage slavery under the political rule of the capitalist class, but narrowly, statically, to today's conditions and struggles.

Lenin, again in "Retrograde Trend," characterizes this view well:

> "It is as though a man setting out on a long and difficult road on which numerous obstacles and numerous enemies await him were told in answer to his question 'Where shall I go?': 'It is desirable to go where it is possible to go, and it is possible to go where you are going at the given moment'!" (Vol. 4, p. 274)

In case there remains any doubt what our Mensheviks mean by "fusion" they oblige us later on (p. 421) by explicitly separating out "fusion" from organizing the political struggle: "Just like we did not break through the middle on the all oppression question, we are not breaking through on the fusion of Marxism with the workers movement." Our Mensheviks are in fact the ones promoting separation, not fusion, by their political narrowness. This is a mistake our Party should not make, and it certainly is one Lenin did not make. Despite our Mensheviks waving around Lenin's essays on fusion, in these very essays he is aiming his fire at exactly the line they are advancing. When Lenin, as they quote him in "Urgent Tasks," is speaking of "vacillation and doubt" (the sin they wish to tag our Party with) he is blasting at economism:

> "Russian Social-Democracy is passing through a period of vacillation and doubt bordering on self-negation. On the one hand, the working-class movement is being sundered from socialism, the workers are being helped to carry on the economic struggle, but nothing, or next to nothing, is done to explain to them the socialist aims and the political tasks of the movement as a whole. On the other hand, socialism is being sundered from the labour movement; Russian socialists are again beginning to talk more and more about the struggle against the government having to be carried on entirely by the intelligentsia because the workers confine themselves to the economic struggle." (Vol. 4, p. 366-7)

Come on Mensheviks, if your aim is to distort Lenin at least you could be a little clever about it.

As if he was speaking to our Mensheviks, Lenin again speaks in the same essay to this same tendency:

> " 'Organise!' *Rabochaya Mysl* keeps repeating to the workers in all keys, and all the adherents of the 'economist' trend echo the cry. We, of course, wholly endorse this appeal, but we will not fail to add: organise, but not only in mutual benefit societies, strike funds, and workers' circles; organise also in a political party; organise for the determined struggle against the autocratic government and against the whole of capitalist society. Without such organisation the proletariat will never rise to the class-conscious struggle; without such organisation the working-class movement is doomed to impotency." (Vol. 4, p. 369-70)

Perhaps realizing they are on shaky ground on the fusion question, the Mensheviks try out a parallel to Lenin's "Left Wing Communism" but, alas, there is no help for them there either. As near as we can figure, their parallel is this: the 60's in this country is like World War I; and today in this country like the period of "Left Wing Communism." They're wrong on two counts. They miss the point that Lenin was, in fact, expecting a new upsurge soon. And he certainly didn't regard the period as less "political."

But basing themselves on this wrong view they begin, "He [Lenin] targeted a number of these new parties who failed to deal with the changing conditions and the new character of the class struggle. This new character was not as thrilling or 'political' as the previous period of upsurge." Having drawn this revealing and wrong parallel, they then go on:"Lenin particularly hit these parties for their failure to be based in the socialized industries and the everyday struggle of our class, failure to work in the bourgeois trade unions and failure to use bourgeois elections as a political platform to expose the bourgeois political parties and their role." (p. 399) Two things should be pointed out—Lenin's answer here was not to limit or curtail communist political activity but to broaden and deepen it. And second, anyone who thinks the situation described above represents the line of our Party or a major deviation that needs to be rooted out is so far "separated" from reality that a little "fusion" wouldn't be a bad idea at all for them.

The Menshevik clipping and curtailing of the real political meaning of fusion is no mere omission. It means separating fusion from politics and it represents—far from a line for merging socialism and the working class movement—a line for *submerging* our Party under the spontaneous level of the working class struggle at any point. This is the purpose to which they try to put the quote from the *Communist Manifesto* on communists having "no interests separate and apart" from the workers as a whole—a purpose and a context quite the opposite from its real meaning and from the context in which it was put and explained in the *Worker* bulletin.

What is stressed in that bulletin is also summed up later in the *Manifesto:* "in the movement of the present [the communists] also represent and take care of the future of that movement." Who can deny that in carrying out our tasks among the masses, in organising them, this is what we need to emphasize today—that in all these battles our Party represents and works for the *revolutionary* interests of our class. Isn't the failure to do this the clearest expression of the failure to carry out real fusion, of the low road? Shouldn't the whole experience of the degeneration of the CPUSA, together with what we know about the pull of spontaneity, especially in an imperialist country, be enough to warn us—to urge us toward the correct and revolutionary path?

The Founding Congress

The Founding Congress of our Party was a great victory, but not for the reasons our Mensheviks give us in their paper. Their reasons amount to economism and to a downright silly glorification—more accurately whitewashing—of their role. The founding of our Party, which we said we were determined would be the second and last founding of the revolutionary Party of the working class in the U.S., was a declaration of war on the bourgeoisie. It concentrated and consolidated the advances made by communists in the class struggle and the struggle between two lines in this country on all fronts—ideologically, politically and organizationally. It forged one Party with one line. This was concentrated in the MPR and *Constitution* and, especially, the Party *Programme.*

But our Mensheviks, as we have said before, wish to present this Congress as if it came out of nowhere and as if it didn't divide into two, especially on the question of economism. From the line of their paper, one can only conclude that they want to go back to the Congress, with the rightism intact and uphold everything. Besides being an impossible dream, this is reactionary and would amount to turning a victory into its opposite.

Their paper introduces the Congress by saying "We would rather not get into a 'who shot John' " (p. 400). This, of course, is a dead giveaway that this is exactly what lies in store and lo! we are not to be disappointed. Playing on people's ignorance of small details of the Congress, they treat the reader to a dizzy and distorted account of a few things, clearly aimed at puffing up their own roles as heroes. (It should be noted that a *thorough* study of Party documents and bulletins adds up to a good refutation of their whole paper.) Even taking their story at face value, their efforts at the Congress are silly. Missing altogether is any sweeping view of the accomplishments of the Congress, and especially any summation of the development of the revolutionary line of the *Programme,* or even an all around view of the MPR (to these, of course, Jarvis' contributions were minimal). Instead we get a picture of their heroic activities of adding a phrase here and there. As to most of these changes—what we said in *Revolution* about the CP(ML)'s Program comes to mind: they have two aspects, trite and wrong.

This is especially so if one wants—as our Mensheviks do—to make a federal case out of them today. For example there is the change they take credit for in altering the *Draft Programme* section on the IWO's from the original version, "While these organizations must be based mainly in the plants and other workplaces their overall role is to apply the single spark method . . ." M. Jarvis claims credit for the change to "These organizations must be based in the plants and other work places, must take an active part in building the fight there and play a leading role in the struggles of the rank and file workers. Their overall role is to apply the single spark method . . ." (RCP *Programme,* p. 109)

There is plenty of correct emphasis given in the *Programme* to the economic struggle, but as experience in building IWO's—and especially in building the NUWO and at its convention, has underlined, the key point about them is their political role in the struggle. They cannot play their role if the core of workers who must form their backbone is not won to understand this and specifically to the question of the working class leading the fight against all oppression. The original version gives this proper emphasis and the second version (in the *Programme*) tends toward eclectically muddling this point. (Nonetheless, the *Programme* can stand "as is"—but the Mensheviks can't.)

Both at the Congress and in this paper M. Jarvis headquartered a move to exaggerate tendencies, which did exist, to downplay the day to day struggle of the workers. It was as if this struggle had just been discovered—by M. Jarvis—and for the first time. That this was new to him is possible (although unlikely), but as we have already pointed out, the RU, both in practice and in polemics, had given proper weight and emphasis to that struggle.

Even in criticizing things that should have been criticized, such as the summation of the May First Workers Movement experience, the tendency was to act as though the problem was "too much politics, not enough economics" instead of the real problem which was a tendency toward a liberal, not communist (strictly Marxist) approach to both economic and political struggle. The purpose of all this, in retrospect, seems to have been to puff up Jarvis' role as the champion of these struggles and, especially, to huff up a big rightist wind. This had to be struggled with to some degree at and to a greater degree right after the Congress. It has persisted, and now this Menshevik paper seeks to blow it up to gale force once again.

Their paper also raises up the question of the "center of gravity," giving M. Jarvis credit for "initiating" this line. The paper carries on about the "center of gravity" and related questions for a while and then ominously poses the question, are the "left idealists" out to reverse this verdict? OK, Mensheviks, we'll bite. It is necessary to sum up this line and the way you blew it up into an economist wind in our Party. First off, to raise this question as this paper does and carry on as if the liquidation of the work in the economic struggle is the major danger facing our Party today would be ridiculous if it weren't criminal. This is once again a case of "many happy returns of the day" to funeral mourners. Once again our Mensheviks are getting sore muscles and bruised feet from lifting so many rocks only to drop them straight down.

Here, while they scream "foul!" for accusing them of pushing economism at the Congress, they once again openly make a big case out of the "center of gravity." But can we find even a *single mention* in their whole paper of the need for comrades to be tribunes of the people? Search as we may, we cannot find it. And with their quoting Lenin, do we find any reference at all, any attempt to sum up and apply the essence of *What Is To Be Done?* to our situation? Not at all.

Perhaps these philistines actually did not read any of the bulletins or articles of the last two years which deal with this and which they omit mentioning in their paper. If they haven't, we wish they'd quit trying to raise their ignorance to an arrogant principle which they try to impose on others. But we are inclined to give them the benefit of the doubt and credit them with greater opportunism than this. Not only are they so driven to tout their own role that they can't help revealing their economism, even more they are out to promote narrowness, pragmatism and rightism in such an all around way that they must jump out and distort Marxism, attack the Party's line, and promote economism which is one big feature of their rightism in this period.

These Mensheviks are once again guilty, just as they were before and after the Founding Congress, of the main deviation which occurred around this "center of gravity" question—turning necessary and urgent work in these struggles into a "special slogan." This was the error pointed to in Comrade Avakian's article in the May, 1976 *Revolution* "The Day to Day Struggle and the Revolutionary Goal". It is worthy once again to look at this article and to quote from an essay by Lenin it referred to which speaks exactly to this question:

> "There is nothing more warranted than the urging of attention to the constant, imperative necessity of deepening and broadening, broadening and deepening, our influence on the masses, our strictly Marxist propaganda and agitation, our ever-closer connection with the economic struggle of the working class, etc. Yet, because such urging is at all times warranted, under all conditions and in all situations, it must not be turned into special slogans, nor should it justify attempts to build upon it a special trend in Social-Democracy. A border-line exists here; to exceed the bounds is to turn this indisputably legitimate urging into a narrowing of the aims and the scope of the movement, into a doctrinaire blindness to the vital and cardinal political tasks of the moment." ("On Confounding Politics With Pedagogics," Vol. 8, pp 452-3)

Actively taking up the economic struggle remains a crucial task for our Party today. And this was very true at the time of the Founding Congress. The advances our Party has made would have been impossible if we hadn't been involved in and led these struggles and, along with this, achieved big progress in the reorganization and concentration of our forces in basic industry.

The 1976 CC Report was correct in pointing out that today the economic struggle "is where in fact the workers, *as workers*, are waging their battles and in the embryonic way they are beginning to develop a sense of themselves as *workers* by fighting against an opposing group of employers, the way the *Programme* puts it." (See page 43. See also *Revolution*, July, 1977.) And since, as the MPR points out, quoting Lenin, our "task is not to concoct some fashionable means of helping the workers" (a criticism that, as we'll see later, applies directly to the Mensheviks with their reformism and gimmickry), this means our Party today must do a lot of our work in these struggles, striving consistently to fulfil all three objectives.

But as the MPR itself and many subsequent documents warned, this cannot be taken to mean that this is all there is to the workers struggle—even the spontaneous struggle today—and still less to mean we should liquidate our Party's independent work. Taking account of this situation cannot mean reducing the Party's role to mere subservience to the workers movement as such. Our attitude toward this must be a revolutionary communist attitude, spelled out by Lenin: "It is the task of Social-Democrats, by organizing the workers, by conducting propaganda and agitation among them, to *turn* their spontaneous struggle against their oppressors into the struggle of the whole class, into the struggle of a definite political *party* for definite political and socialist ideals." ("Our Immediate Task," Vol 4, p. 216. Imagine—"ideals"!)

Even the phrase "center of gravity of our Party's work" does tend to make a separate stage out of our Party's work in the economic struggle. This is something we should sum up and correct, while grasping that the main deviation was not a phrase that appeared once (yes, once—with all the hubbub it's hard to believe) in the MPR. The main deviation was the tendency to turn it into a special slogan. This meant in practice putting forward the erroneous line that everything must be judged in relation to the economic struggle, that the basic connections and links between different struggles against particular abuses lie not in their relation to the overall fight against the capitalist system but in how they "fit into" the "center of gravity" struggles.

Coming off the Founding Congress, due in large part to a deviation headquartered by today's Mensheviks, there was even a tendency to equate being the Party "of the working class" with this "center of gravity." There was a tendency to erroneously take agitation to mean a call to action—a wrong understanding which in practice limits what we do exposures on to what we can organize a struggle around today. There was a narrow tendency to see "Marxist work" as simply bringing light to the current struggles of the working class, and not all around political work.

This latter tendency has been further developed, especially by these Mensheviks, even as they moved off their most blatant economism, into a line that limits political and ideological work to what can be unfolded from particular struggles. This is an expression of their one-sided pragmatic line on the relation between struggle and consciousness. It is true that tendencies toward all these things can be found in some parts of the MPR (this is more true of the CC Report on the Congress which came out afterwards). But it is also true that this is not the main thrust of the MPR, and that other, contrary, statements can be found in it as well. The point is not to negate the MPR, or fail to sum it up as a big advance, but to understand it, as we have said before, as something which was both a product of a process and itself divided into two. This is precisely what our Mensheviks in this paper refuse to do, as they seek to promote themselves and promote rightism.

Our attitude toward errors like the "center of gravity of the Party's work" formulation in the MPR, and on the other hand toward our Mensheviks, can be well summed up in Lenin's words, speaking of the early period when the Russian communists initiated work among the workers:

> "At first it was inevitable that this work should have a narrow character and should be embodied in the narrow declarations of some Social-Democrats. This narrowness, however, did not frighten those Social-Democrats who had not in the least forgotten the broad historical aims of the Russian working class movement. What matters it if the *words* of the Social-Democrats sometimes have a narrow meaning when *their deeds* cover a broad field . . . they go to that class which alone is the real revolutionary class and assist in the development of its forces! They believed that this narrowness would disappear of its own accord with each step that broadened Social-Democratic propaganda. And this, to a considerable degree, is what has happened."

But then he sums up another development:

> "a gross exaggeration of this (*absolutely essential*) aspect of Social Democratic activity, which could bring some individuals to lose sight of the other aspects... It is in this extreme exaggeration of one aspect of Social-Democratic work that we see the chief cause of the sad retreat from the ideas of Russian Social-Democracy. Add to this enthusiasm over a fashionable book, ignorance of the history of the Russian revolutionary movement, and a childish claim to originality, and you have all the elements that go to make up 'the retrograde trend in Russian Social-Democracy.' "("A Retrograde Trend" Vol. 4, pp. 279-80)

(Lest our Mensheviks get too excited, we should point out that Lenin is *not* saying here that line doesn't matter, only practice, as our Mensheviks would have it. He is not denying the importance of rational knowledge as they do—otherwise he would not have bothered to write this work!)

A mistake can be summed up, an erroneous tendency corrected, but as Lenin also put it, "It all goes to drive home the truth that a minor error can always assume monstrous proportions if it is persisted in, if profound justifications are sought for it, and if it is carried to its logical conclusion." (*Left Wing Communism*, Vol. 31, p. 43). This is an excellent description of our Mensheviks' pathetic efforts around the "center of gravity" question in their paper.

To sum up this point, it was correct coming off the Congress to sum up that objectively the struggle of the workers, as workers, is now centered in the economic struggles. But it is definitely wrong and economist to see concentrating there as a separate stage of work and to wall it off from our all around political tasks—even as the phrase "center of gravity" and the policy of concentrating our work in the economic struggle tend to do.*

*In the original text of this "Reply" while the formulation "center of gravity" was criticized and repudiated, it was still stated that it was "generally correct" to concentrate the Party's work in the economic struggle of the workers. At the Second Congress of the RCP, on the basis of deepening the struggle against the revisionist line of our Mensheviks, this was also criticized and repudiated, and it was unanimously agreed that such concentration—which in fact the "center of gravity" formulation was a description of—was incorrect for the same reasons that the "center of gravity" formulation itself was wrong.

At the same time it was stressed that the Party must pay particular attention to uniting with, building and giving political leadership to the economic struggles of the workers as an important part of developing the workers' movement into a class conscious revolutionary movement. But it was also emphasized that this does not mean that the Party's agitation and exposure should center exclusively or even mainly on the economic struggle. For more on this, see especially "Economic Struggle and Revolutionary Tasks," *Revolution*, organ of the Central Committee of the RCP, July 1978 (p. 3) and the "Introduction" to *Revolutionary Work in a Non-Revolutionary Situation*, the Report of the Second Plenary Session of the First Central Committee of the RCP (1976), published as a pamphlet by the RCP in 1978.

Of course, as Lenin pointed out to the economists in *What Is To Be Done?*, if it's quantity (as well as quality) of work in the economic struggle you want, we will gladly compare. The correct line of our Party in many areas (auto is just one example) has given leadership to lots of economic struggles, big and small, and will continue to do so and to a growing extent. In almost every area which was under Menshevik leadership (New York/New Jersey is a good example) work on this front stagnated, too—as a product of the incorrect line. And it was the line of the self-styled NUWO president—not the line of the proletarian headquarters—to downgrade the importance of the miners' contract strike in advance—opposing making an important task of supporting it in the NUWO nationally unless and until it had proved itself to his satisfaction not to be just a routine strike, but a rouser. Aside from being way wide of the mark (shit!) this whole approach failed to base itself on the real political significance of the battle between the proletariat and the bourgeoisie that was focusing even then on the contract battle, because of the nature of the miners' movement in the years preceding. Sorry, again, Mensheviks.

In their summation of the Congress, of course, the authors of this paper from the degenerate Menshevik hindquarters conveniently fail to mention, while they talk about their heroic phrase-adjusting contributions, that the lines over which there was most struggle at the Congress itself were championed there (on the wrong side) by those who are leading members of their headquarters. Even though those lines were defeated there, these forces still persisted, and the further development (degeneration) of these lines was dealt with at the 1976 CC and afterwards.

Comrades can refer to the CC Report that came out reporting on the Founding Congress to see what these lines were and how they were struggled against. They included the line of "everything through the IWO's", which gave rise to the sharpest struggle at the Congress, especially focused in one committee. This line promoted the narrowing down of our Party's work and also tended to negate the need to build the national movements.

In addition some in the Menshevik headquarters raised an empiricist line on the tasks of the Party branches, attempting to change Article 12 Section 1 of the *Constitution* in a way to narrow down the task of constant education concerning the ideological and political line. Besides being struggled against and summed up as empiricist at the Congress, this line is hit at sharply in the second Party Branches article (*Revolution*, Sept., 1977). Though this was not reported on in the Congress summation document, some who are part of this clique also raised up the idea that there was no qualitative leap involved in joining the young communist organization—a line they later developed in a big way in their "youth appeal."

Finally it should be noted that the line for which they "wisely" and "even-handedly" criticize the MPR in a passing reference—that it "failed to explicitly distinguish between economic and political struggle, although that is done without using these particular terms"—was a line M. Jarvis waved the baton for. The passing "criticism" in their paper is the sheerist hypocrisy, since they know well what Jarvis' role was around this, and that Comrade Avakian in particular waged struggle against this erroneous tendency several times leading up to the Congress.

All this, previously summed up by the Party and agreed to by them in words, is of course ignored by this Menshevik summation, while they dish out their petty accounts of this and that wording change as the real essence of the Congress.

At the Founding Congress members of (what has become full-blown as) the Menshevik clique pushed another rotten line that is of considerable significance, especially in light of what has happened since the Founding Congress and especially with the full flowering (weeding) of this clique. That was the line of social-chauvinism—a line that in essence called for support for "our own" imperialists in the international struggle—which of course means capitulating to them in an all around way.

This line was put straight out by some who are now "rank and file" members of the Menshevik camp, in the form of calling for support of NATO and the struggle for "independence" in the lesser imperialist countries in the U.S. bloc—all in the name of fighting against the two superpowers and directing the main blow (though that phrase was not specifically used) against the Soviets. At the Congress itself this line was supported, especially in the committee directly concerned with this question, by that "herky-jerky theoretician," who in typical and revealing fashion dragged up all kinds of documents from the Comintern and the Soviet Union during the 1930s, when they were talking about how the imperialists were divided into so-called "aggressor" states and "peace-loving democracies." The point of this "theoretician" was that our Party should support the same kind of line in regard to the international situation today—once again an indication of this clique's desire and determination to repeat the errors of the Comintern and the revisionist tendencies of the old CP which were the quantity leading up to its leap into utter revisionism (once again, first time tragedy, second time farce). This line was specifically repudiated at the Congress itself and criticized in the CC Report on the Congress. (In this light, note that in their paper attacking the CC Report on China the Mensheviks blast the Four and our Party for what they call failing to uphold "China's foreign policy" (see p. 176)—which means the stuff filling the pages of the *Peking Review* on the international situation. Here is yet another indication of our Mensheviks inching—perhaps "yarding" is a more accurate description—their way toward the CP(ML).

Also of significance in the same direction is the fact that, along with promoting this junk through the use of Comintern and Soviet documents from the 1930s, this "herky-jerky theoretician" pushed essentially the same revisionist stuff through another means—arguing that defense of China was the "cornerstone" of proletarian internationalism today. This was another way of trying to smuggle in the line of directing the main blow at the Soviet Union and capitulating to "our own" bourgeoisie. It was also repudiated at the Congress and criticized in the CC Report on the Founding Congress.

Finally on this point, one of the main scribblers for this bunch of philistines co-authored a critique of the section of the *Draft Programme* on "Life Under Socialism." This critique, while supposedly "improving" this section by focusing more on the class struggle under socialism, actually promoted an erroneous view of socialism and of class struggle. As to the essence of this line and its relevance for the present struggle, we have only to quote the CC Report on the Founding Congress:

> "This line was characterized by the stand of the petty bourgeoisie and tried to paint socialism as an attractive alternative—for the petty bourgeoisie—to the present form of capitalist rule. In reality it put forward not socialism at all—not the rule of the working class, its collective ownership of the means of production and its struggle to transform all of society—but a slicked up version of capitalism, which would give new bourgeois forces a chance to ride on the backs of the workers and exploit them.
>
> "It was essentially revisionist, and as part of its revisionist outlook put forward the 'theory of the productive forces'—reducing the workers to mere producers without class consciousness, without the ability to consciously change the world in accordance with their revolutionary interests as a class."

(As stated this Menshevik dilettante wrote this piece together with another comrade; the other co-author summed up his error and moved forward, while the first has gone further with this erroneous tendency and gone further in his capacity as a "ghost" whose moanings haunt the pages of the papers by the Mensheviks attacking the CC Report.)

The Menshevik paper also criticizes Comrade Avakian's role at the Congress, and challenges the idea he struggled against their rightism. They say, "In the two times he spoke during all the plenary sessions of the Congress, we don't get one word about economism, syndicalism, or overemphasis on industrial concentration." This, too, is a dishonest trick, and they know it—although they hope many others won't.

First it should be pointed out that Comrade Avakian did, to a certain degree, hold back from struggle in the plenaries, not because he was afraid, as is implied (note: our Mensheviks, who claim to have feared open struggle with Comrade Avakian, are now attributing their avowed spinelessness to others), but because for him to wage extensive struggle in the plenary sessions would have meant a major struggle at the Congress, and it was a correct political decision to unite with the overwhelmingly positive thrust so as to preserve the genuine unity and achievements which had been forged.

Secondly, as these Mensheviks know, Comrade Avakian did struggle sharply at the Congress against their rightism. This came up around the previously referred to struggle in a committee that went on around the "everything through the IWOs" line. The wife of M. Jarvis, though not in that committee, had been outside of meetings going to those she considered "her people" in that committee and directly encouraging them to struggle for this wrong line—which they were doing in a very stubborn and arrogant way. This was going directly (and behind their backs) in opposition to the other leading comrades who were heading this committee. (M. Jarvis himself encouraged his wife in this but let her play the more up-front role.)

Comrade Avakian struggled very sharply in the leadership group at the Congress against this line and this behavior. Under these conditions, M. Jarvis and his forces finally agreed to the criticism, but then—supposedly to "unify" the Congress—they suggested that M. Jarvis, not Comrade Avakian, be the one to raise the criticism of the "everything through the IWOs" line on the floor of the Congress. Taking this suggestion at face value, it was agreed to. (It should be noted that people under M. Jarvis' leadership were overheard mumbling at the time—"that hypocrite, this is *his* line he's blasting us for.") Now all this gets turned around by those who know better, into an attack on Comrade Avakian for his "silence." (It is, we suppose, necessary to answer all this tripe, although exposing M. Jarvis and Co. for double dealing is getting about as new and exciting as it was to expose Mayor Daley in Chicago for corruption. All it can produce after a while is yawns.)

It is more revealing to study how these Mensheviks sum up the main distinction that marked the founding of our Party. They say:

> "There was the opening sentence in the Workers Movement section of the Programme that blasted all Trotskyite idealism and metaphysics: 'The working class learns through its day to day struggle.' There was the push in the MPR to unite with the concrete battles of our class, and there was the call in the orientation section of the MPR to rely on, learn from and bring forward our class brothers and sisters, about which there is too little talk today. There was our determination not to be condescending saviours and lecturers, because we saw our class had far too many of these. All these things marked our distinction from every political organization which has existed over the last 20 and more years. It reflected the determination of the RCP to do what had not been done during that period: fuse socialism with the working class movement." (p. 403)

They go on to say "Isolating this contradiction from all other contradictions led to certain problems." Here they once again reveal themselves. The problem was not that this "contradiction" was one-sidedly stressed, but that it's wrong to say, as they do, that this was what "marked our distinction from every political organization which has existed over the last 20 and more years." This was not the essential thing. What about the minor point that we are revolutionary communists, not revisionists, like the CPUSA, which was and is also involved in the daily struggle?

In fact this paragraph, more vividly than elsewhere in this paper, expresses our Mensheviks' open yearning to have a party "just like the party of dear old Mom and Dad"—the CP of "20 or more" years ago—with all its pragmatism intact and all the revisionist tendencies it embodied even before its complete and decisive leap into counter-revolution.

It is this kind of line that the founding of our Party represented a break with—that its line and *Programme* represent a repudiation of—and which gives content to our expressed determination not to go down the path of the old CP into accommodation with revisionism and imperialism. It is precisely for this reason that our current struggle to stick to the high road and repudiate these Mensheviks is a continuation of the actual great victory of the Founding Congress, a struggle which continues our Party on the road of revolution and steering clear of the rocks, so that a Party will not have to be founded for a third time.

There is, of course, no way to reconstruct and return to the old CP even if we wanted to, like our Mensheviks. History moves in spirals, not circles. As Mao puts it, characterizing this outlook:

> "We are opposed to die-hards in the revolutionary ranks whose thinking fails to advance with changing objective circumstances and has manifested itself historically as Right opportunism. These people fail to see that the struggle of opposities has already pushed the objective process forward while their knowledge has stopped at the old stage. This is characteristic of the thinking of all die-hards. Their thinking is divorced from social practice, and they cannot march ahead to guide the chariot of society . . ." ("On Practice," *Selected Readings,* p. 79-80).

Their kind of thinking is the real idealism and rampant metaphysics.

This is the reactionary outlook that also had that Menshevik chieftain M. Jarvis in the CPUSA in the late 1960s. Perhaps this helps to explain the hatred for the revolutionary upsurge of that period that one finds throughout this Menshevik paper. On every imaginable front the CP stood in complete opposition to everything that was revolutionary in the movement of that period and stood for the most blatant revisionism. If you were part of the CP at that time you hated the revolutionary movement and the feeling was mutual. (Of course, the CP is no less revisionist today, but because this is the beginning of a new spiral and there is not yet a mass revolutionary upsurge, the revisionism of the CP does not always stand out so starkly as it did before and as it will, even more fully, in the future.)

Struggle Against Economism

This Menshevik paper also has a summation of the struggle against economism. Difficult, you might think since it actively promotes economism? Undaunted by this problem, our Mensheviks advance the amusing view that it was they—and "their" July 4 campaign in particular— that started this struggle and were responsible for its victory. At one point in commenting on what they call "the absurd view that [the Chair] played a major role in the struggle against economism" (p. 411), they concede that "He did make certain contributions"—such as the "Mass Line" articles and the "Day to Day Struggle and the Revolutionary Goal" article (though they tell us they found it lifeless—small wonder since it squeezed the life out of some of their economism and pragmatism). "But," they go on to say in a stunning statement, "this was after the Party had already broken through on the major line questions."

Most comrades, once they recovered from laughing, would probably voice surprise at the idea that they had "already broken through" on economism as of spring 1976—or that even today it doesn't represent a major problem. But to these Mensheviks, stuck in *real* idealist *apriorism*—their preconceived notion that their work on July 4 made them the conquering heroes of all opportunism—there was simply a minor mop-up operation underway.

This negates the fact that there was a specific struggle in the realm of theory over an economist line, and while practice on July 4 and its summation related to this, it was not identical to this struggle. Articles and documents which they, of course, find irrelevant and lifeless played a major role in this as did struggle on this question throughout the Party. All this they are blind to or seek to deny. This approach is the same one that shows up in their view on China that "class struggle runs through everything"—an eclectic view aimed at negating the key link of class struggle and resurrecting in new form the revisionist formulation "take the three directives as the key link."

The struggle against economism in our Party was a struggle waged before July 4 (in no small part against them), during July 4, and after it, and it had to be raised to a rational level—and without *this* struggle July 4 would not have been nearly so successful, judged by correct, *political* standards. Their view of ideological struggle reveals that these are exactly the kind of people characterized in the Mass Line campaign as putting out the view "fight, fight, fight" (though they don't seem to do too well at that either). Their view of the motion of knowledge is in fact "practice to practice and back to practice again." They actually do not think raising things to the level of rational knowledge is necessary at all in this process and those who do are, according to them, "stuck" at the level of rational knowledge.

A final point on their summation of the struggle against economism. Their paper claims that others were the real supporters of economism and these forces are now the chief supporters of the "left idealist" line. This, as usual, is a gross distortion. Some comrades did not hold these views, especially after the Founding Congress, while others spontaneously made errors, and were encouraged in this by M. Jarvis. The Chair struggled with these comrades as well as with the economist line generally. Over time, these comrades got off it, but M. Jarvis—while sometimes adhering to other forms of rightism—sunk deeper into it. This was because these comrades were making errors, while M. Jarvis had a rightist line, stuck to it and entrenched it in his thinking.

Attempt to Turn July 4 into Capital

Because they consider July 4 the biggest feather in their cap and because to them it sums up what they consider to be the heart of the correct line—the correct concept that small forces can lead big battles—the Mensheviks deal at length and stake a lot on the July 4 campaign. They attribute all kinds of wonders to this campaign—from defeating economism, to establishing the standard for future work (thus their comparison to the NUWO) and, last but not least, to establishing their credentials as great leaders who must not be removed, demoted or even criticized.

Most comrades agree with the correct summation in the 1976 CC Report that the July 4 campaign was a big advance and with what that Report sums up politically as the content of that advance—the working class mounting the political stage to fight a key battle. But most also hold the obviously mistaken view—or so it seems to listen to these Mensheviks—that while some individuals, including some of the departed Mensheviks, certainly played important roles in this, these achievements were mainly due to the correct overall line of our Party, the work of many comrades, and the collective leadership of the Party. Oh well, fooled by "left idealism" again.

This Menshevik paper sets out to reverse these verdicts. Perhaps M. Jarvis has learned from his comrade Hua Kuo-feng. If Hua can turn the example of Tachai into its opposite in China, Jarvis believes he can do the same thing here with July 4. Well, it is not so easy. Comrades can distinguish form from content and right from wrong, and especially since Jarvis lacks state power and since the RCP is under the leadership of a correct line, our Party can persist in its correct summation of the 4th and rebuff these attempts to turn this around.

Their view of this campaign reflects their idea of a perfect action: put the right people in the right place at the right time with the right gimmick and . . . "it'll spin!" This is hardly the essence of the matter. The principal thing in building this demonstration was the line and role of the Party as a whole, including its collective leadership bodies. As to the role of individuals, which they make so much of in this campaign, this becomes more important especially in times of sharp two line struggle. The July 4 campaign did not overall mark such a period, especially on the leading bodies. Some rightist lines did crop up, particularly at the start, but these were struggled with and generally corrected. And these were definitely not taken by the Chair, whose role they seek to contrast with their own heroics.

Since Comrade Avakian's role in this campaign has been made an issue in their paper and elsewhere, it is necessary to go into it a bit. For someone who is overall characterized as drifting, drifting into "left idealist" neverland, it is interesting to note that it was the Chair, not the Mensheviks, who came up with the main slogan for the campaign, "We've Carried the Rich for 200 Years, Let's Get Them Off Our Backs." This slogan, as the Party has summed up, did in fact concentrate the feelings of the masses and provide an important orientation for the whole battle. As a passing point, it should be noted that "thinking up slogans and making speeches" is not just some clever knack, but one important indication of line. Specifically it is exactly an example of correctly combining the general and the particular—returning the ideas of the masses to them in a concentrated form so they can grasp and take them as their own.

On the key tactical question of the campaign—how to handle the threat of troops—our Menshevik master tacticians didn't do so well, with some tending toward retreat to New York, and M. Jarvis not sure but tending to fall into the "we'll march anyway" trap. It was the Chair who came up with the correct tactic of persisting in the line of exposing this as a political attack and expressing confidence that the masses wouldn't allow it. This is again worth pointing out, not only because such "inability to return general line to practice" has been made an issue, but also because it shows that correct tactics themselves are a product of a correct overall line and analysis.

Finally, in regard to the Chair's role in July 4, it should be pointed out that in the divison of labor at the Center he was assigned to other tasks in this period, including giving assistance to others in leading the work around the '76 auto contracts. This work, in contrast to some other efforts in economic struggles in this period—particularly under the leadership of this clique—was a definite advance in applying the mass line and in putting out a line that clearly took up this battle as part of the broader class struggle.

As to stuff about the Chair's "inactivity" in this period we think it best to let concrete actions and leadership stand for themselves. For one thing, comrades should look over the Mass Line articles—including the second and third which were written during the period apparently being talked about—and judge for themselves if Comrade Avakian, who wrote them based on direct and indirect experience in several areas, was getting increasingly isolated from the real questions of the struggle.

It is also worthwhile to speak of M. Jarvis' role in July 4—again since it has been made an issue. He did, in fact have principal responsibility for leading the campaign from the Center and had advanced the concrete proposal for the demonstration. In general he carried out the Party's line and made contributions in this period. However since we are directed by their paper to look at the bulletins to judge the Mensheviks' role, let's do just that. The first bulletin, written by or under the close direction of M. Jarvis, while it should be seen as an early bulletin, does not, on close examination, live up to all the top-line billing it is given. It puts forward the line, advanced by Jarvis in his original proposal, that July 4 will be central for the vets and the unemployed, but not among employed workers. It puts out something very close to a "constituency organizing" approach with something special and palpable to emphasize for everyone. But overall—especially when giving guidance for work among the employed—it tends to portray the 4th as a jobs demonstration. All these, of course, are tendencies which could be, and to a great extent were, corrected through the development of the campaign and the discussion on leading bodies. But—since this is one of the few bulletins M. Jarvis ever wrote, and since their paper says how could he have held economist lines, he proposed July 4 didn't he?—this is worth noting. It is not inconsistent, but perfectly consistent with economism to propose political struggle for others, and economic struggle for the workers.

The second July 4 bulletin (N.B. #2), which reflected collective discussion and a deepening grasp of the correct line, was written not by the Menshevik group, but by the headquarters which is now attacked as "left idealist."

This second bulletin lays out much more fully than the first the political basis for the July 4th campaign and gives guidance much more based on line. Perhaps our Mensheviks will jump to point out that this bulletin several times refers to "building our movement", since the "build our movement line" was criticized later in giving further guidance to the campaign and then in summing it up. But what is in this second bulletin is not the "build our movement line" but a correct emphasis on the fact that, as the bulletin said, "We do *everything* in order to build the movement of our class toward the revolutionary goal and not as things in themselves (gimmicks)."

The erroneous "build our movement line" was the tendency to side-step or downplay the importance of the political battle around the 4th itself—and trying to avoid the controversy that would arise around this—by "selling" the July 4th demonstration on the basis that it would help to build the *already existing* movement of the working class, centered as it is now mainly around economic battles. Clearly, in essence and overwhelmingly in form, this "build our movement line" was narrow and rightist. (There was, to a certain degree, a "left" variant of this "build our movement line" which took the form of simply engaging in discussions about socialism in building for the demonstration—i.e. *only* talking about building the movement for socialism—but this was a very minor error compared to the rightist tendencies and not nearly as serious a problem.)

The second bulletin, while laying out the basis for the specific fight around the Bicentennial, also correctly hits at the above mentioned rightist tendencies, stressing that "if we build the Bicentennial demonstration as a thing in itself and not as part of building the movement of our class, we will be making another form of the same error as doing the center of gravity for the center of gravity's sake—instead of as the main arena now in which we are working to advance the actual struggle of the class, as a class, toward a broad movement against the rule of capital, to carry out the central task."

And, again, "The demonstration is bound to create controversy. But as long as we are really rooted in the deep feelings, needs and hopes of the masses and in their actual struggles, we should not fear this. In fact, as revolutionary communists, we should be far more afraid if our program and ideas created no controversy, because we would then be miserably tailing the masses and caving in to the bourgeoisie."

More "left idealism!" we are sure our Mensheviks will screech, since it is clear that these points—though not written as any kind of polemic—objectively stand as a sharp rebuke to the rightist line of the Mensheviks. (The first July 4th Bulletin does contain a paragraph that starts out talking about how the "center of gravity" is not the same thing as the central task—something Jarvis put in after discussion of this point on the standing bodies. Then, however, the same paragraph in this bulletin ends up turning back on itself with the following two-into-one formulation: "But the Bicentennial work itself serves primarily to advance the struggles of the class, including at the 'center of gravity' where they are presently focused." This tends, again, toward narrowing things and making the main question with regard to different struggles, how do they relate to and build the "center of gravity" battles instead of how do they relate to the building of a revolutionary workers movement against capitalism.) And, the complaints and objections of our Mensheviks notwithstanding, it is also clear that it was the direction given by the Center, especially the "left idealists," to linking *every* battle with the overall fight against the capitalist system and with the long-term goal, rather than taking them up as "things in themselves," that led to the development and deepening of the correct line and the real advances around July 4th. This is an important lesson to sum up, though no doubt it is an outrage to our Mensheviks, who want to treat July 4th not only as a "thing in itself" but *the* thing by which to judge everything else and to which everything else must be related—rather than the overall struggle and the long-term goal.

The sum-up bulletin on July 4th is also highly advertised, so it is worth noting that the draft originally submitted by M. Jarvis (written under his close direction) was so sectarian—attacking "left" and right lines right and left—that it was characterized by those now attacked as "left sectarians" as the "Gloria Fontanez bulletin" (after the ultra-sectarian head of PRRWO). Its effect would have been to disorient and dizzy comrades so badly as to demoralize many. Besides reflecting an outlook, this also reflected the fact it was supposed to serve M. Jarvis' factional purpose in putting some people under attack. The criminal thing is that Jarvis didn't care about the effect on comrades, so long as it suited his purposes. After sharp criticism, this draft was rejected by the Center, which directed a new one to be written. Fortunately, despite all the claims for his virtues at political summation, the Party Center didn't subject the comrades to another sample of M. Jarvis' bulletins on July 4th after the first one.

While July 4 was a major advance, and overall Jarvis' leadership in it reflected and contributed to the correct line of the Party, there was of course even then interference from the incorrect line he and his cronies pushed. This came out in several ways. First, in many ways the normal centralized chain of knowledge and command of the Party was often disrupted and short-circuited by M. Jarvis' reliance on "his own people", particulary the roving team he set up to lead the demonstration. Several regional conferences, especially in the Midwest, suffered from the undermining of Party leadership caused by this method of work—a method which Jarvis popularized and persisted in.

Second, there tended to be an exaggeration of the question of tactics, of how we outmaneuvered the authorities, and to divorce tactics from line—which, of course, is the same error that led the Jarvis bunch to fall into confusion and nearly into disaster around how to handle the threat of troops in the first place. This even took the form of saying, in effect, that the police could not attack us, because of our clever tactics, with the implication that so long as we outfoxed the ruling class it would never be able to launch such an attack—hardly a Marxist presentation of the role of the state! Erroneous tendencies in this direction were common in the popularly held summations of the demonstration among Party members (and some others), but it was also pushed and encouraged by those now constituting the Menshevik headquarters.

We should keep in mind the sum up in the 1976 CC Report. It makes clear that the real significance of the 4th was not tactics. The real "we did it" was the working class entering the political arena to battle the bourgeosie, not "we did it"—the bourgeoisie couldn't stop our demonstration because of our brilliant tactics.

It should also be pointed out that, closely related to this error, this Menshevik headquarters underestimated and even in some cases just plain sabotaged the use of Party propaganda at July 4th, including distribution of newspapers and the Party pamphlet (which they never mention as part of the campaign) at the demonstration.

The way our Mensheviks view July 4 and use it in their paper as the centerpiece in relation to which all sorts of lines, events and people are to be judged represents another negative influence of their line in relation to July 4. As noted before, they have developed a tendency to measure everything in comparison to July 4, rather than against the criterion of how everything contributes to the goal of revolution. In this paper the factional purposes behind this stand out. But more is involved. This has influenced even the methods of work in the Party and a tendency has developed—especially evident in UWOC and youth work, for example—toward "campaign-itis" and "everything aimed toward a big demonstration". This has seriously damaged the method of mass line in the Party's work.

Mao addresses such a tendency (though our Mensheviks' method amounts to a rather puny version of what Mao criticizes) in "On Contradiction": "The dogmatists . . . do not understand that different methods should be used to resolve different contradictions; on the contrary, they invariably adopt what they imagine to be an unalterable formula and arbitrarily apply it everywhere, which only causes setbacks to the revolution or makes a sorry mess of what could have been done well." (*Selected Readings*, p. 99).

In fact in their paper, the Mensheviks only discuss the mass line in relation to the question of "big battles with small forces." July 4 is described as "an excellent living example of the use of the mass line and revolutionary theory", so we anxiously await our lesson. In describing this concept of mass line they state: "Grasping the key issues of concern for the masses, the vulnerable points that the bourgeoisie is trying to cover up (moves to war, unemployment, housing in Philly, etc.) and concentrating these particular phenomena into a general line that concentrates the felt needs of the masses and exposes the class relations of capitalism. This enables relatively small forces to have far greater political impact and influence than their numbers." (p. 409)

To this we reply with all the appropriate profundity it deserves—HUH??? This brilliant contribution to our understanding of the mass line and leading struggle calls to mind Lenin's words "turgid nonsense," an attempt "to palm off a mere *jumble of words* as philosophy." (*Materialism and Empirio-Criticism*, Vol. 14, p. 132).

If our Mensheviks wanted to understand mass line, why not go back to what our *Programme* says:

> "[The Party] takes these scattered and partial experiences and ideas, and by applying the science of revolution, sums them up, concentrates what is correct, what corresponds to the development of society and will move the class struggle ahead. The Party returns these concentrated ideas to the masses in the form of line and policies, which it perseveres in carrying out and propagating in linking itself with and leading the struggle of the masses, and these concentrated ideas become a tremendous material force as the masses take them up as their own and use them to transform the world through class struggle." (p. 59-60)

If we compare our Mensheviks' creative, if turgid, development to what the *Programme* says, we can once again see their line. Their concept of mass line here leaves out science, and especially any attention to the laws of class society. ("Expose[s] the class relations of capitalism" is given no real content or meaning by them, and the more general laws of capitalism are systematically ignored—in this paper and by this Menshevik bunch in general. Certainly they never think of arming the masses with an understanding of these laws, which would be difficult for these Mensheviks, since they lack such knowledge and even a desire to acquire it themselves.) In fact this view of mass line leaves out the masses (especially in the form of downplaying the fact that ideas can become a material force when taken up by the masses). It is a true "heroes make history" (not to mention narrow reformist) line.

The first Mass Line article speaks to this. "It is not a question of a few 'smart people' drawing up a blueprint for 'how society ought to be' and imposing this on reality, but of the masses of people struggling to change the world and in the process learning more about it, and the laws governing it, in order to change it further . . . and on, in an endless spiral."

And more:

> ". . . the Party must not only 'process' the ideas of the masses and raise their experience to rational knowledge, but must continually arm the masses themselves with the science of revolution, to enable ever broader numbers to know and change the world, and develop the struggle of millions, more and more in conformity with the revolutionary outlook and interests of the working class." (See *Revolution,* Dec. 15, 1975 or "Mass Line" pamphlet.)

This real understanding of the mass line, not the chopped and narrow understanding promoted by the Mensheviks, needs to be more deeply grasped and taken up by our whole Party.

The NUWO

Here they again push their "unalterable formulas" line of compare everything to July 4. In giving guidance to building the NUWO the Party Center specifically pointed out the error of equating this campaign with that around the Bicentennial. But this didn't stop the Mensheviks, who treated the convention in particular like another rally. And now their paper tries to take up and roast the campaign to build the NUWO in this light, specifically by comparing it to their view of July 4. We have to reject this method, but should take up the task of summing up the NUWO campaign. A few of their charges need to be answered here.

First off, in contrast to their line that the campaign to form this organization was an idealist flop from start to finish, we should affirm that the formation of this organization represented an important advance in the struggle, one that needs to be built off of in order to develop this organization as a powerful force in the class struggle. We should affirm it both because it is true and because otherwise a real advance will be turned into its opposite.

They call the campaign the campaign of the "four no's": "No line on why form the organization at this time; no line developed to build it; no line and leadership at the convention; no reason why the cadre should be criticized for the way the convention came out." All this, of course, is blamed on the line and leadership of the Chair—in contrast to their July 4 heroes (see p. 415). Any careful study of the Party documents relating to this (including bulletins, the Party pamphlet, the '76 CC Report and parts of the *Worker* bulletin) stands as a clear refutation to this. We urge comrades to do such study, both in relation to the NUWO and the Mensheviks' other distorted accounts of history throughout their paper.

In their summation of this NUWO campaign, their general line of wiping out the role of the bourgeoisie (their role, in this case) stands out most starkly. Here is a campaign waged in the midst of a two line struggle with great factionalism on their part, with many of the leaders of their headquarters running around the country leading such factionalizing around their incorrect line, and we find not even the slightest reflection of two line struggle—simply the Chair's so-called "left-idealism" ruining the campaign. In fact the campaign involved sharp struggle against their line and sabotage—a fact which they try to hide in various ways. We certainly agree with their fourth "No"—no reason why the cadre should be criticized for the way the convention came out—and these Mensheviks *know* it. The criticism was directed at their line and leadership.

This campaign was certainly interfered with by the fact that throughout there were two centers of leadership in the Party. Unified leadership was sabotaged from top to bottom by this clique. They have the nerve to blast the Chair and write "The Party chain of knowledge/chain of command did not function. . ." Their style of going around central and local Party leadership and relying on telephone conversations with "key people" or on their own "road shows" did significant damage to the chain of knowledge and command. Time and again, right down to the eve of the convention, they forced cancellation or postponement of meetings of the Party work team, or when they did show they didn't struggle in these meetings. But all this, we suppose, is also the fault of the Chair's "left-idealism." The fact that this latest Menshevik paper is written to rationalize a split is apparently irrelevant to the development of the campaign. These people know they were out factionalizing, but at least from what they try to push over in this paper, cadre are asked to reject the Marxist theory of contradiction and instead take up the "Deborin school" described by Mao in "On Contradiction": "the Deborin school maintains that contradiction appears not at the inception of a process but only when it has developed to a certain stage. If this were the case, then the cause of the development of the process before that stage would be external and not internal. Deborin thus reverts to the metaphysical theories of external causality and of mechanism." (*Selected Readings,* p. 93) These Mensheviks had a line on the NUWO which they actively pushed. The line was defeatism, rightism, and gimmickry. Their general take was that the NUWO couldn't really be formed. This comes through even in their paper where they say "This is not to say it was wrong to go ahead and build the NUWO. A powerful campaign *could* have *possibly* led to *decent* advances for our class and Party" (p. 417, our emphasis). What a ringing endorsement!

Once the campaign was underway, however, this pessimistic, defeatist view didn't seem to prevent them from attempting to build up their careers by using their positions in it. Although no serious attempt is made in their paper to put out another line on building the NUWO, such a line generally came through in their practice. It amounted to: do a couple things, "single spark" them, and get a reputation (making sure it's not too "left," or "dual unionist"). To them the correct policy of single spark is turned into its opposite—essentially boiling down to press work and other forms of P.R. As our Party has stood for it, the single spark method requires building the struggle internally at the "spark" itself, as well as building broader struggle and understanding.

With their approach, mass line goes out the window and the *political* approach to advanced and active workers of "let's get down politically on the key questions facing our class" goes out the window. All of this was a problem which weakened the (generally successful) Cleveland meeting (to initiate the mass campaign to build the NUWO) and it got worse throughout the campaign—culminating in the convention hype-job to substitute for politics.

Their "get a reputation" approach came through in a number of cases, most notably how they handled the Klanbusters. They plastered about a leaflet and poster with the well known picture of the Ohio Wizard getting punched with the message: Do you want to know what the national workers organization is about? Ask the Klan. While the Ohio action was certainly correct, their approach in this smacks of opportunism (aimed at "getting Blacks"). Besides, the Ohio action was partly initiated by the RSB, a fact which, while hidden in these leaflets, would have been good politically to help raise workers' understanding.

They tried the same "get a rep" and "PR" approach around the Brach strike in Chicago, which took place shortly before the convention. But due to this line, directly under the leadership of M. Jarvis (that great hero of the "center of gravity"), capitulation was practised to a great extent within the strike, especially when it got tough; hence it was not built by relying on the strikers, so ultimately, as our Mensheviks would say, "it didn't spin."

This trend of rightism came out in other ways. One of the self-appointed NUWO "president's" right hand men, on tour on the West Coast, got on TV in L.A. and put out a line on the cancellation of the B-1 saying "They've started cruise missile work in Milwaukee and we're supposed to cheer while our brothers and sisters are laid off in LA." What does that kind of line say about a supposedly political organization of the working class?!

Or take their line on the convention demonstration against the attacks on Black people around school opening and integration in Chicago. This demonstration, on the eve of a very tense opening day of schools in Chicago, with sharp divisions among the masses, was generally a good thing. This was in spite of the confusion spread about the line of the action. (This, too, can be laid at the doorstep of the Mensheviks and the influence of their line. Under M. Jarvis' leadership the line of the Party work team in Chicago was reversed on the most narrow rightist basis to oppose a busing plan that should not have been opposed.)

This demonstration would have been better still if, as a militant demonstration, it had stood out more sharply as a change from what should have been a serious meeting of political discussion. Still it was good, but the self-styled NUWO "president" opposed it from the beginning, using various pretexts to cover his rightism. First he said there would be "no time" for it. Then, in a move that exposed that argument as bogus, he said there should be a demonstration at *two* sites—one targeting layoffs. To have only a *political* demonstration, according to him, would give too "left" an impression of the NUWO.

With this right wing line it is no wonder why at the beginning and once again in their paper, they attack "the potential idealist trip" (p. 416) in the '76 CC Report that says:

> "The key to it we feel is a political question, not the question of do we have the ties and contacts, but the political question of can we bring home to workers who would be the base of this organization and consolidate in their understanding the question of what it means for the working class to take up and lead the fight against all oppression, to infuse its strength, discipline and outlook into every battle and to develop key struggles into campaigns of the class? Because if we can politically solve that question we can develop such an organization." (1976 CC Report, p. 46)

The CC line is exactly the line of "grasp revolution, promote production" as opposed to their line "produce, produce, produce." This is the view that led them to conduct the convention itself as a hype, not a political meeting.

Viewed from the correct line of the CC, the basic purpose of the convention should not have been an extravaganza and a "show," and should not even have been principally a discussion of various campaigns from the point of view of how to carry them out (though this should have been discussed). Instead it should have been a political meeting where some of these campaigns and, even more, the basic stand of the NUWO, should have been mainly discussed exactly from the standpoint laid out in the CC Report—to unify the workers there around a common basic understanding and sense of purpose. There was some unclarity about this point among many leading comrades before the convention (and this is reflected somewhat in the pre-convention bulletin, though it basically emphasizes the correct approach). But this was largely due to inexperience with such a meeting. For the Mensheviks, however, an approach of putting emphasis on political discussion, of politics in command, is "yak-yak" pure and simple.

This kind of political approach was key to forging unity and forging organization. We may ask our Mensheviks, if you can't focus on this kind of basic political struggle at a founding convention of an organization, when the hell can you? And this method of "politics in command," while particularly important in founding the NUWO and at its convention, is also important to the continued functioning of the NUWO with a "life of its own."

If meetings and discussions of the NUWO on all levels are not political meetings focusing on why and how to take certain stands and actions—how in the *political* sense, not just "how to" pass out leaflets, when and where, etc.—the NUWO will never develop. In short, if the meetings are just "organizing sessions" devoted to making concrete, tactical plans for various actions and campaigns, then the advanced workers in particular will be unable to fully take part, their sense of organization as well as class consciousness will not be developed, and they and the NUWO will not play their important role as levers to the class as a whole. This is an important part of the correct dialectical relationship between struggle and consciousness which must operate in the NUWO as well as in the Party. Party members are not the only people who can have rational knowledge, with the workers being only interested in action.

Especially in the light of Menshevik attacks on the Party for "lying to the masses" on matters like China, an interesting footnote to their attack on the NUWO as being built out of Comrade Avakian's head can be found by examining the statements of one of the Menshevik leaders in a letter to NUWO members protesting his removal from the Executive Committee. In it he baits RCP "wrecking activities" and states "the struggle to build a united workers movement and the NUWO grew out of the struggle and work of thousands of hard working people. . . The idea of the NUWO *grew out of the struggle of working people. . .*" (our emphasis). This is quite an interesting statement in contrast to the line he and his ilk put out internally. It appears that this clique's careerism perverts everything about them, including even their concept of "truth."

Their paper accuses the CC of failing to deepen our general line on the NUWO throughout the campaign. Fundamentally, of course, that comes down to a question of deepen *what* line—the correct line or their opportunist line? As a basic response, we once again urge comrades to read the various Party documents during this campaign.

These Mensheviks don't even mention the Party pamphlet, which on a number of questions was and remains an excellent tool in both deepening and popularizing our line both on the objective situation facing our class and on concrete methods of struggle. Each of the bulletins that came out during the campaign took up and gave guidance around new contradictions that had arisen. And after the convention the *Worker* bulletin also took up some of these questions, in large part as a result of experience accumulated by our Party and concrete investigations during the NUWO campaign. It talks about why we must step up our efforts to concentrate on key battles and on being tribunes of the people and goes into the relation between these things today. Doesn't this bulletin take up the question of the single spark method and how it fits into both today's conditions in the class struggle and the long term revolutionary goal? Because they oppose all this, our Mensheviks, of course, are blind to it—or at least they hope others will be.

In defense of what the Mensheviks would call "idealism," it should be (and was) pointed out that the idea of a NUWO is indeed a powerful one, which can be grasped by the masses. All, even most of the workers' experience in the class struggle is not together with us or under our leadership. This is true, no matter how much it may offend the pride of our heroic Menshevik "organizers." For this reason an important and often underestimated part of our work is broadly summing up this experience, including putting out key tasks like building the NUWO. Putting this together with years of life experience, workers can take up these ideas as their own and make them a powerful material force—as indeed many did in building the NUWO.

All this has bearing on why the leadership given in the campaign to the question of building the NUWO "in its own right" and "in the course of struggle" was correct, and why it was correctly stated that during that time "in its own right" was principal. These so-called "breakthrough tools" and their relation during the campaign are attacked by the Menshevik paper. (By the way, their claim that the "all oppression" question was not taken up at that time is easily blown away if comrades look at that bulletin, Vol. 2 #3, and others.)

It should seem quite obvious that building an organization "in its own right" would be the main task in founding it, but apparently this isn't so to our Mensheviks. Apparently from their paper and practice, "T-shirts and beer mugs" are the essence of building this organization "in its own right." Both of these are fine, and the bulletins even gave some guidance on them, but never made them the main thing. The Mensheviks refuse to understand that building the NUWO "in its own right" did indeed involve and, even mainly involved, going into struggles—not mainly to lead and build them broadly, though assistance could be given—but to listen to the experience of our fellow workers, speak to it and get down together with them on why founding the NUWO was a crucial step in that period for the struggle of our class as a whole. This political task was downplayed by them in favor of their "PR" approach. While the relation between these tasks of building the NUWO "in its own right" and in the course of struggle is now different in building the NUWO—and building it in the course of struggle is principal between them—a correct dialectical handling of this question has continued importance to the on-going task of building this organization.

In the light of all this, it is important to sum up some of the code words these Mensheviks used to try to guide the campaign to found the NUWO. For some time in many places they pushed the slogan "Get organized" as the central theme. Besides being an attempt to dump the "all oppression" question—a constant tendency throughout the campaign from Cleveland to the convention and a consistent tendency of the Mensheviks in general—this was blatant *right* idealism. While not wrong to raise under any circumstances, making "get organized" the central slogan really didn't speak at all to the political questions and the real obstacles faced by all active workers. It didn't speak to *why* get organized and for *what.* It tended to make us sound like just another group with a game to run.

This apparently was obvious enough after a while and after some summation, so along came the heavy emphasis on the concept of an "active minority," which soon began to assume the proportions of the key concept to grasp in forming the NUWO. First off, it should be said that although some errors were made in making an empty slogan out of "the masses in their millions" following the Founding Congress, there is no need to flip the other way and make some kind of principle out of being a minority. We should always try to think and act in terms of and rely upon our class as a whole.

Standing on its own and divorced from broader political content, this slogan of "active minority" is not at all helpful. It is helpful if understood precisely in connection with the question of winning a core of workers to a political understanding of the role of the working class in the struggle against all oppression.

This is the way it is treated in the Party pamphlet, for instance when it says:

> "Many illusions spread by the rulers for years are starting to crack, but only a relatively small number of workers have been able to develop a consistent understanding of the nature of the enemy and recognize the struggle as one between two opposing classes. The character of the struggle today is that sometimes the organizers for the workers organizations seem to be leading an army, other times they seem to be leading only a few soldiers." (p. 10)

This is in line with how the *Programme* discusses the IWOs in relation to the "backbone of working class organization"—those workers who "have developed a basic understanding of the nature of the enemy and the class struggle against this enemy." (p. 108) All this helps to give correct political content to the concept of "small forces can lead big battles."

Robbed of this political content, and removed from presenting some basic laws of capitalism, the concept of "active minority" becomes nothing but a replacement for a political approach, a recipe for gimmickry and for bypassing the masses and promoting hackism—splitting a few off from the masses. It is only the logical extension of this line that led the self-appointed NUWO "president" to spread the line that "there are only 5 good organizers in the country."

Overall, the line they put out on the NUWO will almost certainly lead these Mensheviks before long to repudiate the Party's basic line on the IWOs altogether—and thus join a host of other opportunists in doing so. The motive is all the stronger now that the pedestal of their "official posts" is crumbling. While the NUWO will continue to be built, the most these Mensheviks will be left with is a shell organization, an occasional coalition, good for staging periodic extravaganzas. After all from the "Fight Back Committees" to their new "JOIN" this has been the OL(CP-ML)'s approach for years. When the political basis for welding the advanced workers into class concious members of the organization, developing their understanding and sense of organization, is wiped out—nothing is left but such a shell.

A few final words should be said on the NUWO founding convention. First, it is interesting to see that in their summation of it they take no line on the hype job except to hypocritically "defend the cadre" for being "attacked" for it and to say "the plenary sessions were inspiring." (pp. 423-6) In other words they defend the hype—no surprise since they led it and it reflects their line and orientation as petty bourgeois overlords capitalizing on the still low level of the working class movement.

The sum-up bulletin of the convention accurately assessed it. They knew and know that the focus of its attack was not "the comrades" as they feign, but their line and leadership (although they did resort in at least some places under their leadership to directing its spearhead away from them and onto the cadre).

As for their summation of the lack of leadership at the convention, two things should be said. First, the only leadership that would have made them happy was leadership according to their opportunist line—anything else is "bad" or "no" leadership. Secondly, this is the worst hypocrisy. Not only did they sabotage the Party's unified leadership throughout the campaign, but they scheduled a NY/NJ area UWO meeting in such a way that it forced cancellation of the final work team meeting set up to play a key part in planning the convention and the Party's role in it. Then they blame "Avakian's left idealist line" for lack of planning.

Finally it should be pointed out that, although instructed months ago by the Party leadership, their "NUWO leader" never produced even a first draft of a needed bulletin summing up the whole NUWO campaign and pointing the way forward. Since its line was to be based on collective summation, it is obvious why he didn't. Now, based on repudiation of the Menshevik clique and its line, such a task should be undertaken so our work in building this organization can make the needed advances.

'76 CC Meeting

The first thing that strikes you about the section of the Menshevik paper on this subject is, as usual, its pettiness. Here is a meeting in which the Central Committee is broadly summing up the class struggle, concentrating on the question of hewing and keeping to the path of revolutionary struggle in an imperialist superpower, and even according to their own account what we get is a picture of these Mensheviks busying themselves with pious doubts and petty amendments. Such are M. Jarvis' great contributions to Marxist theory. Their eclectic additions are a reflection of their line. They point out (p. 412) that the original draft of the CC Report read " 'But it is the *beginning* of the new spiral—and so the fact that it is an advance is not immediately evident.' This was changed to 'not *always* immediately *so* evident.' "

It is clear from what they write that what they mean by these additions makes them *worse,* not an improvement over the original. They go on to recount some struggles (meatcutters' strike, the rank and file movement in steel to dump Abel, miners' struggles and, of course, July 4). Their purpose is clear. They mean to make the essence of the advance of the new spiral such struggles as these.

But the fact is that, besides the key step of the founding of the Party, what basically marks the advance of the new spiral is exactly "not immediately evident"—in opposition to this line. It requires the *science* of Marxism, not simple and spontaneous perception, to grasp it because there is not a high tide of mass struggle (no matter how important July 4th actually was and how much they want to exaggerate it).

The basic reason the new spiral is an advance is revealed by concrete analysis, Marxist analysis, as in the sentence just before the changed one in the Report, "where things are now is an advance because it is the spiral that will lead to a major change in the relation of forces and will lead to the real prospect of proletarian revolution in this country as well as others." (CC Report, p. 5)

These Mensheviks' understanding is so shallow and non-revolutionary as to be unbelieveable. Are we to go to the masses—particularly workers with any experience in the class struggle—and convince them that this period is an advance because we held a July 4 demonstration, or because the meatcutters struck, even because of the miners' strikes? Most would pat us on the head and think we were crazy, even if well-intentioned. And they should, if that's what we do. Don't we need to bring out what they cannot spontaneously grasp—that which is revealed by the science of Marxism—while not ignoring, of course, the perceptual knowledge the masses have? If we don't do this—then what are communists for anyway?

These Mensheviks write this kind of drivel, glory in the eclectic additions which they inserted and used to defeat the main, revolutionary points, and then pour out phoney outrage that we accused them in the latest CC Report of making "big battles with small forces" principal over the correct understanding of the high road in the last CC Report. The essence of their line just discussed is a perfect example of this approach. Apparently the world view of these careerists is so philistine and bourgeois that they actually believe this period is an advance because they have the opportunity to put themselves at the head of some struggles—which amounts to capitalizing on the still low level of the mass struggle.

While their paper putters around for awhile singing the praises of their petty additions, soon enough it gets around to a headlong assault on the '76 CC Report. Of course this is not done openly, but it is done just the same.

First they skid over the struggle against the right—themselves—at that meeting with the empty phrase "while there were criticisms from the right." They even try to imply elsewhere in this paper that these rightists were people other than themselves. Then they give the impression that their minor additions were the main content of that meeting, and that the real struggle there was against a "one sided and demoralized view", and "ultra-leftist" current, characterized by "vacillation and doubt" about today's objective situation. Of course all this refers to is the majority of the CC's refusal to be fooled by the kind of reformist stuff described above and a determination, clearly reflected in the whole Report, to make genuine and lasting revolutionary advances by facing the situation as it is, grasping its underlying laws and doing revolutionary work on that basis. There is no other basis. Their penny-ante reformist hype just won't cut it.

They then move on to flagrantly attack and try to reverse the verdict on the main and very sharp struggle that did go on at the meeting. This was the struggle (described in the recent CC Report) over whether or not the "Some Points" report was correct "as is", which they try to wish away into non-existence in their paper. The struggle was indeed sharp, with some people from this clique saying things like "I'm not saying the report is revisionist, but..." and then going on to say, in fact, it was.

A significant number of the members of this clique were putting forward that the report "didn't even deal with the right questions." According to them it should have dealt with what they term "summing up practice," i.e., narrow summation, speaking to the development of the struggle in specific sections of industry and so on. This line was sharply struggled against and defeated.

It is obvious that these people were never reconciled to this, worked to undermine the central thrust of the report, and now this comes out clearly in this paper where, in their section on the NUWO, we find the statement "It is here that the question of developments in different industries, society, etc., and the response of different sections of our class (miners, steel, etc.) must be summed up...Attempts to take up these questions at the CC meeting were written off as pragmatic." (pp. 416-17) This is their real summation of the key struggle at the CC meeting—an open reversal of the correct verdict.

The idea that these things were not summed up at that CC meeting is both a lie and a revealing self-exposure by these Mensheviks. In fact the whole Report, in particular "Further Remarks," sums up the experience of our Party in these struggles. Lessons about the problems that arise if we limit ourselves to the daily struggle are summed up from experience such as the miners struggle; lessons about tactics as well as the basic nature of the enemy are summed up from the auto contracts fight.

But such political summation, taken to the level of rational knowledge and generalized so it can be grasped and applied by the whole Party, is not at all "summation" to these Mensheviks. No wonder they attack us for "being stuck" at the level of rational knowledge. They don't want to get there at all. To them to deal at all with ideas, at least in any sweeping political way, is itself "idealism." And their idea of "summation" is to apply their reformist, stagist view of practice and their accompanying "cookbook" view of theory.

Mao spoke well to this question:

> "Fully to reflect a thing in its totality, to reflect its essence, to reflect its inherent laws, it is necessary . . . to make a leap from perceptual to rational knowledge. Such reconstructed knowledge is not more empty or more unreliable; on the contrary, whatever has been scientifically reconstructed in the process of cognition, on the basis of practice, reflects objective reality, as Lenin said, more deeply, more truly, more fully. As against this, vulgar 'practical men' respect experience but despise theory, and therefore cannot have a comprehensive view of an entire objective process, lack clear direction and long-range perspective and are complacent over occasional successes and glimpses of the truth. If such persons direct a revolution, they will lead it up a blind alley." ("On Practice", *Selected Readings*, p. 75)

The Menshevik paper's attack on the concept of the "high road" of revolutionary struggle is blatant and its attempt to pose as the true defender of the high road is laughable. They claim (p. 414) that the recent CC Report redefines the high road and makes it into a call for an idealist and Trotskyite retreat from the class struggle. They say "the ['76] CC Report *always* has 'making every possible link with all struggles against the enemy' or 'waging big battles, together with the masses' as part of the high road. The rectification paper takes this out of the 'high road' formulation and poses it *against* the high road."

While there is no question that we cannot stick to the high road without being a part of the daily struggles (and even the quote they chose to pick at implies this), we should ask ourselves what is the main danger in our Party? Are we mainly failing to pay attention to linking up with these struggles and waging battles? Or is there a greater danger?

Can there be any doubt when they stress "both" leading big battles and preparation for revolution what they mean to be principal? To them, in practice and throughout their paper, from the "fusion" section on, the essence of what they would feebly call the "high road" is these "big battles" and merging with the day to day struggle. There is not the slightest sense of revolution and the danger of revisionism.

Of course these Mensheviks know very well what the essence of the "high road" question is. That is why they jumped out to oppose the whole thrust of the '76 CC Report and why, ever since they were defeated on that, they have tried to redefine it. Isn't it crystal clear if one studies that Report that the whole problem being grappled with there, the essence of the "high road" point is how, in this country today, not to fall into the easy road of reformism and narrow rightism and end up capitulating to the enemy—and instead to do the most for the revolution at every point along the way?

The road these Mensheviks would have our Party follow is more like a rut. It is a well defined groove, worn and channeled by the force of spontaneity and pioneered for us by the old CPUSA. You can close your eyes and do what they're doing. It's very easy. At most what you do is do some good things, accumulate some forces, get mired down further and further in spontaneity and end up capitulating.

Here was a meeting whose whole thrust was trying to begin charting a basically uncharted course—realizing there has never been a successful revolution in an advanced, imperialist country—taking into account the real and significant influence of a labor aristocracy and of the bourgeoisification of a sizeable section of the workers, the danger of war and more—facing all this squarely and looking beneath the surface to chart a course to revolution, basing ourselves firmly on Marxism and the masses. The very thought of this drives these Mensheviks up the wall. With their slide into the rut and their frenzied attacks they have tried to kill our revolutionary Party outright in its infancy—to turn it into a lifeless reformist sect which would degenerate, wither and die. But defeating them is exactly part of the class struggle to stick to the high road, and our Party is determined to do it so we can make our contribution to revolution and communism.

The Theoretical Struggle

First off, their paper attacks self study being the main form of study in the Party, saying it only results in "the rich get richer and the poor get poorer." The thinking behind this, they say is "once again, it's simply 'the idea' which is supposed to make everything flow automatically." (pp. 427-28)

In fact, self-study has historically, and correctly, been considered the main form of study in revolutionary parties. Why is this? Our Mensheviks should know, since they pose as defenders of studying with particular problems in mind when they attack the line of the "Theoretical Struggle" article that theory "in its own right" is principal right now in our Party. Self-study is the main form for study exactly because studying with particular problems in mind, as that article pointed out, is *overall* the main way people's theoretical level develops. Making use of both basic Marxist works, and Party literature such as *Revolution,* such study must go on individually because the problems and questions that arise in different comrades' work and experience are, of course, varied.

There is no substitute for developing the habit of study, no get rich quick schemes to theoretical development so, no matter what promises our Mensheviks may make, they won't be able to deliver. While the Party can and should give comrades assistance in various ways in their theoretical development, the greatest assistance the Party can give now is to smash the anti-theory pragmatic overall line of this clique—whose influence in our Party has been the greatest single obstacle in the past period to raising the theoretical level.

Of course self study can't be the only form, and people cannot be simply told to "sink or swim." For a starting point, certainly, a basic fundamentals class is needed for every new recruit. One thing we should sum up from all this is that we have had shortcomings on this front. Had more people had an even basic grounding in Marxist-Leninist theory, even more would have been able to avoid falling for this clique's anti-Marxist garbage. (It should be said, however, that the fact that the great majority of comrades, despite the pull of spontaneity, rejected these Mensheviks' line does attest to the fact that the Party—and the RU before it—has made significant, if only beginning, progress in waging the theoretical struggle and has accumulated important lessons in waging struggle over line—which should also be summed up more fully.)

But even from the beginning we realized the importance of fundamentals, and this was why everyone was directed to study the Banner book—to get a basic grounding in political economy and the basic method of Marxism. This was to be modified self study, with everyone studying one thing at once and some guidance to be provided. The "Theoretical Struggle" article, with its—correct—emphasis on theory "in its own right" now, was aimed, in part, at stressing the importance at this time of concentrating on getting a grounding in such important fundamentals of Marxism. After a time, when it was summed up comrades were having difficulty and where some of the difficulty lay, some further guidance was provided—the article on commodities in the first *Communist* was written and people were directed in a bulletin to discuss this article in connection with the first chapter of the Banner *Political Economy* book. At the same time, people were directed to forward summations of their progress and difficulties. Admittedly, little of this was done—both because of spontaneity and the sabotage of the Mensheviks.

Around the same time the herky-jerky Menshevik "theoretician" was directed to draw up some further guidelines for study on this book. This he never did. (Some months after this, since he was working on his counter-revolutionary paper on China, he was told he could concentrate on that, not the guidelines—at that time we didn't know his paper would be counter-revolutionary, it was thought it might just be wrong.) Later other forms such as local forums were suggested by the proletarian headquarters. (In some cases the Mensheviks took over this form for their own purposes.) Some attention was given to trying to sum up and popularize experience. For example the article on some comrades' experience in studying the Banner Book appeared in *Revolution* (Sept. 1977).

Throughout this period, despite shortcomings, the Party was trying to sum up experience and give more leadership to study—including the development of a special study plan for middle and upper level leadership cadre, to arm them theoretically and assist them in leading others in studying and waging the theoretical struggle—which these Mensheviks also boycotted and sabotaged. It is the height of hypocrisy for these Mensheviks to pose as the upholders of theoretical development in light of all this, of their sabotage and, of course, as is plain from reading their paper, their anti-theory line.

Comrades should ask themselves from their own experience whether it has been the Mensheviks or the proletarian headquarters that has encouraged the correct attitude toward theory in the Party. Take *Revolution* and *The Communist*, for example. Who has strengthened them and who has ignored and sabotaged them? These have been strengthened in part to assist in the theoretical struggle—writing the article on that subject (*Revolution*, Jan. 1977) which was in part a polemic against the Menshevik line and which they attack, but also other articles on theory, including the theory of knowledge (Workers Viewpoint article, *The Communist*, Vol. 1, No. 2), and such questions as democracy and dictatorship, as well as theoretical principles underlying our line on war and revolution and other key questions of line.

Comrades should also ask themselves who has put forward the line and worked to make the *Worker* newspapers more Marxist in their content, and thus a key tool in the work of the Party and the class struggle?

Other Points

Toward the end of their paper, in their typical scattershot

fashion, these Mensheviks raise a whole series of particular points against the CC Report on Rectification. Answering them all would be like chasing mice across the field—not to mention insulting to comrades who can study the CC Report, the thrust of their paper and deal with these silly arguments on their own. So we'll just direct a few passing remarks at these points, and rely on comrades to recognize and repudiate the revisionist line "running through" these points as well as their whole paper and their whole line.

Jimmie Higgins

The CC Report made the following statement: "We must struggle against the concept of division of labor that reduces basic level Party members to 'Jimmie Higgins'—good for loyal and hard work and little more." Those on the "hot shot heavies" and "big time Party bureaucrats" end of this Menshevik division of labor seem to have been offended by this and appear driven to uphold the CP's line on "Jimmie Higgins workers"—saying attacking it is idealism and denying that the masses are the real heroes (p. 430).

To anyone who knows how the CP used this Jimmie Higgins concept, this is downright criminal. It was used to promote pragmatism and just plain old employee mentality in the ranks of CP members. As we sum up in our *Programme* this kind of method was one big reason revisionism triumphed in the CPUSA. It was the farthest thing in the world from Mao's concept of the masses are the real heroes.

Even the way William Z. Foster writes about Jimmie Higgins is basically no good. It certainly is not based on the view that the masses of oppressed people have always struggled heroically against oppression, but what is fundamentally different now is that with the development of the proletariat and of its Party they can struggle *consciously* and actually put an end to oppression.

The *most* Foster says is that "by infusing him with class consciousness", "the Party enormously increases his efficiency." The image created here is certainly not Lenin's concept of the communist's ideal being a tribune of the people. Neither does this Jimmie Higgins picture Foster creates (let alone the one the CP practiced) give you the model of a communist fighter able to use Marxism to find his bearings independently in the class struggle, or especially in the inner-Party struggle. It treats qualities like loyalty, courage, dedication, etc. statically, metaphysically, and doesn't link them dialectically with the question of line.

The concept of Jimmie Higgins wasn't good when the CP invented it. Lenin's concept of a tribune of the people was far better. This Jimmie Higgins model is far worse now, with the experience summed up by Mao, especially in the Cultural Revolution, about the urgent question of the struggle between two lines in the Party and the key role of the masses in that struggle.

The CPUSA top hacks found the Jimmie Higgins concept useful in keeping the members mired in pragmatism, and when push came to shove it was a nice way to say "Shut up and go to work." This is a lesson our Menshevik hacks seem anxious to learn from their brethren revisionists.

Dizzying Empiricism

"Attack on Results—Cover to Attack Direct Experience" (p. 430) they say, referring to the CC Report's attack on their line of *immediate* results are everything. Seemingly unabashed by the fact they have just finished blasting at us for "sabotaging" the theoretical struggle, here a few paragraphs later they give us more of their empiricist line against rational knowledge, opposing such knowledge with their narrow view of summation. Here is where they take on the *Worker* bulletin on the high plane of theory—by charging (falsely) that the leading comrade in that area of work never left his city to investigate before the CC put out the line on bi-weeklies.

Here, too, they say "anyone who thinks this 'dizzy with success' is a major current in the Party today is very out of touch with the cadre." True, but not out of touch with their Menshevik UWOC and NUWO hacks, about whom this was written. (True, too, the CC Report was written before the self styled "president" was toppled from his NUWO throne, so we may be "out of touch" with the fact that the poor fellow's only dizziness now may be from his fall from what he conceived of as high office.)

Here, too, they ask why make such a fuss about the "immediate results" line, saying "Since the MPR and certainly since the last CC Report it is *generally understood* that results means 3 objectives/3 fronts." [Economic, political, theoretical—our emphasis]!!! What world are you living in? With arguments like these, who needs refutation?

General and the Particular

Here we are told that the CC Report on Rectification has invented a straw argument (p. 432). No one, apparently, ever put forward the line of trying to reduce down the universal—to make the entire general reside in any one or a few particular struggles or exposures (as the Report puts it). Jesus! After subjecting us to page after page of their paper, whose whole method is exactly that—to wander through twisted "facts," for example comparing the NUWO and July 4th campaigns in order to "prove" they're proletarian revolutionaries and the line of the CC is "left idealist"—they've got a lot of nerve to make the statement that no one is trying to reduce the general down to a few particulars!

Then our undaunted Mensheviks proceed with another whopper: "It is true that sometimes *comrades* limit the amount of exposures, ideological work, etc. to only the questions that exist within a particular phenomena" (p. 433, our emphasis). "*Comrades!*" Here we have a real attempt to "blame the comrades" and make this whole thing appear like some innocent spontaneous tendency—coming from a gang which, in the face of sharp struggle, was forced to make considerable self-criticism at the CC meeting, saying not only that they had a *line* against ideological work, but that they organized a *campaign* around "the general resides in the particular" coming off the '76 CC, which they admitted sabotaged its main thrust. Lie, lofty Mensheviks, since you must, but please do better than this!

We will leave it to comrades to judge which represents the most important struggle the Party faces at this time to advance its revolutionary work: the Mensheviks' solution—struggle to get rooted in the particulars of today's struggle—or another kind of "getting rooted" spoken to in the '76 CC Report:

> "[We can] never forget the revolutionary goal. If we do it will affect the smaller battles because they are also dialectically related—whether we understand it or not, whether anyone wants it to be true or not—it is true that what you can achieve in changing the conditions of the masses for example, is related to the big question of how society is going to be organized. There is no way to get around that. If we think we can plug along and just change conditions step by step without running up against the question of changing the whole way society is organized then we have forgotten some very basic things and we need to re-root ourselves in those basics. So while we have to take up these particulars, look at the question of quality within the quantitative buildup, we have to keep in mind always the general, sweeping goal and the big qualitative change that we are talking about." ("Further Remarks," p. 39)

On Trucks

"Steering the truck *Is* Easier When It's Moving"—so they write (p. 434). Since M. Jarvis' motion has landed him and his truck in the swampy marsh, we'll leave it to him to figure out how best to steer in there.

A Few Notes on the "Rush to Judgement" Paper

This little gem of an appendix (p. 148) fairly oozes with Confucian "benevolence" and the conceited tone of the condescending savior who wrote it—and who still tries to play his behind the scenes "kingmaker" role (even not putting his name on the Menshevik roster at the start of their paper—so we'll add it here, Leibel Bergman).

Once again these Mensheviks have produced a scenario that writes the bourgeoisie—in this case themselves—out of the script. This paper sets out to sum up what it pictures as a deceitful and "orchestrated" series of bulletins on China. It is laced with choice little goodies like "Bulletin 2: did not sum up the questions raised in #1" and Bulletin 3 "did not at all discuss the Gang of Four." And why, may we ask, weren't these questions gone into; why was it not possible to organize study and discussion in a different way? Must have been because of the evil sectarians, plotting to keep comrades in the dark, right? Not quite.

The author of this little piece led a conscious and constant stalling "let's bury our heads in the sand" routine to forestall any such development. The appendix to the last bulletin documenting factional activities in Chicago quotes another leading Menshevik crediting this fellow for sabotaging the Center's efforts to take up the question of China in a systematic way and arrive at a conclusion.

Then we have the cute remark "We are told to lie to the masses, and tell close forces the truth only if they promise to lie to the masses." We thought you were a *veteran.* Then you must know that the Chinese Communist Party Central Committee "lied to the masses" for years—saying nothing after it had come to conclusions on the revisionist degeneration in the Soviet Union. Though the situations are not exactly the same, is there nothing to learn from this example? For a veteran you don't seem to know much about the principles of communist organization. Or perhaps you're just a regular old demagogic hypocrite.

Brave Rebels

In the introduction to their whole paper, we find the following note of explanation for why these Menshevik leaders voted at the last CC to go along with the way the China question was taken up. They say in part it was "because of our fear of having to take on The Chairman in a big face to face battle. . ." (p. 144).

This is interesting on two counts: First it is an open admission of cowardice and lack of principle, which certainly establishes your credentials as great leaders. What rebels! What go-against-the-tiders!

Second it is as much as an open admission of the factional intent of your behaviour for some time before and then at the CC meeting—since rather than "take on The Chairman in a big *face to face* battle" you factionalized in a big way for over a year, and then after the CC went back and cooked up a double-dealing, splitting way to try to gain your ends. And why? Because of the "question of principle" of China? Hardly. You openly admitted at the CC that you "don't give a shit about China." If, as was the case, you were determined to go deeper into the swamp, your ass was on the line before the whole Party, and you just couldn't face that thought, could you? In fact you couldn't even face the prospect of criticism from the cadre.

Let's Put an End To It

Given the petty and putrid nature of this clique of philistines, which has been so openly exposed in recent months, many comrades ask how could it arise, how could it gain as much influence in our Party as it did—especially since it is now so hated? The key to understanding this, and to learning still more from their negative example, is grasping how it is that the struggle between two lines in our Party, including this particular struggle, is a product and a key part of the class struggle in society as a whole.

When you think about it, is it even possible to imagine that persevering on the high road of revolutionary struggle in our country could mean anything but constant struggle with the bourgeoisie, including its pull and influence on our own Party and its line? Sticking to the high road, charting a revolutionary course, can only mean struggling not only against the pull of spontaneity but also against revisionism and opportunism of all kinds, a struggle to truly apply the mass line in a correct, scientific sense—joining with the masses, learning from them and assisting in their struggles on the basis of being, as Mao put it "proletarian revolutionary utilitarians", taking "as our point of departure the unity of the present and future interests of the broadest masses, who constitute over 90 percent of the population; hence we are revolutionary utilitarians aiming for the broadest and the most long-range objectives, not narrow utilitarians concerned only with the partial and the immediate." ("Talks at the Yenan Forum on Literature and Art", *Selected Readings,* p. 270)

There are bound to be struggles in our Party in the future to stick to this path, to chart it in the face of new contradictions that arise. These struggles will occur in various forms—from small, daily struggles in every unit over how to proceed, to periodic larger struggles against a full blown bourgeois line and headquarters. There will certainly be struggles against "ultra-leftism," but overall, especially as we continue to become more deeply integrated with the struggles of our class and the masses as a whole, the greater danger, the greater pull will be to revisionism, to the right. This is one reason we should not be surprised at, but should welcome the opportunity to defeat this revisionist, philistine clique and to learn from this struggle.

As we pointed out earlier, the particular starkly apolitical characteristics of this clique are a product of the still generally low level of the struggle, the fact it is the *beginning* of a new spiral. Their philistinism, their utter contempt for genuine revolutionary theory and principles, leads them to attempt to tailor fundamental principles to what they see as the "actual conditions," instead of grasping these principles, using them as a guide in analyzing the conditions, and applying and deepening them in the course of working to advance the struggle from today's conditions to revolution. Failure to concern themselves with all this leads to the positively stunning lack of revolutionary sweep that stands out in their paper.

This, too, is partly a product of their totally anti-Marxist understanding of what objective conditions are. Is it not clear from their paper and their "tactics are everything" practice that by "objective, actual conditions" they mean the most immediate, narrow and superficial phenomena, and that they do not at all grasp the existence of laws, of big forces at work underlying all this which inevitably lead to big leaps and changes in the situation and in the moods and struggles of the masses? A slightly "left" Bureau of Labor Statistics report would be a perfect model of what they mean by analyzing objective conditions; but to them the very real and objective fact of the existence of a new spiral is empty of meaning.

It seems morally unacceptable to them to conclude that conditions are difficult—and this prevents them from grasping the essence of what constitutes the actual advance today and from building on the real advances that are occurring today, including the mass upsurges that are on the horizon and already showing themselves in particular battles. This is why they can and do swing wildly from voluntarism (chanting "we got the power") to determinism, whose confined and rightist view and political program fairly oozes from every page of their paper. They are the ones who are stuck in metaphysics. They do not grasp dialectics, in this case the unity between tough conditions and the real development underlying these conditions, so they cannot grasp the urgent need and possibility of doing revolutionary work in today's non-revolutionary situation. These pragmatists who promote narrowness and capitalize on the backward aspect of today's situation, are the furthest thing in the world from proletarian revolutionary optimists. They are—obviously—the real retreaters and you can't do anything-ers—at least anything revolutionary.

These Mensheviks' particular variant of pragmatism—which flies in direct opposition to and cuts the revolutionary heart out of the concept of high road—has some soil in today's conditions in this country. Some of the specific features of this period enable them to hoodwink some people who have not had experience—at least experience summed up according to Marxism-Leninism—in a revolutionary upsurge. Today we are moving through and beyond a stage where to a degree it appears that to "get things going" depends on the activity of a handful of communists who think up a plan, write up the leaflets and "make things happen."

While such a view doesn't fundamentally correspond even to today's situation, today's conditions can tend to mask the laws and social forces which are actually at work and the real role of communists in the struggle, which stand out all the more clearly in times of revolutionary upsurge—and even to a degree today at high points of mass struggle. This understanding was laid out clearly in the Party *Programme:*

> "Millions of people have become involved in these struggles, entering them for various reasons, with conflicting class viewpoints, and with varying degrees of understanding of the source of the problems and the links between the struggles. Millions more will continue to do so.
>
> "The policy of the proletariat and its Party, in building

> the united front against imperialism under its leadership, is: to unite with those engaging in every such battle; to make clear through the course of these struggles the common enemy and the common cause of the masses of people; to develop fighters on one front against the enemy into fighters on all fronts; and to show how all these contradictions arise from and relate to the basic contradiction between the proletariat and the bourgeoisie and can only be finally resolved through the revolutionary resolution of this basic contradiction—the seizure of power by the proletariat and the continuation of the revolution to the elimination of classes and class conflict." (p. 98-99)

Today's situation may seem to give a degree of credence to these Mensheviks' anti-Marxist petty bourgeois view of methods of leadership, which is having everything in your hands and under your control, or as the Chinese said of Lin Piao, wanting to "have everything under his command and everything at his disposal."

With this line and outlook, it is no wonder that these Mensheviks in their paper evidence such a high degree of hatred for the revolutionary upsurge in the 1960s. Such periods, viewed from a Marxist point of view, underscore even more clearly the true facts of the situation, the real forces at work, the actual role of communists—all of which are absolutely necessary to grasp in order to do correct communist work in *any* situation.

The fact is that the objective conditions, the laws and big forces at work, inevitably will and do throw far more people into motion than our hard work ever can (though such hard work on our part is absolutely necessary and does play a role in this). In periods of upsurge it is absolutely clear that we cannot have everything in our hands and under our control and that is not our basic role. As our *Programme* puts it, people come into motion for many conflicting reasons, and communist leadership means and requires applying the mass line, giving all around political leadership, not only in the concrete struggle but also in the struggle between conflicting lines and ideas among the masses—in short doing revolutionary work.

No, dear Mensheviks, we do not need our "nostalgia for the '60s" to understand this point. Lenin brings out the same points in many of his writings, because such principles reflect real and universal laws of the class struggle. Lenin wrote that in the initial stages of the movement, the communists (Social-Democrats) had

> "to concentrate almost exclusively on economic agitation. Now these functions, one after another, are passing into the hands of new forces, of wider sections that are being

> enlisted in the movement. The revolutionary organisations have concentrated more and more on carrying out the function of real *political* leadership, the function of drawing *Social-Democratic* conclusions from the workers' protest and the popular discontent. In the beginning we had to teach the workers the ABC, both in the literal and in the figurative senses. Now the standard of political literacy has risen so gigantically that we can and should concentrate all our efforts on the more direct Social-Democratic objectives aimed at giving an organised direction to the revolutionary stream. . . Naturally, Social-Democrats will now have to pay greater attention to combating the influence of the bourgeois democrats on the workers. But this very work will have much more real Social-Democratic content than our former activity, which aimed mainly at rousing the politically unconscious masses.
>
> "The more the popular movement spreads, the more clearly will the true nature of the different classes stand revealed and the more pressing will the *Party's* task be in leading the class, in becoming its organiser, instead of dragging at the tail-end of events. The more the revolutionary independent activity of all kinds develops everywhere, the more obvious will be the hollowness and inanity of the *Rabocheye Dyelo* catchwords, so eagerly taken up by the new-Iskrists, about independent activity in general, the more significant will become the meaning of *Social-Democratic* independent activity, and the greater will be the demands which events make on our *revolutionary initiative* . . ." ("New Tasks and New Forces", Vol. 8, p. 215-6)

And in criticising some people who, like our Mensheviks, are truly "stuck" Lenin wrote:

> "Once again, excessive (and very often foolish) repetition of the word 'class' and belittlement of the Party's tasks in regard to the class are used to justify the fact that Social-Democracy is lagging behind the urgent needs of the proletariat. The slogan 'workers independent activity' is again being misused by people who worship the lower forms of activity and ignore the higher forms of really Social-Democratic independent activity, the really revolutionary initiative of the proletariat itself." ("New Tasks and New Forces", Vol. 8, p. 212)

Or again in the same essay, addressing the real question of "vacillation" facing us today:

> "Social-Democracy in Russia is once again passing

> through such a period of vacillation. There was a time when political agitation had to break its way through opportunist theories, when it was feared that we would not be equal to the new tasks, when excessive repetition of the adjective 'class', or a tail-ender's interpretation of the Party's attitude to the class, was used to justify the fact that the Social-Democrats lagged behind the demands of the proletariat. The course of the movement has swept aside all these short-sighted fears and backward views. The new upsurge now is attended once more, although in a somewhat different form, by a struggle against obsolete circles and tendencies." (p. 212)

(This whole essay, obviously, is full of relevant points and worthy of study.)

Does the situation Lenin is describing here exactly fit our situation today? No it does not; he is writing here at the start of a revolutionary upsurge. But Lenin, while he is contrasting different periods here, never promoted and practiced stagism, and never made a principle—let alone a holy crusade—out of narrowing down the political tasks of communists. And Lenin's words here help us grasp principles which enable us today to break with the incredible nearsightedness and narrowness of these Mensheviks. We must grasp the underlying laws of class struggle to do revolutionary work in today's situation. And these laws, together with an understanding of communist methods of leadership and the need at all times to do all around political work, are the principles we can and must draw from Lenin.

In this way we will not only fight better today, but maximize our preparation for the future, exactly along the lines of Lenin's statement quoted in the '76 CC Report: "The task is to keep the revolutionary consciousness of the proletariat tense and train its best elements, not only in a general way, but concretely so that when the popular ferment reaches the highest pitch, they will put themselves at the head of the revolutionary army. The day to day experience of any capitalist country teaches us the same lesson. Every 'minor' crisis that such a country experiences discloses to us in miniature the elements, the rudiments, of the battles that will inevitably take place on a large scale during a big crisis." We must not narrow our sights. We must step up our work in every aspect, including organising the daily struggles of the masses, but above all we should step up our efforts to truly function as communists—as tribunes of the people—so as to continue to truly carry out our central task and united front strategy.

Today in our Party, while we continue and deepen the struggle against the line and influence of this philistine Menshevik headquarters, we must not get bogged down in their pettiness, but build on the excellent atmosphere that is developing among the comrades and set our sights toward the future.

We should fully grasp the opportunity of this struggle and make the best use of these counter-revolutionary teachers by negative example to train ourselves and the masses in the science and method of Marxism-Leninism, Mao Tsetung Thought and the revolutionary line of our Party. We should use this weapon in order to build our Party still more powerfully, in order to grasp the basic trends that underlie today's conditions. Doing so, we can arm the masses and ourselves to wage struggle ever more consciously, so that we will not only weather the storms of difficulty but plunge into the gathering storms of mass struggle in order to advance through them toward the revolutionary goal.